S0-AHV-885

Business and Religion

A Clash of Civilizations?

Edited by

Nicholas Capaldi
Loyola University New Orleans

Published by M & M Scrivener Press
72 Endicott Street, Salem, MA 01970

http://www.mmscrivenerpress.com

First published 2005

1 2 3 4 5 09 08 07 06 05

Library of Congress Control Number: 2005927127

ISBN - 13: 9780976404101
ISBN - 10: 0-9764041-0-9

Conflicts and Trends™ in Business Ethics
Series Editor, Nicholas Capaldi

Printed on acid-free paper by Friesens Printers, Canada

Contents

Acknowledgments

Neither this anthology nor the conference on which it was based would have been possible without the generous support of the John Templeton Foundation. Arthur Schwartz, Vice President for Research and Programs in the Human Sciences at the John Templeton Foundation has been unusually helpful throughout the process.

The idea for this conference and much of its content grew out of a series of discussions with Mark Markuly, a colleague and contributor to this anthology, who has continued to offer his advice and suggestions. Leonard Liggio and Ted Malloch have contributed many helpful suggestions along the way. Dean Patrick O'Brien of the College of Business Administration at Loyola has been unfailing in his support of the Loyola Institute for Ethics and Spirituality in Business. My colleagues William Barnett and Jerry Dauterive were generous with their time and assistance.

Special thanks go to Lyudmila Todorova for her general and editorial assistance. Brandon Thibodeaux and Meredith Capaldi helped with the running of the conference. Amy Keeler, special assistant to the Dean, has been diligent in helping with conference details.

Introduction

Nicholas Capaldi

American culture is confronting a new chapter in its struggle since the late 1960s to articulate an effective business ethics for a pluralistic society. The scandals of Enron and WorldCom constitute egregious examples of the absence or deficiency of ethical decision-making in matters of commerce. This corporate immorality is a reminder of the ineffectiveness of an ethics grounded alone in the rationalism issuing from the Enlightenment, and its ineffectiveness in dealing with the newly forming social relationships of a post-modern global economy. In recent decades, the grounding for ethics in commerce has slowly lost its spiritual roots. As the nation's complex web of relationships or "social capital," which supported ethical decision-making, has eroded throughout the latter half of the 20th century, American jurisprudence has embarked simultaneously on a trivialization of religion throughout society. Mainstream religions have been marginalized from the debate on ethics in general, but especially on the morality of business decisions. Meanwhile, organized religions have exacerbated the breach by adopting adversarial postures toward the overall economic structure, the business community, and even members of their own congregations who work in the business sector.

The United States needs a re-grounding of its moral roots and this will require a more sophisticated understanding of the spiritual roots of business ethics. Loyola University New Orleans has a unique plan and resources for furthering the development of this understanding, both theoretically and practically.

We have established the *National Center for Business Ethics at Loyola University New Orleans*. The aim of the Institute is to show the world that business is a crucial and honorable profession and that commerce is vital to our civilization. It is our hope that business leaders realize that they have the potential to transform the corporate world into a world that promotes excellence, prosperity, and fulfillment. Ethics and spirituality are key factors in making this transformation, and together they can help shape the American and world cultures of today and tomorrow. The Institute is *business centered* not academic-centered: The Institute will learn from and serve the business community; this will enhance our educational mission with students and faculty. Our activities include *lectures, conferences, an online newsletter, a certificate program in the central business district, a national forum* (where business leaders will be invited to lead special seminars and panels to discuss how they have dealt with ethical issues in the world of commerce; participants in the forums will include leaders from business, academe, government, and religious institutions), and a *resource center.*

Our first conference was held June 10-13, 2004, and was entitled "The Ethics of Commerce: An Inquiry into the Religious Roots and Spiritual Context of Ethical Business Practice." It was a gathering of scholars, religious leaders, and CEOs, with papers presented on the perspectives and impact of various religious traditions on the ethics of commerce. The main purpose of this first conference was to publicize and establish the viability of relating spirituality to business ethics. We had already identified and invited a number of business leaders who take spirituality seriously. A special feature of our conference was a series of panels in which business leaders discussed how they have dealt with ethical issues in the world of commerce. We anticipate that a further consequence of the conference will be the establishment of a network for on-going dialogue.

Specifically, we have asked contributors to address the following questions: Is a purely secular business ethics irremediably deficient? Does a substantive business ethics require a religious and spiritual framework? To what extent does current business practice reflect a spiritual dimension? What are the various religious traditions' perspectives on the ethics of commerce? Can the various religious traditions generate a non-adversarial, consistent, and coherent business ethics? Is there a role for religion and spirituality in a global and post-modern business world?

This anthology is the first book to appear in the newly created "Conflicts and Trends™ in Business Ethics" series. That series is, in part, focused upon the extent to which the norms of business practice "affect notions of personal dignity, family, community, education, religion, law, politics, and culture in general" and how those norms are themselves impacted by other cultural practices, including religion.

The Problem

Until recently, many Americans had a spiritual grounding for business ethics anchored in the conceptualization of virtues such as courage, honor, benevolence, or citizenship, as duties revealed through God's laws. Thomas

Hobbes led Western thought and the liberal philosophical tradition in a different but parallel direction by imagining a human motivation grounded in the primacy of rights rather than duties. Human duty was derived and undertaken to secure individual rights. Building on the thoughts of Hobbes and John Locke, the founders of the United States created a political economy with a unique relationship between rights and duties. Rights were grounded in the afterglow of centuries of Western belief in the inherent dignity of the human being in the context of a religious worldview, and duties flowing naturally from the rights of free citizens. As Alexis de Tocqueville noted in his observations of the early republic in the first years of the 19th century, spirituality, religious faith, and the voluntary associations spurred by faith communities, provided an indispensable dimension in the balance between the rights and duties of the citizenry. For most Americans in the first few centuries of the nation, morality in commerce was grounded in a transcendent reference point for decision-making, along with an elaborate network of social relationships to support moral choices.

This religious and spiritual influence endured in many forms through the centuries. In recent decades, however, the grounding for ethics in commerce has slowly lost its spiritual roots. Recent work documents the extent of this breach between religion and business. Research into understanding the perception Christian leaders have of the business enterprise, and the perception business leaders have of the ethical guidance faith traditions and church leaders can offer the practical challenges of business, reveals a radical fissure in communication and worldview. The magnitude of the fissure hampers the development of a sustained dialogue in search of new boundaries for the spiritual re-grounding of business ethics to face the profound problem-solving challenges facing the nation. Indeed, the conflict between commerce and religion is so severe businesses have a difficult time creating organizational structures that allow for spiritual practice and expression to enhance and energize company values, even though the openness to spirituality increases performance. Likewise, the biases of most religious leaders make it impossible for them to bring the religious tradition to bear on the traditional roles and functions of the corporation, which are the points at which business practitioners shape and execute their ethical decisions. Most seminarians and clergy assume those engaged in business are compromising their Christian values as a requirement for success. As a rule, religious leaders consider the Christian value system and a capitalist economic system mutually exclusive. This is one reason, perhaps, why religious leaders demonstrate little understanding of the practical economic issues that allow businesses to thrive. Likewise, interviews with business leaders suggested that most Christian managers considered their pastors and religious traditions largely irrelevant for guidance on the practicalities of their profession.

Despite this cultural disconnect from spirituality, ethics in commerce remains linked to transcendence in the minds of most Americans. According to Daniel Yankelovich, co-founder of the Public Agenda Foundation, the number one reason people are developing a new spiritual search is the lack of trust in the ethics of business leaders. He maintains that 87 percent of the population believes there is a decline in social morality. Organized religion has failed to fill the breach in the ethical challenges of American business, and many American business people have gone looking to a new hybrid of spirituality, and new gurus.

Although secular spiritualities have brought a dignity to the business person's role, heightened the importance of the soul, and encouraged an ethic of inclusiveness, their essential utilitarian approach creates a problem for ethics. As Joan Robinson has suggested, there are three pre-requisites for an economic system: a set of *rules*, an *ideology* to justify them, and a *conscience* in the person to inspire and empower the individual to carry out the rules. The creation of an ideology and the formation of a conscience are complex realities that have historically formed the core of the religious enterprise. If Robinson is correct in believing humans are ideologically motivated, which seems probable based on the latest findings in psychology, then the absence of religion from the ethical discussion does not bode well for the United States. As far back as the 1960s, Robinson lamented that the solutions to haunting moral and metaphysical problems offered by economists are no less "delusory than those of the theologians they replaced." She saw the need for an economics with an ideology based on more than mere monetary values. After more than 40 years of effort, such an ideology has not presented itself. The moral failures of business leaders, and the absence of a coherent ideological system to temper the blind spots and harsh realities of the economic system, create a new urgency in addressing the business ethics challenge.

The Solution

The historic role of Christian religion and spirituality in the United States in the formation of norms for previous eras in U.S. history will be enhanced by an exploration of insights from the two largest non-Christian faith traditions: Jewish and Islamic. This new dialogue will focus on the linkages among these three traditions. For instance, honesty, justice, and concern for the dignity of the poor are of central concern to Christianity, Judaism, and Islam. The international conference inaugurated a dialogue on the common elements of all three traditions, searching for the parameters of guidance on ethical issues in the oral and written Torah, the Christian Scripture, and the Koran and related Muslim writings. The conference allowed scholars to seek out the terrain and boundaries of a religious discussion of business ethics among these Abrahamic traditions. This anthology, therefore, is the beginning of a reconstruction of the understanding of the relationship between religion and commerce.

Origins and Nature of the Clash

The first section of the collection addresses the following issues: In what sense is there a conflict between business and religion? Is this conflict real or apparent? Is the problem more a clash rather than a conflict? Can the clash be resolved?

Machan begins by reminding us that an adequate understanding of commerce would reveal that it is based upon values; values he describes in secular terms as akin to the true (efficiency), the good (moral), and the beautiful. Maibach reinforces the essentially ethical dimension of commerce especially in the founders of the American commercial Republic. At the same time, Maibach raises the alarm about the erosion of the ethical framework.

Markuly summarizes the major research calling attention to the *contemporary estrangement between commerce and religion,* especially the work of Laura Nash. The result of this estrangement, he claims, is the impoverishment of the world of commerce and the rendering of religious teachings on economics irrelevant. There is at the very least a contemporary "disconnect" between religion and business, to use Arbogast's term. Arbogast explores this disconnect as it appears in an important document, the 1986 U.S. Bishops' Letter.

It appears that the estrangement is really a disagreement about something else. It appears to be a political or public policy dispute. More specifically, it is a political disagreement on the diagnosis of social ills and a subsequent disagreement about the cure. As Carden and Arbogast both argue, in the last half of the 20th century, clergy have uncritically accepted the diagnosis that poverty and its attendant ills are primarily the result of the unequal distribution of wealth. As a result, the religious prescription for these ills is the redistribution of wealth through the "coercive machinery of the state." As Arbogast expresses it, Catholic Social Doctrine in particular has a tendency "to focus on symptoms of problems rather than root causes, and to seek immediate remedies for distress at the expense of sounder solutions that play out over time." Specifically, the redistributive policies of the state lead to even greater impoverishment, a consequence ignored by clergy because of their lack of understanding of the economic consequences of public policy. In Arbogast's words, "the American Church has developed a peculiar blind spot towards the importance of economic growth as an enabler of greater justice and equity."

Block's essay is an intriguing attempt on his part to "understand why the Jews, who have benefited so much from capitalism, nevertheless, in the main, reject it in favor of its polar opposite, socialism and government intervention into the economy." After examining a wide range of extant hypotheses, Block concludes that this is still an open question. The value of his examination of these arguments is that they can be extended to other religious groups in the hopes of making us realize that the issue of the "disconnect" may be more complicated than any of us realizes.

Robert Nelson suggests that the "disconnect" is two-sided. Many economists and defenders of the market economy treat economics as if it were a value-free science. While this might be true of some of its statements, the fact is that economists make policy recommendations that presuppose value judgments. He "challenges economists to realize the deficiencies of the 'science' beneath their principles and recognize the 'faith-based' presuppositions buried in the major doctrines of economic schools of thought. In short, public policy requires us to be more self-conscious and self-critical of our value judgments.

There is something worth adding to Nelson's argument. We can distinguish between the body of scientific knowledge built up by economists and the supplementary ideological positions of those famous economists of all stripes who have used the combination of the two (the knowledge and the ideology) to support a wide variety of public policies. Many religiously inspired thinkers would adamantly disagree with some of those ideological positions, especially those based on a reductive, hedonistic, or materialistic conception of human nature. Having decided (usually for good reasons) that those reductive ideological conceptions are false, they have further concluded, wrongly, that there is no reason to study or seriously examine the body of scientific truth.

There is an inevitable tendency on the part of both constituencies to offer caricatures of the other side of the debate. One way of overcoming the caricatures is to realize that advocates on both sides share a great deal in common. This is something to which Schmiesing calls attention. That is why he has chosen to begin the rapprochement by "describing some of the relationships between clergy and businesspeople in the past," in the hopes of illuminating some keys to promoting better clergy-business relations in the future." Schmiesing makes one other point worth noting, and that is that we do not yet have a full blown and adequate account of the long history of the relationship between religion and commerce. There is a tendency to project 20th century disagreements anachronistically into the past. This is a problem we address in Part II.

The conclusions I draw from this first set of papers is that (a) we need to put the relationship between religion and commerce into historical perspective; that (b) an adequate historical perspective might throw light on the origin and validity of the different diagnoses of social ills; and finally (c) that it may very well be the case that neither side had adequately diagnosed our social ills, and therefore that rapprochement might begin with keeping an open mind on this issue, an issue to which we allude but that we do not explore in this anthology.

Regaining Historical Perspective

A plausible account of business practice must be informed by an understanding of the cultural milieu out of which that practice emerges. Western capitalism and its attendant business practice emerged out of a Judeo-Christian cultural milieu and Judeo-Christian ethics inform and are informed by that practice. Consequently, Judeo-Christian ethics is central to our understanding of the practice over which we aspire to theorize normatively. If, per Oakeshott and Hayek, we acknowledge that our capacity for adopting new norms and enmeshing them in our social practices is not infinitely elastic, and that our inherited practice contains or embodies knowledge that we are incapable of recognizing or articulating fully, then Judeo-Christian ethics ought to enjoy a presumptive (although not necessarily conclusive) authority in addressing the open questions of business ethics.

Redpath continues with a concise but eloquent history of the relationship between the metaphysical and religious tradition of the West and all aspects of its culture including business. Alluding to Michael Novak's famous work, *The Spirit of Democratic Capitalism,* Redpath contends that a specific set of "metaphysical teachings helped create the moral and political climate that allowed modern democratic capitalism to arise."

In the "Deuteronomic Double Standard," Norton discusses a provocative topic in the study of Hebrew antiquity. Scholars have pointed to the simultaneous prohibition of lending to fellow Israelites and permission of lending to foreigners as inconsistent and ethnocentric. This paper views the dichotomy in terms of human nature and the comparative advantage of differing economic institutional arrangements-kinship networks versus impersonal markets. The duality is shown to fit with different benefits and costs. Some propositions are developed showing the behavior is not only consistent but also not ethnocentric.

Campbell examines Renaissance Florence in order to show that the richest patrimony is not the fruit of some abstraction, capitalism, or even the free market. It's the bourgeois culture, not the economy, stupid. Or, more carefully, things go best when the economy and the culture are sympathetic to each other, but neither one has the upper hand. Florence, in fact, provides the answers to those critics who never tire of pointing out that the productive capacities of capitalism and free markets to generate material wealth are not enough to win the arguments for a complete social system. The methodology of economics lends itself to such caricatures, but for the lived reality we can return to the inspiring concept of citizenship and classic republicanism created by the bourgeoisie of late medieval and Renaissance Florence.

Liggio offers us a specific example. From the classical world to the present there has been an intimate relationship among family, property, and religion. "The early Christian Fathers were concerned with issues of property and of wealth. Medieval scholastics continued these discussions." Building on the work of Liggio and Chafuen, Pecquet goes on to argue that from "about 1250 to 1650, the Scholastics battled for the moral legitimacy of commerce. Scholasticism constituted the very first classical liberal movement and it shaped western history. Present-day economists have much to learn from the Scholastic monks who studied economics precisely in order to derive moral implications. The Scholastics encouraged traders to ignore inappropriate 'moral' doctrines as well as unjust laws." If Liggio and Pecquet are correct, then there was never a "disconnect" between religion and commerce until the last half of the 20th century!

Some would reject the foregoing claim and argue that Catholic Social Thought beginning with *Rerum Novarum* in 1891 created a gap between religion and commerce. Not so, claims Keckeissen. On the contrary, the social doctrine of the Church and the doctrines of the Free Market are identical! Specifically, with regard to the poor of the developing world, it is the failure of the developed world to honor the principles of the free market such as free trade with no barriers that is contributing to the inability of the developing world to prosper. Politically motivated government intervention into the economy is the root cause.

Jones introduces another dimension to the historical record. Controversy over the Weber thesis aside, research indicates the clear historical connection between religion and capitalism. Rather than being at odds, there has always been a close connection. Wilburn reinforces this contention and carries the argument further. Rather than being a mere historical condition or concomitant, certain aspects of religion may be necessary for the continual functioning and success of a market economy.

Three Bridges

Lapin

It is difficult, if not impossible, to do justice to a Rabbi Lapin presentation. It is more than just an essay; it is more than a collection of witty anecdotes; it is the embodiment and expression of wisdom. Rabbi Lapin elicits the Old Testament view that business is about being successful by satisfying the needs of others. He embeds this insight into a deeply theistic view of the world, exposes the critics of free enterprise as ultimately without a profound sense of the supernatural, and reflects on how the American founders were Old Testament Christians. The secret of the success of Jews in the world of commerce is their connection with the values expressed in the Old Testament.

Beers

Father Beers recognizes that the Catholic tradition is not the unique repository of wisdom on commerce, for "these virtues are part of the holy lives of all people of good will, other Christians, Jews, Muslims, Buddhists, and Hindus." He focuses on identifying what is distinctive in the Roman Catholic tradition of virtues as they are constitutive of the entrepreneurial vocation. After a careful and rich historical review, he argues that in the Catholic tradition of spirituality we find perhaps the clearest and most convincing articulation of the vocation of the entrepreneur in the work of St.

Francis de Sales. He cites de Sales who said that we should not only preserve but to increase "our temporal goods whenever just occasions present themselves and so far as our condition in life requires, for God desires us to do so out of love for Him."

Beers concludes with two references to Germain Grisez who argued that entrepreneurs who have a gift for administering material goods that they should accept that as an element of their personal vocation. "[P]eople with both surplus wealth and skill in management can rightly set up or invest in businesses which provide just wages for gainful work and useful goods and services at fair prices, along with enough profit to compensate them reasonably for their work, which contributes to society's economic common good." Grisez also noted that philanthropy is not restricted to giving to those in need—rather, true philanthropy should promote the elimination of need. The entrepreneur is uniquely able to be philanthropic in that way.

Ahmad

Imam Dean Ahmad provides a careful, concise, and lively history of the importance of commerce in the Muslim world, as well as discussing and rebutting what appear to be conflicts with sound economic practice. More topically, he addresses the issue of what will relieve the Muslim world of its present economic stagnation. His answer is that it must be accompanied by a "return of the civil society institutions that were prevalent in the Muslim world during its glory era from the seventh to the 16th centuries when Islam was the preeminent civilization from Spain to India. In that era, economic infrastructure was generally built not by the state, but by civil society institutions like the *awqâf* (charitable endowments). The economic recovery of the Muslim world will require free markets, just government, and a well-defined and protected system of private property.

He also urges the need to "distinguish the 'free market' from the crony capitalism in which politically influential corporations in the Western world take advantage of the relationship between the American government and Third World dictators to enrich themselves and the dictators at the expense of American taxpayers and potential Third World entrepreneurs who are denied a place in the market."

Applications

A. A Christian (Catholic) Business Ethics

Boileau begins with a direct assault on the notion that a purely instrumental reason can generate a substantive business ethics. If his argument is correct, then much of the literature of business ethics professionals is delegitimated. A substantive business ethics has to stem from a particular ethical tradition. Boileau then proceeds to outline what the general contours of such a substantive ethics would look like from the Christian perspective, with particular reference to scripture. Orsini continues this project by showing how

"St. Antoninus was one of the first teachers of the Church to take away the stigma of the profession of commerce and, instead, point to the potential for spiritual growth in that profession. In his *Summa Theologica,* he even explained the mechanisms for the merchant to grow in perfection: he is to grow in the virtues and conduct all his business in a virtuous manner." Rowntree adds an Ignatian dimension to this project. He maintains that for "the Christian business person, the vocation of business has its roots in the baptismal initiation into the historic Christian community of faith, and grows in this same context. A help to such growth in Christian discipleship takes form in peer groups where members explore and support one another's business vocations."

Edwards makes the case that Christianity in the West is foundational to the free enterprise economic system, with the profit motive optimally tempered by higher, Christian motives. These lead Christians in commercial pursuits toward payment of fair wages, watchcare of those under their authority (i.e., employees), and other demonstrations of Christian virtue in one's calling to the business sector.

These four writers, among many others, have begun, but only just begun, to construct a contentful Christian (Catholic) business ethics. We seem to have moved beyond the idea of a "disconnect" into the beginnings of a constructive and substantive dialogue. Much work remains to be done, but the foundations have been laid.

B. Corporate Governance

Corporate governance is one specific and important focus of contemporary business ethics. Our authors here have raised the question what do the various religious traditions have to offer by way of guidance.

Cavill rehearses the recent corporate scandals and seeks to understand them through the works of the theologian Reinhold Niebuhr. The only people who are shocked by corporate scandals are rational secularists who have somehow managed to convince themselves that it is possible to produce a utopian world. The great Christian insight, and a point emphasized by Niebuhr, is that human beings never lose the capacity to commit sin. This cannot be eradicated by purely naturalistic and rational programs. Only a culture that takes religion seriously, that recognizes both sin and the human capacity for transcendence, can begin to cope adequately with corruption.

Chafuen, a distinguished scholar of Scholastic tradition in economic analysis, begins with a trenchant critique of the misguided and widespread politically correct notion of so much of the corporate social responsibility literature. By drawing on the teachings of the late-scholastics and other Christian authors to date, Chafuen discusses "some of the most prevalent anti-social behavior by corporations, which could be defined as *privilege-seeking through "legal" and "illegal"* means. Specifically, he calls attention to the "dissemination of anti-social ideas." Chafuen's paper reminds us of

Keckeissen's claim that properly understood, the teachings of Christianity, including its critical capacity with regard to corporate governance, is consonant with a proper defense of the market order.

Chafuen's points are reiterated by Johnston, who points out that (a) what we call "corporate governance" "is the application of the fiduciary principle to the management of corporations," that (b) the fiduciary principle is a principle of Christian natural law incorporated into Anglo-American law through the common law tradition, and that (c) "recent business scandals have evidenced widespread deviation from traditional ethical and legal standards." It follows that restoration of confidence in corporate governance requires a return to those traditional principles and not their obfuscation by politically correct mantras. Koslwoski qualifies Johnston's emphasis on the fiduciary role of management with a more detailed examination of the larger social context within which managers operate. Koslowski's point is further expanded by Russello, who, drawing on Pope John Paul II's encyclical *Centesimus Annus* (1991), "argues that the principle of Catholic social thought, known as *subsidiarity*, can be applied to the structure of corporations to give concrete expression to the understanding of a business enterprise as a 'community' organized to attain a series of goods, only one of which is profit for the corporate entity itself."

A different dimension to these problems is provided by Dhir. Dhir appeals to the Hindu tradition, specifically the notion of Dharma. Western Thought, including Western religious thought, has been largely molded by the classical Greek philosophical conception that a good explanation is a deduction from first principles. An ethical argument, presumably, follows the same pattern, with the only question being the identification of the appropriate major premise. However, in other cultures, a good explanation is not the simple application of a rule, but a narrative. We tell stories in order to make an ethical point. Clear analogues to this are the stories and parables in the Old and New Testaments. This has important implications for the pedagogy of business ethics. As many have found, telling stories of good and bad behaviour is a major way of conveying the appropriate norms. Dhir's essay challenges us to develop a larger narrative within which such stories become more meaningful.

Globalization

Globalization is another specific area of concern. Everyone in the world talks about globalization as a major problem for business ethics, but there is little agreement about its meaning and implications, and therefore widespread disagreement about how to address the problems it seems to raise. For our purposes here, globalization is understood to refer to the apparently inevitable spread of the market economy we are familiar with in the West, and its seemingly accompanying institutions, practices, and problems, to the rest of the world. In this context, people have been led to raise many questions, one of which is whether different religious and cultural contexts are a hindrance or a help both to the spread of globalization and to the resolution of its challenges.

Malloch introduces into this discussion the concept of "spiritual capital." His hypothesis is that "spiritual capital is the missing leg in the stool of economic development and entrepreneurial activity, which includes its better known relatives, social and human capital." Echoing Lapin, Malloch reminds us that trust is at the base of business activity and it is "ultimately formed and informed by religio-spirtitual beliefs and traditions."

Our other writers attempt to examine globalization and its relation to religion in specific areas of the world. Legutko examines Eastern Europe, specifically Poland. He offers a fascinating history of how Catholic Poles tried to come to terms with a market economy once it was clear that communism was doomed. John Paul II's encyclical *Centesimus Annus* played a crucial role. Legutko's essay is also an insightful philosophical restatement of the whole problem with which we have been dealing.

Chandler and de La Torre examine Latin America. It is generally assumed among Catholic agencies that poverty in developing countries is the result of a lack of resources. Hence, the obvious remedy is to provide those resources. Rural assistance projects in Latin America often take the form of doing just that, providing tools, seeds, etc. In his study of one such project in Brazil, Chandler documents the fact that some choose not to help themselves even when given outside resources. Twenty households, generally those with the greatest need and fewest means, accepted the package, but during the intervening 42 to 56 days before its delivery failed to prepare their gardens. The reasons cited for their non-participation were numerous, most often verifiably untrue, and frequently absurd ("No one is authorized to use a hoe"). Follow-up data surveys in 2001 and 2003 found that 16 of these 20 poorer households instead had sent their children to ask for garden foods from five especially wealthy households. These transactions occurred exclusively within the community's nominally Catholic households. On the contrary, one hamlet-16 households characterized by high rates of alcoholism, with rare to virtually no participation in community religious gatherings, and widespread endogamy with its resulting high rates of multi-generational autism, mutism, paraplegism, and varying degrees of mental retardation-achieved 100 percent participation. This raises the interesting question, is the Catholic Church spreading the wrong message in Latin America?

Armando de La Torre answers in the affirmative. Specifically, he argues that the wrong message was the doctrine known as liberation theology, and he details how and why liberation theology was promulgated in Latin America. He further details the strong condemnation of liberation theology by Pope John Paul II.

Klein and Khawaja examine the problematic and topical case of the Muslin world. Consistent with Ahmad's contentions, Klein argues that there is no necessary conflict between a market economy and Islam. Klein uses her experience teaching business ethics in Bosnia as a case study to help her argue that it may be free enterprise that, more than any other social and political force, helps promote sophisticated ideas of freedom and democracy in developing nations. Bosnia, she claims, though a "tough case"-given its communist roots and large Muslim population-serves as evidence that free enterprise may be a serious antidote to ethnic and religious hatreds in a war-torn country. In addition, Klein suggests that these past experiences from Bosnia offer a hopeful note for the future of Iraq.

Khawaja offers a more nuanced approach. He argues that the *Quran* espouses what he takes to be an egoistic conception of moral motivation, and an individualistic conception of moral responsibility. Given this, it has little difficulty reconciling its general moral vision with the "enlightened self-interest" necessary for capitalist enterprise. On the other hand, however, the *Quran's* conceptions of divine sovereignty and human vice regency turn out to be difficult to reconcile with the classical liberal conception of rights that undergirds capitalism. The result is an attitude in Islam that is neither overtly hostile, nor obviously friendly toward capitalism, but curiously ambivalent instead: a business-friendly moral psychology combined with a rights-hostile jurisprudence. This ambivalence, he suggests, offers important lessons both to Muslim defenders of capitalism and to secular critics of Islam.

Rai examines India. He begins by offering a broad overview of Hinduism, its similarities and differences from the Abrahamic faiths and other world religions. He goes on to examine how it impacts the practice of business in India, and how it might address the challenges of globalization. Specifically, he suggests that religion not only provides "guidelines for organizational behavior but" it might also act "as a buffer to absorb stress and the other negative fallouts of the globalization process."

Isiramen examines Africa, specifically Nigeria. She makes two important claims. First, she claims that the introduction of western style markets has been accompanied by the delegitimation of Traditional African Religion, and the result has been a cultural disaster. Second, she claims that the religious elements must be reintroduced not only in Africa but globally. Moreover, she understands the religious element in communal terms, not individualistic terms. It is precisely this communal (communitarian?) approach that appeals to so many Western religious critics of the market economy. The Archbishop of Canterbury, for one, claims to speak for the world precisely on these grounds.

Finally, Gregg takes a different stance toward these issues. He is not interested in whether globalization is beneficial or harmful. Rather he seeks to understand how Catholic social teaching, properly understood, should help Catholics to think about, and comprehend, the phenomenon of globalization. He reminds us that before we can apply religion to specific secular concerns we need to remind ourselves what the relationship of our religion to the secular world means from a religious point of view. Gregg's point can and should easily be reiterated from a variety of religious perspectives.

Conclusion

Gordon Lloyd's essay serves as a fitting conclusion to this collection of essays. The issue of globalization is the macro version of the discussion we have been having about whether there is a "disconnect" between religion and commerce in our own society. He does this by engaging in a critique of Rowan Williams, the present Archbishop of Canterbury, and the latter's discussion of globalization. Archbishop Williams sees the 'disconnect' and the overcoming of it in the following way: (a) we need the welfare state because the market is at best amoral, if not immoral, and because individualism is not an acceptable moral vision; (b) the modern welfare state has failed because it has become a soulless entity in need of religious invigoration; and (c) morality has to be imposed on both the market and government by an (or the) established church. Lloyd contests the archbishop's case by maintaining that (a) instead of a misguided welfare state, we need a robust private sector and its power to do good; that (b) "traditional religion should work to reestablish the severed connection between the community and the individual, and the religious ethic and the market spirit; and, finally, (c) that "the only way that traditional religion can provide an ethical guide in the era of globalization is by rejecting, rather than by endorsing, the principles of the welfare state." Many but not all of the writers in this anthology would agree with Lloyd. But, in any case, Lloyd's critique has restated and clarified where the discussion is on the issue of whether there is a mortal combat between religious ethics and the spirit of capitalism.

PART I

ORIGINS AND NATURE OF THE CLASH

Can Commerce Inspire?

Tibor R. Machan

Money, which represents the prose of life, and which is hardly spoken of in parlors without an apology, is, in its effects and laws, as beautiful as roses.
Ralph Waldo Emerson

Aristippus championed only the body, as though we had no soul, Zeno championed only the soul, as though we had no body. Both were flawed.
Michael de Montaigne

Commerce and Its Dubious Reputation

Given its reputation in many of the popular renditions of world religions and philosophies, commerce wouldn't be expected to inspire. Most of those who comment on such matters do not consider engaging in commerce to contain any measure of nobility or moral worth, but merely some practical or instrumental value.[1] For example, the actual transaction in a purchase is taken to be of instrumental importance; however, most people hold that commerce fails to lend our life any dimension of worth.

Many go a lot further and declare commerce outright vicious. Charles Baudelaire, for example, states that, "Commerce is satanic, because it is the basest and vilest form of egoism. The spirit of every businessman is completely depraved." And then he adds, very revealingly, that, "Commerce is *natural,* therefore *shameful.*"[2] And Arthur Miller remarks, a century later and in America where commerce is relatively hospitably treated, that "His was a salesman's profession, if one may describe such dignified slavery as a profession..."[3]

Indeed, one problem with commerce in most cultures is that it is thought to be mundane to the core. There is unease about commerce throughout the religious community in light of what most take to be religion's main concern, namely, striving for everlasting salvation. This is often interpreted to mean, for example, that the rich cannot gain entrance to heaven, that money lenders are the worst lot abusing the temple, that it would not profit one to gain the world but lose one's soul, etc.

Such ideas are not necessarily the best way to understand the relationship between religion and commerce. In especially those faiths that regard the earthly life of human beings vital to care for—or to use an Aristotelian locution, ones that implore us to flourish here on earth—commerce could well occupy a very respectable, honorable role. After all, it is through commerce that we most effectively exercise the moral virtue of prudence vis-à-vis the requirements of our temporal lives. In this respect, as I point out in this discussion, commerce is no less significant for a good human life than medicine or engineering.

Yet, as will be seen, my position is different from the positions of those, such as George Gilder, who hold that commerce lends our lives a measure of worth because it involves a variety of (at least consequentialist) altruism by requiring the commercial agent to pay close attention to what benefits his or her trading partner or customer.[4] This idea, championed among religious defenders of commerce and capitalism, maintains that when we engage in commerce or the profession of business, we are benefiting other people, as well as ourselves, and it is the former that is morally ennobling, with the latter remaining morally suspect but sufficiently moderated so as not to amount to rank greed.[5]

Aristotelian-Thomistic Ethics and Commerce

I argue, instead, that the mainstream position about commerce requires serious reconsideration in light of human nature and the morality of self-perfection or eudemonia.[6] If it is true, as Aristotle, Thomas Aquinas, and some others have held, that a central normative element of our humanity—that is to say, a fundamental ethical responsibility we all have—is to achieve flourishing in our lives, and our lives substantially involve creative, productive connectedness to the natural world that surrounds us, and if commerce facilitates this connectedness, then commerce *qua* self-development and the pursuit of prosperity occupies a far more elevated role in our lives than is testified to by many prominent world views.

Of course, the value of commerce as a means for enriching our lives and enhancing culture can be appreciated even apart from showing that it contains moral worth in and of itself, as a form of human activity. One need but peruse the windows of most stores at a contemporary mall in a thriving commercial society to recognize that they contain creations and products that are awe-inspiring for their combined beauty and usefulness. One might even regard the contemporary mall as a surrogate museum of contemporary culture. It is possible to just wander around, as one does in a museum, and admire the thousands of different items offered up not just for consumption or use, but also for apprehension, appreciation, and admiration. Inasmuch as this is the routine result of commerce, one should join George Mason University Professor Tyler Cowan who argues that free trade is not only efficient and moral but often also quite beautiful, even as it is also destructive of old and outmoded attachments people have formed in their lives.[7]

Why Commerce Is Ethical

But let me now turn to the issue of whether commerce may be constitutive of an ethical, flourishing life, just as moral virtue is constitutive of happiness in Aristotle's and Thomas Aquinas' ethical thought. Within this ethical framework the moral virtues, when practiced conscientiously, help to guide us toward happiness in life, but they are themselves an aspect of the happiness they produce. Choosing to be prudent, honest, temperate, generous, and just amounts to choosing ways of living and the combined result of such choices is likely to be happiness.

Choosing prudently to enhance our lives here on earth, including by means of thoughtful trade, provides us with a source of confidence, efficaciousness, which itself constitutes the flourishing that improves a human life so much.

Of course, there are many adjacent features of commerce that show its beneficial elements: it often is a first step toward friendship, at least a friendship of pleasure or even utility, but sometimes even a friendship of virtue (one often comes to know another person in the course of trading with him or her); romance, too, can commence from a trade relationship; learning, too, is often facilitated by trade, as is aesthetic enjoyment; on the international front, the absence of war between societies the citizens of which are actively trading with each other is a very serious, even inspiring benefit of trade. Such results, of course, can be found quite apart from trade. But that is true of many other ways in which good things come about in human intercourse—for example, athletics, science, education, and politics.

But perhaps the most inspiring aspect of commerce is the realization upon reflection that it is such a widespread contributor to human well being here on earth. It is no accident that every newspaper reports on business in each of its issues, no less so than it does on entertainment, education, athletics, and other positive aspects of human living. More directly, commerce inspires by contributing to one's, one's family's, and associates' well being. Contrary to the view sometimes associated with Aristotle, namely, that retail trade has only instrumental value, there is actually an Aristotelian understanding of commerce that sees it as engendering human self-confidence, pride. When one embarks upon successful dealings, one is demonstrating competence in earning a living within a complicated social framework.

Money as "The Prose of Life"

Martha Nussbaum has argued that, "The Aristotelian holds that money is merely a tool of human functioning and has value in human life only insofar as it subserves these functionings. More is not always better, and in general, the right amount is what makes functioning best."[8] Actually, if this were true, then all human virtues could be demeaned as well, since their worth consists, at least in Aristotle, in their contribution to human happiness. Nussbaum's account clearly suggests that business professionals can only earn moral credit through deeds other than what their profession calls for. These would be *pro bono* contributions such as philanthropic and charitable deeds, funding of libraries, museums, athletic events or art centers, and not contributions as they function in the capacity of business professionals.

This is a mistake. Before I explain, let me turn, however, to the point Nussbaum attributes to Aristotle about money. Here it is Aristotle who was making a mistake, probably because of his general disdain for physical labor and whatever came close to it, such as earning money, as well as his view that only those crafts involving strict determinacy—that is to say, a beginning, middle, and end—are worthwhile. In the case of money-making, there is no determinate conclusion to the task, thus it isn't possible to evaluate it as one can evaluate the work of a tailor, miller, architect, or playwright.

Yet Aristotle fails to note that there are many tasks that resemble money-making, such as farming, exploration, scientific research, and philosophy, none of which involve determinate tasks, but instead, indeterminate, endless activities.

It is also worth noting that being a contributor to human well being, money (or the making of it) is not necessarily "*merely* a tool of human functioning." By Aristotle's own account of the relationship between means and ends—for example in how the moral virtues are means to human happiness—the earning of money can be constitutive of human functioning. To wit, someone who is skilled at making money is an effective contributor to his or her economic well being which, in turn, can contribute to his or her overall flourishing.

Money may be a means of exchange but it is more than that, as well. It is an easily and widely recognized representative of productivity. Money is also a fungible good, like a movie, theater, concert, or any other kind of ticket with which one is able to obtain what one needs and wants. (Professor Walter Williams has called it "a certificate of performance" on a recent radio program.[9]) Obtaining such a ticket enables one to gain the value of seeing a movie, going to a play, concert, or museum, all of them valuable experiences. If money makes this possible, then the activity that gains it cannot be without merit and can, indeed, be constitutive of a measure of success in human living.

Furthermore, an enormous benefit of money is its already mentioned fungibility. Most of us are good at doing this or that, can flourish at our professions, and yet because of earning money rather than engaging in barter, we are able to contribute to the advancement of innumerable other tasks we would not be capable of promoting directly. So, we send money to support the local theater group or orchestra, help some research effort to find a cure for some disease, further our children's and sometimes others' education, promote some idea by giving to a think tank, etc. Money can be earned in tasks at which we are good and then contributed to advance numerous other purposes. (Of course, money can also be spent on frivolity and degradation, yet corruption of any activity is a risk for free moral agents.) Those, therefore, who can help us improve our money earning capacities—that is, our wealth—namely, professionals in business, certainly are justified in taking pride in what they are doing, no less so than are those who can help us improve our health, so that we can then devote ourselves to various other worthy tasks.

Prudence Grounds the Worth of Commerce

Accordingly, I am proposing here that commercial skill or savvy is best understood as an activity that is guided by prudence, which is a moral virtue and is, thus, constitutive of human happiness.[10] Too many thinkers have discounted commerce as a source of inspiration, as a source of ennoblement, even—while electing to credit other endeavors such as art, science, education, and the rest with the capacity to inspire—of possessing the worthy attributes I claim commerce possesses as well. Professional practitioners are worthy persons in these other activities not only because of what they produce. An educator, for example, is honored because of the merits of what he or she does, of his or her calling or vocation, not only because of the valuable results that stem from it. Perhaps this is, in part, because professions such as education, medicine, law, farming, and the like can all be cast as *services to others* and one can, thus, discount the fact that many pursue them for the rewards they bring to the agent—the educator, scientist, artist, attorney, and so forth. But it is no accident that when one considers a profession, one seeks some activity that is self-fulfilling, that realizes one's talents and the vision one has of one's future life, even apart from how others may benefit from it. Some may indeed seek work by asking where one's efforts may be most urgently needed by others, but many ask, also, how their own lives will be enhanced by this work. Many enter a profession because of early affinity for the kind of skill it requires or because some early experience has shown it to be important and personally appealing.

Commerce and the Spirited Life

Accordingly, just as any other worthy craft, skill and profession can inspire, that is to say, result in a spiritually enhanced life—via pride and self-esteem from the knowledge one is doing well at something worthwhile—so has commerce and its professional arm, business, the capacity to produce inspiration.[11] Of course, this may well be thwarted by widespread disdain for the craft or skill, just as the reputation of, say, the performing arts at one time tended to dampen such enhancement for the actors who were the targets of snobbery and derision.

To these considerations someone is very likely to respond along the following lines: "Well, yes, commerce helps one to get what one needs and desires and this is certainly important, but is it really a moral or ethical matter? After all, each of us wants the best for himself—this is only natural. What you've shown is that commerce helps us do this and we shouldn't put it down. OK, but why is it so admirable, indeed moral, to help oneself? After all, even if prudence is a virtue, it is but one of them, and most of the others, when exercised, seem more admirable: courage in saving others seems more admirable than courage in saving oneself, and generosity seems almost totally other-directed..."

This is of course very much a mainstream approach to commerce, not at all in line with the Aristotelian-Thomistic approach I have been urging in this discussion. Actually, prudence is rarely seen as a moral virtue in our neo-Kantian framework on matters of morality,[12] yet in Aristotle prudence is a central virtue— one reason it is often called the first of the cardinal virtues—and Thomas Aquinas continued to treat it as such. "They are called cardinal (Latin: *cardo,* hinge) virtues because they are hinges on which all moral virtues depend. These are also called moral (Latin: *mores,* fixed values) because they govern our actions, order our passions, and guide our conduct according to faith and reason."[13] Another understanding of prudence is "right reason," and that indicates just how fundamental is the moral virtue we are discussing here—the very basis of moral or ethical thinking, given that in the Aristotelian-Thomistic tradition such thinking concerns how one achieves excellence in one's life as a rational animal.[14]

It is because of the neo-Hobbesian materialist ontology that prudence became demoted to a mere inclination, which is how Kant and subsequent moral philosophy tended to treat it.[15]

Some may have reservation about my treatment of Kant who was, in fact, a proponent of commercial society. Kant and Hegel both see the commercial transformation of the world as the act of Sprit in its expression of freedom. Arguably both Aristotelians and Kantians see the nobility of this life.

Christian asceticism, by the way, may be a virtue in a world of extreme scarcity, but it becomes a vice in a world where we *can* overcome poverty; perhaps some members of the religious community failed to note the context within which asceticism made sense; perhaps they are confusing wealth with "spiritual" poverty when we all know that "spiritual" poverty is a psychological condition and not an economic condition. In short, they are confusing a time-sensitive economic condition with religious dogma. They tell us that the pursuit of wealth is bad but then they want us to distribute more of it to the poor. For instance, one could become a saint in the Middle Ages by giving one's wealth to the poor, not, however, by destroying one's wealth. Creating wealth for oneself and others is the modern counterpart.[16]

Religion and Commerce Revisited

Where does this leave us with respect to the issue of the relationship between religion and commerce? As suggested before, it depends on the conception of the good human life that a given faith embraces. If, for example, a faith views the type of earthly life that is proper to us as ascetic and demeans the human body as an obstacle to focusing on what is important, then commerce will naturally occupy a lowly place in that faith. That this is how many understand the relationship is indisputable. Church leaders of many faiths preach the doctrine of unselfishness, self-denial, even self-abnegation from which they derive a view of commerce as representing no more than rank greed in human life.

Adam Smith, the founder of modern economic science and a moral philosopher in his own right made the following poignant observations related to this issue:

> Ancient moral philosophy proposed to investigate wherein consisted the happiness and perfection of a man, considered not only as an individual, but as the member of a family, of a state, and of the great society of mankind. In that philosophy the duties of human life were treated of as subservient to the happiness and perfection of human life. But when moral, as well as natural philosophy, came to be taught only as subservient to theology, the duties of human life were treated of as chiefly subservient to the happiness of a life to come. In the ancient philosophy the perfection of virtue was represented as necessarily productive to the person who possessed it, of the most perfect happiness in this life. In the modern philosophy it was frequently represented as almost always inconsistent with any degree of happiness in this life, and heaven was to be earned by penance and mortification, not by the liberal, generous, and spirited conduct of a man. By far the most important of all the different branches of philosophy became in this manner by far the most corrupted.[17]

On the Wrong Path with Kant

As hinted above, the major philosopher with religious orientation who could well exemplify Smith's point is Kant, even though his work followed Smith's. In Kant the phenomenal—mundane, earthly—life seemed to lack moral significance because it followed the laws of classical physics. In this sphere there is no free will and so there is no genuine choice, which is a prerequisite of morality. (It is Kant, after all, who stressed the importance of the philosophical motto, "'ought' implies 'can'," meaning that only if one is free to choose, it is meaningful to ascribe moral responsibilities to that individual.)

Accordingly, the Kantian approach to ethics stresses the good will, a kind of ineffable spiritual faculty that is free because it is of the noumenal (non-material) dimension of reality. The only reason some room for prudence exists in Kantian ethics is that it represents a needed concern, albeit virtually instinctive, with the well being of the agent.

In this framework commercial savvy is a matter of natural inclination or instinct, not of good will and judgment. The result is that commerce lacks moral significance.

As noted already, an Aristotelian-Thomistic understanding of morality could well cast commerce in a very different light. In Christianity there is room for serious, conscientious attention to flourishing on earth. Jesus became man in part to make this evident to the faithful, or so some have interpreted the faith.

Secular But Not Materialist

Apart, however, from the murky disputes surrounding religious faiths, all hampered, I think, because of the epistemic problem of infirm grounds[18]—faith is more of a commitment to a belief as distinct from belief arising from consideration of evidence and reasoning—the commercial aspect of human social life certainly isn't negligible. Such a practical sphere—no less than medicine, engineering, farming, and other crafts and trades that ought to be done well—deserves respect and so do those who are its conscientious practitioners. With this made possible by rethinking the nature of commerce, self-respect and moral pride shouldn't be far behind.

One hazard, though, of taking such a secular approach to commerce is that it could collapse into sheer reductive materialism, as exhibited in the foundational philosophical work of Thomas Hobbes and the subsequent writings of scientific economists.[19] Indeed, one impetus for Kant's taking morality away from the phenomenal world is that he thought if this was where morality would have to be found, there would be no place for it at all. There is no freedom of choice in classical mechanics, only efficient causation, which leaves no room for making better or worse decisions, despite torturous efforts by some so called "compatibilist" philosophers to reconcile determinism with moral responsibility.[20]

Reconsidering Aristotelian Causation

Instead of accepting the reductive materialist ontology that leaves no room for morality in the realm of nature, a revitalized Aristotelian approach recommends itself. This approach understands that reality is all one system but not all one substance. There are emergent qualities in reality, and human life has developed attributes and capacities that make ample room for significant choices, many of which become subject to moral assessment.

Moreover, this approach understands causality so that not all causes must be of the same type. It is only natural that under the reductive materialist position all causes must be efficient ones, since only one kind of entity exists, namely, matter-in-motion, and thus only one kind of productivity can be found in nature. But if there exists a plurality of beings, some very simple—call them sub-atomistic—and others very complex—call them human—then room may be found for what Aristotelian morality requires, namely, agent causation.

This is the kind of causation ordinarily accepted, one that makes sense of people achieving things: Mozart composing music, Rembrandt creating paintings, Frank Lloyd Wright designing buildings, and Wittgenstein producing puzzling philosophy. Of course, it also makes room for terrorists wreaking havoc, murderers destroying human lives, arsonists making destructive fires, and so on.[21]

Among what such an ontological outlook (that is, one bearing on the *type of being* something is) embraces is, then, humanity's creative capacity. And part of that capacity is to engage in responsible commerce and business. Insofar as it is morally proper for human beings to secure for themselves a prosperous life, their creative capacities may be exercised in service of this objective. How the creative capacities are exercised will, of course, be subject to moral evaluation. Just as in medicine it is generally morally praiseworthy to pursue health, those who do this professionally should also do it ethically—ergo the field of medical ethics. The same is true of other professions that are morally unobjectionable.

So there is a twofold moral issue afoot here: first, the moral standing of the profession and, second, whether the conduct of those who practice it is ethical. This is the same with the profession of business. The main challenge in the theological treatment of this matter is epistemic—how can we know that the tenets of a faith affirming, for example, the significance of one's earthly life are true. The main challenge in the secular treatment is ontological—could there exist a being such that it can choose freely and be morally responsible.

The Secular Spiritual Case Outlined

Since I have made the attempt to demonstrate that the secular treatment can yield a positive answer to the ontological question, I will merely summarize the results. Reality is not all the same but there are fundamentally different types of entities of which it is comprised. Depending on the type of being something is, it will contain different causal powers. In the case of human beings, those causal powers are best understood as creative, so that the human agent can be the cause of some of its own behavior, the cause of its actions. The most evident sphere of such causation is evidently mental—human beings can initiate the process of conceptual thinking. And this is what grounds the quality of their actions and institutions.

The case for this position isn't one that yields deductively certain conclusions but, instead, theses that best explain the phenomena we are aware of, including in association with all varieties of human life. Just as in the case of criminal trials, it is the theory that best explains the evidence at hand that should carry the day; therefore, in such areas of substantive philosophy what explains the phenomena most parsimoniously should carry conviction.[22]

In the absence of an epistemically compelling theological case for a moral perspective on human life and on the field of commerce and the profession of business, and with a secular one available that does reasonable justice to the undeniable moral dimension of human life (which reductive materialists views cannot do), it seems to me that the case pertaining to the spirit—character, values, and highest aspirations—of the individuals embarking upon commerce makes the best sense. It is true, it seems to me, without a reasonable doubt.

Given, then, this conception of spirituality or, rather, *spiritedness*, there is little doubt that commerce and its professional arm, business, can be viewed as every bit as much imbued with spirituality as are medicine, education, science, art, and politics.

Notes

1. See, for more on this, Tibor R. Machan and James E. Chesher, *The Business of Commerce, Examining an Honorable Profession* (Stanford, CA: Hoover Institution Press, 1999).
2. Charles Baudelaire, *The Intimate Journals,* trns. Christophere Isherwood (Boston: Beacon Press, 1957, p. 51). The connection between one's basic philosophical view and what the person thinks of business is clear from the second observation—deeming what is *natural* to be, for that very reason, *shameful.*
3. Arthur Miller, "In Memoriam," *The New Yorker,* December 25, 1995 & January 1, 1996.
4. George Gilder, *Wealth and Poverty* (New York: Basic Books, 1981).
5. See, for example, Rabbi Daniel Lapin, "Judaism, Commerce, and Business," a paper given at "The Ethics of Commerce Conference," June 10-12, 2004, Loyola University, New Or-leans, Louisiana.
6. The most astute modern development of this Aristotelian ethical position is found in David L. Norton, *Personal Destinies, A Philosophy of Ethical Individualism* (Princeton, NJ: Princeton University Press, 1976).
7. Tyler Cowan, *Creative Destruction* (Princeton, NJ: Princeton University Press, 2003).
8. Martha Nussbaum, "Human Functioning and Social Justice: In Defense of Aristotelian Essentialism," *Political Theory,* Vol. 20, No. 2 (May 1992), p. 231.

9. The Rush Limbaugh Program, Friday, November 19, 2004.
10. See, Tibor R. Machan, "Aristotle & the Moral Status of Business," *Journal of Value Inquiry* (forthcoming).
11. Needless to say, all crafts, skills, and professions can be corrupted by misuse and mal-practice. Business is by no means unique in this. See, *op cit.*, Machan and Chesher, *The Business of Commerce.* See, also, Tibor R. Machan and James E. Chesher, *A Primer on Business Ethics* (Lanham, MD: Rowman & Littlefield, 2003), for the professional ethical implications this approach to business yields.
12. Actually Kant liked commerce but as far as gaining moral credit for prudence, his austere conception of deontological morality, wherein anything one is inclined to do would not be morally meritorious, led to the moral evisceration of prudence.
13. http://www.secondexodus.com/html/catholicdefinitions/cardinalvirtues.htm
14. Op. cit. Norton, *Personal Destinies.* See, also, Tibor R. Machan, Classical Individualism, *The Supreme Importance of Each Human Being* (London: Routledge, 1998).
15. Douglas J. Den Uyl, *The Virtue of Prudence* (New York: Peter Lang, 1991).
16. I thank Nicholas Capaldi for pointing some of this out to me.
17. Adam Smith, *The Wealth of Nations* (New York: Modern Library Edition, 1936), p. 726.
18. Gary Wills notes, in a related context, that "Natural reason must use natural tools to deal with this question—philosophy, neurobiology, psychology, medicine." See "The Bishops vs. the Bible," *The New York Times,* June 27, 2004, WK, p. 13.
19. See, for more along these lines, Tibor R. Machan, *Capitalism and Individualism, Reframing the Argument for the Free Society* (New York: St. Martin's Press, 1990).
20. See, for example, Daniel Dennett, *Elbow Room, Varieties of Free Will Worth Having* (Cambridge, MA: MIT Press, 1984). For why this approach is hopeless, see Tibor R. Machan, *Initiative—Human Agency and Society* (Stanford, CA: Hoover Institution Press, 2000) and *The Pseudo-Science of B. F. Skinner* (New Rochelle, NY: Arlington House Publishing Co. Inc., 1074).
21. For more on the scientific thesis about the creative agency of human individuals, see Roger W. Sperry, *Science and Moral Priority* (Columbia University Press, 1983), and his more technical paper, "Changing concepts of consciousness and free will," *Perspectives in Biology and Medicine,* Vol. (Autumn 1976), pp. 9-19.
22. For more, see op. cit., Machan, *Initiative* and Machan, *The Pseudo-Science.*

The Virtues of a Commercial Republic

Michael C. Maibach

As Americans debate the implications of business misconduct, from Enron to Tyco, I fear we have lost sight of the single most important victim of executive malfeasance: not cash or careers, it is our country.

And unless businessmen and women take concrete steps to address this issue, no new government regulations or headline grabbing prosecutions will repair the damage to our nation's foundations. Business actions must deal with the heart of the problem: the systematic education about and restoration of the basic virtues that make business a noble profession.

Understandably, the media and our lawmakers have focused their attention on the most immediate fallout of corporate crime. Enormous wealth has been stripped from millions of Americans because of misdeeds and misinformation; investors no longer know who or what to believe. And the careers of thousands of ethical people at companies like WorldCom and Arthur Anderson have been shattered because of moral failures of a few of their colleagues who abandoned fundamental standards of business conduct.

As terrible as these results are, more significant damage has been done to our country by illegal and unethical acts. For at the core of American citizenship we find the same virtues inherent in commercial life. Indeed, businesses are the nation's de facto classrooms of citizenship.

Across history, the only free societies have been commercial societies. Every day, the work of private enterprise helps create and sustain the environment in which a democratic republic like ours can flourish. While private enterprise doesn't guarantee freedom, it is vital to its establishment and sustenance.

Why is that so? For one simple reason: as human beings, we learn best by doing.

Business life is all about doing, about putting ideas into action in the service of others. Successful enterprises require the very virtues every republic needs instilled in her citizens. Good citizens are not born; they are fashioned by noble habits.

Consider the virtues business men and women must practice every day to be successful:

- Sacrifice - Investing to meet the needs of others.
- Service - The words "May I help you?" ennoble all who say them.
- Teamwork - The success of each depends on all working together.
- Discipline - Good intentions are only as good as timely delivery.
- Persistence - If at first you don't succeed; the customer counts on you.
- Creativity - Expand frontiers and markets expand in your wake.
- Honesty - Trust allows society's wheels to spin, dreams realized.
- Meritocracy - Regardless of background, advance when you perform.
- Pragmatism - If it works, it's good.
- Win-Win Results - True success requires that all parties feel well served.

While imperfect, these classrooms of commerce train citizens to practice ethical behavior. This little bit of magic happens quietly-while people are serving others. The importance of these "habits of the heart" is not to be underestimated. It is said, because it's true, "commerce breeds civility."

Somehow, too many business leaders lost sight of the need for high standards of business ethics. Failing to deal with this oversight simply allows the erosion of the national foundation to continue. Both business schools and national business organizations must take the lead in advancing an understanding of and appreciation for the inherent virtues of commercial life and by doing so, reinforce the practice of those virtues.

First, American business schools must instill these values in their students, the future corporate leaders of the nation. Business schools should offer a course on "Business as a Noble Profession." This will not simply be a "situational ethics" class dealing with day-to-day business transactions. Instead, this must be a semester-long, rich exploration of the important contributions commercial life makes to our nation and its people. It should be a requirement for the granting of an M.B.A. Future executives should begin their careers with a clear understanding of the noble character of their chosen profession.

Second, American business institutions should find ways to recognize and reward ethical businesses. The U.S. Chamber, for example, might institute an annual "Commercial Republic Award," modeled after the Commerce

Department's Baldrige Award For Quality. The Commercial Republic Award would be given to businesses large and small whose CEOs and employees demonstrate a daily commitment to the business virtues listed above.

When the leaders of an enterprise create a culture of integrity and service to others, they build more than a business. They help build a free and prosperous society. Let's see if we can rise to the famous challenge of Benjamin Franklin, to "keep our republic" by restoring faith in and appreciation for the noble profession of business.

Ships Passing in the Night: The Conceptual Disconnects Between American Christianity and Capitalism

Mark S. Markuly

The two great "forming" agencies of world history, Alfred Marshall once said, have been the religious and the economic (Marshall, 1930). Through most of Western history these two agencies have been linked conceptually to one another. In the United States, this relationship has been studied as part of a broader notion of "civil religion," a term popularized by Robert Bellah. Civil religion, with its God language and particular brand of metaphysics, provided a conceptual framework for negotiating the interacting terrain of religion and society from the 17th through 19th centuries. This provided a common language for discussing the validity or invalidity of social and economic "needs," and the justifiability of the costs of responding to those needs (Meeks, 1989, p. 158). Religious and civic economic life shared a language and a common conceptual framework that was supported by a religious apprenticeship that was woven into the maturation process of most faith communities. Together these influences prepared citizens for making ethical decisions, including business choices.

America's civil religion, which has been rooted in a generalized Protestantism, had profound practical implications on the nation's business and economic life. Religion provided a justification for business, so much so that J.P. Morgan called New York City's Protestant clergy to his office during the panic of 1907 to ask them to tell their congregations to leave their money in the banks. But, religion also benefited from the close connection between civic and religious life. As L. Laurence Moore has demonstrated, American religions learned to thrive, in large part, by borrowing ideas from entrepreneurs and applying marketing techniques and technological innovation to their religious visions and missions (Moore, 1994).

American civil religion, with its unique blend of religious and secular symbol and terminology, has taken many forms through the nation's history, and has had a diversity of positive and negative impacts on both religious and economic life. Overall, the relationship has been a helpful one to both cultural institutions. However, after centuries of conceptual linkages, mainstream Christianity and business began a gradual process of estrangement during a 100-year period between the end of the 19th and 20th centuries. Concepts and language are no longer shared. For instance, while religious leaders call for "economic justice," a major economic journal like the Economist dismisses the concept itself as deficient, grounded in –"an almost wholly counterproductive … analytic mindset." Research suggests most business leaders now consider religious leaders as "fuzzy thinkers" about economic issues, while clergy reciprocate with a general attitude that corporate leaders are unethical, or at the very least, compromised Christian believers who have sold their souls to the company store. The multi-million dollar industry of "spirituality and business" literature throughout the 1990s is, in part, a by-product of the inability of more ancient mainline religions to find engaging applications of their religious traditions for the practical and theoretical issues of 21st century capitalism. Once cautious companions with a tense but creative relationship, Christianity and American business are now more like two ships passing in the night. The degree of the conceptual alienation has inspired Harvey Cox to call for a "rebirth of polemics," just to inspire a new level of conversational engagement (Cox, 1999, p. 23). I disagree with Cox and believe polemics will only exacerbate the religious-business estrangement, just as it has further polarized politics. Rather, I think what is needed is a new kind of conversation, a critical theological reflection that brings leaders in religion and commerce into a mutual analysis of each other's basic assumptions about the spiritual value of wealth, work, and the responsibility humans have to each other and the environment. The goal of this conversation would be to discover new concepts and language for exploring the common ground between the life of faith and the world of commerce. I see at least six necessary steps for creating this kind of new conversation.

Step 1: Finding the Real Locus of Disagreement

In *The Spirit of Democratic Capitalism,* Michael Novak (1982, pp. 337-242) surfaces a series of important distinctions for such a conversation. Novak noted that a disciplined theological reflection on economic issues needs to distinguish between three levels of discussion. The first concerns the level of a *general* theology of economics, which explains clearly "critical concepts" about realities like money, capital, distribution, work, scarcity, accumulation, division of labor, and other factors discussed in economics and part and parcel of the activities of the business world. A second level of discussion, the one Novak concentrates on in his book, emphasizes reflection on the broader *systems of political economy* within which every economic system must operate, such as forms of socialism or democratic capitalism. Lastly, theological reflection needs to consider carefully the level of "institutions, practices, and special ethical dilemmas that occur *within* particular systems."

Novak maintains that the lack of clarity between these three levels in most theological and economic discussions has created murky theological positions about economics. An argument that seems directed at one level of theological reflection will actually address another. For instance, objections against transnational corporations might really mask an effort to criticize a free market economic structure, while criticism of particular ethical practices might have the real intent of making a case for the superiority of a different economic system. The confusion between levels of discussion makes it often impossible to discern the real "locus of disagreement." This same dynamic is operative in economic positions. Discerning a locus of disagreement requires a sophisticated conversation between religious leaders and theologians and business leaders and economists, one grounded in the unique historical relationship between Christianity and capitalism.

Step 2: Understanding the Parameters of an Ambiguous Relationship

In a thesis once called "the academic Thirty Years War" (White, 1969, p. 197), Max Weber attempted to articulate one of the first theories on the nature of the conceptual connection between Christianity and modern capitalism (Weber, 1930). Weber sensed the assumptions of Christian belief in the new capitalistic nations, among other things, "inspired an ethical orientation favorable to an acquisitive life-style" (Wuthnow, 1993, p. 20).

Whether Weber's thesis was accurate or not, throughout the 20th century the relationship between economics and religion has become increasingly complex, multidimensional, and controversial. This has resulted in a growing ambiguity in making conceptual connections, resulting in the appearance to most people that religious beliefs and values about money, work, and economic issues spin in different orbits. Robert Wuthnow has explored this ambiguity in greater depth than perhaps any other social scientist (Wuthnow, 1994). He found those who base their ethical decision-making on a theistic moralism are less likely to bend the rules, spin the truth, or cover for someone else in an organization. However, they are only *slightly* less likely to cheat on their timesheet or fudge on reimbursement expenses charged to the firm. While 86 percent of weekly church goers consider greed a sin, only 16 percent say they were taught that wanting a lot of money is wrong and 79 percent said they wished they had more funds (about the same for those in the general labor force, 84 percent). Stewardship sermons are common in nearly all churches, and yet only 25 percent claim to have heard them, 57 percent for weekly attenders. But, less than half of the weekly attenders actually can define the word. Despite the reality that church attenders are more likely to place a higher value on their family and look at work as a way to contribute to their families, they work just as many hours as those who are not religiously devoted.

Some business leaders try to create corporate climates that are supportive of spiritual belief and practice, and, engaging the spiritual needs of workers can enhance and energize company values. But, Ian Mitrof and Elizabeth Denton (1999) have found the disconnect between commerce and religion makes it extremely difficult for businesses to create organizational structures that allow for spiritual practice and expression. Part of the reason for this difficulty, Wuthnow concluded in his study, is due to the compartmentalization American believers make with their beliefs about religion, money, work, and economic issues. When religious teaching impacts economic life, there seems to be a kind of "mental or emotional gloss" that prevents religious teachings on money to impact how people actually live (Wuthnow, 1993, p. 151). The only exception, Wuthnow found, concerned situations constituting blatantly immoral actions, such as embezzlement or falsification of documents. The finely shaded issues, which make up the majority of the ethical dilemmas and the ones most in need of a sophisticated guidance system, are not addressed.

A recent study by Laura Nash and Scotty McLennan (2001) focused on the effect the ambiguity between the issues of God and mammon has had on the perception business and religious leaders have of each other. To estimate the actual influence religious teaching and belief have on specific corporate practices, the researchers identified key factors with ethical and religious implications in the complex web of internal and external relationships that constitute the daily life of a company. Nash and McLennan (2001, pp. 95-117) found that most business leaders consider religious perspectives on economics of little value in maneuvering the complex issues and decisions of a corporation. From the business person's perspective, clergy efforts at applying the Christian tradition to economic issues boiled down almost exclusively to the message of "caring" or "not caring" for the needy. Most business people found this approach simplistic and insulting to the complex decisions of competing values that they must make every day.

On the other hand, Nash and McLennan (2001, p. 102) found religious leaders tended to conceptualize business as nothing more than a "profit machine." In addition, most seminarians and clergy assumed business success required a person to compromise his or her Christian values because the

Christian and capitalistic value systems are mutually exclusive.[1] Overall, the researchers found religious leaders saw business people as a "set of caricatures," either doing evil corporate acts or "taking on the role of Santa Claus" for churches and charities (Ibid., p. 258).

Step 3: Identifying a Relational Model for Religion and Economics

Healing the breach between Christianity and capitalism requires a new level of honesty between religious and business leaders and a new kind of conversation. It will require active listening skills, rigid honesty, and a humble awareness that both sides in this breach do not fully understand or appreciate the value of the other. It will also require surfacing the assumptions forming the foundation of conceptual worlds of both religious and business leaders, as well as theologians and economists.

One of the assumptions deals with the way conversation partners conceptualize the overall relationship between religion and economics. This relationship alone can serve as a locus of disagreement. Patrick Welch and J.J. Mueller (2001) have surfaced four models in economic and religious literature: economics separate from religion; economics in service to religion; religion in service to economics; and religion in union with economics. Identifying the assumptions implicit in each of these models is an essential step in framing the structure of a constructive dialogue.

Most economists and business leaders approach the issue of religion and business from the perspective of "economics separate from religion" or "religion in service to economics," while theologians are inclined to hold the assumption that "economics is in service to the higher values of religion." An example of the effect that the assumptions of a relational model have on shaping a position is found in a work on theology and economics by M. Douglas Meeks. In his attempt to build conceptual bridges between religion and economics, Meeks writes out of the assumptions of a relational model of economics that is in service to religion. He begins his argument by trying to reconceptualize God and the economy, noting the similarities between economic and biblical terminology. But, Meeks sees the correlation between God concepts and the economy as occurring in only three ways, with all three aimed at pointing out the fundamental rightness of a theological critique and the balance it can bring to a fundamental error or injustice of the market mechanism. Few economists and business leaders will be persuaded by the argumentation of Meeks because the assumptions of their relational model will clash with Meeks' model of economics in service to religion, and his real locus of disagreement with the basic elements of the capitalistic system. If clergy adopted Meeks' position and attempted to use it with business professionals in parishes or church organizations, it is unlikely the religious leaders would find an audience.

Step 4: Ground Rules for the Game of Conversation

The problem with Meeks' approach is that it begins with an argument, not a conversation. David Tracy (1987, p.10) has suggested that assumptions are most effectively accessed through a "game of conversation." This game makes room for argument, but moves beyond confrontation, debate, and exam to allow for a process of questioning that can transform conversation partners as they seek to find similarities in what they already experience and understand. At this level, new insights can emerge between divergent positions. At times, one side will convert or moderate its position in light of the "manifestation of truth" they hear in the other position. In other cases, a new synthesis between positions may develop for both parties. If disagreement is not overcome in any way, the conversation partners can still leave with a greater sense of clarity about the true "locus of the disagreements" and a lessened sense of "otherness" in another person's position.

Moving from a position of recognizing a conversation partner as an "other," to openness in finding that one might discover a "similarity-in-difference," requires some strict rules. The first among them is to realize "I belong to my language more than it belongs to me" (Tracy, 1987, p. 50). I am the product of a culture, which has formed me in a worldview and ethos. This makes possible my "view" of reality, but also limits it. Although an easily accepted premise for theologians, this is a difficult concept for economists to grasp unless they have been influenced by the role of cultural issues in economic productivity that has emerged from the Chicago school in economics. A second rule of the game of conversation is to allow the "question" to serve in a primary role.[2] The "question" is the real agent for exposing a position's assumptions and conception of reality.

The game of conversation can expose underlying theological and economic or business management assumptions, move conversation partners from viewing each other as a true "other" to the recognition that differing understandings could yield to a real "similarity-in-difference." But, given the level of estrangement between the religious and economic world, each position probably needs help in seeing some of these "similarities." Fortunately, several recent theorists have tried to do so, challenging the religion/mammon assumptions of both economics and Christianity, and creating a new relational model: "religion and economics as humble learner, not teacher."

Step 5: Challenging the Assumptions of Economics and Business

Modern economics has what Wilfred Dolfsma (2001, p.77) has called in another context a "cold analytical front stage" that is often supported by an "oddly romantic back stage." Economist Robert Nelson provides an insider's exploration of this romantic backstage that should rattle the assumptions of most theoreticians and practitioners of commerce.

The driving force in Nelson's writings center on the question: What are the underlying values of the economics profession and the justifications for favoring those values? He admits most economists consider theologians rather naïve about economics, yet he maintains economists themselves are also naïve about the "character and grounds for their most basic presuppositions." Aware of it or not, economists are actually delivering the religious messages of a secular "economic theology," he says, and, contrary to their attestations of being a science grounded in fact, economists are more akin to priests, taking their own economic religion mostly on faith (Nelson, 2001, p. xx).

Nelson defends his assertion by tracking the evolution of economics from its early years when moral and political philosophers like Adam Smith and John Stuart Mill provided the theoretical and practical orientations for the field. From these beginnings, economics mutated into a profession for more "worldly philosophers," and began a slow withdrawal from issues of morality. During this process, Nelson believes economics actually transmuted into a "religion of the ordinary," a new theological position emerging from the American Christian worldview and many of its religious assumptions. The field of economics "redefined" many theological concepts for more secular purposes in this transmutation. For instance, the Divine Plan governing Christianity's universe was replaced by a belief in Progress—a force operating according to rational principles that was pushing the human race toward the eventual elimination of poverty. The Progressive era in American history became a new moment in salvation history for the United States and a new gospel. Original Sin, the religious concept for explaining the human propensity to sin, was substituted with Material Need, the real cause of hatred, war, social conflict, and most of the human activities traditionally labeled sins. According to this new "economic theology," once Material Need was eliminated the negative behaviors caused by deprivation would discontinue. Meanwhile, the economics of the Progressive era reconceptualized the Natural Law underpinning the foundation for ethics into the Market Mechanism, a social force operating on principles of efficiency and growth, and fueled by self-interest.

Nelson also sees the two chief systems of medieval Christian theology resurrecting in the secularized "theological systems" of a Roman and Protestant "economic theology" (Nelson, 1991, p. 11). The former has been the dominant force in American society, stressing the rational, practical, moderate, and commonsensical. It has a devotion to the rule of law, worldliness, empiricism, openness, utilitarianism, and a respect for property. On the other hand, the Protestant tradition of economic theology is skeptical that reason can improve the human race and is cognizant of the pretense and self-serving nature in the cognitive ability to reason. This tradition, Nelson contends, recognizes the real force directing history does not come from within the person but from without–such as divine intervention or, perhaps the laws of history emphasized by Karl Marx. The Protestant perspective recognizes the fundamental experience of alienation, and favors various forms of asceticism. Its default position is in protest to the status quo. The Chicago school of economics, which Nelson tracks through three generations of educators, is the main example of this perspective, especially in the thought of Frank Knight, who recognized that the core "social and economic problem" is a matter of discovering and defining values.

The iconoclastic perspective of Knight and many in the Chicago school strike at an assumption that is a tenet of faith for most economists: capitalism has the ability to "work" in any society. The problems Russia has had in moving to a capitalistic economy has shattered this article of faith, highlighting the importance of a social structure for supporting capitalism, and the cultural issues involved in a healthy economy. The future of the economics profession, Nelson concludes, is found in theological wisdom, not economic insight, because as the progressive gospel continues to wane, a new "economic religion" will need to fill the vacuum.

Step 6: Challenging the Assumptions of Religion and Business

Nelson exposes and challenges the religious assumptions of economists, offering the practical world of business a level of assumptions that have similarities with theology and a religious worldview. A number of social scientists have provided an equal challenge to the assumptions of theologians and religious leaders. Christians' lack of comfort with the principle of a free market driven by self-interest is a fundamental religious conflict with capitalism. Yet, social scientists Laurence Iannaccone, Roger Finke, and Rodney Stark (1997, pp. 350-364) have made a cogent argument that religion itself operates best in a free market. The Iannaccone, Finke, and Stark thesis is unsettling to those theologians operating out of an "economics serving religion" relationship model, which regards religion as a social and cultural force that provides guidance for the baser instincts ruling the economic realm.

The Iannaccone, Finke, and Stark model is based on the concept of a "religious economy," which they describe as follows:

> A religious economy consists of all of the religious activity going on in any society: a "market" of current and potential adherents, a set of one or more organizations seeking to attract or maintain adherents, and the religious culture offered by the organization(s) (Stark and Finke, 2000, p. 193).

When Iannaccone, Finke, and Stark first proposed in the early 1980s the idea of explaining religion with economic concepts like "consumers" and their activities as responsive to "supply and demand," a large controversy ensued in sociology and theology. But, a decade of research has convinced most social scientists that the concept of a religious economy makes sense in light of the studies conducted by Stark and Finke (2000, p. 218) not only in the U.S., but also throughout the world.

This Stark-Finke thesis, of course, challenges the anti-market assumptions of religious leaders by suggesting the vitality of religion is directly proportionate to the degree religious organizations are allowed (or required) to operate in a "religious" free market. In fact, "religious deregulation ... opens the floodgates of religious innovation" (Stark and Finke, 2000, p. 358). The innovation is fueled by the forces of religious supply-and-demand, with the overall result of a more vital religious culture that better meets the needs of "religious consumers," who are drawn to different religious "products" by self-interest.

According to Stark and Finke, changes in religious practice and commitment are brought about by supply-side changes. New religious movements or organizations, within existing denominations or outside of them, attract adherents and draw people interested in religion to another "supplier."

When a state-sponsored church loses its support from its surrounding culture, a process of desacralization does occur in society. But, contrary to much religious speculation, an attempt to substitute this church-sponsorship with a more generic culturally accepted form of faith does not diminish individual religious commitment. The "deregulation process," as Stark and Finke refer to it, actually results in more religious options and an increase in religious interest and commitment as more motivated religious organizations enter the "religious economy." (Stark and Finke, 2000, p. 200).

Conclusion

The iconoclastic positions of Nelson and Iannacone, Finke, and Stark challenge the romantic backstage of both business and religion. They challenge encrusted perceptions and unsettle the unexplored assumptions that circulate behind the stage curtains. More importantly, they provide a beginning template for a conversation committed to a search for "similarities-in-difference." If leaders in religion and business can begin a discussion as a humble learner of the conversational partner's position, instead of a cocksure teacher of the partner's ignorance of economics or religion, a common new ground is possible.

Educational institutions can do a lot to begin the development of this new relational model. Since the 1970s, it has become customary for seminaries to create "field education" programs as part of the theological and ministerial curriculum. The purpose of these field education assignments is to allow seminarians to ground their theological studies in practical, real life application. Over the course of a four- or five-year master of divinity program, seminarians are assigned to supervised internship programs as chaplains in hospitals, social service agencies, prisons, and parishes. If Christianity is serious about engaging capitalism in a constructive conversation, seminary programs need to add an internship in corporate settings to the ministerial education curriculum. Theology students need to experience the legitimate sacrifice and selflessness required of workers engaged in the complex internal and external corporate relationships identified in Nash and McLennan's research. They will learn corporations are much more than profit machines. Seminarians also need to experience the complexity of decision-making in commerce, perhaps getting experience with board of directors or upper-level executive decisions. They need to understand the full context of such hard choices as allocating funds to infrastructure and inventory, rather than salaries and benefits, or the difficult decision to eliminate positions in order to protect the overall health of the corporation and save the maximum number of jobs as possible.

However, business students also need a different level of engagement with the religion-business issue. It is common for students in undergraduate and M.B.A. programs to do internships with corporations. For a serious conversation with Christianity, business, finance, and economics students need to experience the "collateral damage" of a capitalist economic system. They need to work in social service agencies, hearing the stories and seeing firsthand the effects of economic deprivation. They need to work on case studies of economic development projects in poor neighborhoods, but also meet the community leaders initiating these projects. They need to spend time with middle-aged workers who have lost their jobs to outsourcing, and adults working two or three minimum-wage jobs just to meet their bills. They need to sit in hospitals with mothers and fathers who have deficient medical coverage and are lost in a labyrinth of bureaucratic HMO red tape in their desperate efforts to secure medical attention for their sick child. Wizened by the human pain caused by the economic system, business students will have a better starting point in their discussions with religious leaders and theologians who increasingly use the poor and marginalized as a point of departure for their thinking about issues of economics.

American Christianity and capitalism never had an easy relationship. But they did have enough conceptual connections to maintain a tense but creative relationship that has benefited U.S. society. These two chief "forming agencies" of history are now two ships passing in the night, and only a new kind of conversation will help them see and appreciate each other as they move through the choppy waters of the contemporary world. With this kind of conversation, business leaders and economists and clergy and theologians may find they have more in common than they imagined.

Notes

1. A Christian and an economist by trade, Donald Hay believes in the incompatibility and irreconcilability between Christian values and a free-market system, but

he specifies that the conceptual chasm is really with the free-market Chicago school. Many in the Chicago school have tried to apply the notion of self interest to every aspect of life, including marriage, and their concepts, according to Hay, collide in Christian conceptions of creation, providence in history, and revelation of God's will to humanity. The average religious leader would not make such distinctions. See: Hay, D. (1989). Economics Today: A Christian Critique Leicester, UK: Inter-Varsity Press.

2. Tracy also provides an extensive series of the fundamental questions for the game of conversation that are at the root of the religious quest, pp. 86-87.

Bibliography

Cox, H. (1999). The market as God: Living in the new dispensation. Atlantic Monthly, March.

Dolfsma, Wilfred. (2001). Metaphors of knowledge in economics, Review of Social Economy, March, Vol. 59, No. 1.

Economist (March 13, 2004), p. 13.

Iannaccone, L., Finke, R, & Stark, R. (1997). Deregulating religion: The economics of Church and State, Economic Inquiry, April, Vol. 35.

Marshall, A. (1930). Principles of economics. London: Macmillan.

Meeks, M.D. (1989). God the economist: The doctrine of God and political economy. Minneapolis: Fortress Press.

Mitroff, I. & Denton, E. (1999). A spiritual audit of corporate America: A hard look at spirituality, religion, and values in the workplace. San Francisco: Jossey-Bass.

Moore. L.L.(1994). Selling God: American religion in the marketplace of culture. New York: Oxford University Press.

Nash, L & McLennan, S. (2001). Church on Sunday, work on Monday: The challenge of fusing Christian values with business life. San Francisco: Jossey-Bass.

Nelson, R.N. (1991). Reaching for heaven on earth: The theological meaning of economics. Rowman & Littlefield.

Nelson, R.N. (2001). Economics as religion: From Samuelson to Chicago and beyond. University Park, PN: Pennsylvania State University Press.

Novak, M. (1982, 1991). The spirit of democratic capitalism. Lanham: Madison Books.

Stark, R. & Finke, R. (2000). Acts of faith: Explaining the human side of religion. Berkeley: University of California Press.

Tracy, D. (1987). Plurality and ambiguity: hermeneutics, religion, hope. New York: Harper and Row.

Weber, M. (1930, 2002). The protestant ethic and the spirit of capitalism. New York: Routledge.

Welch, P.J. & Mueller, J.J. (June, 2001). The relationships of religion to economics. Review of Social Economy, Vol. 59, No. 2.

White, L. (1969). The iconography of Temperantia and the virtuousness of technology. In: Theodore K. Rabb and Jerrold E. Seigel (Eds.), Action and conviction in early modern Europe: Essays in memory of E.H. Harbison. Princeton, NJ: Princeton University Press.

Wuthnow, R. (1993). Christianity in the 21st century: Reflections on the challenges ahead. New York: Oxford University Press.

"Disconnected at the Roots": How Gaps in the Catholic Social Doctrine Impede Dialog and Action on Economic Justice

Stephen V. Arbogast

Three years ago, I reviewed the American Bishops' Pastoral Letter *"Economic Justice for All"* as part of a Church History course. It quickly produced a "through the Looking Glass" sensation. I found the bishops' perspective on the economy and on business unnerving, even surreal. Some 30 years of working for an international energy company has instilled some feel for how economies and the global market function. The economic sphere, as discussed by the bishops, was a world I did not recognize.

This realization was swiftly followed by a second—that the Pastoral Letter had failed to stimulate either ongoing dialogue among the church and the business community or tangible changes in the way business operates. I know of no corporations that use the Pastoral Letter as a reference document when they adopt or revise ethics policies. Outside the Catholic universities, leading business schools do not teach from the Letter in coursework on business ethics. Graduate economics courses seldom, if ever, refer to it. Where then is the evidence of the Pastoral Letter having led to enduring dialogue or change?

At its publication, the Bishops' Letter was explicitly put forward as a "teaching document" addressed to a broad audience:

> We write, then, first of all to provide guidance for members of our own Church . . . At the same time, we want to add our voice to the public debate

> about the direction in which the U.S. economy should be moving. We seek the cooperation and support of those who do not share our faith or tradition.[1]

If such was the aim, the Pastoral Letter can only be assessed as having had a negligible impact on the non-Catholic audiences. Confirmation of sorts for this verdict came in "A Decade After Economic Justice for All," in which the National Conference of Catholic Bishops looked back on the Pastoral Letter's impact. Totting up the results, here is what they wrote:

> The economic justice pastoral was an enormous undertaking. Years in preparation, it generated wide discussion, occasional controversy, and much activity...In the years after the pastoral, nine of every ten dioceses conducted education sessions in parishes; 60% strengthened legislative advocacy; more than half held sessions with businesses, labor, or farm representatives; and a majority assessed their personnel policies.[2]

On their face, these are modest results. They are also almost entirely internal to the American Church. Nothing is cited to evidence impact on the public debate. There is also nothing identified in terms of tangible result, legislative or otherwise. The bishops can be excused for putting their best foot forward on the Pastoral Letter's impact; however, an objective assessment would have to conclude that neither effective dialogue with the non-Catholic target audiences—business, policymakers, and economists—nor a major impact on public policy has materialized.

How did it come to be that this Pastoral Letter, so controversial upon its publication, ended up producing such limited results? Partly this can be attributed to the business community's defensiveness, which causes it to treat ethical criticism as attacks to be deflected or ignored. Partially, however, it can also be traced to major gaps in Catholic Social Doctrine (CSD). These gaps are the result of a failure to incorporate fundamental tenets of economics into the Church's thinking. The gaps in question are large ones. Leaving them unrecognized and unresolved is antithetical to both the Church's role as teacher and its desire to influence the public debate. Because CSD evidences little understanding of why business and the economy work as they do, Church criticism and recommendations are easily dismissed as "uninformed." Because CSD does in fact suffer from serious conceptual gaps on economics, its policy descriptions are easily attacked as likely to prove counterproductive. Ultimately, this means that the Church can stir controversy by criticizing but can't be persuasive that it has answers to the issues it raises. Without the ability to persuade those who work in the market place, Church advocacy eventually founders on the rock of ineffectiveness. Then the Church moves on, focusing attention on more prospective matters. Arguably, this is exactly what happened during the last nine years. Faced with a period of staggering corporate scandals, the American Church has largely been a bystander.

This less than satisfactory position can be repaired fairly easily. CSD on economic justice does not need to be dismantled and redone. It must, however, undergo a process of integrating major economic tenets into doctrine. CSD must connect at the root with basic economic theory. Undertaking this process first involves identifying the gaps that must be filled. Foremost, among these is acknowledging that CSD has a blind spot regarding economic growth. Integrating economic growth into doctrine will then compel CSD to reconcile its framework with other core economic tenets, e.g., the need to consider opportunity costs and risk, the role of economic freedom and incentives, the necessity of fiscal discipline, and the unavoidability of adjustment costs. A different understanding of the market economy should emerge out of this process. CSD should come to recognize business as the essential creator of growth; free markets should come to be seen as contributing both to growth **and** the ethical regulation of business. The connection between market efficiency and the ethical behavior of business will come into focus along with the "slippery slopes" that tempt when market inefficiencies arise. The ethical role of regulatory institutions charged with maintaining/improving the market's efficiency will then become clearer. Perhaps most important, fresh Church thinking will be stimulated on the conditions, which allow the poor to emerge from poverty. Said differently, the economic dimensions of the Option for the Poor will be broadened beyond wealth transfer to incorporate creating the necessary conditions for growth and development.

This process of doctrinal integration will have positive practical consequences. For one thing, it should open exciting new vistas of joint advocacy and political action. Numerous actors within the U.S. economy are concerned with business ethics, corporate governance, and the maintenance of efficient markets. Many of these same groups, however, recognize the primary importance of growth and the contribution made by free markets. Instinctively, these bodies have perceived the Church to be uninterested in what produces economic growth and what perfects efficient markets. Consequently, there has been little in the way of effective alliances. By connecting with essential economics, the American Church's possibilities for political alliance on economic justice matters will be substantially broadened. A rejuvenated dialogue will be there for the taking. And within such a dialogue, the Church may then lend its full weight to the specifics of which conditions and protections can best advance the cause of the poor within the market economy.

Disconnected at the Roots—Identifying the Gaps in CSD

We begin then by identifying the essential gaps in CSD as regards economics. Insight into this issue can be gained by asking: "in what way is the Pastoral Letter 'disconnected' from economic principles?"

The beginning of an answer can be found at the outset of Chapter II, "The Christian Vision of Life":

There on display is a basic divide with economics as regards the nature of creation. For the bishops, creation is bountiful:

> God is the creator of heaven and earth; creation proclaims God's glory and is "very good." Fruitful harvests, bountiful flocks, a loving family are God's blessings on those who heed God's word. Such is the joyful refrain that echoes throughout the Bible.[3]

This vision, the Bishops imply, was spoiled by human sinfulness; poverty and suffering result from humanity's selfish nature rather than the difficulties of coping with a harsh natural state:

> Though created to enjoy intimacy with God and the fruits of the earth, Adam and Eve disrupted God's design by trying to live independently of God. Alienation from God pits brother against brother in a cycle of war and vengeance...Sin simultaneously alienates human beings from God and shatters the solidarity of the human community.[4]

This is a familiar and fundamental perspective, grounded in the Bible's opening book. It is seldom noticed, however, that it also establishes a framework at odds with economic theory. For the economist, scarcity is the fundamental condition of nature and society. The condition of scarcity is intrinsic to creation and to the human condition. Economics is about confronting this fundamental scarcity with optimal organization, effort, and creativity. This task is arduous and unfolds over centuries of time. A flavor of the economists' perspective is provided by Robert Heilbroner in his classic work *The Worldly Philosophers*:

> Since he came down from the trees, man has faced the problem of survival...Yet man is not to be too severely censured for his failure to achieve a paradise on earth. It is hard to wring a livelihood from the surface of this planet. It staggers the imagination to think of the endless efforts which must have been expended in the first domestication of animals, the discovery of planting seeds, in the first working of surface ores.[5]

Notice the diametrically opposite views. The bishops emphasize a bountiful creation, which is then damaged and wasted through human sinfulness. For the economist, creation is at best uneven and difficult to master. Man is to be excused to some extent for failing to create a paradise on earth, for the task of providing for the basics has proved difficult enough.

In fact, there should be less of a distinction here than these quotes suggest. The bishops are quoting from Genesis as they establish their foundational framework. In doing so, they fail to mention God's punishment to Adam and Eve upon their expulsion from the Garden of Eden:

> Cursed be the ground because of you! In toil shall you eat its yield all the days of your life. Thorns and thistles shall it bring forth to you as you eat of the plants of the field. By the sweat of your face shall you get bread to eat, until you return to the ground from which you were taken.[6]

This description of nature bears similarities to Heilbroner's; indeed, one could posit that economists see a post-Fall world as it is and deal with it. It is interesting, however, that the Bishops don't cite this passage. By avoiding it and its implications, the Pastoral Letter is able to frame economic issues entirely in terms of sinfulness and the need for moral restoration. But in proceeding in this way, the bishops sidestep the implications of nature's scarcity as the fundamental condition of economic life. One principal implication is that before one can declare the existence of economic rights and distribute the bounty, that bounty must first be created from the post-Fall world's inhospitable nature. What consumes the economist then is exactly what the bishops abstract away—that issues of production must perforce come before issues of distribution and that the benefits associated with changing patterns of distribution must be measured not just in terms of who gives up something for someone else, but whether the community as a whole ends up poorer.

And so we come to the specific disconnects among CSD and microeconomics. This begins with the central response of the economist to a world of scarcity, which is the pursuit of "efficiency." If productive resources are limited, they must be organized optimally—only in this way can production from limited resources be maximized. Free markets are the optimal organization for informing producers what customers want and are willing to pay. Their "optimizing" result-no greater amount of goods can be produced from available inputs at a price customers are willing to pay-in other words, an optimally efficient match of production and customer demand. Finally, the efficient market is dynamic. At each moment there are unsatisfied customers who would willingly buy if prices only declined or goods improved in quality. Incentives for producers to innovate and expand are constantly present.

This sensibility for market efficiency is almost wholly lacking in the Pastoral Letter. There is no conviction of respect for the organizing efficiency of free markets. Instead there is at most a grudging acknowledgement that free markets somehow work; this sense is then swiftly put aside as the bishops turn to their focus, the economic shortcomings of the day. In the process, they reveal a lack of respect for free markets in the alacrity with which they endorse interventions and controls. "Fair prices" as opposed to free market prices are put forth as a policy remedy. Producer "cooperation" is endorsed to ensure that "fair prices" and "just wages" can be achieved. The following excerpts illustrate the point:

> Today a greater spirit of **partnership and teamwork** is needed, competition alone will not do the job . . .[7]
>
> Therefore, the government must act to ensure that this goal is achieved **by coordinating** general economic policy . . .[8]
>
> It is in this light that we understand Pope John Paul II's recommendation that society makes provision for **overall planning** in the economic domain . . .

> what is in question is **a just and rational coordination** within the framework of which the initiative of individuals, free groups, and local work centers and complexes must be safeguarded.[9]
>
> An equitable trading system that will help the Poor should . . . ensure that exports from developing countries receive **fair prices** needed by agreement among the trading partners.[10]
>
> Employers are obliged to treat their employees as persons paying them **fair wages** . . . workers have a right to wages and other benefits sufficient to sustain life in dignity.[11]

The bishops' willingness to embrace market intervention reveals a second critical disconnect, a disregard for "opportunity cost." For the economist, price controls and the like produce sub-optimal results. There may be political, social, or national security reasons for intervening, but economists recognize that such actions come at a cost. The shortfall versus optimal efficiency is the "opportunity cost" of the policy intervention/control. Again, this is a sensibility lacking in the Pastoral Letter. There is little recognition that the proposed interventions carry costs, which should be weighed to assure that "all-in" a better result is being achieved.

The combination of minimal respect for free markets and insensitivity to opportunity costs proves a major problem when the bishops come to making policy recommendations. Take as an example, the bishops' recommendation to establish "economic rights," meaning a right for all citizens, unconnected to work, to some basket of minimum food, shelter, health care, and education. This is put forth without any estimate of cost, any serious proposals as to how it would be funded, and any assessment of the net impact such a massive new entitlement would have on the economy over time. There is, for example, no real consideration of the new entitlements' impact on government deficits and ensuing inflation. Instead, the sensibility is "something is fundamentally right, so people should have it now":

> We believe the time has come for a similar experiment in securing economic rights: the creation of an order that guarantees the minimum conditions of human dignity in the economic sphere for every person.[12]

There is an essential lack of realism inherent in proposals involving massive new costs with no provision for their funding. It, therefore, is not surprising that the bishops' call for a New American Experiment on economic rights has been ignored. Instead, the U.S. instituted welfare reform with the twin objectives of reintroducing welfare recipients into the workforce and cutting governmental expenditure. Well grounded in an assessment of costs/benefits, sensitive to fiscal concerns, and complimentary to a market economy, welfare reform provides a noteworthy contrast to the bishops' approach.

The disregard for or treatment of other key concepts confirms the extent to which the Pastoral Letter is disconnected from economics. The consumer is hardly mentioned in the Pastoral Letter, and then only as a victim of consumerism and a buyer of unnecessary luxury goods. For the economist, the consumer is the prime beneficiary of free markets. Over time, free and competitive markets deliver more and better goods/services at declining prices. This form of utility is largely absent in the bishops' thinking. It, therefore, cannot be weighed in any assessment of policy costs/benefits (which as noted are also not made in the Pastoral Letter). The same is true regarding the treatment of competition. The bishops' perspective is that competition is destructive of human dignity, dangerous, and wasteful. Competition's role in spurring innovation, expanding choice, and creating new industries with jobs while driving down costs and prices, is ignored. Perhaps most illustrative of the bishops' lack of connectedness with the economic sphere is their treatment of risk. Risk is a significant, often decisive factor in the economics of business, and in setting the level of incentives required to induce investment, innovation, and growth. Yet, risk merits a single, fleeting reference in the Pastoral Letter.

Some collective sense of the Pastoral Letter's disconnect with economics can be gained from the following summary:

Market Economic Concept	CSD
Efficiency	
Optimal production from available resources	Not a concern, except where adjustment impacts human dignity
Consumer	
Beneficiary of efficiency via more/better goods @ declining prices	Not seen as beneficiary; focus is on excess of consumerism
Profit	
Signal of strong demand and incentive to invest	Not valued; perceived as rooted in greed and prone to excess
Competition	
Driver of efficiency and innovation	Seen as unnecessary, wasteful and damaging to human dignity
Growth	
Product of efficiency, innovation, and capital accumulation	Not a focus except to allow people to realize productive potential
Distribution	
Based upon contribution to efficiency, innovation, growth	Core Concern; should be based upon need, economic rights, Preferential Option for the Poor

Repairing the Gaps in CSD

What then is the net product of these disconnects as regards Catholic Social Doctrine and economic justice? Cumulatively, these disconnects add up to a blind spot towards economic growth. By neglecting efficiency, the conditions that spur or impede innovation, and the need to weigh costs and benefits carefully when making policy, the bishops ignore the conditions that create growth. As a consequence, the bishops imply that such matters have little to do with achieving a more just economic world.

This perspective should be changed to one **emphasizing the role of economic growth as an enabler of economic justice.** This implies a positive, proactive interest in the conditions that encourage growth and development. It would value the fact that economic growth creates new wealth that can enable reallocation to occur without necessarily making one group poorer to benefit another. It would connect with the fact that growth creates jobs organically while providing incentives for employees to train workers and assimilate immigrants. The Church should want to pursue its economic justice agenda within a context of growth. It is within such environments that general standards can most readily be raised.

Thus, the first CSD gap to be repaired is to incorporate the need for economic growth into Church Doctrine on economic justice. Doing so will prove an immense opportunity. It will force the Church to decide for itself what promotes economic growth and development. In this process, the contributions to development made by fiscal discipline, rule of law, political stability, public priority to education, and openness to international trade will need to be considered and incorporated into Doctrine. A fresh set of insights will then open up as to why certain regions, including such traditional Catholic areas as Latin America, stagnate or even decline (see Argentina) while nations less favorably endowed (see Asian rim) have advanced dramatically.

A special opportunity then awaits the Church in considering what conditions best promote the advancement of the poor. There has been valuable recent work in this area contributed by economists, most notably by Peruvian economist Hernando de Soto. In works such as "*The Mystery of Capital, Why Capitalism Succeeds in the West and Fails Everywhere Else,*" deSoto shines special attention on the lack of legal protection for the property rights of the poor. The essential argument is that the poor find their most basic means for accumulating capital, which is home ownership, blocked by indifferent and corrupt legal systems. Consequentially, there is no incentive to save and no mortgage capital with which to start small businesses. A recent *Foreign Affairs* article put it thusly: "In country after country in the developing world, squatters' rights prevail because the obstacles to obtaining legal titles defeat most of the poor." As de Soto explains,

> In Egypt, the person who wants to acquire and legally register a lot on a state-

> owned desert land must wend his way through at least 77 bureaucratic procedures at 31 public and private agencies...This explains why 4.7 million Egyptians have chosen to build their dwellings illegally. If, after building his home, a settler decides he would now like to be a law-abiding citizen and purchase the rights to his dwelling, he risks having it demolished, paying a steep fine and serving up to 10 years in prison.
>
> Egypt is no exception. In Peru, building a home on state-owned land requires 207 procedural steps at 52 government offices, says deSoto. In Haiti, obtaining a lease on government land–a preliminary requirement to buying–takes 65 steps.[12]

Clearly-defined property rights emerge as a cornerstone of legal and ethical behavior within an economy. They produce positive externalities, which are benefits shared by everyone. Clear titles channel economic activity into the legal market. Utilities can put in services-confident that they know where to bill and their customers have some means to pay. Governments have the necessary information to size and direct services and collect taxes. Local capital markets based upon mortgages can then finance business or an education. When such property rights are thus extended to the poor, the basis is laid for the primary means of upward mobility out of poverty-family business and education for the next generation. Incorporating a concern such as this, property rights for the poor, into CSD would begin a process of grounding the Preferential Option for the Poor into a practical growth-oriented economic framework.

Thinking through how to assist the poor to advance within the market economy will engage the Church in the second major CSD "gap repair." This involves coming to terms with the market economy and integrating market-based perspectives into CSD's ethical framework. The Church's present indifference to growth and to the free markets that foster it contributes to a failure to understand the ethical structure of market economies. This, in turn, handicaps the Church's practical approach to the promotion of economic justice. Market-based solutions that enhance justice go unrecognized and numerous potential alliance possibilities are missed. For these opportunities to become clearer, the ethical construction of the market economy must be examined more closely.

Three distinct steps are involved in this effort:

1. Understanding the ethical contribution of efficient markets.
2. Understanding the legal framework which surrounds developed markets and how this framework advances ethical standards over time.
3. Connecting both efficient markets and today's legal framework to CSD's economic justice concerns.

The key word in this context is "efficient." Markets characterized by efficiency display transparency and competition that discipline many ethical abuses typically of concern to the Church. Efficient markets tend to erode away excess profits. Likewise, they tend to redistribute income from producers to consumers by driving down prices while demanding enhanced quality. Of course, many poor benefit from these trends as consumers—e. g. "low prices every day" at Wal-Mart. It is for exactly these reasons that many businessmen dislike efficient markets. Indeed one can observe two great corrupt themes in a story like that of Enron's—first a desire to "rig" product markets (e.g. California's electricity) and second a desire to manipulate the stock market by providing false financial reports.

Because the contribution of efficient markets is so great, and includes a huge contribution to proper business conduct, the common good of society has a great stake in their protection and promotion. However, efficient markets place all businesses under competitive pressure and punish those who fail. Consequently, market efficiency is always under attack by those who would pursue anti-competitive tactics or consolidate their rivals to extinction. Thus, the legal context around the "efficient" market has come to be characterized by a network of regulatory watchdogs (e.g. SEC, FTC) and independent information sources (e.g. Moody's, S&P). These bodies actively preserve and promote market efficiency. They restrain consolidating forces and maintain standards of required information disclosure; this helps enable the markets' dynamics to continue their intense, creative, and disciplinary work.

Why should this fabric of market-embracing law and disclosure be important to CSD? Because it constitutes the essence of the necessary ethical framework which Pope John Paul II identified as the central ingredient needed if market-based economics were to provide just treatment for their societies. Writing in *Centesimus Annus,* the Pope addressed whether capitalism should be the model for developing countries thusly:

> The answer is obviously complex. If by "capitalism" is meant an economic system that recognizes the fundamental and positive role of business, the market, private property, and the resulting responsibility for the means of production, as well as free human creativity in the economic sector, then the answer is certainly in the affirmative...But if by "capitalism" is meant a system in which freedom in the economic sector is not circumscribed within a strong juridical framework which places it at the service of human freedom in its totality and sees it as a particular aspect of that freedom, the core of which is ethical and religious, then the reply is certainly negative.[14]

As can be seen, the pope clearly appreciates the benefits to be gained from free market capitalism, while also sensing the need to constrain its abusive potential within a strong legal framework. That first line of legal constraint preserves and promotes market efficiency. There next comes a second surrounding framework. These are the laws and regulatory bodies that express society's demands for standards of conduct and principles of wealth distribution. These are the entities, which enforce labor standards, arbitrate industrial disputes, provide essential information to consumers, and which tax and redistribute wealth. Adding this second layer to the first completes a "strong juridical framework . . . the core of which is religious and ethical." In terms of conceptual design, it looks as follows:

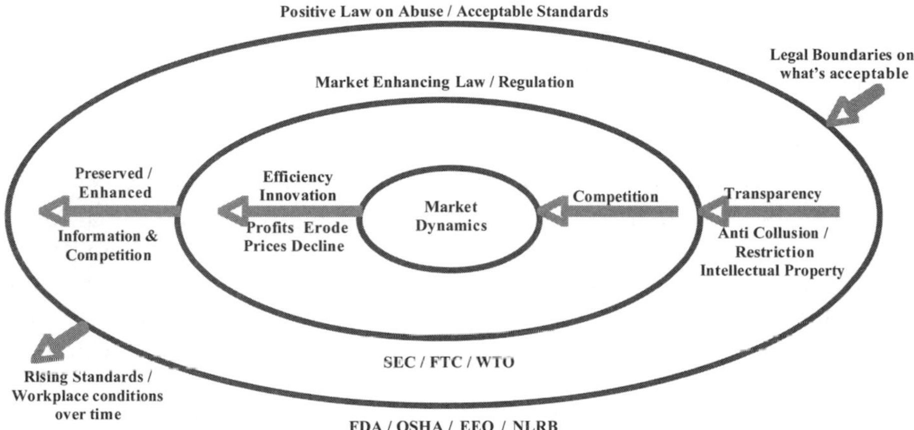

It is within this framework that many of the bishops' wishes for policy changes would need to be worked. Yet, the existence of this juridical framework and the means for influencing it are absent from the discussion of specific economic issues in the Pastoral Letter. This is most unfortunate. Within this framework lie many natural allies for the Church to engage in its pursuit of more just conditions in the economy. Using the above conceptual design as something of a map, new options for promoting economic justice in the public sector can readily be spotted.

Using a Repaired CSD to Advance Economic Justice

Embracing market-based growth and the market's ethical construction will have two practical benefits for advancing the Church's economic justice agenda. First, it will render the Church more discerning about which issues to take on, and in what sequence. Second, it will open up new and diverse political partnerships for the Church to employ, case by case, on specific justice issues.

Actually advancing the Church's agenda requires moving beyond the articulation of general principles. It also requires prioritizing issues in terms of advocacy and political action. This prioritization is, in turn, influenced by, and then the object of, a program of political action in alliance with like-minded groups. This approach has served the American Church well of late on "right to life" issues. Once content to articulate its anti-abortion/capital punishment case in isolation, the Church has learned to team with evangelical groups on the former and liberal elements on the latter. Once re-grounded in market-based economics, a similar Church strategy for effective political action opens up on economic justice.

A particular opportunity for new alliances beacons today in the area of corporate ethics and governance. The Pastoral Letter touched on this matter in writing:

> The question of how to relate the rights and responsibilities of shareholders to those of the other people and communities affected by corporate decisions is complex and insufficiently understood. We, therefore, urge serious, long-term research and experimentation in this area.[15]

Almost two decades later, we know more about these issues. Through the lens of the efficient market, one can see that when corporate management is able to subvert the integrity of accounting information and where boards of directors lack the independence to safeguard corporate controls, the market can be manipulated with severe consequences for shareholders, employees, and communities. Said differently, it is doubtful that WorldCom and Enron would have been able to practice fraud on a "bet-the-firm" scale if their public accountants and Boards had not been suborned.

A renovated structure of accountability has been legislated in the wake of these scandals. Whether it goes far enough is open to question. There remains, for example, no requirement for companies to rotate their public audit firms periodically, and the auditor is still paid by the management it audits. Almost certainly, the reforms enacted to date will be subject to a relentless counterattack alleging they are excessive and too costly. Groups committed to improving corporate ethics will need to sustain focus on these issues. Happily, these groups are more numerous and aroused today. They include investor groups, public pension funds, corporate watchdog organizations, the staffs of the regulatory agencies, and corporations committed to leading on corporate governance. The Church should actively ally with these groups. It is hard to conceive of an issue more conducive to the American Church working out a market-based approach to economic justice and to testing the possibilities for political alliances.

When prioritizing among possibilities for political action, the Church will naturally look for an issue with possibilities for advancing the Option for the Poor. One issue, which should commend itself to the Church's attention, is NAFTA; more specifically, the Church should be interested in how to assure that the economic gains from NAFTA make their way to the grassroots level on both sides of the Mexican-American border.

The Church is well positioned to be influential on this issue. It has grassroots organization on both sides of the border and the ear of many adherents. It also has historic skills in mediating among communities and authorities. This time, a rethink of CSD could also equip the Church with new issues and new allies.

One of these new issues is the competitiveness of Mexico as a supply source for the U.S. market. As a supplier to the U.S., Mexico enjoys a significant locational advantage. Yet, manufacturers increasingly prefer to set up shop near Shanghai rather than in Nuevo Leon. Why? At the risk of oversimplifying, Mexico confronts business with major political risks, poor quality public services, and a less productive labor force. Reports proliferate of shipments pilfered or stolen outright. Electricity and gas are not readily available for new plants or expansions. Insurance is hard to purchase and public education remains a secondary priority. This amounts to a major failure of the Mexican public sector to provide the basic ingredients for economic growth. Of course, the poor suffer the gravest consequences, felt in terms of jobs that don't materialize, legal and physical threats impinging on daily life, and the immigration of loved ones who head north.

This issue is timely. Recognition of Mexico's emerging "competitiveness issue" has surfaced in the wake of NAFTA's 10th anniversary. On the American side of the border, attention is also focusing on devising means to regulate the inflow of new immigrants and so better secure the border. Achieving a more dynamic economic environment within Mexico, especially northern Mexico, is a widely accepted policy goal. The Church can play an important role in bringing about the legal and political reforms, which are essential to achieving this outcome. In the process, the Church can also fight to assure that advances in legal protections include the poor's neighborhoods and property rights. The conjunction of concerns over "Mexican competitiveness" and "Regulating the immigration flow" is tailor-made for measures, which enable the would-be immigrants to compete for jobs and found enterprises in their existing locale. A Church working this agenda from the vantage point of economic competitiveness and enhanced legality on both sides of the border will find a surprising diversity of potential allies-from local community organizers to free trade groups to investors in existing and new plants.

Few issues illustrate the opportunities inherent in formulating a market-oriented CSD like NAFTA. To realize this potential, however, some "role" issues that historically have confused the Church message on economic matters must be sorted out.

Which Role: Prophet, Advocate, or Teacher?

One final problem revealed in the Pastoral Letter is also a key to the Church finding its way to a repaired doctrine of economic justice-this involves a clearer definition of the roles the Church seeks to play and the ways in which these roles interact.

As noted earlier, the Pastoral Letter aspired to be a "teaching document." Yet, its contents were more in keeping with its prophetic and advocacy roles. By prophetic, we refer to its special mission of drawing upon scripture to help identify and protest of unjust conditions experienced anywhere by anyone, but most especially by the poor. As advocate, the Church adopts the cause of those unjustly disadvantaged and fights for immediate redress. The Church then calls upon the faithful to see these causes and adopt the fight as their own. In essence, this is what the Pastoral Letter endeavored to do.

The teaching role, however, is about something broader than the identification of injustice and immediate struggle. In its larger sense, the teaching role begins with a comprehensive understanding of what is true and what works. When these aspects of the Teaching role are neglected, advocacy can be undermined by unrealistic policy suggestions and ineffective action plans. When this happens, the prophetic role can be left stranded-its outcries left to reverberate and then fade in a world of too many problems and not enough solutions. Arguably, this is what the Pastoral Letter ended up achieving.

This paper is then a call for the American Church to revisit the roots of Catholic Social Doctrine in search of greater understanding about what is true economically and what works in the economy. The studied neutrality of the Pastoral Letter, not taking sides in the debate on economic systems, also served to excuse the Church from resolving for itself "what works." It is time to move beyond this. Pope John Paul II has already prepared the way. It does not require an uncritical acceptance of the market to recognize that it provides the soundest foundation from which to advance the cause of economic justice for all.

Notes

1. National Conference of Catholic Bishops (2000). Economic justice for all (p. 27). Washington, D. C.: United States Catholic Conference, Inc.
2. Ibid., p. 5
3. Ibid., p. 32
4. Ibid., p. 32
5. Heilbroner, R. (1961). *The Worldly Philosophers* (p. 7). New York: Time Incorporated.
6. The *New Jerusalem Bible,* Genesis, 3 (17-19). New York: Doubleday, 1985, pp. 20-21.
7. *Economic justice for all,* op. Cit., p. 112
8. Ibid., p. 69
9. Ibid., p. 118
10. Ibid., p. 95
11. Ibid., p. 42
12. Ibid., p. 49
13. Samuelson, R. J. (2001). The *Spirit of Capitalism,* review, January / February, pp. 206-207. New York: Foreign Affairs, Council on Foreign Relations.
14. Neuhaus, Fr. R. J. (1999). *Appointment in Rome* (p. 80). New York: The Crossroads Publishing Company.
15. *Economic justice for all.* op. Cit., p. 116

The Market's Benevolent Tendencies

Art Carden

Introduction

Picture two meals.

The first meal is that available to a Scottish nobleman in the late 17th century. The meal probably includes cheese, dark bread, and meat. Maybe he has seasonal fruits and vegetables and a glass of French wine. The second meal is that available to a Scottish peasant during the same period. The peasant's meal is little more than a thin mixture of sweet milk and oats. The differences between the two were substantial.

Now fast-forward to the year 2004 and picture two different meals. This time, though, picture Bill Gates' dinner, and compare it to Joe Six-pack's dinner. Bill probably has the finest meats, cheeses, breads, fruits, vegetables, and wines that money can buy. Joe may have meatloaf, dinner rolls, canned vegetables, and sweet tea. The differences are trifling.[1]

In sharp contrast to the plight of his forebears, Joe Six-pack enjoys a meal that differs only slightly from the meal Bill enjoys. Where Bill might eat filet mignon with an assortment of sides, Joe might eat a slightly inferior cut of meat with sides that are very similar in every meaningful respect to those

---

*An earlier version of this essay was presented at the Loyola Institute's Annual International and Ecumenical Conference at Loyola University New Orleans, June 10-12, 2004. This research was made possible by a Book Fellowship from the Ludwig von Mises Institute and travel grants from the Institute for Humane Studies' Hayek Fund for Scholars and from the Center for New Institutional Social Sciences. I thank Walter Block, Byron L. Carden, Douglass C. North, John VC Nye, Eric Rovie, and conference participants for comments and suggestions. All errors are mine.

available to Bill. The differences between the goods available to the rich and poor in economic history were substantial, whereas there are few functional differences between the goods available to Bill and Joe. They probably both enjoy their meals in a climate-controlled dining room. Both have stainless steel forks, spoons, and knives. Both have numerous changes of clothes, air conditioning, and cars. Several centuries of capitalism and free markets have generated radically egalitarian outcomes: the difference between rich and poor 300, 200, even 100 years ago meant the difference between who heard the great orchestras and who didn't. Today, it is the difference between who has Bose surround sound and who makes do with Sony and JVC.

The market is a great social equalizer, but merchants and businessmen still have a bad name. Some Christian leaders look down on merchants and on the very process of exchange. It exploits the poor. It produces rampant inequality. It destroys the environment. The free market encourages people to focus on filthy lucre rather than their responsibility to "do justice, love mercy, and walk humbly with (their) God" (Micah 6:8). And so on.

Milton Friedman (1970) wrote that the corporation's social responsibility is to be profitable. Many point to his article as an example of how we are not to think about the social responsibility of business. In our enlightened time, aren't we above and beyond crass commercialism? Aren't we above the narrow pursuit of gain, often at another's expense? Shouldn't we be helping one another? Shouldn't we help people who need...help? Should we eschew the comforts and baubles of modern life to pour ourselves out in service to our unfortunate fellow man?

Maybe. Service to the church is extremely important; however, the institutions and organizations of commercial society are critical to the attainment of various social goals and mores. Production does not occur in a vacuum—it is important for the social critic to realize that the spectacular wealth enjoyed in the western world was not an accident.

The market's bad name among progressive religious scholars is wholly undeserved. It provides hundreds of millions with standards of living that would have boggled the minds of the great kings of yesteryear. In what follows, I illuminate some of the most important aspects of the market economy.

I do several things in this essay. First, I provide a brief overview of market exchange. Second, I discuss its effects. Third, I apply what we know about the market's egalitarian tendencies to the question of globalization. I conclude in section VI.

Demonstrated Preference, Comparative Advantage, and the Benevolence of Trade

The Bible can tell us what one's preferences should be, but it is largely mute on social organization.[2] While lust after unrighteous mammon for its own sake is idolatrous, a world in which everyone pursues his own interests—whatever those may be—while staying within the boundaries prescribed by natural law will be a rich world indeed, providing a great bounty even to the least of these among us.

Ever since Adam Smith (and even before), economists have recognized that specialization and the division of labor are the wellsprings of abundance. The pin factory that Smith so famously observed produced many more pins in a day than someone working alone might have been able to produce in a year.[3] Why?

It's simple: *comparative advantage.* It is usually discussed in the first few chapters of any principles of microeconomics textbook—indeed, Paul Heyne, Peter Boettke, and David Prychitko devote chapter two of their classic *The Economic Way of Thinking* to comparative advantage—and the principle of comparative advantage shows us how specialization allows us to get more wealth using the same input.

Two important principles characterize exchange. The first is increased productivity. The second is that it exhausts all possible mutually beneficial exchanges, as 1986 Nobel Laureate James Buchanan has noted. In other words, the tendency in the market is for all possible exchanges that benefit two parties while harming no one to be made. In the long run, the tendency is for people to find and exploit all situations in which they can make themselves better off. By harnessing the force of self-interest and collating valuable information, the institutions of commercial society have become the modern world's horn of plenty.

But is this *ethical*? Is it in line with the Bible's teachings? Is the crass pursuit of material gain a worthwhile goal? If we drop the unwarranted assumption that the pursuit of self-interest is self-evidently crass, the answer is "absolutely." In an attempt to reformulate welfare economics, Murray Rothbard showed that exchange creates wealth because it allows people to exchange one set of goods and services for a set of goods and services they prefer.

So what are we to say of the effects of state intervention on "social" utility? We cannot say with certainty that intervention "increases" social utility because it involves demonstrable harm to at least one person; conversely, the subjective theory of value prevents us from saying that intervention "decreases" social utility. Extending the analysis in "Toward A Reconstruction," Rothbard (1970, p. 13) takes this up in his follow-up to *Man, Economy, and State, Power and Market*: "The first step in analyzing intervention is to contrast the *direct* (italics in original) effect on the utilities of the participants, with the effect of a free society. When people are free to act, they will always act in a way that they believe will maximize their utility, i.e., will raise them to the highest possible position on their value scale."[4]

It follows, then, that the only welfare conclusion we can reach with *absolute certainty* is that coercive intervention will move the coerced agent to a lower position on his/her value scale. For the coerced agent, the state of the world that obtains in the absence of coercion is necessarily preferred *ex ante* to the state of the world that obtains under coercion.

When all is said and done, our conclusion on welfare analysis is this: the victims of coercion will, with absolute certainty, be moved to lower positions on their value scales, and the resultant changes in relative prices will prohibit such conclusions about whether or not the beneficiaries of coercion attain higher positions on their value scales. Without introducing value judgments, we can't say anything more.

Rich & Poor Yesterday and Today

Ethics and religion center on value judgments and the market is usually condemned on the grounds that it distributes wealth unevenly. This objection is untenable: "income distribution" has no operative meaning. Wealth isn't "distributed" by anyone; as Rothbard (1970, p. 241) notes, "(t)here is no distributional process apart from the production and exchange processes of the market; hence the very concept of 'distribution' becomes meaningless on the free market."

On the changing mode of income distribution as a result of the market process, Rothbard (1970, p. 241) continues: "Since 'distribution' is simply the result of the free exchange process, and since this process benefits all participants in the market and increases social utility, it follows directly that the 'distributional' results of the free market also increase social utility."

Do the facts match the theory? Are people made better off by exchange, commerce, and the pursuit of filthy lucre? To the extent that we can agree on what constitutes being made "better off," the answer is "yes." Donald McCloskey (1995) recorded that income per capita in Great Britain increased by a factor of 12 between the mid-18th century and the modern day. Peter Lindert (1995) and Lindert & Williamson (1983) point out that capitalism has substantially bettered the lot of the least of these among us, making them rich beyond anything we ever could have imagined a mere two decades ago, to say nothing of a few centuries ago.

Critics may point to the "worsening" income distribution—specifically, the top 5 percent of income earners take home a bigger slice of economic pie than they have traditionally—but money incomes may not be the right proxy for what we truly want to measure. As John Nye[5] points out, unequal incomes may not mean unequal lifestyles. The goods that are available to the poor are near-perfect substitutes for the goods that are available to the rich. In other words, they have very similar physical characteristics.

Access to goods rather than incomes *per se*[6] is what matters, and the convergence between rich and poor is most evident at the grocery store. For every high-end item—a fine cut of meat, specialty spaghetti sauce, whole-grain bread, fresh-ground coffee, or fine liquor—there is a cheaper substitute with almost identical physical, temporal, and spatial characteristics. The list of high-end goods for which we can find cheaper substitutes of virtually identical quality is endless; and the common man of today enjoys fineries of which the most powerful kings of yesteryear couldn't dream.

An Application: Globalization[7]

Specialization makes this possible; however, specialization is under attack because of the supposed deleterious effects of globalization. The economics of international trade are straightforward: to the extent that everyone is able to pursue his/her comparative advantage, everyone gets richer. Outsourcing to India yields higher productivity, cheaper products, and higher real incomes for everybody. In the long run, American consumers get better, cheaper products. Poverty-stricken Indians can earn higher incomes in an IT job and no longer face the threat of starvation. Valuable factors of production—labor and capital—can be directed into new lines of production, and a merchandise trade deficit naturally translates itself into a capital account surplus, which means higher investment, higher productivity, and more jobs domestically.

Alas, however, the politics of globalization aren't so simple. Technology jobs pop up all over India and Americans conclude that the sky is falling. Some people lose in the very short run, and those people are very, very visible. Politicians turn this into political mileage. You see your neighbor lose his job because his firm is outsourcing to India, and you conclude that globalization must be "A Very Bad Thing." The long run trend toward lower prices, higher quality, and better service is more subtle. Goods are cheaper. Service is better. You can call an 800 number and speak to a real person. These aren't as apparent as the immediate, concentrated costs of globalization.

Everybody wants to take an ethical stance on globalization. People point to low-wage factory or IT workers and say that globalization is an incomparable evil because people are paid low wages to work under wretched conditions. This reasoning always relies on an irrelevant comparison: wages are "low" and working conditions "wretched" by western standards. By local standards—the relevant comparison—working in a garment factory for 25 cents an hour is a major improvement over your alternatives.

This is instructive: well-intentioned interventions often lead to disastrous results. There was an uproar about Bangladeshi child labor a few years ago that led to outright bans on Bangladeshi imports using child labor. Naturally, a number of factories closed. So what did the child laborers do? They all went to school, right? They were liberated from the bonds of capitalist oppression and were free to "just be kids," right?

Wrong. They went from lives of abject poverty and starvation into factory jobs where they could earn relatively high wages. When the factories closed, some children starved. Others became prostitutes.[8] Those are the unintended consequences that the anti-globalization crowd isn't so quick to see.

In summary, the globalization debate focuses on one side of a cost-benefit analysis. It looks only at the costs, and it often misconstrues some of the benefits (child labor in the third world) as "costs." From a purely utilitarian perspective, outsourcing and globalization are unmitigated goods. Globalization lifts our standards of living while pulling many of the world's less fortunate out of abject poverty.

Institutions & Redistribution[9]

Almost all Christians would agree that the Common Faith contains a common ethical core, as well; in addition to "One Lord, one faith, one baptism, One God and Father of all, who is above all, and through all, and in you all" (Ephesians 4: 4-6, KJV), Christians share a body of common rules that govern human behavior. These are embodied in the Ten Commandments, the Beatitudes, and the Golden Rule.[10] It is uncontroversial to assert that we are to help those who cannot help themselves, that we are to love our neighbors as ourselves, and that we are to refrain from theft, murder, adultery, covetousness, and false witness.

The bone of contention appears not when we ask whether or not we are to love our neighbor as ourselves or whether or not we are to care for the poor, but when we ask how these virtues are to be manifested in the social environment. I will note first that the capitalist revolution that gave rise to the Christian socialist movement of the late 19th and early 20th centuries in fact worked a great benefit to the poor. Second, I will argue that well-intentioned formal institutions designed to redistribute wealth may in fact work to the detriment of the poor.

Formal rules have a pronounced impact on economic performance (North, 1990, 1991, 2004). They consist of the set of "thou shalts" and "thou shalt nots" decreed by the state, and different interpretations of scripture will yield different assessments of what the content of these rules should be. In the libertarian ideal, a state would be an organization that merely protects property rights in exchange for revenue—akin to the insurance company proposed in Hoppe (2001) and enforcing the commandments that "thou shalt not steal" and "thou shalt not kill." In the socialist ideal, a state acts to ensure that everyone has adequate material provision.

Where did Christian socialism come from? Christian socialists' aversion to capitalism stemmed from what they observed in the industrial economies of the United States and Western Europe. At the risk of oversimplifying the matter, the Christian socialists of the late 19th and 20th centuries felt that the unequal distribution of wealth between the proletarian working class and capitalist plutocrats was unacceptable. The plight of *les miserables* cried out for state intervention.

While money incomes were certainly unequal, it does not follow from this fact that the unfettered market wrought unambiguous social injustice. I mentioned above that Lindert (1995) and Lindert and Williamson (1983) show that the industrialization of Great Britain resulted in net welfare increases for the working class. In a collection of lectures delivered at the University of Buenos Aires in 1959 and published posthumously in 1979, Ludwig von Mises noted that the rise of capitalism in the 19th century provided greater opportunities for everyone. As Mises (1979, p. 7) eloquently puts it,

> The famous old story, repeated hundreds of times, that the factories employed women and children and that these women and children, before they were working in the factories, had lived under satisfactory conditions, is one of the greatest falsehoods of history. The mothers who worked in the factories had nothing to cook with; they did not leave their homes and their kitchens to go into the factories, they went into factories because they had no kitchens, and if they had a kitchen they had no food to cook in those kitchens.

He notes that the situation for the children was equally grim: "(T)he children did not come from comfortable nurseries. They were starving and dying" (Mises, 1979, p. 7).

The evidence indicates that the capitalist revolution of the 19th century was a great boon to the daily life of the common worker.[11] Even if this boon is insufficient, it is far from clear that state intervention will succeed in improving the lot of society's less fortunate.

Coercive redistribution is intuitively appealing: what better way to help the poor or advance equality than to take from those who have and give to those who have not? Why wouldn't Christians who believe that we should love our neighbor and care for the poor support redistributive policies? After all, the capitalists of the 19th century and the "robber barons" of the early 20th century certainly possessed the means to provide for those less fortunate.[12]

Economic theory teaches us that people do not act in a vacuum. The fundamental lesson of economics is that people respond to incentives, and a change in formal institutions (such as redistributive intervention) necessarily changes the structure of incentives in the long run and may, in fact, work to frustrate the entrepreneurial mechanisms that produced phenomena like Twelve. While the recipient of government largesse will see his consumption possibilities increase in the short run, the first-order effect of redistributive coercion is to increase uncertainty. Redistribution signals that the state cannot (and will not) credibly commit to respect for and maintenance of property rights. This will decrease the present value of potential investments and, at the margin, lead to lower levels of investment. Lower investment entails a reduction in the rate of economic growth and a potential reduction in future consumption possibilities for everyone.

Second, higher marginal tax rates—which are necessary if we are to effect a redistributive policy—will retard economic growth. High marginal tax rates on labor will reduce one's incentive to supply labor services. This is particularly damaging if we are taxing high-wage occupations. These tend to be occupations in which people are either augmenting a country's technological foundations (research and development, for example) or making entrepreneurial and managerial decisions regarding the allocation of factors of production (executives). Diminishing people's willingness to provide these types of labor services will retard economic growth.

High marginal taxes on capital will produce similar effects. Changing the prospective return to capital will affect investment decisions. Lower investment entails a smaller capital stock, which in turn entails lower future economic growth. The effect manifests itself largely in the form of lower wages: economic theory teaches us that in a sufficiently competitive market workers are paid their marginal value product[13], and their marginal value product will be an increasing function of available capital. Less capital implies a lower marginal value product, which in turn results in lower wages.

What of the incentives for the recipients of state *largesse*? While welfare reforms of the last decade have attempted to address this issue, transfer payments reduce one's incentive to produce by diminishing his/her wage at the margin. To illustrate, consider a situation in which someone wakes up on Monday morning and considers whether or not to work for the week. He can earn $240 by working a 40-hour week at a fast-food job, or he can earn $250 on welfare. If he decides to work, the opportunity cost of a week of labor is $250 in welfare payments, $10 more than what he would earn by working. Even if he can earn $280 by working (and enjoy a positive marginal wage of $30), the incentive to produce is drastically reduced by the possibility of welfare payments.[14]

Conclusions

What do we make of all this? Most importantly, there should be no acrimony between Christianity and commerce. Quite the contrary: the Christian should embrace commercial society because it provides humanity with good things—two good things in particular:

Commercial society makes us rich.
Commercial society makes us equal.

In spite of all this, commercial society is in grave danger. Capitalism has long been lambasted from the pulpits and in the court of public opinion. The great misfortune of it all is that we may very well be strangling the goose that lays the golden eggs.

In summary, Christians and other social reformers must look carefully at the unintended consequences of well-intentioned interventionism. Economic growth is anything but automatic; the phenomenal growth that characterizes the experience of the modern world was the result of a constellation of specific institutional factors, and the most charitable statement we can make about redistributive intervention is that it will necessarily retard economic growth and may harm "the least of these" (Matthew 25:40, KJV) in the long run. Moreover, the near-ubiquity of starvation and stagnation over the history of human civilization—including the 2000 years of the Christian era—certainly tells us that we tend to "get it wrong" far more often than we "get it right," and there is nothing to guarantee that we will "get it right" in the future. If anything, we must proceed with caution.

Notes

1. This example is adapted from Nye, *Economic Growth and True Inequality* (available at www.econlib.org/library/columns/nyegrowth.html) and *Irreducible Inequality* (available at www.econlib.org/library/columns/nyepositional.html). See Gibson & Smout (1995, pp. 248-250) for a detailed breakdown of Scottish diets.
2. Still, the commandments relating to personal interaction are fundamentally libertarian. Though the apostles sought a political revolutionary, Jesus emphasized that His kingdom is not of this world.
3. Smith's classic *An Inquiry into the Nature and Causes of the Wealth of Nations* is available online from the Liberty Fund's Library of Economics and Liberty at http://www.econlib.org/library/Smith/smWN.html.
4. In the next sentence, Rothbard points to a Paretian definition of utility maximization.
5. *Economic Growth and True Inequality* (available at www.econlib.org/library/columns/nyegrowth.html) and *Irreducible Inequality* (available at www.econlib.org/library/columns/nyepositional.html).
6. I am indebted to James Morley for phrasing this point.
7. This section is drawn from private correspondence with Jon Bailey of Washington University's Department of Physics.
8. Nicholas Kristof's op-eds in the *New York Times* have addressed this issue.
9. This section is drawn from section IV of my earlier essay "Christian Ethics, Formal Institutions, and Economic Growth."
10. I stress that this common ethical core represents the *fruits* of salvation rather than the *causes* of salvation, as Paul did in his epistle to the churches in Galatia.
11. Reisman (1996) also discusses the benevolent results of free market capitalism.
12. I ignore for now the obvious ethical difficulties associated with coercion. For a full discussion, see Rothbard (1982).
13. See Mises (1949), Rothbard (1962 [2001]), or any principles of microeconomics textbook for a discussion.
14. The obvious objection to this example concerns the supposed existence of involuntary unemployment. Mises (1949) and Rothbard (1962 [2001]) question the validity of this objection and note that, in the absence of state intervention restricting employment, all unemployment must necessarily be voluntary.

Bibliography

Carden, A. (2004). Christian ethics, formal institutions, and economic growth. Working Paper, Washington University and Ludwig von Mises Institute.

Friedman, M. (1970). The social responsibility of business is to increase its profits. *New York Times Magazine*, September 13, 1970.

Gibson, A.J.S. & Smout, T.C. (1995). *Prices, food, and wages in Scotland 1550-1780.* Cambridge: Cambridge University Press.

Heyne, P., Boettke, P., & Prychitko, D. (2002). *The economic way of thinking.* Upper Saddle River, NJ: Prentice Hall.

Hoppe, Hans-Herman (2001). *Democracy: The God that failed.* New Brunswick: Transaction Publishers.

Lindert, Peter H. (1995). Unequal living standards. In: R. Floud and D.N. McCloskey (Eds.), *The economic history of Britain since 1700*, Volume I (pp. 357-386). 2nd Edition, Cambridge: Cambridge University Press.

_________ and Williamson, J.G. (1983). English workers' living standards during the Industrial Revolution: A new look. *Economic History Review*, 36, 1-25.

McCloskey, D.N. (1995). 1780-1860: A survey. In: R. Floud and D.N. McCloskey (Eds.), *The economic history of Britain since 1700*, Volume I (pp. 242-270). 2nd Edition, Cambridge: Cambridge University Press.

Mises, L. (1949). *Human action.* New Haven: Yale University Press.

_________. (1979 [2002]). *Economic policy: Thoughts for today and tomorrow*, 2nd edition. Chicago: Regnery/Gateway Inc. Online edition prepared 2002. Auburn: Ludwig von Mises Institute.

North, D.C. (1990). *Institutions, institutional change, and economic performance.* Cambridge: Cambridge University Press.

_________. (1991). Institutions. *Journal of Economic Perspectives*, 5, 97-112.

_________. (2004). Markets. In: J. Mokyr (Ed.), *The Oxford encyclopedia of economic history* (pp. 432-439). Oxford: Oxford University Press.

Nye, J.V.C. (2002). *Economic growth and true inequality* [Online]. Available: www.econlib.org/library/columns/nyegrowth.html.

_________. (2002). *Irreducible inequality* [Online]. Available: www.econlib.org/library/columns/nyepositional.html.

Reisman, G. (1996). *Capitalism: A treatise on economics.* Ottawa, IL: Jameson Books.

Rothbard, M.N. 1956. Toward a reconstruction of utility and welfare economics. In: Mary Sennholz (Ed.), *On freedom and free enterprise: Essays in honor of Ludwig von Mises* (pp. 224-262). Princeton: D. Van Nostrand Co. Reprinted 1997 in *The logic of action one: Money, method, and the Austrian school* (pp. 211-254). Cheltenham, UK: Edward Elgar Publishing Ltd.

_________. (1962 [2001]). *Man, economy, and state.* Reprinted Auburn: Ludwig von Mises Institute.

_________. (1970). *Power and market: Government and the economy.* Kansas City: Sheed, Andrews, and McMeel.

The Jews and Capitalism: A Love-Hate Relationship

Walter Block

There is no doubt that at least in some sense, there is a love-hate relationship between Jews and capitalism.

On the one hand, there is a strong tradition of support for socialism, communism, labor unionism, feminism, and affirmative action, within the Jewish community. As well, according to the political aphorism, "Jews have the income of Presbyterians, and yet vote like Puerto Ricans." Jews have a strong tradition of casting ballots for the Democratic Party[1] and have long taken a supportive interest in groups such as the National Association to Aid Colored People, which is also solidly in the corner of this political party.

On the other hand, there can be little doubt that capitalism has been very good to Jews. Many members of this faith have prospered as businessmen. This would tend to incline most people in such a situation in the direction of support for the marketplace. Nor can it be denied that several of their numbers have taken on high profile roles in defense of this system.

Nevertheless, despite these slight exceptions, the overwhelming preponderance of opinion within this community lies in the direction of government interventionism, and dirigisme economics. What accounts for this rather exceptionable behavior? Various theories have been put forth in an attempt to explain this phenomenon. The present paper is devoted to discussing and evaluating several of them[2].

Block, Walter. 2004. "The Jews and Capitalism: A love-hate enigma." *The Journal of Social, Political and Economic Studies,* Fall, Vol. 29 No. 3, pp. 305–326. Republished with permission.

Before embarking on this task, however, we do well to remark on the fact that ordinarily, in most analyses of group behavior, the analyst does not go too far wrong in relying upon the doctrine of quo bono. That is, most human action can be explained in terms of self-interest. But the Jews, it would appear, offer evidence of being a counter example to this general rule.

Support for affirmative action and gun control on the part of the Jewish community are particularly difficult to understand in this regard. When a plan of coerced racial preferences in education is implemented, it benefits groups such as blacks and Hispanics. But who are the people who lose out when such people are chosen? It is hard to avoid the conclusion that Jews are over-represented in this category[3]. As for guns, who has not heard of the Warsaw uprising, and of the vicious treatment these people have suffered at Nazi hands. Surely, if the Jews of Germany, Poland, and other Eastern European countries were heavily armed in the late 1930s, their fate would have likely been less horrific[4]. And this is to say nothing of attacks suffered by Hasidim in neighborhoods such as Crown Heights in Brooklyn, New York. Surely pistols would be of help in quelling such disturbances. Despite the foregoing, Jews as a group have been adamant in championing policies that, it would appear, are directly incompatible with their own self-interest.

Intellectuals & Overrepresentation

Jews are over-represented amongst intellectuals (Seligman, 1994)[5], and intellectuals tend to take on left wing views on economics.[6] This undoubtedly gives at least some impetus to support for socialism from this segment of the population.

There are several plausible ways in which to define intellectuals. One possibility is to include those who earn a living through the use of abstract reasoning, or as wordsmiths, or as "second hand dealers in ideas" (Hayek, 1990, p. 5). Examples of this category would be professors, journalists, clergy, and writers–those who directly or indirectly mold public opinion. A more inclusive definition would add professions in which a high degree of intelligence is required, but where such people are not typically the source of ideas for others. Mises (1972, p. 16) includes "physicians" under this rubric. Others in this category might be physicists, engineers, pharmacists, accountants, architects, etc. An even wider definition would add to this list all of those who think deeply about current events, read widely, keep themselves informed, etc. An operational definition of this third rung of intellectuals would be those who purchase books, keep them at home, frequent libraries, watch news shows on t.v., etc.

Hayek (1990) takes great pains to distinguish intellectuals, in any of these three senses, from experts. The latter are in effect the originators of ideas; the former, the megaphone, or transmission device, with which these ideas are transferred to the general public. His illustration of the economics profession is a telling one. States Hayek (1990, p. 8): "Yet is it not the predominant views of the experts but the views of a minority, mostly of rather doubtful standing in their profession, which are taken up and spread by the intellectuals." Although he does not mention him, reading between the lines one can almost see the name "Galbraith." It is the ideas of this worth which are transmitted to the average man on the street, even though his are in a small minority within the economics profession, most of which strongly disagrees with his perspective on socialism, protectionism, and the evils of the capitalist system.[7]

Whether we choose the narrow, the medium, or the wider definition of intellectual, it cannot be denied that Jewish people are disproportionately represented in these numbers. As for the first category, they are the "talking heads" on television, the professors, the editorialists–in numbers far in excess of their proportion of the population. As for the second, they dominate the professions of medicine, dentistry, psychology, science, etc. And even in the third, when they have jobs as the proverbial "butchers, bakers, and candlestick makers," they are still well read, involved in current events, etc., to a greater degree than their counterparts who follow other religious beliefs.

Early Educational Experiences

Why is it that intellectuals, defined as those who engage in the manipulation of political and economic ideas, oppose free enterprise? Nozick (1997) maintains this is due to the fact that these people, when they were in high school, had the highest grades, and the greatest official recognition, but the job market relegates them to a far lower position in the pecking order than at that time. The result: resentment of the system responsible for not giving them their due.

Van den Haag (2000/2001, pp. 56-57) rejects this thesis on the grounds that one, the business world does reward people on a basis that is proportional to intelligence, and two, "Nozick is quite wrong in believing that superior intelligence is readily rewarded in high schools." Instead, he contends, bouquets are tossed on the basis of athletic prowess.

In my view, Van den Haag's criticisms fall short of the mark. While it cannot be denied that most high school *students* extol athletics over academics, this is not at all the case for teachers. Further, it is equally true that the brainiacs, nerds, and geeks also get their due (if not, perhaps, in inner city high schools, which must be counted as an exception to this rule). There are scholarships, trips to the student versions of the U.N., chess and mathematics tournaments, the debating club, etc. What with the advent of Bill Gates who earns far more than Michael Jordan, the smart kids are coming into their own even the more. Van den Haag is of course correct that athletes and "tough kids" command more respect in some sense, but this is irrelevant to the point Nozick is making, that the highly intelligent high school student is given a strong ego boost by the adult world. Even when the nerd is being physically bullied, he still has a strong sense of entitlement based on his grade scores and other such recognition.

It of course cannot be denied that there is indeed a positive correlation between intelligence and business success (Murray, 1998), but there are enough exceptions to rile intellectuals. Consider only those in this regard earning a relatively modest salary as an associate professors of literature, while the ex high school class bozo makes it big selling toys or burgers and drives around town in a car far more luxurious than theirs. There can be little doubt that Nozick is telling an important part of the story of the disaffection of the intellectuals when he bases it on their high school experiences.

Purposes vs. Effects

Then, too, intellectuals, particularly those not involved in economics (Frey, et. al., 1984, Block and Walker, 1988) often confuse accomplishments with motives.[8] The *goal* of the businessman may well be to maximize profits, something unsavory in the view of the great (economic) unwashed. But this should be seen as distinct from the *effects* of his actions, which are altogether very salutary, particularly to the poor in advanced capitalist nations. This tendency is exacerbated by Jewish, and indeed most religious, focus on intent, not only accomplishments. There is ignorance of Adam Smith's (1776) great finding of the "invisible hand," which leads people to do good for others even though it was not part of their intention to do so.

Further, intellectuals labor under the implicit premise that the morality of the deed ought to be matched by economic reward. That is, the callings of nurses, theologians, doctors, firemen, moralists, clergymen—and of course academics—are all thought to be imbued with a particular moral grace. And yet with the exception of physicians, they are not particularly highly paid. But this too plays into Jewish and indeed all religious precepts, where morality is given a particularly central role.

Too Accurate a Mirror

Mises (1972, pp. 11-16) puts forth a theory to the effect that intellectuals resent capitalism because it is merciless in revealing their failure to make a greater contribution to society. In days of yore, when a man's accomplishments were severely reined in by his place in society, those who failed to garner great wealth or position had a readily available excuse: they were born into the wrong caste, or class, or social position; it was thus not their fault that they rose no higher than they did. None of their fellows, with the same birth disadvantages, likely did any better. States Mises (1972, p. 11, 13): "In a society based on caste and status, the individual can ascribe adverse fate to conditions beyond his own control… Everybody is aware of his own defeat and insufficiency."

Under markets, however, in sharp contrast, none of these excuses held true any longer. "It is quite another thing under capitalism. Here everybody's station in life depends upon his own doing," in the view of Mises (1972, p. 11). A Bill Gates could move from a position of no special prominence to become the richest man in the world. What must his childhood chums think of this meteoric rise?

The stupid ones, Mises (1972, p. 15) tells us, "release these feelings in slander and defamation. The more sophisticated do not indulge in personal calumny. They sublimate their hatred into a philosophy, the philosophy of anti-capitalism, in order to render inaudible the inner voice that tells them that their failure is entirely their own fault." But "the more sophisticated" are precisely the intellectuals we have been discussing. Not for them, merely, a personal attack on the Bill Gateses of the world[9]. In addition, the weaving of a philosophical system which has at its core the evils of the market place, where some, e.g., Gates, rise to heights which are clearly "unfair," insofar as they very much put these "intellectuals" into the shade. In summarizing this point, Mises (1972, p. 18) states: "His passionate dislike of capitalism is a mere blind for his hatred of some successful 'colleagues.'"

Broadway and Hollywood

It is something of a stretch to consider the denizens of Broadway and Hollywood as "intellectuals," even with the broad definition of that term we are employing.[10] Truth, accuracy, and facts are not their stock in trade, as it is, at least ideally, for the intellectual; rather, imagination, communications skills, emotion, and beauty serve as the coin of the realm in these places. Yet, it cannot be denied that quite a high level of intelligence is required to produce movies and plays successfully. In any case, these industries are dominated by members of the Jewish faith, and thus come under our consideration for both these reasons.

Mises (1972, pp. 31-32) explains the communist leanings of these two communities on the basis of the intrinsic risk of the entertainment industry:

> People long for amusement because they are bored. And nothing makes them so weary as amusements with which they are already familiar. The essence of the entertainment industry is variety. The patrons applaud most what is new and therefore unexpected and surprising. They are capricious and unaccountable. They disdain what they cherished yesterday. A tycoon of the stage or the screen must always fear the waywardness of the public…
>
> It is obvious that there is no relief from what makes these stage people uneasy. Thus they catch at a straw. Communism, some of them think, will bring their deliverance.

This has all the earmarks of a good explanation. There is no truer statement than that "no other American milieu was more enthusiastic in the endorsement of communism than that of people cooperating in the production of these silly plays and films" (Mises, 1972, p. 33). This was no less true at the time Mises wrote than at present. Hollywood and Broadway in many ways represent a crap-shoot, with great losses and great profits for different projects, based on an always fickle public. Say what you will about communism, at least it cannot be denied that those who remain in the good graces of the rulers never need fear bankruptcy.

And yet, if it were really true that industries facing high risk would be inclined toward economic adventurism because of that fact, then this ought to apply to others as well. For example, wild-cat oil drilling is a notoriously risky business; there are many dry holes found for every wet one. There have been many business failures amongst the dot.com start-up companies. However, the predilection toward socialism correctly pointed to by Mises in the entertainment industry by no means carries through to oil exploration or new computer firms. Thus, the risk of a business appears to be a poor predictor of left wing ideological support.

Contempt

Another factor that at least in part explains the fevered criticisms of capitalism by most intellectuals is the contempt with which they are held by the leaders of this system, the businessmen. The derisive "pointy headed intellectuals with a briefcase" hurled by former Alabama Governor George Wallace at the bureaucrats of Washington, D.C., during his presidential election campaign, is only the tip of the iceberg in this regard. The leaders of large firms hold the intellectuals in little esteem, and this perspective has percolated into the society at large. In literature, in films, and on the stage, the intellectual is often depicted as absent minded, ineffectual, and physically weak.

In Hayek's (1990, p. 10) view: "It is not surprising that the real scholar or expert and the practical man of affairs often feel contemptuous about the intellectual, are disinclined to recognize his power, and are resentful when they discover it. Individually they find the intellectuals mostly to be people who understand nothing in particular especially well and whose judgment on matter they themselves understand shows little sign of special wisdom."

It is only human nature, under these conditions, for intellectuals to play "pay back" with business leaders. If the latter hold the former in contempt, then this sentiment can be returned, with interest, in the form of rejection of capitalism. It is no accident that in the academic and Hollywood worlds, captains of industry should be portrayed as greedy, grasping, avaricious, and immoral.[11] What with strong "political correctness" sentiment opposed to characterizing in a poor light "protected" groups such as blacks, Jews, women, the handicapped, and other such, it is rare that the villain in most movies and T.V. shows is other than a white male, pre-eminently a white male businessman.

States Mises (1972, pp.19, 20, material in brackets supplied by present author): "What is called 'society' in the United States almost exclusively consists of the richest families. There is little social intercourse between the successful businessmen and the nation's eminent authors, artists and scientists…(the former consider the latter) as people with whom they do not want to consort" and then refers to the "resentment with which the intellectuals react to the contempt in which they are held by the members of 'society.'"

Alternative Explanations

The reason we focus so heavily on the effects of intellectualism in determining Jewish criticisms of free enterprise is that there is a serious question as to whether or not this is a sufficient explanation of the phenomenon. That is, does the intellectualism of the Jewish people swamp their religion, insofar as implications for political philosophy are concerned? To put this in other words, once we have noted that a person is an intellectual, and a Jew, does the impetus of the former toward left wing views exhaust that of the latter? Or, does being a member of the Jewish faith add any more explanatory power to socialist beliefs that are already there, supplied by intellectualism?

It is to these questions that we now turn. We will attempt to discern, when we add "Jewishness" to a person who already is an intellectual, does this further incline him in the direction of socialism?[12] If so, then Judaism supplies an added impetus to dirigisme leanings that is not already in place on the part of intellectuals. If not, then these religious beliefs do not make an independent contribution to market opposition that is not already present in the thinking of the typical leftist intellectual.[13]

Religious Considerations

One hypothesis that could be used to account for Jewish bias against laissez faire capitalism is that it is based upon religious considerations. The theory is that the Old Testament, the Bible, the Talmud, and other formal written aspects of the religion impart receptivity toward the left side of the political economic spectrum to its adherents.[14] For example, the admonition to be charitable, tzedakah, might be used to justify the welfare system. Or the commandment not to "covet" the possessions of others might be considered a warning against "greed," which, in turn, might be seen as the organizing principle of the market. Or the injunction to observe ona'ah might be interpreted as opposition to earning profits above a certain level.[15]

However, the claim that the Talmud is responsible (directly for the religious, and indirectly for the less so) for elevating socialism and denigrating capitalism in this community is countered by the fact that one of the Ten Commandments proscribes theft. If stealing is illegal, it can only be because there is such a thing as a valid system of private property rights; if there were not, it would be logically impossible to engage in any such activity as theft. But private property rights are the bedrock of the capitalist system; if Jewish law promotes this concept, and it most certainly does, then its criticism of markets cannot be a fundamental aspect of the religion.

Historical Political Considerations

Friedman (1985, p. 403) couches the problem we are addressing in terms of a paradox: "Two propositions can be readily demonstrated: first, the Jews owe an enormous debt to free enterprise and competitive capitalism; second, for at least the past century the Jews have been consistently opposed to capitalism and have done much on an ideological level to undermine it."

He offers two explanations for this paradox. The first one stems from historical conditions prevailing in Europe, and especially France, at time of its revolution: only the left, not the right, was willing to tolerate Jewish participation in public life. And second, the Jewish reaction to the stereotype of them by the population at large, that they were grasping, greedy, and concerned with commerce and money-lending. States Friedman (1985, p. 412) of the Jewish reaction to this: "... to deny that Jews are like the stereotype, to set out to persuade oneself, and incidentally the anti-Semites, that far from being money-grabbing, selfish, and heartless, Jews are really public-spirited, generous, and concerned with ideals rather than material goods. How better to do so than to attack the market with its reliance on monetary values and impersonal transactions and to glorify the political process, to take as an ideal a state run by well-meaning people for the benefit of their fellow man."[16]

I have no doubt that both of Friedman's explanations contain more than just a grain of truth. However, the historical one must be taken with a grain of salt: many other groups, besides Jews, have also benefited from free enterprise and yet oppose it. Thus, the historical antecedents relied upon by Friedman can hardly be generalized. For all that, it is not easy to dismiss this as *part* of the explanation, precisely Friedman's point.

Second, Friedman posits that the Jews *could* have accepted the stereotype imposed upon them by society as a whole, and attempted to demonstrate that a concern for money, commerce, profits, etc., contrary to the prevailing view, was actually *beneficial* to society. He (1985, p. 413) replies: "But this reaction was hardly to be expected. None of us can escape the intellectual air we breathe, can fail to be influenced by the values of the community in which we live. As Jews left their closed ghettos and shtetls and came into contact with the rest of the world, they inevitably came to accept and share the values of that world..."

But this response, while a reasonable generalization, is not definitive. Friedman himself is a counterexample. He has for the most part not been "influenced" by the socialist values of the community in which *he* lives.[17] If he could do it, why not others, many others, particularly Jews, who have more than average intelligence, and thus at least the potential to see through the popular socialist nostrums? Second, this answer is incomplete, for it leaves open the question of why the Jews, when they emerged from their ghettos[18], found rampant socialism? Why were they not met with prevailing capitalist ideas?

Minority Status, Persecution

Sowell (1994, p. 231) notes the "remarkable historic achievements of the Jews—a relatively small group of people, spread thinly around the world, and yet so prominent in so many countries and in so many fields that it hardly seems credible that there are fewer Jews in the entire world than there are Kazakhs or Sri Lankans."

There is no doubt that Jews are a minority in virtually every country they reside. Even Israel, the obvious counterexample, is only so on a superficial basis. For while Jews are a majority of this country, it is tiny compared to its neighbors, amongst whom the entire nation is in effect a small minority.

Nor is it rare that minorities would be persecuted. Indeed, Sowell (1998) is replete with cases wherein small populations are brutalized by larger ones[19].

A thesis, then, which emanates from these considerations,[20] is that the Jews have been victimized more often and more deeply than other high earning and intellectually advanced groups, and this biases them in the direction of criticizing markets.

But it is unclear as to why a victimized minority would cleave to the left. Why not to the right, as have the Mormons, who are also a minority, and also have a history of suffering from persecution. Moreover, while to be sure the state of Israel is a minority among its larger national neighbors, this by no means holds true within that country itself. There, Jews are a majority. And yet the internal economic policies of Israel can hardly be considered market oriented (Gwartney, Lawson and Block, 1996).

Income Maximization

According to Rothbard (1973, pp. 66-67): "... why do the intellectuals need the state? Put simply, the intellectual's livelihood in the free market is generally none too secure; for the intellectual, like everyone else on the market, must depend on the values and choices of the masses of his fellowmen, and it is characteristic of these masses that they are generally uninterested in intellectual concerns. The State, on the other hand, is willing to offer the intellectuals a warm, secure and permanent berth in its apparatus, a secure income, and the panoply of prestige."

And, further, Rothbard (1973, p. 69) declares: "This is not to say that all intellectuals everywhere have been 'court intellectuals,' servitors and junior partners of power. But this has been the ruling condition in the history of civilizations..."

This would definitely incline people of the Jewish faith toward statism, not so much because of anything intrinsic to their religion, but simply because they are so heavily over-represented amongst the intellectual classes, and the latter have a predilection in favor of matters governmental. If intellectuals, in general, are drawn toward dirigisme out of considerations of income maximization, and Jews are disproportionately to be found among intellectuals, then this phenomenon alone could account for the leftist bias of that group.

Of course, it cannot be maintained that all employment enjoyed by intellectuals is in the formal civil service, implicit or explicit. This consideration would lead us, presumably, to the conclusion that even if the direction of causation pointed out above were correct, it would not explain much of the phenomenon under consideration. But there are other governmental jobs besides those in the bureaucracy. Teachers and professors, for example, are intellectuals whose paychecks are based on tax revenues. And even those working in private universities are not totally unconnected to the state. For one thing, academics are dependent upon government largesse for fellowships, grants, contracts, etc. For another, given that with the exception of places such as Hillsdale College and Grove City College, a significant percentage of the budget of most ostensibly "private" institutions of higher learning are accounted for by government, it is only a slight exaggeration to say there are no universities not in the public sector.

But the rot spreads further than this, far further. If this explanation imparts to the weltanschauung of academia a leftist bias, it will tend to percolate to other intellectual redoubts, even if there is no direct connection between wealth maximization and the espousal of socialist nostrums. For example, take journalism, both reporting and editorial writing. If most academics favor dirigisme policies, then this applies, too, to professors in schools of journalism. If so, then their graduates likely reflect this political economic perspective. And they, in turn, introduce the general newspaper reading public to this slant.[21]

Nazi Avoidance

There can be little doubt that the Jews have been seared by their exposure to Nazism. As a result, the rallying cry "never again" has become the motto of this community. There is one thing that distinguishes the Nazi society from many if not all others: it was a homogeneous, Christian, white country;

as a result, the Jews have determined that whatever else the United States[22] is and becomes, it shall not resemble that demographic make up (MacDonald, 1998). It is in this context that Jewish support for immigration from non-white European countries, for multiculturalism, for institutions such as the NAACP, for affirmative action (which comes largely at the expense of male white Christians as well as their own group) can be explained.

There is of course no necessary connection between this concern and socialism.[23] The world might well have been a place wherein the desire for race mixing had little or nothing to do with pro or anti-free enterprise sentiment. To explore the reasons why this should have become a rallying cry of the left, not the right, would take us too far afield. Suffice it to say, however, that in the modern political context, there is little doubt that supporters of socialism favor such policies, while opponents do not. Thus, this is yet another phenomenon that impels Jews in the direction of anti-capitalism, even though it stems from issues far removed from economic freedom.

What can be reasonably said about this hypothesis? In my view, we can only say at this point that the jury is still out. It has at least superficial plausibility, in that it accords with the strictures of quo bono. That is, if it were true, this thesis does at least point to a gain that could be garnered by the Jewish community by acting in such a manner.

On the other hand, not a single shred of *evidence* has been adduced in its behalf. Speaking as a Jew myself, one who is reasonably cognizant of the events occurring in this community, I can say that I have never heard any reason to believe that it is true. This hypothesis will be rejected by some, out of hand, as anti-Semitic. That is not at all the position I am taking. As a disinterested observer, as a social scientist, my role is to get that extra one-inch closer to the truth. It is incompatible with this role to reject out of hand *any* hypothesis, no matter how despicable it may sound. All that can be said for this one, at the present time, is that while Jews may conceivably have this motive, there is no evidence that they do, or have acted upon it in this manner.

However, there is something that can be said against it. This hypothesis is rooted in Jewish experience with the holocaust. Therefore, at best, it can explain Jewish behavior *after* that event. But this group of people was highly suspicious and rejecting of free enterprise long before the 1930s. Presumably, there was some cause for *this* state of affairs, which, by the very nature of things, cannot be accounted for by a desire to avoid, or change, homogeneous Christian nations. Further, there are numerous countries that are at least as homogeneously white and Christian as Nazi Germany, and, also, Nordic for that matter, and have not spawned any anti- Jewish holocausts. Iceland, Norway, Sweden, Finland, and especially Denmark immediately spring to mind. It is an interesting hypothesis, which cannot be rejected out of hand on a priori or "racist" grounds, but that does not at all mean we must accept it.

Conclusion

We have come to no firm conclusions concerning the genesis of the support of the Jews for left wing political economic philosophies. There can be no doubt as to the preference for this community of socialistic solutions to public policy challenges, but the causes thereof are less clear. This is an important issue for all those involved in such questions, since members of this religious group are leaders in the academic and intellectual activities concerned with domestic and foreign policy. Hopefully, these remarks will spark research into this fascinating area of study, and make some small contribution to eventually shedding more light on it.

Notes

1. Lilla, 2001; Lefkowitz, 1993; Fuchs, 1956
2. For previous attempts in this regard, see Block 1985, 1990, 1996.
3. Seligman, 1994.
4. Lott, 1998.
5. Seligman (1994) attributes this phenomenon to the higher IQ scores of Jews. Hayek (1990, p. 19, ft. 3) demurs: "... there is little reason to believe that really first class intellectual ability for original work is any rarer among Gentiles than among Jews." However, Hayek (1990, p. 19, ft. 3) continues: "... there can be little doubt that men of Jewish stock almost everywhere constitute a disproportionately large number of the intellectuals in our sense, that is of the ranks of the professional interpreters of ideas. This may be their special gift and certainly is their main opportunity in countries where prejudice puts obstacles in their way in other fields. It is probably more because they constitute so large a proportion of the intellectuals than for any other reason that they seem to be so much more receptive to socialist ideas than people of different stocks."
6. States Hayek (1988 p. 53): "The higher we climb up the ladder of intelligence, the more we talk with intellectuals, the more likely we are to encounter socialist convictions. Rationalists tend to be intelligent and intellectual; and intelligent intellectuals tend to be socialists."
7. A more modern example of this is former President Clinton, playing the role of "intellectual" publicly relying upon the "experts" Card and Krueger (1994) to raise the minimum wage level in order to help unskilled workers, despite the fact that this is very much a minority position amongst economists.
8. The typical sociologist or religion professor guilty of this confusion may have a Ph.D. in these fields, but is no genius when it comes to economic reasoning.
9. Although it is indeed tempting to interpret the anti-trust case of the late 1990s as spiteful acting out against the more successful. For an analysis that in part makes use of this motive, see Anderson, et. al. 2001.
10. See footnote 8.
11. As a case in point, see the movie *Wall Street.*
12. I am indebted to my friend and colleague, Bill Barnett, for impressing upon me

the importance of this question.

13. There are some who would be inclined to argue that "leftist intellectual" is a veritable contradiction in terms. This is a very tempting interpretation. Given that the market is the most moral and economically efficient system known to man, it is hard to credit the good sense, let alone intelligence of anyone who opposes it. As intellectuals are quintessentially those noted for precisely these characteristics, we arrive at the point where we are tempted to disqualify all candidates from the honorific title "intellectual" who persist in their rejection of laissez faire capitalism. But we do not use the term in this manner for the present article. One reason is the fact that a person could reject free enterprise not out of stupidity, but rather evil; this might well leave his claim to intelligence intact. Another is that were we to automatically disqualify all Marxists and their ilk from the rank of intellectuals, we would need another word to describe those who favor socialism and yet write books, give speeches, serve as faculty members of universities, or in any other such way earn a living through the promotion of these ideas. Thus, the term "intellectual" is not a pejorative, indicating accuracy of analysis. Rather, if refers to those who, from *any* perspective, deal with social and economic ideas in their professions. Sowell (1980, pp. 331-332) defines intellectuals "as the social class of persons whose economic output consists of generalized ideas, and whose economic rewards come from the transmission of those generalized ideas. This in no way implies any qualitative cognitive judgment concerning the originality, creativity, intelligence or authenticity of the ideas transmitted. Intellectuals are simply defined in a sociological sense, and a transmitter of shallow, confused or wholly unsubstantiated ideas is as much of an intellectual in this sense as Einstein." Precisely.
14. For the view that the claims of liberation theologians to the effect that the Old Testament of the Jews was not receptive to markets and private property is mistaken, and that this mistaken analysis is due to a reading of these texts divorced from the economic and sociological conditions under which they were written, see Liggio, 1997.
15. For an analysis of this concept, see Block, 2002
16. For a critique of Friedman's thesis, see Frankel (1985, pp. 429-442). Frankel (1985, p. 436) rejects Friedman's mention of the makeup of the French parliament as "a-historical," and objects to his reliance on fighting stereotypes as based upon the Nazi Sombart's (1913) analysis. Friedman (1985, pp. 443-446) replies that he does not at all rely upon Sombart, and that Frankel provides no evidence to back up his "a-historical" charge. In this debate, I concur entirely with Friedman.
17. For an exception to this statement, see Block (1999), Rothbard (2002).
18. This word is sometimes used to describe the home of the blacks in American inner cities in the northeast. But this is misleading. The Jews in Europe during those times were prohibited by law from living outside the areas specifically reserved for them. Nothing of this sort applied to blacks in northern American cities, certainly not after 1865.
19. Although see Diamond (1999) where the exact opposite occurs; namely, small advanced populations overcome ones that are less well economically developed. For a critique of this book, although not on this ground, see Block (1999).
20. I am not attributing this to Sowell.

21. As but two small yet revealing instance of this phenomenon, consider the fact that about 90 percent of the journalists covering the Nixon-McGovern presidential election favored the latter, while the former won in a landslide. Further, there is the almost total refusal of crime reporters to mention the race of perpetrators.
22. This also applies to other nations in which large numbers of Jews reside; e.g., Britain, France, etc.
23. This does not apply to affirmative action when carried out on a coercive governmental basis, as opposed to being adopted by private interests, voluntarily. See on this Epstein (1992), Block (1982), Block and Walker (1985), Williams (1982).

Bibliography

Anderson, W., Block, W., DiLorenzo, T., Mercer, I., Snyman, L., & Westley, C. (2001). The Microsoft Corporation in collision with antitrust law. *The Journal of Social, Political and Economic Studies, 26,* 1, 287-302.

Block, W. (1999). The Gold Standard: A critique of Friedman, Mundell, Hayek, Greenspan. *Managerial Finance, 25,* 5, 15-33.

Block, W. (1996). The Mishnah and Jewish dirigisme. *International Journal of Social Economics, 23,* 2, 35-44.

Block, W. (1990). Jewish economics in the light of Maimonides. *International Journal of Social Economics, 17,* 3, 60-68.

Block, W. (1985). The Jews and capitalism. *Vital Speeches of the Day, LI,* 9, 283-288.

Block, W. (2002). Review of Diamond, J. (1999). *Guns, germs and steel.* New York: Norton; in *Ethics, Place and Environment, 5,* 3, 282-285.

Block, W. (2002). Ona'ah. *International Journal of Social Economics, 29,* 9, 722-729.

Block, W. (1982). Economic intervention, discrimination and unforeseen consequences. In: W. Block and M. A. Walker (Eds.), *Discrimination, Affirmative Action and Equal Opportunity* (pp. 101-125). Vancouver: The Fraser Institute.

Block, W., & Walker, M. A. (1988). Entropy in the Canadian economics profession: Sampling consensus on the major issues. *Canadian Public Policy,* XIV, 2, 137-150.

Card, D., & Krueger, A. B. (1994). Minimum wages and employment: A case study of the fast-food industry in New Jersey and Pennsylvania. *American Economic Review, 84,* 4, 772-793.

Diamond, J. (1999). *Guns, germs and steel,* New York: Norton.

Epstein, R. A. (1992). *Forbidden grounds: The case against employment discrimination laws.* Cambridge: Harvard University Press.

Friedman, M. (1985). Capitalism and the Jews. In: W. Block, G. Brennan and K. Elzinga (Eds.), *Morality of the market: Religious and economic perspectives* (pp. 401-418). Vancouver: The Fraser Institute.

Frankel, S. H. (1983). Modern capitalism and the Jews. *Oxford Centre for Postgraduate Hebrew Studies.* Reprinted as: Comment on Milton Friedman's 'Capitalism and the Jews'. In: W. Block, G. Brennan and K. Elzinga (Eds.), *Morality of the market: Religious and economic perspectives* (pp. 429-442). Vancouver: The Fraser Institute.

Frey, B. S., Werner, W. P., Schneider, F., & Gilbert, G. (1984). Consensus and dissension among economists: An empirical inquiry. *American Economic Review, 74,* 5, 986-94.

Fuchs, L. (1956). *The political behavior of American Jews.* Glencoe, Il.: Free Press.

Gwartney, J., Lawson, R., & Block, W. (1996). *Economic freedom of the world,* 1975-1995. Vancouver: The Fraser Institute.

Hayek, F. A. (1990). *The intellectuals and socialism.* Fairfax, VA: Institute for Humane Studies. Reprinted from *The University of Chicago Law Review, 16,* 3, Spring 1949.

Hayek, F.A. (1989). *The fatal conceit: The errors of socialism.* Chicago: The University of Chicago Press.

Lefkowitz, J. P. (1993). Jewish voters and the democrats. *Commentary, 95,* 4, 38-41.

Liggio, L. P. (1997). Market and money in Jewish and Christian thought in the Hellenistic and Roman ages. In: K. R. Leube, A. M. Petroni, and J. S. Sadowsky (Eds.), *An Austrian in France: Festschrift in honour of Jaques Garello* (pp. 283-294). La Rosa. Originally published in T. J. Burke (Ed.), *The Christian vision: Man and morality.* Hillsdale, MI: The Hillsdale College Press, 1986.

Lilla, M. (2001). *The reckless mind: Intellectuals in politics.* New York: New York Review Books.

Lott, Jr. J. R. (1998). *More guns, less crime: Understanding crime and gun control laws.* Chicago: University of Chicago Press.

MacDonald, K. (1998). *The culture of critique: An evolutionary analysis of Jewish involvement in twentieth-century intellectual and political movements.* New York: Praeger.

Mises, Ludwig von (1972). *The anti-capitalist mentality.* South Holland, IL: Libertarian Press.

Nozick, R. (1997). Why do intellectuals oppose capitalism. In *Socratic Puzzles,* Cambridge: Harvard University Press.

Rothbard, M. N. (1973). *For a new liberty.* New York: Macmillan.

Rothbard, Murray N. (2002). "Milton Friedman Unraveled," *Journal of Libertarian Studies*, Vol. 16, No. 4, Fall, pp. 37-54; http://www.mises.org/journals/jls/16_4/16_4_3.pdf

Schumpeter, J. A. (1942). *Capitalism, socialism and democracy.* New York: Harper, p. 198.

Seligman, D. (1994). Of Japanese and Jews. In: *A question of intelligence: The IQ debate in America.* New York: Citadel, Carol Press, pp. 118-135.

Sombart, W. (1913). *The Jews and modern capitalism.* London: Unwin.

Sowell, T. (1980). *Knowledge and decisions.* New York: Basic Books.

Sowell, T. (1994). *Race and culture: A world view.* New York: Basic Books.

Sowell, T. (1998). *Conquests and cultures: An international history.* New York: Basic Books.

Van den Haag, E. (2000/2001). The hostility of intellectuals to capitalism. *The Intercollegiate Review, 36,* 1-2, 56-63.

Walker, M. A., & Block, W. (1985). *Focus on employment equity: A critique of the Abella Royal Commission on Equality in Employment.* Vancouver: The Fraser Institute.

Williams, W. (1982). On discrimination, prejudice, racial income differentials, and affirmative action. In: W. Block and M. Walker (Eds.), *Discrimination, affirmative action and equal opportunity.* Vancouver: The Fraser Institute.

Doing "Secular Theology": Business Ethics in Economic and Environmental Religion

Robert H. Nelson

The field of business ethics, as I will suggest in this paper, should incorporate a new field of study of "secular theology." This involves the exploration of secular ideas to reveal their underlying religious content. It is not that such issues have not been explored previously. Indeed, there is a long tradition of religious interpretation of secular events and ideas, dating at least as far back as Alexis de Tocqueville (1856) who wrote about the French Revolution as a modern "religious revolution."

But a more systematic approach is needed. The new field could be seen as a brand new area of theology inquiry, the formal study with traditional theological methods now addressed to "secular religion." It is not necessary for a person to be deeply religious to engage in such efforts. I am myself mostly a secular person, although I have long had a strong interest in theology.

What is a "secular religion?" It might help to start with an example. Michael Crichton is the best-selling author of *The Andromeda Strain, Jurassic Park,* and other best-selling novels. In September 2003, Crichton gave a speech to civic leaders in San Francisco at the Commonwealth Club. His topic was environmentalism and his main theme was that it is a real religion. It is an unusual religion, however. Crichton captured the irony in describing environmentalism as today "the religion of choice for urban atheists." As

Crichton was saying, some people believe deeply in a religion even when they might deny that they subscribe to any form of religious belief.

Clearly, under this definition, a religion does not have to have a God or a belief in a hereafter. Such a definition, to be sure, encompasses some faiths traditionally regarded as valid religions—there are forms of Buddhism, for example, that do not have a God. Environmentalism for many of its faithful also falls in the category of a religion without a God. As Crichton was also saying, environmentalism fills a role in the life of true believers that is typical of religions of the past, including traditional Jewish and Christian faithful. It provides, for example, a vocabulary and a basis for making moral judgments, including the morality of business actions. Indeed, the ethical judgments of environmental religion are likely to be among the most widely influential in American society today.

For Christians, it was good and evil; for environmentalists today, it is a morality of "natural" and "unnatural." Consider the example of environmental morality as applied to business (and other) actions that may contribute to world climate change. A well known economist, Robert Mendelsohn (1999, 2000) of Yale University, argues that a moderate degree of climate change would probably be a good thing for many parts of the world. In places such as Siberia, and even many regions of the United States, a certain amount of warming of the climate would produce more benefits than costs. But that is not the point for environmental ethics. Environmentalists believe that we should not be changing the climate in principle, whatever the specific benefits and costs.

Human beings—and their business activities—should not play God; the climate should be determined by "natural" forces. It is reminiscent of the old religious attitudes to usury. The charging of interest might be beneficial economically as a way of rationally ordering the priority of business investments, but the Bible said it was wrong, so Christianity for many centuries took the position that usury must be prohibited, whatever the economic calculations.

For environmentalism, the places closest to moral perfection are wilderness areas. A wilderness is a place, as the Wilderness Act of 1964 says, "untrammelled by man." It is in effect a church or cathedral of environmental religion. A person goes to a wilderness to reinforce and recommit to the highest values of unaltered nature. As a consequence, one might note, the business world can never reflect the highest ethical values in environmentalism because business is a product of intense human action–very far removed indeed from a wild place where human impacts are at a minimum.

There are many more parallels between environmentalism and traditional religion. The connection was obvious to John McPhee, a leading American non-fiction writer who once followed the environmentalist David Brower for several months. Brower was the director of the Sierra Club in the 1950s and

1960s and by many accounts the most influential environmental advocate of the second half of the 20th century. In a book *Conversations with the Archdruid*, McPhee (1971, p.79) wrote that Brower preached "sermons" very much in the manner of Billy Graham. Graham probably won more individual converts, but McPhee suggests that Brower had more political and policy influence on American society.

The messages of Brower and Graham were surprisingly similar. Evil was triumphing over the earth. For Brower, morally corrupt men and women were destroying nature; they were defacing God's Creation. Only a moral renewal among human beings could turn things around. It would be necessary for all Americans—in fact, eventually for the entire world—to see the light. The pursuit of economic growth and development for its own sake must henceforth be renounced. Rather than a force for the good, the rising level of GNP measured the spread of natural loss—of evil—in the world. As a leading instrument of modern economic advance, and thus of the ongoing destruction of the natural world, business must therefore be ranked in such an environmental religion as exhibiting a lower order of ethics in American society. In the most favorable interpretation, it may be an unfortunate necessity.

Environmentalism thus graphically illustrates a key point. It is possible to have a powerful western religion without the formal features of Christian or Jewish religion. I first realized this working at the Interior Department headquarters in Washington, D.C. I was a career economist in the Office of Policy Analysis of the Office of the Secretary of the Interior. My office functioned in some ways as an in-house think tank for the Interior Department, and I found the work so interesting that I remained for 18 years.

I knew in advance that interest-group pressures would be important but I was surprised by the importance of ethical ideas to the policy-making processes (Nelson, 1987). The Interior Department was a leading battleground in a fierce struggle to define the moral—shall we say secular religious—values expressed in American public life. That was a main reason why environmental politics often became so nasty. Economic compromises are not as difficult; it is always possible to compromise by dividing an economic pie. But when the correct religion is at issue, it tends to be much harder to split the difference.

The Interior Department, as I came to realize, is the keeper of some of the main religious symbols of the American nation. These include the Lincoln Memorial, the Grand Canyon, Yosemite Valley, the Gettysburg battlefield, endangered plant and animal species, and so forth. Land use management in these and many other places is about the interpretation of theology. If Catholic prelates must decide today who is to be allowed to take communion, Interior Department employees must decide what particular uses will be allowed in a wilderness area.

In one dispute in the early 1980s, when James Watt was the Secretary of the Interior, he wanted to drill for oil underneath a wilderness area. The land surface would not have been affected; the oil drilling would have taken place outside the wilderness area and the angle of the drill could be slanted to enter only the wilderness subsurface. Watt thought that there should be no objection to drilling in these circumstances but environmentalists strongly disagreed. It was really a theological issue—whether the penetration of an oil drill even 500 feet below the land surface might "desecrate" a wilderness. This was an example of how environmental religion may become central to determining ethically acceptable business actions, based on an implicit environmental ethics—grounded in environmental theology—applied to business actions.

It was not only Interior Secretary Watt; environmentalists also had major problems with the way members of the economics profession thought about the natural world. An economist might see a valuable "natural resource" where an environmentalist would see a sacred cathedral of nature. Bryan Norton is a distinguished environmental philosopher. In 1991, he authored a paper in *Environmental Ethics* on the subject of "Why Environmentalists Hate Mainstream Economists." Although Norton did not specifically discuss the economic role of business, it would seem to follow that environmentalists should hate mainstream businessmen equally as much, since they are the ones who put economic ideas into practice.

Although I have often criticized the economics mainstream, I do have a Ph.D. in economics. From my experience at the Interior Department, I would agree with Norton that economists and environmentalists often have a difficult time in getting along. The reason, as I ultimately came to conclude, is that economics and environmentalism reflect much different religious understandings of the world. Economics is a religion and environmentalism is a religion—if in both cases a secular religion—and they differ profoundly in their theological prescriptions for ethical business actions and for other conduct of public policy. Economics, for one thing, is a religion of economic progress, while environmentalism finds its highest values in nature "untouched by human hand" where any signs of economic progress are at a minimum.

At some point my intellectual curiosity got the better of me and I decided to write about this new form of religious disagreement in American society (actually, it was not altogether new). I eventually wrote two books, one published in 1991, *Reaching for Heaven on Earth: The Theological Meaning of Economics,* and a second in 2001, *Economics as Religion: From Samuelson to Chicago and Beyond.* I also published a number of professional and popular articles on the subject of environmental religion.[1] I consider this past work to be part of my own contribution to the needed future task of "doing 'economic theology.'"

What specifically is an "economic theology?" Marxism is one of the best examples; in fact, a great number of people have previously said explicitly that Marxism is a religion.[2] The characterization of Marxism as a religion is not just sociological—that it is organized in the manner of a religion, and inspires followers whose behavior exhibits a religious zeal. Rather, Marxism has an actual theology with a moral system and a vision of the salvation of the world based on the tenets of this theology. Admittedly, like other secular religions, there is no God. There is, however, a close equivalent to God, the economic laws of history. Economic history in Marxism is omniscient and omnipotent. According to Marx, everything important in the world—ideas, institutions, culture, and also business organization—is determined by the particular economic stage of history at this moment.

In the end, according to Marx, the workings of economic history will lead inevitably to the arrival of heaven on earth. As in the Bible, the coming of heaven is preceded by a great cataclysm—in Marxism, seen as the final stage of class warfare and the triumph of the proletariat. Marxism, as one might say, is a Book of Revelations, rewritten for modern times in secular imagery. As Crichton says with respect to environmentalism, it is a remapping of Christianity onto a more modern religious landscape.

Marxism is not the only economic religion. Indeed, there have been a host of economic theologies, including social Darwinism, American progressivism (the "gospel of efficiency"), old fashioned European socialism, and others. As I explore in my two books on the subject, since the Enlightenment, many people have believed in ideas of economic progress as new forms of religious faith. Moreover, while there are new elements introduced, the roots of economic religion lie in Judeo-Christian sources. Secular and traditional religion both offer, for example, a vision of history as leading along a path of salvation to a new heaven on earth. Just as Christian schools of theology have differed on the details of salvation, economic schools have had competing interpretations of the best routes of economic progress. Indeed, it is possible to draw direct parallels from earlier Christian schools to current economic schools; the economists now carry on the old theological debates in modern economic language.[3] As in environmentalism, the tenets of an economic religion will also yield a business ethic, ranging from the Marxist view to the strong ethical approval among the followers of Herbert Spencer.

Since the middle of the 19th century, most economic theologies have focused on the ending of economic scarcity. It reflected a wider view, what might be called the economic explanation for the existence of sin in the world. In the Bible, evil came into the world when Adam and Eve ate the apple in the Garden. In economic religion, there is a new understanding of original sin. Human beings have lied, cheated, stolen, and otherwise so often behaved badly throughout history because they have been driven to it by a state of severe economic deprivation.

Over the course of human history until very recently, most people lived in severe poverty; many children died before five, and few people lived past 50 years. If it was a matter of stealing food for your baby or letting the baby die, most people would steal. Nations, as economic theology similarly taught, fought wars with one another because they were fighting for control over economic resources necessary to survival. It was not simply that they liked to fight. This was the central premise of economic theology-that the existence of sin in the world historically had a material basis.

Then, if this assumption is true, it opens up the possibility of a wonderful and glorious future. By the mid-19th century it was becoming apparent that a new economic era was arriving. With modern science and industry, poverty might actually be abolished throughout the world. As it seemed, a new era of full abundance would be arriving. It followed from the tenets of economic theology that sin would then be abolished; heaven would arrive on earth, based on economic progress. Stated in its simplest terms, if evil reflects economic circumstances, and economic circumstances can be perfected, the problem of evil in the world is solved. Growing material abundance will not only make us rich but spiritually transform us. As the leading agent of economic growth and development, business in economic religion has an exalted role to play; business becomes a main instrument of human salvation. The officers of a successful business corporation will be among the chosen in the eyes of an economic god.

That is to say, economic progress—based significantly on the workings of the modern business corporation would mean a great moral advance in the human condition. Economists like to say that they are genuine scientists. Hence, as professionals they should usually keep their moral convictions under wraps. Indeed, an explicit confession of a moral ground for economic reasoning might be professionally discrediting. On a few occasions, however, leading economists have been explicit about their own secular faith. John Maynard Keynes (1930, p. 372) once declared that economic growth would "lead us out of the tunnel of economic necessity into daylight." Keynes regarded the pursuit of self-interest as a crude and unpleasant human motive but it was only a temporary necessity. Within perhaps as few as 100 years, he prophesied, humanity might be "free at last" to discard the base institutions of a market economy, based on the unworthy motive of private greed.

Richard Ely was a founder of the American Economic Association in 1885 and also a leading member in those days of the social gospel movement. Like other social gospellers, he transposed the traditional Christian message to this world. For him, heaven was not to be sought in the hereafter but right here on earth. As Ely (1889, p.73) stated, there must be "a never-ceasing attack on every wrong institution, until the earth becomes a new earth, and all its cities, cities of God." Ely saw the activities of professional economists as central to this crusade; economists would become the leading priesthood of the modern age.

Economists were so important because it was their responsibility to provide the scientific understanding for the achievement of economic progress. Ely even argued that economics departments should be located in schools of theology. If this idea sounds odd to most economists today, it followed logically enough from Ely's beliefs. Economists were the ones who had the expert knowledge to save the world—and therefore the field of economics must be truly the most important subject in theology (Bernstein, 2001).

Ely's religious motives in founding the American Economic Association reflected wider religious roots of American progressivism as a whole. The progressive era has been labeled a secular "great awakening" (Fogel, 2000). The progressive goal was to save the world here on earth. There has been much written and today there is wide agreement on such matters among professional historians (Ross, 1991). In my own writings, I bring these arguments closer to the present time. I argue that economics today as well still has a religious underpinning. The economists of the second half of the twentieth century adopted a strictly scientific posture but in reality they were yet another priesthood—in this case the proselytizers for a "neo-progressive" gospel of economic efficiency.

The religious elements of contemporary economics are mostly left implicit, so it is necessary to probe beneath the surface to find them. Yet, without certain religious assumptions, even some of the main "scientific results" of modern economics would not hold. Almost all economists today argue, for example, that the market system is the most efficient way of organizing an economy. However, this conclusion holds only if certain (secular) religious assumptions are made.

The free market, one can say empirically and without any element of religion entering, is the greatest engine of economic change in human history. If there is some new and better technology, or a superior method of organizing business, the old methods will be swept aside by the market pursuit of profit. But what about the losers in this process? There are many people who are driven out of business by the forces of competition or workers who lose their jobs. They not only lose income; many of them will feel very badly. As a result of their displacement by the market, they may have to move to a new region and perhaps make new friends all over again. Their sense of self pride and confidence may be deeply and even permanently wounded.

In standard economic theory, however, the costs of these business failures simply do not enter into the social calculation. In the business ethics of economic religion, corporate leadership need not be concerned with such transitional social losses. Economics is entirely focused on the question of whether a new outcome is better than the old state of affairs; transaction and other temporary costs thus are to be ignored. This is important because, if such costs were counted, it would be impossible in principle to defend the vaunted efficiency of the market system.

How do economists explain their—and businesses'—usual ignoring of potentially large transitional costs? In the end, the answer is theological. Economic progress will bring us to heaven on earth. The market is the best and fastest route of economic progress. So society should leave the market alone to work its miracles of economic growth and development. This is very much like Christianity. In the traditional Christian faith, the events of this world are transitory; the important goal is to reach heaven in the hereafter. It would be folly to sin gravely today, at the risk of an eternal future in hell. So an ethical businessman should focus on the glories of the long run, and in fact there is a religious obligation to neglect any temporary diversions from the road of economic progress, however large the short run stresses and strains in society might be.

Few economists, admittedly, are aware that they are making such strong ethical arguments in their professional writings. A focus on long run progress is simply second nature for an economist with intensive training in the methods of analysis and reasoning of the economics profession. When I have attempted to bring up such arguments, economists do not offer a refutation. They simply have little interest in ethical argumentation which they mistakenly consider to be outside their own province. Leading economists work in a university environment and a social culture more broadly where religious and ethical questions are not taken seriously; religion is seen as a matter of personal belief necessarily outside any professional dialogue. Evangelical Christianity may be sweeping across America today but you would never know it at the University of Maryland.

There is a strong argument for change in this respect. The modern age thought that old religious superstitions had been overcome. In truth, there has been little modern decline in the importance of religion. Instead, the forms of religion have merely changed; the most important modern gospels have often denied that they represented a religion at all. As a result, the religious presuppositions—the underlying theological assumptions and religious lines of argument—remained implicit in the social sciences and received little formal attention. It is now the task of "doing 'secular theology'" to correct this mistake. It will be necessary to bring the modern forms of theology—including the business ethics of economic religion—explicitly to public light and scrutiny (Nelson, 2004).

If such studies were undertaken, as I have argued, it would also serve to emphasize the theological continuity of modern religion with earlier forms of religion. Contrary to the assumption of the 18th century, there was no new great era of modern "enlightenment"—with the major exception of the natural sciences—in which the understandings of the past by comparison must be regarded as the dark ages. Many modern men and women thought that theology had receded into ancient history. They had transcended religion. At the beginning of the 21st century that view now appears mistaken. Religion seems as important as ever—sometimes tragically so in places such as the Middle East. Religion may once again demand the attention of leading scholars, recognizing the diverse forms in which religion can come. Radical as it may sound, that could mean incorporating theology again across the full range of the university curriculum, and putting departments of theology back at the center of university life.

Because economic progress has been the modern path of salvation, economists have been the pre-eminent priesthood in areas of public policy. Economists are the sources of the most influential verdicts on business ethics of our time. If environmentalists judge morality by a standard of naturalness, economists judge it by a standard of efficiency. However, the religion of economic progress encompasses all the social sciences. In matters of individual behavior, the "science" of psychology has been perhaps more influential. The religious role and functions of psychology were explored in a 1977 book, *Psychology as Religion* (Vitz). I have yet to find a book on "Sociology as Religion" but it would be an apt title.

Much as Richard Ely advocated at the end of the 19th century, the study of the subject of economics has in fact been located in the modern school of theology. In the 20th century, social science was in essence the new theology, and the teachings of the social sciences lay at the center of university life. Where old fashioned schools of theology still could be found, as at Princeton Theological Seminary, they had been banished to the margins of university intellectual life.

If the modern age has seen the impoverishment of theology, the post-modern age may witness a revival. In at least the most economically successful parts of the world, the miracles of modern science and economic organization have succeeded in eliminating poverty and in fact almost any significant economic deprivation. In the future, given the modern accomplishment of the satisfaction of most material wants, the state of human welfare will be determined less and less by the physical conditions of existence, and more and more by the spiritual possession of a sense of meaning and purpose for each individual.[4]

That is the province of religion. It should be possible to learn more about this subject in the university world of the future. In the process, the field of business ethics, among other moral issues, will surely be reworked and rethought. Doing secular theology will also mean doing the business ethics of secular religion.

Notes

1. See, for example, Robert H. Nelson, Environmental colonialism: 'Saving" Africa from Africans. *The Independent Review* (Summer 2003); Robert H. Nelson, Does

'existence value' exist?: An essay on religions, old and new. The Independent Review (March 1997); Robert H. Nelson, Calvinism minus God: Environmental restoration as a theological concept. In L. Anathea Brooks and Stacy D. VanDeveer (Eds.): *Saving the seas: Values, scientists and international governance* (Maryland Sea Grant College, 1997); Robert H. Nelson, Environmental Calvinism: The Judeo-Christian roots of environmental theology. In Roger E. Meiners and Bruce Yandle (Eds.): *Taking the environment seriously* (Lanham, Md.: Rowman and Littlefield, 1993); and Robert H. Nelson, Unoriginal sin: The Judeo-Christian roots of ecotheology. *Policy Review* (Summer 1990).

2. *The Encyclopedia of the World's Religions* contains a chapter on Marxism. See R. C. Zaehner (1977). Dialectical materialism. In Zaehner (Ed.): *The encyclopedia of the world's religions.* New York: Barnes and Noble Books.
3. This is a main theme of Nelson, *Reaching for Heaven on Earth.*
4. See also Fogel, *The Fourth Great Awakening & the Future of Egalitarianism.*

Bibliography

Bernstein, M. A. (2001). *A perilous progress: Economists and public purpose in twentieth-century America.* Princeton, NJ: Princeton University Press.

Crichton, M. (2003). *Remarks to the Commonwealth Club.* San Francisco, California, September 15, 2003.

Ely, R. T. (1889). *Social aspects of Christianity and other essays.* New York: Thomas Y. Crowell.

Fogel, R. W. (2000). *The fourth great awakening & the future of egalitarianism.* Chicago: University of Chicago Press.

Keynes, J. M. ([1930] 1963). Economic possibilities for our grandchildren. In: J. M. Keynes, *Essays in persuasion.* New York: Norton.

McPhee, J. (1971). *Encounters with the Archdruid.* New York: Farrar, Straus and Giroux.

Mendelsohn, R. (1999). *The greening of global warming.* Washington, D.C.: AEI Press.

Mendelsohn, R. (2000). The peculiar economics of global warming. *The Milken Institute Review,* Second Quarter 2000.

Nelson, R. H. (1987). The economics profession and the making of public policy. *Journal of Economic Literature,* March.

Nelson, R. H. (1991). *Reaching for heaven on earth: The theological meaning of economics.* Lanham, MD: Rowman & Littlefield.

Nelson, R. H. (2001). *Economics as religion: From Samuelson to Chicago and beyond.* University Park, PA: Penn State Press.

Nelson, R. H. (2004). What is 'economic theology.' *The Princeton Seminary Bulletin, No. 1.*

Norton, B. G. (1991). Thoreau's insect analogies: Or, why environmentalists hate mainstream economists. *Environmental Ethics,* Fall.

Ross, D. (1991). *The origins of American social science.* New York: Cambridge University Press.

de Tocqueville, A. ([1856] 1955). *The old regime and the French Revolution.* Garden City, NY: Doubleday.

Vitz, P.C. (1977). *Psychology as religion: The cult of self-worship.* Grand Rapids, MI: William B. Eerdmans.

Why Is There a Conflict Between Business and Religion? A Historical Perspective

Kevin E. Schmiesing

Businessmen and clergy were the first Europeans to set foot in much of what would become the United States, but the relationship between the fur traders and the missionaries was not always harmonious. The missionaries, one French priest complained, were compelled to "escape the contempt" generated among Native Americans by the "negligence" and "avarice" of those "who have heretofore held the trade of this country."[1]

Antipathy between clergy and businessmen is a venerable American tradition. It is, in fact, a common phenomenon within the history of Christianity more broadly, which some would trace to Christ's own sayings on money and his violent overturning of the moneychangers' tables in the temple in Jerusalem. An attempt to understand the historical conflict between business and religion must take into account longstanding tensions between businesspeople and clergy.

Observation of the often tense, sometimes hostile, relationship between Christian clergy and the business leaders of their congregations is not novel. Yet the problem so often noticed has proved intractable. While others have detailed the ways in which contemporary religious leaders and business leaders view each other, what remains lacking is an explication of the historical dimensions of the problem. Such an enterprise is an ambitious one, and this essay offers only an anecdotal beginning.[2]

Robert Keayne

While French missionaries and traders plied the St. Lawrence valley, colonists of British descent were forming communities on the eastern seaboard. For the British colonists, the evangelizing and profit-making missions were thoroughly mixed. The New England Company, formed in 1628, declared its purpose to be the "propagation of the Gospel of Jesus Christ and the particular good of the several Adventurers." At least 25 of 41 of the company's identified subscribers were merchants, and the Puritans who migrated to New England hailed from some of the most commercial regions of Old England. In 1630, by decree of the General Court, the shareholders of the company became the citizens of the state; the following year the franchise was expanded to include all male church members. In this way, the company became the polity, which was coterminous with the church.[3]

The lineaments of clergy-business interaction in colonial New England are highlighted in the case of Robert Keayne (1595–1655), an affair immortalized by the accounts given in Massachusetts Governor John Winthrop's journal and Keayne's own *Last Will and Testament*. Legendary Harvard historian Samuel Eliot Morison granted Keayne a place in American institutional history by noting that the 1642 dispute between magistrates and deputies over the case of Goody Sherman's sow—in which Keayne was implicated—led to the development of bicameralism in the Massachusetts (and hence the national) legislature.[4]

More revealing for our purposes is the censuring of Keayne three years earlier by the government of the colony.

Robert Keayne was a London merchant who expressed early interest in the colonization of New England. He was a financial supporter of the Plymouth Company in the 1620s, but his interest went beyond a thirst for economic gain. He was a regular churchgoer and paid close attention to sermons, as his volumes of notes attest. Keayne came to the New World himself in 1635, a move whose motivation Winthrop described as being for "conscience's sake, and for the advancement of the gospel here."[5]

Keayne assumed prominence in Boston, joining the church and selling manufactures imported from England. In 1639, however, his standing in the community was called into question: he was charged in General Court with "taking above six-pence in the shilling profit; in some, above eight-pence; and, in some small things, above two for one."[6] For this offense, the court fined Keayne £200.

Keayne was also called before the church, where he "did, with tears, acknowledge and bewail his covetous and corrupt heart." At the same time, he made "some excuse for many of the particulars, which were charged upon him, as partly by pretense of ignorance of the true price of some wares, and chiefly by being misled by some false principles." Stopping short of excommunication, the church severely admonished the merchant, "for selling his wares at excessive Rates, to the Dishonor of God's name, the Offence of the

Generall Cort, and the Publique scandal of the Cuntry."[7]

Against Keayne stood the imposing figure of Reverend John Cotton (1585–1652). Cotton's moral authority was preeminent. Cotton declaimed the "false principles" that had deformed Keayne's business ethic:

> 1.That a man might sell as dear as he can, and buy as cheap as he can. 2. If a man lose by casualty of sea, etc., in some of his commodities, he may raise the price of the rest. 3. That he may sell as he bought, though he paid too dear, etc., and though the commodity be fallen, etc. 4. That, as a man may take the advantage of his own skill or ability, so he may of another's ignorance or necessity. 5. Where one gives time for payment, he is to take like recompense of one as of another.[8]

As Cotton's list of condemned principles indicates, the Keayne case intersected with a historical debate among Christian moralists concerning the concept of the "just price," and, by implication, the role and moral obligations of the businessman. Roughly speaking, the debate broke down between two sides, one of which viewed the just price as what later economists would call the "market rate," the other arguing that considerations other than the market must factor into the setting of prices. Cotton was presumably familiar with the longstanding debate, but his list of false principles does not make clear exactly where he stood. Principle (1), for instance, indicates that Cotton did not consider the market price to be inherently just. Principle (3) on the other hand, with its language "though the commodity be fallen," implies that the merchant ought to base the price of goods on the market.

Historical differences on the question of pricing, moreover, cannot be seen as a simple case of clergy-business division. The debate over just price was one that took place primarily among moral theologians—not between business advocates on one side and theologians on the other. As long as clergy could not agree among themselves as to the moral obligations of merchants, the traders of goods—even and perhaps especially those who were most conscientious—were bound to be frustrated in their attempt to live up to the moral standards of the church.

That ambiguity with respect to business obligations obtained in New England is evident in the accounts of both Winthrop and Keayne. Winthrop noted the mitigating circumstances that led many magistrates to sympathize with the merchant:

> 1. Because there was no law in force to limit or direct men in point of profit in their trade. 2. Because it is the common practice, in all countries, for men to make use of advantages for raising the prices of their commodities. 3. Because (though he were chiefly aimed at, yet) he was not alone in this fault. 4. Because all men through the country ... were guilty of the like excess in prices. 5. Because a certain rule could not be found out for an equal rate between buyer and seller, though much labor had been bestowed in it, and divers laws had been made, which, upon experience, were repealed, as being neither safe nor equal.[9]

These remarks are telling. Winthrop frankly acknowledged that Keayne's business practices were typical, that there was no law against them, that a "certain rule" for setting prices could not be attained, and that experience showed that any attempt to regulate prices by law was doomed to fail. Yet Keayne and his colleagues were expected to understand that some, undefined, rates of profit were excessive and that charging whatever price the market could bear was, in some, undefined cases, an offense against the community and the church—though, in other cases, there was nothing wrong with it.

The government of Massachusetts put few legal constraints on the conduct of trade, but the leadership of the colony assumed that moral constraints would do the necessary work. The difficulty lay in the fact that not only the positive but also the moral law concerning price was not clearly defined. As might be expected, the businessmen of Massachusetts were perplexed by the obligation to follow a rule that was not really a rule. In a climate of such vagueness, enforcement could not but seem arbitrary and vindictive rather than equitable and just.

That was Keayne's view, which, despite his earlier appearance of repentance, he elucidated in his *Last Will and Testament.* He rued the fact that "any act of mine (though not justly but by misconstruction) should be an occasion of scandall to the Gospell and pfession of the Lord Jesus." In Keayne's account, the charges against him had originated in a duplicitous customer who accused Keayne of charging him 10 penny rates for eight-penny nails. Though eventually vindicated by the testimony of the messenger who delivered the nails, Keayne had by that time become a magnet for accusations of over-pricing by troublesome clients. The accusers won over enough of the court to sustain the censure and fine.[10]

The instigator of the charge then made another claim against Keayne, which was similarly refuted by the evidence. The merchant intended to sue for slander, but Reverend Cotton "advised him to forbear because of his recent troubles, and await a more seasonable time for the counter-suit." Keayne recounted that, following this incident, Governor Winthrop had indicated that he would initiate a revocation of the original conviction. Winthrop died before that could come to pass, however, so Keayne requested as part of his last will that Winthrop's intention be fulfilled.[11]

Despite his run-ins with the authorities, Keayne continued to prosper as a merchant and retained the respect of his fellow colonists, serving in several public offices. He came into final disgrace, however, when he was convicted of drunkenness, prompting his resignation from the Boston tribunal.[12]

A devout Puritan and successful tradesman, Keayne's relationship with the leaders of the church was complicated. He counted ministers among his friends and relatives: Reverend John Wilson, a prominent Puritan clergyman, was his brother-in-law. John Cotton, though enunciating the "false principles" that had led Keayne astray, also advised him wisely concerning Keayne's proposed counter-suit.

At the same time, Keayne displayed frustration with what he viewed as the meddling of clergy in affairs that were not in their purview. Keayne scolded Reverend John Eliot for his unwanted intervention in a land purchase that the merchant made from the natives. The affair prompted Keayne to suggest that, in matters temporal, lay Christians may have as much wisdom as their ecclesiastical superiors. He urged the clergy "to harken to the advice and counsell of there brethren and to be as easily pswaded to yeeld in civill and earthly respects and things as they expect to prvayl with any of us, when they have a request to make to us for one thing or another."[13]

Keayne's testament shows that he remained dedicated to his faith and well disposed toward the clergy to the end of his life. Among his final contributions to the community and church were funds designated for a town hall, which were to include "a gallery or some other handsome Roome" for the meetings of church leaders. Winthrop remembered him as a man who had a reputation as "a hard dealer in his course of trading," but who also "was very useful to the country."[14]

Cornelius Vanderbilt

More than two centuries later, clergy and businessmen continued to interact in similar ways. Perhaps no period in American history has been as closely identified with the activities of business as that occurring between the end of the Civil War and the rise of progressivism in the final decade of the 19th century. Conventionally referred to as the Gilded Age, its central figures are equally conventionally called robber barons. As these appellations indicate, the typical portrait of the Gilded Age businessman in the American historical imagination is that of an unscrupulous executive in a big business, hungry for power and money and willing to exploit other human beings to reach his goals. "This is a government of the people, by the people and for the people no longer," President Rutherford B. Hayes bemoaned, a decade after the Gettysburg Address: "It is a government of corporations, by corporations and for corporations."[15]

This portrait is lent gravity by well-known episodes such as the Credit Mobilier scandal in which illegal ties between business leaders and Grant administration officials were uncovered. The era was characterized, too, by gigantic undulations in the business cycle, punctuated by severe depressions in 1873, 1887, and 1893. Violent encounters between management and labor drew attention to the growing pains of a form of capitalism that continued to overturn traditional relationships between workers and their craft and between workers and the owners of productive capital. Against this backdrop, the spectacular and unprecedented wealth amassed by a handful of the most notorious capitalists such as Jay Gould, J. P. Morgan, and John D.

Rockefeller provoked consternation and accusations of injustice and immorality.

Indisputably, the scale of the largest businesses continued to increase. During the 1860s, Singer Sewing Machine became the first multinational company based in the United States by opening offices in Britain and continental Europe. The rise of a managerial class was signaled by the establishment of the first school of business at the University of Pennsylvania in 1881. In 1879, the first trust was formed as a way of combining companies without running afoul of legal hurdles preventing the owning of corporation shares by another corporation. In 1889, New Jersey became the first state to legalize such corporate shareholding, and the popularity of holding companies boomed. The rise of business reached across racial boundaries, with the number of African-American-owned businesses catapulting from 4,000 to 50,000 between 1867 and 1917.[16]

Meanwhile, the rise of organized labor stimulated the formation of business organizations to counter it. The National Association of Manufacturers, heretofore concerned with promoting trade, shifted its focus to the suppression of union organization. By the end of the century, the traditional antagonism between business and government had settled, as powerful business leaders came to see the government as a useful tool for ensuring stability, furthering special interests, and enabling competition by preventing monopolies.[17]

Christianity, meanwhile, was, as in all periods, both declining and increasing. As the conventional view has it, religion was too comfortably allied with business to offer any serious criticism of the wealthy class: "For Protestantism in particular this period [1880s] was a time when the Gospel of Christ was felt to be in full harmony with the Gospel of Wealth."[18] The alliance of religion and business was recognized by clergy at the time. In 1878, Reverend Matthew H. Smith contended, "whoever wrote the history of American business would also have to write the history of religion."[19] Another contemporary, Jonathan Blanchard, acerbically described the relationship thus: "With a $10,000 gag in his mouth, a man must be a rare prodigy of faith if he can speak otherwise than gingerly of the sins of the donors."[20]

In accord with this view, some business advocates celebrate what they perceive as the triumph of business concerns over religious concerns that occurred during the period. "America, up until the industrial revolution, was far more concerned with the conduct of life rather than business," Peter Krass claims; "God still came before Mammon and the almighty dollar." By the 1890s, however, "The industrial leaders had an audience as Mammon usurped God."[21]

The possibility for genuine friendship between clergy and even a seemingly recalcitrant and imperious business mogul was demonstrated by the case of Reverend Charles Deems (1820–1893) and Cornelius Vanderbilt (1794–1877). Deems was a longtime friend of Vanderbilt's second wife and, at some point late in his life, Vanderbilt inquired about the minister, wondering if he might call on the couple. Informed of the Commodore's remark, Deems was diffident. "I have never run after rich people," he said. "I have not avoided them, but when a man, conspicuous for wealth or position, desires to know me, he must seek me."[22]

Vanderbilt did invite the minister, but Deems was wary, for Vanderbilt had a reputation for being unfriendly toward religion in general, and clergy in particular. Deems' instincts were confirmed in his first meeting with the Commodore; he had the impression that Vanderbilt was nothing but a greedy robber baron, who made no use of his fortune for the betterment of society. Vanderbilt nonetheless seemed taken by Deems and the two visited often. Deems never asked Vanderbilt for money, which was surely a mark in his favor, since Vanderbilt was notoriously annoyed by "clerical beggars." In the words of a biographer:

> His most persistent applicants for money were clergymen, and for them he felt an aversion not unmerged with contempt. As a rule he dismissed them abruptly, sometimes rudely, and once, when he had been annoyed persistently by a needy parson, he presented him with a free ticket to the West Indies and never heard of him again.

Word eventually came to the Commodore, however, that Deems hoped to buy an existing church for his expanding congregation. Vanderbilt offered to fund the purchase.

"I fired up in a minute," the minister recalled, because he suspected that Vanderbilt wished to use him as a mouthpiece for Vanderbilt's views, or perhaps to use the building itself for business purposes. Vanderbilt reassured him that his motives were pure. "After the discharge of my lightning," Deems recounted, "I felt that a sort of April shower was coming." Tears welled in Deems' eyes as he saw the working of Providence through this unbelieving railroad magnate.

"Commodore, if you give me that church for the Lord Jesus Christ," he said, extending his hand, "I'll most thankfully accept it."

"No," Vanderbilt replied. "Doctor, I wouldn't give it to you that way, because that would be professing to a religious sentiment I don't feel. I want to give you a church. That's all about it. It is one friend doing something for another friend. Now, if you take it that way, I'll give it to you."

"Commodore, in whatever spirit you give it, I gratefully accept it, but I shall receive it in the name of the Lord Jesus Christ."

In the execution of his gift, Vanderbilt displayed at once his legendary practical sense and his inscrutability. Deems wanted the church owned by trustees, but Vanderbilt insisted that it be Deems' personal property. "No, you hammer away at some of them fellows about their sins," the

Commodore said, "and they'll turn around and bedevil you so that you will have to quit. I'm going to give it to you yourself."

"And from that day forth," Deems testified, "he always treated me as one gentleman treats another who has done him a very great favor."

The minister and the mogul grew to be very close friends in the years following and the friendship produced another, grander act of charity on the part of the Commodore. Vanderbilt once expressed his admiration for Deems' learning and for the value of education more generally. This was something of a revelation, since Vanderbilt had been known for taking pride in his success despite his lack of formal training. It was widely thought that Vanderbilt considered education worthless, or worse.

Deems told the Commodore as much. "You are one of the greatest hindrances to education that I know of," he said.

"Why, how so?"

"Why, don't you see," Deems replied, "if you do nothing to promote education, to prove to the world that you believe in it, there isn't a boy in all the land who ever heard of you, but may say, 'What's the use of an education? There's Commodore Vanderbilt; he never had any, and never wanted any, and yet he became the richest man in America?'"

Vanderbilt had been considering building a monument to President Washington at a cost of one million dollars. Deems suggested, "Such a monument will not add one iota to Washington's fame.... Suppose you take that money and found a university."

The seed, once planted, grew in Vanderbilt's mind. Vanderbilt's first inclination was to found an institution connected to the Moravian church, the denomination to which his ancestors belonged. No one in that communion being found suitable to head the endeavor, the matter was entrusted to a friend of Deems', Bishop McTyeire of the Southern Methodist Church. Encouraged by the prospect of helping to heal the divisions opened by the war of the previous decade, Vanderbilt agreed to build the school in the South. In 1873, McTyeire set about founding the university, to be located in Nashville. Vanderbilt was immensely pleased with the gift and its result, expressing his satisfaction in one of the last statements of his life.

Conclusion

It is inherently difficult to draw clear and consistent lessons from historical occurrences, especially from two anecdotes such as these, widely separated by time and context. Each of the relationships examined here does, however, point to factors that contribute to fruitful businessmen-clergy interaction. Two are noted here.

First, businesspeople will be more inclined to respect the moral authority of clergy when the churchmen are perceived to be speaking from positions of knowledge rather than ignorance. This does not mean that religious leaders should say nothing about the moral dimensions of business life, but that when they do so they should demonstrate a grasp of the realities of the subject. John Cotton condemned Robert Keayne's pricing, for example, but he did not offer practical and realistic guidance as to how Keayne should have gone about setting a fair price.

Second, religious leaders must view businesspeople, especially wealthy ones, as more than sources of revenue. Vanderbilt, understandably, had no time for clerics whose sole objective was to tap his treasury. In contrast, Vanderbilt initiated contact with Reverend Deems and Deems, far from pursuing Vanderbilt's money, was at first suspicious about the motives of the benefactor. As a result, he gained Vanderbilt's respect, friendship, and, eventually, his financial support.

Both of these issues were among those cited in a recent study of the contemporary state of the relationship between Christianity and business.[23] Business-religion conflict is not only rooted in historical tensions between businesspeople and clergy; these tensions are persistent. Overcoming traditional conflicts, it seems, is a challenge that must be perennially engaged.

Notes

1. Father Paul leJeune, S.J., to Reverend Father Provincial of the Society of Jesus in the Province of France, "Relations of What Occurred in New France..." (1634), in *The Jesuit Relations and Allied Documents: Travels and Explorations of the Jesuit Missionaries in New France, 1610–1791,* vol. 6 (New York: Pageant Book Company, 1959), ed. Reuben Gold Thwaites, 145.
2. Two analyses of contemporary business-clergy relations are Laura Nash and Scotty McLennan, *Church on Sunday, Work on Monday: The Challenge of Fusing Christian Values with Business Life* (San Francisco: Jossey-Bass, 2001); and Robert A. Sirico, *The Entrepreneurial Vocation* (Grand Rapids, Mich.: Acton Institute, 2001).
3. Bernard Bailyn, *The New England Merchants in the Seventeenth Century* (Cambridge, Mass.: Harvard University Press, 1955), 17; Stephen Innes, *Creating the Commonwealth: The Economic Culture of Puritan New England* (New York: W. W. Norton & Company, 1995), 61, 206–7. Church and state in Massachusetts remained distinct, however: clergy were not permitted to hold political office.
4. Bernard Bailyn, "The *Apologia* of Robert Keayne," *William and Mary Quarterly* 7 (October 1950): 568; Samuel Eliot Morison, *Builders of the Bay Colony* (Boston: Houghton Mifflin, 1930), 92–93.
5. Bailyn, "Apologia," 571; *Winthrop's Journal: History of New England, 1630–1649,* 2 vols. (New York: Charles Scribner's Sons, 1908), ed. James Kendall Hosmer, I: 316.
6. Bailyn, *Merchants,* 41; *Winthrop's Journal*, I: 315.
7. *Winthrop's Journal,* I: 317; Robert Keayne, *Last Will and Testament,* quoted in Bailyn, "Apologia," 573.
8. *Winthrop's Journal,* I: 317.
9. *Winthrop's Journal,* I: 316.
10. Bailyn, "Apologia," 573–4; Keayne, *Last Will,* quoted in Bailyn, 573.

11. Bailyn, "Apologia," 574–5.
12. Bailyn, "Apologia," 577.
13. Bailyn, "Apologia," 582–3; Keayne, *Last Will,* quoted in Bailyn, 583.
14. Keayne, *Last Will,* quoted in Bailyn, 582; *Winthrop's Journal,* II: 65–66.
15. Quoted in John Micklethwait and Adrian Wooldridge, *The Company: A Short History of a Revolutionary Idea* (New York: Modern Library, 2003), xiv.
16. C. Joseph Pusateri, *A History of American Business,* 2nd ed. (Arlington Heights, Ill.: Harlan Davidson, 1988), 297, 302; Thomas C. Cochran, *Business in American Life: A History* (New York: McGraw-Hill, 1972), 153–4; John Sibley Butler, *Entrepreneurship and Self-Help Among Black Americans: A Reconsideration of Race and Economics* (Albany: State University of New York Press, 1991), 147.
17. Cochran, *Business in American Life,* 164, 210.
18. Paul A. Carter, *The Spiritual Crisis of the Gilded Age* (DeKalb, Ill.: Northern Illinois University Press, 1971), viii, 136–7.
19. Quoted in Cochran, *Business in American Life,* 186.
20. *Christian Cynosure* 4 (February 15, 1872): 1, quoted in Carter, *Spiritual Crisis,* 139.
21. *The Book of Business Wisdom: Classic Writings by the Legends of Commerce and Industry* (New York: John Wiley and Sons, 1997), ed. Peter Krass, xiii.
22. This recounting of the Deems-Vanderbilt relationship is based largely on W. A. Croffut, *The Vanderbilts and the Story of Their Fortune* (Chicago: Belford, Clarke, 1886), 132–141. See also Wheaton J. Lane, *Commodore Vanderbilt: An Epic of the Steam Age* (New York: Alfred A. Knopf, 1942).
23. Nash and McLennan, *Church on Sunday,* 124, 153, *inter alia.*

PART II

REGAINING HISTORICAL PERSPECTIVE

The Metaphysical Foundations of the Ethics of Commerce

Peter A. Redpath

Metaphysical and moral principles are the first and ultimate measures of all theoretical human knowledge and practical human choice. As such, we cannot possibly divorce speculation about education, art, science, politics, or commerce from reflection upon metaphysics, ethics, and human nature. As a classical metaphysician would say, "*agere sequitur esse*" ("the way a thing operates follows from the way it exists"). Existence is the first principle of all action. And all action, in some way, reflects its subject's way of existing.

Transferred to the domain of human behavior, this metaphysical principle translates thus: People and the things and human faculties that activate human actions are first principles of these actions, including of human education in general, philosophy, and business activities. How we answer the questions about who we are, where we came from, why we are here, and where we are headed influences the way we understand all human action, including our understanding of commerce.

Ancient Philosophical Reflections about Metaphysics and the Ethics of Commerce

No surprise, then, that as far back as Plato's classic work *The Republic* (Bk. 2, 368A–383E and Bk. 1, 343A–347E), we find sophisticated philosophical reflection about the relation of commerce to such moral and metaphysical questions. These appear, for example, in Plato's attempt (1) to answer for his brothers Glaucon and Adeimantos the query of how cities originate and grow and (2) to explain to the sophist Thrasymachos the difference between the arts of shepherding and money-making.

In his discussion with Glaucon and Adeimantos, Plato (427–347 B.C.) maintains that cities originate from our self-knowledge of the neediness of our human nature, from our evident knowledge that we human beings (1) are weak, not omnipotent; (2), as individuals, do not tend to be able to live as well as we can as when we cooperate with other human beings in mutual self-improvement; and (3), as individuals, lack a lot of things, including commerce with, and cooperation of, many skillful people, that we need to possess to live a superior human life. In short, in Plato's view (*ibid.,* Bk. 2, 369 A–C), the city's "real creator . . . will be our needs."

The way we act, in short, follows from the way we exist. And, given the evident awareness of our natural neediness, Plato maintains that cities grow through commerce with, and cooperation among, skillful people. He adds that our first and chief need is to provide food to enable us to maintain our existence and live. Next comes our need for housing. Third is our need for clothes and footwear.

Given this order of needs, Plato immediately concludes that, to supply these needs, at a minimum, to survive, a city will have to have five primary industries: (1) farmers, (2) home builders, (3) weavers, (4) shoe-makers, and (5) other artisans who provide for bodily human goods (examples would be physicians and teachers of trades).

Beyond this, Plato (*ibid.,* 369 C–370 B) says that a city will need a division of (1) labor (because we all have different natural abilities and skill levels) and (2) times of employment (because "if one lets slip the right season, the favorable moment in any task, the work is spoiled").

At a bare minimum a city's continued existence will also require development of secondary industries. These industries include transportation, communication, and free-trade networks. For a city cannot long survive, much less flourish, if (1) its primary artisans must also be tool-makers and distributors, (2) it lacks adequate means for such artisans to communicate a knowledge of their work, and (3) these primary and secondary artisans lack the ability freely to transport and market their wares.

Hence (*ibid.,* 370 B–Bk. 4, 427 C), the city will also need an economic sector to manufacture and distribute money, a market exchange, shopkeepers, and employees. If it wants to become a luxurious city, it will have to develop leisure industries to provide luxury items. This will have to include a network of international trade and a sophisticated political order to engage in, and handle the complexities of, internal affairs and international commerce. This will include military and educational institutions for training political leaders to coordinate all these activities, development of a legal code to regulate commerce and internal and international affairs, and laws related to educational formation, marriage, religion, and entertainment.

In his discussion about the nature of justice with the sophist Thrasymachos, Plato (*ibid.*, Bk. 1, 336 B–343 A) adds more precision to our awareness of how to engage in philosophical reasoning about this, and any, issue. Thrasymachos maintains that, precisely speaking, justice is "the advantage of the stronger," or, as we might say today, "might makes right." In opposition to Thrasymachos, Socrates (470–399 B.C.) claims that, precisely speaking, justice is "the advantage of the weaker," or, "right makes might." In defense of his claim, Socrates cites the example of the shepherd, whose business, according to Socrates, essentially involves "considering the good of sheep."

When Thrasymachos (*ibid.*, 343 B–344 E) attempts to ridicule Socrates' claim by arguing that the chief aim of shepherds is to fatten sheep to kill them, Socrates (*ibid.*, 345 A–347 B) replies that, precisely speaking, the arts of shepherding and money-making are essentially distinct because they necessarily refer to (1) two essentially different relationships and (2) two essentially different goods produced by two essentially different human faculties. Hence, just as, precisely speaking, the art of medicine refers to the specific sort of knowledge (the medical art) that a person's medical faculty produces that improves a specific sort of body (a potentially or actually "sickly body"), so, precisely speaking, the money-making art refers to a person's money-making knowledge that a person with money-making ability applies to a potentially or actually economically-deprived body.

The Human Person, Human Faculties, and the Ethics of Commerce

Socrates' discussion with Thrasymachos about the essential difference between the arts of shepherding and money-making is quite revealing because it indicates that Socrates understood necessary principles of human action to involve relations that necessarily exist between human faculties and specific differences in specific subjects that move these faculties to act (such as a body's color moves the human eye to see, or its sound the human ear to hear). While Socrates *qua* Socrates is not essentially Socrates the shepherd or money-maker, Socrates the shepherd or money-maker is Socrates possessed of a qualified knowledge, an artistic knowledge, that, in some way, an actually or potentially deprived healthy animal or economic body has activated in him through a specific difference in this respective body that necessarily relates to this artistic quality of mind.

I make the point about the proper way precisely to understand the nature of principles of human action because, precisely speaking, human commerce is a human action and, precisely speaking, a main job of the philosopher is to study first principles, indeed, all such principles. The philosophical art deals, among other things, with precision related to first principles.

Ciceronian, Aristotelian, and Medieval Reflections about the Human Person

Another precision I want to add to those Plato has already made to the question at hand is one that Marcus Tullius Cicero (106–43 B.C.) (*De officiis*, 2.157, p. 61, ed. M. T. Griffin and E. M. Atkins, trans. Atkins) makes in his celebrated work *On Duties.* There Cicero tells us that fellowship with other human beings is another inclination consequent upon our human nature.

While Plato might be right that our inclination to join together with other people to form cities is a natural result of our evident awareness that, by nature, we are weak, Cicero maintains that a more fundamental natural inclination leans us toward socializing with other human beings. Hence, he tells us: "[I]t is not in order to make honeycombs that swarms of bees gather together, but it is because they are gregarious by nature that they make honeycombs. In the same way, but to a much greater extent, men, living naturally in groups, exercise their ingenuity in action and reflection." From this common principle of animal and human nature, Cicero concludes:

> [U]nless learning is accompanied by the virtue that consists in protecting men, that is to say in the fellowship of the human race, it would seem solitary and barren. In the same way, if greatness of spirit were detached from sociability, and from the bonding between humans, it would become a kind of brutal savagery. And so it turns out that the bonds between and the sociability of men take precedence over any devotion to learning.

Were this not the case, were we human beings only inclined to join together with other human beings for individual benefit to satisfy individual needs, Cicero (*ibid.*, 2.158, p. 61) tells us that, if through some sort of magical wand, a talented intellectual were to acquire the means to fulfill all life's necessities and acquire all human comforts, this person "would drop all his business and immerse himself completely in learning and knowledge."

Cicero maintains that just the reverse is true. He says: "[I]t would not be like that: he would flee from loneliness, seeking a companion for his studies; he would want both to learn and to teach, both to listen and to speak." Hence, Cicero concludes that we must prefer "every duty whose effect lies in preserving the bonding between men and their fellowship" to the duty "limited to learning and knowledge."

In making these sage observations, knowingly or not, Cicero follows Aristotle's (*Metaphysics,* Bk. 1, Ch. 1; *Ethics,* Bk. 1, Chs. 1, 2; *Politics,* Bk. 1, Chs. 1, 2) equally sage observations that, by natural inclination, all human beings desire to (1) know, (2) develop arts and sciences, (3) socialize, and (4) thereby form cities to improve our lives, and, (5) through cooperative living with friends, become happy. For the same reason, St. Aurelius Augustine (354–430) (*Confessions,* trans. with an intro., W. S. Pine-Coffin) later tells us that we human beings "learn better under a spirit of curiosity than under fear and compulsion" because we have a natural desire to express our thoughts, to communicate with others. And, still later, St. Thomas Aquinas (1224/25–1274) (*Summa theologiae,* 1–2, 94, 2, respondeo) tells us that natural law's first precept is: "Do good and avoid evil."

Cicero (*De officiis,* 1.107, p. 61; 1.153, p. 59; 1.160, p. 62; 2. 11, pp. 66–67) maintains that all human beings have a natural inclination to develop arts, sciences, and virtue in general because we have a natural duty toward human fellowship in which and through which we become happy. Intellectual and moral virtues, in short, are a result of a natural call to duty. By nature, Cicero thinks, that, because we all have a share in reason, we human beings have a natural love for other human beings and the gods that surpasses our love for all other kinds of things. This love for all things human and divine naturally impels us toward initiative, entrepreneurship. Hence, just as, because bees are naturally gregarious toward other bees, they naturally incline to build honeycombs, so, because we human beings are naturally gregarious toward other human beings and divinity, we human beings naturally incline to (1) listen and speak, (2) teach and learn, and (3) exercise our ingenuity in action and reflection.

Business Education as Training in Intellectual and Moral Virtue

Education is the art of using our knowledge of the nature of things around us and ourselves to (1) liberate ourselves from the slavery of ignorance, bad choice, and disordered delight and, thereby, (2) improve our lives. More precisely, human education is the art of using knowledge about ourselves and things around us to develop excellent human habits of judging, choosing, reasoning, and enjoyment.

As such, human education is an art whereby we improve ourselves in our ability to acquire, develop, and mature in human knowledge and use of human freedom. Education, in short, is training in the arts of wisdom and prudence in natural fellowship with other human beings.

Business is the product of human education. As such, business education is the result of training in intellectual and moral virtue. Hence, Michael Novak (1996, p. 115) is absolutely correct and speaks in the best of classical tradition of thinkers like Cicero when he tells us in his little book *Business as a Calling*:

> Business has a vested interest in virtue. It cannot go forward with realism, courage, wisdom, honesty, integrity without a highly motivated and virtuous work community. It cannot endure without leaders and colleagues in whom many key virtues are internalized. In this and in many other ways, business is dependent on the moral and cultural institutions of a free society: families especially, schools, and public civil life. A nation's moral culture is even more fundamental than its physical ecology.

Creation *ex nihilo,* the Incarnation, and the Modern Ethics of Commerce

Even more fundamental than a nation's moral culture, however, is its metaphysical culture. What we hold to be the first and most universal truth about everything measures and influences what we hold to be true about all other things, including our views of ethics, science, and culture. Democratic capitalism's rise within Western culture was no accident. We can already see the intimations of its existence in the works of pagan philosophers and orators like Plato, Aristotle (384–322 B.C.), and Cicero. Ancient cultures, however, could not have produced the principles of modern democratic capitalism for the same reason that priest-scientist Stanley L. Jaki (1986) convincingly demonstrates they could not have produced modern physics: they lacked the metaphysical principles to do so.

As Jaki notes, ancient cultures teem with a cyclical view of time and history. Such a view tends to develop an escapist attitude within people: a hostile attitude toward time, a psychic determinism, and a general pessimism about human nature and human activities in nature and society. Such a metaphysics creates a hostile environment within which to attempt to develop a Newtonian understanding of time, the experimental scientific method, institutions of higher learning, or of democratic government.

For this reason, Jaki maintains that Christian metaphysical teachings about Creation ex nihilo and the Incarnation were largely responsible for the development of modern science. I concur with Jaki about this and add that, for similar reasons, these same metaphysical teachings helped create the moral and political climate that allowed modern democratic capitalism to arise. So does Western historical development.

In making this last claim, I do not think I am going beyond theses that Novak (1991) maintains in his classic *The Spirit of Democratic Capitalism.* I am simply filling in some historical and metaphysical details. Modern democratic capitalism and modern democratic government are mutually dependent. Such government and the political theory behind it was largely the result of metaphysical and moral principles developed by Christian natural law theorists like John Locke (1723–1790) and Montesquieu [Charles Louis de Secondat, Baron de la Brède et de Montesquieu] (1689–1785). That Adam Smith (1723–1790) was inspired by a Christian metaphysic and ethic is no more an accident than was the similar inspiration behind the scientific work of Galileo Galilei (1564–1642) and Sir Isaac Newton (1642–1727).

The later Middle Ages and Renaissance were periods of incredible initiative, enterprise, and entrepreneurship precisely because of the metaphysical impact that Christian doctrines about Creation and the Incarnation started to have upon European culture after the famous papal condemnation of 1277, issued through Parisian Bishop Stephen Tempier, of many currently-circulating metaphysical, and other scientific, teachings. This condemnation, in turn, was chiefly motivated by metaphysical and moral thought and views about human nature and ethics that had arisen within cathedral schools and Catholic universities in Europe going back to prior centuries.

Ancient pagan culture did not develop the Madisonian principle of limited government upon which we base the separation of powers that lies at the heart of modern political economy and democratic capitalism. Modern Christian thinkers developed it from principles they inherited through Sts. Thomas and Augustine and other church doctors and fathers from principles they received from Moses and Jesus Christ, Socrates, Plato, Aristotle, and Cicero.

Christianity, Limited Government, and the Modern Ethic of Commerce

The modern principles of limited government are rooted in the cardinal moral virtues that Western culture inherited mainly from the moral teachings of Socrates, Plato, Aristotle, and Cicero, which presuppose the Greek philosophical view that human beings are rational and social animals. St. Thomas Aquinas (S. t., 1–2, 91, 4, respondeo) synthesized this teaching with Catholic moral theology in his treatment of the variety of law in question 91 of the First Part of the Second Part of his *Summa theologiae*. In so doing, apart from ancient Greek natural law doctrine and views about human nature, he depended upon the theological work of St. Augustine and Jewish Scriptures.

In article 4 of this question, St. Thomas examines whether we need a divine law beyond natural law and human law. Referring to *Psalms* 18:8, St. Thomas replies that we need such a law for four reasons: (1) because law directs us to actions proportionate to our end; (2) because human judgment is uncertain, especially regarding singular and contingent matters; (3) because (a) people are able to make laws about things we are able to judge, (b) we can only judge exterior personal movements, not interior human acts, and (c) full virtue demands that we be right in both areas; and (4) because, as St. Augustine says in *On Free Choice* [*De libero arbitrio*], (Bk. 1, Ch. 5), human law is unable to punish all evil because, if it were to attempt to do so, it would withdraw much good from the political order and impede, not help, the common good, which we need for human discourse.

If we want to go beyond Sts. Thomas and Augustine, we can trace the Madisonian principle in Western culture to Moses' (*Exodus*, 7:1–5) dealing with Pharaoh and to Jesus' (*Matthew*, 22:15–22) teaching that we have to give to God the things that are God's and to Caesar the things that are Caesar's.

Novak (1991, pp. 77–80) tells us that Adam Smith designed his economic views as closely as possible "to fit human character," "to unleash human creativity." According to Novak, Smith thought: "The key to the wealth of nations lies in human creativity more than in any other source." The key to that lies in "the natural system of liberty."

Beyond this, Novak observes that, in his famed *An Inquiry into the Nature and Causes of the Wealth of Nations,* Smith came up with "the bold and original idea," new, at least, for that time, that "intelligence" (*caput* in Latin) was the main cause of "sustained economic development." Novak adds that Smith was motivated to develop a new understanding of economics because he envisioned it as the best means to achieve abolition of famine, raise up the poor's standard of living, and banish material suffering from all humankind.

In short, like all Christians, Smith held that this universe in which we live is not cyclical in time. It displays novelty, and human beings are free agents. These facts are a cause of hope in the future. As a Christian, Smith knew that human beings are created in the image and likeness of God. As such, we possess free choice of will and, in some sense, are masters of our own destiny that is part of a providentially guided world. Smith was a product of modern Europe, culture largely developed over centuries through the metaphysical sacrifice of Franciscan love for the poor, and a higher educational system built on the shoulders of Benedictines, Dominicans, Franciscans, and Jesuits. Within 200 years of their founding in 1574, the Jesuits alone had established about 650 colleges in Europe.

Modern Corporate Success and the Ethic of Commerce

As Novak (1996, pp. 54–133) correctly observes, the American political order essentially depends upon business. And, among other things, as he tells us, sound business depends upon (1) wealth creation through a sector of the body politic separate from the government, (2) a political climate that encourages inventiveness, and (3) good business habits. Successful business ventures require moral virtues: the courage to take initiative and risk, and to trust; the willingness to sacrifice now, to forego short-term profit and to budget for future, and larger, rewards; a sense of justice displayed in teamwork, honesty, integrity, and respect for others; and the marks of practical intelligence that result from prudence: foresight, practical realism, and inventiveness.

No wonder, then, that he (*ibid.,* pp. 42–45) tells us business leaders are among the largest group of church-goers in the United States, third after the clergy and military.

Attempts to explain the success of modern business in terms of greed are inadequate on historical, political, moral, and metaphysical grounds. Such attempts fly in the face of the metaphysical principle of *agere sequitur esse.* Moreover, greed does not produce the climate of social cohesion that a sound political economy needs in order to flourish. Justice does this. And, as ancient Greeks like Socrates, Plato, and Aristotle well understood, we cannot sustain justice without prudence, temperance, and courage.

Furthermore, we cannot sustain prudence, temperance, justice, or courage in a metaphysical climate rooted in pessimism, skepticism, cynicism, and doubt. Hence, to fail to recognize the crucial dependence of political economy upon definite metaphysical principles that can support the ethic upon which it is essentially grounded dooms such an economy eventually to contribute to producing bad moral habits in citizens that will eventually bury the economic order and the political order it helps sustain. Hopefully, Americans of this generation will display the prudence not to make such a devastating metaphysical mistake. *Verbum sat sapientiae.*

Bibliography

Aquinas, St. Thomas (1224/25–1274). *Summa theologiae.* 5 vols. Ed. Piana. Ottawa: Collège Dominicain d'Ottawa, 1941.

Aristotle (384–322 B.C.). Ethics. In: Richard Mc Keon (Ed.), *The basic works of Aristotle.* New York: Random House, 21st printing, 1968; first published in 1941.

_________. *Metaphysics.* In: Richard Mc Keon (Ed.), *The basic works of Aristotle.* New York: Random House, 21st printing, 1968; first published in 1941.

_________. *Politics.* In: Richard Mc Keon (Ed.), *The basic works of Aristotle.* New York: Random House, 21st printing, 1968; first published in 1941.

Augustine, St. Aurelius (354–430). *Confessions.* W. S. Pine-Coffin (Trans.). Baltimore, Md.: Penguin Books Inc., 1964 repr.; first published Harmondsworth, Middlesex, England: Penguin Books, Ltd., 1961.

Cicero, Marcus Tullius (106–43 B.C.). *De officiis* [On Duties]. M. T. Griffin and E. M. Atkins (Eds.), Atkins (Trans.). Cambridge, England: Cambridge University Press, Cambridge Texts in the History of Political Thought, 2001; first published in 1991.

Jaki, S. L. (1986). *Science and creation: From eternal cycles to an oscillating universe.* Edinburgh: Scottish Academic Press, revised and enlarged edition.

Novak, M. (1996). *Business as a calling.* New York: The Free Press, Simon & Schuster, 1996.

_________. (1991). *The spirit of democratic capitalism.* Lanham, Md. and New York: Madison Books and London, England: IEA Health and Welfare Unit, Institute of Economic Affairs [distributed by National Book Network].

Plato (427–347 B.C.). *Republic.* In: Edith Hamilton and Huntington Cairns (Eds.), *The collected dialogues of Plato: Including the letters.* New York: Random House, Bollingen Series 71 [distributed for the Bollingen Foundation by Pantheon Books], 1961.

The Deuteronomic Double Standard: Human Nature and the Nature of Markets

Seth W. Norton

Introduction

The Deuteronomic command regarding usury (Deuteronomy 23: 19-20) has drawn unparalleled attention from the widest range of political leaders as well as clerical and theological luminaries. Conflicting interpretations have dominated during different periods, constituting a remarkable evolution. The evolution has been lengthy, lasting more than two millennia.[1]

The present is not like the past. Controversies over the meaning of the text no longer garner much attention among scholars of business, economics, or ethics. The triumph of capitalism and secularism has rendered sacred exegesis irrelevant and at most the subject of a quaint history. However, the absence of controversy over sacred texts in general should not diminish this particular text. The length and intensity of interpretative battles attest to its importance in bygone centuries. My contention is that the centrality of the text to present issues is undervalued. My point is that the ambivalence of the Deuteronomic commandment or what has been called the "Deuteronomic Double Standard" is not a double standard at all. The text contains the foundation of the comparative institutional choice between economic institutions—the family, in a broad sense, and the market, also in a broad sense. Because implicit interest rates are inherent in nearly all exchange and production, the message of Deuteronomy applies to nearly all commercial life, not simply financial capital. Moreover, several ethical issues related to commercial life are linked to the ambivalence of the Deuteronomic commandment.

The Double Standard

The Old Testament contains a number of texts that proscribe lending. The Deutronomic command is particularly troublesome, however, because it appears to have an ethnocentric quality. The text bans usury among the Hebrew brotherhood and yet condones or, some would say, commands lending at interest to foreigners.

Nelson (1969, p. xx) contains the amplified text:

> Deuteronomy 23: 19. Thou shalt not lend upon usury (*neshek*) to thy brother (*l'ahika*); usury of money, usury of victuals, usury of anything that is lent upon usury:
>
> Deuteronomy 23: 20. Unto a stranger (*nokri*) thou mayest lend upon usury; but unto thy brother thou shalt not lend upon usury, that the Lord thy God may bless thee in all that thou settest thine hand to in the land whither thou goest to possess it.

Nelson (1969, p. xix) also notes that the tribal or ethnic component of the commandment was limited. Privileges and proscription of kinship included resident strangers (*toshab*) and sojourners (*ger*). Thus, the text extends beyond the narrowest kinship ties.

Controversy

It seems unlikely that any single sacred text that refers to economic affairs has generated as much controversy as the Deuteronomic commandment. In the West, intermittent controversy existed for more than two millennia with a major cessation only occurring in the last two hundred years.

The controversy has included a wide range of participants: local clerics, church hierarchy, popes, reformers, jurists, and even heads of state. For example, in the German Reformation, the controversy touched the raw conflict between the radical element that sought to undermine civil authority and establish a communalistic society wherein no usury or even private property would exist and the conservative reformers who did not favor a social revolution. The latter sought to curb the social unrest. The theological issues focused on the continued relevance of the Mosaic Law to commercial activity, but the practical implications were even more profound. Theological conflict bordered on the causes of insurrection and justification of rebellion.

Middle Ages

The spread of Christianity throughout the Roman world and beyond led to a universalism in world views and in wide ranges of economic life. The new Christian world conveniently tried to stress the brotherhood of believers. Consequently, for centuries, lending at interest of any kind among communicant Christians was viewed as inconsistent with the faith and worthy of punishment. The idea of brotherhood–the kinship of the ancient Hebrew society-was replaced by bonds of faith and religious citizenship so that lending at interest among the broad community of faith came to be viewed as sin. It was grounds for denial of sacraments and other punishments as well as forced restitution through the quasi-civil fiats of ruling clergy. The tradition was heartily endorsed by leading clerics and theologians, including St. Jerome, Innocent III, Peter Lombard, and Thomas Aquinas.

There were some countervailing pressures. St. Ambrose followed a Christianized, literal reading of the text by applying the ban on interest to all of the Christian community, but permitting lending at interest by Christians to non-Christians. More importantly, commercial pressure on clerics to redefine the ban on usury, to expand the exceptions, and to accept novel contracts with interest terms attached were common for much of the medieval period, but came to the fore in Italy in the 15th century and more broadly in the 16th century. Popes Martin V and Calixtus III proved amenable to condoning "novel contracts."

Modern Capitalism

The tension between the radical and conservative reformers identified above highlights a period of ferment in the German Reformation. Radical reformers favored aggressive action against those who practiced usury, princes, and more generally, civil authority. Sabbatical and Jubilee practices were highlighted.

Conservative reformers did not reject the brotherhood concept and at times were sympathetic with the anti-commercial populism. However, as violence and the threats of violence developed in the 1520s, conservative reformers moved away from the radicals. Conservatives tended to associate the ban on usury with the ancient Hebrew polity and argued the Old Testament would not be a model for modern civil society. While Luther was somewhat ambivalent regarding usury and trade in general, other conservative reformers—Bucer, Melanchthon, and Zwingli laid the foundations for a break with the long-held teaching on usury.

John Calvin marked many turning points in European thought. His writings on usury laid the foundation for the role of capital in commercial life. Calvin went beyond the German reformers in limiting the applicability of Hebrew civil law to the commercial world of his day. In particular, Calvin stressed the social benefit of usury linked to commercial life and the benefits of voluntary agreements that benefit all parties and harmed no one. Widespread commercial lending seemed to be well within the boundaries of Christian faith and practice.

Calvin's view spread. England was an early adopter of liberalized lending policies. The liberalization corresponded to a commercial boom. The value of free flowing capital seemed legitimate. Jurists such as William Blackstone added formal and powerful legitimacy in opinions and writings. Other European nations followed. Jews in France under pressure from Napoleon officially sanctioned a view with Calvinist and nationalist leanings. Catholics in England and throughout Europe did the same, and some even emphasized the long-run compatibility of Catholic teaching with lending at interest and other features of capitalist economies.

A General Problem

The length and at times intensity of exegetical and real wars over usury and capitalism's decisive triumph obscure the grand questions of the text. The Deuteronomic commandment addresses more fundamental issues than whether lending is permissible in light of the text. Foundational questions regarding human nature and human relations and the core institutions that enhance human well-being are contained in the text. In short, the text deals with the central issues of economic life.

Discrete Exchange

To understand the breadth of meaning in the text, it is crucial to examine the nature of exchange. Ian Macneil (1978) provides a delineation of exchange. It is common to think of buying and selling in the simplest textbook treatment of those processes–essentially, a spot market. Macneil places such behavior under the rubric of "discrete exchange." That category corresponds to exchange at an instant in time with no reference to the past and none to the future. There is, naturally, no financing with the transaction. Macneil (1978, p.855) gives the example of a cash payment for gasoline at a station on the New Jersey turnpike by a motorist who rarely travels that route.

The model of discrete exchange is useful because such exchanges occur frequently in everyday life. However, the model is more useful as a contrast to prevalent forms of more complex exchange. For example, much of modern exchange entails recurring transactions, extensions of liability, and negotiable and contingent payment. In such transactions, a finance charge is virtually always present. Interest payments are implicit in much of exchange. Indeed, Macneil's observation is that modern economies are dominated by complex exchange and contract law has evolved to address the role of law in such exchanges.

While the prevalence of complex exchange is greater today than in the ancient or medieval world, it merits noting that elements of complex contracts that clerics dealt with in usury controversies often had some of these features. For example, consider the case of Father Jeremiah O'Callaghan, a traditionalist Irish cleric, who disciplined a retailer "... whose time price was much higher than his ready-money price" (Nelson 1969, p. 124). The transactions that the retailer offered were not discrete transactions unless the exchange was of the "ready-money" type and there were no other intertemporal features to the exchange. Routine exchanges were likely to entail nondiscrete features in the pre-industrial world. Doubtless they are more common today. In short, the Deuteronomic text seems to address the core of market exchange behavior and prohibitions against market behavior.

The Adam Smith Problem

A more general reading of the Deuteronomic text show remarkable affinity to another putative text-based inconsistency. The "Adam Smith problem" refers to the inconsistent treatments of human nature in Adam Smith's famous works, *The Theory of Moral Sentiments,* Indianapolis, IN: Liberty Classics (1759) [1982], and *An Enquiry into the Nature and Causes of the Wealth of Nations,* Indianapolis, IN: Liberty Classics (1776) [1981]. The former stresses the human propensity for benevolence stemming from sympathy for others, while the latter stresses the human propensity for trade stemming from self interest. The conflict is amplified by Smith's observations that both qualities of human nature and behavior are universal.

Scholars in economic thought have devoted considerable attention to this inconsistency.[2] It does not have the length, visibility, and direct impact on commercial life as the controversies surrounding the Deuteronomic text, but the controversy has an important niche in the history of economic thought. The relevance of the Adam Smith problem is that reconciling the conflicting stories of human motivation provides insight into the ambivalence of the Deuteronomic text and its relevance to the ethics of commerce.

Scholars have tried to find consistency in the ostensibly inconsistent themes in Smith's works. Otteson (2002) provides a detailed history of economic thought and coherent analysis and resolution of the Adam Smith problem. The conflicting texts can be reconciled by two principles, (1) the evolution of both morals and markets, and (2) the "familiarity principle."

Otteson notes that the evolution of morality and markets both stem from the human propensity to trade for mutual benefit. In the process of trade and in the underlying specialization of production that leads to trade, markets emerge as an unintended order with rules and beneficial outcomes consistent with the innate human desire for a better life. Similarly, Otteson sees a nearly identical evolution in the area of morals that leads to consensual standards of morality.

The evolution of morality and markets may have considerable relevance for tracing the exegetical wars over the Deuteronomic text. Perhaps the evolution of the interpretations of the text and the attendant laws, judicial opinions, and contracts that stemmed from them conform to the Smithian evolution. One way to interpret the theological and civil debate over the text is the evolution of thought to accommodate the evolution of market institutions. Whatever merit the evolution of the morality of economic institutions has in intellectual history, it misses the fundamental unity of the text. Indeed, the purely evolutionary view treats part of the text—the tribal or family component-as obsolete. The unity of the text lies in the complementary features of the tribe/family and the market. Otteson's second theme, the "familiarity principle," is most relevant.

Otteson's analysis is in the same tradition of Coase's (1976) discussion of the Adam Smith problem. The familiarity principle is Otteson's appellation for Smith's observation in *The Theory of Moral Sentiments* that benevolence varies directly with people's familiarity with others. Humans tend to be naturally altruistic towards their closest family, then less so towards distant family, and even less so towards neighbors, friends, and colleagues, and very little toward strangers.

Altruism, "benevolence" in Smith's terms, is a wonderful thing. It is a human virtue by nearly any standard. However, benevolence is limited. People sacrifice for those they know best and much less for others. Much human interaction with those we know is altruistic whereas human interaction with those we do not know is motivated by self interest. Smith asserts people will sacrifice to save unknown people caught in great tragedies, but they will not sacrifice very much. However, people are well disposed to benefit others by mutually advantageous trade even when, or primarily when, those people are complete strangers, unknown and perhaps unknowable.

A Two-Edged Sword Not a Double Standard

The unity of Smith's two classic works permits a reinterpretation of the Deuteronomic text. The term double standard is misleading. Indeed the role of trading with strangers but applying benevolence or altruism to tribal "brothers" is remarkably consistent with Smith's unified view of human nature. The medieval exegesis simply is outside of Smith's framework and fails to recognize the consistency of the text with the maximum possible benefits of human interaction.

Consequences

Reading the Deuteronomic texts in light of Smith's observations changes interpretative foundations. A Smithian view of the text underscores the benefits of trade. Second, it presents a rough framework for analyzing the ethics of commerce.

The Power of Markets

The most direct implication of a Smithian reading of the text is that the power of markets is affirmed. The sacred text affirms the precept that what people are reluctant to provide out of altruism they may provide out of self interest. The ancient Hebrews were permitted to generate economic benefits for foreigners through trading and financing the trading with strangers. More generally, the gains from trade combined with the limits of altruism underscore the ethical mandates not to fetter markets without other compelling ethical interests. Ronald Coase (1976, p. 544) provides a cogent summary of this theme.

> The great advantage of the market is that it is able to use the strength of self interest to offset the weakness and partiality of benevolence, so that those who are unknown, unattractive, or unimportant, will have their wants served.

The Benefits of Credit: An Example

Much of ancient opposition to lending and the restrictive interpretation of the text treated mutually voluntary trade that included interest as inherently exploitive—either bereft of benefits or disproportionately unbeneficial. The evolution of modern commerce should be *prima facie* evidence against that view, but common social critiques of market exchange, e.g. Meeks (1989), echo the sentiment of medieval exegesis. Simply stated, social critiques of market exchange with interest components ignore the benefits of market exchange—particularly for the poorest of the world's peoples.

Modern empirical analysis, e.g. Norton (2003), provides rigorous evidence for the benefits of market institutions and processes. Some simple descriptive statistics provide further relevant evidence. The benefits of credit provision—often seen as nefarious in medieval thought and contemporary social criticism, can be seen by looking at the role of credit provision and world poverty. Table 1 contains descriptive statistics.

Table 1. Benefits of Private Credit Provision

Category	Human Poverty Index	Survival to Age 40
Low Provision	39.9	33.5
Medium Provision	30.7	19.4
High Provision	10.6	7.1

N=55. High and low are one standard deviation above and below the sample mean for the value of credit to the private sector as a percentage of GDP. The credit data are for 1980-95. Data are from Demirgüc-Kunt and Levine (2001). The poverty and survival data are from the United Nations (1997) and are for 1990-95. The mean estimates are significantly different at the .001 level or lower.

The data in table 1 show the arithmetic means for well-established poverty measures—the United Nations Human Poverty Index and for one of its easily interpreted component measures. The index is a ranking of largely nonindustrialized countries based on an index of human deprivation with respect to education, nutrition, sanitation, and mortality. Higher levels indicate more deprivation—poverty. One problem with the index is the difficulty in interpreting its scale. Its component measures are the percentages of a country's population that suffer some index of human deprivation. An example is the component of the poverty index that is also shown in table 1—the proportion of country's population that does not survive until the age of 40. The data are available primarily for the poorer countries of the world and thus do not reflect the simple advantages of infrastructure, human capital, or even geography that are generally associated with North American, Europe, and the richest of the Asian countries.

The critique of lending focused on its excesses or excessively high rates, but ignored any corresponding benefits. To the extent providing commercial credit enhances productive activity and the benefits of trade, we should expect the poverty measures to be reduced where credit is more abundant. Accordingly, table 1 contains mean poverty measures in countries with high, low, and intermediate provision of credit to the private sector from banks and other financial intermediaries. The credit measure is total credit provided to the private sector as a percentage of GDP. The data are from Demirgüc-Kunt and Levine (2001).

The mean poverty measures in table 1 show a strong pattern of reduced poverty where private credit is more readily available. The poverty index is nearly four times higher (more poverty) in countries with low private credit availability than in those countries with high credit availability. Similarly, the percentage of the population not surviving until the age of 40 in low credit availability countries is more than four times the percentage in countries with high credit availability. Because the sample countries are primarily among the poorer countries of the world and include some of the poorest countries of the world, the benefits of credit for the world's poor must be considered when examining social critiques of lending and markets. The data are unequivocal. Credit availability is linked with reductions in poverty and mortality.

The Benefits of Globalization: Another Example

A second set of statistics bears on the question of the benefits of market exchange more generally when human differences are common. Otteson and Coase both view the advantages of markets as a substitute for altruism when ethnic or other differences tend to diminish benevolence or purely altruistic exchange.

It is straightforward to posit the hypothesis that markets should render greater benefits in polities where altruism is limited because of social heterogeneity. Recent research, e.g. Easterly and Levine (1997), Knack and Keefer (1997), Norton (2000), shows that growth enhancing institutions and even the trust of other citizens are retarded when ethnic fractionalization is present. Moreover, domestic trade is also likely to be attenuated when fractionalization is present (Easterly and Levine, 1997). However, one implication of Adam Smith, at least as interpreted by Coase and Otteson, is that markets in the form of international trade should be more beneficial to citizens in more ethnically fractionalized countries than in more homogeneous countries.

Table 2 contains poverty data as it is linked to world trade. The same poverty measures are used as in table 1, but comparisons are made between counties with above average ethnic fractionalization and countries with below average fractionalization.[3] The implication of the familiarity principle is that trade—in this case openness to world trade-should reduce poverty but should do so more where the poverty reducing benefits of altruism are restricted due to ethnic fractionalization. The categories of open and closed are obtained from Gallup, Sachs, and Mellinger (1999).[4]

Table 2. Benefits of Trade and Ethnic Fractionalization

	Homogeneous Countries		Ethnically Fractionalized Countries	
Trade Status	**Poverty Index**	**Survival**	**Poverty Index**	**Survival**
Closed Countries	30.9	19.4	42.0	30.1
Intermediate Countries	22.2	12.6	37.7	27.5
Open Countries	17.5	11.2	16.7	10.5

N=35 for the low fractionalization subsample and n=40 for the high fractionalization subsample. Trade status data are from Gallup, Sachs, and Mellinger (1999). Poverty data are from United Nations (1997). Data are for 1990-95. The difference between estimates for the closed and open countries is statistically significant at the .10 level for the low fractionalized countries and .0001 for the highly fractionalized countries. All other differences in means are significantly different at the .05 level, except for the closed versus intermediate trade countries for the survival measure in the highly fractionalized subsample.

The mean poverty values are shown in table 2. Two points are salient. First, trade openness is associated with lower poverty levels. The ubiquitous critiques of globalization are not evident in these data. The poverty index is a lot lower in countries open to trade compared to countries that are closed to trade. That pattern is evident for both types of countries. Second, the magnitude of the difference between open and closed countries is much greater for ethnically fractionalized countries than ethnically homogeneous ones. While trade within countries may be inhibited by lack of trust or the absence of market friendly institutions, trade from abroad generates much greater benefits in the ethnically fragmented countries. For example, in ethnically homogeneous countries the percentage of people surviving to the age of 40 is only about eight percent more in open countries than closed countries. However, in ethnically heterogeneous countries, the gap is much greater. The percentage of the population in closed, ethnically fractionalized countries that does not survive to age 40 is about 30 percent, while the comparable percentage for ethnically fractionalized countries that are open to international trade is only about 10 percent.

The data in tables 1 and 2 show that credit and trade benefit the poor. Poverty and mortality are lower where credit is more readily available and the benefits of trade are greater in more ethnically fractionalized countries. The benefits are greater where trust and altruism are likely to be lower. Thus, the lending and trading opportunities permitted in the most literal reading of the Deuteronomic text are consistent with behavior that helps the world's poor.

General Framework for Ethics

The Deuteronomic text on lending underscores the value of benevolence for people in close daily proximity and the power of markets in more anonymous interaction. One evident implication is the power of markets in ameliorating human deprivation as the poverty index and mortality data in table 1 and 2 show. However, the two-edged sword presents a more important feature. It lays the foundation for framing ethical dimensions—the issue of the comparative advantage of institutions for solving problems—benevolence through family or clan versus free exchange through anonymous markets. One simple implication is that ethical decisions must somehow entail (1) selecting the appropriate domain for human action and (2) devising rules that are consistent with advantages of the appropriate institution.

These are not original propositions. They are delineated quite well by Hayek (1988, p. 18) and amplified by Vernon L. Smith (2003, p. 465). Consider the quotation from Hayek with Vernon Smith's interpretative inserts in parentheses.

> ... we must constantly adjust our lives, our thoughts, and our emotions, in order to live simultaneously within different kinds of orders according to different rules. If we were to apply the unmodified, uncurbed rules (of caring intervention to do visible "good") of the ... small band or troop, or... our families.... to the (extended order of cooperation through markets), as our instincts and sentimental yearnings often make us wish to do, we would destroy it. Yet if we were to always apply the (competitive) rules of the extended order to our more intimate groupings, we would crush them.

Hayek and Smith are clearly saying something about the efficacy of family or clan versus anonymous markets. The edited text from Hayek is consistent with the controversial text from Deuteronomy. For kin and those with whom we are familiar, benevolence dominates. It has its own rules, not the same rules as the unfettered market. Presumably, reciprocity is instrumental. Presumably, a sense of community is also present. For non-kinship or unfamiliar parties, market exchange dominates with rules, norms, and practices that sustain market exchange and differ from the benevolent rules of kinship and community. Their domains are separate and Hayek seems to suggest that the separation is in the best interest of human well-being.

Caveats about Markets

Demonstrating a powerful and beneficial effect of open trade policies strongly affirms their advantages or more precisely the limits of benevolence. That these results do not conform to the anti-globalization motif makes the communication of the benefits of markets an essential task. However, despite the evident benefits of trade, it does seem likely that prohibitions against market exchanges that meet the wants of some members of the community at the expense of third parties would naturally fit with the consensual standards for the ethics of commerce.

Far more relevant from the Hayek/Vernon Smith perspective is the danger of using market exchange and its attendant rules for activities that are more appropriately handled by the family or extended kinship. Coase (1976, p. 544) cites child rearing as an example. Coase seems to affirm the view that much of child rearing and certainly ultimate responsibility for child rearing belong in the family/kin domain. Others would disagree, but a curious agenda for the ethics of commerce emerges. What are the ethics of offering market solutions for child rearing? Is corporate day care an ethical employment benefit, or is failure to provide those services an ethical provision? What about offering products in the market that clearly undermine parents' effectiveness in child rearing activities? How does the necessity to maintain freedom of contract and the formation of public policy interact with these choices?

The intent to this paper is not to resolve this issue or countless related ones. The intent is also not to discuss whether public policies or business policies should rule on these issues. The central point of the Deuteronmic text and the Hayek/Vernon Smith text is that nonmarket exchange through family and kinship ties is the right domain for many types of human action, and the power and triumph of markets should not destroy such exchanges.

Caveats about Benevolence

Corresponding warnings about benevolence also exist. One feature is the emotional purity or sentimentality of benevolence should not lead to the conclusion that markets do not enhance human well-being. Whatever the magnitude of benefits of housing provided by altruistic nonprofit construction firms, a lot of beneficial housing construction is provided through the market. Policies that circumscribe market behavior for the provision of goods widely held to be essential to life would hardly seem ethical.

More importantly, benevolence may be wonderful within the family or clan, but it is partial, i.e. discriminatory. As Coase notes, the provision of goods via benevolence will more likely go to some privileged subset of the community. It hardly seems unethical for that to be the case. Providing for our families and friends and those we deem disadvantaged is natural and common. However, the ethics of institutional choice must countenance the inherent partiality of benevolence and simultaneously recognize the impartiality of markets. Limiting the domain of market exchange to expand the domain of family/kinship exchange necessarily raises the possibility of more partiality.

Concluding Thoughts

The Deuteronomic commandment on usury is rich. The long controversies it engendered and the variety of arguments regarding the text underscore it richness. Moreover, an examination of the complexities of exchange clearly point to a lot more than what might commonly be thought of as usury.

The richest feature of the text is that is shows the appropriateness of both benevolence in nonmarkets and anonymous market exchange as alternative sources of human problem solving. The implication of the text and similar expositions by Adam Smith, Hayek, and Vernon Smith indicate that the ethics of commerce should be related to alternative forms of coordination and cooperation.

There are many religious issues in the ethics of commerce. Issues of disclosure and fraud come to mind as do the pricing of precious life-saving chemical entities. The discussion above does not address many specific business issues. The fundamental contention is that the role of comparative institutions is foundational to ethical issues.

Part of ethical behavior entails fitting behavior and institutions with the special capabilities of alternative institutions. Lending versus giving and markets versus family and clan are not necessarily substitutes. They are in fact complements in human problem solving and enhancing well-being. Affirmation of this simple point is one foundation for the ethics of commerce.

Notes

1. Benjamin Nelson (1969) provides a thematic yet detailed account of the scholarly and practical aspects of usury. Views of clerics, theologians, jurists, public officials, and traders are included. The accounts in this chapter come primarily from Nelson. For a strictly economic interpretation of usury laws, see Glaeser

and Scheinkman (1998).
2. The inconsistency and scholarly contribution to the meaning of the inconsistency are discussed in Coase (1976) and in greater detail in Otteson (2002). Both Coase and Otteson tend to view the inconsistency as a misinterpretation of human nature and human context. Both Coase and Otteson view the two sides of human nature identified by Adam Smith as complementary.
3. The ethnic fractionalization data are the standard used in empirical research. The data are the Atlas-Narodov-Mira data. The data are from Taylor and Hudson (1972). See Norton (2000) for a description.
4. Gallup, Sachs, and Mellinger (1999) describe the openness measure for a large sample of countries for the period 1965-1990. The categorization is based on average tariff rates less than 40 percent, quotas and licensing must cover less than 40 percent of imports, the "black market premium" must be less than 20 percent, and export taxes should be moderate.

Bibliography

Coase, R. H. (1976). Adam Smith's view of man. *Journal of Law & Economics, 19,* 529-546.

Demirgüc-Kunt, A. & Levine, R. (Eds.) (2001). *Financial structure and economic growth.* Cambridge, MA: MIT Press.

Easterly W. & Levine, R. (1997). Africa's growth tragedy. *Quarterly Journal of Economics, 112,* 1201-50.

Gallup, J., Sachs, J. D., & Mellinger, A. (1999). Geography and economic development, Center for Economic Development. Harvard University.

Glaeser, E. L. & Scheinkman, J. (1998). Neither a lender nor borrower be: An economic analysis of interest restrictions and usury laws. *Journal of Law & Economics, 41,* 1-36.

Hayek, F. A. (1988). *The fatal conceit.* Chicago: University of Chicago Press.

Knack, S. & Keefer, P. (1997). "Does social capital have an economic payoff? A cross-country investigation. *Quarterly Journal of Economics, 112,* 1251-87.

Macneil, I. (1978). Contracts: adjustment of long-term economic relations under classical, neoclassical, and relational contract law. *Northwestern University Law Review, 72,* 854-905.

Meeks, M. D. (1989). *God the economist.* Minneapolis, MN. Fortress Press.

Nelson, B. (1969). *The idea of usury: From tribal brotherhood to universal otherhood.* 2nd Edition. Chicago: University of Chicago Press.

Norton, S. W. (2000). The cost of diversity: Endogenous property rights and growth. *Constitutional Political Economy, 11,* 319-37.

Norton, S. W. (2003). Economic institutions and human well-being: A cross national analysis, *Eastern Economic Journal, 29,* 23-40.

Otteson, J. R. (2002). *Adam Smith's marketplace of life.* Cambridge: Cambridge University Press.

Smith, A. (1759) [1982]. *The theory of moral sentiments.* Indianapolis, IN: Liberty Classics.

Smith, A. (1976) [1981]. *An enquiry into the nature and causes of the wealth of nations.* Indianapolis, IN: Liberty Classics.

Smith, V. L. (2003). Constructivist and ecological rationality in economics. *American Economic Review, 93,* 465-508.

Taylor, C. L. & Hudson, M. C. (1972). *World handbook of political and social indicators.* New Haven, CN: Yale University Press.

United Nations. (1997). *Human development report.* New York: Oxford University Press.

What Does America Owe to Florence?

William F. Campbell

Introduction

Bertrand de Jouvenel once delivered a challenge to the United States which is still relevant:

> We can and we must spell out public policies for the control of all those forms of pollution with which we are debasing our environment and for the creation of harmonious cities, but we shall not achieve very impressive results unless education at the very earliest stage breathes into our conscience reverence for the earth's bounty, on which we depend, and regard for beauty as Man's only lasting achievement.
>
> Surely the United States as the richest country of our world, should take the lead. When Italy held this position, in the late Middle Ages and during the Renaissance, it gave the world what is still our richest patrimony. Is it not time for her heirs to emulate her?[1]

We have perhaps filled our end of the bargain on pollution, but we are still in arrears on the creation of harmonious cities and the fostering of beauty. The purpose of this presentation is to link together the themes of beauty, wealth, and poverty. In the words of Edmund Burke, "To make us love our country, our country ought to be lovely."

More importantly, I wish to argue that the richest patrimony is not the fruit of some abstraction, capitalism, or even the free market. It's the bourgeois culture, not the economy, stupid. Or, more carefully, things go best when the economy and the culture are sympathetic to each other, but neither one has the upper hand.

Florence

Florence, in fact, provides the answers to those critics who never tire of pointing out that the productive capacities of capitalism and free markets to generate material wealth are not enough to win the arguments for a complete social system. For example, Eugene Genovese in his defense of southern conservatism claims that modern capitalism undermines "the foundations of civilized life by atomizing individuals and that undermines the inspiring concept of citizenship created by the bourgeoisie in its great days."[2]

The answer to Genovese's problems of atomization and alienation is to realize that the atomized individual is a straw man as far as real-world institutions go. Yes, it is true that the methodology of economics lends itself to such caricatures, but for the lived reality we can return to the inspiring concept of citizenship created by the bourgeoisie.

The classical republicanism of late medieval and Renaissance Florence was combined with a great respect for those kind of markets which Genovese approves: "markets, especially in earlier times, have served as meeting places for face-to-face exchange of goods and had a civilizing function."[3]

The lecture that I gave used videos that combined art, music, and pictures. I will try to describe as best I can the impact that these videos were designed to engender by using the words and explanations that led to their being selected in the first place. If a picture is worth a thousand words, I hope that a few thousand words can suggest a few of the pictures.

The first video of Florence is to acquaint you with the sheer beauty and magnificence of the city. The city's motto was "Più bello che si può" (as beautiful as possible) which was used in many contracts for artistic performance. The music for this segment draws on this motto. *Ne Piu Bella di Queste* was composed by Heinrich Isaac who was born in the Low Countries but moved to Italy. He composed for the Medicis from 1484 to 1495. It is a song in praise of Florence bursting with civic pride.[4]

Since the video provides a literal overview of the city, I would like to draw attention to certain of the images and locations that are more prominent. The best picture of Florence as a whole as it appeared in the early Renaissance is the chain map of Florence which captures the smallness of the city-state, its beauty, and its fortifications against the despots of Milan, the Visconti, as well as the intended protection against the powerful, centralized monarchies of France, the Holy Roman Empire, and occasionally even the Papacy. In the chain map you will also see tightly joined together the Baptistery, the Bell Tower, and the Cathedral.

The Baptistery was dedicated to Saint John the Baptist, one of the patron saints of the city of Florence; the Cathedral was dedicated to the Virgin Mary. Saint John the Baptist and the Virgin Mary were not only conjoined in the scriptures, but also in the coinage of the Florentine Republic, the gold florin. Ironically, although the florin was a numerical measure of wealth, it was also symbolically a celebration of poverty. On one side was represented the lily of the Virgin at the Annunciation and on the other side, John the Baptist, the patron saint of Florence. This gave rise to a local saying: "St. John will have no cheating." Because of its stability it became the currency of Europe.

The florin was first minted in 1252 after the first defeat of the Ghibellines (feudal nobility and powerful merchants) by the Guelph party (an emerging but cultured middle-class with commercial origins). They had been pitted against each other since 1215.

Again in 1266 after the battle of Benevento, the Florentines expelled the Ghibellines. The Guelfs were then divided into the Black party (bankers, merchants, and artisans) and the White party (declining nobility). Dante (1265-1321) was part of the White party and they were also forced into exile.

John the Baptist's Romanesque baptistery in the Piazza del Duomo was built from 1059 to 1150 under the patronage of the Arte di Calimala, the Wool Merchant's guild. The first set of doors was sculpted by Andrea Pisano (c. 1290-1348) in 1330. He was commissioned to do the first set of doors on the south side. Pisano completed the project with scenes from the Baptist's life, the four Cardinal Virtues, and the Four Theological Virtues. Notice that the Bible, pagan philosophy, and Christian theology go hand in hand even in these medieval days before the Renaissance.

The competition between the potential sculptors was to be judged on the basis of how well they could do the Sacrifice of Isaac, a theme which resonated with the Florentines who were declaring their liberty from the tyranny of the Milanese. Gian Galeazzo Visconti suddenly died in September of 1402. The last minute escape of Isaac spared by the hand of God was similar to the escape of Florence from the Milanese. The competition panels of Ghiberti and Brunelleschi displaying the Sacrifice of Isaac still exist and can be seen in the Bargello.

Ghiberti was also chosen to do the third set of doors for the Baptistery. Tradition says that Michelangelo called them the "Doors of Paradise." This time there was no competition. Ghiberti was assisted by Leonardo Bruni in choosing the themes for the panels from the Old Testament. The scenes chosen from the Bible have both religious content and political content. For example, David slaying Goliath has the little David (Florence) slaying the giant Goliath (Milan). This theme was also picked up in later famous sculptures by Donatello, Verocchio, and Michelangelo himself.

The Campanile or Bell Tower of Florence adjoins the Cathedral. *Campanilismo,* or loyalty to the local, characterized Florence as well as Siena. The bell tower or campanile in this case was designed by Giotto c. 1334 and perhaps completed by the same Andrea Pisano who executed the first set of doors for the Baptistery. The sculptures are said to depict "in the lower zone the life of man from his creation to the development of civilization through the arts and sciences; and in the upper zones the planets, which influence the virtues, the liberal arts, and the sacraments that discipline and sanctify man."[5] In short, we have a coherent order and integration of human and divine knowledge.

The Cathedral, aptly named Santa Maria del Fiore, Saint Mary of the Flowers, captures the name of Florence as well as the beautiful images connected with Mary. The name Florence connotes all the meanings of flowering and flourishing. It is interesting to note that the motto of the city Glasgow in Scotland was "Let Glasgow Flourish." Glasgow at the time of Adam Smith and the Scottish Renaissance was not far from the population of Florence at the time of the Renaissance after the plagues—40,000.

Poverty Series

Although there was a new emphasis on wealth in Florence, it did not easily capture the day. The traditions of poverty in classical Greece, Rome, and early Christianity intertwined secular and religious concerns. There was an ideal of poverty that had to be challenged before riches became intellectually and spiritually respectable.[6]

Certainly no one can quarrel with the ideal of poverty as long as it is purely voluntary. The important question is whether the monastery doors are closed or opened on the world, who came in and who came out. In the orthodox Christian traditions, the vows of poverty, chastity, and obedience were counsels of perfection; they were also taken voluntarily. They were chosen because men and women aimed at perfection. They were spiritual athletes and thus had to be ascetics, i.e. persons in training to achieve their highest goals. In comparison to athletes, whether physical or spiritual, most men are comparatively free. Ordinary people do not achieve the highs and the lows of human excellence and degradation which only asceticism can produce.

The music for this series of paintings is Josquin Desprez's (c.1440-1521) *Ce Pauvre/Pauper sum ego,* performed by The King's Singers. The video is only a minute and a half; the lyrics are:

This poor beggar of God

has neither benefice nor employment

that is valuable or helpful to him

except what he carries with him.

I am poor.

Because of the lyrics, I will start with the Christian tradition, but we shall see that this tradition had a major influence on the secular intellectuals through the joint combination of Christianity, Greek, and Roman exemplars.

In this video we essentially establish the Triumph of Poverty. There are many paintings of St. Antony of the desert who gave away his worldly wealth. He was an inspiration to the Franciscan and Dominican Friars.

There are many portrayals in frescoes and mosaics of the Franciscan tradition. He is shown giving his cloak to the poor and renouncing all his earthly goods, marrying Lady Poverty, and despising money.

It is not hard to see how St. Francis could become the hero of the flower children of the Sixties when one notes that St. Francis apparently was opposed to the care of the body. He was described by a contemporary: "his habit was sordid, his person contemptible, and his face unkempt."[7]

The severity of the Franciscans was moderated—not without great battles, schisms, and heresies—by Pope Gregory IX who "set aside the Testament and the extent of the practical difficulties in carrying on business with the lack of all possessions shows in the roundabout way an agent had to be appointed to accept necessities for the Friars' daily life."[8] The lay persons associated with such orders were often called *oeconomicus* which takes us back to the older concepts of economics as prudent household management. The economists will have their day.

The Dominicans were the main competing monastic order. Here again vows of poverty were deemed all-important. A more detailed history and visual portrayal of the Dominicans is the subject of other videos which I have prepared using the frescoes of Fra Angelico at the monastery of San Marco in Florence.[9]

Also within each order there was violent competition between what came to be called, the Observants (the strict poverty tradition) and the Conventuals (those who believed that poverty applied only to the individual (no private property rights) and not to the monastic order as a whole (bequeathed wealth and donations could lead to a very comfortable lifestyle).

Ironically, both the sensible saints discussed by Raymond de Roover, Bernardino of Siena, Franciscan, and Antonino of Florence, Dominican, were Observants and not Conventuals. But both these two strict ascetics, St. Bernardino and St. Antonino, understood quite clearly that poverty had to be voluntary and, even then, could be a source of pride. Furthermore, they were opposed to the Spiritual Franciscans, or Fraticelli, who demanded absolute poverty and had an apocalyptic criticism of all worldly activity since the millennium was soon to be on its way.

The final pictures on the pro-poverty side are of three persons intimately involved with Florence: Dante, Petrarch, and Boccaccio. First of all we see Dante and Petrarch in Andrea del Castagno's fresco, *Nine Famous Men and Women,* in the Villa Carduci just outside of Florence.

These humanist links with poverty are extensive, if usually ambiguous. For example, Dante could be baptized as either a quasi-Franciscan or a "civic humanist" by Matteo Palmieri, Leonardo Bruni, and Manetti for his role as a Florentine patriot in holding office and fighting in the battle of Campaldini, the crucial battle between Florence and the city of Arezzo.

The Franciscan interpretation of Dante is supported by his treatment of avarice and usury. Although Aristotle had claimed that, "nobility is inherited wealth and virtue," Dante found it convenient to leave out "wealth" and emphasize "virtue." Humanist intellectuals of a Stoic persuasion were inclined to a Franciscan view of the dangers and temptations of riches and avarice. *Paupertas* was not restricted to religious men.

But Boccaccio was even sterner than Dante. He criticized Dante for marrying; according to Hans Baron, Boccaccio considered "marriage as the greatest danger to a man of learning." Boccaccio claimed "the Florence of his own day had preserved nothing of the 'honorable poverty' which he admired in early Roman times."[10]

How do we come to understand these brilliant intellectual humanists? Dr. Johnson's Dictionary defines a "patron" as "commonly a wretch who supports with insolence, and is paid with flattery." Those humanist intellectuals who were either excluded or excluded themselves from being true monks or friars were dependent on such patronage for their uncertain incomes. I am reminded of Mike Uhlmann's second law: "The public is quite prepared to bite the Invisible Hand even as it is being fed by it."

Dante and Petrarch, for example, went further than asserting that money does not buy happiness, or that wealth can be a trap or snare that corrupts man. It stands in the way of true happiness and virtue. Dante redefined virtue to not include riches.

Although most humanist intellectuals of the time had neither wealth nor *a fortiori* inherited wealth, they were endowed with the sin of pride and perhaps envy, to desire the esteem of nobility. Therefore the only angle they had was to claim virtue. Furthermore, they had nothing but contempt for the slovenly, boorish, and bellicose virtues of the feudal, quasi-military regimes; nor could they admire the aggressive, entrepreneurial skills of the urban bourgeois classes. Ironically, many of the latter only aped the land-owning aristocracies once they had risen to wealth; their desire was to acquire land or public office, more permanent fixtures of honor than mere wealth.

Petrarch (1304-1374) was opposed to riches, marriage, and family. Living in seclusion, he would usually come out to help out tyrants and revolutionaries, but not those of free republics like his native Florence. He refused to assume the Rectorship of the Florentine studio or university when it was offered to him.

The Civic Humanist understanding of Dante can be seen in Bruni's biography of Dante. He compared him favorably to the stay-at-home, Petrarch. "Among the stay-at-homes, who are withdrawn from human society, I have never seen one who could count to three. A lofty and distinguished mind does not need such fetters... Standing apart from the interchange of ideas with others is characteristic of those whose inferior minds are incapable of understanding anything."[11] In the early stages the ideas of a not-so-voluntary poverty were held as a badge of natural honor and virtue by the humanist intellectuals; they were shared, as Hans Baron has argued, by Dante, Petrarch, and Boccaccio. They joined the ideals of Franciscan poverty and Stoic poverty in a manner which denied the golden mean of the Aristotelian tradition. The spirit of the poverty tradition left the monastery, opened all doors before it, and attempted to take over the whole world, culminating in the theocracy of Savonarola, as we shall see later.

Humanist Background to the Medici

For our final video on wealth and civic humanism, we shall go back in time to trace the kinds of "civic humanism" which nurtured the wealth and created beauty that so angered our fiery Dominican, Savonarola.

The "civic humanism" of Florence reaches backwards to the period before Cosimo Medici. There is another humanist tradition which extends from Coluccio Salutati (1331-1406), Leonardo Bruni (1369-1444), Matteo Palmieri (1406-75), through Cosimo Medici (1389-1464), and reaches an extravagant height in Poggio di Bracciolini (1380-1459). The emphasis in this tradition is on wealth rather than poverty.

Let us take a look first at Salutati who can be seen in Masaccio's painting of the *Raising of the Son of Theophilus* in Florence. He was Chancellor of Florence for 31 years after he had studied law at the University of Bologna. He was the first intellectual favorable to the active life, wealth, republicanism, and marriage. He wrote *De Fato et Fortuna* (1396-1397) in which he was attempted to reconcile God's overall Providence with the free will and responsibility of individual human beings. Florence's archenemy, Duke Giangaleazzo Visconti reportedly remarked that one letter by Salutati "was worth a troop of horsemen."[12]

The Stoic and Franciscan contempt for riches was questioned most trenchantly by Leonardo Bruni who translated and commented on the Pseudo-Aristotelian Economics for none other than Cosimo Medici. Wealth is the lifeblood of the city. The reason that wealth was so important was that it made possible the life of charity. The possession of external goods makes possible acts of charity, the greatest of Christian virtues and the mother of all the other virtues.

Bruni's opinions were shared by the humanist Matteo Palmieri (1406-1475). Palmieri stressed the importance of the sharing of one's money rather than the idle hoarding of cash balances; the virtuous man is characterized by the virtue of liberality, and the miser is the one who suffers from avarice.

Cosimo Medici

Although this is not the place to fully elaborate on the morality play of the rise and fall of the Medicis, I would like to discuss one of the important religious symbolisms used by the Medicis. The Adoration of the Magi is rich for both its range of artistic interpretations and also its spiritual message.

The artwork is based on the *Adoration of the Magi* by Benozzo Gozzoli and focuses primarily on the chapel in the Medici-Riccardi Palace in Florence. The music used in the video presentation is by a 20th century Argentinian composer, Ariel Ramirez. In his *Navidad Nuestra* (1964), he included a movement, "Los Reyes Magos" (The Wise Kings). This version is sung by José Carreras.

Benozzo Gozzoli probably also did the *Adoration of the Magi* in San Marco which was used to decorate Cosimo's private chapel. San Marco was founded in January 1436 by nine friars from the Observant Dominicans who came from San Domenico, Fiesole, which had just been dedicated in October 1435. San Marco was dedicated in 1443, and right after that Cosimo began to build his palace.

If we are allowed a prayer for this part, I would like to quote from a Sermon for the Compagnia de' Magi on Holy Thursday by Pier Filippo Pandolfini in 1476.

> May the splendour of that star which from Orient led the three Magi to adore and contemplate the divine majesty, light up our minds and lead us all to the true glory and supreme happiness. And in order that better and more deservedly we be harkened to, let us offer this evening to Jesus Christ, imitating the holy Magi, the gold from the treasure of our minds...let us give him our souls…let us offer him the incense of our prayers... begging him devoutly that by virtue of his most holy body and precious blood, of which this evening we make special mention, he may have mercy on all this family.[13]

There are many, if not most, who assert that Cosimo Medici was the downfall rather than the apogee of classical republicanism. He was the founder of a crypto-tyranny or despotic government while maintaining outwardly republican forms.

Dale Kent provides a good antidote to the trashing of Cosimo Medici. He argues that the biblical account of the Magi "provided a perfect metaphor for the spiritual journey of the wealthy and powerful toward true devotion, the submission of the kings of the earth to the supreme authority of the word of God, incarnate in his Son. The story of the Magi presented this basic and familiar spiritual lesson in progress from pride to humility, from preoccupation with the things of this world to acknowledgement of the infinity of the next."[14]

Florence provides a rich depository of imagery and thought for a society like ours which in its own way grapples with the same issues and problems—albeit less elegantly.

Conclusion

Both wealth and poverty were sung and celebrated by the Florentines. Christian and classical themes were easily conjoined together by both religious and secular thinkers. The complexity of the culture and the need to keep in tension both the religious and commercial strains is the legacy for us. The fact that the tension often broke down is no reason for discouragement, but should be a challenge for us today to recapture the vitality of thought and culture of Florence in its golden age.

Notes

1. Bertrand de Jouvenel, "The Stewardship of the Earth" in *The Fitness of Man's Environment* (New York: Harper Colophon Books, 1970), p. 117.
2. Eugene Genovese, *The Southern Tradition: The Achievement and Limitations of an American Conservatism,* Cambridge, Mass: Harvard University Press, 1994, p. 38.
3. *Op. cit.,* p. 15.
4. As the liner notes states, it "reads in places like something commissioned by the Tuscan Tourist Board." *An Evening at the Medici's: Festival Music of Florence,* MCA Classics, London Pro Musica, Director, Bernard Thomas.
5. Francesca Flores D'Arcais, *Giotto,* New York: Abbeville Press, 1995.
6. I am deeply indebted to the article by Hans Baron, "Franciscan Poverty and Civil Wealth As Factors in the Rise of Humanistic Thought," *Speculum,* Vol. XIII, No. 1, January 1938, pp. 1-37.
7. Mulhern, *op. cit.,* p. 102
8. Mulhern, *op. cit.,* p. 104; also see Leff, *Heresy in the Later Middle Ages* Vol. I, p. 66 for a discussion of the latter.
9. Although the development of Scholasticism out of the Dominican tradition of St. Thomas Aquinas has been amply developed in the history of economic thought, there is no consensus as to the economic teachings of Aquinas and the subsequent traditions. I personally believe that the Schumpeter-De Roover-Rothbard-Chafuen line of classical liberal interpretation is more correct than the others, but I also feel that there is a tendency to make the economic issues which are often quite narrow matters involving contracts into larger entities like classical liberalism.
10. Baron, *op. cit.,* p. 17.
11. Hans Baron, *In Search of Florentine Civic Humanism: Essays on the Transition from Medieval to Modern Thought,* Volume 1, Princeton: Princeton University Press,1988, p. 18.
12. Cf. treatment by Ronald G. Witt in *The Earthly Republic: Italian Humanists on Government and Society,* University of Pennsylvania Press, 1978.
13. Quoted in the luminous article by Rab Hatfield, "The Compagnia De Magi," *Journal of the Warburg and Courtauld Institute, 33,* 1970, p. 131.
14. Dale Kent, *Cosimo De' Medici and the Florentine Renaissance,* New Haven: Yale University Press, 2000, p. 305.

Property in Roman Religion and Early Christian Fathers

Leonard P. Liggio

Religion formed the foundation of law and property rights in the Greek and Roman religion and the law based upon it. The early Christian fathers were challenged by zealots who claimed that poverty was not merely a special vocation but applied to all. The early church fathers' responses are an important body of analysis.

The great English legalist in the age of the American revolution, Sir William Blackstone (1723–80), defined property as "that sole and despotic dominion which one man claims and exercises over the external things of the world, in total exclusion of the right of any other individual in the universe" (Blackstone, [1765–69] 1962, II, I, p. 2).

Property is an institution of the human person from the first record of his customs. "The law finds the institution of property in existence, as well at the earliest as at all later stages of growth, and, far from creating its varieties, is occupied only in defining, maintaining and validating them" (Noyes, 1936, p. 18).

Sir Henry Sumner Maine (1822–88), in his *Ancient Law* ([1861] 1986), described the common legal customs of the Indo-European peoples, drawing on his judicial experience in India. The Indo-European legal history that has received the greatest study is that of the ancient Greeks and Italians.

History professor at the Sorbonne, Numa Denis Fustel de Coulanges (1830–89), *The Ancient City: A Study of the Religion, Laws, and Institutions of*

Greece and Rome (1864), provides an analysis of the classical legal institutions. The Indo-Europeans did not believe that after life there was no afterlife; rather, they looked on death not as a termination, but as a change of life to a second existence. In a religious tradition in which the souls of the dead remained near the living families, the graves of the dead members of the family and their daily remembrance by the head of the family were of central importance.

Each Greek and Italian family possessed its own religion because each had its own particular ancestors to whom daily respect was offered. The family altar and fire were the focus of religion of each family. Observance of the daily rites was necessary for the happiness of the dead ancestors and thus of the success of the living family. The family home and land were an extension of the family ancestors. "The members of the ancient family were united by something more powerful than birth, affection, or physical strength; this was the religion of the sacred fire, and of dead ancestors. This caused the family to form a single body, both in this life and in the next" (Fustel de Coulanges, [1864] 1956, p. 42).

Marriage was the first institution of each domestic religion. The wife became a priestess of her husband's domestic religion and, should she die, the widower could no longer perform his priestly functions. The worship of the ancestors and the domestic fire was transmitted from male to male, but was shared by the wife. By the sacred ceremony of marriage,

> [The husband] is now about to bring a stranger to this hearth; with her he will perform the mysterious ceremonies of his worship; he will reveal the rites and formulas which are the patrimony of his family. There is nothing more precious than this heritage; these gods, these rites, these hymns which he has received from his fathers, are what protects him in this life, and promise him riches, happiness, and virtue. And yet, instead of keeping to himself this tutelary power, as the savage keeps his idol or his amulet, he is going to admit a woman to share it with him (Ibid., p. 43).

By the sacred ceremony of marriage the wife is ordained and adopted into the domestic religion as a necessity for her to become a priestess of the sacred fire of her husband's ancestors. The marriage ceremony at the sacred fire culminates in the husband and wife sharing a wheaten loaf:

This sort of light meal, which commences and ends with a libation and a prayer; this sharing of nourishment in presence of the fire; puts the husband and wife in religious communion with each other, and in communion with the domestic gods (Ibid., p. 46).

> The institution of sacred marriage must be as old in the Indo-European race as the domestic religion; for the one could not exist without the other. This religion taught man that the conjugal union was something more than a relation of the sexes and a fleeting affection, and united man and wife by the powerful bond of the same worship and the same belief. The marriage ceremony, too, was so solemn, and produced effects so grave, that it is not surprising that

> these men did not think it permitted or possible to have more than one wife in each house. Such a religion could not admit of polygamy (Ibid., pp. 47–48).

Fustel de Coulanges notes:

> There are three things which, from the most ancient times, we find founded and solidly established in these Greek and Italian societies: the domestic religion; the family; and the right of property–three things which had in the beginning a manifest relation, and which appear to have been inseparable. The idea of private property existed in the religion itself.
>
> Every family had its hearth and its ancestors. These gods could be adored only by this family, and protected it alone. They were its property. Now, between these gods and the soil, men of the early ages saw a mysterious relation. Let us first take the hearth. This altar is the symbol of a sedentary life; its name indicates this. It must be placed upon the ground; once established, it cannot be moved. The god of the family wishes to have a fixed abode . . . (Ibid., p. 61).

He shows the role of religion in property:

> It did not matter whether this enclosure was a hedge, a wall of wood, or one of stone. Whatever it was, it marked the limit, which separated the domain of one sacred fire from that of another. This enclosure was deemed sacred. It was an impious act to pass it. The god watched over it, and kept it under his care . . . This enclosure, traced and protected by religion, was the most certain emblem, the most undoubted mark of the right of property.
>
> Let us return to the primitive ages of the Aryan race. The sacred enclosure, which the Greeks call *eoxos,* and the Latins *herctum,* was the somewhat spacious enclosure in which the family had its house, its flocks, and the small field that it cultivated. In the midst rose the protecting fire-god. Let us descend to the succeeding ages. The tribes have reached Greece and Italy, and have built cities. The dwellings are brought nearer together; they are not, however, contiguous. The sacred enclosure still exists, but it is of smaller proportions; oftenest it is reduced to a low wall, a ditch, a furrow, or to a mere open space, a few feet wide. But in no case could two houses be joined to each other; a party wall was supposed to be an impossible thing. The same wall could not be common to two houses; for then the sacred enclosure of the gods would have disappeared. At Rome the law fixed two feet and a half as the width of the free space, which was always to separate two houses, and this space was consecrated to 'the god of the enclosure' (Ibid., pp. 62–3).

Each family home is a domestic temple, which gives a sacred character to the land, which surrounds and encompasses it. The family is consecrated master and proprietor of the land of the domestic divinities. The right of private property is a sacred right.

"What is there more holy," says Cicero, "what is there more carefully fenced round every description of religious respect, than the house of each individual citizen? Here is his altar, here is his hearth, here are his household gods; here all his sacred rights, all his religious ceremonies, are preserved"

(Cicero, *Pro Domo,* in Fustel de Coulanges [1864] 1956, p. 64).

The boundary of each property was marked by an upright post or stone, a *terminus* which was considered divine as part of the family religion:

> The employment of *Termini,* or sacred bounds for fields, appears to have been universal among the Indo-European race. It existed among the Hindus at a very early date, and the sacred ceremonies of the boundaries had among them a great analogy with those which Sculus Flaccus has described for Italy. Before the foundation of Rome, we find the *Terminus* among the Sabines; we also find it among the Etruscans. The Hellenes, too, had sacred landmarks ... (Fustel de Coulanges [1864] 1956, p. 68).

> To encroach upon the field of a family, it was necessary to overturn or displace a boundary mark, and this boundary mark was a god. The sacrilege was horrible, and the chastisement severe. According to the old Roman law, the man and the oxen who touched a *Terminus* was devoted–that is to say, both man and oxen were immolated in expiation. The Etruscan law, speaking in the name of religion, says, 'He who shall have touched or displaced a bound shall be condemned by the gods; his house shall disappear; his race shall be extinguished; his land shall no longer produce fruits; hail, rust, and the fires of the dog-star shall destroy his harvests; the limbs of the guilty one shall become covered with ulcers, and shall waste away' (Ibid., p. 69).

> Plato, *Laws,* VIII, p. 842 states: 'Our first law ought to be this: let no person touch the bounds which separate his field from that of his neighbor, for this ought to remain immovable. ... Let no one attempt to disturb the small stone which separates friendship from enmity, and which the land-owners have bound themselves by an oath to leave in its place' (Ibid., p. 69).

The Gospels

In the Gospels, Jesus makes various references to wealth. Some of the parables speak of the value of investment in property, trade, and human capital as examples of spiritual investment. Many of the recommendations of Jesus are aimed at those who wish to join his circle of disciples to live a rigorous life. Often they are counsels of perfection, and not aimed at ordinary believers who live their everyday life in their family, their work, and their prayers. These counsels of perfection are calls to a special vocation of a spiritual life; it is the counsels of perfection—chastity, poverty, and obedience—which are followed by the members of religious orders—monks, friars, canons regular,[1] brothers, and nuns—in the Orthodox, Catholic, Anglican, and Lutheran churches.

In particular, Jesus' counsels of perfection can be found in several of the Gospels. In Luke 18:1–8, Jesus recommends persistent prayer to God. In Luke 18:9–14, Jesus recommends the quiet prayer of the sinner (tax collector) standing far off in the Temple as opposed to the self-congratulatory prayer of the Pharisee. Christian tradition interpreted Luke's next verses (18:15–17) to enjoin the perfection of obedience like little children (also, Mark 10:13–16 and Matthew 19:13–15). Similarly, in the second counsel of perfection regarding celibacy in Mark 10:1–12 and Matthew 19:1–2, Jesus declares: "All receive not this word but they whom it is given. … He that can receive it, let him receive it."

Then the matter of poverty for the perfect is addressed in Luke 18:18–30, Mark 10:17–31, and Matthew 19:16–30. The rich man seeks Jesus' counsel on going beyond the normal commandments. Jesus declares:

> If thou wilt be perfect, go sell what thou hast, and give to the poor; and thou shalt have treasure in heaven; and come, follow Me. … And Jesus seeing him become sorrowful, looking round about, said to His disciples: Amen, I say to you: How hard shall they who have riches enter into the kingdom of God. And the disciples were astonished at His words. But Jesus answering again, said to them: Children, how hard it is for them that trust in riches to enter the kingdom of God. Again I say to you: It is easier for a camel to pass through the eye of a needle than for a rich man to enter into the kingdom of heaven. And when the disciples heard this, they wondered the more, saying among themselves: Who, then, can be saved? And Jesus looking on them, said: With men it is impossible, but not with God; for all things are possible with God.

A minority interpretation among scripture scholars notes that "the eye of the needle" was the name given to the pedestrian gate, which would require the camel to pass through on its knees; something that would require extra effort.

Jewish and Christian Thought on the Market and Money in Hellenistic and Roman Ages

If one examines the Old Testament, one finds references to issues such as private property. In the earliest books of the Old Testament, when the Hebrews arrived in the Holy Land, land was distributed to them as individual holdings, and they were enjoined under penalty of sin from moving boundaries from the land or changing the boundaries. That would amount to theft as in coveting a neighbour's goods. In the Old Testament, there is an emphasis that one should not make an idol of property, just as one should not make an idol of poverty; that material goods should not come before one's obligations to God.

In the Old Testament, there are references regarding the unjust taking of property. In Isaiah 1:23, the prophet warns princes not to consort with thieves or give corrupt judgments. This is preceded, in Isaiah 1:22, by the statement: "Thy silver has become dross; thy wine has become mixed with water." Isaiah is warning here against the dilution of currency, and we see that in many other places in the Old Testament, the prophets are condemning this dilution in the rules (in essence, inflation), and treating it as a major form of theft alongside the princes' taking-away of private property. Ezekiel 22:18–22 used the evil of debasing coin as an example for princes to address in their individual reformation.

The Old Testament prophets placed great emphasis on defending the individual family's right of property against the state. Ezekiel warns against the oppression whereby the property owned by the individual Jew is taken by the ruler. This is a major theme that then continues in the early Christian literature.

During the Hellenistic and Roman periods, there was a division in Judea between the Sadducees (who were from the priestly caste and mainly lived in Jerusalem) and the Pharisees and the other pious people in the countryside. The Sadducees oversaw the collection of taxes, and were the object of the criticism directed at the rich (tax collectors). The Pharisees were developing a belief in immortality of the soul and bodily resurrection, and a strong sense of the role of oral tradition in addition to the written Bible. When one comes to the birth of Jesus and his emergence in public life, Jesus is articulating the language of the Pharisees, while not their legalistic practices. Jesus' public ministry was supported by the wealth of his friends and disciples. Wealth was not condemned as it was necessary to support Jesus' public ministry; people were not condemned by failure to use their wealth to support Jesus and his disciples. This use of wealth was a special calling.

In the Epistles of Paul, we find a continuity of Stoic ideas, some of which are very similar to Christian ideas. In particular, Paul refers to the Stoic idea of the importance of self-sufficiency—the importance of people having their property in order to be self-sufficient and working to achieve enough property to support their family. If Christians do not work to achieve that necessary wealth, they are lacking in the necessary Christian grace.

A leading father of the early church was the Athenian-born Clement of Alexandria (AD150–215). Alexandria was the great city of the Eastern Mediterranean. Founded by one of Alexander the Great's generals, Ptolemy I Soter (367–283BC), Alexandria became the centre of Greek philosophy associated with its great library. Ptolemy II Philadelphus (309–246BC) asked 70 scholars of the city's large Hebrew community to translate the books of the Bible into Greek. They created the *Septuagent* Greek Bible (270BC).

Titus Flavius Clement of Alexandria was head of the Christian school in which Origen was one of his pupils. Clement left Alexandria during the persecution of Emperor Septimus Severus. He approved private property and the accumulation of property in his *Who Is the Rich Man that Is Saved?* in which he analyses Mark 10:17–31. He did not encourage ordinary Christians to pursue an ascetic ideal of giving up one's possessions. Clement argued that riches and goods are the means that can benefit our neighbour. They have been provided by God for the good of humankind to be used by those who know how to use them.[2]

Clement was not impressed with the argument that poverty equaled holiness. He noted that if poverty equaled holiness, then proletarians, derelicts, and beggars, and some who have few virtues and are ignorant about God, would be the best candidates for religious life simply because they had no money.[3]

The Christian father Lactantius (AD260–340) emphasized that the concept of abolition of private property was unacceptable to Christians. He noted that it was Plato who introduced the notion of community of property rooted in the unnatural idea of community of wives. As a Christian Father, Lactantius calls out to the Christian world that it must first protect private property if it wants to protect the family from all the assaults of the state. Lactantius joined other philosophers in considering private property as a distinguishing quality of humankind, as opposed to animals. Lactantius explained the interconnection between private ownership and the virtues that come from it, the sound families it produces, and how the assault on private property is an assault on Christian virtue.

Wealth exists, according to the Old Testament, to be used productively and wisely, and this theme is continued in the New Testament. In I Timothy 1:3, there is a strong statement about the responsibility of the family to produce wealth and thereby to care for its own. In order to defend the family, it is imperative to defend private property. Lactantius stated: "for ownership of things contains the matter of virtues and of vices, but community holds nothing other than the license of vices" (Lactantius 1871).[4]

St. Augustine of Hippo (AD354–430) responded to his close friend from Syracuse, Hilarius, regarding the remarks of some Christians in Syracuse: "That a rich man who continues to live richly cannot enter the Kingdom of Heaven unless he sells all he has, and that it cannot do him any good to keep the Commandments while keeping his riches."

Augustine responded at great length in order to supply Hilarius with arguments to rebut this idea. Augustine declared:

> Listen, now, to something about riches in answer to the inquiry in your next letter. In it you wrote that some are saying that a rich man who continues to live richly cannot enter the Kingdom of Heaven unless he sells all that he has, and that it cannot do him any good to keep the Commandments while he keeps his riches. Their arguments have overlooked our Fathers, Abraham, Isaac, and Jacob, who departed long ago from this life. It is a fact that all these had extensive riches, as the Scripture faithfully bears witness, yet He who became poor for our sake, although He was truly rich, foretold in a manner in a truthful promise that many would come from the East and West and would sit down, not above them, not without them, but with them in the Kingdom of Heaven. Although the haughty rich man who is clothed in purple and fine linen, and feasted sumptuously every day, died and was tormented in Hell, nevertheless, if he had shown mercy to the poor man covered with sores who lay at his door, and was treated with scorn, he himself would have deserved mercy. And if the poor man's merit had been his poverty, not his goodness, he would surely not have been carried by Angels into the Bosom of Abraham, who had been rich in this life (Augustine [fifth century] 1951, p. 340).[5]

Augustine continues his analysis of the example of our father Abraham, and then supposes that the Christians of Syracuse probably say that the patriarchs did not sell all they had to give it to the poor because the Lord had not commanded it. Augustine says:

> We believe that the Apostle Paul was the minister of the New Testament when he wrote to Timothy, saying, 'Charge the rich of this world not to be high-minded, nor to trust in the uncertainty of riches, but in the Living God, who giveth us abundantly all things to enjoy. To do good, to be rich in good works, to give easily to communicate to others. To lay up on store for themselves a good foundation against the time to come, that they may hold on to the true life' (1 Tim. 6.17–19), in the same way as it was said to the young man, 'If thou will enter into life.' I think when he gave those instructions to the rich, the apostle was not wrong in not saying, 'Charge the rich of this world to sell all they have and give to the poor and follow the Lord', instead of, 'Not to be high-minded nor to trust in the uncertainty of riches.' It was his pride, and not the riches, that brought the rich young man to the torment of Hell because he despised the good poor man who lay at his gate; because he put his hope in the uncertainty of riches and thought himself happy in his purple and fine linen and sumptuous banquet (Ibid., pp. 342–43).

Augustine said that it was unlawful to steal to give alms. The medieval *Decretals* imposed a penance of three weeks upon a man who commits theft because he is hungry.

The Christian Father, Salvian's (AD405–95) major work, *De Gubernatione Dei* (The government of God) was completed in about AD450 in Marseilles. Salvian asks: "What is a political position but a kind of plunder? There is no greater pillage of poor states than that done by those in power." He continues to speak of tax collectors by speaking of those strangled by the chains of taxation as if by the hands of brigands. "There is found a great number of the rich whose taxes kill the poor" (Salvian 1947, pp. 100–101).[6] Salvian continued:

> What towns, as well as municipalities and villages, are there in which there are not as many tyrants as tax collectors? Perhaps they glory in the name of tyrant because it seems to be considered powerful and honored . . . What place is there, as I have said, where the bowels of widows and orphans are not devoured by the leading men of the city, and with them almost all Holy Men? . . . They seek among the barbarians the dignity of the Roman because they cannot bear barbarous indignity among the Romans (Ibid., pp. 134–5).

The Roman emperors appointed the rich as tax collectors who were responsible from their own wealth for the annual tax burden. The system was built around the collection and the avoidance of taxes. To escape the tax burdens, and the tortures associated with tax collection, many people fled from their farms and from the cities, and lived in the countryside or in the wilderness. Many of these were very religious people, and some of the early monastic communities, as in Egypt, evolved from these refugees from taxation. Many rich and poor fled taxation by moving to the areas ruled by the Germanic tribes which had migrated into the Roman provinces. Salvian declared:

> Thus, far and wide, they migrate either to the Goths or to the Baghudi, or to other barbarians everywhere in power, yet they do not repent having migrated. They prefer to live as free men under an outward form of captivity, than as captives under appearance of liberty. Therefore, the name Roman citizens, not only greatly valued but dearly bought, is now repudiated and fled from–and it is considered not only base but ever deserving of abhorrence. And what cannot be a greater testimony of Roman wickedness than that many men, upright and noble and to whom the position of being a Roman citizen should be considered as of the highest splendor and dignity, have been driven by the cruelty of Roman wickedness to such a state of mind that they do not wish to be Romans? . . . [t]hey, who suffer the insistent, and even continuous destruction of public tax levies, to them there is always imminent a heavy and relentless proscription. They desert their homes, lest they be tortured in their very homes. They seek exile lest they suffer torture. The enemy is more lenient to them than the tax-collectors. This proved by this very fact that they flee to the enemy in order to avoid the full force of the heavy tax levy (Ibid., pp. 136, 138).

The limited narrative of the writings on religion and property rights opens the doors to a rich literature. They formed the basis of the writing of the medieval Scholastic authors.

Notes

1. A canon regular is a religious cleric destined to those works which relate to the divine mysteries, unlike monastic orders. In canon law, Jesuits, Theatines, and Oratorians come under canons regular concept as they are living by a rule but are not monks or friars.
2. *Clement of Alexandria: Quis dives salvatur?* (Who is the rich man that is being saved?) in Barnard (1897, pp. 1–66).
3. Ibid.
4. Lactantius, *Works* in (Roberts and Donaldson (Eds.), 1871).
5. Augustine of Hippo, *Works,* vol. XI, *Letters,* vol. III, *Letters* 156 and 157, in *The Fathers of the Church* (1951).
6. Salvian, *De Gubernatione Dei* (The government of God), *Writings of Salvian,* trans. Jeremiah O'Sullivan in *The Fathers of the Church* (1947).

Bibliography

Barnard, P. Mordaunt (1897). *Clement of Alexandria: Quis dives salvetur*. Cambridge: Cambridge University Press.

Blackstone, Sir William ([1765–69] 1962). *Commentaries on the laws of England.* Boston, MA: Beacon Press.

Fustel de Coulanges, Numa Denis ([1864] 1956). *The ancient city: A study of the reli -*

gion, laws, and institutions of Greece and Rome. Garden City, NY: Doubleday Anchor Books.

Lactantius (1871). Works. In: Roberts, Alexander and James Donaldson (Eds.) *Ante-Nicene* Fathers. Edinburgh: T. & T. Clark.

Noyes, C. Reinold (1936). *The institution of property.* New York: Longmans, Green & Co. Augustine.

Salvian. De Gubernatione Dei (The government of God). *Writings of Salvian. In The Fathers of the Church.* Trans. by Jeremiah F. O'Sullivan. New York, Cima Pub. Co., c1947.

Perestroika in Christendom:
The Scholastics Develop a Commerce-Friendly Moral Code

Gary M. Pecquet

Introduction

Morality matters. The moral values embraced by a culture inevitably shape its destiny for better or worse. For almost 12 centuries between 325 and 1517, the Roman Catholic Church commanded a virtually uncontested role in shaping the moral values of Western culture. Yet, the Church canon regarding the morality of commerce changed markedly after the 13th century. The early Augustinian-Platonic view contrasted the morally ideal with the imperfect, morally suspect requirements of successful living. The Church discouraged practical worldly pursuits placing all hope upon the hereafter. In contrast, Alejandro Antonio Chafuen (2003) has shown that beginning in the 13th century, the Late (Thomistic) Scholastics applied an Aristotelian-natural law approach to moral reasoning. This moral technology rejected the conflict between morality and long-term practical success, gradually developing a commerce-friendly moral code.

The following pages present a case study demonstrating the contrasting

* The author wishes to acknowledge the helpful comments of the following people: William Barnett, Nicholas Capaldi, Alejandro Chafuen, P. J. Hill, John Levendis, Leonard Liggio, Clifford Thies and Chris Walker.

moral technologies held by the Church. Historically, the battle for the moral legitimacy of commerce was not between religious and secular philosophy. Religious and secular thinkers can be found among both the pro and anti-commerce crowds. The case for the moral legitimacy of commerce depends upon the technology adopted to discover and apply moral principles.

St. Augustine's Heavenly City vs. the Earthly City

Rome declined economically, culturally, and militarily from the third century onward. Economically, the increasing demands of the Roman welfare state placed greater demands upon the rural tax base. Population declined as tax rates increased requiring yet even heavier taxes upon the shrinking tax base. Emperors debased the coinage. Inflation soared and periodic price controls failed to work. By the fourth century, Rome tied peasants to the land and forbade professionals to change their crafts in order to prevent tax evasion.

The Emperor Constantine ended the persecution of Christians and extended legal privileges to the clergy. He conferred tax-exempt status to Christian clergymen, but tried to prevent Church office from becoming a convenient tax loophole (Johnson, 1985, pp. 76-78). In 325, the first Church Council at Nicea, chaired by Constantine, prohibited members of the clergy, but not laymen, from charging usury (interest) on loans.

Culturally, Rome's Pagan (mostly Platonist) philosophers proposed no practical remedies. Instead, they accepted decline as inevitable, condemning pleasure while advising followers to abandon practical pursuits. Platonist philosophers contrasted an ideal perfect "world of forms" with the lower physical world of the senses. This disconnected abstract reasoning from real world observations and divorced moral "ought"s from practical "is"s.

Before converting to Christianity, St. Augustine (354-430) studied the contemporary Platonist Philosophy. The Augustinian-Platonist approach to morality did not try to reconcile the moral commandments with the practical requirements of successful living. The purpose of moral rules was to highlight the depraved nature of man and thereby induce guilt and lead people to salvation.

In his *City of God,* St. Augustine contrasted the pursuits of this world with the Heavenly City. Augustine discouraged practical worldly pursuits since Christian hopes depended upon God's Heavenly City. Augustine understood that commerce was socially useful. Nonetheless, Augustine advised Christians to abstain: "Let Christians amend themselves, let them not trade." Augustine actively entertained a hypothetical plea that a man may be a moral and honest trader, but in the end he rejected that plea: "For they that are traders ... attain not the grace of God" (Irwin, 1996, p. 17). St. Augustine even admonished against the pursuit of scientific knowledge as the "lust of the eyes." Since human nature was corrupted by original sin and human beings were dominated by uncontrollable demonic passions (anger, greed, lust, gluttony, sloth, envy, and pride), attempts to improve man's plight on earth seemed hopeless, at best, and examples of hubris at worst.

The Moral Basis for the Feudal/Guild System

Charlemagne established the infamous guild/feudal system throughout Christendom. Each town sponsored local craft guilds (blacksmiths, carpenters, and other small manufacturers) and restricted entry into these fields, passing membership from father to son. All trade was to be carried out in regular town markets where prices were regulated and market speculation was prohibited.

The Church Council at Njmegen in 806 A.D. broadened the doctrine of *turpe lucrem* (illicit gain) to apply to everyone and cover all violations of Charlemagne's extensive regulations and applied the restrictions to clergy and laity alike. Accordingly, Church doctrine condemned numerous activities and attitudes necessary to a healthy, prosperous economy.

(1) Barter and trade were not forbidden, but subjected to important restrictions: trade had to satisfy "natural needs." Luxury goods were sinful and this impeded foreign trade and innovation.
(2) Moreover, trade had to be conducted at "just" prices, as determined by the town guilds. This restricted competition.
(3) The charging of any interest on a loan constituted the sin of usury. This inhibited raising capital and achieving economies of scale.
(4) Attempting to monopolize the market for a particular commodity constituted the sin of "engrossing." In practice, this impeded merchants wishing to expand their markets and realize economies of scale.
(5) Market speculation on commodities, called "forestalling," was also a taboo. This required the various town currencies to exchange at legally prescribed rates, despite their metallic contents and supply and demand considerations. This again erected trade barriers between towns.
(6) Finally, even the desire to improve one's economic well-being (upward social mobility) was considered sinful "avarice." A person was supposed to passively accept the station in life that he or she inherited. Nobles were supposed to live as nobles, craftsmen as craftsmen, and peasants as peasants.

Undoubtedly, many participated in the underground rural trade, but Church and state tainted merchants with a capital scarlet "C" for commerce.

Perestroika in Christendom

Joseph Schumpeter (1954) described how the late-medieval Catholic Church assisted economic development by promoting learning and scholarship in its monasteries. Why did the Church change its long-held suspicion of knowledge and trade? Competition and self-interest.

By the 11th century, Islam challenged the theological monopoly held by the Catholic Church. Muslims enjoyed a more open society and had access to a greater variety of consumer goods, better medicinal herbs and spices, and the wisdom of the ancient Greeks. Christendom sought *perestroika* towards knowledge and commerce, not unlike the quest by the former Soviet Union to acquire the latest technological developments from the West..

An expanding economy and population base could help the Church to compete with Islam and increase its own domain—provided that its own moral authority was not undermined. Potentially, the Church could share in the prosperity through increased contributions and the increased value of its extensive landholdings (between 30-40 percent of all productive lands in Europe).

The rediscovery of Justinian's *corpus juris civilis* sparked a revival in commercial law. In 1156, a commission of legal scholars met in the Italian city of Pisa for the purpose of forging a commercial law code. Despite this revival, Peter Lombard (d. 1160) expressed the predominant 12th century view of commerce in contending that a merchant could not practice his profession without sinning—consigning all merchants to the same "living in sin" status as common adulterers.

The Church needed a new moral technology to align its commercial doctrine with the requirements for economic prosperity. But this required independent thinkers to challenge the orthodoxy and heretics risked chastisement and death. We beneficiaries of modern prosperity owe much to the courageous 13th century trailblazers for *perestroika.*

During the early 13th century, the Western monasteries acquired copies of the works of Aristotle. Aristotle's arguments impressed the next generation of theologians on a wide-range of topics—including commerce. A series of 13th century philosophical-theological commentaries defended commerce in general and profit-making in particular. These works included the Dominican professors Albert Magnus (Commentary, 1244-1249), and Peter of Tarentaise (who later became Pope Innocent V) (Commentary, 1253-1257), and the Italian theologian St. Bonaventure (Commentary, 1250-51; Rothbard, 1995, p. 48). One of Albert Magnus' students became the greatest Christian-Aristotelian. His name was Thomas Aquinas.

Summa Theologica: A Christianized Version of Aristotelian Philosophy

Thomas Aquinas' *Summa Theologica* (written between 1265 and 1273) presented a comprehensive Christianized version of Aristotelian philosophy. The *Summa* retained all of the theological dogmas of Christianity including the doctrine of "original sin," but packaged them differently to create moral space for the quest of knowledge and trade.

To Aquinas, there was no contradiction between a valid philosophical system of nature (science) and the theological "truths" of Christianity. Since the supernatural and natural ends were not mutually exclusive, man could and ought to use his reason in order to discover God's design for the universe. Historian Charles Van Doren (1991, p. 121) summed up this outlook:

"Human beings were placed here by a loving God on an earth teeming with beings and full of intellectual puzzles, equipped with a superb mental apparatus (especially if you were a Thomas Aquinas) for dealing with those puzzles. Had God not meant for man to think? Had he intended man to pass through the earthly city with blinders, and with his eyes on another existence in the future?"

The *Summa* linked economics and ethics bridging the infamous "is-ought" gap through the natural law doctrine.

The Natural Law Doctrine as a Technology for Moral Reasoning

Thomas Aquinas believed that God's plan directing creation to its final teleological end constituted eternal law. He defined the natural law as the sharing of rational creatures in God's eternal law. There were two kinds of natural law: the *analytical* natural law and the *moral* natural law. *Analytical* natural laws pertained to positive, predictable cause and effect relationships (sometimes referred to as the "laws of nature"). In biology, the analytical natural law embraced the growth and development of organisms and the propagation of species (Chafuen, 2003, pp. 19-20 and Rommen, 1998, pp. 40-41).

On the other hand, the *moral* or normative natural law laid down principles for human behavior based upon "right living," such as "thou shalt not steal." It was possible to violate these moral laws, but not without suffering adverse consequences (Chafuen, 2003, p. 20). Aquinas believed that principles for right living could be derived from the study of nature as well as scripture.

The biological laws of growth and development bridge the "is-ought" gap by providing a standard for evaluating moral natural laws. The Genesis command to "be fruitful and multiply and replenish the earth" refers to expanding both the quantity and quality of human life. This Genesis command provides a meta principle that is necessary to properly apply the Ten Commandments. For example, the Hebrew commandment, "Thou shalt do no murder," never prohibited killing in self-defense. Nor did "sinful covetousness" prohibit the desire to get rich through legitimate trade. But the principles that advance human life are universal. Non-Christians can derive moral laws (akin to the Ten Commandments) without the help of scripture. Aristotle's *Nicomachean Ethics* developed a similar standard for measuring the moral natural laws called eudiamonia, which defines human happiness in relation to "right living." Modern Aristotelians prefer the phrase "human flourishing," which encompasses individual and societal long-range human well-being.

The Scholastics believed that the way to determine the difference between virtue and vice was to determine what actions were "reasonable" based upon cause and effect relationships (or the analytical laws of nature) in the context of human flourishing (Chafuen, 2003, pp. 20-27). Obeying the moral natural law requires reasoned judgment, rather than blind obedience. Blindly pursuing hedonistic pleasures leads to negative consequences (drunkenness, unwanted pregnancies, the destruction of property, etc.). Blindly following ethical precepts or commandments without contextual understanding can be equally disastrous (enabling sloth, appeasement of tyrants, extreme asceticism, etc.). As an act of free will, human beings are able to study and gain the knowledge needed to properly apply moral principles. This willing choice to participate in the natural law constitutes a morally meritorious act (*Participatio legis aeternae in rationali creatura.*) (Chafuen, 2003 p. 19). With this beautiful doctrine, Aquinas did not merely permit practical intellectual inquiry into moral and philosophical matters; he elevated learning into a form of worship.

The Scholastics applied "reasonableness" and "right reason" in interpreting Church doctrines on a case-by-case basis. This closely resembled the "reasonable man" standard used to settle disputes under the common law. Since trade benefits both parties, the expansion of the freedom of contract in most cases will be "reasonable." Under common law, case-by-case dispute settlement evolved a commerce-friendly set of procedural and substantive rules (Trackman, 1983, pp. 61-73). In a similar fashion, the Scholastics' interpretation of the canon according to "reasonableness" in the context of human flourishing supported the moral case for expanding the freedom of contract. For example, an analytical (positive) examination of economics reveals that market-determined prices tend to clear excess quantities supplied or demanded. A normative conclusion would argue that buyers and sellers justly trade at market prices, rather than at an arbitrary predetermined price.

The Scholastics Battle for the Moral Legitimacy of Commerce

The Scholastic natural law approach struck the moral foundations of the feudal/guild system. Aquinas embraced Aristotle's golden mean (pleasure in moderation). This weakened the condemnation of luxury goods paving the way for later Scholastic economists to adopt the goal of consumer satisfaction as an indispensable foundation for economic analysis. Production and trade also required competition, profits, and the free play of market prices. The guild system allowed artisans to increase the price of finished goods as compensation for their labor, but in 1188, the bishop of Ferrara shifted the justification of profits away from the production cost of added labor to the needs of the merchant's family. Aquinas recognized that supply and demand often produced price discrepancies for the same goods in different towns and defended entrepreneurs who practiced arbitrage by buying in the low market for resale at a higher price. He even argued that merchants may morally sell goods at high prices to a starving city and had no obligation to disclose the news that additional shipments may be *en route* because future arrivals were uncertain events (De Roover, 1957, p. 133).

Aquinas concluded that profits were an appropriate intermediate goal for business, but the final goal ought to serve a Godly purpose (i.e. to provide for the merchant's household, to help the poor, to improve the merchandise, to ensure that essential supplies are provided, etc.) (Chafuen, 2003, p. 115). Following the *Summa,* many of the moral objections to entrepreneurship, profit, market speculation, and trade quickly evaporated. The condemnations of usury and currency markets proved a bit more troublesome.

Even when the canon initially imposed an obstacle to conducting business, such as the prohibition of usury, the Scholastic method of case-by-case application of the natural law inevitably narrowed, cast into another context, or outright repudiated the rule. For example, Aquinas actually strengthened the Church's arguments against usury by adding Aristotle's objections to the practice. But Scholastics had already developed an exception to sinful usury called *interesse,* which derived from the Latin word *interno* meaning "to be lost." Lenders were entitled to receive compensation if they incurred a loss (cost) since in these cases lenders did not demand "more than was given" (Homer and Sylla, 1991, p. 73). Over time, Scholastics carved out exceptions to usury by allowing lenders to be compensated for risk, to charge penalties for late payment, and eventually allowed lenders to charge borrowers for the foregone earnings that the lender lost by losing the opportunity to use the funds himself. Eventually the Scholastics reduced the scope of sinful usury to what economists call "the pure time value of money," and even that became a matter of individual conscience.

Even though Aquinas wrongly attributed the value of money to the state, rather than supply and demand forces, subsequent Scholastics corrected the error by developing monetary theory. In 1307, Franciscan Alexander Bonini defended spot monetary exchange markets by arguing that the weight and content of the coins, not the state, determined their value. Currency futures markets posed a problem for subsequent 14th and 15th century Scholastics. They considered market speculation and compensation for risk to be legitimate reasons for currency futures prices to vary from spot markets, but price differences due purely to time delays continued to be regarded as sinful usury. To distinguish the two components for currency premiums, they slowly advanced monetary theory. The climax came in a monetary treatise *De Cambis* (1499) written by Cardinal Cajetan that justified futures markets and permitted lenders to charge *lucrum cessans* (opportunity cost interest described above) on loans made to businessmen (Rothbard 1995, p. 100).

During the 14th century, a most surprising development took place throughout Italy, the intellectual heartland of Christendom. An unprecedented volume of trade broke out! Merchants handled so much volume that new methods for conducting business had to be invented. Foreign exchange markets emerged. The first check was written in Pisa, Italy. Business insurance introduced by the Florentines two centuries before now became commonplace (Schweikart, 2000, pp. 26-27). To keep pace, double-entry accounting developed.

In 1494, Luca Paciolo, a priest from the very ascetic Franciscan order, delivered the *coup de grace* in the battle for the moral legitimacy for commerce. Paciolo codified accounting practices into a popular book creating a start-up guide for aspiring entrepreneurs. Paciolo embraced the morality of profit by writing, "If the loss exceeds the profit (may God protect each of us who is a really good Christian from such a state of affairs)" (Hunt and Murray, 1999, p. 240).

Eventually, the Scholastics removed every one of the medieval moral objections to commerce, opening trade between fiefdoms and dooming the local guild/feudal system. Scholastics also used the natural law approach to critique public officials and anti-commercial public policies, such as protectionism, oppressive taxes, monetary debasement, and corruption. It may be claimed that the Scholastic reforms merely responded to changing economic circumstances, but it is more reasonable to argue that the moral reforms acted as the prime mover by ratifying the formerly suppressed underground transactions outside of the medieval guild system. By the beginning of the 16th century, most of the arts and crafts were manufactured in the countryside, outside of the guild structure.

Scholasticism as an Intellectual Movement

The introduction of Aristotle into Christendom by the *Summa* compares with the modern-day collapse of Marxism in the Soviet Union, except that the Scholastic revolution took centuries to complete. As an intellectual movement, Scholasticism proved to be one of the most successful, and least remembered, in Western history. Scholasticism persisted for several centuries beating back the arguments of opponents to pave the way for modern commercial society.

A few contemporary scholars rejected the Scholastic approach. Duns Scotus (1290-1350) argued that "just" prices were determined by a cost-plus normal-profit formula, rather than the free play of supply and demand. The Scholastic schools exposed Duns Scotus' views as typical examples of fallacious reasoning (De Roover, 1958, 424). The term "dunce," a corruption of that errant medieval scholar's name, still brands erroneous students today. Another dissenter, Marsiglio de Padua (1275-1342), believed that justice had no rational foundation, morality had to be accepted on faith and the head of state could not be questioned; but these views made little headway until the rise of the nation-state centuries later.

What made Scholasticism such a powerful force in behalf of economic freedom? The strength and effectiveness of Scholasticism as an intellectual movement came from three factors:

(1) The financial backers of the monasteries—the multinational Catholic Church had a financial interest in the prosperity of all Christendom. Usually, nations or trade groups with an agenda to benefit the interest of one segment at the expense of the general public fund most economic research. Compared to most present-day economic practitioners, the Scholastics were much closer to being independent, truth-oriented social scientists—at least in regards to economic matters. This allowed Scholastic economists to freely discover the economic/moral principles that promote general prosperity.

(2) The moral vision—in order for any social movement to endure over centuries, it must satisfy both the individual self-interest of the participants **and** appeal to a moral vision. Utopian communistic schemes appeal to a moral vision, but invariably fail because they do not enable people to serve their individual interest harmoniously. Private markets are practical paths to prosperity, but, according to neo-conservative writers, supposedly lack an inspiring moral vision. The *partici - patio* doctrine provided the missing moral dimension to markets. Scholastics studied economics precisely to uncover moral implications. This motivated them in a way that modern "welfare economics" cannot.

(3) The Scholastic method—practical implementation of Scholastic economic analysis to actual cases often at the personal level. The Aristotelian-Thomistic scholars recognized that human concepts were based upon real world observations. This implied an inductive approach to human knowledge including the moral natural laws and their application. The purpose of morality was not only to achieve an eternal reward in the hereafter, but also to lead successful lives on earth. The Scholastics also read the Scriptures, but by also studied the analytical laws of nature. This enabled them to produce consistent, common sense moral guidelines.

Conclusion: Moral Technology Today

St. Augustine rejected human flourishing as the standard for ethical behavior. He branded merchants with the scarlet "C," and placed the Church in perpetual conflict with prosperity.

The Scholastic method applied moral codes based upon reasonableness standard in the context of human flourishing. This led them to question Church dogmas and the moral claims made by earlier churchmen. The

Summa provided a moral technology capable to establishing a commerce-friendly moral code.

Present-day secular philosophers reject the natural rights approach with the claim that an "ought" cannot be derived from an "is." Instead, they seek a *secularized* Heavenly City by deriving "ought"s from "isn't"s, such as Marx's Utopia around the dialectal corner or John Rawls's "veil of ignorant" unborn spirits. By adopting global, end-state, social justice norms, present-day secular philosophies reject the commerce-friendly method of moral discovery. The secular left firmly brands a scarlet "C" on businessmen, not unlike the ninth century Churchmen!

The Scholastics liberated people from the guilt-onus of impractical medieval moral precepts, and opened the way for a commerce-friendly culture. Shouldn't we Scholars be doing the same today?

Bibliography

Chafuen, A. (2003). *Faith and liberty: The economic thought of the late-Scholastics.* New York: Lexington Books.

De Roover, R. (1958). The concept of the just price: Theory and economic policy. *The Journal of Economic History, 28,* 418-429.

De Roover, R. (1957). Joseph A. Schumpeter and scholastic economics. *Kyklos, 10,* 115-146.

Homer, S. & Sylla, R. (1991). *A history of interest rates.* New Brunswick: Rutgers University Press.

Hunt, Edwin S. & Murray J. (1999). *A History of Business in Medieval Europe.* New York, Cambridge University Press.

Irwin, D. (1996). *Against the tide: An intellectual history of free trade.* Princeton: Princeton University Press.

Johnson, P. (1985). *A history of Christianity.* New York: Atheneum.

Rommen, H. (1998). *The natural law: A study and social history and philosophy.* Indianapolis: Liberty Fund.

Rothbard, M. (1995). Economic thought before Adam Smith: An Austrian perspective on the history of thought. Volume 1 Edward Elgar, Northampton, MA: Edward Elgar.

Schweikart, L. (2000). *The entrepreneurial adventure: A history of business in the United States.* Orlando, FL: Harcourt and Brace.

Schumpeter J. (1954). *History of economic analysis.* New York: Oxford University Press.

Trackman, L. (1983). *The law merchant: The evolution of commercial law.* Littleton, CO: Fred B. Rothman & Co.

Van Doren, C. (1991). *History of knowledge: Past, present and future.* New York: Vallentine Books.

The Concern of the Church and the Unconcern of the Free Market

Joseph Keckeissen

Conscious that half the world lies in extreme poverty, recent Holy Fathers have been urging all Catholics and others to adopt whatever measures are necessary to eliminate this misery. The proletarianization of huge multitudes of persons in the subhuman favellas of the world is a somber, accelerating phantom. Our question is why are not the free market people in accord with the pope in his great crusade. This poverty exists, and the free market folks know it, and they also know that libertarian principles are being disregarded on a worldwide basis. Why don't they seem to be interested?

On another occasion, I tried to demonstrate my intuition that the formal principles of the church and the standard tenets of free market capitalism (notably of the Chicago and especially the Vienna versions) are along the same lines, whether the point in question is the dignity of the human person, the need for a climate of liberty, limitations on the intrusion of governments, the inviolable right to private property, the blessings of free enterprise and free commerce, or the beauties of cooperation (what the church dubs solidarity). The church version, more staid and otherworldly, is so to say dressed in gown and surplice, as befits her heaven-oriented mystique, while that of the free market appears more in coat and tie, or if you wish, blue jeans, to reflect its this-worldly concerns. But in essence, I submit, they both speak the same principles.

If so, why aren't the two in accord when the subject is world poverty? To explain this discrepancy, I offer the thesis that we, free marketers, principally dedicate our efforts to promoting our pet themes, and not much more. Each one of us advances his stuff in discrete articles, sporadic laments, mathematical bla, or not much more than a feeble "I told you so." Our concerted social communication is just about inaudible. Some groups like the Foundation for the Future of Freedom are energetically voicing their convictions that freedom is being jeopardized, and they do so valiantly and effectively, but they mostly limit themselves to themes relating to freedom, neglecting other vital practices that are the cause of poverty, like the rise of prices, poverty-promoting interventionism or our incredibly unstable and intolerable monetary system.

An addendum or second thesis is that we free marketers seem to be all head and no heart. We expound marvelous theoretical truths, but when the world is not observing our dictums, we hardly shrug our shoulders. We are passively morose in things human. "Let them eat cake," we seem to say.

So our theme is that if we-believers in liberty-would perk up and whistle, shouting our time-honored convictions from the housetops, all of them, and at the same time show some open evidence of humanism, we would be in accord with the Pope, concerned with him over the hunger and misery of the Third World, or more directly over the anti-capitalism of the Third World. Some evidence of our neglect of our doctrine, that has fatal repercussions on poverty, follows.

The World Is Replete with Impoverishing Price Distortions Brought about by Government Programs

Government intervention makes some prices higher, thus hurting the consumers of the world, and other prices lower, thus lambasting the producers of the world. It is the Third World consumer and the Third World producer who are most impoverished by this intervention. The world economy becomes lopsided.

Free market theory is quite clear on the cause of price distortions, especially those of basic commodities. We might enumerate some of these causes.

Agricultural controls lead the list. Here we have the example of the United States coddling for more than 70 years our agricultural millionaires, now at the rate of a billion dollars a day. Assuring them that prices will be high, the government promotes excess production and guarantees high prices even to the extent of buying and storing any excess product. This has resulted in overproduction with its consequent dumping on the world market. In the case of cotton, world prices are lowered and the squeeze is put on the naturally more efficient tropical producers. Brazil estimates this lowering of price at 12 percent. This subsidized production is uneconomic, although profitable to its beneficiaries and its political sponsors. The struggling farmers of the Third World are sacked from competition. Here we can mention the 20 million dollars regaled to 30 wealthy sugar producers of Florida, or the European Union artificially creating the beet sugar market, subsidizing it so as to deprive the tropical sugar producers of their natural world outlets. On the other hand, tariffs, quotas, and controls all serve to raise the prices of essential goods. Examples abound as steel imported from Europe, or lumber from Canada. The idea: enrich our guys and impoverish the Third World.

Our free market doctrine has always condemned these practices, and it is clear that they really hurt the overseas poor. And yet we remain silent over and beyond an occasional learned article. We insist on them at trade meetings. Do we not recall that, in a capitalist society, prices should normally decline secularly, as was experienced in the late nineteenth century? Economic efficiency alone should make for lower and lower prices that would benefit all classes of society, and much more the starving section.

Monetary Insouciance Has Distorted and Raised World Prices

One of the great causes of the blunted growth of the world economies is our unbridled monetary system. Bretton Woods failed, floating exchanges failed; even currency boards succumbed when politicized. Without a stable monetary system, we can have no sure progress. Values will always be topsy-turvy. Solid decisions can't be made. Prices will run awry. Sleepily we permit the reigning monetary moguls to continue their interventionist steering of our monetary system, directing billions of dollars created from nothing to whatever crisis comes along. The Fed policymakers, both in times of acceleration and of slowdown, continue their unabated issuance of fiat dollars, always with contemptuous disregard of the only functional system that the world has seen, the gold standard, that at one time authoritatively inserted discipline into monetary affairs, a system that impeded infinite price rises and would have prevented our recurrent business slumps with their accompanying unemployment and underproduction, as well as have demanded saner policies of the politicians of the Third World.

We hardly protest any more that our system is piloted, not by the market, but by bureaucrats whose main objective is to distort the signals of the market. We continue to accept the inflationary doctrine of "lender of last resort," notwithstanding that we now have trillion dollar banking enterprises that the reigning ideology will consider "too big to fall." This concept, as shown by the late Murray Rothbard, was foisted upon us so as to enrich the banking profession, and we seem contented to allow it full sway as it continues to create ever more moral hazard. Allan Greenspan is ever multiplying dollars, and, with negligible opposition. He raises interest rates by slowing the growth of money, and then lowers them by opening the money sluice. We let him and his minions in the financial press tell us one day that we have to watch out for harmful deflation, and on another for imminent price inflation. Interest rates are left to the mercy of a bureaucracy that ignores the fact that the fundamental function of interest is to orient business towards producing either more consumer goods or more capital goods. This process creates fiat money not backed by anything real, in contrast with every act of genuine savings being an act sacrificing some real good or service that remains available in the capital inventory. It lowers the rate of interest, as more liquidity is pumped into the economy, and blurs the distinction between investing in consumer goods (when interest rates are rising) or in production goods (when interest rates begin to fall). The lower rates of interest resulting from the availability of the new money cause many investment projects to appear profitable, which would not appear so at the truer market rates. Much of this investment sooner or later appears unsustainable and results in capital wastage. This again is the signal for a recession that is needed to wash away the muck of wasted capital.

We listen to frequent pronouncements, totally contradictory to the Mises/Hayek cycle theory. We have completely neglected to rely on the markets to create Purchasing Power Parity to set the value of the relations between currencies. The inflation indexes these days falsely tell us that there is no serious inflation because they omit relevant prices... they include rents, which are at the moment relatively low, and omit housing which is at an all time high. The rise in the Dow stock prices do not count for inflation, bubbles notwithstanding. They are said to be caused by speculators and not by money creation.

We entrust huge supplies of money to the hands of the World Bank and the IMF to conduct repeatedly unsuccessful bailouts of country after country with meek response. Our financial press ignores completely the fact that the money supply is growing like Topsy. It offers frivolous logic to explain the recent boom and bust, but never speaks of the spectacular growth of the circulating medium. It says that whatever goes up must come down, marvelous metaphysics, or talks of greedy speculation, or psychological euphoria, or whatnot, but never a word about the creation of new unbacked fiat money. And our guys are mostly silent, or uninterested, or saying stupidities like "Money doesn't matter." Our monetary system is in such bad shape, that any day now, a generalized revolt against the dollar could provoke an international plunge into economic chaos and despair. Yet few and rare are the voices that are informing us of this fact horrible to envision.

How can we expect adolescent nations to devise an orderly monetary system that promotes their growth and prosperity, when our own system, on which they depend, is so fraught with error? We can in no way serve as a model for them. We are asleep at the wheel; we are about to crash or fall into the next precipice.

Were we to be congruent with our theory and publicly exposing all these errors day in and day out, we would be pushing for something sound, like the gold standard was in its day. We would be screaming about the international effects of a dollar that has lost 95 percent of its value during the course of the 20th century. And how that is one of the fundamental causes of stagnation in the Third World, and most assuredly, how the immense debt of the Third World, which has the Holy Father very much preoccupied, is a result of our loose monetary system.

Government Hijacking of the Credit Markets

Uncontrolled deficits are the bane of the Third World, and one of the chief obstacles to its progress. But what an awful example the first world offers! We allow our governments to amass huge deficits, financed by debt, when politically they can't further raise taxes or inflate. The government thus competes in the financial markets for the scarce financial capital that would otherwise be employed in advancing private production and prosperity. This reflects an enormous opportunity cost, the out-pricing of private wealth-enhancing investments in productive projects. Mises considered this to be disloyal competition on the part of government finance. It is treason against the creative productivity of a free market. It squanders capital in wasteful projects and current expenses, and impedes productive investment. The debt of the United States has now reached astronomic levels, as has that of the individual states.

This propensity to create debt by the developing nations has become so massive that it could be blanked out only by a humiliating national bankruptcy or a precedent-setting process of forgiveness. Why are we so reticent to discuss these matters? There has been infinite irresponsibility both on the part of the local political actors, as well as of the international banks that have been encouraged to provide ever more government-backed financing. Finance should rather be limited to sound entrepreneurial projects, rather than capital-wasting government outlays.

This is another field in which the free market economists have been less vocal than they should be. Were we to be insisting on this point much more vocally, we would be in line with the papal admonitions, and would be turning the tide towards healthy growth investments and away from government boondoggles.

We Are Not Promoting the Entrepreneur

Our ingrained wisdom asserts that it is the entrepreneur who, by means of economic calculation, bountifully services the consumers of the world with ever more and better offerings. Free market literature abounds on this point (see Mises, Kirzner, Schumpeter). Why are we not decrying the fact that entrepreneurs in the Third World are either not functioning, or not allowed to function? Our great universities seem to have exchange programs with students of the Third World. Why are not these programs producing more salutary effects?

The Unemployment Debacle

Our two-centuries-old theory tells us that outsourcing is well in accord with the law of association of Ricardo. We are not only not revering Ricardo, we are opposing him. The big guns in our economy are attributing not only actual unemployment, but also the definitive loss of jobs to this newest effect of worldwide globalization, outsourcing, or the hiring of overseas foreigners for their cheaper labor cost, accompanied by transfers of capital overseas as well. Paul Craig Roberts, himself a stalwart supply-sider, is a most noteworthy instance of this reversal of our principles, arguing that Ricardo's law does not cover the movement of factors. He has reverted to protectionism against outsourcing.

This discussion, however, seems to neglect one important point. Are not American wages relatively too high? Is not American labor over-priced? Were not American wages forcibly raised during an entire century by means of monopoly privilege granted by government and by legitimatized blackmail in our labor negotiations? Should not our wages be allowed to adjust to the real market forces of the new globalization? Free market doctrine seems to demand this adjustment. We never seem to blame the labor unions for their hostility to progress over the many years and their opposition to the Third World laborers.

Labor unions have already begun to see the light. In the European Union, they have recently been forced by circumstances to accept wage cuts and workplace simplifications in order to reduce the threat of wholesale transfers of facilities to the newly incorporated countries of Eastern Europe. It was unheard of that Spanish labor bosses might conceivably ever agree to a five percent cut in wages or that IG Metall, Germany's labor giant, accept modifications in its traditional contracts. "Spanish wages, though well below German levels, are more than double those in Slovakia, where VW has been expanding manufacturing capacity." These corrections, theory should tell us, are beneficial to all in the long run.

Furthermore, it is just not true that China and India are the fundamental cause of the loss of American jobs? Rising medical insurance premiums, elevated labor costs due to new rules adopted in the Clinton administration, labor-economizing technology, and improvements in productivity are also fundamental causes of these modifications. The rise in productivity in the first quarter of 2004 shows in part the reasons for the losses in employment. Firms, not yet experiencing the post-recessional reductions in costs and prices, want to hold down their prices and thus boost their prospects of profits. These factors alone can explain our unemployment at 5.6 percent. Lamentations over globalization are really not in order. It is about time that we deglorify our overprotected labor market.

All this seems fair play. Doesn't justice demand that all players abide by the same set of rules? Privileges for American labor are out of order in a globalized world. Let American labor compete with the rest of the world, and let it conserve only those privileges earned by its proven higher productivity. It is interfering in the Free Trade negotiations to protect its bailiwick at the expense of newcomers. Freedom in the world labor market would be a great boon to the workers of the undeveloped world. Give them a break. Give them a chance to honestly compete.

Consumer Spending (Consumerism)

Austrian theory directly contradicts the Keynesian paradigm, which overplays consumption and the so-called marginal propensity to consume. For the Keynesians, and even the Republican Bush administration and its Central Bank, consumer purchases are what sustain an economy. This idea is flatly contradicted by the Mises-Hayek doctrine, whereby it is production that is the essential factor in growth of the Domestic Product.

Production, when not netted out, accounts for two-thirds of economic activity and far outdistances consumption. Production depends on true savings, and each act of savings always implies a reduction in consumer spending. Consumption is merely the result of production. It is the dessert at the end of the production process. Consumption is but a waste of capital. And it has a huge opportunity cost.

In addition to waving the consumption flag, as the savior of a tottering economy, the moderns fail to note that American consumer debt has reached extraordinary and unsustainable heights. Just this year it is up 6.7 percent from a year earlier. The asset value of housing in the American economy has been looted in order to increase consumption. Savings is at an all-time low. These situations cannot last. We cannot continue on consuming more than we produce. We are paying for this gluttonous level of consumption principally by the creation of debt. How much longer will our creditors continue to amass credits in our favor before pulling out? The day may soon be upon us that they determine to cash in their dollar securities, causing a monetary landslide whose effects are difficult to conceive.

The papal admonitions against excessive consumption are well known. The church, otherworldly as she must tend to be, decries the modern penchant for excessive consumption, calling it consumerism. The Austrians, as just stated, consider unnecessary consumption an obstacle to progress. There, though on different logical paths, the two sources converge. If the first world would really consume less of the unnecessary goods that it demands today, would there not be a greater quantity of savings and investment?

Would not the lengthened path of this new investment make capital goods ever more productive and ever more abundant and cheaper? Would not the Third World also have a stake in this? Are not the third-worlders also stakeholders in our economy? But we waste relatively little energy in expounding the negative aspects of consumption.

Cooperation vs. Solidarity

We preach that our system is that of cooperation, but reject as ideologically perverse any reference that the Holy Father makes in favor of solidarity, when he laments the fact that we have barred the Third World from participating in the benefits of world capitalism. Is not cooperation just about the same as solidarity? Are they both not forms of treating others with justice and respect?

The recent Holy Fathers since John XXIII have pleaded that the capitalist world take the Third World under its wing. Perhaps they were a little off a sound economical base in suggesting that the Third World solution depended on three different factors:

- that the high consumption of the first world is a cause of the poverty of others;
- that the richer countries had the obligation to share their gains with the poorer ones; and
- that it is urgent that the accumulated debts of those countries be forgiven, so that they might have a fighting chance to reach prosperity.

The Holy Fathers are not economists, and their economic suggestions might not be the most practical. The late Lord P.T. Bauer has shown us that poverty results principally from wrong attitudes and unsavory government intervention. Also, if the debts are forgiven without correcting the cause of such great wastage of capital, very little positive gain would be experienced. Notwithstanding Friedrich Von Hayek's misgivings on the use of the term justice, most capitalists, I presume, would agree that a just world means that all involved get a fair shake. Certainly, free market doctrine accepts that simple principle. And what does a fair shake imply? Cutting out special privileges for our own farmers and labor unions, letting the capitalist system reduce the prices-as it should do, buying from the cheaper source (the Third World) rather than from privileged suppliers, etc. Are not all these capitalist norms? Is not that the cooperation of the market, and in turn, solidarity? Why are we not insisting on returning to this pure free market doctrine?

If the believers of free markets would start a universal chant to:

- eliminate tariffs and all sorts of barriers to trade,
- convert the monetary system into something healthy and stable,
- harangue against distorted prices, like those of OPEC oil,
- reduce the government's craze for aggrandizement, etc.,

the free market would be a much better economic partner with the Third World, and would be in unison with the Pope in decrying the senseless poverty and proletarianization of the other half of the globe. We would be pushing for more productive investments there, creating more outsourcing and letting the other guy also make some profits. We would be allies and not resentful critics of the papal doctrine. The Third World products would have a gateway into the developed world; the evils of monetary inflation would be held in check; the free market would not be crimped of its potential to capitalize the undeveloped. We might beget a healthful feeling for the plight of the undernourished other half. We would be then allied with the papal pleas for a better world.

In retrospect, if we be allowed to make a comparison between the free market outlook and that of the Holy Fathers, it would seem so evidently clear to anyone that the church's position is far more noble, generous, healthy, and sound, whereas the free market approach seems selfish, unconcerned, hard-hearted, and ice-cold, notwithstanding the fact that its very principles, continuously neglected, eminently coordinate with that of the church. Oh, Free Market, get with it. Push for your stuff with all your might, and you'll see that you and the See of Peter are close allies, as they should be, in the fight for a more prosperous world.

The "Conflict" Between Business and Religion: Where Does It Come From?

Harold B. Jones, Jr.

Since the Conference on Ethics and Spirituality in Business, I have had several email exchanges with Frances Eddy. In one of her notes she told me this: "When faced with a multitude of options of 'what to do next,' there is usually a strong pull to do what is less demanding or more pleasant, or to follow a distraction, etc. Today, I was able to demonstrate some dominion in doing client work and taking care of other responsibilities in a more orderly fashion." Such self-disciplined behavior came more easily, she said, on the days when she had devoted "more than superficial attention or minimal time at the beginning of the day to spiritual thinking."

She worked harder and more efficiently, that is to say, on the days when she put her devotional life ahead of her work. Her clients were better served when the way in which she met her obligations to them had been deliberately molded by her efforts to be conscious of God.

I have not asked Frances about this, but I am going to assume she does not charge more on the days she begins with prayer. If that is true, and if her clients had some way of knowing which days these were, those would be the days on which they would want her to work on the tasks for which they pay her. She is doubtless superior to her competitors even on the days she gets out of bed late, stubs her toe, mutters something unkind (not that she ever would), and completely neglects her devotions. Her more spiritual self, though, is a better worker than her less spiritual self, and given their choice, her clients would prefer to have their jobs done by the better worker.

Speaking more generally, it might be suggested that there is a positive correlation between the quality of one's religious life and the quality of one's work. Genuflecting then to the doctrines of economics, it might be added that there will be a greater demand for a superior level of service. Meeting this demand will enhance the wealth not only of the person who delivers the service but also of those who benefit from it.

If that is true, the much talked-about "conflict" between business and religion may be more apparent than real. It is entirely possible that the disciplines associated with economic success are not merely similar to but spring from the disciplines associated with religious commitment. Perhaps the internal logic of capitalism and the internal logic of faith are in perfect accord and their so-called "conflict" is the byproduct of historical processes that are threatening to both. It is the purpose of the present essay to examine this possibility in more detail.

The Intrinsic Religious Orientation

Of Ronny Heaslop in *A Passage to India,* C. S. Forster says the man agreed with religion when it endorsed the national anthem and disagreed with it when it attempted to influence the way he lived. He shook off questions about the struggle between Christianity's moral code and his personal lifestyle by saying he did not think it was well to talk about such things; each of us has to work out his own faith. What Heaslop did not like about religion was the discipline with which it was associated. He had no difficulty with the God of "God Save the King." It was the God of the Ten Commandments he wanted to avoid. For Ronny Heaslop, "faith" was an external thing. It was something about which he had opinions, perhaps even very strong opinions, but it was not something he had internalized. Religion was valuable as a means of self-justification and perhaps even as source of comfort in times of distress. It could never be regarded as the source of rules about how to live.

The psychologist Gordon Allport described attitudes of this kind as an Extrinsic Religious Orientation. At the far opposite extreme, Allport said, is the Intrinsic Religious Orientation (IRO). For persons with an IRO, religion is more of a master than a servant in the economy of life. Their faith is a source of motivation, and in an ever-expanding awareness of what their faith implies, they find guidance about how to act on the basis of that motivation. They see the narrow, short-term concerns arising from fear and random desire giving way to a wider view, confidence replacing anxiety, and discipline gaining the upper hand on impulse. They are the persons to whom William James, in his famous Gifford Lectures of 1901-02, referred as "twice-born." For them, faith has become not a means to an end, but an end in itself.

The old saw about "being so heavenly minded as to be of no earthly good" is not an accurate characterization of persons with an IRO. Questionnaire research has shown that those who believe in a disciplined religious life are more likely than non-believers not merely to go to church, but also to be meaningfully involved in secular activities. Studies have found a strong positive correlation among the IRO, church attendance, and various types of self-reported, non-spontaneous helping behaviors.

Other studies have shown that religious convictions, church attendance, and meaningful secular involvement are correlated with an internal locus of control. People with an internal locus of control do not believe they are in control of what happens to them, but they do have a sense of power over the way in which they respond to what happens to them. They tend to have higher aspirations, to respond more favorably to challenges, and to be more persistent than persons with an external locus of control. The IRO seems thus to be associated with the tendency to think of oneself as in control of one's own life. The economic significance of this is suggested by the fact that those who think of themselves as in charge of their own lives tend to be happier with their jobs, more successful, and financially better off than those who think of themselves as the victims of circumstance.

The IRO has been found to correlate with intrinsic motivation and college GPA, scores on standardized tests of intellectual capacity being held constant. It also correlates with a sense of personal responsibility. Subjects with a strong IRO have scored better on a variety of measures of psychological well being and were found to have a greater sense of purpose in life. The sense of life purpose, in turn, is correlated an emphasis on the importance of salvation; low scorers emphasize pleasure, excitement, and comfort.

Allport thought of the ERO and IRO as being at the opposite ends of a continuum. Questionnaire research indicates that they may coexist. The extent to which their relative strength within a given personality depends upon individual choice has yet to be researched, but stories of lives changed in a conversion experience are suggestive. James' "twice born" terminology may be better than Allport's "Intrinsic Religious Orientation."

James' examination of historic cases points in the same direction as modern psychological research: other things being equal, the deeply religious person is likely to be a more effective human being than the one who keeps God at a distance. The ceteris paribus of the statement needs to be stressed, for other things are seldom equal. Intelligence plays a part, and so does talent. The role of opportunity cannot be overstressed. The argument is simply that a particular person with particular gifts and in a particular situation is likely to deal more effectively with life when under the influence of a deeply held faith.

Society is a collection of individuals, so a society in which a large number of persons have a meaningful faith is likely to be exploiting its opportunities more effectively than one whose members are untouched by religion. Society may be more than a collection of individuals, in the same way that a house is more than a collection of bricks, but it would be nonsense to suggest that one can build a strong edifice out of crumbling blocks or a red home out of brown bricks. A society's effectiveness is heavily dependent on the effectiveness of the persons who make it up. While this effectiveness may transcend, it must of necessity include an economic dimension. A society under the influence of widespread religious enthusiasm is likely to be doing better with the things of the world than a society whose attention is focused entirely on the things of the world.

The Weber Thesis

The German sociologist Max Weber, though neither the first nor the only, is the best known of those who have examined this case in detail. He described the individual in whom religious faith and effective economic behavior intersect as an "ascetic." The term comes from a Greek word that means "one who exercises" and suggests among other things "anyone who lives with strict self-discipline and abstinence" (*Webster's Twentieth Century Dictionary,* Unabridged, 2nd ed., p. 108). The self-control that springs from a desire to use one's life in the service of higher purposes and with an awareness of ethical consequences, Weber said, provides renewed assurances that one is obeying God. Asceticism might therefore be described as an expression of an IRO. William James made a detailed examination of asceticism as an element of the twice born personality.

At its simplest level, Weber's argument was simply that through its association with the ascetic disciplines, religious faith has been a powerful stimulus to economic progress. The English economist R. H. Tawney disagreed, but only because he missed Weber's point. Tawney was incapable of distinguishing been Christianity and the institutional church; the asceticism in which Weber was interested always arose as part of a challenge to the complacency of the religious mainstream. During the Middle Ages, the challenge came in the rise of new monastic orders; in the 16th century it came as Protestantism; in the 17th century it came as Puritanism in England and Jansenism in France; and in the 18th century it came as the Evangelical Revival. All these movements were associated with economic change.

The particular ascetic discipline that most interested Weber was work, to which the members of radical movements applied themselves with an intensity born of the conviction that God had called them to it. The Weber thesis is associated with the term "Protestant Ethic," but Weber understood the relationship between vocation (from the Latin vocare, to call) and labor was not uniquely "Protestant." Long before the Reformation it had been the distinctive trait of Western monasticism and as such had played a role in laying the foundations of Western prosperity.

Between the seventh century and the ninth century, Benedictine monks were the driving force in European economic progress. They were literate, they kept accounts, they worked according to a daily timetable and an accurate calendar, they produced surpluses, and they invested their surpluses in new construction, livestock, and feed. They also experimented with new methods, and their farms were centers of technical innovation and economic efficiency.

In the 11th and 12th centuries, Cistercian monks took over for the increasingly worldly Benedictines. Hoping to avoid the temptations of civilization, they founded their houses far from castles and towns and devoted themselves to clearing land and draining swamps. The acreage they added to Europe's productive capacity was the foundation of the late medieval economic expansion with which Rosenberg and Birdzell begin their story in *How the West Grew Rich*. Cistercian abbots were in no way less aggressively businesslike than the merchants who in the 13th century began to replace them as the leaders of Western economic progress. They did all they could to lower their labor costs, and monasteries might be closed down so that the monks could be moved to an area offering a potentially higher rate of return.

The so-called "Protestant Ethic" was a descendant of the ethic that made the monasteries productive. The Rule of St. Benedict was "poverty, chastity, obedience." The monks were not allowed to spend their earnings on themselves, they were not permitted to have women, and they were expected to comply with the orders of their Superior. In the 16th century, the monastic rule became the common property of every Christian who wanted to claim it. For the radical Protestants, "poverty" became living well within one's means, "chastity" became faithfulness to a single spouse and the raising of God-fearing children, and "obedience" became working hard at whatever life happened to demand.

The monk believed he had been called to serve God by withdrawing from the world to live in a monastery. Radical Protestants believed they had been called to serve God by means of faithfulness in whatever line of work they found themselves. John Calvin said that doing one's best religiously meant filling the position one had actually been assigned, namely one's occupation. A century later, clerics like John Angier and William Perkins urged the Puritans to so spiritualize their earthly employment that it might become a source of good works.

The importance of this insistence upon serving God by means of diligence in one's daily tasks cannot be overemphasized. The laboring classes have had a long record of doing no more than was absolutely necessary for subsistence. Writing just before the dawn of the Evangelical Revival, Daniel Defoe said that Englishmen would work until they had their pockets full and then go spend their money in the pub. When he asked such men about their intentions, Defoe said, they usually replied that they planned to drink for as long as they could afford to before returning to work. The first European manufacturers found that workers responded to an increase in piece rates by maintaining their previous income with the production of fewer pieces. Adam Smith said high wages led to hard work, but this was in the last quarter of the 18th century and in England, where the Evangelical Revival had already begun to exert its powerful influence.

There is little historical evidence that the relationship between increased wages and increased effort is as universal as economists and psychologists might like to suppose. The willingness to work seems in the first instance to have been the byproduct of a heightened religious awareness. It is true that by the 20th century people had begun think of work primarily as a means to consumption. The trinkets on which they set their hearts, however, could never have become widely available if it had not been for the earlier appearance of a willingness to work even in the absence of trivial incentives.

In 1753, Henry Fielding suggested that the morals of able-bodied paupers should be improved by sending them to a workhouse to learn a trade. Even as he wrote, the poor were coming under the influence of the evangelicals, whose message about the joys of another world led to a greater diligence in this one. The case of James Lackington is instructive. He was the son of a drunkard and apprenticed to a shoemaker when he became a Methodist. He borrowed five pounds from the Methodist Lending Society and proceeded to make himself a wealthy bookseller. Later in life he said that if he had never heard the Methodists preach, he would have ended his days as a poor, ragged, dirty cobbler.

The Attack on Christianity and Capitalism

The history of the next century and a half was the experience of James Lacking "writ large." Under the influence of repeated religious revivals (the three "Great Awakenings"), America and England led the way, and the remainder of the West followed at a distance. The poverty and economic stagnation of pre-industrial society gave way to rapid progress, child labor began to disappear long before there were any laws against it, and the common man came to enjoy a standard of living unknown even to kings a few centuries before.

For most of the 19th century, people understood the relationship between the ascetic disciplines and economic progress. It was, said John Maynard Keynes, a period during which morals, politics, and literature conspired with religion to encourage frugality, investment, and the production of wealth. Church leaders were likely to be staunch defenders of capitalism: Henry Ward Beecher (Harriet Beecher Stowe's little brother and a noted preacher) attacked the railroad strikes of 1877 as a violation of Christian principles. Alfred Marshall said that religious motives were more intense than economic and devoted a few pages in his *Principles of Economics* to the effect of the

Reformation on economic progress. Russell H. Conwell's lecture on "Acres of Diamonds" described financial success as the result of Christian attitudes; Conwell delivered the lecture more than 6,000 times; admissions proceeds provided the funds with which to found Temple University.

The mood, however, was beginning to change. The law-abiding industry springing from religious conviction produced an abundance that made it easy to set aside religious conviction. Commenting on the course of events in early America, Cotton Mather said that religion had produced prosperity, and prosperity was now destroying religion. In England, John Wesley observed that as soon as people became Methodists they became industrious and frugal; their industry and frugality led to wealth, and wealth led to spiritual complacency. That turned out to the story of the 18th and 19th centuries. Christianity exerted a directing influence on Western civilization at least until the 1880s. By the time of Russell Conwell's death in 1925, however, the old religious disciplines seemed antiquated.

There were few who were willing to admit that the faith's offense lay what it demanded of them. It was argued rather that religion was the byproduct of an outmoded approach to life and that its demands were therefore inappropriate. John Dewey said the findings of biology cast doubt on the doctrines of sin, redemption, and immortality. Biology has in fact nothing to say either one way or the other about the doctrines of Christianity, but Dewey and his collaborators were looking to science as a substitute for religion, and they insisted upon setting the two at odds.

The new faith was a faith not so much in science as in the inevitability of widespread abundance. The progress of 150 years convinced many that progress was natural and that every delay was the result of some defect the law could be used to cure. Christianity insists on the limitations of human nature and therefore on the limitations of human legislators; capitalism insists on the reality of limited resources; they were attacked in the same breath. After seeing the slums of Glasgow, the novelist Sinclair Lewis said that God should damn both the economic system that would permit such poverty and the religions that would stand for it. Like other "reformers," he lacked the wisdom to thank God and capitalism for the comforts he enjoyed. He insisted instead on condemning both Christianity and the economic system for the discomforts that remained.

The interesting thing about this new indignation is that it never led to action. Timothy Smith and his student, Norris Magnus, chronicled the personal involvement of Orthodox Christians in the campaigns first against slavery and then against the despair in America's slums. There is no similar story about the authors who condemned capitalism and Christianity for the world's ills. Lewis, for one, never used any of the vast fortune generated by his books to relieve so much as a single soul; he would not even help the members of his own family. His life was a string of affairs with women young enough to be his daughters. He could haughtily discuss the failures of religion; he could not accept the disciplines associated with a vital faith. He wanted to take the position of God in judging the world but was unwilling to listen to God's call in the concrete realities of his own life.

Among educated persons, the extrinsic religious orientation (see above) was coming into vogue. The clergy of long-established denominations, as Adam Smith observed, are more likely to adopt the attitudes of the educated classes than to accept the disciplines of personal commitment. This is the background against which we must understand the role of Reinhold Niebuhr and Archbishop William Temple in the 1930s' crusade against capitalism. Neither offered a noticeable challenge to the atheism of 1933's widely talked about "Humanist Manifesto." Both were insistent on legislation to reign in the behavior of private businessmen. They were less interested in religion than in using the powers of the state to impose their vision on the future.

This is not to suggest that those who pointed to the ethical infractions of business were entirely mistaken. The list of merchants and industrialists who could be considered for canonization is a short one. The same could be said, however, of political leaders. The "injustices" of Western capitalism were nothing when compared to the brutalities of the Soviet Union and Nazi Germany. One of Temple's colleagues praised the spirit of comradeship and zest for public service in the former; Niebuhr offered a word of commendation for the latter in his famous *Moral Man and Immoral Society.* Neither Temple nor Neibuhr suggested Christian conversion or obedience to the precepts of the gospel as a means to the amelioration of society's problems. Both wanted to adapt religion to the demands of the interventionist state. These men and their intellectual heirs have been less concerned about business and religion than in subjecting both business and religion to the whims of an overreaching political authority.

Conclusion

Perhaps it is time for well-meaning individuals who talk about the "conflict" between business and religion to examine their premises. Neither psychology nor history points to a disagreement between the disciplines of religion and the disciplines that lead to success in business. This essay has considered only the role of Christianity, but Weber's writing and the work of psychologist David C. McClelland point to Rabbinical Judaism, Zen Buddhism in Japan, and Jainism in India as blessings on the economic life of the communities that have embraced them. Business and religion do not threaten each other. Both are threatened by the complacency that accepts abundance as the natural order of things and questions the need for any form of personal discipline.

Capitalism Beyond the "End of History"

James R. Wilburn

The teaching of business ethics has been embarrassingly lacking in a coherent and self-confident understanding of the moral roots of capitalism. Faculties who teach ethics in professional schools have too often resigned themselves merely to updating their students on the most recent court interpretations of sexual harassment, racial discrimination, or asbestos liability, rather than wrestling with the nourishment of moral character. Further, in the last century, the related field of economics largely abandoned its earlier classic study of economics as moral philosophy, being usurped by deterministic mathematicians. Spiritual leaders, on the other hand, have typically lacked the basic vocabulary of commercial enterprise necessary to be taken seriously.

Added to this scandalous paucity is a more recent arrogance about the future prospects of capitalism. Humankind seems eternally vulnerable to declaring some passing phenomenon to be a major hinge in history, generalizing an experience particular to a time or place or group and giving it cosmic significance to describe an entire age. Acquiescing to belief in some final denouement after the fall of the Berlin Wall, some have proclaimed an ultimate, climactic, conquest by liberal democracy and free-market economics in what Francis Fukuyama (1989) called a kind of Hegelian (perhaps more aptly a Marxian) "end of history."

Others foresee the death of the nation state and its evolution, according to Philip Bobbit (2002, p. 667), into a "market state," assuring us that "early in the twenty-first century, it seems not unlikely that virtually all major states will accept for themselves the fundamental assumptions that Margaret

Thatcher and Tony Blair urged for Britain and that Bill Clinton and George W. Bush urged for the United States." Offering further assurance, Michael Mandelbaum (2002) maintains that three ideas-peace, democracy, and free markets-have now "conquered the world." With an optimism that is rare for one whose grasp of history and human experience is far broader and deeper than most, Michael Novak ([1991] 2001, pp. 184-185) sees "signs that the twenty-first century will be marked by a new approach to the philosophy of humankind, a new vision of the nature and destiny of man," because former socialist regimes are "now discovering the moral practices of a free society." Even Pope John Paul II has found in capitalism's progress an important spiritual emphasis on human creativity that validates humankind's fundamental right to economic initiative. Thus, according to Novak, "We are all capitalists now, even the pope."

I want to suggest a less optimistic prognosis for the future of democratic capitalism (what the 18th century might have called a "commercial republic"), and then make some brief observations about where I believe our emphasis should be to nourish ethics in business and ensure the future of capitalism.

Hostility to Capitalism

There are two reasons why I hesitate to join the sanguine celebration of the triumph of free institutions. One is the persistent, deep hostility toward business, especially toward those who are resolutely successful. There were academic leaders who declared, even as the dust of "Nine-eleven" still hung over Manhattan, that America got what it deserved because of its long history of economic exploitation. In addition, there are those who, for immediate political gain, continue to cant *ad nauseum* the need for confiscatory taxation of those who are economically successful as the absolute first principle in their book of virtues. Add to this zealotry the continuing absence of business leaders among heroes portrayed in fiction, the network news, or the movies (portrayals like "Schindler's List" should not be such a rare exception), and the prospects are still less heartening.

The perennial denigration of those who benefit from economic liberty is long standing and well studied.[1] To some extent it survives as a relic from ancient times when economic gain was a zero-sum pursuit won only at the expense of others. More recently, many economic historians have themselves been socialists, and in the last century social scientists like Herbert Spencer and William Graham Sumner did unwitting damage to business in all its forms under the rubric of Social Darwinism. Only recently have economists tardily developed any theory of social capital while others, in their zeal for the scientific method, often ignored the moral implications of their conjectures.[2] Given the disappearance of the family farm, there even persists a surprising strain of Jeffersonian agrarianism in such a gifted and serious writer as Victor Davis Hanson (1996. p. xvii) who recently wrote "that the entire cargo of our current unhappiness–materialism, crime, spiritual emptiness–is in inverse proportion to the number of people who are both rural and agrarian."

Added to these sources of intellectual hostility is the primitive and age-old opposition of pure envy. Marching under the banner of "social justice" (a phrase which tends to release individuals from responsibility to be ethical persons), are some leaders bent on gaining power rather than achieving virtue, and such righteousness requires a Satan easily found in capitalism. As a sociological phenomenon given cachet as the "New Class," Daniel Bell and others have focused on the "knowledge industry" comprised of professors, writers, and media celebrities who resent the influence of (in their perception, less sophisticated) business leaders. That the Ten Commandments would warn against envy seven times should help us not to be surprised that it is alive and well. In the global arena, envy's threat to capitalism finds further expression in the votes by Third World dictators in the United Nations, worldwide terrorism, and the fierce hostility by reigning monarchs to liberty in any form.

Second, and perhaps even more disturbing than this continuing and ferocious hostility to capitalism, is the loss of vigilance that attends its incredible success in providing material benefits. What disturbs me most about writers like Mandelbaum, Bobbit, and Fukuyama is their hubris. If, as Solomon warns, "pride goes before a fall," it is tempting to adapt the poets' universal warning to read, "Whom God wishes to destroy, he first makes rich." There is no guarantee that this experiment in liberty will be more than a passing interlude to an otherwise dreary life on earth if those who benefit most from its bounty do not understand its moral justification and learn to defend it steadfastly. Capitalism's greatest challenge may be how to stay awake on a full stomach.

Moral Framework of Capitalism

None can question the capability of free markets to produce incredible material abundance. But the need to be clear about the virtues of the market and how it relates to the moral culture of a civil society remains an imperative. That capitalism's enemies have completely ignored its spiritual roots is not surprising. But as a former businessman, business school dean, and economic historian, I am more concerned about illiteracy among its friends and those who benefit most from its bounty.

To begin with, most who have written about the sins of capitalism have completely ignored its triune nature, the interdependent economic, political, and moral-cultural systems that are so essential and mutually supportive that none of the three is sustainable without the others. To rescue economics from a purely utilitarian and materialistic realm, one can begin by remembering that the Anglo-American conception of liberty, as Michael Novak has understood, has always focused on "the inner form of the law derived from reason, law, duty, or a well-ordered conscience." Liberty, whether economic, political, or spiritual, is indivisible and the expansion of human liberty, as Lord Acton understood, is in fact "the key to the design of Providence for human history" (Novak, ([1991] 2001, p. 190). Acknowledging the moral culture which is critical to sustaining the free markets of liberty brings the more recent notion of "rational choice" closer to the religious reflection that, in fact, makes a free market work. But this understanding is not new. It rather is a rediscovery of origins. Adam Smith, though typically recognized as the incomparable economist, was first of all a moral philosopher. He attempted to explain moral sentiments through what seemed to be the universally accepted attribute of human sympathy that, in turn, leads us to be concerned about the fortunes of others' happiness even though we personally derive nothing more than the pleasure of seeing it. (James Q. Wilson, in *The Moral Sense,* has surveyed recent biological and psychological studies of human behavior and discovered them to be compatible with and explicative of Smith's earlier work.)

When Adam Smith pursued the sources of a market's ability to improve the life of a community, whether a nation or the world, he concluded, in one of the most revolutionary books ever published, that a market's power is in its capacity to pool the practical intelligence of many people (seen as persons and not merely as consumers) for the benefit of all. The market thus accumulates the social intelligence of many citizens to provide the maximal benefit to the entire social fabric.

From Adam Smith in 1776 through the appearance of John Stuart Mill's *Principles of Political Economy* in 1848, economics continued to be studied as a division of moral philosophy. But during the 20th century, economics, as other fields, was captured by a school of social scientists eager to apply to human behavior the scientific method that had proven well suited to inanimate matter. They tended toward condescension, if not outright contempt, toward economics as moral philosophy. No publication more completely reflects this phenomenon than the textbook of Paul Samuelson, simply titled Economics, which, for 50 years, was the economic Bible to thousands of young American college students. In it, Samuelson warned against any return to the "mystical principles" of Adam Smith's economic theories which, he said, had done "almost as much harm as good in the past century and a half."

Not until the emergence of the so-called "Austrian School" of "classical liberals," was the study of economics, at least among some, restored to its place among the liberal arts, enriching its science with the insights of moral philosophy. Led by such luminaries as Friedrich von Hayek and Ludwig von Mises, the Austrian School (Hayek preferred the designation "Whigs") took advantage of cross-cultural studies of social trust, individual initiative, patterns of cooperation, values, choice, and other moral habits. Von Mises, in fact, opened his classic work *Human Action: A Treatise on Economics* with the observation that "Choosing determines all human decisions. In making his choice man chooses not only between various material things and services. All human values are offered for option." Von Mises restated crisply what had been lost. As mere science, economics had no tools with which to account for the free will that is as basic to understanding economic choice as it is to understanding moral philosophy. Thus, by recognizing the centrality of the human subject, the Austrian School focused on the importance of "human capital."

At the University of Chicago where, since 1975, 13 winners of the Nobel Prize in economics were either faculty members or received their doctorates, further doubts arose about the economic determinism and scientific management that pervaded the Progressive Movement. Key to the shift from Samuelson's enclave in Cambridge, Massachusetts, to the "Chicago School" was Chicago's founding father, Frank Knight, who was professor and resident sage in Chicago from 1928 to his death in 1972. Although he did not consider himself a Christian, in his evolution from a microeconomist to a moral philosopher he viewed the core social and economic problem to be a "discovery and definition of values," incapable of discovery simply through a purely rational explanation analogous to the laws discovered by the physical sciences. Though uncomfortable with Catholic ideas of natural law, Knight nevertheless believed that individuals inevitably operated within some social culture where religion was a significant source of self- identity and action. For him private property was justified by something akin to the Christian view of fallen human beings plagued by original sin (In *Economics as Religion,* Robert Nelson's chapter on the Chicago School is even titled "Frank Knight and Original Sin").

By the early 1990s, as communism began to crumble and capitalism appeared to emerge victorious, Pope John Paul II issued his encyclical, *Centesimus Annus* (Hundredth Year), in which he extolled the free market as the most efficient instrument for utilizing resources and effectively responding to human needs. While explaining the moral foundations of a market economy, he repudiated any idea of a possible compromise between capitalism and socialism and confirmed his strong desire to end the divorce between religion and economics. The economic and political changes sweeping Eastern Europe produced "new things" belonging to the 21st century, including a new definition of wealth. "Value" and "wealth," John Paul argued, are products of human creativity, found in the human mind, not in the ground.

To be sure, the encyclical is not a blank check endorsement of every kind of capitalism (i.e. not of libertarianism, for instance). Properly circumscribed within a strong juridical framework, it should be placed at the service of human freedom in its totality. In this context, poverty becomes a matter primarily of exclusion from the opportunities of producing and exchanging goods and services. According to the pope, the task of a free society is to encourage "trust in the human potential of the poor and consequently in their ability to improve their condition through work or to make a positive contribution to economic prosperity" (Weigel, 1999, pp. 615-616).[3]

No one since Adam Smith, British historian Paul Johnson has noted, has done more to reconnect economics to its moral roots than Michael Novak. Questioning his own earlier suspicions of business and free markets, he began to call for the development of a theology of the corporation and a coherent philosophical structure to buttress democratic capitalism, a venture that was to occupy much of his energies during the next several decades. He discovered that democratic capitalism thrives in a special kind of culture "in which high values of individual responsibility, social cooperation, and the voluntary spirit have for centuries been nourished." Economic systems, Novak came to understand, are not merely materialistic, but a "way of life with love for liberty, noble behavior, highly developed character, for justice and compassion." Thus, "sustained economic growth does not consist solely in material abundance; it springs from and it continues to demand the exercise of moral character of certain sorts. Should such character disappear, so would sustained economic growth" (Novak, 1977, p.17).

Christian and Evangelical Roots

Jacques Maritain, carefully warning in his classic work, *Christianity and Democracy,* that no one is "required to militate in favor of a particular form of government simply as an expression of Christian faith," nevertheless noted that "there is hardly a less developed area in the tradition of Christian thought, whether in philosophy or in theology, than the relation of Christianity to economics." Indeed, he maintained that "the democratic impulse has arisen in human history as a temporal manifestation of the inspiration of the Gospel." This is not to suggest some militant fundamentalism claiming God to be on the side of capitalism. However, even such a secular economist as Frank Knight seems to postulate a view of human nature that is decidedly Protestant in outlook. Indeed, his disciple James Buchanan ([1947] 1982, pp. 246-247) observes that Knight "can be explained, phenomenologically only through recalling his roots in evangelical Christianity."

Thus, from Adam Smith to Wilhelm Röpke and Jacques Maritain, in the work of Michael Novak and now from Pope John Paul II, the key elements of a coherent moral rationale for capitalism are being developed and now need to inspirit both the teaching of business ethics and the understanding by business leaders of what it is that they are up to. Without expanding each theme in detail here, it seems to me that we should be prepared at least to give voice to several of these key ideas which have proven valid and which are candidates to become more clearly defined in the intellectual resources of as many business leaders as possible. Among these I would list the following:

Capitalism Acknowledges and Accepts Human Nature

Not the least of these spiritual insights is capitalism's close reading of human nature, its understanding of the reality of human sinfulness (though seldom stated by practitioners in the technical jargon of theology). In fact, it may be one of the most providential coincidences of history that free markets developed within the context of a Judeo-Christian world view whose sacred literature, if the early chapters of Genesis are to be taken seriously, is drenched in the tragic impulse and cosmic destruction of the human will to power. Because democratic capitalism assumes and understands the temptation to tyranny, for its own self-preservation it diffuses the control of political regimes through the apparatus of economic and political markets. The Constitution consequently reflects a clear caution in trusting imperfect humans. When the local grocer places on the cash register the humorous slogan, "In God we trust—all others pay cash," he is acknowledging the pessimism engendered by ageless experience with the human race. Neither individuals nor assemblies, especially assemblages of elites, should be unreservedly trusted. And unitary systems are perpetually vulnerable to being captured and put into service by ruling individuals, at best by benign elite groups, and at worst by committed tyrants.

Capitalism Constantly Reforms and Remakes Itself

To be forced by the practical demands of the profit motive to acknowledge this reality of human nature, has in turn bred radical reform, a kind of self-critical repentance, capable of challenging and destabilizing even its own institutions and accounting for capitalism's continuing habit of reform. As its free markets permit citizens to "vote" with their dollars, it is the economic expression of the political regime of representative government. This is not to conclude that it is, at heart, essentially motivated by Christian humanistic impulses. But it is to declare that it is nevertheless better than the authoritarian forms which have so often clothed their intentions in humanistic, sometimes even Christian language. Its surprising ability (at least surprising to Marx, Schumpeter, and others) to constantly remake itself is unquestionably related to the instinctive habit of a market to orient its attention constantly to the expressed needs of its "customers" (citizens). Thus the most successful reform leaders have come from the ranks of business leaders themselves rather than more righteous political reformers.

Bertrand de Jouvenel finds it ironic that "the intellectual community has become harsher in its judgment" while the business community "was strikingly bettering the condition of the masses, improving its own working ethics, and growing in civic consciousness." He concludes that the "capitalism of today is immeasurably more praiseworthy than in previous days," and wonders whether the intelligentsia itself has experienced such an improvement (Jouvenel, 1954, p. 120).

Concern for the Poor

Beyond its creative response to human sinfulness, capitalism's child, industrialization, made possible the existence of a population never before permitted to survive, literally creating an entirely new group of people who could find work away from the starvation of rural subsistence. This was closely followed by an increased concern for the poor. Before industrialization, multitudes either did not survive childhood, or were out of sight in rural hovels barely existing and thus not subject to attention by literature and the charitable organizations funded by industrialism. All stocks in multinational corporations may not be owned by widows and orphans, as George Babbitt might have claimed, but it nevertheless is instructive that while a lawyer and priest passed by on the other side of the road, a Samaritan merchant, who had the resources as well as the inclination, stopped to make provision for the victim of wayside robbers in Jesus' parable. (He was a good illustration that the production of wealth takes priority, both in terms of time and attention, over its distribution.)

Corporate Community

Much neglected is the positive good that the modern corporation accomplishes by way of creating and sustaining community. People devote a major portion of their lives to its welfare, form lasting relationships through its endeavors, and express compassion and connection during its activity. In commercial pursuits, individuals daily encounter opportunities to grow in patience, in authentic respect for a variety of flawed children of God, and together accomplish truly spiritual growth in a thousand daily exchanges never possible in earlier, more rural, lonely, and insular lifestyles. Even the suffering experienced in a downsizing or an acquisition is something similar to the experience of death or divorce, or the kind of personal tragedy we associate with the breaking of family connections. The purpose of gathering people together in a corporate setting is much more than making a profit. It finds meaning as a fellowship inclined to meet the needs of others.

Alexis de Tocqueville (2000, p. 637) wrote that "trade is the natural enemy of all violent passions," and that it "loves moderation, delights in compromise, and is most careful to avoid anger." And Samuel Gregg (2003, p. 28) has noted that while commercial relations are not a substitute for the kind of self-giving we expect in healthy families, nonetheless there often is a kind of calming, almost civilizing potential of commercial activity.

Pursuing this theme in *Centesimus Annus,* Pope John Paul II employed almost Hayekian insights when he observed how humans, simultaneously fallen and redeemed, encounter in business the ethical ambiguities characteristic of the human predicament more than anywhere else, and thus have the opportunity to learn, in community, to become what they never could become in isolation.

Imago Dei—In the Image of God

In his encyclical the Pope focused on two major themes. One is the ability to build community. But equally important is a reverence for the worth of individuals as co-creators with God, in God's own image. Thus, central to capitalism is not only the acknowledgement of human sinfulness, but also reverence for the incredible potential of humans to create, to dream, to risk, and to find excitement and reward in bringing something new into existence. Giving birth to a new business is as awesome and inspiring as a great painting or piece of music. In contrast to Marx's labor theory of value, the pope probes the interiority of human action to link the creation of wealth to the value of knowledge and human creativity. As countries like England and Japan both demonstrate eloquently, wealth does not flow from natural resources but from the human mind. It flourishes from the investment of intellectual capital through the capacity of business leaders to come to an understanding of the needs of others and to create practical, efficient, and effective ways to meet those needs. Indeed, our system of patents and copyrights, described in Article 1, Section 8 of the U.S. Constitution, codifies this reality and was a historic development breaking with the past and critical to the growth of the American political economy (Novak, 1997).

Business Ethics and the Moral/Spiritual Culture

Generally and sadly, neither religious leaders nor business practitioners are well prepared to defend the capitalism that Fukuyama, Mandelbaum, and Bobbit seem to feel has prevailed. Many religious leaders in fact agree with the delusions of Paul Tillich who said, "Any serious Christian must be a socialist." Too often they lack the appropriate vocabulary or even the world-view, let alone the ability to read a balance sheet or to deal satisfactorily with a strategic business analysis. Michael Novak longingly observed that "their professional vocabulary, for the most part, so misses the point that it is painful to listen to them."

In addition to the need for greater understanding by religious leaders, it is my contention that business leaders themselves need to become more capable of appreciating and verbalizing the spiritual nature of their endeavors. Business leaders must not become so wrapped up in the demands of their enterprises, or so intimidated by writers, newscasters, and entertainment celebrities, that they let others define the agenda. Immersed in the practical world of business, leaders of commerce have not been trained to think like philosophers. They know from experience what works in practice, but they have difficulty verbalizing how it works "in theory" because the hands-on demands of their day denies them the leisure of the "theory class." Preferring what works to what is neatly symmetrical, they undervalue the landscape of the ideas that have huge consequences for their future.

Consequently, to return to my place of beginning, rather than leaving the teaching of business ethics to legal scholars, on the one hand (who may only help business leaders to understand the most recent regulatory interpretations), or theologians and philosophers, on the other (who lack understanding of the world of business), we need to prepare our business schools and mediating institutions to nurture the moral understanding and spiritual culture which provide the soil in which capitalism can take root and flourish. This requires far more than cheap and vapid slogans or Sunday-school pietism. Business leaders themselves need to engage in a serious study of the Christian and evangelical roots of capitalism. Only by nurturing, often through the mediating institutions between citizens and the government, the inner moral gyroscope which is required for a system of free markets to develop and sustain itself, can its blessings be guaranteed to the next generation.

"Understanding," Victor Hugo wrote, "is gained in quiet contemplation, but *character* in the rush of life." Those who practice business in the "rush of life" are no less responsible for understanding and defending their way of life than the professor or philosopher in quiet contemplation.

Notes

1. See for example, Doug Bandow (1994), Samuel Gregg (2003), F. A. Hayek (1954), Ernest Van den Haag (2000).
2. For an excellent treatment of this period in the history of economic thought, as well as the re-discovery of the moral implications of the study of political economics by the Austrian School and the Chicago School, see Robert H. Nelson, *Economics as Religion: From Samuelson to Chicago and Beyond* (University Park, Pennsylvania: Pennsylvania State University Press, 2001).
3. For an additional similar consideration of poverty, see Richard John Neuhaus, *Doing Well and Doing Good: The Challenge to the Christian Capitalist* (New York: Doubleday, 1992), especially chapter eight, "The Potential of the Poor."

Bibliography

Bandow, Doug (1994). *The politics of envy.* New Brunswick, NJ: Transaction Publishers.

Bobbit, Philip (2002). *The shield of Achilles: War, peace, and the course of history.* New York: Alfred A. Knopf.

Buchanan, James M. ([1947] 1982). Foreword to Liberty Press edition of Frank Knight, *Freedom and reform: Essays in economics and social philosophy.* Indianapolis, IN: Liberty Press.

Fukuyama, Francis (1989). The end of history? *National Interest, 16,* 2-18.

Gregg, Samuel (2003). Markets, morality, and civil society. *The Intercollegiate Review,* Fall 2003/Spring 2004, 23-30.

Hanson, Victor Davis (1996). *Fields without dreams: Defending the agrarian idea.* New York: The Free Press.

Hayek, F. A. (1954). *Capitalism and the historians.* Chicago: University of Chicago Press.

Jouvenel, B. (1954). The treatment of capitalism by continental intellectuals. In: F. A. Hayek (Ed.), *Capitalism and the historians.* Chicago: University of Chicago Press.

Mandelbaum, Michael (2002). *The ideas that conquered the world: Peace, democracy, and free markets in the twenty-first century.* New York: Public Affairs.

Novak, Michael (1977). An underpraised and undervalued system. *Worldview,* July/August. Reprinted in Younkins.

Novak, Michael (1991). The great convergence: A new consensus in favor of economic and religious liberty. Crisis, December, 1991. Reprinted in Younkins, E. W. (Ed.). *Three in one: Essays on democratic capitalism.* New York: Rowman and Littlefield, 2001.

Novak, Michael (1997). *The fire of invention: Civil society and the future of the corporation.* Lanham: Rowman and Littlefield.

de Tocqueville, Alexis (2000). *Democracy in America.* J.P. Mayer (Ed.), G. Lawrence (tans.). New York: Perennial Classics.

Van den Haag, Ernest (2000). The hostility of intellectuals to capitalism. *The Intercollegiate Review,* Fall/Spring 2000/2001, 56-63.

Weigel, George (1999). *Witness to hope: The biography of Pope John Paul II.* New York: HarperCollins.

PART III

THREE BRIDGES

An Explanation for Jewish Business Success

Rabbi Daniel Lapin

I was trying to think of something I could tell you that absolutely nobody but a rabbi would ever tell you. And so I thought I would ask a question that, frankly, I believe has never been asked before at a Catholic educational institution. The question is: Why is it that Jews are so good with money? I think this is a field that warrants some analysis because there is no question that Jews have been disproportionately successful with money.

You can't fail to notice that representatives of a people constituting at maximum 2.3 percent of America's population occupy about 70 to 100 of the names on the Forbes 400 list, instead of what you would expect statistically, which is about eight or nine people. And this is not just in America. It is throughout the world. In Europe you had—even in times of stress—the Rothschilds building banks in England. In Asia—you had the Sassoon family building empires in India. Additionally, it is surely too much of a coincidence for any rational person that almost without exception throughout the history of modern mercantile activity, it is truly difficult to think of any country that has created an indigenous capital market, any country at all, outside of–to use an old-fashioned word—Christendom.

It is too much of a coincidence that America, which has certainly built the greatest engine of prosperity that the world has ever known, is a country that was based almost more on the Judeo side than the Christian side of the Judeo-Christian system. It is for this reason that Abraham Lincoln and later the British historian Paul Johnson referred to America as the "almost chosen people." If anything, if one looks at most of the contemporary writing of the founders, one can arrive at the conclusion that the founders of America were Old Testament Christians.

And therefore I thought it would be beneficial to research whether there is anything intrinsic to Jewish culture that explains this conspicuous, but nonetheless unmentionable success with commerce that this people of the Book seems to possess. Naturally, I needed to start by refuting and debunking the false explanations—at least four I was aware of—while approaching them with academic rigor and an open mind.

The first explanation was that Jews ruthlessly cheat their way to the top. There was some support given to the theory by the Old Oxford English Dictionary which defines one of the meanings of the word "Jew" as a verb, as in "to jew" somebody. There is one problem with this explanation and it has to do with whether honesty is the best policy in business. I think complete flexibility is probably the best policy in business for the short term. As for the longterm, honesty is the best policy because it is directly correlated with reputation. As long as people communicate with one another in that marvelous, invisible network of social cooperation called the business world, honesty becomes absolutely crucial. And in my travels to research my work across the country, I ran into too many people of non-Jewish background who spoke fondly of many years of business partnerships and countless happy transactions with Jews. So it seemed to me that while there was no question that Jewish representatives could be found in the world of dishonest business, this was not an adequate explanation for the conspicuously disproportionate success of Jewish business.

That brought me to the second explanation. It was a profoundly racist explanation, but a sufficient number of people believing it to warrant my work at refuting it. It basically said that the Cossacks killed all the poor Jews, leaving the rich to escape and breed.

For those of you who are pondering the validity of this possibility let me explain that it requires the discovery of a Jewish money gene—to put it bluntly—and such is not the case. Such a gene has not been discovered. But even if that claim were true, how do you communicate this to your children? Is there nobody who has ever been disappointed with the way a child came out? It does not seem a reasonable explanation. And so for reasonable people who reject a flagrantly racist proposition that somehow business acumen gets passed on genetically, the number of possible explanations was rapidly diminishing.

The third possibility seemed very plausible for a while. This possibility said that Jews with great determination devotedly advanced one another's interest. Now, I am sure that none of you have experienced any kind of backstabbing intrigue and political ruthlessness in the running of your churches; however, let me tell you that anybody who has any experience whatsoever serving on the board of any Jewish synagogue will immediately burst out into uncontrollable and hysterical laughter at the thought of so much Jewish cooperation. It was manifestly absurd to suppose that Jews devotedly advanced one another's interests. Jews are just like other people except perhaps even more so. And that does not explain in any way Jewish business success.

The most famous story is that of the Jew marooned on a desert island for 25 years. When the Coast Guard finally rescued him, he said, "Before we leave, let me show you around...this is the cave I've been living in; this is where I do my fishing; this is a synagogue I built...and that's another synagogue I built." The Coast Guard said, "Excuse me. How many of you are on the island? Are we rescuing anyone else?" The Jew responded, "No, just me." "But there is this synagogue and that synagogue?" the Coast Guard wondered. "Yes," said the Jew, "This one is the synagogue I go to, and that one is where I wouldn't be seen dead in."

Another famous story is that of the Israeli Prime Minister Golda Meir who, in one of her meetings with the United States president, indicated that she felt her job was tougher than his. The president said, "Mrs. Meir, let me just remind you that I am the president of 200 million people. You have only two million in your country." To this she responded, "Mr. President, there is one thing you forget. You may be the president of 200 million people, but I am the prime minister of two million presidents."

The only other explanation that was entertained—in addition to dishonesty, genetics, or mutual support—was intelligence. After all, Jews score conspicuously high on the I.Q. rating. This explanation was a bit more difficult to study and analyze but in the final analysis not impossible to refute. The fact is that there are—if you look at the bell curve of I.Q. distribution in the population—people with an I.Q. that is just too low for them to function effectively in business. In exactly the same way there are people with an I.Q. that is so high that they are not any good at business either. Bill Gates is a once-in-an-epoch phenomenon. The overwhelming majority of highly successful business professionals in America are people who fall into that broad midrange of acceptable intelligence. The Sam Waltons of the world would not have ever made it in the upper reaches of academia.

As a matter of fact, there is an interesting study showing that 60 percent of Fortune 500 companies are headed by people without advanced degrees. There are probably many other correlating factors, but it is interesting to note that those companies headed by people with advanced economic degrees under perform those headed by people without advanced economic degrees. It is probable that super intelligence is a detriment to business success. Have you ever heard the phrase "too smart for your own good?" It is truly difficult to think of any likeable character—all the people in entertainment, for example—whose characteristic is brilliance and intelligence. Somehow that does not necessarily make for likeable people. The super brilliant have to work twice as hard at being nice and being likeable. And if there is one thing we know about business, it is that people prefer to do transactions with others that they know, like, and trust. And so it soon became clear to me that the notion that Jews are successful because of abnormally high intelligence was highly improbable because such intelligence would in reality be a detriment to business success.

The question remains then what does account for Jewish success in business, and is it possible that certain traits were implanted into America as a result of its comfortable relationship with the Old Testament?

I would like to suggest that perhaps one of the most important cultural aspects of being Jewish that contributed more than anything to Jewish economic success is something that America did adopt. It is something that distinguishes America even from other parts of former Christendom like Western Europe. Because I remember still—while studying in England as a boy, somebody said in my presence, "Oh, pay no attention to him, he's just a merchant." In the years before World War II and even right into the early 60s, the attitude in England towards business was one of contempt. If you actually worked for a living, it was shameful in English society. To be a self-made man was embarrassing; it meant you worked. Far better to have inherited your wealth. If you have read the charming novels of P.G. Wodehouse, you know that while being humorous, satirical caricatures, they nonetheless do indicate what it was that England valued in society, and it certainly was not the self-made man.

However, in the early days of America there was merit in earning a living. You must remember that in the good old days, all the way through the 1800s and into the 1900s, children were raised with a notion of doing well, as well as doing good. There is a very well-known Jewish principle that God's presence never rests on anybody who does not possess four characteristics: self-discipline, wisdom, humility, and wealth. Wealth is a virtue. You will remember the Horatio Alga stories which today would bring gutfuls of laughter from the educated elite. It was not until, regretfully, a Jewish socialist by the name of Matthew Josephson coined the term in the 1920s that the commercial giants of the 19th century were referred to as the "robber barons." We were well into the 20th century before economic success was viewed as evidence of malfeasance and wrongdoing.

Today there is a danger of sliding into a dangerous trap. We all are aware of the wrongdoings in the corporate world. However, it may be appropriate to remind ourselves that there are millions of professionals actively engaged in the field of business in the United States of America today. And after a fairly lengthy period of the most rigorous investigation and the most aggressive prosecution in recent history, we have discovered a limited number—perhaps in the order of hundreds—of wrongdoers. Therefore, there are several orders of magnitude difference between the people who were and who have been doing wrong and that countless multitude of American business professionals who go about their daily lives conducting their business in sincerity, honesty, and nobility providing the goods and services that the entire world desires. Let us remember the good as well as the bad. Because if we lose the battle of ideas, if we allow this notion to prevail, that somehow economic success is de facto evidence of wrongdoing, we will rapidly find ourselves in the same position as Germany today.

I dare say there are many other explanations for why it is that the country that gave the world the term "economic miracle" in the years 1945 to 1965 is now plummeting to the bottom of economic productivity. But I can only tell you what the *German Business Week* magazine says. *German Business Week* magazine polled and tested the attitude among young Germans between 1965 and 1995 in how they felt about business, entrepreneurship, and money. Whereas in 1965 the overwhelming majority of young Germans were eager to become young entrepreneurs, seeing business as a good force in society, by 1975 only 17 percent of young Germans felt positive about business, and by 1990 the figure had plummeted right off the graph to statistical insignificance.

This cannot be totally disassociated from Germany's lackluster economic performance. Why is that? It is 50 years ago that a couple of really interesting things happened. First, a man called Roger Bannister, a young 19-year-old medical student, ran the mile for the first time in all of human history, in under four minutes. Second, at about the same time a man called Edmund Hillary climbed Mount Everest for the first time in human history. Those are interesting enough facts, but what is more interesting is to look and see how many people ran the mile in under four minutes in the first 12 months after May 1954. Nearly a hundred athletes ran the mile in the first 12 months after Roger Bannister did it in under four minutes.

The question is why did no other runner perform this feat before Bannister so he could have gone down in the history books? The answer is simple. Nobody ran the mile in under four minutes before Roger Bannister because nobody thought it could be done. It is as simple as that. Doctors predicted that the human organism would die in the attempt. In fact, Bannister collapsed onto the ground as he breasted the rope, and everyone thought he was dead. But he was very much alive. Similarly, although none had done it before Hillary showed it could be done, thousands have since scaled Everest.

Human beings are curious organisms. We are driven by our minds. In fact, if we wanted to ask ourselves if we are primarily physical and material beings with a little touch of the intangible and the spiritual or if we are perhaps primarily spiritual beings with a little touch of the material, I think among those two choices we would have to agree that we are primarily spiritual beings. Our essence is in our minds, hearts, and souls.

If you think about it, almost anytime you are hiring somebody for your company, you are hiring spiritual qualities, not material qualities, unless you are hiring fashion models or ditch diggers. I can't think of too many areas in which someone's body matters in the slightest. We have come to realize that in business we are hiring people for their persistence, loyalty, integrity, courage, and for their ability to keep going even when things are tough. And the interesting fact is that there is not a single laboratory instrument in the world that can measure any one of these qualities. We can measure everything physical but nothing spiritual. That is almost the best definition of spiritual that exists.

We can take a fetus and tell if it is going to be black or white, male or female, tall or short, we can tell if it is going to have a tendency towards obesity or a tendency towards fitness. But all that information is worthless because nobody cares. Those are material things, while we care about the spiritual things. And that is the single most important contribution to Jewish business success, in my opinion, and to American success in creating the world's greatest engine of prosperity, and ultimately the avenue to understanding a Jewish approach to business ethics. Specifically, this is the Old Testament concept that in business you are succeeding in direct proportion to the extent that you believe you are acting selflessly.

I am sure many of you have encountered those rather sad kinds of business groups, where people show up the first Wednesday of every month for breakfast to exchange cards and to promote one another's business. I have looked at those groups very carefully. They do not produce a fraction of the business that is produced at a weekly meeting of your local Rotary club, at a board of director's meeting of the local art gallery or symphony orchestra. The reason is that none of us really likes dealing with people who are totally self-interested. But if I meet somebody at a Rotary club and we have the same goal of raising money to eradicate polio in India, I would be interested. This is somebody I could be friends with. This is somebody I could come to know and to trust. Because this is the kind of people that human beings are: we do better when we are focused on the good, when we are focused on other people rather than when we are focused upon ourselves. And the Jewish approach to business is driven by this basic idea that business is a way of becoming obsessed with the needs of other people.

To understand the Jewish approach to business we need to take a look at its theological origin. In Jewish tradition a question is asked, and the question is: Does God want us to be rich? The answer in Jewish tradition is that the good Lord is very preoccupied and that is not at the forefront of his mind; *however,* what he does want is for human beings to become obsessively preoccupied with the needs and welfare of other human beings. And if you succeed in discovering and supplying what others need, then you should not be surprised that you are rewarded with a great, wonderful blessing called wealth.

So Jews were never ever handicapped by the theological notion that somehow wealth was a vice or evidence of wrongdoing. Rather to the contrary, it was the notion that wealth was a reward, not necessarily on an individual basis, but rather on a group basis, for a group of people who commit to one another and create a moral legal framework in which property and rights are preserved and in which trust and integrity are rewarded. It should come as no surprise that what emerged was the United States of America–essentially, an Old Testament vision of society.

Although one of the practices of Jewish religious observance that people are most familiar with has to do with dietary regulations, kosher food, there are many more laws in the Torah about the ownership and treatment of your own and other people's property. The respect for ownership of property emerges as a very basic principle, a very realistic assessment of human nature which says people care most for the things that they own and, an understanding that the best way to get the things you want is to be absolutely obsessive about giving as many other people the things that they want.

And so you have, for instance, the time-honored Jewish profession of the peddler. My great-grandfather was a peddler. He would roll into town and knock on a door asking, "Do you have anything you don't need?" The people would say, "Yes. There is an old table in the basement we are going to get rid of." "How much are you going to have to pay the city to cart it away?" my great-grandpa would ask, and the response was, "Well, the city charges about five dollars to cart it away." Here my great-grandpa would propose, "I'll give you five dollars if you let me take the table away." Great-grandpa would spend a dollar on nails and paint to fix up the table and knock on another door, "Hi. Anybody need a table?" In reality, of course, grandpa would knock on quite a few doors, but eventually somebody would say, "Oh, sure. We have a daughter getting married, a young couple who needs a table." He would say, "Well, how much were you going to spend on a table?" "We priced about 20 dollars on a table," the family would respond. Here great-grandpa would make another proposition, "I have a used one for 10 dollars."

So the first family is 10 dollars better off, the second family is 10 dollars better off. And guess what? Great-grandpa has four dollars in his pocket as well. It is no wonder that the Jewish peddler traveling through the cities during the 19th century was a welcome figure. He was not looked upon as a predator. Because if you multiply great-grandpa's activities in the village and he had spend three or four days in the village knocking on all the doors, at the end of the day when he left the village, somehow miraculously, everybody felt the village was better off, as we have seen in the sort of economic microcosm. By the way, I think it will not escape anyone's attention that I have just described the revenue model of one of the most successful Internet companies ever, called "E-bay." E-bay is nothing but 10 million great-grandpas. Because if you build connectivity and you figure out how to help other people, you have a successful business model. In other words, other people are our wealth, and obsession with other people is the key to pleasing God and the key to reaping the benefits of God's benevolence. And the entire focus of business ethics is the concern for other people.

The whole idea of the corporate shield is a very penetrable one in Jewish philosophy. The idea of the corporation is real but never as a shield from behind which damage can be wreaked on human beings. Business must always be the consequence of relationships between human beings, not the cause. This core principle is the source of wealth and also the source of the ethics that drives the creation of wealth because, fundamentally, we are a people of a spiritual nature rather than of a physical nature. And it is precisely through this approach unique to America that the creation of wealth is so visibly connected to fundamental principles of Old Testament philosophy.

The Virtue of Commerce in the Catholic Tradition

Rev. John Michael Beers

The Entrepreneurial Vocation

Oskar Schindler, the celebrated subject of Thomas Kenneally's historical novel and Steven Spielberg's movie, "Schindler's List," is portrayed in both as saying that his father often stated that an entrepreneur needed only three people in his life: a good accountant to increase his wealth, a good physician to preserve his health, and a good priest to forgive him his sins. While I have no background in economics or medicine, I am a priest and, so, I would like to address in this paper the last of these three, namely the spiritual dimension of the entrepreneurial vocation.

The entrepreneur's vocation in no way excludes the religious, rather it is a unique opportunity both to grow in holiness and assist others in their common vocation. *Commercium* makes possible *communio,* in the language of Pope John Paul II's personalist phenomenology. Conversely, there must be a community in order for commerce to exist and to flourish; simply to have any meaning, commerce cannot exist in a vacuum. As the phenomenologist understands, the phenomena of our existence are of the greatest significance; it matters greatly that we exist here and now, in this place, in relationship with these persons of our present experience. So, too, the entrepreneur has unique relationships with unique opportunities both for doing well and doing good.

Oskar Schindler, a man raised in the Catholic faith, a faith that he embraced and lived to his very death, is an excellent example of the entrepreneur who sees his work in business and commerce as his particular vocation to holiness. His vocation was neither to the priesthood, nor to medicine; rather, his life's work was in business. The priest and the doctor have other and different relationships to persons; it is obvious that the phenomena of their vocations are significantly different from the phenomena encountered by the entrepreneur. As the phenomena of their vocations are fundamentally different, so, too, their holiness is realized in fundamentally different ways. Their end, common to us all, which is union with God, will be attained differently, consistent with the phenomena of their different vocations.

Because of his success in business and his courage to exercise heroic virtue in risking everything, including his own life, Oskar Schindler made possible not just the livelihood of his employees, a good which should be obtained by every moral entrepreneur, but also the very continuation of life itself for thousands of Jews during the Second World War. Precisely because he was a successful entrepreneur, Oskar Schindler had a unique opportunity for doing extraordinary good in the context of the ordinary circumstances of the entrepreneurial vocation. Such an opportunity would not be given to a priest, a doctor, a teacher, a military officer, a monk, a bureaucrat; rather, this was a unique opportunity to do good given to and realized by an entrepreneur.

Oskar Schindler was an extraordinary man, who lived in extraordinary times. What of the ordinary vocation of the entrepreneur? Is it any less a vocation to holiness and virtue? I should like to argue that the entrepreneur has always been called to holiness and that the virtues of commerce are foundational to the Judeo-Christian tradition. I would like to consider what is distinctive in the Roman Catholic tradition of virtues as they are constitutive of the entrepreneurial vocation, though in no way is our Catholic tradition the unique repository of wisdom on virtues, nor surely on commerce for that matter; rather, these virtues are part of the holy lives of all people of good will, other Christians, Jews, Muslims, Buddhists, and Hindus.

Oikonomia, Commercium, Communio

Anyone who has spent an hour in my classroom knows the value I place by etymology, so let's consider the full meaning and origins of several words significant in our discussion.

"Economy" comes from the Greek *oikonomia,* a term that means literally "the law for the household," perhaps better "the good ordering of the home." Interesting is the theological use of this term in the phrase "divine economy," which refers both to the relationship of the persons of the Trinity and to the relationship of God to man. When this latter relationship is as it should be, then the household of God and man is truly in good order because the "law for the household," in biblical terminology, the Covenant, is rightly observed. It can be said that "God and man at table are sat down."

Of course, the most common use of "economy" bespeaks the good ordering of business and the financial well being of people, but the theological sense always remains, at least in the background. If society is in chaos, as during the barbarian invasions, or earlier still during the period of persecution and martyrdom, there is little likelihood of having a tranquil, spiritual life. Under such circumstances, religion is a luxury.

It is significant that the first councils meet and the first creeds are written only in the fourth century when Constantine brings persecution to an end with the recognition of the Church as a legal entity capable of entering into the economic life of the Empire. Constantine's recognition of the Church was not to make of Christianity the "state religion," as is commonly said, but mistaken all the same. How else could the vestal virgins still be gainfully employed fully a century later if Constantine had outlawed paganism in the early fourth century? In fact, it was still argued in the Roman Senate as late as the fifth century whether the time had finally come to extinguish that sacred fire tended by the vestal virgins that served literally as the "focus" of the entire Roman Empire.

Rather, Constantine's recognition of the Church was entirely economic; the emperor recognized the Church as a legal entity capable of owning real estate. This had great implications for the Church. From this point on, the Church was no longer obliged to celebrate the liturgy in hiding or in private homes. Owning real estate meant that the Church could now build churches on a scale like that of the synagogues and temples, in fact, often appropriating material from those temples, as they, in time, did eventually fall into disuse.

The doors of St. John Lateran, the cathedral church of the Bishop of Rome, were originally those of the Temple of Jupiter Stator, the gift of Constantine himself to the pope. The papal altar of the Constantinian basilica of St. Peter came from the Temple of Antoninus Pius. This practice survived well into the Renaissance as Bernini used the bronze that had covered the dome of the Pantheon to form the baldachino over the papal altar in the present St. Peter's. The Pantheon itself today bears little resemblance to a pagan temple with its Christian artwork and altars. It was providential that Constantine had elevated the architectural style of the basilica to the level that it enjoyed by the fourth century as this served not only as the model for grand, new churches, but also many of the already standing basilicas would in time be converted to ecclesiastical use.

The most significant consequence of Constantine's recognition of the Church as a legal and economic entity was the end of persecution, because the Church now had corporate recognition as a participant in the empire's economy. Thus, the Church with all her members enjoyed the corporate rights of citizenship. The well being of the home was extended to God's household; the Divine Economy was supported and fostered by the secular economy.

In the events of the past 15 years alone, we see a parallel in the end of the Church's persecution in Eastern Europe concurrent with the collapse of communism and the socialist economy. This was anticipated by Karol Cardinal Wojtyla (later Pope John Paul II), when he preached to the papal court in 1977 a series of sermons published after his election to the papacy as "Sign of Contradiction." There he observed, clearly reflecting his personal experience, that a free market (he does use the Marxist terminology "Capitalist") economy alone allows for the free exercise of religion, while socialism stifles all religion. As the economy goes, so goes religion.

The terms *commercium* and *communio* are both similar and inter-related. Literally, *commercium* means an exchange of rewards, the seller receives payment for his merchandise and the buyer enjoys the use of or the benefit provided by his purchase. In turn, *commercium* facilitates *communio* which is the unity of persons who come together for a common enterprise. *Communio* is at the very heart of Pope John Paul II's personalist philosophy. During his lengthy pontificate, he has had the opportunity of observing two anniversaries of Pope Leo XIII's "Rerum Novarum." Too often the latter encyclical, "Centesimus Annus," tends to overshadow the earlier "Laborem Exercens," in which the Holy Father advances themes of personalism to portray the subjective dimensions of labor as supremely important, indeed as "the essential key to the whole social question" (no. 3).

The encyclical concludes with a section entitled "Elements for a Spirituality of Work." Here the Holy Father portrays Christ as the "man of work" who preached a "gospel of work" (no. 26) to encourage all men to become co-creators with God, participants in God's plan for the universe (no. 27). In "Centesimus Annus" and especially in his homilies for the feast of St. Joseph the Worker, the Holy Father emphasizes the relation of work to human dignity, underlining his observation in "Laborem Exercens" that "in the first place work is for man, and not man for work" (no. 6).

Within the *communio* of men, as a consequence of *commercium,* private ownership of property is made possible and realized. At least for the past century, papal teaching has maintained that private ownership, even of productive goods, is a natural right, a right that belongs to man by virtue of his dignity as a person and not because of any concession by public authority. This right is proper to man because he is spiritual, intelligent, free, and responsible for his own livelihood and destiny. So, too, each man is responsible for the support and government of the family he decides to form and bound to contribute personally to the common good.

In "Mater et Magistra," Blessed John XXIII states that "the right of private property, including that pertaining to goods devoted to enterprises, is permanently valid. Indeed, it is rooted in the very nature of things, whereby we learn that individual men are prior to civil society, and hence, that civil society is to be directed toward man as its end" (no. 427).

St. Francis de Sales and the Universal Call to Holiness

I should like to suggest that in the Catholic tradition of spirituality we find perhaps the clearest and most convincing articulation of the vocation of the entrepreneur in the work of St. Francis de Sales. The third chapter of the first part of the "Introduction to the Devout Life" is entitled: "Devotion is Possible in Every Vocation and Profession," where de Sales writes:

> When he created things God commanded plants to bring forth their fruits, each one according to its kind, and in like manner he commands Christians, the living plants of his Church, to bring forth the fruits of devotion, each according to his position and vocation. Devotion must be exercised in different ways by the gentleman, the worker, the servant, the prince, the widow, the young girl, and the married woman. Not only is this true, but the practice of devotion must also be adapted to the strength, activities and duties of each particular person. I ask you, Philothea, is it fitting for a bishop to live a solitary life like a Carthusian? Or for married men to want to own no more property than a Capuchin, for a skilled workman to spend the whole day in church like a religious, for a religious to be constantly subject to every sort of call in his neighbor's service, as a bishop is? Would not such devotion be laughable, confused, impossible to carry out? Still this is a very common fault, and therefore the world, which does not distinguish between real devotion and the indiscretion of those who merely think themselves devout, murmurs at devotion itself and blames it even though devotion cannot prevent such disorders.
>
> No, Philothea, true devotion does us no harm whatsoever, but instead perfects all things. When it goes contrary to a man's lawful vocation, it is undoubtedly false. "The bee," Aristotle says, "extracts honey out of flowers without hurting them" and leaves them as whole and fresh as it finds them. True devotion does better still. It not only does no injury to one's vocation or occupation, but on the contrary adorns and beautifies it. All kinds of precious stones take on greater luster when dipped into honey, each according to its color. So also every vocation becomes more agreeable when united with devotion. Care of one's family is rendered more peaceable, love of husband and wife more sincere, service of one's prince more faithful, and every type of employment more pleasant and agreeable.
>
> It is an error, or rather a heresy, to wish to banish the devout life from the regiment of soldiers, the mechanic's shop, the court of princes, or the home of married people. It is true, Philothea, that purely contemplative, monastic, and religious devotion cannot be exercised in such states of life. However, besides those three kinds of devotion there are several others adapted to bring perfection to those living in the secular state. Examples in the Old Testament are Abraham, Isaac and Jacob, David, Job, and Tobias, and Sarah, Rebecca, and Judith, and under the New Covenant, St. Joseph, Lydia, and St. Crispin lived

> lives of perfect devotion in their workshops, and St. Anne, St. Martha, St. Monica and Aquila and Priscilla in their families, Cornelius, St. Sebastian, and St. Maurice in the army, and Constantine, Helena, St. Louis, Blessed Amadeus and St. Edward on their thrones did the same. There have even been many cases of people who lost perfection in solitude, which for all that is most desirable for perfection, and have kept it in the midst of crowds, which seem to offer little help to perfection. "Lot," St. Gregory says, "who was so chaste in the city defiled himself in the wilderness." Wherever we may be, we can and should aspire to a perfect life. (DeSales, 1966, pp. 36-38)

I think we can hear an echo of the first Latin Father of the Church, Tertullian, who in his "Apology" (42) writes at the end of the second century: "We Christians don't turn our backs on the world; we are present in the forum, at the baths, in the workshops, the bazaars, the market places and public squares. We are sailors, soldiers, farm hands, businessmen."

Following the model of the New Testament, the early Christians worked at all the normal occupations of their time, with the exception of any professions that might present a danger to their faith like interpreters of dreams, diviners, or temple-keepers. They were involved in all the activities of the forum, the market place, and the army. At the beginning of the second century, the anonymous patristic text, the Letter to Diognetus, put it well: "As the Soul is in the body, so the Christian is in the world."

It is clear why Pope Paul VI, in "Sabaudiae Gemma," recognized St. Francis de Sales for his great influence on the Second Vatican Council, in particular the clear advance of what was called the "Universal Call to Holiness," generally recognized as the particular contribution of the young Polish bishop, Karol Wojtyla.

The Way of the Lord Jesus

I should like to return to St. Francis de Sales for his recommendations particular to the entrepreneur. He devotes the third part of the "Introduction to the Devout Life" to "Instructions to the Practice of Virtue." In chapter 15 he writes:

> Philothea, our possessions are not our own. God has given them to us to cultivate and he wants us to make them fruitful and profitable. Hence we perform an acceptable service by taking good care of them. It must be a greater and finer care than that which worldly men have for their property. They labor only out of self-love and we must labor out of love of God. Just as self-love is violent, turbulent, and impetuous, so the care that comes from it is full of trouble, uneasiness, and disquiet. As love of God is sweet, peaceable, and calm, so also the care that proceeds from such love, even if it is for worldly good, is amiable, sweet, and agreeable. Therefore let us exercise this gracious care of preserving and even of increasing our temporal goods whenever just occasions present themselves and so far as our condition in life requires, for God desires us to do so out of love for him. (DeSales, 1966, pp. 134-135)

My former colleague at Mount Saint Mary's College and Seminary, in Emmitsburg, Maryland, Dr. Germain Grisez, in "The Way of the Lord Jesus," develops both Salesian thought and the teaching of the Second Vatican Council in a way that is most appropriate to contemporary circumstances. As de Sales exhorts people in business to invest their capital in a way that makes the livelihood of others possible, providing true welfare for them and for their families, and as Pope John Paul II sees in such labor made possible by the investment of capital by others the provision for the dignity of man, Grisez writes:

> Sometimes, although its owners could give away property or money, they have such a gift for administering material goods that they should accept that as an element of their personal vocation. For example, people with both surplus wealth and skill in management can rightly set up or invest in businesses which provide just wages for gainful work and useful goods and services at fair prices, along with enough profit to compensate them reasonably for their work, which contributes to society's economic common good. (Grisez, II, 1993, p. 813)

Grisez cites "Gaudium et Spes" (65): "It is wrong to allow one's resources to remain unproductive when they could be put to work contributing to the economic development of one's community." Certainly relevant to the current Enron woes is this observation by Grisez:

> In investing savings, one must consider potential return and be careful about safety, so as to serve the purpose which justifies using the money in this way rather than in meeting someone's more or less urgent present needs. However, one also should try to avoid turning over the management of one's savings to people who will use them in unjust or otherwise immoral activities, and should try instead to invest in something morally acceptable. (Grisez, II, 1993, p. 817)

> In any community, good example and sound admonition, manifesting moral truth and love of neighbor, are the most basic and powerful means of fostering virtue. Even large and diverse communities can be inspired by the stories of saints and heroes who provide relevant models and do their best to make them known. (Grisez, II, 1993, p. 843)

As I came in from the airport for this conference, I was struck by the great testimony to Catholic philanthropy that is evident in Xavier University, established by the saintly woman from Philadelphia, St. Katherine Drexel, who embodied the Catholic tradition of the corporal works of mercy: to feed the hungry, to give drink to the thirsty, to clothe the naked, to shelter the homeless, to visit the sick, to ransom the captive, and to bury the dead (cf. Mt. 25:34-40, 1 Cor. 3:16). Her philanthropy was made possible solely because of the great economic stewardship and business acumen of her father. She could have died a wealthy woman on Society Hill, but instead she devoted her life and her wealth to those in need.

Philanthropy is not restricted to giving to those in need—rather, true philanthropy should promote the elimination of need. The entrepreneur is uniquely able to be philanthropic in that way.

Not all of us are called, as de Sales forcefully reminds, to the religious life of Katherine Drexel, nor are we capable of the heroic virtue of Oskar Schindler, but all of us are called to holiness and ultimately to union with God. The entrepreneur finds himself uniquely able as he makes the livelihood of others possible such that their families are thereby fed, clothed, and sheltered. Through fruitful and productive commerce, in the exchange of goods, no one need go hungry, thirsty, naked, homeless, or sick, be reduced to crime, or die denied the dignity of a life well-lived.

Bibliography

De Sales, Francis (1966). *Introduction to the devout life,* trans. John K. Ryan. New York: Harper and Row.

Grisez, Germain (1993). *The way of the Lord Jesus, vol. II: Living a Christian life.* Quincy, Ill.: Franciscan Press.

Islam, Commerce, and Business Ethics

Imad-ad-Dean Ahmad

Introduction

Islam is the only major world religion founded by a businessman, although, in a sense, Judaism, Christianity, and Islam all trace their origins to another businessman, Abraham, the ancestor of Moses, Jesus, and Muhammad, peace be upon them all. Islam has never had any hostility to the profession of the merchant. In the traditions called *hadîth* (sayings of the Prophet and his companions, distinct from God's direct revelation to Muhammad, called the *Qur'ân*), the Prophet is reported to have said, "The truthful and trusty merchant is associated with the prophets, the upright, and the martyrs."

I shall begin with an introduction to the notion of spirituality in Islam using a story of the creation of Adam, a story familiar from the Bible, although the Qur'anic version differs in certain significant details. I shall then turn to the Islamic perspective on commerce, its value, the importance of property rights and contract, the laws that govern commerce, and the place of commerce in man's spiritual life. Finally, I shall offer an observation as to what it will take to sell the concept of free markets to the modern Muslim world and the Third World in general.

Theologically, man requires property in order to fulfill his function as the *khalîfah*, God's vicegerent on earth. The word *khalîfah* is used in Muslim history to refer to the temporal leader of the Muslim community (the "caliph"), but in the Qur'an it refers to every individual man and woman as God's agent, or steward, on earth. Legally, property has been sanctified in Islamic law. Morally, theft, fraud, and injustice of all kinds have been prohibited by the *shari'ah*, the Islamic law. Practically speaking, the objective of *falâh*, prosperity, cannot be achieved without respect for economic realities.

The historical success of Islam in providing the framework for a thriving world economy from the seventh to the 15th centuries is a matter of historical record, but it does not answer the question of whether Islam in particular, or religion and spirituality in general, are helpful to or necessary for the ethical conduct of business in the modern world. Modern institutions have allowed for corporate activity on an unprecedented scale, impossible in the era before the development of the modern corporation. I shall conclude by examining the advantages and disadvantages of those institutions, the moral challenges they pose, and my opinions as to how religion and spirituality are necessary to deal with them.

The Khalifah

Let me begin with a small sermon and some Qur'anic exegesis.

> Behold thy Lord said to the angels: "I will create a vicegerent on earth." They said, "Wilt thou place therein one who will make mischief therein and shed blood? Whilst we do celebrate Thy praises and glorify Thy holy (name)?" He said: "I know what ye know not" (Qur'an 2:30, trans. Ali).

God is telling the angels he will create mankind and make him His agent on earth. The angels don't understand and ask why He would place the earth under the agency of a being endowed with free will, having the choice whether to obey or disobey God and therefore with the ability to create bloodshed and misery that the world might become a terrible place, while the angels are incapable of disobedience to the Lord. In other words, the angels are as baffled by the "problem of evil" as are some modern philosophers.

God asks the angels to describe the nature of things and they confess that they only know what God tells them; they have no ability to independently struggle to acquire knowledge (2:31-32). Adam, however, is able to state the nature of things (2:33). Adam's free will is inseparable from his ability to acquire knowledge. Thus, it is essential to God's plan to give agency over the earth to a being capable of free choice. Now comes the most startling part, God tells the angels to bow down to Adam (2:34), indicating that this being who can *choose* to obey Him is superior to creatures that obey Him of necessity. Man is superior; the angels are like any other creature that obeys God's will by its nature, a planet swimming in its orbit, a rock rolling down a hill, or the rain falling from the clouds. Their obedience is without moral merit.

In the company of the angels was Iblis, who refused to bow down (2:34). Iblis is not an angel, obviously, if he can disobey God's command. Iblis is another creature with free will called a *jinn* in the Qur'an. Jinns are like humans in that they have free will, but different in that they are not made of clay but of some alien nature described by the Qur'an as "smokeless fire."

Another section of the Qur'an adds a significant detail: "God said: 'What prevented thee from bowing down when I commanded thee?' He said: 'I am better than he: thou didst create me from fire and him from clay'" (7:12).

Satan (as Iblis is henceforth called) reveals his nature in this response. If he had instead said, "I bow down to no one but You," that would have been a positive response. Instead he asserts superiority over man on the grounds of his material nature, a petty arrogance reminiscent of the racist who professes superiority because of the color of his skin. Men and jinns are volitional beings that God shall judge on their morality, not on their material nature. Thus, God curses Satan (7:13-15), yet when Satan asks for respite, the all-merciful God immediately grants it (7:15).

Satan is neither grateful for this mercy nor repentant of his arrogance. He threatens to use the time God has granted him to lead men astray (15:62).

> God said: "Go thy way; if any of them follow thee verily Hell will be the recompense of you (all) an ample recompense.
>
> "Lead to destruction those whom thou canst among them with thy (seductive) voice; make assaults on them with thy cavalry and thy infantry; mutually share with them wealth and children; and make promises to them. But Satan promises them nothing but deceit.
>
> "As for My servants no authority shalt thou have over them." Enough is thy Lord for a Disposer of affairs (15:63-65).

In Islam, the devil is "the Whisperer." He can put suggestions into our hearts, but if we choose to follow him, that choice is ours, not his. Therefore, we have full responsibility for our actions.

Adam and his wife are invited to dwell "in the garden and eat of the bountiful things therein" as they will but warned not to approach the tree, not of knowledge, but of "harm and transgression" (2:35). When Adam and Eve listen to Satan and eat from the tree, they are evicted from the Garden (2:36, 7:21-22). The Qur'an does not dump the blame on the woman. Adam and Eve share the responsibility. Both ask for mercy (7:23) and God turns in mercy towards them (7:37-38).

The biggest difference between Islam and the Judeo-Christian tradition is that, in Islam, there is no original sin. All this is preamble, a microcosm of our life on earth, but made simple. There is only one rule for Adam and Eve, stay away from the tree of harm and transgression. While our lives are more complicated, the principle is the same. The rules that govern our lives are also designed to keep us from harm and transgression.[1]

The Virtues of Commerce

We see from the Qur'anic narration of the story of Adam that life on earth is not a punishment, but a trial. Man is not a being born into a state of sin punished by consignment to a world in which toil is misery, but a rational, volitional being placed on a stage in which he has blessed with the opportunity to demonstrate his moral worth.[2] Reward or punishment, whichever he may deserve, will come as the consequence of his own choices, not as an inherited punishment for the acts of his ancestors. "Every soul shall have a taste of death: and We test you by evil and by good by way of trial: to Us must ye return" (21:35).

This is the Qur'an's answer to the problem of evil: evil, like good, in this life is a test. God knows what is the best way to test us, whether we will be faithful, not to abandon hope in bad times and not to become arrogant in the good times, but to remain true at all times.

> Now when trouble touches man he cries to Us; but when We bestow a favor upon him as from Ourselves he says "This has been given to me because of a certain knowledge (I have)!" Nay but this is but a trial but most of them understand not (9:49)!

When we suffer in this world we say "Why is God punishing us?" and when something good happens we think we are so great, but God says we are wrong on both counts, the bad and the good are both tests.

The call to prayer is a call to success, *falâh. Falâh* means success both in this life and the next. In their prayers of supplication, Muslims routinely pray for "the good in this life and the next." The Qur'an never argues against self-interest, rather it takes it for granted that man seeks his self-interest and seeks to explain to man what is in his true self-interest.

> There are men who say: "Our Lord! give us (thy bounties) in this world!" but they will have no portion in the hereafter.
>
> And there are men who say: "Our Lord! give us good in this world and good in the Hereafter and defend us from the torment on the fire!"
>
> To these will be allotted what they have earned and God is quick in account (2:200-202).

The merit of a man is not measured by the amount of his wealth (nor his poverty, for that matter) but by how he acquired whatever wealth he has and what he shall do with it now that he has it.

Property is a necessity for man to fulfill his calling as *khalîfah.* The freedom of action by which we are tested is hampered by the absence of property. You are not as free, in the sense that you are not as empowered, if you have no property. Property is an extension of the self that leverages our freedom of choice and therefore provides the best opportunity for testing our morality.

Historically, Islam has been favorable to the merchant, beginning with the Prophet Muhammad (peace be upon him), who was a merchant, and his wife Khadijah (may God be pleased with her) who was also a merchant. Indeed, she was the wealthier of the two, and he worked for her before their marriage. It was, in fact, because she was so impressed by his strong business ethics that she proposed marriage to him, 15 years before he received the call to prophethood. Although she was 15 years his senior, he admired her character so much that he accepted her proposal.[3]

Property is strongly protected in Islamic law. The punishment for theft is very severe. In his farewell pilgrimage, the Prophet said to the assembled pilgrims: "O Men, your lives and your property shall be inviolate until you meet your Lord. The safety of your lives and of your property shall be as inviolate as this holy day and holy month" (Haykal, 1976, p. 486).

> O Men. Harken well to my words. Learn that every Muslim is a brother to every Muslim and that Muslims constitute one brotherhood. Nothing shall be legitimate to a Muslim which belongs to a fellow Muslim unless it was given freely and willingly. Do not therefore, do injustice to your own selves (Haykal 1976, p. 487).

A Contractual Conception of Commercial Law

The Qur'an holds contracts in very high regard. It has already been noted at this conference (Khawaja, 2004) that the Qur'an even uses contract as a metaphor for our relationship with God, referring to the great bargain man obtains in entering a contract with God which will render him a huge profit.[4]

The Qur'an contains some details of contract law. This is further testimony to the importance of contracts as, contrary to what you may have heard, the Qur'an contains few laws and little legal detail. The legal structure of Islamic law comes from the legal precedents of the early community and from the jurisprudential analyses of the legal scholars through a process called *ijtihâd*. This word comes from the same root as *jihâd*, which means "struggle" in general, and *ijtihâd* means the struggle of the individual scholar to understand the law.

In Islam, the law is analogous to the "natural law" of the physical sciences, something to be discovered rather than invented.[5] The natural law is whatever it is, whatever God has ordained it to be, and the physicists' theories are their articulation of their understanding of that law. So in Islam, the word *sharî`ah,* which is usually translated as Islamic law, literally means "the path to the well." Like the path to the well, like the natural laws of physics, Islamic law is whatever it is, and like the map to the path to the well, like the theories of the physicists, the struggle of the scholars to understand, is the jurisprudence of Islam, called the *fiqh*. The books of jurisprudence written by these scholars contain their conclusions as to God wants us to do, after looking at the Qur'an, the practice of the Prophet, after considering what is equitable, what is in the public interest, etc.

The overall view of human relations in Islam is contractual. Within the broad scope of the law as to what is permitted and what is prohibited, all else is determined by contract among ourselves, by mutual agreement.

The adoption of democratic formalisms that has been properly urged upon Muslims will not relieve the Muslim world of its economic stagnation if it is not accompanied by a return of the civil society institutions that were prevalent in the Muslim world during its glory era from the seventh to the 16th centuries when Islam was the preeminent civilization from Spain to India. In that era, economic infrastructure was generally built not by the state, but by civil society institutions like the *awqâf* (charitable endowments). The economic recovery of the Muslim world will require free markets, just government, and a well-defined and protected system of private property.

Today we speak of "globalism," but in the Muslim era trade was international and a Muslim could travel from one end of the Muslim world to the other without a passport. A non-Muslim only needed a letter of introduction to travel freely throughout that period.

Of course, Islamic society, despite its wonderful dynamism, was not utopia. The Muslims had to contend with the same problems we have to contend with of overweening government. Government would perpetually exceed its allotted boundaries. The scholars were often the brakes on that government. The scholars in those days were completely independent of the government. The founders of all four Sunni[6] schools of Islam were persecuted for refusing to be co-opted by the government. Ibn Malik rejected the Caliph's proposal to use his political power to give Malik's magnum opus a privileged status among the books of law. Abu Hanifa was imprisoned for refusing to accept a judgeship. Ibn Hanbal was tortured for refusing to endorse the state-sanctioned doctrine.

Early on the Muslim governments began to insist that the scholars were no longer qualified to engage in this process of *ijtihâd,* independent critical thinking, and should simply blindly imitate the decisions of previous scholars. This process of blind imitation was called *taqlîd,* and gradually, after many centuries, as later generations of scholars without the intellect or the courage of the early schools caved in to the pressure, accepted government positions, and unsurprisingly rubber-stamped the government's decisions. It is to this that I attribute the Muslim civilization's gradual decline over the centuries to its present unenviable state.

Despite these problems, Muslim society remained remarkably vibrant for a long time because of its liberality. For example, in the matter of religious tolerance, the Qur'an explicitly commands that religious minorities, particularly the Jews and Christians (5:43), have their own legal systems under Islamic law. For example, Christians, who needed wine in their sacraments, were exempt from the absolute prohibition on wine applicable to all Muslims.

Thus, there was a pluralism hardwired into the system in the concept of the protected minority, the *dhimmi.* The *dhimmi* was not really an equal citizen in the sense that all American citizens are equal. Yet too much should not be made of this. Non-Muslims sometimes reached ranks equivalent to prime minister. While a non-Muslim could not become Caliph, naturalized Americans cannot become President. A *dhimmi* paid a special tax in lieu of military service, but that tax was much smaller than the tax Lincoln imposed on persons seeking exemption from service in the Civil War.

Most important to a minority living in a given society is to be free to practice their religion, to earn their living, and to relate to their families unimpeded. For the most part of Muslim history, this is what religious minorities were allowed to do. In the West, Spain is often put forth as a romanticized example of a glorious period of tolerance, and certainly it was compared to what was happening elsewhere in Europe, but it was similar to what was the practice throughout the Muslim world. When the *Reconquista* occurred and the Jews and Muslims were driven out of Spain, the Jews as well as the Muslims sought refuge in the Muslim world.

Corporatism and Public Choice

The limits to contract under Islamic law, it appears to me, are: that contracts must be voluntary; they must be entered into by informed consent; they must be among real persons; they must not impose costs on persons who have not entered the contract; and no agreement to commit an unconscionable act is binding.

How does commerce today differ from the heyday of Muslim civilization? In most respects they are remarkably similar. The *hawala,* a kind of bank permitting remote payments, was the beginning of modern credit. Instead of carrying heavy and easily stolen gold, Medieval Muslims used paper checks to make payments in international trade. When the Crusaders invaded the Muslim lands they quickly learned of Muslim innovations in credit transfer and the Knights Templar emulated many of the ideas, introducing them into Europe.

There are two issues that stand out as differences: *ribâ* (usually translated as usury) and the status of fictitious persons (corporations). Most Muslim scholars throughout history have interpreted any form of interest on a loan as *ribâ.* I disagree with this interpretation. I have argued elsewhere that ribâ means any unconscionable overcharging (whether on an interest rate or a spot price), and charging a market rate of interest does not constitute *ribâ.* (See Ahmad 1996 for a full discussion.)

The idea of a corporation as a fictitious legal person was not part of medieval Muslim law. They did have various kinds of organizations. Business partnerships, for example, existed and were similar to the limited partnerships in American law. There were also trusts of various kinds, for example a trust for the property of an orphan. I have already mentioned the charitable trusts that played an important part in the development of hospitals, clinics, roads, irrigation systems, and schools. People would write a charter for an endowment, donate assets dedicated for a specific purpose, and appoint its initial board. These organizations were perpetual, but they were considered to be property, not legal persons. Orphans' trust funds were the property of the orphans and endowments were the property of the people who set them up. It is people who have freedom of choice; it is people who are the *khalifah;* it is people who are held responsible for their actions. Corporations have no consciences.

The problems of corporations are well dealt with by public choice theory. The bigger an organization becomes, the more divorced the interest of the various stakeholders become from one another. In a one-man operation, labor, management, and the owner is the same person. It is simply impossible for the worker to slack off on management or for management to cheat the owner, or for the owner to be oblivious to the working conditions. In a small family enterprise such things become theoretically possible, but remain unlikely because the common interests of the family are strong, the individuals engaged in the enterprise are too intimate with one another to allow things to go beyond certain limits. When you get to organizations the size of Enron the problem becomes enormous, and thus we have developed complex rules of business ethics, rules of governance and accounting in an effort to develop transparency and accountability. Such rules did not develop in the Muslim world because the state-imposed protections given to fictitious corporations were not there. The fact that some individual or individuals must retain personal responsibility for the actions of an organization put a natural limit on the size of commercial enterprises.

Thus, if modern state-protected forms of corporate organization (fictitious persons) are to exist in the Muslim world, then safeguards that attempt to deal (however imperfectly) with the problems such institutions generate will have to be developed. The existence of corporations certainly leverages the productivity of commerce, the problems of corporations (limited liability, for example), which after all are artificial creations of the state, must be addressed. For example, limited liability is a privilege given to corporations that seems to violate the spirit of individual responsibility that we associate with true free enterprise.

When the colonial powers conquered the Muslim world they dismantled the civil society institutions and turned their functions over to the state. The state was the only corporate entity they permitted in the Muslim world, yet, because of its monopoly on the use of force, the state is the corporation most susceptible to the abuses engendered by the public choice dilemma. Add to this the view that the cultural bias that sees a corporation as the private property of its founder or CO, and you can understand why the Muslim world is plagued with dictators. We must find a way to overcome that cultural attitude but it is naive in the extreme to think it can be overcome by turning on some light switch. Ellen Klein's (2004) observation about teaching democracy in Bosnia can be applied to teaching good corporate governance in the Muslim world in general: "It's a messy and painful process like any birth." As recent events have demonstrated, the idea that one can march an army into a country and, within months, set up a healthy democracy is a fantasy divorced from the real world.

I think the most effective way to deal with these issues is to "plant seeds" among the intellectuals of the society to explain the need for these institutional issues to be addressed and to tie them to the principles and precedents of that culture and especially the Muslim religion, to let them evolve a spontaneous order that accommodates these ideas and accept the fact that it may take a while and there may be many wrong turns and failed experiments en route. It took Britain a long time to establish a liberal democracy and even building on the shoulders of the British, America had to go through the Articles of Confederation before writing the Constitution, and then have a civil war before giving the vote to black men, decades more before giving the vote to women, and more decades before giving it to 18-year-olds. (Iran is the only country that gives the vote to 16-year-olds.)

The Role of Religion and Spirituality

Is there a role for religion and spirituality in a global and postmodern business world?

When Muhammad was a young man, before he had received the call to Prophethood, he co-founded a group called the "League of Ethical Businessmen," intended to encourage the merchants of Mecca to be honest in their dealings and to share with the poor a part of their wealth. His efforts there may have added to his personal reputation for honesty and generosity, but whatever influence the league may have had on others, it pales against the influence Muhammad has had on history as a prophet. In his book, *The One Hundred Most Influential Men in History,* Michael Hart rated Muhammad at the top of the list, not for founding the League of Ethical Businessmen, but for establishing a religion that to one degree or another impacts the lives of 1.3 billion people in many ways, including their business ethics.

If there were no role for religion and spirituality in the modern world, it would be because other forces have squeezed them out, either assuming their role or making fulfillment of their purpose impossible. Have institutional safeguards and state regulation made ethical self-regulation obsolete? Hardly. Enron is only the tip of an ugly iceberg.

Have the scale and competitiveness of global markets today made it impossible for religion to fulfill its role in inspiring good business ethics? On the contrary, unless people have faith in markets they will either collapse or be made impossible by popular pressure and/or political interference. Consider the hope that market interventionists have placed in environmental issues. The same people who once openly pushed socialism have in the face of that ideology's undeniable failure sought to bring it back by calling it environmental protection. These people are called "watermelons," green on the outside and red on the inside. Human actors who voluntarily embrace their appointment as God's stewards on earth will avoid the actions that make them vulnerable to such predators.

In the first few hundred years of Islamic history, Muslim legal scholars developed a sophisticated and detailed commercial law in which all agreements are by voluntary, informed consent within the limits of the law. The general limits put on commercial activity by the Qur'an are of four kinds: the prohibition of theft, of fraud, of taking unfair advantage, and of engaging in a generally prohibited activity. Thus, as extramarital sex is prohibited, so is prostitution, which is only a commercial example of a prohibited act. The act is prohibited because of its social and personal consequences, not because it is commercial.

Theft, being an example of the initiation of coercion is not a free market activity. Similarly, few would argue that fraud is admissible in a free market. An agreement made without the informed consent of both parties is no agreement at all, and the attempt of one party to impose it on another is just a variation on theft.

While we may call on the state to enforce violations of these standards, the fact is that a society in which we *had* to call on the state in every case would be a dysfunctional society. Only where the strength of moral imperatives makes the need for coercive enforcement the exception rather than the rule can economy be expected to flourish. If we had to sue to enforce every clause of every contract we entered into, commerce would grind to a halt. This self-enforcement is the hallmark of the religious society, by which I mean a society of religious people, those people for whom the enforcer is not Hobbes' Leviathan but Divinity.

The prohibition on unfair advantage is more controversial. What constitutes an unfair advantage? A contract between A and B, the enforcement of which you might favor if you were A, but would oppose if you were B, would be a contract that fails the fairness test. A boatman who sees a man drowning offers him a ride to the shore not for his usual fare of $2 but in exchange for all his worldly goods is clearly at an unfair advantage. Because it is more difficult to obtain a general consensus on this, it is even less desirable to rely on litigation here. Legal determination of fairness is possible, but the efficiency of the market will be severely impaired by frequent resorts to the courts to make such determinations. A willingness on the part of the people not to impose contracts on others that they would deem unfair if imposed upon them is a spiritual issue best enforced by a sound conscience.

Because the above issue is controversial among market liberals, I want to make the point very clear. I am not claiming that the moral duty to help others is enforceable by the state. In any case, that is a different issue from the question of the enforceability of an unfair contract. Denying the enforcement of a contract between a drowning man and the boatman who demands all the wealth of Fortune's victim is not a violation of market principles, but rather recognition that there *is no market* in the hypothetical example. Markets regulate prices better than the state can, but only where they exist, that is, where there is competition. Had six boatmen been present near the drowning man, the price they would have asked would have been reasonable. The boatman in my example can be unreasonable only because of the absence of a market. Thus, we have identified at least three cases where overcharging is possible: by coercion, by fraud, and by the *absence* of a market.

The category of generally prohibited activities is the most controversial. Conservatives may have no problem with general principle, but may disagree as to which activity should be prohibited, depending on their own choice of religion or moral code. Most Christians would seek to prohibit polygyny (marriage to multiple wives) but allow liquor sales, while most Muslims would hold the opposite view. Libertarians would oppose state intervention prohibiting any such activity, leaving it to individual conscience. This is the area where religion and spirituality must fill the gap that market regulation in a free society cannot fill. In addition to avoiding force, fraud, and unfairness, the religious businessman will not engage in pandering. If market research shows that the four most profitable enterprises in a potential market are, in order of decreasing profitability: recreational drugs, gambling, prostitution, and health-care, he will choose health-care. He will not make the excuse that since his customer has voluntarily chosen a course harmful to the self, his pandering has no moral significance.

Conclusions

It has been correctly noted that many leftists who oppose globalization are really opposed to freedom of trade in itself and not any real or imagined side effects. However, to ignore real harm that is being done under the cover of globalization is to drive the mass of humanity that is victimized by those crimes into the arms of those leftists.[7] Muslims have no inherent sympathy for either atheistic Marxism or anti-market socialism. However, leftists have confused the issue by associating imperialism with capitalism. On my first visit to Turkey, I found that when we spoke of free markets to students they never argued with us over any of the economic issues. They only demanded to know why did the liberal thinkers not speak out against imperialism. It is a faint defense to assert that Edmund Burke and Ludwig von Mises opposed imperialism, as that was a long time ago. They want to know about what's happening in our time: Why didn't market proponents speak out against American support of the Shah of Iran, or of Saddam Hussein's aggression against Iran; or of the Mubarak regime in Egypt; or of the Israeli occupation of the West Bank and Gaza. They want to know what does the philosophy of liberty have to say about the decision of the American government to invade Iraq and depose its former ally on the pretext that he had weapons of mass destruction and fanciful links to persons who did wish us ill but who came from another country entirely.

We have to become good salesmen by becoming sensitive. When we talk about free markets we must broaden our attention beyond the evils of price controls. Even the most conservative of Muslim scholars, Ibn Taymiyyah, was opposed to controls over prices set by market forces (i.e., absent a monopoly). He quoted the Prophet who, when a natural disaster caused the price of a particular commodity to soar, rebuffed the pleas of his people to fix the prices of the commodity. The Prophet's response was, "Allah grants plenty or shortage; He is the sustainer and real price maker (*musa`ir*). I wish to go to Him having done no injustice to anyone in blood or in property"(Islahi 1988, p. 94). In other words, "God has set one price and you want me to set another?"

Selling free markets to Muslims is easy. We need to address the politically sensitive issues that have been attached to the issues of economic reform. We need to distinguish the "free market" from the crony capitalism in which politically influential corporations in the Western world take advantage of the relationship between the American government and Third World dictators to enrich themselves and the dictators at the expense of American taxpayers and potential Third World entrepreneurs who are denied a place in the market.

The pattern of which I speak is well characterized by the following example given by Lederer (1961, pp. 14-17). In the late 1950s, the largest recipient of aid per capita in the world was Laos (intended to distance the Laotians from Communist China). That money did not provide a rising tide to float all the Laotian boats. Rather, a small elite became enormously wealthy, spending their money not in trade with their fellow Laotians, who had nothing to sell them, but in buying luxury goods beyond the reach of the Laotian masses. All Laos knew of the government corruption engendered by the American aid, and the population responded to the Communist propaganda that capitalized on it. In the next election the Communists won a resounding victory.

That pattern is still repeated around the world, notably in the Muslim countries. Now, in Iraq, in the name of the war on terrorism, major American corporations are becoming wealthy on American tax money while displacing the masses of Iraqi engineers (a disproportionate part of the Iraqi people are engineers) that could be doing the job using Iraq's own "dead capital."[8] The effort to establish an environment of commercial laws and business ethics that could revive and deploy dead capital would be much assisted by putting on the front burner opposition to crony capitalism and neoimperialist policies that contribute to keeping the capital of the Third World in its morbid state.

Good salesmanship requires that we relate the benefits of free markets to the needs of the people we wish to embrace them. A recognition of their spiritual and religious heritage and its links to the principles and history of the development of markets and a frank admission of where we have betrayed those principles are indispensable to the propagation of the blessings of commerce and good business ethics.

There is a parable about a man who had four wives. He loved the fourth the best and would dress her in the finest clothes and shower her with gifts. He loved the third a great deal and would boast of her to his friends. He loved the second somewhat, but never gave her the time and attention she deserved. The first he had lost affection for and never paid her any attention. One day the man learned that he was dying. He turned to his fourth wife and asked if she would accompany him into death. "No way," she replied. "When you're dead, I'm out of here." The man was crushed by this response. He asked the third wife if she would accompany him into death and she said she would not, that when he was gone she would find another man to marry. Disappointed, he turned to his second wife and asked if she would accompany him into death. She said, "I love you a lot, but what you ask is impossible. When you are dead, all I can do is to bury and praise you." Finally, he turned to his first wife and asked if she would follow him into death and she replied, "Nothing could separate me from you," and he became ashamed of the way he had neglected her.

His fourth wife was his body, and when he died it would turn to dust. His third wife was his possessions, and when he died they would belong to someone else. His second wife was his friends and family, and when he died all they could do is to bury him and mourn his loss. His first wife is his soul, mind, and spirit, the very essence of his self. In Islamic law a man may only have more than one wife if he treats them equally, and that is the key to understanding this parable.

While we are on this earth we should take care of everything: our bodies, our property, our friends and family, and our mind and spirit. This is summed up in the Muslim proverb attributed to the Prophet's cousin Ali Ibn Abu Talib: "Work for this life as though you are going to live forever; work for the next life as though you will die tomorrow."

Notes

1. "O ye children of Adam! We have bestowed raiment upon you to cover your shame as well as to be an adornment to you but the raiment of righteousness that is the best. Such are among the signs of God that they may receive admonition! O ye children of Adam! let not Satan seduce you in the same manner as he got your parents out of the garden stripping them of their raiment to expose their shame: for he and his tribe watch you from a position where ye cannot see them: We made the evil ones friends (only) to those without faith." (7:27-28)
2. "When they do aught that is shameful they say: 'We found our fathers doing so';

and 'God commanded us thus': say: 'Nay God never commands what is shameful: do ye say of God what ye know not?' Say: 'My Lord hath commanded justice; and that ye set your whole selves (to him) at every time and place of prayer and call upon him making your devotion sincere as in his sight: such as he created you in the beginning so shall ye return.' Some He hath guided: others have (by their choice) deserved the loss of their way: in that they took the evil ones in preference to God for their friends and protectors and think that they receive guidance. O children of Adam! wear your beautiful apparel at every time and place of prayer: eat and drink: but waste not by excess for God loveth not the wasters. Say: Who hath forbidden the beautiful (gifts) of God which He hath produced for his servants and the things clean and pure (which He hath provided) for sustenance? Say: they are in the life of this world for those who believe (and) purely for them on the Day of Judgment. Thus do We explain the signs in detail for those who understand. Say: The things that my Lord hath indeed forbidden are: shameful deeds whether open or secret; sins and trespasses against truth or reason; assigning of partners to God for which he hath given no authority; and saying things about God of which ye have no knowledge." (7:28-33)

3. Although pre-Islamic law put no limits on the number of wives a man could have and Islamic law, although it limited and regulated polygyny, did not prohibit it completely, nonetheless, Khadijah was Muhammad's only wife as long as she lived.
4. See e.g., Qur'an 9:111, 61:10, 2:245, 57:11, 64:17, and 5:12.
5. It is pertinent to point out here that the Islamic civilization was dynamic in its development of the physical sciences as well as the legal sciences. See, e.g., Ahmad (1992) and Sarton (1927).
6. 85-90 percent of all Muslims belong to the Sunni denomination of Islam, which primarily consists of four schools Hanafi, Shafi, Malaiki, and Hanbali. (The Wahabis, who have gotten much press recently, are historically a radical offshoot of the Hanbali school.) The rest are mostly of the Shi`a denomination.
7. See, e.g., Chaufen (2004).
8. See DeSoto (2000) for a detailed explanation of the notion of "dead capital," that the poor of the world actually possess resources that they are unable to mobilize.

Bibliography

Ahmad, I.A. (1992). *Signs in the heavens: A Muslim astronomer's perspective on religion and science.* Beltsville, MD.

Ahmad, I.A. (1996). Riba and interest: Definitions and implications (22nd conference of American Muslim Social Scientists (Herndon, VA, Oct. 15-17, 1993), Minaret of Freedom Institute Preprint Series 96-5. Bethesda: Minaret of Freedom Institute. [Online] Available: http://www.minaret.org/riba.htm.

Ali, A.Y. (1987). *The holy Qur'an: Text translation and commentary.* Elmhurst, NY: Tahrike Tarsile Qur'an, Inc.

Chaufen, A. (2004). Corporate responsibility: Traditional teachings for a current issue (Loyola Institute for Ethics and Spirituality in Business International Ecumenical Conference June 10-12, 2004), in press.

DeSoto, H. (2000). *The mystery of capital.* New York: Basic Books.

Haykal, M.H. (1976). *The life of Muhammad, trans.* Isma'il Ragi al-Faruqi. USA: North American Trust Publications.

Islahi, A.A. (1988). *Economic concepts of Ibn Taymîyah.* Bradford-on-Avon: Islamic Foundation.

Khawaja, I. (2004). Islam and capitalism: A non-Rodinsonian approach, (Loyola Institute for Ethics and Spirituality in Business International Ecumenical Conference June 10-12, 2004), in press.

Klein, E. (2004). Free enterprise as an enterprise in freedom abroad: A Bosnian experience, (Loyola Institute for Ethics and Spirituality in Business International Ecumenical Conference June 10-12, 2004), in press.

Lederer, W.J. (1961). *A nation of sheep.* New York: Fawcett World Library.

Sarton, G. (1927). *Introduction to the history of science. I. From Homer to Omar Khayyam.* Washington, D.C.: Carnegie Institute of Washington.

PART IV

APPLICATIONS

A. A Christian (Catholic) Business Ethics

Can Theology Help Us in Applied Ethics?

Rev. David A. Boileau

Sometime in the mid-1980s, on the occasion of one of the first colloquia on the contribution of theology to business ethics, Richard De George made this statement: "If the theologians want to contribute to business ethics, then they must cease to be theologians, if they want to produce good theology, then they can contribute nothing to business ethics."[1] I think we should take a strong objection to this statement and to the type of rationality that produced it.

What I am proposing for your consideration is that theologians can free themselves and us from the historical limits of fragmented modern rationality, thanks to their hermeneutic relationship with a living tradition, which precedes modernity and its rationality.[2] The theological tradition is older, different, and just like poetry, literature, and contemporary art, it can give different perspectives on our existence.

My colleague from Louvain, Dr. Johan Verstraeten says:

> Thanks to a hermeneutic relationship with biblical and patristic texts which open a world of meaning different from the world interpreted by modern rationality, and thanks to a different comprehension and interpretation of the human being as moral actor, the moralist theologians who have a relationship with their narrative tradition, can engage in a semantic operation which permits them to make a critique of all moral and ethical relativism too dependant on modern hermeneutics, which reduces moral problems to ethico-technical questions. ...Management cannot be understood without posing questions about the meaning of work, or about business as a sphere of human endeavor, etc. The greatest obstacles to an adequate ethics are the hermeneutic givens

> which deform our perception and our understanding of reality and of ourselves. As with the inhabitants of Plato's cave, the ethics-experts take their technocratic and manipulative world-view to be an objective representation of reality.[3]

Is not a malady of our times the fact of our inability to understand the complexity and the semantic richness of human life? Neither ethical relativism nor the so-called "objective" analysis of experts cannot and do not help. Verstraeten, among others, calls for a more fundamental remedy. A hermeneutic *metanoia* through the intermediary of the intellectual appropriation of texts and narrative is needed:

> The theologians who have a hermeneutic relationship with biblical narratives, as well as all moralists who know how to get to the source of poetic texts, in the Aristotelian sense of the word, become capable of reinventing and reinterpreting professional reality. The texts they have read have given them metaphors and metaphorical narratives which are not simply anaphoric, that is to say metaphors which see reality in an old light. The reading of texts permits them to "see" the world through diaphoric metaphors, fundamental metaphors (root metaphors) which create, by their impertinent addition, possibilities for new interpretations. They have introduced their readers to new and different presuppositions, and thus have created the capacity to enrich the interpretation of professional reality with meanings that are personal, convivial, fraternal, and holistic, so often absent from instrumental reason, as with the new modes for being which are the precondition of new ways of behaving.
>
> Let us replace, for example, the dead metaphor of Adam Smith's "invisible hand," which dominates neo-classical economics, with the living metaphor of the "invisible handshake," image of biblical solidarity. ...The invisible hand expresses a mechanical and deistic interpretation of the world in which individuals' self-interest is orientated toward the common good by means of an imagined mechanical providence, whereas the metaphor of the handshake refers to an organic and fraternal world where everyone is linked and where the social dimension of human behavior is not lost from sight.[4]

Let me sketch out for you how I see the problematic nature of moral relativism. We can define Modernity by three elements: the identification of truth with certitude; the conception that the world is a closed system, understood by itself by theoretical knowledge; and skepticism of religion as something mythological and magical. In the Western world, we have devoted ourselves to 500 years of positive science. It is still with us; nonetheless, there is a postmodern world arising.[5]

Of course, the first element, truth as certitude, thus an instrumental causality, has produced a tremendous technological transfer. However, positivism is intrinsically limited and these limitations cause us ethical problems.

One ethical problem is that the differentiation found in moral relativism has produced fragmentation in human life. MacIntyre calls this situation a theatre of social life, where each person plays different parts, but obeys different moral imperatives. If this is the case, how can I focus on the tension in moral life between particular moral acts and a fundamental ethical (or metaethical) choice, which is the starting point of a human's moral being?

Another ethical problem is the dominance of instrumental or manipulative rationality. Quoting again from Verstraeten we read:

> Instead of finding an existential project full of meaning, professionals and managers are trapped in a certain pattern of destruction and of existential non-sense. Relative to this tendency, moral relativism, and the reflexive ethics which accompanies it, are themselves too tributary to instrumental rationality to be capable of operating as critical judgments.[6]

A third problem is that applied ethics, despite its differences, attempts to get beyond the limits of these particular meanings by integrating elements of a formal, universal ethics. The moral relativists, though subjected to an instrumental rationality, cannot avoid looking for a rational justification for their technical, bureaucratic, or political claims, which are, supposedly, expertly made.

So, we have the **principle of autonomy**, which is reduced to mean everyone's freedom to choose his/her own ideals or to live according to his/her own desires; the **principle of no-harm**; and sometimes as well the **principle of beneficence**. Do not these three principles form the basis of all professional codes?

Again, Verstraeten points out the problem:

> The problem is not so much the choice of these principles in itself, but their interpretation and the reduction of their meaning to a few abstract ideas having a tendency to caricature the meaning of human actions. Autonomy is a positive value and a necessary condition for making adult moral judgments. But when it is reduced to an individualist ideology which has no limits save those which permit others to live according to their own individual moralities, autonomy risks being deprived of its semantic and human complexity. The hermeneutic problem is thus posed: how can one prevent principles which are rich and valuable in themselves from being reduced to meanings which impoverish the sense of human life, or which express only a certain sentimentality?
>
> Furthermore, the use of these three formalized principles brings with it a procedural mode in which the how of moral judgment becomes ultimately more important than its content. In this procedural morality, the ARBITERS are no longer [EACH AND EVERY] responsible individuals, but experts and commissions giving depersonalized responses.
>
> Although this may be inevitable in a complex society where the "cage" of bureaucratic rationality has been imposed, the unilateral dominance of this type of procedural ethics does not do justice to the complexity of reality, nor to the complexity of personal decisions or the tragedy of perplexing situations.[7]

The decisive aspect of moral judgment appears when a particular conviction is made as to right living and a conception of the hierarchy of values with which conviction is linked. These two aspects are not the result of objective reasoning, or of formal argumentations, but the expression of a conviction, of *pistis,* of confidence in a tradition.[8]

Now, the theologian comes not from abstract rationality but is conscious of his/her dependence on a particular tradition. The theologian can contribute in a two-fold manner. First, he/she will express the priorities and values of his/her interpretive community. Second, the theologian will unmask the illusion, which consists in the belief that in ethical and moral matters a scientific objectivity is possible, and that a hierarchy can be determined that is totally independent from tradition.

I am going to demonstrate, or at least suggest, that the liberation of existential nonsense in professional life is only possible to the extent that theological and philosophical thinking permit us to open the closed hermeneutic horizon in which we live. Because of their hermeneutic relationship with a living tradition that precedes modernity and its rationality, Verstraeten claims theologians can free themselves from the historical limits of fragmented modern rationality.[9] He also claims that a rational approach advocated in and by modernity gives short shrift to a person's make-up and moral quality. Consequentialist calculations or rationalistic principles do not determine a person's development as a moral being. I can also indicate one interpretation: a responsibility toward oneself and others, based on a fundamental meta-ethical choice that engages the entire person as a narrative whole, and that, beginning with the discovery of what is understood as obedience, could be described as responsibility to a vocation.[10]

This idea of a vocation shows how the origin of a responsible moral life ultimately finds its existential foundation in the inner discovery of oneself and of that which transcends oneself. The development of a well-understood inner life is the precondition of a personalized moral life. However, modern man only understands him/herself in a mediate role, brought about by his/her conquest of the world, through his/her work, or through the objects he/she produces or consumes.[11]

Moral relativism does not help us at all in this situation. It is precisely this alienation from the inner life that is the source of an existential agony, which is expressed through professional activity. Thus, Verstraeten claims that: The liberation of Man from such alienation requires a stronger remedy, such as the hermeneutic *metanoia* described above. Moral theology, insofar as an ethico-hermeneutic contemplation, can play a role in this respect and contribute to the deconstruction of the concept of business or professional life as false transcendence. Furthermore, in combining moral and spiritual life, and by aiding individuals in the discovery of the inner life, theology can set guideposts for a new consciousness of the self that rejects the illusion of an illusory immortality and that liberates workaholics from the resulting power games.[12]

Theological narratives move us beyond the limits of jurisprudence and the demands of justice. Our modernistic "professionals" cannot get beyond their rationalism. If I am only my profession, my possessions, or my grade-point average, then the context of moral principles is put aside and the principles become abstractions or skeletons. Levinas calls this situation "a lack of fundamental questioning." Professor Verstraeten reminds us that "the parenthetic nature of narratives puts the reader in a position of having to choose: he is called on to assume a responsibility, which goes beyond the morality of his professional role."[13]

Furthermore, Verstraeten states that through the confrontation with and the intellectual appropriation of biblical narratives the professional limits of our responsibility are opened toward a limitless and concrete responsibility, since this responsibility is always incarnated in the response to the concrete face of him/her who calls to us. Formal responsibility has no reality without concrete involvement and vice versa. The consequences for professional morality are evident: the professional class "actors" are obliged to leave the cocoon of the obligations of their roles, expressed in their code of conduct, and they are at the same time called upon to weigh the structural, social effects of their decisions and the tears that bureaucracy is incapable of seeing.[14]

In the final analysis, it is our suggestion that moral relativism, in its guise of a rational ethics of experts, loses sight of the fragility of moral decisions, especially in the case of tragic choices. Tragic cases fill the business/professional world, and are not solvable by rational arguments or prudence. A strictly moral solution is no longer possible. Only the opening of religious and narrative perspectives can make any sense of it, thus the domain of theology or of narrative philosophy.

With Verstraeten, we can conclude that there are no sufficiently convincing arguments for excluding the modest contribution of theologians to the debate over professional or compartmental ethics. The time is ripe for putting an end to the prejudices of a poorly understood modern rationality and, in fact, for reversing, in a certain sense, the campaign to demythologize narrative ethics.

Contrary to the a priori exclusion of theologians, one would do better to plead for a *perichoesis* between a well-understood rationality and a hermeneutic approach to reality inspired by a metaphoric and narrative imagination. Rationality guards us against all temptation of ir-rationalism, particularism, partisanism, "fidéism," or fundamentalism. Whereas, the metaphoric and imaginational perspectives, opened by poetic and religious texts, as well as a culture of the inner life, which integrates the possibility of *a lectio, meditatio,* and *contemplatio* of biblical narratives, can contribute better to vanquishing the fragmentation and instrumentalists derailments of modern rationality that empty life of its human meaning.[15]

Let me begin this section with a plea for an intellectual lay-religious Christian. The Christian texts, as we now have them, have to be freed from the monopoly of the cults. Traditionalism and pietism cannot truly comprise an adequate rationality. Faith solely in the name of a tradition or in the name of a form of devotion is not a sufficient reason to exist. Today, we live in a climate of critical reflection, thus nothing that does not bear the mark of thinking can either long appeal or long endure. Being postmodern means we must answer to the demand for a critically self-rationalized rationality. To be Christian, to have an intrinsic Christian identity, means we base ourselves on an intellectual and reflective appropriation of the confession of faith and the message bound up with it. Our source and point of departure lies in a "reflective" approach to the Scriptures. Let us locate it among the approaches that every Christian has or is using in their reading of the Bible.

First, there is the "fantastic bible," the so-called sacred history. It is the child's bible, the one mother reads to you after supper. It is the bible as "story." We read or have read to us the bible mediated by images. This stage is of enduring worth. It gives fundamental enrichment for the succeeding stages. The images and stories of the Bible are a means of orientation just like the streets and buildings of our towns.[16] Now, put away the things of a child, for the fantastic but also naïve relationship with Scripture is therefore to be transcended and taken up in critical reflection. It is time now to be an adult.

The second stage is that of the "historical bible." This stage of historical and literary-critical investigation is in fact inexhaustible and can keep one busy an entire lifetime. We have within us an essential desire to understand what has happened. The arguments appearing in the textbooks show a painful lack of support from modern exegesis. However, this stage contains the danger of making the scriptures an archaeological fossil with nothing to say to us today. Levinas criticized this approach to Judaism when he said: "Fifty centuries were put on cue cards: one immense Hebrew epigraph, written in bundles dedicated to hearing their historical witness, and this only in order to situate the point where their influences cross. What a graveyard! The graves of one hundred and fifty generations!"[17] We would deprive our Judeo-Christian texts of any ability to give meaning to existence if we considered them only as archeological fossils. So, this stage is also insufficient. These historical facts alone can never furnish us with truths to live by. Some distance must be taken from the "historical" look at the Bible and then approach it with the great existential questions of our existence.

Finally, we come to the third stage. We want the Bible to tell us how to live. One submits to the Word in order to receive insight for living. The Bible as life-giving word shows how it can be a modality of human existence. Our relation to the Bible can never be purely instrumental or functional. An adult approach to the Bible culminates in relating oneself to it as "founding word," as a word where inner truth founds and supports my very existence. Such a founding word is more than edifying a priori; it puts me in relation to what guards my existence, gives breath and depth to it, guides it, and holds it open.[18] There must always be personal reflection and critical imagination of that which has been read. Biblical texts call for the reflective resources of thinking readers so that the enduring insights and values contained there can continue to nourish souls. We can approach Plato, Aristotle, and Thomas purely from a philological and historical-critical approach. This is not so with the Bible. It is not the case that what is in the Bible is true because it is in the Bible; rather, it is in the Bible because it is true. We have to bring the intrinsic truth-values of Scripture into science for us today. There are fundamental metaphysical, anthropological, and ethical insights found within the Scriptures. They are truths that give life.[19]

In line with Levinas, we might also designate this reflective, philosophical conception of how to read Scripture as the "reading of the Bible without images." To read the Bible in the way one reads a picture book or comic strip is to give an imaginary or anecdotal meaning to texts and stories, by which we then populate our imaginary world in all its curiosity with "strong stories" and "exact facts." Such a reading pays no attention to the meaning suggested in those texts and stories that greatly exceeds their purely historical truth. To reduce the Bible to some sort of cartoon strip, full of rich imagery and fascinating stories, would be to take no account of the numerous interpretations and a whole culture of thought that exist thanks to the text and around the text, and that is always in reflective redefinition and renewal. The reading of the Bible as a "religious picture book" is superficial and thoughtless; in the end, it mummifies the life-giving text. It passes shamelessly over the spiritual life of a tradition, which is not at all a simple repetition of biblical texts but, to the contrary, a reflective commentary and deepening that ceaselessly gives rise to thinking.[20] For Levinas, Biblical thinking is an original thinking, thus, it has a hermeneutic all its own.

G. E. Lessing thought that revelation has a pedagogical function whose necessity is only historical. In order to realize the very particular and indispensable contribution of Judeo-Christian Scripture (whose source is Jerusalem), one must take them as a starting point in the conviction that they are not leftovers of a completely bygone time but bearers of a living culture crucial for reaching a truly human and meaningful existence. Hence, do the Scriptures deserve to be addressed at the same level of reflection as the other great texts of western culture? For the original and enduring, or better, always new and irreducible meaning of Judeo-Christian Scripture to nourish souls, they must once again nourish *brains*.[21]

As Levinas explains, a Talmudic spirit always approaches the texts of the Bible and tradition as the evidence and source of a specific way of thinking that is taken completely seriously only by pursuing one's own thinking through and beyond. To relate to this thinking reflectively, to read the Bible reflectively is first to listen honestly to the text itself. It is to avoid immediately rejecting its suggestions, and instead accept them without prejudice, from a philosophical standpoint. Such a reading seeks always the "objective and communicable credibility" of the text. In short, Scripture contains completely original and irreducible insights, which, via a philosophical standpoint, can be made generally available to human souls!

In our time, texts from Scripture are quickly cast aside on the ground of their place within a particular faith-confession. The text is rejected before and without having been read, thus and without the echo of a thinking at least as radical and founding as the thinking to be heard, for example, in the fragments of the pre-Socratics. Even within the Greek philosophical texts, biblical texts can and must come to power, not because they belong to the bible, but due simply to the great degree to which we recognize ourselves through them and can think them.[22]

Now, biblical thinking also rests on a certain kind of spirituality. Levinas clarifies this specific spirituality, which he calls that of "strict application." His clarification is found in comparing this spirituality of "strict application" with that of the "emergent source" that strives after an immediate and emotional intuitive contact with the truth of Scriptures. He contrasts a subjective, idealist spirituality with an objective, realist spirituality. The "emergent source" is based on inner feelings, driven by a sort of "spiritual" hunger for depth-experience.[23]

Levinas classifies the account here not on the object-pole of the feeling, in other words, the immediate and lived contact with a concrete reality, but rather, and even exclusively, on the subject-pole, on attachment as the lived experience of oneself. There is a movement here of self-coinciding and interiorization; the subject is its own living and experiencing life. Feeling is thus above all an "inward-movement" to the immenseness of inwardness intimacy within oneself. We can therefore designate feeling as an ongoing dynamic of "introversion," back into oneself (*vers soi*).[24]

This inward dynamic of feeling is also bound to a metaphysical significance. It can get beyond the subject to the "subterranean" ground that supports and inspires everything. Immanence is then the avenue to transcendence to and via my self-affection to and in the wholly Other, which is closer to me than I am to myself (*intimior intimo meo* to cite Augustine). However, most people do not go this far; there is a lack of fundamental questioning. Therefore, it is necessary to submit this spirituality of an emergent feeling of God to serious reconsideration. Does it not appeal to a highly subjective and uncontrolled rush of forces and passions?

A very different sort of spirituality, which focuses on the object-pole of feeling, is that of "strict application." It begins not from the subject itself and its inner experience, but from the "object," the "other" that comes over us from "elsewhere." This does not involve an immediate, inner feeling but a process of study in which one is confronted with what is other than oneself. We do not discover this "otherness" but find it. We can therefore call this confrontation an experience in the strict sense of the word: we meet with something that we have not found in ourselves and could not possibly have found there. We strike against something that resists and breaks through the project of supporting and pursuing our own preferences, expectations, and interpretive scheme. Precisely for this reason, the "meeting" with the other is disappointing with respect to what we had expected or to the desires we had harbored. It brings something radically new, unexpected, and therefore painful into our existence, and in that way dispossesses us and places us in question. This is also why we often feel a temptation to flee from the confrontation with the "other." We would rather not go there or remain there; we would rather be left undisturbed in our identity and stability, and would rather abide in the security of the "same."

In order to give real content and meaning to this "exteriority" that we thus encounter, one needs to apply oneself, and this requires time. Those who quickly define and relate the "other" to themselves as if receiving an immediate welling-up will never truly discover the content that this other "reveals." It must be humbly and scrupulously, with receptiveness and patience that we encroach upon the "other." This is so that through our respectful and devoted listening, but thorough and penetrating thinking and meditation, its "mystery" can slowly reveal itself without betraying itself or scraping and bowing before shameless eyes. We can call this listening "real learning."

This spirituality is in contrast to the spirituality of the emergent source and is called the "spirituality of strict application." The biblical tradition does not come from the inner alienation of the subject, but presents itself as an unambiguous alterity preceding the subject. The word of scripture requires that the bearer dedicate him/herself to something that comes from the outside. That "something" does not easily surrender its secret. To enter into the "mystery" is not an easy exercise; on the contrary, it is hard work demanding much time and the resources of one's thinking. It is not attractive or fascinating. It is a struggle, raising argument against argument, but slowly developing into a stubborn, unconquerable idea. The Word is a hard nut that can be cracked only with the most religious attention.[25]

This makes it clear that "learning" and "study" play a crucial role in the development of a mature faith. A "religion of adults" does not permit itself to be seduced by and enclosed in the first moment of a charming but still hazy discovery. A religion of adults transcends and consolidates this first discovery by deepening it rigorously, but without wishing to achieve immediately new insights or world-shaking results. One must want to be a Christian with his/her whole heart, but one must not *only* desire, as if driven by some naïve élan or spontaneous rush of heart, or any surprising tide of Spirit. To be a Christian consciously, or a conscious Christian, is possible only if one also applies oneself to Scripture. This application must be more than a simple reading, more than pious credence or hasty "edifying reading." It must be the *ascesis* of patient and thorough study that seeks critically not only for understanding but also, and foremost, to discover and develop a vision that can support spiritual life. To apply oneself in this way is to re-read constantly and re-appropriate the revelation from which and by which the human adventure can be judged and receive meaning. This returns me to my plea for a reflective faith and an intellectual lay Christianity.

This intellectual approach to the Scripture is not without intensity or passion. On the contrary, one must do it with "heart and soul." Thus, we must be completely filled with the text on one hand and completely present to the text on the other. It is a form of mystical experience for an intellectual application, which thinks steadily through, critically tests, and investigates. Thinking is a form of rationality that is itself a specific sort of experience and feeling. By reasoning, I create an active enthusiasm and thus awaken a passionate one. Yet again, all the enthusiasm of the approach itself, this "transportment" as Levinas says, presents itself as a "mysticism of disenchantment."[26]

During the hard work of applying our hearts and minds, we are moved and exquisitely hurt by the "bewildering new insights." The foundation of our daily existence trembles and we all too gladly flee. In this respect, the study of texts and tradition is not always free of ambiguity. Some people make this somewhat timely and yet untimely appeal to traditions or "sacred texts," wisdom, or formative experiences, to defend an already calcified way of life and thinking. The moment a reflective approach to Scripture appears to involve having their established insights and convictions put in question, the moment it challenges "the same," they find all manner of reasons and rationalizations to avoid applying themselves in that way. However, those of us who find the (mad!) courage to see this disenchantment all the way through are rewarded with new horizons that in turn fulfill spiritual desire in new ways.

A concrete reading that desires to come to the heart of the text precisely out of respect for the message that lies hidden there is possible only through a sort of violence done to the words. Meaningful words covered in layers of use and convention, once they have been brought back across history to the light of day, already possess and deliver considerable "food for thought," which the inexhaustible richness of Scripture helped discover.

At this point, it is useful to remind ourselves of Marcel Lègaut's distinction between "remembering" and "recollecting."[27] To remember a tradition or a text is something much more concretely active than simply calling up the past again. To remember a tradition creatively is not only to preserve or protect a text, but also to open it up so that its originally grounding experience can again be a source for thinking and living. The tradition registered in and through memory is delivered by remembering over from the domain of concrete implements (the text) to the domain of insight and meaning giving.

By wrestling with Scripture in its objective expression, the subject remains in a lively awareness of God's exteriority and "holiness" (*sanctus*—originates from *sancire*: "to split, or separate"). I experience a presence that lies outside the limits of inner, so-called "spiritual" life through the discipline of faithful adherence to that which does not spring from the depths of my own inner experience but which comes over me and addresses me. God's exteriority and holiness remain outside precisely because He is God! However, through applying myself strictly to Scripture, I can come wondrously near this wholly transcendent God. Levinas even goes so far as to say that this approach to Scripture, this thinking study, can lead to an intimacy with God as great as that of prayer.27

These remarks on the spirituality of strict application make it finally possible to situate a reflective-philosophical reading of Scripture. As "mediator" between Word and life, it has neither the first word nor the last. It does not begin from itself but rests on the "pre-given" resources of tradition flowing from Scripture, as the "other" in which reason confronts itself. Scripture is itself a fact of experience so that the approach reason makes to the text is a lived experience in the true sense of the word. In this sense, we can speak of an "inspired rationality" out of which develops and unfolds a rational force not simply based on itself but bound to the heteronomous origin of the Word. Inspired rationality is an obedient rationality, holding itself open to what comes from "elsewhere."

In authentic artistic activity, the artist often has a sense of not being the author of his or her own work. Artistic activity can be experienced as a "calling," a being called and animated by an inspiration, which one does not create but discovers. Artistic inspiration involves the consciousness of a radically alien intervention in human activity and self-determination. It is the experience of a subterranean "en-spirit-ment," which not only comes from elsewhere, but also is much greater and deeper than my limited ego and its meager capacities. One can also speak of "enthusiasm" or "possession," referring to a sense of being stricken to the very marrow by something "other." The artist does not resist this "infiltration" but surrenders to it completely, grateful for the great gift of befallen inspiration.[28] However, this heteronomous activity does not at all take away the creative activity and role of the artist. To the contrary, inspiration awakens in us the impulse to create. It is the work of the artist to manage and work this impulse out, which requires one to respect (and in a sense master) the specific laws and conditions of his/her craft and technique in order to bring indeed that inspiration to expression. Inspiration overwhelms the artist without doing violence.

Insofar as it is inspired, the reflective approach to Scripture has a heteronomous origin, but as a human activity, it is nonetheless the work of the person and takes place according to the particular laws governing rationality. As heteronomous source of a reflective approach to the text, Scripture does not exclude the autonomous capacities of rationality, but in fact calls them to develop their proper fulfillment and with enthusiasm. Scripture itself is not without thought, but rather a specific form of thinking: it literally "gives" to thinking. Just as inspiration does not rule out the artistic activity and craft of the artist, but to the contrary, supports and makes it possible, so Scripture as a "way of thinking" does not rule thinking out, but challenges it, thus displaying a degree of faith in its capacities to give its best to the effort of making the message of the text available in and through thought.

Inspired wisdom also does not have the last word. The reflective approach to Scripture, however uplifting and enthusing it may be, does not occur simply for itself. To the contrary, a reflective approach to Scripture seeks to nourish, support, and guide such an engagement, and in that way resists or compensates for the one-sidedness of the so-called "postmodern" spirit of the times. Persons truly realize their humanity only if they allow themselves to be claimed by this "sense," thus, transcending themselves.

Of course, not every surrender or action is responsible, not every engagement is meaningful, and not every involvement or attachment is good. What follows then is an irrational circuit of attachment to attachment, action upon action, and enthusiasm on enthusiasm. What I have tried to do in these pages is protect the purity of an involvement with Scripture.

A reflective approach to Scripture seeks to protect and promote precisely this inner freedom, grounded in rational insight. A faith that is experienced heart and soul in personal engagement can become established and grow to maturity and depth only if it consciously resists all cheap consumption and the rapid diversion of interest toward only what sparkles with newness rather than what is simply true. A reflective, philosophical approach to Scripture cannot in its turn become an endpoint. No less so than the historical literacy approach to Scripture, the reflective philosophical approach runs the risk of becoming an "objective and detached study" in which we apply our understanding apart from the insights by which Scripture can yield instructions to live by. One can misuse the reflective approach to Scripture and avoid confronting one's own life with the message to be found in Scripture. However, one can just as easily open oneself to the help it offers in a "truth that sets us free." This requires one to confront, eye to eye, directly the kernel of the text that reflection has laid bare.

Conclusion: Source of Thought and Life

The reflective approach to Scripture comes after a source for thinking that is at once an experience and a tradition: Scripture. The response of the believer following this approach is born by the enthusiasm of lucid insight. The engaged believers surrender themselves precisely in order to make their faith true and to experience it in that way. It makes possible a mature and free answer to the Word. At the same time, this is also a bearing witness to God Himself, to the Wholly Other, which is also the marvelous Proximity in the Scripture to which we apply our thinking.

My objective throughout was to point out a method of reflection, a hermeneutic on the Scriptures for ethics. This involves a "thinking" approach to the Scriptures. Following Levinas and his general hermeneutical concept, we can apply it to a few particular biblical texts and see what the "bible gives to thought." Jesus' proclamation of an ethically qualified God showing the passion of God and the ethical radical requirements of biblical ethics can be shown by an analysis of the "Good Samaritan" (Luke 10, 30-37). In Genesis (12, 10-20), we find Abraham and Sarah displaying our responsibilities for future generations. In St. Matthew's Gospel (19, 16-22), we see that the comparison of prohibition and taste in ethics are the bipolarity found in Christian, biblical ethics. Again in I Kings: 21, the story of Namoth and his vineyard brings up, foremost, the seriousness of evil as inflicted injustice. Many aspects can be discerned: evil doing on a human scale; desire and evil doing; evil doing and complicity; the justification of evil doing; and finally, the lethal gravity of evil. The prophet by his actions takes evil seriously, coming from and speaking for a God who is angry. Nevertheless, a God who provides the healing peace of forgiveness that allows us to escape and get beyond the weight of judgment and introduces confession as a condition of forgiveness.

Professor Verstraeten has already been footnoted and quoted. My other colleague is Professor Roger Burggraeve. He is Leuven's resident on Levinas. One should see his article "Prohibition and Taste: The Bipolarity in Christian Ethics,"[29] with a quote from which I would like to close:

> Ethics is not a simple matter, it is a complex field wherein orientations, commandments and prohibitions, suggestions, examples and experiences all play a role. ...Reducing ethics to obeying commandments and prohibitions leads to a rejection of ethics, while a narcissistic absolutizing of taste leads to a destruction of ethics in as far as it results in the aestheticism of pure taste and in arbitrariness. Only an ethic that remains normatively modest by focusing its attention on the essential delimiting rules that protect basic values opens perspectives towards a creative meaningful life as a 'lively adventure.'

Notes

1. R.T. De George: "Theological Ethics and Business Ethics," *Journal of Business Ethics,* (Vol. 5, 1986, pp. 421-432).
2. D. McCann: "Umpire and Batsman: Is it Cricket to be Both?," *Journal of Business Ethics,* (Vol. 5, 1986, 6, pp. 445-452).
3. J. Verstraeten: "Dépasser La Morale Sectorielle: La Contribution D'Une Éthique Herméneuteque et Théologique," *Revue D'éthique et de théologie Morale* (Le Supplement, no. 213, Juin 2000, pp. 83-104 p. 94).

4. *Ibid,* pp. 95-96.
5. Antoine Vergote: *Modernité et Christianisme,* CERF, Paris, 1999, p. 189.
6. Verstraeten, *op.cit.,* p.88.
7. *Ibid,* pp. 89-90.
8. Cf. J. A. Selling, "In Search of a Fundamental Basis for Ethical Reflection," *Ethical Perspectives,* 1, 1994, (1. p.13-21).
9. See footnote #3 above.
10. *Ibid,* p. 97. (Here, Professor Verstraeten is commenting on a remark by Vaclav Havel.)
11. Dupré, L.: *Transcendent Selfhood,* (the Seabury Press, 1976).
12. See: Verstraeten, *op. cit.,* p. 101.
13. *Ibid,* p. 102.
14. *Ibid,* pp. 102-103.
15. *Ibid,* p. 104.
16. E. Levinas: *Ethics and Infinity* (trans. R. A. Cohen, Duquesne University Press, 1985, pp. 21-22).
17. E. Levinas. *Difficult Freedom, Essays on Judaism* (Baltimore, The John Hopkins University Press, 1990, p. 268).
18. E. Levinas: *Ethics and Infinity* (pp. 17-19).
19. *Ibid,* pp. 116-117).
20. E. Levinas, "Lire la Bible sans images," in *Esprit,* 1990, no. 6: 120.
21. Cf. G. E. Lessing, *Die Erziehung des Menschengeschlechts* (1790).
    See also: Cf. E. Levinas, *L'au-delà du verset. Lectures et discours talmudiques,* Paris: Minuit, 1982, p. 165 note 2: "The written Torah is the name for the forty-eight books of the Jewish biblical canon. In the more restricted sense, the Torah is from Moses: the Pentateuch. In the widest sense of the word, the Torah is the whole of the bible and the Talmud with their commentaries and even including the collections and homiletic texts of the Haggadah."
    See also: Cf *Ibid.,* p. 165: "The Talmud is comprised of discussions between learned rabbis which took place between the first century before the common era and the sixth century afterward. Historically, these discussions as spirituality in the Temple is replaced by centers of study, thus from cult to study. These discussions and lessons concern above all the portion of Revelation bearing prescriptions: rites, morality, the law, but in their own way also the form of parables about the whole spiritual universe of humankind: about philosophy and religion."
22. See also: "Entretiens Emmanuel Levinas–Francois Poirié," in F. Poirié: *Emmanuel Levinas. Qui êtes-vous?,* Lyon: La Manufacture, 1987, pp. 110-111.
23. E. Levinas: "Reality and its Shadow," trans. S. Hand in the *Levinas Reader,* pp. 130-132.
24. J. Wahl: *Existence humaine et transcendence,* (Neuchâtel, 1944, pp. 30-34). Note: this is Levinas' friend.
25. E. Levinas: *Difficult Freedom,* pp. 6, 27-29, 123-124, 137, 139-139, 213-214, 220.
26. E. Levinas, *De Dieu qui vient à L'idée,* Paris: VRIN, 1982, p.57.
27. E. Levinas, *Beyond the Verse,* p. 88.
28. E. Levinas, *Reality and It Shadow,* pp. 132-133.
29. R. Burggraeve: "Prohibition and Taste: The Bipolarity in Christian Ethics," *Ethical Perspectives* (Vol. 1, No. 3, 1994, pp. 130-144).

The Sources and Spiritual Basis of Catholic Business Ethics

Jean-Francois Orsini

"Business Ethics," "Corporate Social Responsibility," "Business Governance," all those are very familiar notions evoked nowadays in business schools. Unfortunately, the Catholic views of many of the concepts covered are basically invisible in the most common courses on these subjects taught in secular business schools, as well as—and that is cause for serious alarm—in Catholic business schools.

What is readily obvious is the chasm between courses of management—also called "administration" in business schools—which do not want to scare students or "organizational behavior" in those, which have scholarly pretensions—and of business ethics. Actually, in those schools dedicated to impart the rudiments of business tools, after courses of management teaching how to deal with employees, courses of marketing teaching how to deal with customers, and courses of accounting teaching how to deal with money, are offered (oftentimes on an elective basis) Business Ethics courses whose message is "Oh! By the way. Do not forget to be ethical." Once the discourses on subjects of management, marketing, and accounting have been presented, the student is supposed to graft on them a totally new discourse, that of ethics. And the student is pretty much supposed to do it on his/her own because, typically, professors of business ethics are not particularly well trained in management, marketing, and accounting.

Catholic business ethics starts with a sound theology of work. And there are few places with better elements of a philosophy of work than in Pope John Paul II's 1981 encyclical "Laborem Exercens," itself a 90th anniversary celebration of the great seminal social encyclical "Rerum Novarum." Many issues that management scholars struggle with find an elegant and edifying resolution in this encyclical. It is really incredible that there has been so little recognition and celebration of this fact in academic, Catholic, and professional circles. Without going too far in illustrating that claim, let us simply remind ourselves that some people find immoral that a human being can use another human being for his/her own purpose. Now this is exactly what is going on in an employment contract. Does the payment of money entirely void the immorality of submission of one human being to another? To answer positively and without additional consideration to that question rings somewhat shallow, doesn't it? The difficulty vanishes when one takes to heart the distinction made by Jacques Maritain between the "person" and the "individual." The person is a wholesome creature who operates at the level of Grace; the individual is only part of a whole, which is Society and needs to function amidst that whole. The individual operates at the "level of Creation." It is proper and necessary that to fulfill his/her obligation, the human being as an individual operates in cooperation with other human beings and therefore accepts an operational submission in order to carry out his/her tasks, according to the principle of division of labor.

Starting from the beginning, the book of Genesis, several teachings are readily given on work, within the first events that define those who preface mankind: Adam and Eve. As soon as they are created "in the image of God…male and female" (Gen.1:27), they are told to "be fruitful and multiply, and fill the earth and subdue it" (Gen. 1:28). This requirement of fruitfulness is called by Pope John Paul the "transitive" element of work. According to the transitive element of work, work is about applying oneself on something and modifying that something to increase its value. This something that one applies himself/herself to is exterior of oneself; it can be a tree that will be transformed in a board or a piece of furniture, or it can be a music sheet that one uses to play on an instrument, or a set of data that one collects in the surrounding world for the purpose of producing a research report.

This thing exterior to oneself is also called Capital and the effort applied to transform it is called Labor. Indeed anything of value, the tree, the music sheet, and the money that is paid for a researcher to conduct his work are all of value. They are all Capital. In work, Labor is more important than Capital because it is more alive and is more human. Capital may have been the product of past human work. But now this music sheet sits on the shelf and will not be of much value if new work is not originated using that music sheet. For philosophers, let us say that Capital is Potentiality and Labor is Act. God is pure Act. To act is better than having potentialities.

"Work is the key to the social question," the pope tells us. By that, he means simply that the essence of work has the above-mentioned special meaning in this dialectic between Capital and Labor. He also teaches that lessons to be derived from the nature of genuine work reach further than this dialectical lesson.

What the human at work applies to the exterior thing, some embodiment of Capital, are skills, talents, and virtues. Skills are acquired after much experience; talents are most often personality traits that no other human being possesses in the same fashion or degree, which makes for the work of each person unique. But the application of one's virtues is what *all* human beings do in one manner or another when at work. This is the true social dimension of work. To use virtues at work is a necessary aspect of the human condition.

Before we address the virtues, let's go to another element of work because that it also amplifies what is to be understood by the importance of the virtues in work.

Genesis also tells us, by way of Adam and Eve who are being chastised for their Original Sin, that Adam would win his bread "by the sweat of his face" (Gen. 3:19). St Thomas Aquinas tells us in the *Summa* that human creatures would have worked in Paradise, had there not been the Fall. The mere fact that Adam will have to work is therefore not a punishment. The punishment is that now Work has become toil. While beginning toil, it has not yet lost its other aspects.

By exercising his virtues at work, Man is not only expiating his Sin, but is on the path of gaining his redemption: "Be perfect as your heavenly Father is perfect," Matthew 5:48. The virtues are the tools of the search for perfection, as well as the benefits gained on the way to this perfection. The virtues include both the theological virtues of Faith, Hope, and Charity and the cardinal virtues of Prudence, Justice, Temperance, and Courage.

The piece of furniture, the music played on an instrument, and the written research report are objective elements of work. It is what Man has positively to show for in his work, the direct primary product of his work. But, there is also a subjective element of work. This element is what Man the worker becomes by applying his virtues. After work, not only is the work done, the piece of furniture made, the melody played, etc., but the human worker is also more done as a person. He/she has grown in the virtues. He/she has become more perfect.

In subduing the earth and multiplying, Man is following God the Father, allying himself to the great work of Creation. In working by the sweat of his face, Man is following Our Lord Jesus Christ in his expiation of all sins. Man is contributing to the Second Person of the Trinity's mission of redemption.

No wonder only Man works. Pope John Paul tells us, "Work is one of the characteristics that distinguishes Man from the rest of the creatures." Physics explains to us that a machine can work. It can be said that animals can also work in their own way, but the Work of Man is really touching the Trinitarian mystery!

One can derive by reduction a secular version to the theology of work. Man suffers but builds his muscles, acquires more skills and produces goods. The grain dies so that it can germinate. This secular vision of work also includes then a positive and a negative dimension of work. Man's work is his cross on which he redeems himself to come out as a more perfect being.

Now with all these elements of work, we have all we need to shed the necessary light on the importance of the virtues at work.

The Personal Prelature of Opus Dei is very involved in promoting the importance of the theological virtues at work. Indeed, prayer at work increases Charity and Hope, especially when the work is anguish-filled. Meditating on Our Lord's work is conducive to growing in Faith. Naturally, Grace is the only mode of growing in the theological virtues. The Catholic who wishes to grow in these virtues at work must follow the teachings of the Church relative to staying in the state of Grace and growing in Grace.

The cardinal virtues are different. Not as noble as the theological virtues but more materially connected with the physical nature of the human worker and of the tasks at hand. Virtues are habits. They are good "stable dispositions to act in a certain way." The opposite of virtues are vices. Virtues are therefore eminently germane to the psychological and mental capacities of the human worker. When the social sciences approach to business school discourse of management invokes the psychology of the worker, it sorely misses the mark when excluding the virtues.

The cardinal virtues are named such because they are the four virtues on which all the other virtues "hinge." The cardinal virtues are capable of offering a wholesome view of Man the worker. The social sciences of management are seats of bickering between the psychologists and the sociologists. Even many schools of psychology are at odds with one another.

There cannot be an ethics of business before there is an ethics of management, and there cannot be an ethics of management before there is an ethics of workers. And there cannot be an ethics of workers before there is a whole moral philosophy of Man at work and Man at work doing good. Materialistic business ethics is widely ignoring these essential levels of analysis resulting in a discipline limited to a laundry list of disconnected issues included more as a way to follow the fashions of the time, rather than following any sound moral or ontological basis.

Now it behooves us to offer a glimpse on how the cardinal virtues can be indeed immediately effective in directing Man at work to be a more efficient modern manager and white-collar worker.

A study of successful businessmen asked them one central question: "what do you consider the most important thing for being successful in business?" A whole variety of possible answers were offered in the multiple-choice questionnaire. One of the answers was even jokingly: "Marrying the boss's daughter." Well, the number one answer offered by these businessmen was "good judgment." Now, people have to be instructed on the fact that nowadays the word "prudence" has lost much of its original meaning, with a negative connotation of pusanimity. Its original meaning as a virtue is really captured by the phrase "good judgment." Indeed, one dimension of the virtue—and it has many dimensions to be discovered in St.Thomas' *Secunda Secundae of the Summa*—is the proper alignment of means and ends. If a businessman wants to succeed at a material goal, he should be able to attain it if he finds the proper means to reach these proper ends. Well, working with means and ends corresponds to most of the responsibilities of managers. Peter Drucker, the most famous of management consultants, developed the concept of "Management by Objectives."

The annual meeting annals of Industrial Psychologists complained that they had no "construct" (they talk like that) for "effort." Indeed psychologists are paid by corporations not for making the minds of employees whole, but to find ways for employees to be harder at work. Now, in the *Summa,* St. Thomas tells us that being capable of hard work is a sub-dimension of the virtue of Courage. To be courageous is to be capable of taking risks to achieve a "hard good" (*bonum arduum*). The highest risk to be incurred is to lose one's life. Courage is still displayed when the risk is not so high, risking being fatigued, for example. However, different jobs require different hardships: there are physically exhausting jobs, physically dangerous jobs, mentally demanding jobs, financially dangerous jobs etc., etc.…all these difficulties require a related virtue of courage to complete them.

There are chapters that can be said about these virtues as well as the other cardinal virtues of Justice and Temperance.

Pope John Paul II said about the end of the Cold War that what made communism fall of its own weight was that it had a flawed anthropology. Naturally, the pope was not talking about anthropology as presented in typical university departments of anthropology. He was talking about what he already said in the encyclical "Redemptor Hominis," specifically that the most important element of the human person was his/her relationship with his/her Creator, a Creator who also loved His creature so much that He assumed for Himself the Human nature. As he did so, we can all verify what is the proper manner to fulfill one's human condition. Similarly, the post-modern economic world and its most prized temples, which business schools have come to be, will have to adopt a Catholic ethics and philosophy of work if it is not to collapse.

But before secular universities discover the perennial wisdom of scholasticism applied to management, it would be a great progress to witness the business departments of Catholic universities start adopting the vision, instead of being passively mesmerized by the fashionable trends at secular universities.

As Cardinal Ratzinger taught us that the values of this modern world are most typically economic values, it is essential to penetrate the economic culture with Catholic values, not only for the preservation of the souls of all involved in that modern culture, but also for the survival of society. Priests and bishops should be preaching in season and out of season the importance of the virtues in the economic world.

"The object of gain is that by its means man may provide for himself and others according to their state. The object of providing for himself and others is that they may be able to live virtuously. The object of virtuous life is the attainment of everlasting glory" (St. Antoninus, *Summa Theologica,* I. 1,3,ii). St. Antoninus was one of the first teachers of the Church to take away the stigma of the profession of commerce and, instead, point to the potential for spiritual growth in that profession. In his *Summa Theologica,* he even explained the mechanisms for the merchant to grow in perfection: he is to grow in the virtues and conduct all his business in a virtuous manner.

Calling, Character, Community: Spirituality for Business People

Rev. Stephen C. Rowntree

Introduction

The very name of our conference sponsor, the Loyola Institute for Spirituality and Ethics in Business, testifies to the positive connotation in our day of the term "spirituality." Actors, singers, movie producers—among others—have claimed a piece of the spirituality action. New Age Spirituality, at least, seems to be associated with a growing market for music tapes, CDs, DVDs, books (traditional and audio), incense, candles, oils, workshops, retreats, and so forth. Cynics might see "spirituality" as our individualistic, consumer society's answer to the rigors of old-time religion characterized by creed, cult, and code.

As with anything, spirituality can be misused. The spiritualities associated with figures such as the Desert Fathers, St. Benedict, St. Francis, St. Clare, St. Dominic, St. Catherine of Siena, St. Theresa of Avila, John of the Cross, and St. Ignatius of Loyola are styles, we might say, of being Christian, and not alternatives to it.

The spirituality I know best is Ignatian spirituality, as is fairly predictable since I am a Jesuit. St. Ignatius of Loyola (1492-1556) bridged the late medieval and early modern periods. His *Spiritual Exercises* represent the fruits of his intensely personal conversion experiences in which God directly taught him the personal meaning of the Christian creed: creation, sin, redemption by Christ's death and resurrection, and the Church as the ongoing work of God's Spirit in the community and the world.[1] When Ignatius shared the fruits of his experiences with others, the process was intensely personal and individual: the director directing the exercises met daily one-on-one with the individual making the exercises. The exercitant reported to the director how he/she had been affected by the materials for prayer (mainly scripture passages) provided on the previous day. In view of how God had touched the exercitant, the director suggested new content for the day's prayer. The full exercises were designed to last 30 days: days spent separated from one's ordinary circumstances. They were usually made in a retreat house (often today called a "spirituality center") in complete silence and solitude except for conversation with the director and two or so "days off," as it were (called "days of repose").

Often the aim of these exercises was to help the person freely to make a major life decision such as choice of vocation. In defining the term "spiritual exercises," Ignatius observes their purpose to be "the conquest of self and regulation of one's life in such a way that no decision is made under the influence of any inordinate attachment" (SE, # 23). In putting matters this way, Ignatius assumed that the norm or standard for this decision to be God's will revealed in a general way in the Christian economy of salvation and individualized to the retreatant. However innovative and modern the method in its focus on the individual's personal relation with God, the content, as noted, was the Old and New Testaments, as understood by the Catholic Church.

Much could be said about how Ignatian spirituality might be relevant for "the ethics of commerce." First, I believe it suggests we get personal and think of how it is relevant to the "the ethics of business men and women." And among many possible themes, I'd like to focus on three: (1) the Christian calling, (2) the Christian character, and (3) the Christian community of business men and women.

Christian Calling

Ignatius's *Exercises,* focused as they are on making major life decisions in the context of the invitation to follow Christ, would be most relevant to discerning whether God has given one the gifts and call to a vocation in business or commerce, and what specific form this call has taken. The time of decision ("election," in Ignatius' term) comes in the second week. In the first "week," one experiences at a deep, personal level what it means to be a sinner, but a loved sinner. The second week (most often extending over 10 or more days) focuses on the life of Christ, especially the call to his followers to accompany him in poverty, humiliation, and suffering. After experiencing Christ's general call, the exercitant is in position to discern the particular way God is calling him or her. Week three, focused on Christ's passion and death, brings home the cost of following one's call, yet the incredible love of God revealed in Christ's dying for each of us.

I think that for those already engaged in commerce/business, Ignatian spirituality suggests how business men and women might name and claim their work as their personal living out of God's call to them. I choose to pass over the somewhat complicated history of how Christian theologians gradually came to recognize that, as with most callings, commerce involved both temptations to sin (to avarice, dishonesty, unfair dealings), and opportunities to serve (by supplying essential material needs).

The place of commerce in God's plan for the world can be interpreted in a variety of terms. I think of it from the perspective of the modern tradition of what we might call "Catholic political economy" (especially as found in papal, conciliar, and other official teachings, beginning with Leo XIII's 1891 *Letter on the Condition of the Working Class* [Latin title: *Rerum Novarum*].

This tradition takes God's purposes in creating human beings in a material world as its starting point. Humans are made for union with God in this life and the next ("made to know, love, and serve God in this life and to be happy with Him in eternity," in the words of the old *Baltimore Catechism*). All other creatures are intended by God as help to humans' achieving their ultimate end. Creatures are to be used insofar as they help to achieve this end and to be renounced insofar as they hinder achieving it:

> Man is created to praise, reverence, and serve God our Lord, and by this means to save his soul. The other things on the face of the earth are created for man to help him in attaining the end for which he is created. Hence, man is to make use of them insofar as they help him in the attainment of his end, and he must rid himself of them in as far as they prove a hindrance to him. ("Principle and Foundation," SE, #23)

The general form that obstacles to our union with God take, according to Ignatius, are "inordinate attachments" (SE, #21). By this he means loving and holding on to things of lesser value in preference to those of greater. For example, money and power can be used for good purposes (e.g. to support one's family, to help the needy, to alter unjust situations, and so forth), but if they become ends desired for their own sake, they easily become obstacles or alternatives to union with God.

Catholic political economy affirms material sufficiency, other things being equal, as a help to union with God. Thus we find repeated St. Thomas' claim (echoing Aristotle's) that dire, grinding, demoralizing material poverty often distracts persons from attending to God. Hence we can infer that God wants all humans to live a materially decent life. The world is badly "out of joint" in that billions of people live in absolute poverty (according to the standard definition, living on less than $1 per day). Those of us who have more often immeasurably more than we need or can even use, are insistently exhorted to help those in need. A harsh judgment is portrayed in the New Testament for those who don't assist the poor, especially those whom they encounter at close hand. (See, for example, Luke's parable of Lazarus and the Rich Man [16:19-31], and Matthew's scene of the last judgment [25:31-46]).

How best to alleviate material poverty, an urgent task God calls us to, is debated. If we ask what economic structure has best succeeded in overcoming mass poverty, I take the answer to be "market economies," or "the free enterprise system." The weight of historical evidence, distant and recent, shows that these systems, involving as they do free trade between nations based on an international division of labor, can best assure material sufficiency for those still impoverished.

I thus find God's purpose of providing the material prerequisites of a decent life to all to be realized most effectively by the inner dynamic of free enterprise: knowledge-based product and process innovation, the continual effort to produce goods and services at the lowest cost, free entry to and exit from markets, capital markets that finance business investment (including venture capital that encourages innovation and new enterprises), ever finer division of production and cross-border supply chains, foreign direct investment, and so forth, undergirded by legal and regulatory regimes which constrain its abuses and facilitate its functioning with low transaction costs.

I suggest we all think of our jobs and professions, diverse as they surely are, as calls, ministries, gifts of service for the whole human community. In this horizon, we can think of the work we love and do well, our accumulated skills and developed talents as God's gifts to us for serving our brother and sister humans.

Many of us, for sure, might have difficulty seeing our daily work as call, vocation, or gift of service. The pressure to support a family, the jobs available in a particular place, wage differences, and so forth, surely account for most job choices—none of which feels like God's call. But I don't think it completely fanciful to see God working in the apparent accidents and contingencies of our work lives. Wherever we end up in the world of work is a place where we can serve our brothers and sisters in some way they think worth spending money on.

St. Paul, for one, reminds his hearers that the lowest and meanest jobs are important, and those holding them graced and called:

> As a body is one though it has many parts, and all the parts of the body, though many, are one body, so also is Christ....Now the body is not a single part, but many. If a foot should say, "Because I am not a hand I do not belong to the body," it does not for this reason belong any less to the body....Indeed, the parts of the body that are weaker are all the more necessary, and those parts of the body we consider less honorable we surround with greater honor. (I Cor. 12: 12, 14, 22)

Both the highest and lowest of us would do well to take this truth to heart and to reflect it in how we think and act toward one another.

Christian Character

So far, I have given what might appear to be a blanket endorsement of free markets for their ready provision of products and services for which people are willing to pay. Certainly for some, obtaining what they desire at the lowest cost seems to be a very good thing, at least most of the time. Of course, many recognize legitimate reasons for not allowing everything to be bought and sold that people desire: e.g. babies, sex, votes, body parts, political offices, hard drugs, and weapons of mass destruction.

Ignatian spirituality with its strong insistence that union with God is our ultimate good, can be read to endorse, as noted, market economies as the best means to insure for everyone the material needs helpful for this end. However, given our ultimate end, many things we desire (which may be perfectly legal) are bad for us, and things we may not desire at all would be very good for us.

It was from this perspective that once upon a time the Catholic social tradition advocated reconstructing society to make it a Christian society, one more consonant with God's Kingdom, present and to come. In such a society one can easily imagine legal enforcement of the closing of businesses and factories on Sunday, and a ban on the production and distribution of sexually explicit materials (with or without artistic value). The category of legally permissible "harmless wrongdoing" might not exist at all. For any "harmless" to others moral wrongdoing would not be harmless to wrongdoers, but might prevent them from achieving their ultimate end, a harm far worse than any loss of property or physical injury.

For many easily stated reasons, the attempt to reconstruct our current American society to make it a Christian society closer to God's Kingdom is not a good idea. For one thing, given the diverse forms of belief and unbelief, such an effort would undermine the right to religious freedom of non-Christians. The failed experiment with legal prohibition of alcoholic beverages suggests the general form of what would result from trying legally to enforce Christian norms.

Ignatian spirituality (as well as all forms of Christian spirituality, and others) must continue to remind us that many things we could buy on the market are not conducive to our achieving union with God. And many things we cannot buy would be very conducive to our achieving this goal. What is required for Christian consumers (individually and communally) is to test their purchases by the ultimate standard: will this purchase bring me closer to God or will it be an obstacle? This may sound terribly rigorous as a general rule. Catholic political economy has long been comfortable saying it is permissible to live according to the general standard of one's social class.

Thus "keeping up with the Joneses," in general merits no censure. However, union with God as our ultimate end renders far less important, even to the point of relative unimportance, power, wealth, and prestige, which so many seek as ultimate goods.

The Synoptic Gospels portray the primacy and ultimacy of God as our ultimate end in Jesus' challenge to his disciples (and to us): "What does it profit a man if he gain the whole world and suffers the loss of his soul" (Mark 8:36)? And Jesus says this in the context of a call to his disciples to follow him shouldering their crosses in imitation of Him: "Whoever wishes to come after me must deny himself, take up his cross and follow me. For whoever wishes to save his life will lose it, but whosoever loses his life for my sake and that of the gospel will save it. What profit is there..." (Mark 8:34-36).

Jesus here is portrayed as appealing to the hearer's self-interest in the language of commerce. The challenge posed is not to forget self and attend to others, but to serve one's authentic self-interest. We are most authentically God's beloved children called to be conformed to His only son's suffering, dying, and rising so that we might be united with Him eternally. As John reminds us, "perfect love drives out fear" (4:18), but we will be accountable before God for how we have lived our lives. And the criterion for judgment, as Matt. 25:31-46 reminds us, is how we responded to our fellow humans in need.

I'm not sure whether any specific business ethics follows from this vision of our ultimate nature and destiny. But it surely does provide motivation for adhering to legal and ethical standards as they have been articulated for the kind of ministry or service God has called one to. And surely it calls for one to see all people one encounters as fellow forgiven sinners and beloved children of God. New Testament texts repeatedly call on us to take on Christ's way of acting, thinking, and feeling, i.e. to develop a certain kind of *character.*

The New Testament authors did not, in general, understand the solidarity of God's children redeemed by Christ and sanctified by the Spirit to require abolishing social distinctions, even a distinction as odious to us as master and slave. But Paul, for one, insisted that in Christ these distinctions were abolished: "Here there is not Greek or Jew, circumcision or uncircumcision, barbarian, Sythian, slave, free, but Christ is all in all" (Col. 3:11). And, "For through faith you are all children of God in Christ Jesus. For all of you who were baptized into Christ have clothed yourself with Christ. There is neither Jew nor Greek, there is neither slave nor free person, there is not male or female; for you are all in Christ Jesus" (Gal. 3:26-28). Thus one's subordinates, one's superiors, one's customers, one's competitors, one's regulators are to be seen as fellow members of Christ's body (potential if not actual), and to be treated as such.

The Christian in the marketplace sees his/her work, salary, co-workers, everything in the horizon of God's creation, its redemption from sin, and its sanctification by Christ's suffering, dying, rising, and outpouring of the Spirit. So the style of Christian spirituality that is Ignatian as a practice and way of life would make us people who, while remaining ourselves with our unique histories and personalities, take on Christ's way of thinking, feeling, and acting—so our fundamental character gradually becomes more Christ-like. And so our life's work and our lives themselves continue Christ's healing, helping, serving and thereby building up the Body of Christ.

In light of this challenge, we all fall short. We are always sinners who are tempted to choose the lesser good over the greater good, to make idols of power, wealth, and prestige. What progress we manage to make in developing a more Christ-like character is always due to God's action in us when we choose to accept it.

The conflict between good and evil takes social forms, and we are called to struggle against unjust social structures. But this same struggle plays itself out in our own individual lives. The call to repent is always one we need to hear.

Christian Community

The ancient moralists, as well as contemporary psychologists and sociologists, underscore the important role our social environments play in our moral and religious development. As helpless, dependent infants we learn basic trust when our parents respond to our cries for help. We become children with a conscience, an internalized sense of moral right and wrong, because we come to care about our parents' approval and disapproval. And we care about their approval and disapproval because they first cared for us.

But the role of social context in our moral and spiritual character formation is not limited to family. Parents, especially parents of teenagers, know how pervasive the influence of their children's peer groups is. The same also is true, perhaps to a lesser degree, perhaps not, for adults.

For sure, Christ knows us and loves as the unique individuals we are. The Spirit graces and inspires us with gifts for service. But ordinarily we come to know of this through participation in the community that is God's people. Becoming a disciple whose character conforms to Christ's requires a nurturing, challenging community which proclaims, celebrates, and lives the love of God revealed in Christ as the highest value, the "pearl of great price," the "treasure hidden in a field."

Granted, the actual Christian churches, perhaps especially our local one, may seem far from this picture. But for Christians, God continues to become incarnate in the nitty-gritty of our sinful humanity, just as God became incarnate in Christ who "had to become like his brothers in every way that he might be a merciful and high priest before God..." (Heb. 2:17). Just as

Christ's divinity could only be seen in his humanity by the eyes of faith, the Spirit's continuing work through the Christian churches is not evident to the naked eye.

Christ's gift of Himself, intensely personal and individual ("Who do you say I am?") is mediated by the Church and our acceptance of this gift takes visible form in being baptized—a sign both of our individual commitment and a ritual of initiation into this very community.

The churches need to nurture and fortify all calls and vocations, including the ministries of those who work in the world of commerce. The Woodstock Business Conference (WBC) is one example of what this looks like. My acquaintance with the WBC is still second-hand. The following is a description of its basic content and structure drawn from a summary of conference documentation done by Donald Lee, Esq., who works in the financial services industry.

The WBC describes itself as a "national movement of spiritual and social renewal for the business community." This movement seeks to apply Ignatian spirituality to participants' work experience. It began in 1992 with questions posed by a pilot group of business leaders:

What difference does it make and for whom, if business leadership is seen as a call for excellence, a call to do God' will?

How does a business run by a committed Christian differ from any other?

These questions had emerged during a series of three "Business Vocation Conferences," (held in 1889, 1990, and 1991) organized by the Woodstock Theological Center. A fruit of these three conferences was the founding of the Woodstock Business Conference, which was a network of business leaders organized in local chapters. The chapters were designed as places where peers could support peers (compare the myriad Twelve Step programs where peers help peers to overcome their addictions for some sense of the power and popularity of "peer ministries") (Woodstock Business Conference, 2004).

Chapters meet monthly for approximately one and one-half hours, and involve prayer, reading of the mission statement, scripture readings and reflection, and a discussion of a topic based on previously distributed materials (Woodstock Business Conference, 2004).

I'm sure that a little research would discover many such efforts—some parish-based, some denomination-based, and others independent of formal church structures (such as the WBC)—designed with similar aims, whereby business men and women minister to one another.

Conclusion

In these brief reflections, I have proposed an interpretation of one style of spirituality for business people: The work of earning our daily bread, a commission from God for all of us becomes our call (vocation) and ministry when we can discern how we can best serve our brothers and sisters given the graces and gifts God has graciously bestowed on us. Christian business people also share the general task initiated at Baptism constantly to repent, and constantly to seek to put on the mind of Christ so we can be in some sense other Christs, doing in our time and place what Christ did in his. Christian call and Christian character formation can happen only in the context of Christian tradition and nurturing Christian communities in which business men and women can help one another daily to think, feel, and act in the business world as authentic disciples more and more becoming conformed to the image of Christ; hence, "A Spirituality for Business People: Call, Character, and Community."

Notes

1. To be referred to as SE by section number.

Bibliography

Ignatius of Loyola. (1951). *Spiritual exercises.* Lewis J. Puhl. (Trans.), Westminster, MD: Newman.

Woodstock Business Conference. (2004). *Affirming the relevance of religious faith to business practice* [On-Line]. Available: http://www.georgetown.edu/centers/woodstock/wbc-in.htm.

"Mankind Was My Business:" An Examination of a Christian Business Ethic and Its Application to Various Ethical Challenges

James R. Edwards, Jr.

Perhaps the best-known, best-loved tale of a businessman's redemption is Charles Dickens' *A Christmas Carol*. Dickens' (1994, p. v) "Ghost of an Idea" was to spread the Christmas spirit throughout society, throughout the year. That spirit comes directly from the celebration of the birthday of Jesus Christ.

Ebenezer Scrooge's business model relates well to an inquiry into the religious roots of ethical business practice. Scrooge's harshness toward his clerk, Bob Cratchit, down to the deprivation of sufficient coal to stoke the office fireplace, illustrates Scrooge's business ethic of profit at all costs. The old skinflint—"a tight-fisted hand at the grindstone, Scrooge! a squeezing, wrenching, grasping, scraping, clutching, covetous, old sinner!" (Dickens, 1994, p. 2)—fixated on profit and gain, personifies the "win at all costs" mentality of cutthroat business tomes that populate the bestseller lists.

Scrooge's core motives arise from his deformed character. But early on, Scrooge learns that man is ultimately measured by a different standard. The ghost of his long-dead business partner, Jacob Marley, visits Scrooge wearing the "chain I forged in life" made "link by link, and yard by yard," a fetter fashioned "of my own free will" (Dickens, 1994, p. 20). Scrooge says "you were always a good man of business, Jacob." But with new eyes, Marley exclaims

> Business! . . . Mankind was my business. The common welfare was my business; charity, mercy, forbearance, and benevolence, were, all, my business. The dealings of my trade were but a drop of water in the comprehensive ocean of my business! (Dickens, 1994, p. 22).

Such alarming truth contrasts starkly with the parameters of Scrooge's economy.

Similarly, Revelation 3:15-16 has shocked and convicted Christians feeling comfortable about the way their lives are going.

> I know your deeds, that you are neither cold nor hot; I would that you were cold or hot. So because you are lukewarm, and neither hot nor cold, I will spit you out of My mouth. Because you say, "I am rich, and have become wealthy, and have need of nothing," and you do not know that you are wretched and miserable and poor and blind and naked . . . . (Ryrie, 1978, p. 1900).

As Scrooge learned, life consists of much more than account balances, stock portfolios, and material gain—and everyone's life is under God.

This paper gives a Christian perspective on ethical business practice. Drawing an analogy from Dickens' Scrooge, it examines the biblical view of free enterprise. Next, it identifies two cornerstone principles from Scripture. Then it applies those principles in a variety of contemporary business situations.

Scrooge, Christianity, and Profit

Dickens' tale reflects the Judeo-Christian ethics of Western culture. That culture achieved greatly in human progress, promoting liberty and human rights, the entrepreneurial free market and the rule of law. The undergirding Christian ethic checks the excesses of the market, as well as the excesses that can turn liberty into license. This "form-freedom balance," in theologian Francis Schaeffer's (1982, p. 25) term, reached its foremost stage in the United States.

Former *Christianity Today* editor Harold Lindsell, in *Free Enterprise: A Judeo-Christian Defense* (1982), argues that the Bible institutes a private property-based free enterprise economic system. Yet biblical free enterprise does not equal cutthroat capitalism. In the Christian economic model, individuals use the marketplace talents God has given them to honor Him. Lindsell (1982, p. 69) explains:

> The free enterprise system of the Old Testament did have some controls. P reviously we said there is a free enterprise viewpoint which goes back to the Enlightenment, even as socialism does, which makes private property an absolute without any controls whatever except the laws of the marketplace. Socialism, contrariwise, has controls without room for free enterprise. The Milton Friedman type of free enterprise has all freedom and no adequate controls. The Old Testament form of economic freedom took into account the sin-

ful nature of man and placed some controls on economic activity. Basically the controls called for altruism as an indispensable component of free enterprise.

Regarding the profit motive, God says in Deuteronomy 8:18 that "He gives the power to create wealth." The key is whether profit becomes god over God. Christian business expert Larry Burkett (1998, p. 55) says, "Every Christian in business, employer and employee alike, should work to maximize profits, but not to the exclusion of other key elements of a biblically based business."

The principle implied in Scrooge's meeting with Marley's ghost is, "For what will a man be profited, if he gains the whole world, and forfeits his soul?" (Matt. 16:26a, Ryrie, 1978, p. 1474). The cost of one's soul lost for eternity is a price too high.

The Ghost of Christmas Past shows Scrooge Mr. Fezziwig, who apprenticed him. Fezziwig's kindness rekindles within Scrooge warmth unfelt in ages. Scrooge observes, "He has the power to render us happy or unhappy; to make our service light or burdensome; a pleasure or a toil" (Dickens, 1994, p. 43).

In the end, Scrooge's character is transformed. Scrooge anonymously sends the Cratchits a prize turkey, donates a huge sum to a private charity, and attends church. He gives Bob Cratchit a healthy raise in salary and pledges "to assist your struggling family." And (Dickens, 1994, p. 113), "Scrooge was better than his word. . . . He became as good a friend, as good a master, and as good a man, as the good old city knew . . . ." All were merely outpourings of a renewed heart.

A Christmas Carol is a metaphor for Christian business ethics. With a rightly focused heart, newly imbued with Christian character, Scrooge adopts Fezziwig's management model.

Christianity gives a "more excellent way" to pursue one's calling. The biblical model of Ephesians 6:9 provides a practical way to love neighbor and love and honor God in the workplace. John Beckett of R.W. Beckett Company finds this to be true, as Christian business consultant Larry Julian notes in *God Is My CEO* (2002):

> [C]ompassion and accountability complement each other. . . . As John sees it, "Compassion without accountability produces sentimentalism. Accountability without compassion is harsh and heartless. Compassion teamed up with accountability is a powerful force—one which we have found can provide a great incentive to excel." (Julian, 2002, p. 104).

Christianity provides morally right principles for ethical business practice.

Cornerstone Christian Principles for Commerce

In which economy is one ultimately responsible: the "profit of dollars" economy of Scrooge's former self or the "profit for eternity" economy of the transformed Scrooge?

Burkett, in his bestselling *Business by the Book,* sets forth principles derived from the critical commandments that Jesus cited: "And you shall love the Lord your God with all your heart, and with all your soul, and with all your mind, and with all your strength," and "You shall love your neighbor as yourself" (Mark 12:30-31, Ryrie, 1978, p. 1529). These two central principles involve one's ultimate accountability unto God and one's relation to other people.

First, everyone lives under authority, *accountable to God* for how he/she conducts himself/herself. That accountability extends to loving God and neighbor in the mundane duties of business. Burkett (1998, p. 10) warns that reflecting Christ in business practices "will cost you money. . . . Anyone operating in a manner that glorifies Christ will be faced with many opportunities to suffer." But the real bottom line is the bottom line for eternity.

Submission to God's authority shows Him love and honor. Proverbs 3:6 says, "In all your ways acknowledge Him, and He will make your paths straight" (Ryrie, 1978, p. 941). Colossians 3:23-24 instructs, "Whatever you do, do your work heartily, as for the Lord rather than for men; knowing that from the Lord you will receive the reward of the inheritance. It is the Lord Christ whom you serve" (Ryrie, 1978, p. 1802).

The second principle, *loving one's neighbor,* is best known from the Golden Rule. Matthew 7:12 says, "Therefore, however you want people to treat you, so treat them, for this is the Law and the Prophets" (Ryrie, 1978, p. 1456). Treating others as one would like to be treated is the essence of loving one's neighbor as one loves oneself. As an ethic of commerce, Burkett relates this principle to fairness toward employees, customers, and creditors.

One manifestation of love for neighbor is "servant leadership." In Mark 10:43-45, Christ says "whoever wishes to become great among you shall be your servant" (Ryrie, 1978, p. 1525). Jesus provides a perfect model of servant leadership. Luke 22:26 says, "[L]et him who is the greatest among you become as the youngest, and the leader as the servant" (Ryrie, 1978, p. 1590). The Apostle Paul in Ephesians 5:1-2 writes, "Therefore be imitators of God, as beloved children; and walk in love, just as Christ also loved you, and gave Himself up for us, an offering and a sacrifice to God as a fragrant aroma" (Ryrie, 1978, p. 1785). The servant leader's life is characterized by living for Christ and emulating Christ.

The Principles Applied

How might the fundamental principles of wholly loving God and one's neighbor apply in business?

Take an executive's fiduciary duty to the shareholders of a publicly traded company. These business leaders owe a duty to maximize profits. ServiceMaster's chief executive Bill Pollard says: "God and business do mix

. . . and profit is a standard for determining the effectiveness of our combined efforts. For us, the common link between God and profit is people" (Julian, 2002, p. 14). This business model has resulted in "stellar growth and profitability with 20 years of record growth" (Julian, 2002, p. 21).

In Conoco's 1998 initial public offering (Julian, 2002, pp. 79-86), chairman and CEO Archie Dunham knew that an acquisition could result in thousands of employees seeing their jobs eliminated. But the IPO was successful on Wall Street, thus being true to investors, and employees kept their jobs, thus being faithful to "love your neighbor."

How do employees compare with customers and shareholders? Burkett (1998, p. 52) says a Christian business is "to supply the physical needs of those who depend on it: your own family and your employees." Citing I Timothy 5:8 and James 5:4, Burkett (1998, p. 52) reasons, "God holds us responsible for providing for those under our authority." Employees hold a special position under the employer's authority. They depend on the employer to make wise decisions, to keep the business solvent. Just as employees stand accountable to their employer to give an honest day's work, so employers stand accountable to God to care for those under their watchcare. For example, Burkett (1998, p. 52) offers guidance for fair pay: "[A] good rule of thumb is to consider whether you would be willing and able to live on what you're paying the people under your authority."

What about in serious challenges? Burkett (1998, pp. 52-54) relates a real-world example of an employer who strove to honor Christ in his business. Among other things, he created a benevolence fund to help meet the special needs of his employees. The economy went bad, while interest rates stayed high, and he needed operating funds to run the business. The employees raised the necessary funds and made their boss an interest-free loan, keeping the firm afloat.

Similarly, Julian (2002, pp. 186-191) tells of a travel management firm that lost a major client, leaving the company short on revenue. The company president faced laying off 30 employees. Struggling prayerfully, she decided the training invested in those 30 employees was worth the short-term rise in payroll, meaning better efficiency and profit margins in the long- term, over losing experienced employees and later having to invest in training new employees. She gave her staff the facts and asked for 10 percent more productivity. The grateful employees came through with 24 percent higher productivity.

Circumstances may require severe measures. A company cannot hemorrhage revenue interminably; no one is helped if the company goes out of business in order to save a relative few jobs in the short term, when laying off a few employees could save the company from bankruptcy. However, layoffs should be a last resort, similar to radical surgery in order to save a life, rather than a routine course of action.

Sharing the pain would seem a desirable course, if possible. Business owners (and certainly top executives) signal solidarity with employees and middle managers by taking pay cuts along with everyone else. Highly-paid executives in large corporations demonstrate that those working for the company are all in it together when they take significant pay cuts in economic hard times.

Also, biblical principles would imply that persons laid off be rehired once conditions allow it; after all, they showed loyalty to the company and trusted management's leadership. If they are good employees, the firm owes them a higher degree of loyalty than to untested new hires.

Some industries may be unable to look beyond the short-term bottom line. Can a business in a sector with tight profit margins and employing low-skill labor survive by paying its workers above-market wages?

Ritz Carlton Hotel Company chief executive Horst Schulze heads "an industry leader in employee satisfaction, customer satisfaction, and profitability" (Julian, 2002, p. 167). Ritz Carlton has an employee turnover rate of 29 percent in an industry that routinely has 100 percent annual employee turnover. According to Schulze (Julian, 2002, p. 169), "'Our industry is notorious for getting bodies to fulfill a function—do things,' he says. 'I think it is irresponsible and in a sense immoral. . . .'"

The fast-food industry is notorious for thin profit margins and disregard for employees. Burkett counseled the owner of a chain of hamburger restaurants on how to improve quality of service by improving the way employees were treated. The business faced constant employee turnover, low and falling quality of work, and increasing customer complaints (though profits remained good). Burkett advised: Raise wages to reduce employee turnover and to attract better workers. The owner raised starting wages 40 percent, gave experienced workers 20 percent raises, instituted a scholarship program tied to length of service, and started a profit-sharing program based on quality improvement.

> As a result of the changes Roland made, the college-bound students flocked to his businesses, and his personnel problems virtually disappeared. . . . These incentives attracted better employees, who worked hard and treated customers better.
>
> In the short run, Roland's profits declined, but within a year they were higher than ever and now they exceed the national average for all similar businesses. (Burkett, 1998, p. 138)

These examples show that biblical principles, while contrary to common business practices, prove themselves in the real world.

A related matter is dumping employees for the cheapest workers the labor market will provide. Burkett (1998, p. 162) acknowledges that long-term employees are likely to be older and earning more. "Pure economics would dictate replacing them with younger, more aggressive (and lower-paid) employees," he writes. Pure economics also would rationalize outsourcing and offshoring. But Burkett (1998, p. 163), citing Proverbs 3:1-4, says, "In the ethics of a Christian, kindness and justice play predominant roles, and the practice of dumping long-term employees is neither kind nor just."

Some corporatists advocate free-wheeling global labor competition, without regard to the effects upon loyal employees. They break faith with the free market's "virtuous circle," whereby all parties benefit in a set of mutually beneficial transactions.

Western free enterprise developed this "win-win" phenomenon. In the virtuous circle, as opposed to a vicious cycle, businesses continually compete for workers by raising wages, offering better benefits, and improving working conditions. This constantly pushes better productivity through such tools as technological breakthroughs, mechanization, efficiency gains, and better management. Productivity gains[1] allow businesses to reward hard-working employees through wage hikes. All wage increases improve sales through higher consumption—putting more money in the pockets of employee-consumers.

Increased wage rates have modest effect on overall costs; profit has a much more pronounced effect. Adam Smith (Skinner, ed., 1974, pp. 200-201) says:

> In reality high profits tend much more to raise the price of work than high wages. . . . That part of the price of the commodity which resolved itself into wages would, through all the different stages of the manufacture, rise only in arithmetical proportion to this rise of wages. But if the profits of all the different employers of those working people should be raised five percent, that part of the price of the commodity which resolved itself into profit would, through all the different stages of the manufacture, rise in geometrical proportion to this rise of profit. . . . In raising the price of commodities the rise of wages operates in the same manner as simple interest does in the accumulation of debt. The rise of profit operates like compound interest.

Scripture does not grant the right to gain on the backs of ill-treated employees, calling into question cutthroat market decisions.

To be sure, there is room in a prudential sense for the global economy to shift sectors so that jobs in one sector might have net movement out of the country while new jobs in other sectors are created to employ people who have lost their jobs. But former Reagan Assistant Treasury Secretary Paul Craig Roberts explains how new phenomena break faith with the virtuous circle.

Roberts (2004) says, "As a result of outsourcing, offshore production and Internet hires, the U.S. recovery is creating jobs for foreigners, not for Americans." Roberts notes that "the necessary conditions under which free trade produces mutual gains to the participant countries . . . have been destroyed by the international mobility of factors of production." Adam

Smith's version of free trade, benefiting both sides, rests upon comparative advantage. Roberts (2004) writes:

> The flow of factors of production to absolute, in place of comparative, advantage vitiates the economic case for free trade. What we are witnessing is the redistribution of First World income and wealth to developing countries blessed with excess supplies of labor.

Yet some corporations maintain Christian-based policies. Eli Lilly and Company (2004), a leading pharmaceutical manufacturer, retains a corporate culture that values its employees as the company's most valuable assets. Lilly's commitment to its employees shows in several ways. For one, *Fortune* magazine frequently lists Lilly as one of America's 100 best companies to work for. Second, the company has a no-layoff tradition. In 2002, Lilly eliminated 700 positions, but gave affected employees first opportunity at newly-created or vacant positions. Those taking lower-paying positions received their current salary for two more years (Associated Press, 2002A).

The Hershey chocolate company in Pennsylvania has displayed a corporate culture built on Christian principles (Pearlstein, 2002, pp. A1, A14). Hershey has nearly half the U.S. chocolate market share, while providing some of the highest wages and most generous benefits in the industry. These labor costs add negligible amounts to consumer prices. Hershey, Lilly, and others built a strong middle class with strong communities, which helped inspire a spirit of civic responsibility and unity. They advanced the virtuous circle.

By contrast, Pharmacia Corp., in anticipation of its acquisition by Pfizer, "slashed" the pensions of thousands of its employees and "made changes that will prevent workers who are already vested for pensions from taking retirement funds when they leave." The acquisition would mean thousands of job cuts. Not helping public relations was the fact that Pharmacia's eight top executives "will get $110 million in severance and pension benefits when the acquisition is complete." Its pension tactics are "becoming typical as employers nationwide continue to reduce benefits for employees" (Associated Press, 2002B).

Immigration can challenge the Christian approach to commerce. The present situation in the United States, whereby the immigrant (and nonimmigrant, or temporary) inflow has reached sustained, historically high levels, with immigrants typically lacking skills and education, is changing the dynamics in the American economy. Sustained mass immigration of predominately unskilled aliens (and an extremely high proportion of illegal immigrants) puts foreign workers in direct competition with the most vulnerable American workers.

American workers—particularly the lowest skilled and least educated—suffer as an artificially enlarged labor pool holds down wages. A landmark National Academy of Sciences study (Edmonston & Smith, 1997, pp. 5-28, 5-

34), documented that 44 percent of the wage loss between 1980 and 1995 of workers with less than a high school diploma is directly attributable to immigration.

This harmful effect reflects simple supply and demand. Having a lot of something—cotton, steel, would-be laborers—makes its value fall. The more limited something's supply, the higher its cost. Thus, the fees of a talented architect or doctor rise because that person's time is limited; one cannot add hours to a day, so one must pay a premium price for that professional's time.

An ever-increasing supply of low-skilled laborers pressures employers who would prefer the virtuous circle model to hold down costs radically, especially when some competitors employ illegal aliens. Census Bureau figures (Camarota, 2003, p. 1) show that approximately half the immigrant arrivals since 1997 are illegal aliens, and the net increase in foreign-born employment during the most recent recession grew by 1.7 million while native-born employment fell 800,000 (Cohn, 2003, p. A7).

Competitive unfairness (Hoppe, 2002, pp. 75-97) occurs when employers of foreign workers privatize the benefits (by paying these workers far less than the market otherwise would bear) while socializing the costs of the foreign workers and their families.[2] A scrupulous Christian employer, trying to honor God by treating his employees fairly, would face unfair competition from employers who oversubscribe immigrants in the current American immigration situation (large volume, low skills). The latter employers could underpay their workers, force their immigrant workers to public hospitals' emergency rooms for taxpayer-funded care instead of providing health insurance, force American taxpayers to subsidize low-paid immigrants through public assistance and other welfare benefits, and the like.

Hiring illegal immigrants makes things even worse. While knowingly employing illegal aliens is a felony, the U.S. government has increasingly shirked its duty to enforce employer sanctions laws. Unscrupulous operators unfairly and unlawfully gain competitive advantage over law-abiding businesses. In some sectors, business owners have been forced into a morally untenable position. They must either break the law to hire illegal aliens or risk being driven out of business by competitors who do so.

This dilemma confronts a small business operator who testified before Congress. Matthew J. Reindl (2002, p. 1) said he spoke "for the tens of thousands of law abiding small business owners, who are being adversely affected, many forced to close, because of illegal hiring practices of employers." His family-owned woodworking business, Stylecraft Interiors, employs legal immigrants among its workforce, pays its taxes and a fair salary, and provides health insurance benefits. "However, if illegal immigration continues to drive our selling price down, I fear we will not be able to provide health insurance to our employees in the future. In fact, I may even be forced out of business" (Reindl, 2002, p. 3). Reindl (2002, pp. 5-6) calculated that legitimate employers bear costs 78 percent higher than lawbreaker employers, while the federal government loses nearly $186 in taxes per week when employers pay "off the books."

A *Los Angeles Times Magazine* article (Dickey, 2003) chronicles the microeconomic consequences of mass illegal immigration. A California motel maid who is a U.S. citizen must compete directly with immigrants, many illegally present. She supports her three children as a single parent on $300 per week pretax wages. She is stuck earning $7.50 per hour and cannot ask for a raise because of the intense competition of "willing worker" illegal aliens—younger and cheaper who will not complain about pitiful working conditions.

Mass immigration, particularly of illegals, has driven native-born blacks out of jobs such as California janitors and auto body repairmen, while driving down wages substantially. Radio host Terry Anderson cites examples such as a black 17-year-old from South-Central Los Angeles who applied for a job at McDonald's and was turned down because he did not speak Spanish (Dickey, 2003).

Government subsidy by other means, with privatized benefits and socialized costs of hiring foreign labor, is not limited to unskilled jobs. Nonimmigrant visas such as H1B and L-1 have become popular with high-technology firms as a way to reduce labor costs and even to displace qualified American workers. In the wake of the "dot-com" debacle, many foreign workers who held these skilled-worker temporary visas and populated Silicon Valley have returned home to establish branches of the business there and to hold positions there at much lower wages (Thurm, 2003).

Clearly, Christians sometimes live within unjust systems in which it is impossible to take moral actions without suffering. At the very least, business owners should seek to change those unjust systems and not perpetuate them. For example, most business owners are members of some kind of business association. Many national business associations lobby Congress forcefully and incessantly for more and more labor importation. Business owners have a moral responsibility to work to ensure that those who speak for them in the halls of government seek just systems.

Conclusion

A Christian business ethic will almost necessarily contrast with secular business ethics. This is because of the different bottom lines at issue. Loving God with heart, soul, strength, and mind and loving neighbor as oneself result in different priorities, different practices, different profit motives, and different principles.

Christian business principles can lead to long-term business success. A Christian business ethic dictates dependability, truthfulness, honesty, and fairness. A business characterized by dependability and the like might well attract repeat customers and build long-term client relationships.

Divergent motivations are distinct:

> There is a vast difference between a man who goes to work every day to serve God and a man who goes to work every day to make money [alone]. . . . If a man sells insurance chiefly to make money, he will work to sell his client what will bring him the greatest commission. But if a man sells insurance chiefly to serve God, he will work to sell his client what will best meet the needs of that client. The primary motive for work does matter! (Sartelle, 2004, p. 55)

A non-Christian business ethic is principally concerned with the temporal and with glorifying self; a Christian business ethic is principally concerned with the eternal and with glorifying God.

It has been said (Gregg, 2003/2004, p. 27) that, "[a]bove all, . . . man is Homo religiosus" and "much more than homo economicus." The options for behavior boil down to the difference between the old Scrooge and the new Scrooge. The former Scrooge did what he thought was good business. But as Proverbs 14:12 (Ryrie, 1978, p. 957) says: "There is a way which seems right to a man, but its end is the way of death." The transformed Scrooge still succeeded in business, but his bottom-line priorities had changed. The later Scrooge management model is rooted in the Christian business ethic of accountability to God and love of neighbor.

Notes

1. However, business commentator Robert J. Samuelson in the March 19, 2003, Washington Post explains how "fixations with certain economic statistics," productivity in particular, can misguide. Samuelson notes how during the Great Depression some business sectors had great productivity gains, how certain "productivity gains of the late 1990s were more statistical than real," and that "efficient production of what's unneeded . . . is still wasteful" (p. A31).
2. The 1997 National Academy of Sciences report, *The New Americans,* documents the net cost to society of immigrants with less than a high school education and bears out the fact of socializing immigrants' costs, particularly by admission of many foreign workers at the low end of the economic spectrum.

Bibliography

Associated Press. (2002A). *Eli Lilly plans to shift 700 jobs next year* [Online]. Available: online.wsj.com/article_print/0,,SB1039655262611902433,00.html.

Associated Press. (2002B). Pharmacia cuts pensions for thousands of workers [Online]. Available: online.wsj.com/article_print/0,,SB1038166489807059188,00.html.

Burkett, L. (1998). *Business by the book: The complete guide of biblical principles for the workplace.* Nashville: Thomas Nelson Publishers.

Camarota, S.A. (2003). Immigration in a time of recession: An examination of trends since 2000. *Backgrounder* (November). Washington: Center for

Immigration Studies.
Cohn, D. (2003). Feeble economy, tighter borders don't stem immigrant tide. *Washington Post* (March 10).
Dickens, C. (1994). *A Christmas carol.* New York: Barnes & Noble Books.
Dickey, F. (2003). *Undermining American workers: Record numbers of illegal immi - grants are pulling wages down for the poor and pushing taxes higher* [Online]. Available: www.latimes.com/features/printedition/magazine/la-tm-immmigration29jul20215420,1,7044553.story?coll=la-headlines-magazine-manual.
Edmonston, B., & Smith, J. (Eds.) (1997). *The new Americans: Economic, demographic, and fiscal effects of immigration* (prepublication edition). Washington: National Academy Press.
Eli Lilly & Co. (2004) Highlights [Online]. Available: http://www.lilly.com/about/highlights.html.
__________. (2004) History [Online]. Available: http://www.lilly.com/about/history.html.
Gregg, S. (2003/2004). Markets, morality, and civil society. *Intercollegiate Review,* 39 (Fall/Spring), 23-30.
Hoppe, H.-H. (2002). Natural order, the state, and the immigration problem. *Journal of Libertarian Studies,* 16, 1, 75-97.
Julian, L. (2002). *God is my CEO: Following God's principles in a bottom-line world.* Avon, Mass.: Adams Media.
Lindsell, H. (1982). *Free enterprise: A Judeo-Christian defense.* Wheaton, Ill.: Tyndale House Publishers.
Pearlstein, S. (2002). A bitter feud erupts over Hershey plant. *Washington Post* (September 2).
Preserving the integrity of Social Security numbers and preventing their misuse by terrorists and identity thieves, Hearings before the Subcomm. on Social Security of the House Comm. on Ways and Means and the Subcomm. on Immigration, Border Security, and Claims of the House Comm. on the Judiciary, 107th Cong., 2nd Sess. (statement of Matthew J. Reindl).
Roberts, P.C. (2004). *The jobs problem* [Online]. Available: www.chronicles-magazine.org/News/Roberts/NewsPCR011504.html.
Ryrie, C.C. (1978). *The Ryrie study Bible: New American standard translation.* Chicago: Moody Press.
Samuelson, R.J. (2003). Economic Darwinism. *Washington Post* (March 19).
Sartelle, J.P. (2003). Whatsoever you do. *Tabletalk* (July).
Schaeffer, F.A. (1982). *A Christian manifesto.* Westchester, Ill.: Crossway Books.
Skinner, A. (Ed.) (1974). *The wealth of nations.* Baltimore: Penguin Books.
Thurm, S. (2003). *Indian immigrants return home where software jobs await them* [Online]. Available: online.wsj.com/article/0,,SB10715311423454200,00.html.

PART IV

APPLICATIONS

B. Corporate Governance

Corporate Corruption: How the Theories of Reinhold Niebuhr and the Ethical Practices of Joseph Badaracco May Help Understand and Limit Corporate Corruption

James Cavill

We have all observed in recent years the destructive consequences of corporate corruption. After the unethical and/or illegal actions are exposed, they are followed by moral pronouncements from various sources and a rush to propose legislation supposedly to prevent such actions ever happening again. Unfortunately, these occur after the damage has been done. Corporations and lives are ruined, jobs and great financial losses occur.

I am interested in the attempt to empower individuals in corporate structures faced with unethical behavior by others to understand its cause, determine to act, and be able to pursue justice and proper behavior in a manner that saves both the organization from harm as well as the individuals involved.

The thesis of the paper is that the theories of Reinhold Niebuhr and the practical methodologies described by Michael Badaracco in his book Leading Quietly can improve our understanding of how corruption can develop in corporate structures as well as provide some methodology for employees who are attempting to deal with the unethical behavior of others in such situations.

The understanding we need to find encompasses the ideal of justice that Niebuhr regarded as one approximation of the law of love in a world in which perfect love always remains an "impossible possibility."

Niebuhr provides an understanding of the principles regarding the character of humanity and how this character operates within human structures. From the Gifford lectures, Niebuhr's analysis of sin, power balances and imbalances, and the pursuit of justice within the context of human sin is most applicable to our current corporate problems.

Badaracco is another form of ethical pragmatist. Badaracco proposes practical actions in the modern world designed to empower individuals in situations where the unethical holds sway over the ethical.

Corporate Corruption

There is no question that throughout the world and particularly in the United States, ethical issues have created crisis within a number of major corporations and industries.

We need only review the recent allegations and legal prosecutions involving some form of corporate corruption against individuals holding positions of trust within corporations or industries. This is a problem of serious dimensions. The destruction of WorldCom, Adelphi Corporation, and, of course, Enron Corporation due to financial corruption were only the most prominent.

In describing the mutual fund and securities industry, John Markham, business reporter for MSN Money, is quoted as saying that "there seems to be a culture of corruption in much of the mutual fund industry."[1] Mercer Bullard, a former Securities and Exchange Commission member is quoted as saying that "Half the industry is probably implicated in one way or another."[2]

The incidences of corporate corruption occur in new industries and old, financial and manufacturing, and vary from subtle manipulation for financial gain to outright theft.

Sadly, as a corporate vice president of Safety-Kleen Corp., a one and one-half billion dollar lubricants and solvent services company, I saw firsthand the destruction of this profitable and viable company. Following Safety-Kleen's hostile takeover by a subsidiary of a large Canadian corporation, within 18 months of the takeover, Safety-Kleen was in Chapter 11 bankruptcy. The three top officers sent to manage Safety-Kleen from the takeover company were indicted by the SEC for various fraudulent activities. One aspect of the culture prior to this bankruptcy was the institution of a culture of secrecy about the decisions and activities of the company.

The existence of these corporate practices causes widespread harm. In addition to the job loss and financial losses, many people now believe that neither corporations nor the stock market operate in the best interests of the average shareholder or individual. Cynicism extends to the whole corporate activity, not just those specifically engaged in illegal activities.

Reinhold Niebuhr

Two important aspects of Niebuhr's theories are particularly relevant to our question today. The first is the reaffirmation of the existence of sin, or evil and the nature of that evil. The second is the organization and structure of society and the existence of power relationships within human social structures resulting in the necessity for power equilibrium.[3]

The corporation is a product of the Enlightenment and the development of capitalism. The corporation is seen as a product of science and reason and a tool in the inevitable progress of man. Since the mid-19th century, the corporation has become more than an entity. Various legal expansions of the limited liability aspects of the corporation and the recognition of the corporation's right to operate as a person under the law have promoted the development of immense corporations capable of conducting business around the world. While much of this has contributed to the well-being of humanity, Niebuhr reminds us that:

> Since the dawn of modern history, the advances of science, the phenomenal increase of wealth and comfort which the applied sciences have made possible, the revolutionary changes in government and industry and the expansion of commerce to the point where it now in circles the globe... all these developments were conducive to the support of the renaissance of the spirit of human optimism. It is not easy to understand that the perennial problem of Man's existence in history, which is sin and evil, all will reappear in every level of historical achievement even when the changes in the condition of life are so great as to create the illusion that now conditions have eliminated the perennial problem of sin and evil. (Niebuhr, 1943, p. 181)

We should view the corporation as neither a demon to be destroyed nor a panacea for all problems, but as another part of human social history with potential for both virtues and vices.

For Niebuhr, the greatest sin is when persons take on the belief in self over belief in God, self-love. Niebuhr believed in the ability of the individual to give unselfish love, agape, but had no such belief when people formed into community of any form. Niebuhr believed that human structures could judge conduct that violated the principles of the brotherhood of man and the principles of justice in love. However, this form of judgment needed to understand that sin and evil grows, develops, and becomes more complex as structures, including corporations, develop, grow, and become more complex. (Niebuhr, 1943, p. 122)

Niebuhr strips modernism and the corporation of their uniqueness and their blind belief in eternal goodness and progress. The modern corporation is a product of the optimism within modernism combined with the development of commerce. From Niebuhr, we can conclude that the corporation will still bear within it the problem of sin arising out of man's nature, particularly man's nature as it operates in structures. We can also surmise that this problem will not be understood with the depth and power it requires.

For Niebuhr, power was the ultimate governing element in community. While roundly criticized for this belief, Niebuhr's belief serves our purposes. Niebuhr wrote that "no human community is, in short, a simple construction of conscience and reason. All communities were more or less precarious harmonies of vital human capacity. They are governed by power." (Idem, p. 255) There are two aspects to power for Niebuhr: the coercive and organizing power of government, and a balance of the vitalities and forces in any given social situation. These two aspects of power are known as "the central organizing principle" and the "equilibrium of power principle." (Idem, p. 257) For Niebuhr, no moral or social advance can redeem society from its dependence on these two principles. There is always some tension between the two. For Niebuhr, the spiritual and physical faculties of man are able to create endless varieties of types and combinations of power from that of pure reason to that of pure physical force.

Corruption of organizations, including corporations, arises, for Niebuhr, from two power issues, which place human brotherhood in peril. The first of these is the will to dominate, which results in imperialism or slavery; the second is when interests come in conflict with interests and mutual dependence is destroyed. For our study of the corporation, Niebuhr would have us understand that the corporation is simply another structure representing human power relationships, which brings within it the existence of sin as much as it brings ethical morality.

For us and for Niebuhr, the concern is with the relation of the structure of justice and the various forms of communal organization, including the corporation, to the principal of brotherhood. For any hope of accomplishing this, there must be a balance between the forces of organization and the forces of change. The key for Niebuhr is that distortions of power lead to injustice. Niebuhr wrote "The domination of one's structure, or vitality, by another is avoided most successfully by equilibrium of powers and vitalities. With this equilibrium weakness does not invite enslavement by the strong."(Idem, p. 265) Lack of this equilibrium is the problem in many of the corporate scandals. Without equilibrium, no moral or social restraints are possible.

The development of equilibrium is a "principle of justice" insofar as it prevents domination and enslavement. But the principal of equilibrium can also be a principle of anarchy and conflict if unresolved tensions exist too long. Domination or enslavement, terms describing the extremes of control, as well as unresolved tensions, will exist as power imbalances within corporate structures as a tendency for decision makers to be able to operate without ethical checks and balances.

Using Enron as an example of this, both the Arthur Anderson accounting firm and the legal firm of Wilson and Elkins of Enron had provided an accounting and legal approval to the special entities which individuals had used to gain great personal profit, but which eventually led to the destruction of the company. Both firms made such decisions while in a disequilibrium of power with the Enron management. Both Arthur Anderson and Wilson and Elkins had been co-opted by the large retainers and fees granted by the very same people seeking approval of the special entities. The existence of self-love and the presence of power imbalances destroyed the company.

We would like to believe that sin and evil do not exist or are psychological aberrations or bad education. Niebuhr has us understand that human beings sin and can do evil in varying forms and degrees. Thus the structures developed by humankind will contain individuals and groups who can commit evil, not just isolated groups, but most human structures. Whatever the motivations expressed, sin will arise from an excess of self-love, of human beings' placing themselves before God. There will be a lack of humility and critical self-awareness and understanding of their place in creation.[4]

Niebuhr's solution to the problems of power and disequilibrium was government acting as "an organizing center." (Niebuhr, 1943, p. 269) Niebuhr knew that government power could be abused, but for Niebuhr the state was divinely recognized and abuses could be curbed in a democratic society. I disagree. Government in our modern democratic state can contain its own inertia without resorting to abuses. While government will play an important role, it must be less than Niebuhr envisioned. Governments are much more process oriented and are subject, in our modern era, to subtle abuses by interest groups, which create imbalances of power or paralysis, which destroys equilibrium.

Governments can also develop laws attempting to set boundaries in social organizations, including corporations. For example, in the United States under the Sarbanes-Oxley Act, the Securities and Exchange Commission has brought in regulations on the conduct of the Board of Directors and, as noted by the commission, "The principle and aims of Sarbanes-Oxley is to strengthen the responsibilities of lawyers as gatekeepers."[5]

While I am sure these regulations will catch some crimes and prevent others, they do not deal with human sin as part of the attempt to balance the equilibrium of power within the structure. They impose a process from without. The laws create more emphasis on the status quo creating an overemphasis on the organization of power, but will permit few vitalities and new groups to be able to rapidly expand and develop and nurture the corporations' growth. This leads to timidity and stultification. Niebuhr himself said that "The place of the law tended to destroy vital elements in segments of society in the name of order." (Niebuhr, 1943, p. 268)

Let us now look at one alternative methodology that originates within the body of the organization experiencing some form of unethical behavior.

Leading Quietly

There must be the opportunity for change in ethical human conduct itself, which will correspond to the needs expressed by Niebuhr for equilibrium and justice. The most successful changes could be engendered within the organization itself by increasing the ability of individuals within the corporate structure to influence ethical behavior or correct unethical behavior. I like one idea for these changes, which is found in Joseph Badaracco's *Leading Quietly*.[6]

The significance of this book is that it is an attempt to provide a methodology for individuals to use within organizations to create ethical change. As such, it utilizes the understanding of power structures within organizations as provided by Niebuhr and combines it with a desire for individuals to act ethically and forcefully in the face of unethical or questionable behavior by more powerful entities within the organization.

Badaracco deals with the strategy and tactics of an individual in an immediate ethical crisis. Badaracco observes that "the most effective leaders are rarely public heroes...They don't spearhead ethical crusades. They moved patiently, carefully and incrementally. They do what is right for their organizations, for the people around them and for themselves inconspicuously and without casualties." (Idem, p 8.) Badaracco does not deny the necessity for heroes and great people but essentially is concerned with the unsung, non-heroes of our society who get things done. Badaracco believes that many big problems can only be resolved by a long series of small efforts. Quiet leadership often turns out to be the quickest way to make an organization and the world a better place.

In the pyramid structure of life, great figures occupy only a small portion of the top. The great majority of people are in the middle. They do their work, act responsibly, and take care of the people around them. Quiet Leadership emerges when someone, typically a manager in an organization, faces a difficult ethical challenge and resolves it in a practical, responsible way. These quiet leaders transcend the world in that they refuse to accept unethical behavior or behavior destructive to the organization. They do not place themselves on a superior ground, based upon some presumed understanding of a more perfect order. They recognize some need within themselves to act, but the quiet leader also recognizes that situations have moral ambiguity. They consider all the aspects of the issue including their own personal wants and needs. Badaracco predicts that individuals in difficult situations should expect their motives to be mixed and confused and these may be useful in dealing with the problem. (Idem, p. 18)

Badaracco offers solid advice in a number of specific areas. Each chapter of the book is involved in some tactical aspect that an individual utilizes when attempting to change the situation. Individuals attempting to stop or mitigate unethical behavior must learn to drill down into the technical and political aspects of the situation searching for imaginative ways to bend the existing rules, not break them, while understanding how to compromise ethically for the prevention of greater destruction. It is important for the individuals seeking to solve an ethical problem in this way to move gradually and seek these compromises when necessary. (Idem, p. 80)

It is important in *Leading Quietly* to understand that small, incremental steps with careful analysis at each step are the heart of the system. Badaracco notes, "The vast majority of difficult, important human problems—both inside and outside organizations—are not solved by a swift, decisive stroke from someone at the top. What usually matters are careful, thoughtful, small, practical efforts by people working far from the limelight. In short, quiet leadership is what moves and changes the world." (Idem, p. 9)

Finally, Badaracco discusses the three quiet virtues that are required for an individual to utilize quiet leadership properly. People with these virtues will use the tools responsibly and effectively. As with Niebuhr, human nature counts. Badaracco agrees. He states it is necessary to "look beyond what quiet leaders do and see who they are." (Idem, p. 170) The virtues of restraint, modesty, and tenacity are characteristics of individuals who utilize quiet leadership in a responsible manner.

Proper interpretation of the rules of quiet leadership is vital. Rules are not made to be broken. A compromise reached, when necessary, must not be a sellout of basic principles. The guidelines for quiet, ethical leadership are not excuses for doing nothing or taking improper shortcuts. Badaracco notes: "There are times when a direct course of action is clear, when compromises betray important values, and when leadership means taking a stand and paying the price. The quiet leaders understand that some situations require direct and forceful courageous action and a few even call for heroism. It is critical to have a sense of when and how the tools of quiet leadership should be used and to understand their limits and risks." (Idem. p. 8) In recognizing an ethical problem, understanding it and taking careful, intelligent actions, both the individual's moral center and the organization remain intact.

Conclusion

In their own way, both Niebuhr and Badaracco are pragmatic problem solvers who seek to illuminate our understanding of the nature of humanity and its structures. Both authors seek to allow for change within the context of an ethical sense of justice and rightness. As we see corporations destroyed by corrupt behavior, we hope that individuals can accept the hard concept of sin and evil existing in the dynamic of power relationships within corporate organizations. This recognition will provide a specific spur to both the recognition of unethical behavior as well as a spur to act against it.

From Badaracco, our acceptance of a pragmatic, ethically-based methodology to begin the process of correcting unethical behavior can only be advancement in bringing ethical behavior to unethical practices.

If someone in Enron Corporation could have understood what the ethical implications were of the off-the-books entities and had been able to utilize a process and methodology as described by Badaracco within the corporate structure early enough to prevent their formation, there is the chance that the thousands of employees who lost their life savings and their jobs might, just might, be still happily employed.

Notes

1. Markham, J. (2003). *How Mutual Funds Stole Your Money,* (Online) Available: http//www.msn/com/money/11/12/2003,1.
2. Ballard, quoted in Markham, 2.
3. Niebuhr, R. (1943). *The Nature and Destiny of Man, Volume 2, The Destiny of Man,* From the Gifford Lectures, New York: Charles Scribner's Sons, 157.
4. Niebuhr, R. (1941). *The Nature and Destiny of Man, Volume 2, The Nature of Man,* From the Gifford Lectures, New York: Charles Scribner's Sons, 261.
5. Rubin, S. (2003). SEC's New Foot Soldiers, *The New York Times, Legal Post,* November 12, 2003, Quote from William Donaldson, Chairman of the Securities and Exchange Commission, 2.
6. Badarocco, J.L. (2002) *Leading Quietly,* Boston: Harvard Business School Press, 3.

Bibliography

Badaracco, J.L. (2002). *Leading quietly*. Boston: Harvard Business School Press.

Markham, J. (2003). *How mutual funds stole your money.* [Online] Available: http//www.msn./com/money/11/12/2003

Niebuhr, R. [1941] (1964). *The nature and destiny of man. Volume 1: The nature of man.* From the Gifford Lectures, New York: Charles Scribner's Sons.

Niebuhr, R. [1943] (1964). *The nature and destiny of man. Volume 2: The destiny of man.* From the Gifford Lectures, New York: Charles Scribner's Sons.

Rubin, S. (2003). SEC's new foot soldiers. *New York Times, Legal Post,* November 12, 2003. Quote from William Donaldson, Chairman of the Securities and Exchange Commission.

Corporate Social Responsibility: A Traditional Catholic Perspective

Alejandro Antonio Chafuen

The moral and legal obligations of those who are involved in business have been studied from very early ages. The late scholastics (13th-16th centuries) wrote volumes about the duties of the businessperson (Chafuen, 2003). Their analyses of business practices differed little from their analysis of any other interaction between two human beings. The emergence of the notion of the modern corporation created new questions. In this paper, I work with traditional concepts of the corporation, the social, and the meaning of responsibility. It brings the three concepts together, using them to build a model to develop meaningful indicators, and lists seven principles of Corporate Social Responsibility. Although the analysis can be helpful for those working within other traditional Judeo-Christian frameworks, the paper is framed within a Roman Catholic tradition.

The Corporation

Seen as the greatest invention by some and pilloried by others as promoting irresponsible behavior, the notion of the corporation is at the center of the Corporate Social Responsibility (CSR) debate in the developed world. The Corporation has been evolving through centuries. By limiting the risks of investors, it encouraged the pooling of resources and increased the incentives for risk taking in creative activity, revolutionizing production as no other effort of human interaction. As this is a topic that has global dimensions, we need to be aware that the reality, if not the notion, of the corporation is very different in other parts of the world.

Of the great moralists of the 20th century, Oswald Von Nell-Breuning, S.J., is one of the most influential amongst those who studied the corporation. In his analysis of joint-stock companies, he warned about the dangers of severing the link between ownership and management and the weakening of the sense of responsibility. Notwithstanding, Nell-Breuning acknowledged that abolishing limited responsibility, anonymous societies, would lead "very likely to even greater immorality and corruption" (Utz, 1964, p. 323).

Nevertheless, thinkers from different ideological perspectives continue to express their doubts. Matthew Fox, who carries considerable weight among the religious left, attacks the principle of "limited responsibility" as a major cause behind the "lack" of corporate social responsibility. Irving Kristol, a leading voice of the "neo-conservative" movement in the United States of America, argued that "the trouble with the large corporation today is that it does not possess a clear theoretical—i.e., ideological—legitimacy" (Barry, 1998, pp. xii-xiii).

Robert Hessen has been one of the most consistent defenders of the corporation. In his words:

> The essence of capitalism is the inviolability of individual rights, including one's right to use or invest one's wealth as one chooses, and one's right to associate with others for any peaceful purpose and under any terms of association that are acceptable to all parties concerned. (Hessen, 1979, p. xiii)

He accepts the legitimacy of giving limited liability for some but not for all. Those who have strategic control of the assets should be liable for all the potential harm they might do. Hessen criticized those who use the legal figure of the corporation as a shield for their action. Nevertheless, most CSR activism is not directed against these "fake" corporations, but against public corporations with deep pockets involved in non-politically correct products or services.

Man's responsibility to his neighbor precedes the existence of the state. They precede even family bonds. It is sufficient for two people to meet, even by chance and for a few moments, for new duties to arise. (Balmes, [1846-1850] 1944, p. 144.)[1]

Father Balmes uses an example that can be turned into a business case. A group of sailors, who jointly own a ship, encounter a shipwrecked person. The duty to help is a human duty. They could have a policy for their enterprise to aid shipwrecked persons, yet, even if they don't, each of the sailors would have the right to use elements that belong to the corporation, say life-preservers, to fulfill their responsibility.

Hessen (1979, p. 41) writes that "The rights of any organization or association, including corporations, are the rights it derives from the individuals who create and sustain it." The same can be said about their duties and responsibilities. In traditional Christian ethics, individuals have the duty to be socially responsible. It does not follow automatically that groups of people, or their organizations, also need to be socially responsible. But it makes sense. Hessen cautioned that:

> People rightly fear that corporations, alone or in clusters, can exercise political power and manipulate the government in order to obtain special favors and privileges at the expense both of other companies and of consumers . . . There is no justification for allowing any private individual or business organization, including corporations of any size, to achieve its goals by means of political power. (Hessen, 1979, p. 111)

Hessen argues that "Corporations should not be absolved from any of the responsibilities or liabilities that apply to individuals or to other organizations, either business or nonbusiness," and his conclusion is completely consistent with traditional ethics: "The proper principle of liability should be that whoever controls a business, *regardless of its legal form,* should be personally liable for the torts of agents and employees." (Hessen, 1979, p. 20)

The Social

If the notion of the corporation needs clarification, so does the concept of the "social." While some abuse the term to mean their own view of what is beneficial to the commonwealth, a narrow school of individualist writers negate the social dimension of human beings. This was not the case of some of the great champions of the free society such as Von Mises, who used the term "social cooperation" to describe the essence of the market economy. Henry Hazlitt, while preferring the term "mutualism," sided with Mises: "Because *social cooperation* is the great means of achieving nearly all our ends, this means can be thought of as itself the moral goal to be achieved." (Hazlitt, [1964] 1998, p. 356)

F.A. Hayek wrote an important essay where he described the abuse suffered by the term. He would accept only two uses for the term social: one as meaning "peculiar to society" or "arising out of a specifically social process." In that sense, he wrote that "**we have an urgent need for the word.**" (Hayek, 1967, p. 242). The other is "when 'social' is used in the sense of 'serving the interests of society'" to which Hayek concludes "it certainly raises a problem, but provides no solution." (Hayek, 1967, p. 243)

As the term has been so abused, Hayek tried to avoid it as much as possible. He would have asked "what is different between corporate responsibility and corporate *social* responsibility?" If people would have a clear notion of the social aspect of the human person, I would agree 100 percent with him, and would gladly join in a crusade to avoid the word. But, as people do not have a clear meaning of the social dimension of human action, I choose to retain it, work with the "language market" and use the term in the same ways accepted by Hayek.

CSR should be regarded as a topic of social ethics. Social ethics distinguishes the reciprocal ties between persons in relation to the common good. The common good is the set of conditions and legal frameworks that are conducive to the healthy development of the human person. The social moralist question is if a particular institution is fulfilling its natural function in civil society. It also asks how those responsible, in order to seek the common good, should distribute rights and duties among the members of that institution (Utz, 1964, pp. 361-362).

The existence of the "social" creates special questions. Why not pollute where there are no rules or there is no enforcement? Why not define the period of profit maximization as five years and therefore be ready to bribe and blackmail to obtain privileged conditions?

Another topic that creates confusion is the analysis of CSR from the point of view of social justice. True social justice is a justice *that goes beyond court - room justice: the efforts of civil society to help build a just social order* (Chafuen, 1985). A false concept of social justice: *taking from the "rich" to give to the poor,* is much more prevalent today. CSR should be seen as the efforts of the corporations in favor of true social justice. As the term of social justice is even more equivocal than social responsibility, I seldom use it, even in its appropriate meaning.

As the human person is a social being, the need for solidarity is essential for preserving the free society. It is needed to reduce inequality before the law, and the unjust inequalities that result from governments privileging the few at the expense of the many, who are kept satisfied with populist policies.

Responsibility

The notion of responsibility is essential for the free society. The word comes from the Latin word for *responding, answering.* It is always the person who, as an individual or as a representative of a corporation, should know what he or the corporation should be accountable for. Some CSR campaigns end up by weakening personal responsibility. Responsibility presupposes freedom. "The first striking mark which distinguishes moral values from all other personal values is the fact that man is held responsible for them" (Von Hildebrand, [1953] 1972, p. 171). The *Catechism* states that "Freedom makes man responsible for his acts to the extent that they are voluntary" (*Catechism* #1734). It further adds that "imputability and responsibility for an action can be diminished or even nullified by ignorance, inadvertence, duress, fear, habit, inordinate attachments, and other psychological or social factors" (*Catechism* #1735). These statements also apply to the human person acting in a corporate environment and to corporations as such.

What is the difference between personal and corporate responsibility?

The corporation, being composed by different persons, does not have a conscience. One could speak of a "culture" or an "ethos" in a corporation. Yet those responsible for a corporation should try to pay attention to the views of those who are members. It is possible to argue that the more a corporation is owned, or led, by a single member of a family, the more CSR will mirror PSR (Personal Social Responsibility).[2]

Defining the limits of responsibility is "one of the most difficult in ethics" (Hazlitt, [1964] 1998, p. 192). Hayek, concerned that the notion of social responsibility was weakening personal responsibility, wrote that "The essential condition of responsibility is that it refer to circumstances that the individual can judge . . .without too much strain of the imagination" (Hayek, 1960, p. 83). It is still an open question if the current CSR movement will help define the limits of responsibility, or create more confusion.

Responsible entrepreneurs don't have easy answers, as Francois Michelin wrote "The head of the business has to navigate in a fog of uncertainty. He is forced to take action in real life circumstances, and that is precisely where the problem lies" (Michelin, 2003, p. 61). A safe rule is to apply to corporate responsibility the principles of personal responsibility. When "somebody acts with a bad intention, then he is held responsible" (Von Hildebrand, [1953] 1972, p. 171); "in order to prove that a person is not to be held responsible for something, we need only show that it was beyond the sphere of his free influence" (Von Hildebrand, [1953] 1972, p. 172). We should apply these same principles in most cases of persons acting on behalf of corporations.

Solidarity

The principle of solidarity should guide persons and corporations. Also articulated in terms of "friendship" or "social charity," is a direct demand of human and Christian brotherhood. "Solidarity is manifested in the first place by the distribution of goods and remuneration for work. It also presupposes the effort for a more just social order where tensions are better able to be reduced and conflicts more readily settled by negotiation" (*Catechism* #1940). Solidarity has a personal, national, and international dimension. "International solidarity is a requirement of the moral order; world peace depends in part upon this" (*Catechism* #1941).

CSR touches upon all of these, and other issues mentioned in points 1940 and 1941 of the *Catechism*. One needs to keep in mind, however, that as Karol Wojtyla, who later became John Paul II, wrote, solidarity does not mean having to agree with current regulations. Quoting Wojtyla,

> [O]pposition is not inconsistent with solidarity. The one who voices his opposition to the general or particular regulations of the community does not thereby reject his membership; he does not withdraw his readiness to act and to work for the common good.

And he adds,

> It would be too easy to quote endless examples of people who contest—and thus adopt the attitude of opposition—because of their deep concern for the common good (e.g., parents may disagree with the educational system or its methods because their views concerning the education of their children differ from those of the educational authorities). (Wojtyla, [1969] 1979, p. 286)

If we follow Wojtyla's argument, persons, acting on their own, or as stewards of a corporation, could be acting in a socially responsible way when opposing public education, an animal rights agenda, or a particular position on climate change. One would be hard-pressed to find any CSR activist today calling for opposition to any of the above causes.

The Corporation, Not the Same in All Places

The prevalence of the limited liability public corporation as a major legal structure for the world of production in developed economies, such as that of the United States, gave birth to the notion of Corporate Social Responsibility as a "topic" and also to the *modus operandi* of the activists. In most parts of the world, businesses are owned or controlled by a single family and usually by a single person. The Spanish term for CSR is Business Social Responsibility (or *responsabilidad social empresaria,* where *empresa* refers to "enterprise" or "business."). While in emerging economies CSR analysis is "imported" from the developed world, the empirical analysis focuses more on business and even "family business" responsibility.

In most of the less developed world, the "person" of the corporation is a completely different being from the one that exists in the United States. Those who control management seldom respect minority ownership rights, even when they are family members. I have yet to find a serious study on CSR that takes this radical difference in consideration.

Some of the best books on CSR coming from other cultures, such as that of Méndez Rivas (2003), emphasize the efforts conducted by the families who own the businesses on behalf of their staff and society at large: efforts that go beyond their contractual obligations. CSR is, in those cases, nothing more than the responsible behavior of owners who chose to benefit segments of society above and beyond the narrow needs of their business.

The huge differences in corporate governance and ownership in other parts of the world is aptly described, and with abundant empirical research, in *Corporate Governance in Development: The experiences of Brazil, Chile, India, and South Africa* (Oman, Charles P. Ed., 2003). The situation is especially problematic in South America where "ownership concentration and the quasi-absolutist exercise of power by family/controlling shareholders is a fundamental characteristic of Brazilian corporate governance structures" (Oman, 2003, p. 66).

As very few have the chance to become stockholders of those enterprises, the activities of those who wish to influence them to act in a certain way toward social goals and institutions are very different from those in the United States. They put pressure not as stockholders, but as "stakeholders" and especially as customers. In countries with weak rule of law, CSR activists might try to use corrupt officials to further their cause, but so could the businessman to overbid them in buying bureaucrats.

Becoming Owners to Promote CSR

CSR is strongest in countries with developed capital markets. People of different ideologies try to buy sufficient shares of companies in order to influence their behavior according to their notions of CSR. But to attract resources to their cause, they need to have a policy based on a list of actions deemed socially responsible. The Christian Brothers religious order, for example, is practicing what it preaches on transparency when listing its do's and don'ts of the investment policy it uses to manage a $4 billion portfolio. Most of the guidelines, such as not investing in companies that produce artificial birth control products, are completely consistent with traditional Roman Catholic ethics. Other policies, such as not investing in companies that manufacture tobacco products, while being open to investing in companies that produce pornographic material as long as it does not represent more than 50% of their sales, seem more curious. Even today, in the Social Doctrine of the Catholic Church and in its Catechism, production and consumption of tobacco and alcoholic products have no special condemnation. Only its abuse and over-consumption does. Traditional Christians are much more condemning of pornography, yet this is not the case for the Christian Brothers.

The Need to Develop Indicators

Some of the conflictive issues of CSR will never be settled as there will always be strong differences in people's opinion on religious, social, and legal issues. There is, however, a profusion of anecdotal arguments in the CSR debate. In order to come with sound ethical and religious principles on CSR there is a need to develop proper indicators.

In Japan, Integrex, a Tokyo-based independent research firm, provides CSR rankings focusing on corporate integrity, ethics compliance, and transparency. Integrex sends questionnaires to approximately 3,600 listed companies in Japan, of which 877 have qualified for CSR evaluation. MHCi, another company, produces a different index that takes into account 50 different indicators. It works globally, and has analyzed the largest 100 companies in the U.K. In Europe, ASPI Eurozone® is one of the most widely used indicators.

As with any new index, time, improved analysis, and refinements will help separate the good indices from the bad. Huge volatility in the measurements, or lack of useful correlations, should encourage us to look for ways to refine them. Are the weaknesses the result of weak logic, weak inputs, or a weak rule of law?

Recent scandals at Enron and Shell, companies that promoted the concept of CSR, and might have scored well in the eyes of some activists, show that there is still much to learn when trying to measure CSR.

As a guide to develop, or judge CSR indexes, I developed the following model in a table format. It could also be developed as a function of the type: CSR=$F(n, x, y, z)$, where CSR is a function of the nature of the business (n), the actions and impact in its relationship with the internal players (x, or first degree of responsibility), external players (y, second degree of responsibility), and the far removed players (z, third degree of responsibility).

Table 1: The Different Degrees of Responsibility

n	**First degree of responsibility (x)**	**Second degree of responsibility (y)**	**Third degree of responsibility (z)**
Nature of Business: (some businesses are involved in products deemed anti-social)	Internal players: a) shareholders b) staff		
		External players: a) customers b) suppliers c) creditors d) government authorities e) neighbors	
			Far removed players: a) beginning of supply chain b) "downstream" product impact c) "Planet"

A few examples might help explain this model.

The Nature of the Business (n)

Take the case of a business that has as its main activity the production of good and services that are deemed anti-social. It is well known that "drug lords" have been very generous with local communities, but no matter how "socially responsible" they are with their profits, few would rank them high in a social responsibility index. But one does not need such extreme; those who evaluate CSR and are convinced that killing babies in wombs is bad would never give a good CSR grade to Planned Parenthood, or other abortion providers. On the other hand, extreme environmentalists, guided by a narrow definition of sustainable development, would regard oil companies that are based on fossil fuel exploration and extraction (an unsustainable activity) as irredeemable. Even from the point of view of traditional Christian ethics, the topic of the *nature* of the activity is not so easy to deal with. There is a passage in the scriptures, that of the unfaithful administrator, where part of the message is to "make good use of ill-gotten gains." (Luke 16:9)[3] The case of the Christian Brothers mentioned above, where they have harsher policies against the sellers of tobacco than pornography is a case in point about how difficult it is to come up with CSR guidelines even for people who share fundamental principles.

First Degree of Responsibility (x)

I contend that to be truly socially responsible, a corporation first needs to behave responsibly with its most intimate society: the owners, or shareholders, and the workers. **In simple terms, the social function of a business can only be fulfilled if it produces more than what it consumes.** The main responsibility toward owners and staff is that of respecting all just contracts. In traditional moral philosophy, this would pertain to commutative justice. There is an area, however, that pertains to distributive justice: the rules that determine how much each participant gets from goods held in joint ownership. There are no simple rules of commutative justice for determining dividends, giving key jobs to family members, and prizes and rewards to management. As a result, many owners have been victims of injustice by controlling managers.

One can provide many examples, both from private and public companies. Royal Dutch/Shell Company, for example, which has been championing CSR and ranked high by many for its "socially responsible" donations, had its top management faking its accounts of known oil reserves. The magnitude of their falsity dwarfed all their combined donations throughout their history. Apart from the legal aspects, such accounting fraud is socially irresponsible.

Second Degree of Responsibility (y)

Once a company fulfils its obligations to its intimate society, it has to fulfill its responsibility toward external players: customers, suppliers, creditors, government authorities, and neighbors. In different degrees, all these players are relevant to the profitability of the corporation. As with x, the first rule is to comply with all the just laws and contracts. But as the number of people impacted by the corporation grows, the more one needs to take into account other factors. Not seeking government privileges, for example, can in many circumstances, be seen as going against profits, owners, and workers. Nevertheless, for society as a whole, seeking privileges can be detrimental to all. Customers, suppliers, creditors, government authorities, and neighbors also interact with many other businesses, and the self-centered behavior of a corporation can affect external players in a detrimental fashion.

Third Degree of Responsibility (*z*)

This last level of responsibility, at least according to my reading of traditional ethics is, curiously, one that dominates the discussion of CSR. How the activities of a corporation might be affecting "the planet" gets more attention in many cases than defrauding staff and shareholders. A company that buys sugar from a middleman or a cooperative is asked to ascertain than no child labor is used to plant or harvest the product. In the same manner, if someone uses a product of a corporation in a manner not intended by the seller, by nature of the use or by its abuse, then the CSR inquisitors flock to them with their attacks. Sniffing glue to get a "high," or over-consumption of alcohol, tobacco, or hamburgers, are good examples.

I am not aiming at negating the importance of "far removed" players by regarding them as third in the line of responsibility. Due to the nature of its production process, a corporation involved in nuclear energy, for example, has to be concerned with the impact of its operation on the planet. If people are using a product I produce in an anti-social manner, it is a matter of human decency, essential to social responsibility, that I try to do something to mitigate the problem, even if it affects profits. And if in the early stages of my supply chain, we find abuses to human rights or criminal endeavors, I should be concerned and evaluate the impact on society, and not just on profits. Public corporations should also be concerned.

In addition, all the players mentioned here (x, y, z) and not only the internal players (x), help, through civil society, to establish the rules of the game that make profits, and the social function of the corporation, possible.

Conclusion

It is clear in my analysis that I do not find anything wrong in the concept of CSR itself. I find many things wrong with current notions of the corporation, responsibility, and the "social."

Is there any hope that we will gain in better understanding of CSR? If one has to judge by the preponderance of CSR efforts which are actually a weakly veiled attempt to attack the free enterprise system, one would be tempted to arrive at a pessimistic conclusion. For each serious student of the topic, there are hundreds who approach the issue for a spurious motive.

I think, nevertheless, that the emergence of indicators will help make the debate more serious. The major area for potential improvement is in less-developed countries and will depend on the emergence of a rule of law based on limited government and respect for private property. Corporations can play a positive or an obstructionist role in this regard. In all likelihood, their corporate behavior will depend on the nature of their comparative advantage. If they depend on privilege, they will likely act as obstructionists; if they are fair competitors, they will play a positive role. Many will be in the middle.

Those who are concerned with CSR are rightly concerned about corruption. Indicators of economic freedom and corruption, for example, clearly show that free-markets are a major deterrent of corruption (Chafuen and Guzman, 1999; Gregg and Schenone, 2004). Advocates of CSR, especially corporations, should do all in their power to promote the free enterprise system, so I share the bewilderment of Rev. Robert Sirico:

> Even more puzzling than the anti-capitalist bias among the clergy is the bias found among capitalists themselves. In misguided attempts to achieve a high level of "social responsibility" for their companies, some business leaders have succumbed to false views of the marketplace. While creating wealth for society through their successful businesses, they simultaneously support causes antithetical to economic growth, free enterprise, and human liberty. Why does the rhetoric of "corporate social responsibility" seem to have such an anti-capitalistic bias? (Sirico, 2001, p. 15)

It will be up to those who work in the field of social and economic studies, and those who aim for the moral high ground by basing their recommendations on truth, to be effective in their pressure for corporate behavior that is truly social and respectful of human dignity.

With such divergent views about what constitutes social behavior as those that exist for example, in the guidelines used by Christian, and others, on corporate behavior on issues of family and health, can there be an agreement on some aspects of CSR? The following seven CSR principles might provide some direction:

- Say "no" to privilege seeking
- Practice impeccable accounting
- Be careful in choosing partners
- Be meticulous in the observance of just laws
- Promote protection and enhancement of just laws
- Begin by being responsible with workers, clients, and yourself
- Pay attention to all owners, not only to the most vocal

Several of these principles depend on the understanding of some of the terms used, such as the concept of "just" law, which due to the space assigned to this essay, can't be dealt with here. But for those who are familiar with traditional social doctrine, especially Roman Catholic doctrine, the meaning is clear.

Samuel Gregg (2001), one of the most lucid experts of Catholic Social Thought, has written that:

> The emergence of stakeholder theory illustrates that boards of directors as well as executives must have some consciousness of the direction and character of public policy debates. This will require a more active engagement with the world of ideas on the part of corporate leaders, not least because the promotion of stakeholder notions such as 'corporate social responsibility' and 'ethical investment' has spawned an unprecedented debate about ethics and corporate life. Yet when it comes to developing a sound moral ecology within corporations, there is no substitute for abiding by long-established conventions, observance of the rule of law, and an enhancing of understanding of nature of ethics.

Unless we move in the direction pointed by Gregg, much of what it passes as CSR will actually be corporate anti-social behavior. Without moral clarity, and a solid understanding of business and economic reality, CSR will become a good sounding but empty word.

Notes

1. *Antes de examinar los derechos y deberes que se fundan en el orden social conviene advertir que independientemente de toda reunión en sociedad, y hasta de los vínculos de familia, tiene el hombre obligaciones con respecto a sus semejantes. Basta que dos individuos se encuentren, aunque por casualidad y por breves momentos, para que nazcan derechos y deberes conformes a las circunstancias.* (Balmes [1848-50], 1944)
2. Pompeo Piva argues that there is a strong connection between individual responsibility and "social" responsibility. "Individual responsibility by its own nature, tends to produce a communion of responsibility: it is a journey, in a sense, from the *me* to the *we*, not to the *we* of the organic community of pre-modern era, but the *we* of the post-modern solidarious community in which one assumes freely his responsibility. The moral norm is the fruit of the community of responsibility." (Piva 2004, 79)
3. "And I tell you, make friends for yourselves by means of unrighteous mammon, so that when it fails they may receive you into the eternal habitations." Or more direct in Latin, *"Et ego vobis dico: Facite vobis amicos de mammona iniquitatis, ut, cum defecerit, recipient vos in aeterna tabernacula."* (Luke 16:9) (The Navarre Bible, 1998)

Bibliography

Balmes, J. [1848-50] (1944). *Curso de filosofía elemental.* Barcelona: Balmesiana.

Barry, N. (1998). *Business ethics.* London: Macmillan.

Chafuen, A. A. (2003). *Faith and liberty.* Lanham: Lexington Books.

Chafuen, A. A. (1985). Justicia distributiva en La Escolástica Tardía. *Estudios Públicos,* Santiago, Chile, *18,* 5-20 [Online]. Available: www.cepchile.cl/dms/archivo_796_979/rev18_chafuen.pdf

Chafuen, A., & Guzmán, E. (1999). In: O'Driscoll, Holmes and Kirkpatrick (Eds.), *Economic Freedom and Corruption.* In 2000 *Index of Economic Freedom,* Washington, D.C.: The Heritage Foundation-Wall Street Journal. Spanish version [Online]. Available: http://www.atlas.org.ar/economia/chafuen_guzman.asp

Gregg, S. (2001). *Corporate obligations should reflect stakeholders' best interests* [Online]. Available: http://www.onlineopinion.com.au/view.asp?article=1342

Gregg S., & Schenone O. (2004). *A theory of corruption.* Grand Rapids: Acton Institute.

Hayek, F.A. (1967). *Studies in philosophy, politics and economics.* Chicago: The University of Chicago Press.

Hayek, F.A. (1960). *The constitution of liberty.* Chicago: The University of Chicago Press.

Hazlitt, H. [1967] (1998). *The foundations of morality.* Irvington-on-Hudson: The Foundation for Economic Education.

Hessen, R. (1979). *In defense of the corporation.* Stanford: Hoover Institution Press.

Méndez Rivas, Charo 2003, *Responsabilidad Social de Empresarios y Empresas en Venezuela durante el Siglo XX,* Caracas: Strategos Consultores.

Michelin, F. (2003). *And why not? Morality and business.* Lanham: Lexington Books.

Novak, M. (1996). *Business as a calling: Work and the extended life.* New York: Free Press.

Oman, C. P. et al. (Eds.). 2003 *Corporate governance in development: The experiences of Brazil, Chile, India, and South Africa.* Washington: CIPE-OECD.

Piva, P. (2004). *Sogno un imprenditore cristiano,* Milano-Genova: Marietti.

Sirico, R. (2001). *The entrepreneurial vocation.* Grand Rapids: Acton Institute.

Utz, A. F. [1958] (1964). *Etica social.* Barcelona: Editorial Herder.

Von Hildebrand, D. [1953] (1972). *Ethics.* Chicago: Franciscan Herald Press.

Wojtyla, K. [1969] (1979). *The acting person.* Trans. Andrzej Potocki. Dordrecht: D. Reidel Publishing Company.

___________ (1994). *Catechism of the Catholic Church.* United States Catholic Conference, Inc. Libreria Editrice Vaticana.

___________ (1998). *The Navarre Bible.* Dublin, Ireland: Four Courts Press.

Natural Law and the Fiduciary Duties of Business Managers

Joseph F. Johnston, Jr.

"...the laws of commerce ... are the laws of nature, and consequently the laws of God."
Edmund Burke, 1795

Introduction

The news media in recent years have been filled with stories of business scandals involving massive failures of corporate governance. These failures reflect widespread deviation from traditional ethical and legal standards on the part of the directors and officers who manage corporate affairs. Investigations of the derelictions underlying recent corporate disasters have uncovered startling examples of fraud, self-dealing, and neglect.

These episodes have raised once again two fundamental questions: to what standards should managers be held, and what are the historical and conceptual bases for these standards? In this paper, I hope to show that the legal standards applicable to managerial behavior are traceable to deeply rooted moral standards; and that these fundamental moral standards are the basis of the fiduciary principle that underlies the duties of corporate managers. Further, I will argue that the fiduciary principle is a principle of natural law that has been incorporated into Anglo-American law through the

---

I am grateful to Alan Ullberg of the District of Columbia Bar for his helpful comments.

common law tradition. I conclude that it is only by vigorous adherence to this tradition that abuses of trust can be prevented.

The Nature of Fiduciary Duty

Professor Austin Scott, who for many years was the leading American scholar in the field of trust law, wrote in 1949 an important article showing that the "fiduciary principle" extended far beyond the law of trusts to include many relationships including the duties of agent to principal, attorney to client, guardian to ward, and executor to legatee. As we will see, the fiduciary principle also includes duties of corporate managers to the corporation and its shareholders. Scott defined the term "fiduciary" to mean "a person who undertakes to act in the interest of another person."[1] In most fiduciary relationships, the fiduciary is given control over some aspect of the life or property of another (the beneficiary) with the expectation that the fiduciary will exercise that control for the benefit of the beneficiary. The salient elements of a fiduciary relationship are "'the actual placing of trust and confidence in fact by one party in another and a great disparity of position and influence between the parties to the action.'"[2]

Underlying the fiduciary relationship is the element of trust, which is a necessary condition of social harmony and of the proper functioning of organizations. Indeed, trust can be regarded as a "pre-contractual" element in all social arrangements. In fiduciary relationships, because of the fiduciary's position of dominance and control over some aspect of the life or property of the beneficiary, the latter must necessarily trust the fiduciary to give proper consideration to the beneficiary's interest. The fiduciary relationship thus gives rise to an ethical obligation of loyalty on the part of the fiduciary. This aspect of the moral law is regularly enforced by courts of equity.

The fiduciary principle is of great antiquity. It is clearly reflected in the provisions of the code of Hammurabi (circa 1700 B.C.) that set forth the rules governing the behavior of agents entrusted with property. Virtually every source of primitive law deals with the entrusting of property for safekeeping, pledges of good faith, and other indicia of trust.[3] In the Judaeo-Christian tradition, the religious roots of the fiduciary principle can be traced to the Old and New Testaments. In the Old Testament, the Lord told Moses that it is a sin not to restore that which is delivered unto a man to keep safely, and penalties must be paid for the violation (Leviticus 6: 2-5). Other examples include the fraudulent betrayal by Jacob of Isaac's trust to obtain his father's blessing (Genesis 27); the requirement to redeem pledges (Exodus 22:26); and prohibitions against unjust weights (Deuteronomy 25: 13-16). The New Testament contains a particularly clear example of the fiduciary principle in the parable of the unjust steward (Luke 16:1-8). An employer had accused his steward of wasting his goods and threatened to fire him. Knowing that he might soon be looking for a job, the steward decided to advance his own interest by agreeing with his employer's debtors (some of whom might later employ the steward) to release them from their obligations to the employer upon payment of a fraction of what they owed. The steward, who was entrusted with the management of his master's property, thus violated a fiduciary duty by serving his own interest rather than those of his master. St. Luke states the underlying principle clearly: "No servant can serve two masters." (Luke 16:13. See also Matthew 6:24 ["No man can serve two masters."]) This principle is particularly appropriate, of course, when one of the masters is oneself. It has often been said by the courts that the fiduciary duty of loyalty is based upon the Biblical precept that no person can serve two masters.[4]

The ethical norms arising from relationships of trust and confidence are not limited to western societies. Chinese history, for example, reflects a similar fiduciary principle. One of the three basic questions of self examination attributed to Confucius is the following: "In acting on behalf of others, have I always been loyal to their interests?"5 The Chinese concept of "Tao" was in some respects similar to the western concept of natural law, in that it reflected a natural order that served as a basis for law and as "a moral link between enacted law and transcendent principles."[6] Chinese rulers were deemed to have "a fiduciary responsibility to maintain harmony between the human and natural worlds."[7] The fiduciary principle was recognized in the codification of Chinese law under the Qing Dynasty (1644-1911),[8] and is recognized in modern Chinese law.[9]

Roman jurists incorporated the ethical obligations of the fiduciary principle into law, most notably in mandatum (the relationship of commission or agency), which involved an undertaking by the mandatory (agent) to act for the benefit of the mandator (principal). Cicero pointed out the link between the ethical inequity of breach of trust and the legal consequences:

> In private business, if a man showed even the slightest carelessness in his execution of trust [*mandatum*]—I say nothing about culpable mismanagement for his own interest or profit—our ancestors considered that he had behaved very dishonorably indeed. In such cases a trial for breach of trust was held, and conviction on such a charge was believed to be every bit as shameful as conviction for an offense such as theft.[10]

Anyone who betrays such a trust, Cicero added, "is undermining the entire basis of our social system."[11]

Feudal relationships in medieval Europe were based on mutual trust and loyalty. The fiduciary principle was integral to the feudal law. Indeed, the very essence of the basic feudal contract was "faith" or "fealty" (*fidelitas*). The modern trust has its origin in the medieval English device of the "use," under which a feoffor gave legal title to property to a "feoffee to uses," for the benefit of the feoffor or a third party (the "*cestui que use*").[12]

As the medieval use developed into the modern law of trusts, the ancient rule encompassed in the fiduciary principle that no man can serve two masters was enforced by courts of equity in England and later in the United States. In the leading case of *Keech v. Sandford*,[13] the trustee held a profitable lease in trust for an infant beneficiary. On renewal of the lease, the lessor refused to renew without a covenant, which the infant could not enter into, so the trustee took the renewal for himself. The court held that this was a breach of trust. The rule in *Keech v. Sandford* is not confined to trustees. "'Whenever a person clothed with a fiduciary or quasi fiduciary character or position gains some personal advantage by availing himself of such character or position, a constructive trust is raised by courts of equity, such person becomes a constructive trustee, and the advantage gained must be held by him for the benefit of his *cestui que* trust.'"[14]

The English law of fiduciary obligation was carried forward into American law. A leading American case is *Michoud v. Girod*, which involved a purchase by an executor of property from the estate. The Supreme Court held that the purchase would be set aside at the instance of the beneficiary. The Court suggested that "[t]he general rule stands upon our great moral obligation to refrain from placing ourselves in relations which ordinarily excite a conflict between self-interest and integrity. It restrains all agents, public and private . . . "[15]

Although 19th and early 20th century jurisprudence reflected a trend toward positivism and away from "moralistic" concepts of law, the moral element in law has always been present. Dean Roscoe Pound observed:

> In fact, the ethical element in application of law was never excluded from the actual administration of justice .... A great and increasing part of the administration of justice is achieved through legal standards. These standards begin to come into the law in the state of infusion of morals through theories of natural law. They have to do with conduct and have a large moral element. The standard of due care in the law of negligence, the standard of fair competition, the standard of fair conduct of a fiduciary, the Roman standard of what good faith demands in a particular transaction, ... all involve an idea of fairness or reasonableness.[16]

With respect to fiduciary relations, he cited Joseph Story's treatise on equity jurisprudence for the proposition that courts enforce the fiduciary duty of good faith "'in aid of general morals.'"[17]

The best-known modern decision embodying the fiduciary principle is Judge Cardozo's opinion in *Meinhard v. Salmon*.[18] In this case, defendant Salmon held a 20-year lease on a hotel in New York City. Salmon entered into a joint venture with Meinhard, the plaintiff, to renovate the building. Salmon was to have sole power to "manage, lease, underlet and operate" the hotel. When the lease was about to expire, Salmon negotiated with the lessor, who also owned some adjacent property, and obtained in his own name a new long-term lease on the entire tract. Salmon never informed Meinhard of these negotiations. Meinhard bought suit asking that the new lease be held in trust as an asset of the joint venture. The court concluded that Salmon held the old lease as a fiduciary, and therefore Meinhard had a right to share in the "pre-emptive opportunity" presented by the new lease. Judge Cardozo's opinion contains a paragraph that has been quoted an infinite number of times by lawyers and judges in cases involving fiduciaries:

> Joint adventurers, like copartners, owe to one another, while the enterprise continues, the duty of the finest loyalty. Many forms of conduct permissible in a workaday world for those acting at arm's length are forbidden to those bound by fiduciary ties. A trustee is held to something stricter than the morals of the market place. Not honesty alone, but the punctilio of an honor the most sensitive, is then the standard of behavior. As to this there has developed a tradition that is unbending and inveterate. Uncompromising rigidity has been the attitude of courts of equity when petitioned to undermine the rule of undivided loyalty by the "disintegrating erosion" of particular exceptions. Only thus has the level of conduct for fiduciaries been kept at a level higher than that trodden by the crowd. It will not consciously be lowered by any judgment of this court.[19]

The facts of *Meinhard v. Salmon* reflect the basic elements of a fiduciary relationship: Meinhard was a woolen merchant who had entrusted his money to Salmon, a real estate operator, and Salmon was in control of the business with exclusive powers of management. Thus, as Judge Cardozo analyzed the case, Meinhard's dependency on Salmon was clear. The relationship imposed upon Salmon a duty of loyalty that went beyond the strict terms of the contract. It is principally the vulnerability of the beneficiary (in this case the passive partner) to the abuse of power by the manager that gives rise to the need for fiduciary rules of conduct. The result in *Meinhard v. Salmon* can be criticized on the ground that Meinhard was not a "vulnerable" plaintiff, but rather an experienced businessman who voluntarily ceded control over the operation of the venture to Salmon. Meinhard could have protected himself in the partnership agreement, but failed to do so. Nevertheless, Judge Cardozo's opinion shows the extent to which courts will protect passive associates from overreaching by managers. This tendency reflects the basic principles of fiduciary conduct, which, as I will argue below, are derived from the natural or moral law. *Meinhard,* moreover, illustrates a crucial point in the relationship between law and economics. Without the protection of fiduciary duties, passive investors will be reluctant to invest in risky projects. Adherence to high fiduciary standards is therefore essential to the success of our system of managerial capitalism.

The Fiduciary Obligation as a Principal of Natural Law

The foregoing recitation of the history of fiduciary obligation demonstrates that fiduciary responsibility stems from fundamental moral principles of trust, which are inherent in certain human relationships. As we have seen, many human societies have recognized the fiduciary principle. As Timothy Fort and James Noone conclude, "If many cultures repeatedly articulate the same norm, that norm is evidence of a 'natural law' that all persons must take into account in making moral judgments. For example, the fact that all world religions, as well as higher primates, have a social rule of reciprocity indicates that this norm may be stitched into our moral nature."[20]

The literature on natural law is so vast that it is impossible to do more than give a brief and inadequate summary in this paper.[21] Further, any attempted definition of "natural law" is bound to be arbitrary. As a working start, however, I will define natural law as a system of principles for the guidance of human conduct, derived from the nature of man as a free, rational and social being, and ascertainable independently of specific positive law as enacted in any given polity. In the history of jurisprudence, "natural law" theory is generally contrasted with "legal positivism" which asserts that law is merely the will of the sovereign and has no intrinsic connection to any moral order. In today's world, the will of the sovereign means the power of the state. It was obvious to St. Thomas Aquinas, on the other hand, that law is more than the will of the sovereign: "in order that the volition of what is commanded may have the nature of law, it needs to be in accord with some rule of reason, ...otherwise the sovereign's will would savor of lawlessness rather than law."[22] The abandonment of this fundamental insight by modern positivist and pragmatic legal theories has invited the very lawlessness that Aquinas warned against. The difference between these two views of law is critical: if there is no natural or "higher" law, then there is no conceptual basis for arguing that any human law is unjust.

Under natural law theory, humans are by nature social beings with a capacity for cooperation through the development of moral rules to constrain individual behavior. Because man is both a rational and social being, he is able to think about the basis of his mutual relationships with others and to derive through the use of his reason the principles of human association in the *polis*.[23] The application of reason to human conduct is the essence of the rule of law. Given the rational and social nature of man, practical reason shows that we need certain norms ("oughts") to live together as humans. As Aristotle noted, "he who bids the law rule may be deemed to bid God and Reason alone rule, but he who bids man rule adds an element of the beast . . . The law is reason unaffected by desire."[24] The Stoic philosophers constructed from these principles a universal system based on the concept that all men have received from nature the gift of reason, and law is right reason as applied to the regulation of human behavior. Perhaps the most famous formulation of the Stoic concept of natural law is in Cicero's *Republic*:

> True law is right reason in agreement with nature; it is of universal application, unchanging and everlasting; it summons to duty by its commands, and averts from wrongdoing by its prohibitions.... We cannot be freed of its obli-

> gations by senate or people, and we need not look outside ourselves for an expounder or interpreter of it. And there will not be different laws at Rome or Athens, or different laws now and in the future, but one eternal and unchangeable law will be valid for all nations and all times, and there will be one master and ruler, that is, God, over us all, for he is the author of this law, its promulgator, and its enforcing judge.[25]

The concept of "nature" in natural law theory does not refer to materialistic biology but "to the rational nature of each individual man [and] to man's endowments of intellect and free will, on which rest the dignity, liberty, and initiative of the individual person; . . ."[26] For man, as a free, rational and social creature, the order of being becomes an "order of oughtness, a moral order,..." because the light of reason, inherent in our nature, if properly followed, tells us what rational and free creatures ought to do and avoid.[27] The natural law is prescriptive and not merely descriptive. The Latin word "*naturalis*" suggests a necessary condition or presupposition of social order. The function of justice is to establish and preserve a fair, predictable, and stable order of human relationships. The human social order depends upon the recognition of basic principles of possession, reciprocity, and obligation. From these requirements can be derived a number of general principles that form the basis for contractual and other obligations. "Thus there is a *naturalis possessio* at the root of all property. There is a *naturalis obligatio,* which may or may not be legally protected, but which is the necessary prerequisite of all obligations."[28]

In the centuries following Cicero, the Roman jurists formulated a system of jurisprudence, which, in its essential characteristics, adhered to the Stoic premise that law should correspond to natural and universal justice. The Institutes of Justinian, published in the sixth century A.D., restated the basic principles of natural justice: "The precepts of law are these: to live honestly, not to injure anyone and to render to each person what is due."[29] From the precepts of natural justice, it follows that injuries are to be rectified, promises fulfilled, stolen property restored, and quarrels adjudicated. The fiduciary principle is also derived from the principles of natural justice. All stable and collaborative social institutions require trust and loyalty among the members. The "institutionalization of trust" is therefore essential to life in society, and to associations, corporations, and other groups within society. And the institutionalization of trust requires, *inter alia,* that lives and property entrusted to another be faithfully respected. This is the essence of the fiduciary principle. The fiduciary principle also follows from Justinian's formulation of natural law precepts obliging us to act honestly and to give to each his due. For example, if property has been entrusted to us, we must secure it from harm and, if it is lost through our faithlessness, we must restore its value, together with any improper gain which we may have received from the use of it.[30] These rules of natural justice apply to those who manage a private enterprise or association, as well as to public officials. As indicated by Aristotle's reference to "God and Reason" and the passage from Cicero's *Republic*, quoted above, classical concepts of natural law are closely connected to religion. During the Middle Ages, Christian thinkers developed a theory of natural law that was based on divine law. As St. Thomas Aquinas expressed it, "this participation of the eternal law in the rational creature is called the natural law."[31] In short, natural law in the Western tradition assumed that moral obligation was inherent in human nature as part of the divine order. Even modern interpretations of natural law, which are not specifically theist in origin, assume that there is a "higher law" whose principles are superior to those of positive law.[32]

The specific content of natural law has, of course, been much debated over the centuries. Under virtually any interpretation, however, it is sufficiently broad to include the fiduciary principle. Aquinas specifies a number of precepts of "practical reason," which can be derived from the nature of man as a rational and sociable being, and the requirements of a rational social order. Most basic of these is the preservation of human life. Other precepts of practical reason include the ownership of property and the prohibition of theft and fraud. Aquinas also includes an important aspect of the fiduciary principle: "goods entrusted to another should be restored to their owner."[33] This can be seen as the application of trust (*fides* or good faith) to the institution of property.

Hugo Grotius, the noted 17th century natural law theorist, derived natural law from the nature of man as a rational being and man's need to maintain social order.[34] The maintenance of social order requires adherence to certain basic principles: abstaining from what is another's, the obligation to fulfill promises, and the making good of a loss incurred through our fault (the bases, respectively, of property, contract, and tort). Another principle is "the restoration to another of anything of his which we may have, together with any gain which we have received from it; . . . ."[35] This principle, together with that of *fides* (good faith) that underlies it, is at the heart of fiduciary obligation.

Underlying natural law theory is a universally felt need to justify statutes and legal decisions, and this process of justification requires principles of right and wrong. Legal positivists have long argued that there is a sharp conceptual separation between morals and law. But natural law, history, and common sense dispute this conclusion. While it is true that not all moral principles are reflected in positive law, it is also true that many moral principles are embodied in law. Some obvious examples are duty of parents to children, obedience of children to parents, the duty not to kill an innocent person, truthful speech, fidelity to one's given word, respect for the dignity of others, and the obligation of loyalty to one who has reposed trust and confidence (this last point being particularly relevant to the subject under discussion here). Of course, the basic norms that constitute natural justice are quite general. In practice, more specific rules can be obtained only by a consideration of various circumstances. The variety of possible circumstances explains the diversity of positive laws. In spite of the apparent victory of positivism over natural law jurisprudence in the first half of the 20th century, lawyers and judges, as Roscoe Pound showed, have continued to rely on norms such as good faith, restitution, and other equitable doctrines of the "higher law." Under all natural law theories, law is conceived as an objective basis of rights and duties, originating not in the arbitrary will of the sovereign but from a natural order reflecting the essential dignity and freedom of human beings. As the American Declaration of Independence states, the "laws of Nature and of Nature's God" establish certain self-evident truths about the rights of man. Indeed, natural law theories always tend to re-emerge precisely when freedom is threatened. When the positive legal order becomes unjust, men return to the self-evident truths of the moral law, which place limits on arbitrary government.[36]

The Fiduciary Principle and the Duties of Business Managers

The fiduciary standards of good faith and honest dealing apply to business as well as to personal relationships. This was the case in Roman law and continues to be true today.[37] As Edmund Burke said, "the laws of commerce... are the laws of nature and consequently the laws of God."[38]

As in the case of other social institutions, the law imposes obligations upon those who manage business enterprises, designed to ensure that the managers have regard for the interest of the members who have entrusted their assets to the venture. (The term "managers," as used here, includes both directors and officers of corporations.) These obligations are reflected in concepts applied by the courts, such as "loyalty," "due care," "good faith," and "fairness." What we now call "corporate governance" is the application of the duties associated with these concepts to the management of corporations. As discussed above, these concepts are derived from natural law principles and are a part of the "institutionalization of trust" that is essential to the survival of all human associations.

American courts have long held that corporate directors are fiduciaries.[39] The relation is a fiduciary one because the shareholders have given control over the corporation's assets to the directors with the expectation that the directors will exercise that control for the shareholders' benefit. The United States Supreme Court in *Pepper v. Litton* traced the duty of a corporate manager back to its ancient roots in the natural or moral law:

> He who is in such a fiduciary position cannot serve himself first and his *ces - tuis* second. He cannot manipulate the affairs of his corporation to their detriment and in disregard of the standards of common decency and honesty. He

cannot by the intervention of a corporate entity violate the ancient precept against serving two masters.[40]

The law of Delaware has become the principal source of corporate law in the United States because a majority of large corporations are incorporated in Delaware. Delaware has also established a highly regarded chancery court system with judges having special competence in corporate litigation. Under Delaware law, directors stand in a fiduciary relation to the corporation and its shareholders. The fiduciary nature of directors' duties has been consistently reaffirmed by the Delaware courts.[41] The courts of other states are in accord.[42] As in the case of any fiduciary duty, the obligation of a corporate director or officer to the corporation and its shareholders is greater than a mere obligation to perform one's contracts and to avoid injuring others. It involves affirmative duties of good faith, loyalty, care, and disclosure.

Good Faith

The duty of good faith (*bona fides*) requires honesty of intention in dealing with others, and avoidance of conduct that is unconscionable or seeks to take undue advantage of the actor's superior knowledge of relevant circumstances to the detriment of another. Good faith is at the heart of all fiduciary duties, and is derived from principles of natural law.[43] It is a term traditionally used to designate the mental state of honest conviction as to the truth of a proposition or the morality of an action.[44] In connection with responsibility of a fiduciary, "good faith" takes into account the fiduciary's intentions as well as the degree of his attention to duty.

A recent decision of the Delaware Chancery Court shows the continuing importance of good faith in performing the duties of corporate directors. A shareholder suit against directors of the Walt Disney Company alleged that the directors breached their fiduciary duty when determining the compensation and terms of termination for the former president of the company. The complaint charged that, after a tenure of barely one year, the former president left the company, receiving severance pay and other benefits exceeding $140 million. The facts alleged in the complaint indicated that the directors' approval of the compensation arrangement, which carried with it obvious financial risks to the company, was perfunctory and uninformed. In refusing to dismiss the case, the court said that the alleged conduct of the directors amounted to "deliberate indifference." Such conduct would constitute a failure to act "honestly and in good faith."[45]

The beneficiary in a fiduciary relationship is particularly vulnerable to deception, which is an obvious manifestation of dishonesty. Illustrations of fraudulent conduct are a depressing feature of corporate life. When, for example, the chief financial officer is directed by the chief executive officer to falsify the company's financial statements to conceal its poor financial condition, he should of course refuse to do so, since his primary duty is to the company and its shareholders, who deserve to be told the truth, not to the CEO. Ignoring this simple rule has led to a great deal of mischief and personal tragedy.

Duty of Loyalty

The duty of loyalty is simply a restatement of the basic moral principle that a person who undertakes to act for another must refrain from placing his/her own interest ahead of the other's interest. In the corporate context, it requires that the directors devote "an undivided and unselfish loyalty to the corporation," and that "there shall be no conflict between duty and self-interest."[46]

The loyalty rule that was generally applied to corporate fiduciaries by American courts in the 19th century followed the strict doctrine of trust law that any transaction between a trustee and the trust is automatically voidable at the behest of a beneficiary, whether or not the terms were fair.[47] As modern corporate capitalism developed, it became evident that a rule making every contract between the corporation and a director or his affiliate automatically voidable at the instance of the corporation was impracticable. Faced with the reality that corporations often needed to do business with directors or their affiliates, state legislatures adopted "safe harbor" statutes providing that a contract or other transaction between a director and his corporation, or between corporations with interlocking directors, is not voidable simply because there is a fiduciary relationship between the parties if there is disinterested approval or if the interested person can prove that the transaction is fair to the corporation.[48] The duty of loyalty has by no means been abandoned. It has merely been modified to take into account the needs of a dynamic economy in which business people with many interests must deal with each other. The fiduciary principle remains applicable because the action taken by the directors must be taken in good faith and conform to the fiduciary standards of loyalty, due care, and candor.

Duty of Care

The virtue of prudence has deep roots in the moral law. From classical to early modern times, it was considered to be one of the "cardinal virtues," along with justice, courage, and temperance, and was often identified with "practical reason." Prudence involves the qualities of foresight, deliberation, and judgment that are needed for clear-sighted, objective decisions.[49] In law, the standard of reasonableness or prudence has been adopted by Anglo-American courts to bring an element of objectivity into decision-making in matters involving alleged negligence or "nonfeasance."

The duty of prudence, or "duty of care" as it is usually called today, is often cited in fiduciary law sources as an intrinsic aspect of relationships of trust and agency. The duty of care can be viewed as a corollary of the duty of loyalty because loyalty demands that the fiduciary bring a disinterested focus to his responsibilities and exercise prudence in carrying out his trust. In its classic formulation in corporate law, the duty of care provides that "[a] corporate director or officer has a duty to the corporation to perform the director's or officer's functions in good faith, in a manner that he or she reasonably believes to be in the best interests of the corporation, and with the care that an ordinarily prudent person would reasonably be expected to exercise in a like position under similar circumstances."[50] This standard is commonly referred to as the "prudent man" rule. It has long been recognized, however, that there are numerous risks inherent in the decisions that directors and officers are required to make, and that these decisions should not be subjected to second-guessing by courts merely because the decisions turn out in hindsight to have been unwise or unsuccessful. Accordingly, courts have developed the "business judgment rule," under which a director or officer who makes a business judgment will be held to have fulfilled the duty of care if he or she acted in good faith; was disinterested; was reasonably informed; and rationally believed that the action taken was in the best interests of the corporation.[51] The courts have been careful to impose limits on the business judgment rule. Directors will not be permitted to take advantage of the rule, for example, if they were not sufficiently disinterested[52] or if they were not adequately informed.[53] In addition, the business judgment rule does not apply to failure of the directors to exercise proper oversight over the corporation's business.[54]

A faithful fiduciary in short, must be informed, and must act rationally, in order to fulfill his/her trust. The requirement of the business judgment rule that directors must be adequately informed is consistent with the doctrine of classical Greek philosophy that no one can act properly without sufficient knowledge—a fundamental axiom of prudence or "right reason" that is implicit in the Aristotelian-Ciceronian concept of natural law.

Duty of Disclosure

Courts have recognized that directors and officers of corporations have a fiduciary duty to disclose material information when they seek shareholder action.[55] Whether or not there is a request for shareholder action, moreover, directors who knowingly disseminate false information that results in corporate injury or damage to stockholders violate their fiduciary duty and may be held accountable.[56] The analytical basis for the duty of disclosure (or "duty of candor" as it is sometimes called) is the principle that, in communicating with the shareholders, the directors have the same fiduciary duty to exercise due care, good faith, and loyalty as in other corporate transactions. In short, "the *sine qua non* of directors' fiduciary duty to shareholders is honesty."[57]

As is well known, corporate managers also have duties of disclosure under the federal securities laws. Rules of fiduciary obligation are important in determining whether federal disclosure obligations exist in certain circumstances, for example, where "insider trading" is involved.[58]

Statutory Modification of the Duty of Care

In recent years, many states have adopted legislation permitting shareholders to adopt a provision in the corporate charter designed to eliminate or limit the personal liability of directors for money damages for breaches of the duty of care. These statutes represent a significant limitation on the traditional duty of care. They were deemed necessary by state legislatures because of the extraordinary rise in the frequency and severity of litigation in the U.S. by shareholders against corporate directors seeking to hold them responsible for negligent mismanagement even though they did not participate directly in the wrongdoing. The legislators feared that the potential liabilities were so serious that many capable people would be reluctant to serve as directors.[59] The limitation of liability statutes, however, generally do not apply to corporate officers, who are the day-to-day managers of the corporate business, and, more significantly, they contain specific exceptions for conduct graver than negligence such as breach of the duty of loyalty or acts involving bad faith, fraud, or other intentional misconduct. Accordingly, notwithstanding the limitation of liability statutes, the most important features of the fiduciary duties of business managers remain applicable and are regularly enforced by the courts.

The Fiduciary Principle Is Not Explainable in Contractarian Terms

Some "law-and-economics" scholars have argued that fiduciary duties are contractarian and may be modified or eliminated by contract even in the absence of a statute.[60] But this position is analytically and historically unsound. While it is true that many aspects of the trust relationship can be varied by agreement, the basic fiduciary duties of good faith and loyalty cannot.[61] Indeed, as Deborah DeMott has written, "fiduciary obligation sometimes operates precisely in opposition to intention as manifest in express agreements."[62] In corporate law, while there is a narrow exculpation provided by the statutory provisions permitting limitation of liability for the duty of care, the fiduciary duties of good faith and loyalty cannot be eliminated by contract. The reason is that these fundamental legal duties are not contractual: they have a moral origin and a moral function. There is a natural justice "that is binding on all men, even on those who have no association or covenant with each other."[63] Many social roles carry with them obligations that are noncontractual and are part of the social structure, not objects of negotiation. These include the role of a fiduciary. Someone may agree or not agree to become a fiduciary, but once he/she has entered into the role, he/she is not free to abandon the essential norms that attach to it. Contract law itself is dependent on principles of honesty, good faith, and fair dealing which are rooted in natural law. The basic reason why contract and fiduciary rules are treated differently is that each party to a freely negotiated contract is expected to act in his/her own interest (subject, of course, to implied obligations of good faith and fair dealing) whereas the beneficiary in a fiduciary relationship is dependent on the fiduciary and is unable to monitor effectively the fiduciary's self-interested behavior. The contractarian position is based ultimately on principles of wealth maximization and economic efficiency. But the rules of fiduciary conduct (like many other rules of human behavior) are based on moral principle, not economic efficiency. Courts have generally understood that, as a Delaware case recently expressed it, "*homo sapiens* is not merely *homo economicus*."[64] Consequently, most judges do not see themselves as maximizers of wealth, but rather as "engaged in a process of trying to understand and protect the values embodied in the law."[65]

The foregoing analysis applies to corporate directors and officers as well as to other fiduciaries.[66] The prohibition against managers contracting away their fiduciary duties would be a sensible conclusion even if the contractarian position were accepted, because an *ex ante* waiver of the duty of loyalty by public shareholders would have to be based on informed consent and there is no way to disclose in advance to the shareholders all of the possible conflicts of interest that could arise.

The corporation is a historical institution that is the product of centuries of social, cultural, and legal as well as economic forces. It is not, any more than a university, a mere "bundle of contracts." The courts did not develop fiduciary rules to reflect the self-interested preferences of economic actors, but to implement values of trust and confidence through the application of traditional moral norms. Public shareholders, who cannot effectively bargain with corporate managers, rely on these fiduciary rules when they invest, and fundamental fairness (itself a feature of natural justice) requires that they be observed. The fiduciary principle, of course, applies to closely held business entities as well as to public corporations. See the discussion of *Meinhard v. Salmon*, above.

Shareholders and Stakeholders

Corporate managers today face growing pressures from two directions. On the one hand, shareholders demand that managers pay more attention to increasing shareholder value. On the other hand, advocates of corporate social responsibility hold that managers have obligations not just to the corporation and its shareholders, but also to employees, creditors, and other "stakeholders," including the communities in which they operate.

"Stakeholder" proponents argue, for example, that the social responsibilities of managers include environmental protection, sustainable use of natural resources, and power sharing with workers. Most of the countries of continental Europe have a political climate that favors the stakeholder model. This point of view is linked to welfare state policies that emphasize social welfare responsibilities and the need for extensive government regulation of the economy.

During the 1980s, a number of states in the United States adopted statutes, generally referred to as "non-shareholder constituency statutes," that permitted (but did not require) corporate directors to take into account the interests of various "stakeholders"—such as employees, customers, suppliers, and communities–in making decisions on behalf of the corporation.[67] These statutes were a response to the takeover movement of the 1980s. They were designed to protect local companies from being swallowed up by outsider raiders, rather than a conscious effort to move the law toward a stakeholder paradigm. In any event, the constituency statutes, to date, have not been construed so as to create duties to other constituencies equivalent to fiduciary duties to shareholders.

Proponents of the "stakeholder" model of corporate governance assert that employees, creditors, suppliers, customers, and communities all make "firm-specific" contributions to the company, so that directors should have responsibilities to all of these constituencies. Under the traditional shareholder-value model, corporations conduct business with a view to enhancing corporate profits and shareholder gain. This is the position taken by a great majority of American cases. This position gives the directors a single channel of fiduciary accountability and a clear focus on increasing the value of the business over time. In economic theory, the shareholder-value model promotes economic efficiency because shareholders, as residual claimants, have the greatest incentive to maximize the profits of the firm and should therefore be the beneficiaries of the bottom-line duties of managers.[68]

If the stakeholder model means that managers have a duty to employees, creditors, and other stakeholders that is equivalent to the duty owed to shareholders, the difficulties of serving multiple masters are obvious. In many situations, the interests of shareholders and stakeholders will conflict. Suppose, for example, that management decides to close a clearly unprofitable plant. Shareholders will benefit from the closure, but some employees and the local community may suffer. Without the guidance provided by the principle that long-term shareholder value comes first, it will be difficult for managers to make a decision. If the interests of all stakeholders must be given equal consideration, the directors will either decide to do nothing or will make a political compromise rather than a business decision. As a practical matter, this means that directors will be able to cite the interests of some constituency as a reason for not acting, thereby serving their own vested interest in preserving their jobs. Simply put, stakeholder theory sounds good in social theory but will not work in practice.

This analysis does not imply, of course, that non-shareholder constituencies have no legal remedies. The corporation has a variety of enforceable legal relationships with employees, creditors, suppliers, and other third parties. In addition, managers are obligated to obey the law and to establish procedures for oversight over the company's compliance with environmental, safety, labor, and other governmental regulations. The managers and the stakeholders are thus tied in an interlocking web of relationships and statutory protections that effectively protect the third parties.

In addition, and more significantly for the purposes of this paper, the conclusion that managers in most cases do not have fiduciary duties to stakeholders does not mean that they have no ethical duties to them. Men and women do not cast off their ethical responsibilities by becoming corporate managers. They are morally obligated to treat the company's employees with respect, to avoid jeopardizing the health or safety of customers, and not to deceive the public. These duties follow from elementary natural law principles, such as the duties to avoid harming others (*non fit injuria*), to act honestly, and to give to each person his/her due. Companies whose managers regularly fail to meet these moral obligations will not survive over the long term. Corporate managers, moreover, are constrained not only by their traditional moral duties, but also by their reputational interest in adhering to accepted standards of conduct. Directors and officers are not anxious to be branded as slavedrivers or polluters.

There are limits, however, to the freedom of corporate managers to devote corporate assets to eleemosynary purposes. Shareholders, as the residual risk takers, have entrusted their funds to the corporation for the purpose of gaining profit. This creates a relationship of trust, which, in law and in equity, takes precedence over the inclination of managers to be charitable with other people's money. It is entirely justifiable that corporate managers should consider the legitimate interests of employees, customers, suppliers, and other constituencies, including the community, but only so long as there is a rational and perceptible nexus between actions favoring other constituencies and long-term shareholder benefit.

Sensitivity to environmental and social concerns is good business judgment. It would be unfair, however, to demand that business enterprises clean up the world's environmental messes or provide poor relief, elementary education, police protection, and other "public goods" at the expense of their shareholders. These are political problems to be addressed by government under the rule of law, not passed on to corporate managers, who have not been elected by and are not accountable to the voters at large. It is for this reason, among others, that managers' fiduciary duties of loyalty and care run to their companies and shareholders, not to the public. To hold otherwise is to create a confusion of roles that can only be harmful both to corporate and to political governance.

Conclusion

This paper has summarized the basic fiduciary duties of corporate directors and officers, and has argued that these duties have their origin in principles of natural law. Recent corporate governance scandals reflect a widespread failure to adhere to these traditional duties of good faith, loyalty, and care.

The factual record of governance failures is replete with examples of self-dealing and conflict of interest on the part of management, in which directors either participate or acquiesce. These examples invariably evidence a violation of the ancient rule by which an agent is not permitted to prefer his/her own interest to that of the principal, where the two conflict. The parable of the faithless steward in Chapter 16 of St. Luke's gospel is a paradigm case. The most obvious common feature of recent managerial misdeeds is the financial interest of managers in increasing the value of their stock options and bonuses by manipulation of the corporate earnings through fraudulent accounting techniques. A related example is "insider trading," in which managers use a corporate asset (confidential information about expected events) to make a personal trading profit. Another common abuse is the loan of corporate funds (sometimes amounting to tens of millions of dollars) to top executives for personal use.

A common element in these transgressions has been the failure by boards of directors to exercise their duty of care. This duty, under American law, is not especially rigorous, since a finding of liability requires grossly negligent behavior or obvious inattention to duty. Yet in many recent cases of corporate disaster, boards have failed to uncover behavior, which even a minimum investigation would have shown to be damaging or illegal, and have awarded options, bonuses, and other forms of executive compensation in amounts that would have made Croesus blush. Officers and directors are not the only responsible parties. Outside accountants have sometimes ignored signs of financial fraud, influenced by reluctance to lose opportunities for additional lucrative business from the corporation. Recent administrative settlements have revealed that some major banks have aided and abetted fraudulent corporate activity in order to protect lending or other profitable relationships. All of these recent abuses are violations are of basic moral principles and well-established legal duties worked out by legislatures, courts, and commentators over the centuries.

The American system of free market capitalism has been a powerful engine for the production of wealth, and it would be unwise to impair the effectiveness of this system through unnecessary government regulation. Yet increased regulation is the inevitable result of massive corporate scandals that capture the attention of voters and their elected representatives. A far better solution is for shareholders, who are the owners of corporations, to insist that those they hire to manage the business adhere to longstanding fiduciary standards of conduct, based on the traditional moral law and enforced by courts in accordance with regular and established procedures. There are some recent signs that major institutional shareholders (particularly pension funds) are beginning to use their power and influence to guard the corporate guardians and enforce the ancient rules.

Notes

1. Austin Scott, *The Fiduciary Principle,* 37 CAL. L. REV. 539, 540 (1949). Scott's definition has been criticized as placing undue emphasis on voluntary assumption of the duty by the fiduciary. This definition does not work in the case of a constructive trustee or in certain other cases in which courts impose fiduciary duties, such as actions by a majority shareholder in a corporation that may affect minority shareholders. *See* Deborah A. DeMott, *Beyond Metaphor: An Analysis of Fiduciary Obligation,* 1988 DUKE L.J. 879, 910-11 (1988).
2. Morris v. Resolution Trust Corp., 622 A.2d 708, 712 (Me. 1993). "'[A]t the heart of the fiduciary relationship lies reliance, and *de facto* control and dominance.'" United States v. Chestman, 947 F.2d 551, 568 (2d Cir. 1991), *cert. denied,* 503 U.S. 1004 (1992).
3. See KOCOUREK & WIGMORE, SOURCES OF ANCIENT AND PRIMITIVE LAW 404-11, 483-87, 665-71 (1915, reprinted 1979)
4. Pepper v. Litton, 308 U.S. 295, 311 (1939); United States v. Miss. Valley Generating Co., 364 U.S. 520, 549, 550 n. 14 (1961).
5. 1 THE ANALECTS OF CONFUCIUS ¶ 4 (A. Waley trans., Vintage 1938).
6. Karen Turner, *Rule of Law Ideals in Early China?* in BASIC CONCEPTS OF CHINESE LAW, at 24 (Tahirih V. Lee ed., 1997). See C.S. LEWIS, THE ABOLITION OF MAN, 56 (N.Y. 1955), analogizing the Tao to natural law.
7. Turner at 43.
8. THE GREAT QING CODE 162 (William C. Jones Trans., Oxford 1994) (providing for criminal punishment for one who receives deposit of property of another and consumes such property without authority).
9. See BASIC PRINCIPLES OF CIVIL LAW IN CHINA 317 (William C. Jones ed., 1986) (recognizing "contracts of entrustment"), and at 321 (obligation of brokers to act "honestly, justly, in good faith, and not in a way contrary to the notion of fairness.")
10. Cicero, *In Defense of Sextus Roscius of Ameria,* in CICERO: MURDER TRIALS 87 (Penguin 1978) (footnote omitted).
11. *Ibid.*
12. See R. H. Helmholtz, *The Early Enforcement of Uses,* 79 COLUM. L. REV. 1503 (1979).
13. Chancery, 1726, Sel. Cas. Ch. 61, 25 Eng. Rep. 223.
14. Walter G. Hart, *The Development of the Rule* in Keech v. Sandford, 21 LAW Q. REV. 258, 259 (1905).
15. 45 U.S. 503, 555 (1846). The Court cited examples of the general rule from Roman law as well as from English law. *Id.* at 559-60.

16. Roscoe Pound, *The Ideal Element in Law* 86 (Liberty Fund 2002 [1958])[footnotes omitted].
17. *Id.* at 87, note 60, citing 1 JOSEPH STORY, EQUITY JURISPRUDENCE (1835) (Arno Press, 1972) § 431, as well as sources in Roman law.
18. 164 N.E. 545 (N.Y. 1928).
19. 164 N.E. at 546.
20. Timothy L. Fort & James J. Noone, *Challenges to Corporate Governance: Bundled Contracts, Mediating Institutions, and Corporate Governance: A Naturalist Analysis of Contractual Theories of the Firm*, 62 L. & CONTEMP. PROBS. 163, 198-99 (1999) (citations omitted).
21. For recent treatments of the subject of natural law, see J. BUDZISZEWSKI, WRITTEN ON THE HEART: THE CASE FOR NATURAL LAW (1997); ROBERT P. GEORGE, IN DEFENSE OF NATURAL LAW (OXFORD 1999); RUSSELL HITTINGER, THE FIRST GRACE; REDISCOVERING THE NATURAL LAW IN A POST-CHRISTIAN WORLD (ISI Books, 2003); Alasdair MacIntyre, *Theories of Natural Law in the Culture of Advanced Modernity*, in COMMON TRUTHS: NEW PERSPECTIVES ON NATURAL LAW (Edward B. McLean ed., 2000); HEINRICH A. ROMMEN, THE NATURAL LAW (Liberty Fund Reprint 1998).
22. ST. THOMAS AQUINAS, SUMMA THEOLOGICA, Q.90, Art. 1 (Modern Library 1948).
23. See ARISTOTLE, POLITICS, Bk. I, Ch. 2, at 1253a; POLITICS, Bk. III, Ch. 16, at 1287a (THE BASIC WORKS OF ARISTOTLE (Random House, N.Y., 1941)); SAMUEL PUFENDORF, OF THE LAW OF THE NATURE AND NATIONS, Bk I, Ch. VI, at 76 (London 1717) (natural law is "that which is so exactly fitted to suit with the rational and social nature of men, that human kind cannot maintain an honest and peaceful fellowship without it; . . .") The need to counteract the desires of human rulers with the reason of law is the philosophical basis for the separation of powers and the American system of constitutional law. See EDWARD S. CORWIN, THE "HIGHER LAW" BACKGROUND OF AMERICAN CONSTITUTIONAL LAW 8-9 (Cornell 1955).
24. POLITICS, Bk. III, Ch. 16, at 1287a.
25. CICERO, REPUBLIC, BK. III, § XXII, at 211 (Loeb Classical Library, William Heinemann, Ltd.,1961).
26. ROMMEN, *supra* note 21, at 135.
27. ROMMEN at 158.
28. ALESSANDRO PASSERIN D'ENTRÈVES, NATURAL LAW: AN INTRODUCTION TO LEGAL PHILOSOPHY 33 (1994).
29. *"Juris praecepta sunt haec: honeste vivere, alterum non laedere, suum cuique tribuere."* J. INST., I.
30. See HUGO GROTIUS, THE LAW OF WAR AND PEACE 12-13, 25 (1925); JOHN FINNIS, NATURAL LAW AND NATURAL RIGHTS 288 (1980) (profits received without justification and at the expense of another must be restored).
31. ST. THOMAS AQUINAS, SUMMA THEOLOGICA, Q. 91, Art. 2. See David Novak, *Law: Religious or Secular?*, 86 VA. L. REV. 569 (2000). Novak argues persuasively that both the classical and the Christian approaches to natural law are based on a divine order that is discovered, not invented, by men. *Id.* at 579. If law is to order our desires in a way that serves the common good, that law cannot be the product of the desires of those who need to be governed by it, but must have a

transcendent base. *Id.* at 594. See Harold J. Berman, *The Religious Foundations of Western Law,* 24 CATH. U. L. REV. 490 (1975).

32. EDWARD S.CORWIN, THE "HIGHER LAW" BACKGROUND OF AMERICAN CONSTITUTIONAL LAW (Cornell 1955).
33. AQUINAS, Q. 94, Art. 4, at 641. Aquinas makes the point that, because of the complexity of human relationships, when one descends from very general precepts to more specific rules, conditions and exceptions multiply. For example, there might be an exception to the precept of fiduciary obligation if the owner were to reclaim weapons for the purpose of fighting against his/her own country. This is a classic example of conflict of obligations requiring practical reasonableness (itself a principle of natural law) in accordance with experience.
34. GROTIUS, THE LAW OF WAR AND PEACE 11-14 (Indianapolis 1925). Grotius also held, however, that natural law was consistent with divine law.
35. *Id.* at 13. *See also,* Samuel Pufendorf, supra n. 23, Book III, Chap. IX.
36. See RUSSELL HITTINGER, INTRODUCTION TO ROMMEN, THE NATURAL LAW, xii (Liberty Fund 1998). *See also* HORACE, DICTUM, Epis. I, x, at 24 ("*Naturam expelles furca, tamen usque recurret.*") (You may expel nature with a pitchfork, yet she will always return).
37. See Cicero, De Officiis, Book III, xvii (obligation to act honestly and in good faith derives from nature and applies to buying, selling, and other commercial relationships).
38. Edmund Burke, "Thoughts and Details on Scarcity" (1795) in WORKS, Vol. II, 180 (N.Y. 1837).
39. *See* Pepper v. Litton, 308 U.S. 295 (1939); Twin-Lick Oil Co. v. Marbury, 91 U.S. 587, 588-89 (1875) ("That a director of a joint-stock corporation occupies one of those fiduciary relations where his dealing with the subject-matter of his trust or agency, and with the beneficiary or party whose interest is confided to his care, is viewed with jealousy by the courts, and may be set aside on slight grounds, is a doctrine founded on the soundest morality, and which has received the clearest recognition in this court and in others.")
40. 308 U.S. at 311.
41. *See, e.g.,* Guth v. Loft, Inc., 5 A.2d 503,510 (Del. 1939); Smith v. Van Gorkom, 488 A.2d 858, 872 (Del. 1985); Paramount Communications v. QVC Network, 637 A.2d 34, 43 (Del. 1993).
42. *See, e.g.,* Francis v. United Jersey Bank, 432 A.2d 814, 824 (N.J. 1981); Alpert v. 28 William St. Corp., 473 N.E.2d 19, 25-26 (N.Y. 1984).
43. ROMMEN, supra n. 21, at 24.
44. See THE CATHOLIC ENCYCLOPEDIA (1914 ed.), www.newadvent.org/cathen/066412a.htm.
45. In re The Walt Disney Company Derivative Litigation, 825 A.2d 275, 289(Del. Ch. 2003).
46. Guth v. Loft, Inc., 5 A.2d 503, 510 (Del. 1939).
47. Twin-Lick Oil, 91 U.S. at 588. *See also* Harold Marsh, Jr., *Are Directors Trustees?,* 22 BUS. L. 35 (1966) and cases cited therein.
48. A typical "safe harbor" statute is § 144 of the Delaware General Corporation Law. *See also* Model Business Corp. Act §§ 8.60-8.63 (1984 & 1994); A.L.I., PRINCIPLES OF CORPORATE GOVERNANCE: ANALYSIS AND RECOMMENDATIONS § 5.02 and Reporter's Note (1994) (hereinafter "A.L.I. PRINCIPLES"). The safe har-

bor statutes are often unclear and their precise legal consequences have been much disputed.

49. See Josef Pieper, THE FOUR CARDINAL VIRTUES 12-17 (N.Y. 1965); and DOUGLAS J. DEN UYL, THE VIRTUE OF PRUDENCE (N.Y. 1991).
50. A.L.I. PRINCIPLES § 4.01(a). See Briggs v. Spaulding, 141 U.S. 132, 152 (1891).
51. *See* CORPORATE DIRECTOR'S GUIDEBOOK 11, 2d ed., Section of Business Law, A.B.A. (1994); A.L.I. PRINCIPLES § 4.01(c). The business judgment rule is often stated as a "presumption" that directors and officers have acted properly, which the plaintiff must rebut by showing that one or more of the elements of the rule are not present (for example, that they were not disinterested or were not adequately informed). *See* Smith v. Van Gorkom, 488 A.2d 858 (Del. 1985).
52. *See* Treadway Cos. v. Care Corp., 638 F.2d 357, 382 (2d Cir. 1980); Lewis v. S.L. & E., Inc., 629 F.2d 764, 769 (2d Cir. 1980).
53. Smith v. Van Gorkom, 488 A.2d 858 (Del. 1985).
54. *See In re* Caremark Int'l Inc., 698 A.2d 959 (Del. Ch. 1996); A.L.I. PRINCIPLES § 4.01(c) and cmt. c at 174-75.
55. Stroud v. Grace, 606 A.2d 75, 84 (Del. 1992); Arnold v. Soc'y for Sav. Bancorp, 650 A.2d 1270, 1276 (Del. 1994).
56. Malone v. Brincat, 722 A.2d 5, 9 (Del. 1998).
57. Id. at 10. *See* Eric A. Chiappinelli, *The Moral Basis of State Corporate Law Disclosure,* 49 CATH. U. L. REV. 697 (2000).
58. The breach of a fiduciary relationship may give rise to a "misappropriation" of confidential information for purposes of establishing liability under § 10(b) of the Securities Exchange Act of 1934. *See* United States v. O'Hagan, 521 U.S. 642 (1997). For a comprehensive analysis of the "misappropriation" theory, see Stephen M. Bainbridge, *Insider Trading Regulation: The Path Dependent Choice Between Property Rights and Securities Fraud,* 52 SMU L. REV. 1589 (1999).
59. James J. Hanks, Jr., *Evaluating Recent State Legislation on Director and Officer Liability Limitation and Indemnification,* 43 BUS. L. 1207 (1988).
60. John H. Langbein, *The Contractarian Basis of the Law of Trusts,* 105 YALE L.J. 625 (1995); Frank Easterbrook and Daniel R. Fischel, *Contract and Fiduciary Duty,* 36 J.L. & Econ. 425, 427 (1993) (arguing that fiduciary relationships "have no moral footing; they are the same sort of obligations, derived and enforced in the same way, as other contractual relationships."
61. RESTATEMENT (SECOND) OF CONTRACTS §193 (1981): "A promise by a fiduciary to violate his fiduciary duty or a promise that tends to induce such a violation is unenforceable on grounds of public policy;" RESTATEMENT (SECOND) OF TRUSTS §222(2)(1959) (exculpation clause not effective to relieve trustee of liability for breach of trust committed in bad faith or with reckless indifference to interest of beneficiary). There are many decided cases to the same effect. *See* Scott, *supra* n.1, at 542. It is noteworthy that the remedies for breach of fiduciary duty are generally equitable, not contractual.
62. Deborah A. DeMott, *Beyond Metaphor: An Analysis of Fiduciary Obligation,* 1988 DUKE L.J. 879, 887 (1988); Victor Brudney *Contract and Fiduciary Duty in Corporate Law,* 39 CORPORATE PRACTICE COMMENTATOR 749, 760 (1998).
63. ARISTOTLE, RHETORIC I, 13, 1373 b.
64. In re Oracle Corp. Derivative Litigation, 824 A.2d 917, 938 (Del Ch. 2003).
65. RAYMOND A. BELLIOTTI, JUSTIFYING LAW 126 (1992).

66. Paramount Communications Inc. v. QVC Network, Inc., 637 A.2d 34, 51 (Del. 1993) ("the Paramount directors could not contract away their fiduciary obligations.")
67. See Morey McDaniel,*Stockholders and Stakeholders.* 21 STETSON L. REV. 121 (1991); Mark E. Van der Weide, *Against Fiduciary Duties to Corporate Stakeholders,* 21 DEL. J. CORP. L. 27 (1996).
68. The literature on this subject is extensive. On the stakeholder side, see Margaret M. Blair and Lynn A. Stout, *A Team Production Theory of Corporate Law,* 85 VA. L. REV. 247 (1999). On the shareholder value side, see Mark E. Van Der Weide, supra. For a British view favoring shareholder value, *see Modern Company Law for a Competitive Economy: the Strategic Framework,*" 44 (Company Law Review Steering Group (1999); and Elaine Sternberg, CORPORATE GOVERNANCE IN THE MARKETPLACE, 2d ed. (Institute of Economic Affairs, London, 2004).

The Common Good of the Firm as the Fiduciary Duty of the Manager

Peter Koslowski

Realizing the common good is usually seen as the task of government and as an obligation for politicians, not for the managers of large corporations. The common good is a concept that is used constantly, that is made concrete rarely, and that is viewed as an empty concept more and more often. It seems to be a difficult obligation to work for the common good and to consider the effects of one's own action for the public good if, in a market society, everyone has the right to follow his or his/her self-interest or private good.

Nevertheless, the concept of public interest is indispensable, particularly indispensable for politics. The right of a politician to follow his or his/her private interest and that of his/his/her immediate clients in his/his/her office is defended by no one. The role description of the politician incorporates that he or he/she works for the common good in his/his/her action and not for his/his/her party's good. The demand for public interest is his/here no empty concept but something like a general clause that applies to all actions of politicians.

Politicians can consider their self-interest and strive for fame, prestige, and career as a side effect of their intention to realize the public good, but they cannot view the common good as the side effect of the realization of their self-interest.

In a market society, the reverse causation is effective it is often said. The shareholder and the manager of a corporation realize the common good of public efficiency as a side effect of the pursuit of their self-interest and profit so that in a market society the demand to realize the common good does not hold.

According to the invisible hand thesis of economics, the common good is not realized in the market by intending it but by the working of the invisible hand of the market that turns selfish interests into efficiency and wealth creation. The kernel theorem of the invisible hand theory is that the common good of efficiency and wealth creation is realized in a market society as a side effect of the pursuit of self-interest. It is, however, not clear how far this theorem is taken by Adam Smith as a description of fact or as a normative statement.

The Common Good of States and the Common Good of Other Social Groups and Business Corporations

It is characteristic for the theory of the common good that it does not confine the demand for realizing the common good to the state. Every community or organization has its common good and its task to realize it.[1] The idea of the common good of groups shows that the common good is not only a concept for the totality of the common good of the whole of state and society but at the same time it is a totality of totalities that is structured internally. Every community or organization, be it a business corporation, a university, or a school, is not only characterized by the private interest of each of those working in them but also by the interest of all working in these institutions. All are interested in the prospering of their institution and the continuation of this situation since the continuation of the whole institution and this/hereby of all the groups in it is endangered if certain individuals or groups in this institution are damaged in their good. The solidarity of the interests and of the common good of the groups or stakeholders in an organization makes it impossible to define the good of an organization only by the good of a single group or only some individuals.

The connectedness or solidarity of the groups and individuals in an institution holds, however, not only for their connectedness within an institution. It also concerns, although to a lesser degree, the different individuals or institutions working in the same field—be this field a shared profession or a shared industry.

Recent research in business ethics shows that this/here is a common good of an industry and of a profession besides the corporate good of the corporation. The corporations of an industry or the individuals of a profession are connected in their prosperity and share a common interest in the well-being of the industry or profession. If, e.g., certain firms damage the consumers they damage by doing so the reputation of the whole industry. The member of a profession like a medical doctor damages the reputation of the whole profession by damaging a client or patient. By his/her "unprofessional" behavior, he/she not only damages the consumer or client but also the other members of an industry or a profession.

On the higher level of the economy of a region or continent, even of the whole world economy, a similar connectedness of the common goods holds true. Economies are connected in their common good even if this is so to a decreasing degree of intensity depending on the measure of remoteness of groups from each other. No part of humanity can prosper in the long run if another part of humanity is in desperate need.

The structure and sequence of communities result in a structure and sequence of the common goods of groups that correspond to the specific connectedness of the members of these groups. Their common good and joint interest are caused by the closeness of the humans in their respective groups and by the subsidiarity of the tasks of groups and organizations. The public interest of smaller groups and institutions is the subsidiary condition of the common good of the whole of society and vice versa. The political union or state can only prosper if the intermediary social institutions like families, corporations, etc. prosper.

Modernity as the Emancipation of Self-Interest?

The era of modernity is often seen as the epoch of the emancipation of self-interest in which the demand for a consideration of the common good in the individual pursuit of interest has become obsolete. Modernity seems to have no need for the motive of intending to realize the common good. Some thinkers of Public Choice theory and its model of democracy go so far to say that even the political order of the democratic state cannot be understood in categories of the common good but must be seen as the mere result of the composition of individual self-interested votes and of self-interested politicians. Public Choice theory is an important innovation if it is understood as a critical theory of the actual motivation of politicians and as a critique of the naive idea that politicians have different and *per se* better motives than the decision-makers of the private sector. Public Choice theory becomes, however, problematic if it excludes *a priori* the possibility that politicians try to find out and to realize the common good.[2]

Adam Smith who is considered by some social scientists the founder of modernity has stated only as a fact, not as a norm, that it is not from the benevolence, but from the self-interest of the butcher, brewer, or baker that we expect to get what we need for food. This statement by Adam Smith[3] seems to be interpreted by some of today's economists to be a normative statement describing how it *ought* to be. They contend that it is not only a fact that we depend on the producer's self-interest, but it is normatively demanded that we ought to depend only on the producers' self-interest for being provided with goods.

From the textual base and from the synopsis of his two works, *The Theory of Moral Sentiments* and *The Wealth of Nations*, it must be concluded that Adam Smith took his statement only as a statement of fact and not of normative content. The butcher is free, of course, to provide his services also for the common good, even for philanthropic or altruistic reasons. The market cannot rely on these higher motives but it does not exclude them as a norm that these higher motives ought not to be realized. The exasperation of the self-interest theorem to a normative principle would make the "Adam Smith Problem" of how Smith's ethical and economic theory is compatible, unsolvable. Since Smith has written both treatises, they must be reconcilable in his mind. The market coordinates self-interested action. The content of the motives of self-interest is left open by the price system. Common good orientation is as possible as narrow self-interest, and possible are also mixed motives and an over-determination of human action by various self-interested and common good motives.

The Public Interest of Institutions and the Increase of the Responsibility for the Public Interest to the Degree of the Power of Those Managing the Institutions

Every organization and institution possesses its specific common interest or good common to the organization. It has the task to realize the interest of the organization as a whole. The obligation towards the orientation on the public interest increases with the increasing impact of decisions and with the decision-maker's increasing power since the side-effects, the positive and negative side-effects of an action, increase with the action's impact. The acting persons are obliged to consider the public interest in those ranges of action that are relevant for the public interest. The fact that the decision problem becomes more difficult and complex by the duty to consider the public interest must not imply that the increasing complexity of the decision frees the decision-maker from the consideration of its side-effects on the public interest. The increasing complexity of decision-making only implies that in judging the success of a decision in itself and in considering the public good the difficulty of the task has to be taken into consideration.

The obligation to include the side-effects of one's decision-making on the public good increases with increasing power. This increasing obligation to consider the public good indicates that power itself is a moral phenomenon. The more power a person possesses the more the person must consider the side-effects of his or his/her decision-making. The idea of the public interest points to this relationship between power and the duty to consider the public good.

As Roman Herzog has demonstrated,[4] it has been Thomas Aquinas who has introduced two insights to political philosophy by his idea of the common good: first the insight that sovereignty and the exercise of political power do not have their criterion of action in themselves but refer to a higher authority and are therefore a constraint in their freedom, and secondly the insight that the state *and* the individual are bound by the common good. Thomas Aquinas starts from monarchy in his theory of the common good and binds the ruler to an authority outside of the ruler's own will and self-interest. The ruler cannot only follow his free and sovereign will. He is not only directed by his own interest but by the higher authority of the common good and is constraint by it in his will and sovereignty. His office or duty is to further the common good. Government is not this/here to increase the self-interest of those governing.

The idea of the common good leads to the development of the modern idea of office. The political office is obliged to realize the common good, it is not this/here to increase the power or advantage of the office holder and his self-interest. It is not only the self-interest of the state, the *raison d'état,* or the sovereignty of the prince or king and his self-interest that matter. The office, particularly the political office, bears in itself the obligation to good governance and is bound by the effect of the decisions on the common good.

The idea of office that is concluded from the idea that power is bound by the public good does not only constrain political, but also economic, cultural, and religious power. The idea of office shows that power is a moral phenomenon and therefore always related to the common good. Not only political power is an office that is not only defined by the sovereign will of the one in power and that is subject to what is demanded by the realization of the common good. The same holds true for the holder of an economic, religious, and cultural office and its concomitant power.

The obligation to include the idea of the common good in the individual decision-making of economic, religious, and cultural power as well as in those of political power follows from the fact that the individualist decision-making processes of the market and of democracy cannot function without such a consideration of the public good since frictions in the economic and political realm are the consequence if they are based on self-interest only.

The need for the consideration of the common good in the market and in democracy arises first from the problem of the aggregation or composition of individual decisions determined by self-interest to a market price and to a political decision. The phenomena of market failure and of democracy failure describe such frictions of coordination in the market and in democracy. The need to consider the common good also arises on the other hand from the fact that the holder of economic and political responsibility are not only the agents of the principals that give them the agency power but also of those, even if so to a lesser degree, that they do not represent but whose life is influenced deeply by their decisions. The holders of an office must consider the common good of the institutions which they direct beyond their mere agency duties to those who gave them the power to manage or to govern their principals. Fiduciary duty is more then agency, then acting in the interest of one's principal. It is the duty to act for the good of the whole institution, of the entity for which one has been authorized to act by the principals.

The Obligation of Managers to Realize the Common Good of Their Corporations

The obligation to consider the common good is not only valid for the politician. The politician is not only the agent of his/his/her constituency and party but is always at the same time the representative of those that did not vote for his/her. Likewise, the manager of a large firm is not only the agent of those who employed him-the shareholders or owners of a firm-but also the fiduciary of those who work under his leadership by virtue of his being the fiduciary of the whole firm. The obligation to realize the common good of the institution is therefore also valid for the manager of the large firm.[5] It is his or his/her fiduciary duty towards the firm the manager works for.

The fiduciary duty defines the duties of the manager as the duty to good faith, the duty to loyalty towards the firm, the duty of care and prudence, and the duty of disclosure.[6] In fulfilling these duties, the manager is not free to follow his/her own interest or the shareholder's interest at the cost of fulfilling the fiduciary duties towards the firm. Rather, the shareholders invest the managers with their office to further the good of the whole corporation, and not only their, the shareholders', own good. It is a kind of self-binding on the side of the shareholders and the managers that is instituted by the law of fiduciary duty that goes beyond mere shareholder and manager interest.

The duty of loyalty in the fiduciary duties obliges the manager to the undivided and unselfish loyalty to the corporation, not to the shareholders. It is more then mere contract, namely an obligation towards the firm as a whole.

The duty to care and prudence obliges the managers to act in the interest of their corporation, not in the interest of themselves or of the firm's shareholders.

The duty of disclosure obliges the managers not to take advantage of knowledge confidentially acquired in the course of their work for the firm or of knowledge given to them by the shareholders about the firm. Their fiduciary duty of disclosure excludes the use of this knowledge as insider knowledge for making insider deals in the pursuit of their duties as managers of the firm or as private party. The prohibition of making use of insider knowledge or the duty to disclosure follows from the fiduciary duty of the manager towards the firm and the shareholders, but not to the shareholders only.

The manager is not only the agent of his/her principals, be they shareholders or single owners, and he has more duties than those of realizing the interest of the shareholder group in profit maximization only. The managers must consider the interest of the whole firm which includes taking into consideration the interests of other stakeholders when they realize the legitimate shareholder interest in return on investment. By maximizing shareholder value, the manager must at the same time realize the common good of the entire firm.[7] The manager's task to realize the maximum productivity of the firm cannot be secured by the market, competition, and the price system alone. The manager must realize productivity even where the power of competition does not force him/her to do so as e.g. in imperfect markets or in developing nations. This indicates that the productivity of the firm is a kind of common good of the firm beyond mere profit maximization.[8]

The decision-maker of an institution cannot dispense him- or his/herself from the responsibility for the common good of the institution by pointing to the duty towards the shareholders only. Referring to a narrow principal-agent relationship instead of the full fiduciary duty towards the whole firm can include an element of exculpation from responsibility. Every kind of principal-agent relationship or of acting for the sake of someone else and of someone else's goals leads to a reduction in the moral obligation since, by the agency relationship, the responsibility for actions is divided between the principal and the agent and can be shifted forward and backward between them.

The danger of such a reduction of the total responsibility of management for the common good of a firm can be demonstrated in the exaggeration of the shareholder value principle as the only goal of the firm. The theory that it is the task of the firm to increase the value of the firm and its shares for the owner of the firm only and that the management success is only measured by the attainment of this goal reduces the complexity of the management's obligation towards the common good of the firm.[9] All other goals of groups of firm members are rendered to be only means for the final end of the return on the owner's investment. The effect is that the management can exculpate itself from the responsibility towards the other groups of the firm.

The manager is not only the agent of the owners but at the same time the steward of all groups in the firm and the fiduciary of the firm as a whole. The distinction between agency and fiduciary duty, between being an agent and being a fiduciary, holds true even more for the politician who has a democratic mandate. The politician cannot be seen as the agent of his/her immediate constituency only. He/she must accept that he/she has the duty of office or the fiduciary duty towards the common good, the duty to represent all voters. Politics and management are a fiduciary office that does not only include the duty towards furthering the interests of the principals, be they shareholders or voters or constituency, but that implies beside the immediate agency relationship with the principal the fiduciary duty and duty of stewardship towards the common good of the firm. The interest of the principal, of the voter or the shareholder, and the interest of all people concerned, of the total voting population or of all employees of the firm, must be considered at the same time. This/here is no unlimited autonomy of the voter or of the shareholder as principals to define the duties of their agents, the politician or the manager. The manager's fiduciary duty is not only an obligation towards the shareholders, even it is primarily so, but also towards the corporation as a whole.

By giving agency power to a member of parliament or a minister or to a manager, the person invested with this power, the politician or the manager, cannot be obliged to neglect the common interest and to realize only the interest of his or his/her immediate principals. In the market, the consumer, the shareholder, and the manager representing them as well as in politics the voter and the member of parliament representing the voter must understand their right to decide to be an office and fiduciary duty that aims at the common good of their institutions. The politician or the manager cannot understand themselves as autonomous lobbyists or agents only of that segment of the constituency or the firm that voted for them or employed them.

The idea of the common good and of the boundness of decision-makers in government and in economic institutions by the fiduciary duty towards the good of their institutions is not an idea imposed from the outside and in a normativist way on the principals' and the agents' individual self-interest, be they voters and politicians in the political arena or shareholders and managers in the market. The idea of the common good does not impose a situation of heteronomy on them. Rather, the idea of the common good demands the inclusion of the public interest in the enlightened self-interest of those that have power to decide. Powerful decision-makers can only realize their own and their principals' self-interest if the institutions they direct are flourishing. Decision-makers cannot reply to the objection that the common good of their institutions is not realized by replying that they acted only as agents of their principals. The politician cannot exculpate himself/herself in cases of government failure by answering that he/she only acted in the interest of the voters that gave him/her their vote. The manager whose firm is becoming smaller and smaller while it pays high dividends to shareholders cannot justify his or his/her action by pointing to the fact that the interest of the shareholders have been realized. Fiduciary duty is more then mere agency for someone else.

The idea of the common good implies that the general, entire, or total interest of an institution is fulfilled. The total interest of an institution is to be derived from the nature of the task of the institution. The neglect of the common good leads to a violation of the total good of an institution. It leads therefore to functional friction and to the incomplete fulfillment of the task of the institution.

The idea of the common good of an institution shows that institutions cannot reach their optimal performance and due diligence without anticipating their common good in the self-interested decisions of the people acting in them. The interest on the realization of optimal performance and due diligence leads to acknowledging the inevitable task to consider as well the common good as the self-interest of its member in the governance of institutions, be they political or economic.[10] The purely individualistic pursuit of goals in the market or in democracy without consideration to the common good of the polity or the firm in the individual interests of those who have to make far-reaching decisions causes a suboptimal performance of the institution in question, the firm or the polity.

Notes

1. Cf. Gundlach (1959), col. 738.
2. James Buchanan, in a recent paper, does not discard the common good principle completely but retains it as a regulative principle. He contends that by the imposition of the constraint of the non-discrimination principle on all political decisions, politicians would be forced to think about "approaches of the true consideration of the common good interest" (my translation of the German version of the paper). Cf. James M. Buchanan: "Gleiche Spieler, anderes Spiel. Wie bessere Regeln der Politik auf die Sprünge helfen / Mit geeigneten Anreizen zum Gemeinwohl" (Same players, different game. How better rules help politics to get started / With the right incentives to the common good), *Frankfurter Allgemeine Zeitung,* Nr. 80, 3 April 2004, p. 13 (page "The Order of the Economy"). The non-discrimination principle that political decisions that discriminate against certain group or favor interest groups at the cost of all becomes a constraint on politicians that enables them to take the common good into consideration. The political process is his/here seen as a process that includes the consideration of the common good.
3. Adam Smith: *The Wealth of Nations,* in: *The Works of Adam Smith,* Vol. 2, 1811-12, Re-print Aalen (Otto Zeller) 1963, Book 7, chap. 2, 21.
4. Herzog (1974), col. 256.
5. Cf. H. Alford and N. Naughton: "Working the Common Good: The Purpose of the Firm," in: S. A. Cortright and Michael J. Naughton (Eds.): *Rethinking the Purpose of Business. Interdisciplinary Essays from the Catholic Social Tradition,* Notre Dame, Indiana (University of Notre Dame Press) 2002.
6. See the paper by Joseph F. Johnston: "Natural Law and the Fiduciary Duties of Business Managers" in this volume.
7. This need for a constraint on self-interest applies also to the stakeholder theory of the firm. One might be tempted to think that the stakeholder approach is closer to the common good idea than the shareholder approach since it includes, ideally, all stakeholders in the firm whereas the shareholder group is only one group of the firm. The stakeholders may, however, form coalitions against the shareholders or form other coalitions against other stakeholders, coalitions that do not represent the common good of the firm. The shareholders as the outside controlling institution of the firm may have to enforce the common good of the firm against stakeholder coalitions that are not in the interest of the long run survival of the firm.

8. Cf. also L. A. Tavis: *Power and Responsibility: Multinational Managers and Developing Country Concerns,* Notre Dame, Indiana (University of Notre Dame Press) 1997.
9. Cf. P. Koslowski: "Shareholder Value and the Purpose of the Firm," in: S. A. Cortright and Michael J. Naughton (Eds.): *Rethinking the Purpose of Business. Interdisciplinary Essays from the Catholic Social Tradition,* Notre Dame, Indiana (University of Notre Dame Press) 2002.
10. Confer for the part of political governance of the common good problem P. Koslowski: "Public Interest and Self-Interest in the Market and the Democratic Process", in: Bernard Hodgson (Ed.): *The Invisible Hand and the Common Good,* Berlin, New York, Tokyo (Springer-Verlag) 2004.

Bibliography

Alford, H., & Naughton, N. (2002). Working the common good: The purpose of the firm. In: Cotright, S. A., & Naughton, M. J. (Eds.), *Rethinking the purpose of busi - ness. Interdisciplinary essays from the Catholic social tradition.* Notre Dame, Indiana: University of Notre Dame Press.

Buchanan, J. M. (1954 a): Social choice, democracy, and free markets, *Journal of Political Economy,* 62, 114-123.

Buchanan, J. M. (1954 b): Individual choice in voting and the market, *Journal of Political Economy,* 62, 334-343.

Buchanan, J. M. (2004). Gleiche Spieler, anderes Spiel. Wie bessere Regeln der Politik auf die Sprünge helfen / Mit geeigneten Anreizen zum Gemeinwohl (Same players, different game. How better rules help politics to get started / with the right incentives to the common good), *Frankfurter Allgemeine Zeitung,* 80, 3 April 2004, p. 13 (page "The Order of the Economy").

Buchanan, J. M., & Tullock, G. (1962). *The calculus of consent.* Ann Arbor: University of Michigan Press.

Dahl, R. A. (1987). Dilemmas of pluralistic democracy: The public good of which public. In: P. Koslowski (Ed.), *Individual liberty and democratic decision making. The ethics, economics, and politics of democracy.* Tübingen: Mohr Siebeck.

Downs, A. (1968 [1957]). *Ökonomische Theorie der Demokratie.* Tübingen: (J. C. B. Mohr [Paul Siebeck]) 1968 (engl. 1957).

Evangelischen Kirche in Deutschland, Ed. (1991). *Gemeinwohl und Eigennutz—Wirtschaftliches Handeln in Verantwortung für die Zukunft; eine Denkschrift der Evangelischen Kirche in Deutschland.* Gütersloh: Güterslohis/her Verlagshaus Gerd Mohn.

Gundlach, G. (1959). Artikel "Gemeinwohl," *Staatslexikon der Görres-Gesellschaft,* Freiburg i. Br. (His/herder), 6th ed., col. 737-740.

Hayek, F. A. V. (1968). *Der Wettbewerb als Entdeckungsverfahren.* Kiel: Institut für Weltwirtschaft.

His/herzog, R. (1974). Artikel "Gemeinwohl II," in: J. Ritter (Hrsg.): *Historisches Wörterbuch der Philosophie.* Darmstadt: Wissenschaftliche Buchgesellschaft, Vol. 3, col. 256-258.

Hibst, P. (1991). *Utilitas Publica–Gemeiner Nutz–Gemeinwohl. Untersuchungen zur Idee eines politischen Leitbegriffes von der Antike bis zum späten Mittelalter.* Frankfurt a.M. u.a. (Peter Lang).

Hirschman, A. O. (1970). *Exit, voice and Loyalty: Responses to decline in firms, organiza - tions and states.* Cambridge, Mass.: Harvard University Press.

Jänicke, M. (1980). *Zur Theorie des Staatsversagens, Aus Politik und Zeitgeschichte (Das Parlament)*, 14, 29-39.

Jetzer, M.(1975). *Öffentliches Gut und Externalität. Ein Paradigma des Marktversagens,* Diss. rer. pol., Zürich.

Kahn, A. E. (1966). The tyranny of small decisions: market failures, imperfections, and the limits of economics, *Kyklos*, 19, 23-45.

Kettern, B. (1992). *Sozialethik und Gemeinwohl. Die Begründung einer realistischen Sozialethik bei Arthur F. Utz.* Berlin: Duncker & Humblot.

Koslowski, P. (1982). *Gesellschaft und Staat. Ein unvermeidlichis/her Dualismus.* Mit einer Einführung von R. SPAEMANN. Stuttgart: Klett-Cotta.

Koslowski, P. (1987). Market and democracy as discourses. Limits of discursive societal coordination. In: P. Koslowski (Ed.), *Individual liberty and democratic decision making.* Tübingen: Mohr Siebeck.

Koslowski, P. (1997). Subsidiarität als Prinzip der Koordination der Gesellschaft. In: K. W. Nörr, Th. Opper¬mann (Hrsg.), *Subsidiarität: Idee und Wirklichkeit. Zur Reichweite eines Prinzips in Deutschland und Europa.* Tübingen: Mohr Siebeck, S. 39-48.

Koslowski, P., Ed. (1999). *Das Gemeinwohl zwischen Universalismus und Partikularismus* (The Common Good between Universalism and Particularism). Stutt¬gart: Frommann-Holz¬boog.

Koslowski, P. (2001). *Principles of ethical economy.* Dordrecht: Kluwer Academic Publishers.

Koslowski, P. (2002). Shareholder value and the purpose of the firm. In: Cortright, S. A., & Naughton, M. J. (Eds.), *Rethinking the purpose of business. Interdisciplinary essays from the Catholic social tradition.* Notre Dame, Indiana: University of Notre Dame Press.

Koslowski, P. (2004). Public interest and self-interest in the market and the democratic process. In: Hodgson, B. (Ed.), *The invisible hand and the common good.* Berlin, New York, Tokyo: Springer-Verlag.

Matz, U. (1985). Aporien individualistischis/her Gemeinwohlkonzepte. In: A. RAUSCHIS (Hrsg.), *Selbstinteresse und Gemeinwohl. Beiträge zur Ordnung der Wirtschaftsgesellschaft.* Berlin: Duncker & Humblot, 321-357.

Mishan, E. (1971). The postwar literature on externalities. An interpretative essay. *Journal of Economic Literature*, 9, 1-29.

Nawroth, E. (1994).Art. "Gemeinwohl", in: F. Geigant u.a.: *Lexikon der Volkswirtschaft.* Landsberg: Verlag Moderne Industrie, 6th ed., 325-326.

Rendtorff, T. (1994). Gemeinwohl und Eigennut –Perspektiven für den Dialog zwischen Kirche und Wirtschaft, In: P. Bocklet, G. Fels, H. Löwe (Hrsg.), *Der Gesellschaft verpflichtet. Kirche und Wirtschaft im Dialog.* Köln: Deutschis/her Instituts-Verlag, 145-164.

Runciman, W. G., & Sen, A. (1965). Games, justice and the general will. Mind, 74, 554-562.

Schelling, T. C. (1974). On the ecology of micromotives. In: Marris, R. (Ed.), *The cor - porate society.* London: Macmillan.

Schelling, T. C. (1978). *Micromotives and macrobehavior.* New York: Norton.

Sen, A. (1970). *Collective choice and social welfare.* San Francisco: Holden Day.

Smith, Adam (1963). *The wealth of nations.* In: *The works of Adam Smith,* Vol. 2, 1811-12, Reprint Aalen (Otto Zeller).
Tavis, L. A. (1997). *Power and responsibility: Multinational managers and developing country concerns.* Notre Dame, Indiana: University of Notre Dame Press.
Tullock, G. (1970). *Private wants–public means. An economic analysis of the desirable scope of government.* New York: Basic Books.
Tullock, G. (1971). Public decisions as public goods. *Journal of Political Economy,* 79, 913-918.
Utz, A.-F. (1958). *Sozialethik. Mit internationaler Bibliographie. I. Teil: Die Prinzipien der Gesell¬schaftslehre,* Heidelberg (F. H. Kerle) / Löwen (E. Nauwelaerts).
Weisbrod, B. A. (1964). Collective-consumption services of individual-consumption goods. *Quarterly Journal of Economics,* 78, 471-477.

Subsidiarity as a Business Model

Gerald J. Russello

Introduction

This is an exciting time to be working within the tradition of Catholic Social Thought. Modern Catholic Social Thought, or "CST," began with Pope Leo XIII's 1891 encyclical on "the social question," which is known under the title *Rerum Novarum*. But it has been the pontificate of Pope John Paul II that has inspired a wave of new thinking by Catholic scholars seeking to apply CST to contemporary social, political, and economic questions. Indeed, CST has now shifted from its concerns in the early 20th century over the growth of the state and of the relations between the state and the Church, to focus increasing attention on the business world and the new economic forms created by the "global economy."

Americans, and not just Catholics, are conflicted about the role corporate organizations should play in the nation's political and economic life. On the one hand, the dot-com bust and the subsequent revelations of corruption across several industries have revealed a dark underbelly of the "creative destruction" of capitalism. Once-respected companies like Enron and professional partnerships such as Arthur Andersen have become by-words for greed and the neglect of public responsibilities for private interests. On the other hand, the boom that preceded the bust confirmed America as an investor nation. More Americans are participating in the stock market, either directly or through intermediaries like 401(k) plans or mutual funds, and the forces of globalization are sweeping aside other forms of economic organization. The issues being debated range from the structure of corporation to their global social responsibilities, and cross the usual political and economic categories. In his 1991 encyclical, *Centesimus Annus,* which marked the 100th anniversary of *Rerum Novarum,* Pope John Paul II reaffirmed the traditional Catholic support for private property while at the same time rooting a respect for capitalism in broader theological reflections on the nature of work and the dignity of the person. There should be no doubt now, if there ever were, that the personal initiative and enterprise, linked to making a profit, that is the heart of the free market system is considered a good in Catholic thought. In the words of *Centesimus Annus,* "[t]he modern business economy has positive aspects. Its basis is human freedom exercised in the economic field, just as it is exercised in may other fields" (*Centesimus Annus,* par. 32).

But this acceptance was not unqualified, and these qualifications continue another theme of CST: applying limits to business conduct based on traditional Catholic moral principles. *Centesimus Annus* goes on to say that "the purpose of a business firm is not simply to make a profit, but is to be found in its very existence as a community of persons who in various ways are endeavoring to satisfy their basic needs, and who form a particular group at the service of the whole of society" (*Centesimus Annus,* par. 32). This community certainly includes the employees and managers of a business firm. But this community also includes the shareholders and possibly other constituencies who may have claims (moral or legal) on the business enterprise.

The explosion in writing about the implications of CST has resulted in varying conclusions about what the tradition actually says about business conduct and organization. Michael Naughton and others, for example, have tried to reconceptualize the role of profit-maximization in the businesses corporation. Scholars like Amy Uelmen are developing critiques of common-law rules based on a Trinitarian "theology of communion." And economics has not escaped this current wave of Catholic critique. Recent work in economics has supported the CST conclusion that profit need not be the only sole economic criterion of success. Professors Stefano Zamagni and Luigino Bruni, for example, have developed a critique of "utilitarian" economics by focusing on the economic effects of reciprocity and happiness. "Economics," Bruni writes, "neglects something important which affects people's happiness" (Bruni, 2004, p. 22). Its reduction of the person to a *homo economicus,* while useful for some limited purposes, fails to capture the full complexity of modern economic relationships. Zamagni has characterized conventional economic thinking as embodying "a limited conception of personal well-being and the common good which takes little account of human capacities for moral sentiments going well beyond the limited accounting of personal and immediate gains" (Zamagni, 2003, p. 1). That is to say, modern economics fails to capture human actions such as altruism that have economic effects. Other scholars have explored the importance of social capital and "relational" goods that are not captured in the standard profit-maximization economic models.

As Mark Sargent has discussed, CST "is by definition a sphere of prudential judgment in which we try to discern the meaning of our faith for complex questions of social and economic life. It thus allows for disagreement, change, and development in understanding" (Sargent, 2003, p. 2). Sargent has characterized the schools that dominate CST in America in shorthand as the "right" and "left" wings. The core principles of CST are the same, but are interpreted quite differently. The work has been interesting, but as Sargent notes, "much groundwork needs to be done before we can construct a CST theory of the corporation and a CST-inspired method of resolving problems in the law of corporations" (Sargent, 2003, p. 3).

The right wing, represented principally by Michael Novak, sees CST through what I would call a Cold War lens. The great danger to human freedom, on this view, is state power and its potential control of individual freedom. Novak and others hold that intermediary institutions such as corporations serve as bulwarks against state power and protectors of individual liberty. The corporation, because of its dynamism, size, and wealth, is among the best protectors of individual freedom against state power. Therefore, state power (primarily in the form of taxation or regulation) over the corporation and its activities should be limited. Further, Novak has contended that corporations have a theological foundation. The corporate form provides "signs of grace" through and in which busy modern people live out their faith. Stephen Bainbridge has updated this critique. He has employed the methods of law and economics to demonstrate that traditional corporate rules, such as the shareholder-maximization principle, remain sound both in economics and in terms of CST (Bainbridge, 1993, p. 1423). These scholars have interpreted the Catholic tradition, and especially Pope John Paul II's writings on the economy, as an endorsement of the American-style free market. While controversial, thinkers like Novak and Bainbridge have made an important contribution to CST by recognizing that the business world and its operations now must be centers of theological reflection for Catholics.

What Sargent calls the left wing, on the other hand, has a less positive view of the corporation as a sign of God's incarnational presence. It sees CST as providing a reasoned basis for the government to interfere with business arrangements for the common good. In particular, while thinkers like Novak generally endorse current corporate forms, the left wing believes that the proper application of Catholic social principles would result in a different kind of economic system. This work has resulted in calls to abolish the legal "personhood" of the corporation (Quigley). The CST theory of property, drawn from Aquinas, also stresses that property, while privately owned, must be made available for common use. Some have interpreted this injunction to mean that owners hold property in trust, and cannot use it to exploit others (Small, 2003, p. 2).

As with the right wing view, this view has its own theological basis: because corporations cannot act morally, the law should not treat them as persons, with all the concomitant protections that personhood brings. As Quigley has argued, "[t]hough there has been much discussion about making corporations morally or socially responsible, their legal DNA prevents them from acting like humans and having the chance to act in moral ways" (Quigley, 109). Therefore, the form should be abolished to allow "the full panoply of ethical and social responsibility" embodied in CST to act directly upon the individuals engaged in business conduct rather than indirectly through the corporate form.

While CST is still only just beginning to articulate a distinctive voice, it is part of a larger set of conversations about the place of Catholic thought in the modern and postmodern world. The last 20 years have witnessed a crisis in liberal political theory; its assertions of the "autonomous" individual with many rights and few obligations and the "neutral" state that offers no substantive vision of the common good has received a great amount of criticism, on both normative and empirical grounds. Philosopher John Gray, for example, has declared that "[i]t is evident that liberal political philosophy . . . has reached a dead end in which its intellectual credentials are negligible and its political relevance nil" (Gray, 1995, p. 66). Catholic theorists such as Robert P. George and John Finnis have engaged liberal political theory from a Catholic natural law perspective, and have tried to articulate a vision of political order that contains within it the promotion of substantive human goods. And in a specifically American context, the work of John Courtney Murray and other Catholic thinkers has been invoked to compare the Catholic vision of a democratic culture with a secularist, liberal one (Murray, 1960; Gould, 1992).

Examining CST and corporate issues is another aspect of the same conversation. The development of modern American corporate law has been in tandem with larger currents in American intellectual life (Millon, 1990, p. 201). The most influential statement of American corporate understanding is found in the 1919 case of *Dodge v. Ford Motor Co.,* in which the court (p. 684) declared "a business corporation is organized and carried on primarily for the profit of the stockholders." Since then, shareholder profit-maximization has been considered the cornerstone–indeed, the only logical organizing principle–of corporate structure. The contrasting positions of Adolf A. Berle and Gardiner C. Means and of E. Merrick Dodd remain the touchstone for the debate. Berle and Means contended in their 1933 classic, *The Modern Corporation and Private Property,* that the corporation existed to serve its shareholders' profit interests; duties to shareholders should be emphasized and management conflicts of interest reduced to serve this goal. The focus on the shareholders' interests excluded most public-oriented activities of the corporation, though some "corporate charity" was considered appropriate, but only if it contributed to the ultimate good of the shareholders. This argument was famously updated by Milton Friedman (1972, p. 177) when he compared using the corporation's resources for any other purpose tantamount to theft. Dodd took the opposite approach. He believed that as an entity chartered by the state, a corporation had a public dimension that could not be captured only by looking to the shareholders' interests (Dodd, 1932, p. 1148). Because management worked for the corporation as an entity and not directly for the shareholders, wealth maximization need not be the only governing principle for their decisions.

This long-running debate has set the stage for the task of current scholars exploring these issues from within the Catholic tradition. Whether the resources of CST can (or should) accommodate, cooperate with, or transform the structures of the modern business economy remains the subject of much controversy. In this paper, I focus on the Catholic concept of subsidiarity, which is one of the more familiar elements of CST. I will break it into some of its characteristic features, to see whether they can be used to help understand the contributions CST may be able to make to these larger debates.

Subsidiarity

Subsidiarity makes its first recognizable appearance in the 1931 papal encyclical Quadragesimo Anno. The encyclical describes subsidiarity as a principle of proper governance and envisions it as a series of authorities in widening and overlapping circles of responsibility. But the appropriate level of authority for a given function is more than just an administrative convenience: "[j]ust as it is gravely wrong to take from individuals what they can accomplish by their own initiative and industry and give it to the community, so also it is an injustice and at the same time a grave evil and disturbance of right order to assign to a greater and higher association what lesser and subordinate organizations can do. For every social activity ought of its very nature to furnish help to the members of the body social, and never destroy and absorb them" (*Quadragesimo Anno*, par. 79). Indeed, the encyclical goes on to define subsidiarity as a "fundamental principle of social philosophy."

As Robert Vischer notes, while the enunciation of the subsidiarity principle was somewhat new, it represented a longstanding Catholic social vision rooted in a "complex web of family, social, religious, and governmental ties" that served to support the exercise of the individual's responsibility in society (Vischer, 2001, p. 109). And it is still most often used as a defense of decentralized government authority or as an explanation of the circumstances under which government can act upon private enterprise. As a general matter, this interplay between government and private industry has strong support within the Catholic tradition. Pope John Paul II (*Centesimus Annus*, par.

15) has written that "[t]he State however, has the task of determining the judicial framework within which economic affairs are to be conducted, and thus of safeguarding the prerequisites of a free economy, which presumes a certain equality between the parties, such that one party would not be so powerful as practically to reduce the other to subservience." Governmental authorities are needed at several levels: to co-ordinate the activities of the lower levels of government with one another, with a view to the common good, and to make sure that private transactions are governed by certain "prerequisites," which at the very least seem to imply a rough equivalence in bargaining power. However, the underlying ethic of subsidiarity lends itself to application to economic organizations and not just to relations among levels of government or between the state and private entities.

The American bishops made extensive use of the term in their controversial 1986 pastoral letter, *Economic Justice for All.* The themes in that letter are not directly germane to the discussion here, as the thrust of the bishops' argument there was to set out the Church's teaching that the government has the responsibility to undertake tasks that are beyond the reach of individuals, and in particular that the government has the responsibility to care for those less fortunate. But the bishops did (*Economic Justice for All,* par. 298) call for "new institutional mechanisms for accountability that also preserve the flexibility needed to respond quickly to a rapidly changing business environment." In particular, the bishops called for new worker-management relationships, and more responsiveness by corporate managers to non-shareholder constituencies (*Economic Justice for All,* par. 303).

Five years later, *Centesimus Annus* returned to the subject of subsidiarity. That encyclical (*Centesimus Annus,* par., 48) defined it as follows: "a community of a higher order should not interfere in the internal life of a community of a lower order, depriving the latter of its functions, but rather should support it in case of need and help to co-ordinate its activity with the activities of the rest of society, always with a view to the common good." This definition was later included in the *Catechism of the Catholic Church.* The *Catechism* (par. 1894) also added that "in accordance with the principle of subsidiarity, neither the state nor any larger society should substitute itself for the initiative and responsibility of individuals and intermediary bodies." Here again the thrust in the discussion of subsidiarity is primarily on the relation between public institutions and the private sector, specifically, on providing smaller spheres of participatory governance where such local control is feasible. However, in its invocation of "societies" the language of the *Catechism* can be adapted to look at structures wholly within the world of private initiative.

With this background, I want to examine whether subsidiarity can be used to examine how corporate organizations are structured or to help define what, if any, the purposes of the corporate form should be. To do this, I want to focus on three characteristics of subsidiarity, which I will call (1) scope, (2) structure, and (3) purpose.

Scope

By scope I mean how we consider whether a corporation or business association is the "right size." Large corporations routinely come under fire merely for being too big, and criticizing their power is a long-standing American tradition. But corporations have never been as large as the largest of contemporary entities, or had their economic reach and cultural influence, which rival that of some smaller countries. The world has never seen, really, anything like Wal-Mart or ExxonMobil or Coca-Cola or JP Morgan Chase. To be at all effective, therefore, CST needs to address the questions the existence of these entities raise for economic ordering. But it should not be forgotten that most corporate entities are still family-owned or extremely small. There is some value in creating a corporation, and a CST analysis should not be distracted by the size and power of a handful of corporations from focusing on some of its advantages.

The Catholic understanding of subsidiarity does not criticize size per se. In the governmental use of subsidiarity, encyclicals such as *Pacem in Terris* endorse international action and agreements to solve international problems. The encyclical explicitly cites to "[t]he same principle of subsidiarity which governs the relations between public authorities and individuals, families and intermediate societies in a single State, must also apply to the relations between the public authority of the world community and the public authorities of each political community. The special function of this universal authority must be to evaluate and find a solution to economic, social, political and cultural problems which affect the universal common good" (*Pacem in Terris*, par. 140). The European Union has explicitly adopted a form of subsidiarity for its political arrangements. There does not therefore seem to be a prohibition within subsidiarity on the size of a corporate form. And it may be that just as with international agencies, some economic areas can be handled efficiently only by a large multinational or other corporation. Size becomes, in the words of *Quadragesimo Anno*, a "disturbance of right order" only when a larger collectivity assumes the functions of lesser entities or, implicitly, when its size becomes a hindrance to its own functions. Where that dividing-line may be is unclear. Nor is it clear whether CST would require corporations to reject expansion or growth opportunities if they violate other substantive principles.

The first step in looking at the scope of an activity, from a CST perspective, is to asses whether a larger structure within the corporation is subsuming functions that could be better left to smaller entities within it. At an organizational level, this process can involve programs designed to decentralize particular functions of the corporation, while retaining large-scale management decisions to the Board of Directors. The emphasis in subsidiarity is to determine the appropriate level of activity that furthers the flourishing of the corporation's workers, while still maintaining profitability. In other words, the issue of scope must take into account what is proper to the human person, and not to impersonal economic forces. *Laborem Exercens* (par. 15) is quite clear on this point, stressing the "priority of labor over capital," and warning that "excessive bureaucratic centralization" can extinguish the meaning that people put into their work. Such centralization can engender the feeling in employees that they are mere "production instrument[s]" rather than human persons. Bureaucracy and alienation, of course, can occur not only in socialist states but also in large companies. *Centesimus Annus* reminds us that people jointly pursuing projects share in a "community of work." To be a community of work means to treat individuals as persons, and not solely as means to profit for the shareholders. Therefore, one can anticipate a stage in an organization's growth where it can no longer respond, or even recognize, the needs of the members of the overlapping communities that make up its existence. So while CST may not oppose exceedingly large business associations on that basis alone, the size of an activity poses unique problems from a CST perspective. Therefore, analysis of this characteristic of subsidiarity could potentially encompass a range of issues, from human resources policies to job responsibilities, to see whether the scope of the corporation's intended conduct serves, even unintentionally, to strangle the sense of self-worth of the individual employee or manger.

This is not a question of neglecting profit. While there is a debate on how important profit should be to the life of a business, there is no question that profit is a criterion for success. But shareholder profit is not the only criterion; if it were, there would be no principled objection to the argument that bigger is better, if being bigger could attain larger profits for the shareholders. Granting primacy to profit also runs the risk of denigrating the individuals within the business firm: "It is possible for the financial accounts to be in order, and yet for the people—who make up the firm's most valuable asset—to be humiliated and their dignity offended" (*Centesimus Annus,* par. 35). Profit, then, must yield to considerations of human dignity.

The second step in considering scope is whether particular industries or economic sectors are at a greater risk of interfering with the "internal life" of their own constituent parts. For example, the ownership of news organizations by an entertainment conglomerate may pose difficulties for the proper functioning of the news organizations. The ability of the latter to achieve its function may be restricted by its inclusion within the larger entity. Or a mortgage company owned by an international financial consortium that has most of its customers in a specific geographic area may run the risk of having the individual mortgages "stripped" off and sold like other commodities, thus harming its reputation in the community and perhaps causing harm to the homeowners it serves. Or one could look to the growth of law firms and accounting firms from small, city-based partnerships to multinational limited liability structures with global clients. There is a significant literature, some of it anecdotal, that such growth has harmed not only the practice of those professions, but also the emotional and professional lives of those working under such conditions (Kaveny, 2001). Therefore, an analysis of the proper scope of a corporate organization needs to take into account the details of that economic sector and the various factors that go into the relevant business.

Structure

The second characteristic of subsidiary I have called structure. It deals with translating the general statements of CST into concrete proposals for corporate organization and governance. While CST refrains from endorsing any particular model of economic ordering, and while it has criticized both capitalism and socialism, it still must offer guidelines for what is and is not in accordance with Catholic principles for it to be effective in the larger conversation. As Sargent (2003, pp. 36-37) has noted, the realm of practical solutions is where CST has not yet fulfilled its promise.

What I am calling structure is usually captured by one of two debates. The first is the call for more democracy in corporate governance. This usually means more worker involvement or more shareholder control of what were previously considered issues of internal corporate governance. So, for example, religious orders and others have made frequent use of their voting power as shareholders to bring out issues of social importance. Scholars have proposed structures such as Employee Stock Ownership Plans (ESOPs) and other devices to achieve the goals of greater economic distribution of corporate property, and increased corporate democracy goals. The second is the so-called "stakeholder" debate, which argues for greater responsibility by corporate management, enforceable in law, to constituencies other than the corporation's shareholders. More shareholder involvement may in fact be a good thing, and is not inconsistent with subsidiarity, but neither is it absolutely necessary from a CST perspective. As Bainbridge notes, the corporation is one of the most hierarchical of organizations. There is no principled objection, as I see it, within CST to the hierarchical nature of the corporation per se and therefore to the restriction of shareholder involvement only to certain classes or categories of decisions.

Similarly, I do not want to continue the debate of whether other constituencies need to be recognized by management. There are objections to this position. Imposing legal obligations on directors for non-shareholder constituencies runs contrary to basic corporate law in America that the fiduciary duties of directors do not run to others outside of shareholders. The few stakeholder statutes that have been passed have generally been ineffectual. Nevertheless, some scholars have argued that a business' "common good" must include not just shareholders but other groups as well, and that the corporation's managers must incorporate those other groups into their decision-making. Like a politician who has responsibility not just for those who voted for him/her, but for all the voters, "the manager of a large firm is not only the fiduciary of those who employed him/her but also those who work under his leadership" (Koslowski, 2004, p. 6). Understanding the manager's "office" as a servant of the firm rather than the shareholders alone necessarily implies that the manger's duties include the totality of interests that make up the common good of the firm. The manager, as Pius XII implied, must respect the individual autonomy of the workers; as Calvez and Naughton (2002, pp. 7-8) have argued, this requires "employers and entrepreneurs to create workplace conditions that allow employees to develop."

I want to focus instead on a preliminary debate. Those working within CST should consider, in terms of structure, the way we envision the corporation. In the popular mind, the corporation is considered a "legal fiction," that is, a legal personality in which the directors act for the shareholders who have risked their equity for the corporation. This conception dates from the early decades of the 20th century when changes in law and business caused a movement from understanding the corporation as a state-chartered entity towards a view that understood the corporation as a "natural entity" established by the incorporators and shareholders, with only minimal state involvement (Millon, 1990, pp. 214-16). In contemporary scholarship, and increasingly in judicial opinions, that conception has been displaced by a view that treats the corporation as a "nexus of contracts." The contractual definition provides that "most organizations are simply legal fictions which serve as a nexus for a set of contracting relationships among individuals" (Jensen and Meckling, 1976, p. 310).

On the contractual view, therefore, there is no "corporation:" there are only individual contractual relationships that exist for the benefit of the contracting parties. Contractarian theory posits autonomous individuals who seek to make the most advantageous bargain. The emergence of the nexus of contracts theory provided an argument as to why corporations should not be deemed to have "public" character or any public responsibilities aside from profit-maximization. If the corporation is not a separate entity, and exists only to serve the profit-maximizing interests of the contracting parties, it cannot have any independent responsibilities to do anything else. Some CST scholars, such as Bainbridge (2002), have defended this model. The underlying assumption of the contractarian position posits freely-negotiated contracts for wages, services, or products. The underlying issue, however, is whether this "minimalist" understanding of contract captures the complexity present in some CST pronouncements, for example, *Rerum Novarum*'s (par. 43-45) assertion of "natural justice" that should condition the contracting parties' actions.

The mainstream of CST retains the older view of a corporation as a separate legal entity that has an independent existence from that of its shareholders. Even considered as a legal entity, however, the rights given to the corporation–immortality, primarily, but also limited liability and the separation of ownership and control-are still problematic from a CST perspective. They deviate in significant ways from Catholic anthropology, which sees the person as mortal, whose liability for sin and moral failing is personal, and who therefore must seek forgiveness and redemption, and whose life is integrated and oriented toward the common good and eventual life with God. These differences present a temptation for the corporation to act in ways that would not be considered moral if engaged in by a person.

But there is an additional structural consideration. In the modern financial world, the existence of an identifiable group of "shareholders" is not as clear-cut. In a mutual fund, for example, the owners of the mutual fund shares have a sometimes-fractional interest in actual companies. The mutual fund votes on their behalf, and they are more interested in the returns on the particular portfolios in which they are invested rather than, in most cases, the underlying companies. The investor in a mutual fund is different from the investor who purchases stock directly in a particular corporation. While the latter may be concerned about receiving profits from that company, and may be more interested in tracking the decisions of the company's board (thus exercising control over the board's actions), the mutual fund investor is in a different position. The mutual fund investor is "essentially a customer of the fund's management," and looks at the mutual fund as a means of managing investments rather than as a means of asserting his or her identity as a voting shareholder in an identifiable corporation (Carter, 2003, 10).

CST has not yet developed an understanding of the implications of these types of institutions. First, the individual mutual fund shareholders may have different goals or moral views from those of the mutual fund that votes a company's shares on its shareholders' behalf. If, as *Centesimus Annus* teaches, the question of how and where to invest is a moral choice, the choice must lie both with the individual mutual fund shareholders, as well as with the fund itself. Even if shareholder profit maximization is the proper goal, it is not clear whether corporate action that raises the value of the mutual fund company's shares always directly translates to the value of the shareholders' shares.

Purpose

Ultimately, Catholic social teaching directs us to consider the purpose of any human institution, and economic institutions are no exception. To quote again from *Centesimus Annus* (par. 35), "The purpose of a business firm is not simply to make a profit, but it is to be found in its very existence as a community of persons who in various ways are endeavoring to satisfy their basic needs, and who form a particular group at the service of the whole society." That is to say, part of the very purpose of the business entity is service to "basic needs." This does not mean that a company can disregard profit, nor does it mean that a company must bankrupt itself in social philanthropy. But it does impose some objective moral limits on corporate activity while at the same time providing two goals at which its manager should aim: satisfying needs and furthering the common good.

Dennis McCann has argued that while CST has not yet formed its own fully-articulated view of the corporation, "it may help clarify which, among competing theories of business, are the most consistent with the overall agenda of Catholic social thought" (McCann, 2002, p. 181). In this attempt at clarification, McCann turns to management theorist Peter Drucker, and specifically to Drucker's definition of the purpose of a business: "to create a customer." To do this effectively over time, Drucker enunciates several characteristics of a successful business that McCann contends are consistent with subsidiarity: decentralization, treatment of the customer as a "person" with which the corporation can build relationships, and that the structure of the corporation should be centered around building those relationships. In short, the "managerial hierarchy" envisioned by Drucker "is at the service of those who serve the needs of customers, and in that it is justified-entirely in keeping with the principle of subsidiarity-just so far as such service and support is actually required" (McCann, 2002, p. 184).

This is fine as far as it goes, but I would amend McCann's description in at least one respect. CST contains within it a substantive notion of the common good and the "needs" of individual persons that the corporation aims to fill. The critique CST has articulated against a certain adulation of capitalism is based on precisely this point. Untrammeled production can create a culture of consumerism and materialism, which is harmful to a full sense of the human person. Before allowing customers to be created, a "comprehensive picture of man which respects all dimensions of his being and which subordinates his material and instinctive dimensions to his interior and spiritual ones" must be recognized and accepted (*Centesimus Annus,* par., 36). Corporations do not need to find customers when they market things that people do not need, nor by innovating to create even more needs. In this sense, Drucker's contention that marketing and innovation are central concerns for the business enterprise is troubling from a CST perspective. Some needs are not recognized as legitimate by the Catholic tradition, and corporations that create or incite those needs are acting contrary to the common good.

Conclusion

The modern corporation is in significant ways the institutional parallel of the modern view of the person. The corporation maximizes profit for its shareholders. The liberal individual maximizes happiness or desire-satisfaction. The corporation engages in contracts to further its goals, and has no legal obligations to the wider society. The liberal individual engages in relationships or associations to further his or her own personal goals and can disengage from those attachments at any time.

CST presents important challenges to this model, by placing the individual into a larger network of relationships and duties. While concurring in the preservation of freedom and the beliefs in a free market, both the left and the right wings of CST reject the autonomous view of the person and the understanding of the corporation as an institution that has no goals other than those of the self-interest of its shareholders. Indeed, both wings see the corporation as having a public function. The public character of the corporate form creates certain public responsibilities. For the right wing, those responsibilities include the protection of individual liberty from state encroachment. For the left wing, those responsibilities may include the engagement in certain socially responsible acts.

While originally applicable to governmental relations with the private sector, subsidiarity can provide a method to analyze corporate conduct. This paper has tried to show that the principle of subsidiarity provides some guidance for assessing corporate forms and conduct. By looking at the scope, structure, and purpose of business corporations, CST can critique their satisfaction of basic, authentic, human needs and their contribution to achieving the common good.

Bibliography

Bainbridge, S. (2002). The bishops and the corporate stakeholder debate. *Villanova Journal of Investment Mgmt, 4,* 2-37.

__________. (1993). In defense of the shareholder wealth maximization norm: A reply to Professor Green. *Washington & Lee Law Review, 50,* 1423-1447.

Bruni, L. (2004). The "technology of happiness" and the tradition of economic science. *Journal of the History of Economic Thought, 26,* 19-43.

Calvez, Y. & Naughton, M. (2002). Catholic social teaching and the purpose of the business organization. In: M. Naughton and S.A. Cortright (Eds.), *Rethinking the purpose of business: Interdisciplinary essays from the Catholic social tradition* (pp. 3-22). Notre Dame: Notre Dame University Press.

Carter, D. (2003). Mutual fund boards and shareholder actions, *Villanova Journal of Investment Mgmt, 3,* 6-39.

Catechism of the Catholic Church (1995). New York: Image.

Dodge v. Ford Motor Company (1919). 170 N.W.2sd 668 (Michigan Supreme Court).

Friedman, M. (1972). *An economist's protest: Columns in political economy.*

Kaveny, C. (2001). Living the fullness of ordinary time: A theological critique of the instrumentalization of time in professional life. *Communio, 28,* 771-819.

Dodd, E. (1932). For whom are corporate managers trustees? *Harvard Law Review, 45,* 1145-1161.

Gould, W. (1992). The challenge of liberal political culture in the thought of John Courtney Murray. *Communio, 19,* 113-144.

Gray, J. (1995). *Enlightenment's wake.* London: Routledge.
Jensen, M. & Meckling, W. (1976). Theory of the firm: Managerial behavior, agency costs, and ownership structure. *Journal of Financial Economics, 3,* 310.
John XXIII. (1963). *Pacem in Terris* [Online]. Available: http://www.vatican.va/holy_father/john_xxiii/encyclicals/documents/hf_j-xxiii_enc_11041963_pacem_en.html.
John Paul II. (1991). *Centesimus Annus* [Online]. Available: http://www.vatican.va/holy_father/john_paul_ii/encyclicals/documents/hf_jp-ii_enc_01051991_centesimus-annus_en.html.
__________. (1981). *Laborem Exercens* [Online]. Available: http://www.vatican.va/holy_father/john_paul_ii/encyclicals/documents/hf_jp-ii_enc_14091981_laborem-exercens_en.html.
Koslowski, P. (2004). The common good of the firm as the "office" of the manager. *Paper presented at the International Ecumenical Conference,* June 10-12, 2004, Loyola University New Orleans.
Leo XIII. (1892). *Rerum Novarum* [Online]. Available: http://www.vatican.va/holy_father/leo_xiii/encyclicals/documents/hf_l-xiii_enc_15051891_rerum-novarum_en.html.
McCann, D. (2002). Business corporations and the principle of subsidiarity. In: M. Naughton and S.A. Cortright (Eds.), *Rethinking the purpose of business: Interdisciplinary essays from the Catholic social tradition* (pp. 169-89). Notre Dame: Notre Dame University Press.
Millon, David. (1990). Theories of the corporation. *Duke Law Journal,* 201-262.
Murray, J., S.J. (1960). *We hold these truths: Catholic reflections on the American proposition.* New York: Sheed and Ward.
Pius XI. (1931) *Quadagesimo Anno* [Online]. Available: http://www.vatican.va/holy_father/pius_xi/encyclicals/documents/hf_p-xi_enc_19310515_quadragesimo-anno_en.html.
Quigley, W. (204). Catholic social thought and the amorality of large corporations: Time to abolish corporate personhood. *Loyola Journal of Public International Law, 5,* 109-124.
Sargent, M. (2003). Competing visions of the corporation in Catholic social thought (on file with author).
Small, G. (2003). *Contemporary problems in property in the light of the economic thought of St. Thomas Aquinas.* Congresso Tomista Internazionale [Online]. Available: http://e-aquinas.net/pdf/small.pdf.
United States Catholic Bishops (1986). *Economic justice for all: Pastoral letter on Catholic social teaching and the U.S. economy* [Online]. Available: http://www.osjspm.org/cst/eja.htm.
Vischer, R. (2001). Subsidiarity as a principle of governance: Beyond devolution. *Indiana Law Review, 35,* 103-142.
Zamagni, S. (2003). Happiness and individualism: An impossible marriage. *Paper presented at "The Paradoxes of Happiness in Economics,"* University of Milano-Bicocca, Italy, March 2003.

The Hindu Executive and His Dharma

Krishna S. Dhir

Introduction

Throughout the history of the modern corporation, the separation of ownership from control has produced a set of enigmatic corporate problems, including those relating to the legitimacy of its authority, the efficacy of its bureaucracy, and the efficiency of its functioning (Dhir, 2003a). Smith (1776) questioned the ability of professional managers to manage the interests of joint stock company shareholders. Berle and Means (1932) described the structure and behavior of corporations in terms of the separation of ownership and control. Their work influenced subsequent scientific inquiry relating to structure and performance. Jensen and Meckling (1976) saw the potentially divergent interests of shareholders and the corporate managers as the fundamental issue in corporate governance. Moral and ethical dilemmas arising from conflicts between individual obligations and social responsibilities continue to plague contemporary corporate executives, who get inadequate guidance from professors of ethics for informed decision-making. In this article, we discuss insights offered by the Hindu philosophic literature, describing the Hindu executive's orientation toward resolution of corporate moral and ethical dilemmas. We present a paradigm for the virtuous decision-making behavior with applications. This paradigm describes dilemmas in terms of time-constrained decision-making necessitated by conflict between individual obligations and social responsibilities. The conflict unexpectedly requires decisions in an uncertain situation with inadequate time for research. First, we explore the scale of the problem and the nature of dilemmas.

Public Trust and Expectation

The confidence that corporate managers are good individuals, who can be trusted, fosters investment. In 1989, 52.3 million individuals in the United States owned stocks, either directly, or through mutual funds, retirement savings accounts, or defined pension plans. By 1998, this figure had already risen to 84 million individuals. These included 33.8 million Americans whose ownership was limited only to stocks in which they had invested directly. These figures may suggest a high degree of investor confidence in contemporary corporate managers. However, media reports on prevailing social and environmental impact of corporate activity are disappointing. In the aftermath of the Enron debacle in January 2002, the *Business Week*/Harris poll revealed that only 33 percent of Americans believed large companies had ethical business practices, and just 26 percent believed they were straightforward and honest in their dealings with consumers and employees. Earlier, *New York Times*/CBS News had found that in 1995, 55 percent of the American public believed that "the vast majority of corporate executives were dishonest," and 59 percent opined that, "executive white-collar crime occurred on a regular basis." Public trust had been severely compromised even though over 90 percent of the *Fortune 500* companies had ethical codes of conduct reminding their employees and stakeholders of their shared beliefs and values, and what was expected of them in terms of responsibilities and behavior (Wulfson, 1998).

The separation of ownership and control creates conditions that give rise to corporate dilemma. Votaw and Sethi (1973) explain that corporate dilemma results "from the collision between accepted traditional values and contemporary reality." Ethical breaches of trust are a conspicuous feature of the contemporary society, worldwide. Corporate executives are criticized for not fulfilling their responsibilities to the stakeholders. The AACSB International—Association to Advance Collegiate Schools of Business – describes these responsibilities as follows:

> In addition to providing a return to owners, business is charged with other straightforward tasks–acting lawfully, producing safe products and services at costs commensurate with quality, paying taxes, creating opportunities for wealth creation through jobs and investments, commercializing new technologies, and minimizing negative social and environmental impacts (AACSB, 2004, p. 10).

Although at first reading the above charge to the business executive seems "straightforward" enough, the execution of the tasks is not necessarily easy. It is reasonable to expect that products are safe. However, consider the dilemma of a corporate executive who discovers that a product potentially has a flaw or a defect, which is not entirely established but one that could potentially harm the customer. What should this executive do? What action should the executive take? What model of ethics should inform the executive? Both options, one of recalling the product, and the other of not doing so, challenge the executive. The executive may consider communicating with consumers about potential difficulty with the product. Would that be ethical? The flaw in the product is not established. The assets belong to another, and the consequences are borne by others as well. Product withdrawal may compromise opportunities of jobs and investments, and the returns to the owners. It may happen that the potential flaw was no flaw after all. On the other hand, the product may indeed be flawed. Would the executive not be wise to withdraw the product immediately before it harms someone?

There are a number of instances where corporations have recalled products from the marketplace without awaiting verification. Proctor and Gamble recalled the Rely product in 1980. Johnson & Johnson withdrew Tylenol in 1982. In these instances, the executives decided on actions that left the market open to their competitors. However, they acted to protect human welfare and save lives. In these cases, the companies were not certain that the products were flawed. However, they did not have adequate time to eliminate the uncertainty through research. They realized that they faced a genuine moral dilemma. They did not solve the dilemma, but they resolved it. Solving it would require that they fulfill their obligations to all parties involved. They did not do that. They opted to fulfill the obligation of social responsibility at the expense of other obligations. In these examples, the executives demonstrated the courage to act in protecting human welfare even in the midst of incomplete information, and showed integrity and humility in communicating with consumers about possible difficulties with a product (Williams and Houck, 1992). How are we to explain such decision-making behavior? What are the available models of ethical behavior that might guide an executive? A brief review of the literature is in order.

Literature Review

Epstein (1998) offers a sweeping review of the development of business ethics and corporate social policy. In the evolving literature on *ethical* decision-making, one can discern emergent interest in *virtuous* decision-making behavior as well (Beck-Dudley, 1996; Dhir, 2003a; Pincoffs, 1984; Williams and Houck, 1992). Virtuous behavior is demonstrated in the courage to act in protecting human welfare even with incomplete information about the potentially significant cost to the decision-maker. Dhir (2003b) has presented a paradigm for the study of the virtuous decision-making behavior, and identified the constituent elements of such decision-making process.

Ethical behavior need not necessarily be virtuous or courageous. It may very well be motivated by self-interest. Unethical behavior can also demand courage. However, virtuous behavior is both ethical and courageous. Philosophers (Rorty, 1986; Walton, 1986), psychologists (Deutsch, 1961; May, 1975), and theologians (Tillich, 1951) have explored the role of courageous behavior in the face of threats to one's own well being. Certain works suggest that in the context of helping others, courageous behavior may be based on a motivating purpose or mission of life (Cuff, 1993), and a desire to avoid cowardice (Asarian, 1981) and be fearless (Finfgeld, 1999). Nevertheless, various models suggested for the study of ethics are predominantly rule-based or rule-directed. Managers may practice with a narrative case, forewarned of the presence of an ethical dilemma. This approach is characterized as "quandary ethics" (Pincoffs, 1984). In practice, however, decision-makers do not usually have the benefit of forewarning. They identify problems, formulate solutions, and implement plans, while performing under varying degrees of stress, engaging in parallel sets of concomitant activities, and interacting with a number of people over a range of decisions, all within a time constraint. Loe, Ferrell, and Mansfield (2000) have reviewed various normative and positive models of ethical decision-making. Normative models seek absolute truths about a decision. Positive models seek to explain actual decision-making behavior (Hunt and Vittell, 1986; Thorne and Ferrell, 1993). Unfortunately, these models prove inadequate in their capacity to explain *virtuous* behavior (McCracken, Martin, and Shaw 1998; Bartlett and Preston, 2000).

Inadequacy of Theories

Two major theories of principle, the deontological and the utilitarian, dominate the contemporary discussion on ethics and moral obligations. The deontological approach studies the decision-making behavior in terms of binding obligations, as in duty (Kant, 1965). The utilitarian approach studies the decision-making behavior in the tradition of Bentham (1970) and Mill (1971), stressing the importance of utility over beauty or other considerations. The literature offers additional theories of principle that are equally inadequate for our purpose. For instance, Hobbes' non-utilitarian theory of egoism (Hobbes, 1914) suggests that individuals behave in self-interest. The egoist asks, "What is in it for me?" If there is no benefit to the individual, then there is no reason to behave ethically. Clearly, Hobbes' theory is of little help in understanding virtuous decision-making. The decision-making behavior demonstrated by executives dealing with the withdrawal of Rely and Tylenol are not be explained by the deontological or the utilitarian approaches, either. Unfortunately, these theories fall short of explaining behavior emanating from considerations of virtue.

Hindu Ethics and the Western Response

The Hindu philosophic literature offers an alternative theory. Central to this theory is the concept of *dharma,* or virtuous or righteous conduct. This concept offers us an opportunity to re-examine the nature of moral dilemma. In both classical and contemporary Hindu literature, dharma is explored through narratives, or telling of stories. These stories are rich in accounts of moral dilemmas, most of which remain unsolved. Such dilemmas arise when an agent—an individual, a group, or an organization—faces two or more obligations, but circumstances are such that the fulfillment of one violates one, some, or all of the other obligations. The decision-maker is faced with irreconcilable alternatives. The actual choice from among the alternatives becomes either irrational or based on grounds other than morals. This condition has provided Hindu writers with the opportunity of taking creative license of nesting stories within stories to explore in delightful detail the many aspects of moral dilemma and *dharma,* offering challenges and opportunities to their protagonists. The Hindu ethics requires the protagonist to be virtuous. For this, the protagonist must first recognize the nature of the difference between the irreconcilable alternatives, and then make a choice based on what wisdom can be mustered. It does not demand reconciliation. It only seeks resolution.

Western philosophers have generally had problems with Hindu treatment of dilemmas. Moral philosophers in the West have generally denied that moral dilemmas are possible. According to them, a genuine dilemma does not exist. An adequate moral theory is supposed to eliminate such dilemma. That is to say, such dilemmas are not genuine. According to them, the existence of a dilemma suggests that two or more principles are being applied simultaneously when the applicability of one principle should rule out the application of others. As stated by Kant:

> [B]ecause two mutually opposing rules cannot be necessary at the same time, then, if it is a duty to act according to one of them, it is not only not a duty but contrary to duty to act according to the other. It follows, therefore, that a collision of duties and obligations is inconceivable (Wendel, 2000, p.137).

In Book I of Plato's *Republic,* Cephalus defines "justice" as speaking the truth and paying one's debts. However, suppose one borrows a gun from a friend promising to return it by a specified time. Should the individual keep the promise of returning the lethal instrument if, in the interim, it becomes evident that the owner is intent on committing mayhem? Kant sees morality as objective, independent of human feeling, and applicable to all. Kantian ethics would return the gun as promised. The Hindu thought would take issue with such action. Hindus describe practically every moment of human existence in terms on an ongoing struggle to resolve dilemmas. For instance, in the *Bhagavad Gita,* Krishna argues that keeping of a promise, or even truthfulness, cannot be an unconditional obligation when in conflict with the avoidance of unjust and criminal acts. Telling the truth, protecting the truth, and keeping of a promise, are strong obligations. However, saving an innocent life is a strong obligation as well. According to Hindu thought, genuine dilemmas exist, are paradoxical, and are seldom solved. They may be resolved or dissolved, but not solved (Dhir, 2003a). Let us explore this point further.

The Concept of *Dharma* and the Nature of Action

The term *dharma* is complex and has many meanings in the various Hindu writings. It deals with law and custom governing the development of individuals and with the proper relationships between different groups of society. In the context of this essay, *dharma* refers to the basic principles of virtuous and righteous conduct. According to Manu, the author of *Manusmriti,* the term *dharma* includes the concepts of (1) law, usage, custom; (2) moral merit, virtue; (3) duty, prescribed code of conduct, obligation; (4) right, justice; (5) piety; (6) morality, ethics; (7) nature, character; and (8) an essential quality, characteristic property, and attribute (Patwardhan, 1968, p. 80). The precise meaning of *dharma* is derived from the context of its usage. *Adharma* is the opposite of *dharma,* or devoid of *dharma.* Aiyar has described *dharma* as follows:

> *Dharma* is the cohesive element, and on the human plane, it is the principle of organization. From the standpoint of the individual, it is the implementing of the intellectual perception of his proper place and duties in the social cosmos; from the standpoint of the group, it is reason or intelligence... [that is] the basis of social life... (Aiyar, 1968, p. vii).

Sometime after 300 B.C., Kanada developed the *vaisheshika* (particularity) system of *dharma,* describing it as a property belonging to the person, not the action performed. It is particular and depends on the person's proper place and duties in the social system (Radhakrishnan and Moore, 1960, pp. 416-418). The *dharma* of the eldest brother relative to his younger brother is not entirely the same as that of the younger brother relative to his elder brother. The dual quality of *dharma* in terms of individual obligations and social responsibility is evident. It is apparent that *dharma* consists of both qualities that belong to the individual and those that belong to the group.

If dilemmas are paradoxical and are seldom solved, what is an individual to do? To resolve a dilemma, the decision-maker, group, or organization must be able to *recognize* the conflict between *individual obligations* and *social responsibilities.* Acquisition of knowledge is an essential prerequisite for such recognition. Knowledge is the basis of enlightened wisdom. It is noteworthy that to explain the significance of *dharma* and its relationship to *karma* or action, the *Bhagavad Gita,* uses the metaphor of war—a forum for action. Arjuna commands the Pandava army, which awaits his orders to engage the vast Kaurava army across the Kurukshetra battlefield. The Kauravas are his kin. Seeing his friends and relatives at arms against each other, Arjuna is overcome by a deep sense of despondency, a sense of inaction. Would it not be *adharma* to kill his kindred for the sake of the kingdom? With doubts clouding his mind, he laid down his arms. He was no coward. His was a morally-conscientious decision. He tells his friend and charioteer, Krishna, that he would not fight. He explains that he saw nothing worthwhile in waging war with his own community divided in two opposing forces. He argues that the principle of the good of community should rule his action. Arjuna foresees the disastrous consequences of extinction of the community resulting from war. Along with the community, age-old traditions would be destroyed and lawlessness will prevail. Krishna counters by reminding Arjuna of two essential aspects of action (*karma*) performed by an agent. First, one cannot attain freedom from action through abstention or inaction, for no one, indeed, can remain even for a moment unengaged, without doing work due to the impulses born of Nature (*prakriti*) (Radhakrishnan and Moore, 1960; More, 1995, p. 192). Performance of action is inextricably tied with the biological fact of life. Performance of action is a necessary condition for continuity of life.

Second, Krishna explains how individual and social elements of *dharma* come together in action that eliminates dissonance. He emphasizes that it is important to behave in a manner consistent with *svadharma,* or one's own *dharma.* Whereas *dharma* is a social phenomenon, svadharma refers to the mode of individual existence in the context of the society. The concept of *svadharma* is closely related to that of *svabhava,* or one's nature. *Svabhava* is a personalistic concept, while *svdharma* is not. However, *svadharma* presupposes *svabhava.* An agent is bound to act in manner that is dictated by the agent's nature. It follows that there would be some correspondence between what the agent is disposed to do and what he is expected to do. To the extent to which these two converge, there exists harmony between the agent and the society (Radhakrishnan and Moore, 1960; More, 1995, pp. 97-98).

The Paradigm of Virtuous Decision-Making Behavior

We now formulate a new paradigm for the analysis of virtuous decision-making behavior based in the Hindu ethics and illustrate it by applying it to the case of a corporate whistle-blower. The process of *virtuous* decision-making is evident when an agent—an individual, a group, or an organization including corporations—attempts to ameliorate a dilemma in which action is demanded of an agent who is unexpectedly presented a situation of conflict not of his or her own making. The conflict is between (i) the agent's self-interest and *individual obligations,* often with relatively low associated costs or risks borne by the agent, and (ii) interest of others, raising the issue of the agent's *social responsibility,* often with relatively high associated costs or risks borne primarily for the benefit of others. The agent may have little advance warning of the emergent situation, the timing may be awkward or inconvenient, the time available to make a choice may be limited, and the choice made may have significant consequences for the agent or for others. To be virtuous, the agent must first *recognize* the dilemma; that is, there are (i) conflicting obligations or responsibilities to be met, and (ii) no solution that would satisfy all demands of the situation. The agent must make an *informed* choice, with awareness of the consequences posed by the alternative actions available to him or her for all parties affected. *Enlightened wisdom* facilitates the decision-making process. Therefore, *knowledge* is a prerequisite for virtuous decision-making.

Let us now examine how this paradigm may be applied. Consider the actions of the scientist-executive Jeffrey Wigand, who exposed corporate deceit and wrongdoing in spite of threats to his life and career. Dr. Wigand was vice president of research and development at Brown & Williamson from 1989 to 1993. He states:

> I realized after ten months with the company that I had made a mistake. I was making a lot of money. I had a wife, and two daughters, one of whom required extensive medical coverage, and I wasn't ready at that time to bring the wrath of the tobacco industry on my family and me. So I looked the other way until laboratory testing showed a controversial pipe tobacco additive, called Coumarin, to be a lung-specific carcinogen in mice and rats... (Shainbaum, Fitzgerald and Palko, 2001, p. 106).

In 1993, he took issue with the Brown & Williamson's continued use of Coumarin in pipe tobacco. They terminated him. In 1994, the CEOs of seven major tobacco companies swore at congressional hearings on the effects of tobacco that nicotine was not addictive. Wigand had a confidentiality agreement with Brown & Williamson. He decided to expose the perjury. He broke the confidentiality agreement with his former employers and appeared on *60 Minutes* with Mike Wallace in 1996. He talked about the smoking issues. He also described the harassment of his family with death threats. Initially, CBS shelved the interview, fearing a lawsuit from his former employer. Personal fallout from the stress included a divorce from his wife that same year. The interview was subsequently aired. Brown & Williamson sued Wigand for breach of confidentiality. However, with the settlement between the tobacco industry and the states, this suit was dropped in 1997.

Wigand recognized that he had a dilemma. Conflict existed between (i) his personal well being, security of his family, and continuity of his career, and (ii) obligations to others, including (a) his confidentiality agreement with Brown & Williamson to protect their secrets, and (b) obligation to the society in terms of savings human lives and protecting human health. He faced relative safety in complying with the agreement he had with Brown & Williamson and grave danger to his well-being in talking to CBS News. Dr. Wigand made an *informed* choice of protecting human life over protecting the secrets of his former employer, though paid a heavy price for it. His training as a researcher with specialized knowledge of sciences facilitated his informed choice. Dr. Jeffrey Wigand, as a scientist-executive, exhibited behavior that had all the hallmarks of virtuous decision-making: defiance, strength, courage, bravery, skill, loyalty, and honor.

Conclusion

The separation of ownership from control has produced a set of enigmatic corporate problems. These include problems relating to efficiency in corporate management, vitiating effects of corporate bureaucracy, and legitimacy of corporate hierarchy. This describes dilemmas in terms of conflict between individual obligations and social responsibilities. The contemporary discussion on the ethics and moral obligation of decision-making is dominated by two major theories of principle, the deontological and the utilitarian. Unfortunately, these theories fall short of explaining behavior emanating from considerations of virtue. In this article, we have discussed insights offered by the various Hindu philosophic and religious literatures. These offer clues to the Hindu executive's philosophic orientation toward resolution of corporate moral and ethical dilemmas. A new paradigm is suggested for the analysis of virtuous decision-making behavior, along with illustrative applications.

Bibliography

AACSB International (2004). *Ethics education in business schools.* St. Louis, MO: AACSB International.

Aiyar, C.P.R. (1968). Preface. In Patwardhan, M.V. Manusmriti: *The ideal democratic republic of Manu.* Delhi, India: Motilal Banarsidass.

Asarian, R.D. (1981). The psychology of courage: A human scientific investigation. Doctoral dissertation, Duquesne University. *Dissertation Abstracts International, 42,* 2023B.

Bartlett, A., & Preston, D. (2000). Can ethical behavior really exist in business? *Journal of Business Ethics, 23,* 199-209.

Beck-Dudley, C.L. (1996). No more quandaries: A look at virtue through the eyes of Robert Solomon. *American Business Law Journal, 34* (1), 117-132.

Bentham, J. (1970). *An introduction to the principles of morals and legislation.* London, U.K: Athlone Press.

Berle, A.A., & Means, C.G. (1932). *The modern corporation and private property*. New York, NY: Commerce Clearing House.

Cuff, W.T. (1993). *The experience of courage and the characteristics of courageous people.* Doctoral dissertation, University of Minnesota. *Dissertation Abstracts International, 53,* 5408B.

Deutsch, M. (1961). Courage as a concept in social psychology. *Journal of Social Psychology, 55,* 49-58.

Dhir, K.S. (2003a). The corporate executive's *dharma*: Insights from the Indian epic *Mahabharata.* In: O.F. Williams (Ed.), *Business, religion, and spirituality: A new syn -*

thesis (p. 122-138). Notre Dame, Indiana: University of Notre Dame Press.
Dhir, K.S. (2003b). Emerging paradigms of health care decision-making behavior. In: Jack Rabin (Ed.), *Encyclopedia of public administration and public policy.* New York: Marcel Dekker.
Epstein, E.M. (1998). Business ethics and corporate social policy. *Business and Society, 37* (1), 7-40.
Feinfgeld, D.L. (1999). Courage as a process of pushing beyond the struggle. *Qualitative Health Research, 9* (6), 803-815.
Hobbes, T. (1914). *Leviathan.* London, U.K: J.M. Dent.
Hunt, S.D., & Vitell, S. (1986). A general theory of marketing ethics. *Journal of Macromarketing, 6* (1), 5-16.
Jensen, M.C., & Meckling, W.H. (1976). Theory of the firm: Managerial behavior, agency costs and ownership structure. *Journal of Financial Economics, 3,* 305–60.
Kant, I. (1965). *The metaphysics of morals, 1,* trans. J. Ladd. Indianapolis, Indiana: Bobbs-Merrill.
Loe, T.W., Ferrell, L., & Mansfield, P. (2000). A review of empirical studies assessing ethical decision-making in business. *Journal of Business Ethics, 25,* 185-204.
May, R. (1975). *The courage to create.* New York, N.Y: Norton.
McCracken, J., Martin, W., & Shaw, B. (1998). Virtue ethics and the parable of the sadhu. *Journal of Business Ethics, 17,* 25-38.
Mill, J.S. (1971). *Utilitarianism.* New York, N.Y: Bobbs Merrill
More, S. (1995). *Krsna: The man and his mission.* Pune, India: Gaaj Prakashan.
Patwardhan, M.V. (1968). *Manusmriti: The ideal democratic republic of Manu.* Delhi, India: Motilal Banarsidass.
Pincoffs, E. (1984). 'Quandries and virtues,' quandry ethics: 1971, *Mind, 80* (32), 552-571.
Radhakrishnan, S., and Moore, C.A. (Eds.) (1960). A source book of Indian philosophy, Second Edition. Princeton, NJ: Princeton University Press.
Rorty, A.O. (1986). The two faces of courage. *Philosophy, 61,* 151-171.
Shainbaum, B., Fitzgerald, S, and Palko, M. (2001). *Hope and heroes: Portraits of integrity.* Toronto, Canada: London Street Press.
Smith, A. (1776). *An inquiry into the structure and causes of the wealth of nations.* London: Cannon (Modern Library).
Thorne, D.M., & Ferrell, O.C. (1993). Assessing the application of cognitive moral development theory to business ethics. *Journal of Business Ethics, 10,* 829-838.
Tillich, E. (1951). *The courage to be.* New Haven, CT: Yale University Press.
Votaw, D., & Sethi, S.P. (1973). *The corporate dilemma: Traditional values versus contemporary problems.* Englewood Cliffs, NJ: Prentice-Hall.
Walton, D.N. (1986). *Courage: A philosophical investigation.* Berkeley, CA: University of California Press.
Wendel, W.B. (2000). Value pluralism in legal ethics. *Washington University Law Quarterly, 78,* 113-213.
Williams, O.F., & Houck, J.W. (Eds.) (1992). *A virtuous life in business.* Lanham, MD: Rowman and Littlefield Publishers.
Wulfson, M. (1998). Rules of the game: Do corporate codes of ethics work? *Review of Business, 20*(1), 12-17.

PART V

GLOBALIZATION

Spirituality and Entrepreneurship

Theodore Roosevelt Malloch

The social and business sciences are replete with a mature literature and treatments, both empirical and theoretical, on the role of entrepreneurship in economic development.[1] The concepts of social capital and human capital are by now rich and extend beyond economics to management, human resources, political science, and sociology. Indeed, both have become in recent decades important, twin pillars in capitalism and democracy at the individual, corporate, societal, and global levels.

Less developed by far is the emerging concept of *spiritual capital* and its attendant impact on entrepreneurial behavior. The concept is pregnant with possibilities drawing on the intersection of economics and religion and such classic works as R.H. Tawney's (1998) *Religion and the Rise of Capitalism* and Max Weber's (1905) *The Protestant Ethic and the Spirit of Capitalism,* as well as more recent political economy thinking on economics and development. But does "spiritual capital" pass the so-what test? Is it possibly the hidden motivation in economic booms as far apart as Ireland and Singapore? How exactly does religion affect economic behavior at both the macro and micro levels? Is it a secret ingredient in the very nature of entrepreneurship? Can we fully demonstrate the relevance, validity, and potential of the notion that spiritual mores and underpinnings demonstrably affect economies? Firms?

Here is the *hypothesis*: In the ultimate sense, spiritual capital is the missing leg in the stool of economic development and entrepreneurial activity, which includes its better known relatives, social and human capital.

Entrepreneurship derived from the French, originally meant the acts of persons who managed a company and assumed the risks of business. The verb came from the same as: *to undertake*; it therefore suggested proactive behavior. J.B. Say, the French economist at the outset of the 19th century used the word for those who shifted economic resources out of an area of lower and into an area of higher productivity and greater yield. But that action was shaped by the culture and delivered in *trust*. Trust was at the base of business activity and it was ultimately formed and informed by religio-spirtitual beliefs and traditions.

Social Capital

In *In Good Company*, Don Cohen and Laurence Prusak (2001) examine the role that social capita—a company's "stock" of human connections, such as trust, personal networks, and a sense of community—play in thriving organizations. Social capital, it turns out, is so integral to business life that without it, corporate action—and consequently productive work—is not possible. Social capital involves the social elements that contribute to knowledge sharing, innovation, and high productivity.

The World Bank (1985, p. 29) defines social capital as "the norms and social relations embedded in social structures that enable people to coordinate action to achieve desired goals." Robert Putnam, the Harvard political scientist, describes it similarly. "Social capital," Putnam (2001) writes, "refers to features of social organizations such as networks, norms, and social trust that facilitate coordination and cooperation for mutual benefit."

In Cohen and Prusak's (2001, p. 14) recent seminal study, social capital consists of the "stock of active connections among people, the trust, mutual understanding, and shared values and behaviors that bind members of human networks and communities and make cooperative action possible." Social capital makes any organization or any cooperative group more than a collection of individuals' intent on achieving their own private purposes.

The term*first* appeared in print in 1916 in the context of academic debates on the decline of America's cities and close-knit neighborhoods. In present decades, sociologists have given the term more credentials. Glenn Loury used the phrase in 1977[2] to describe sources of certain kinds of income disparities, and Pierre Bourdieu[3] described it as one of the forms of capital that help account for individual achievement. Chicago sociologist, James Coleman,[4] has also employed this concept throughout his *opus* of contributions.

As yet, most of this literature has little to say about *how* managers or entrepreneurs can actually increase an organization's stock of social capital. And most recently, Nan Lin's trilogy on social capital: theory of social structures and action; theory and research; and foundations of social capital, has further refined what has become a more and more widely used social construct now in popular parlance.[5]

In the realm of politics, Robert Putnam's landmark 1993 book, *Making Democracy Work,* convincingly demonstrated that the political, institutional, and economic value of social capital is substantial. In 2000, Putnam brought out *Bowling Alone,* a scholarly and provocative account of America's declining social capital. Numerous findings of comparative economic studies by the World Bank and United Nations corroborate Putnam's thinking; i.e., some regions of the globe lag behind while others thrive due to their social capital.

It seems apparent that in the same sense some firms thrive as a result of their stored social capital, while others fail for its lack. But what is the origin of such stocks within a firm? Mission statements and goals carried on laminated cards or placed in hallways don't produce values *per se.* In entrepreneurial firms, founders' values often carry exceptional weight for numerous generations to propel companies to extraordinary results. In past centuries and decades, many of these grew out of religious impulses or were grounded in the spirituality of their founders. Such companies as ServiceMaster, Herman-Miller, and Mailboxes etc., are more recent examples of this same phenomenon.

Human Capital

The term "human capital" first appeared in a 1961 in an *American Economic Review* article, "Investment in Human Capital," by Nobel-prize winning economist, Theodore W. Shultz. Economists have since loaded on much baggage to the concept but most agree that human capital comprises skills, experience, and knowledge. Some, like Gary Becker (1978),[6] add personality, appearance, reputation, and credentials to the mix. Still others, like management guru Richard Crawford, equate human capital with its owners, suggesting human capital consists of "skilled and educated people."[7]

Newer conceptions of **total human capital** view the value as an investment. Thomas O. Davenport (1999), in *Human Capital: What It Is & Why People Invest It,* looks at how a worker performs depending on ability and behavior. For him, the choice of tasks also requires a time allocation definition. The combination of ability, behavior, effort, and time investment produces performance, the result of personal investment, THC = A&B x E x T, where a multiplicative relationship enhances the outcome.

Davenport further elaborates a worker investment notion, describing what it means to work in the relationship nexus between the employee and the employer. He explains in mostly anecdotal, company specific detail, how companies that treat workers as investors can attract, develop, and retain people. These people both get much value from their organization—and give so much in return that they create a *competitive advantage* for their firms.

A further quantitative refinement in this field is the so-called business case for ROI in human resources. Works such as *The HR Scorecard* by Jack Phillips (2001), among others, put forward a measurement case for viewing the employee as a human asset. It has become almost trite to recite the fact that in both economic development and in firm behavior—the most important assets are the human ones. In firms that grew out of a spiritual formation there is typically a great commitment to so-called "people development," as workers are viewed as stewards and co-owners who deserve and need constant nurturing.

Spiritual Capital

When you do a thorough web search not much comes up on the topic *spiritual capital.* In Amazon.com, an index search of all categories, books included, yields much the same result. It turns up *Seven Capital Sins* by Bishop Fulton Sheen, *Witchcraft and Welfare in Puerto Rico,* and an out-of-stock pamphlet on capital cities and urban planning. So why bother? Is this a virgin field or a foolish endeavor? Can the development literature fill in any of the gaps and provide an adequate framework on spiritual capital? Is the study of entrepreneurship a hot-bed of spiritual capital?

In the last two decades, more recent debates in development macro-economics have revolved around debt management and relief, the appropriate role of the price mechanism, trade policy, the effect of policies in developed countries on the rest of the world, and the transition from closed or centrally planned economies to open market ones. At the micro-level, questions concerning choice of planning techniques have continued with a renewed debate on whether capital-intensive projects and globalization produce the most growth. There has also been at the UNDP in particular, an emphasis on human economic development in a broadly defined sense.[8] Few studies to date have asked how entrepreneurship is originated or sustained. The religious basis of entrepreneurship is anecdotal at best. Some comparative studies have argued that entrepreneurship surfaces in many globalizations around the world most notably in places like Bangalore, India, as a result of Hinduism; Chile, where evangelical sects have proliferated; and of course in offshore Chinese communities.[9]

But development is not just a goal of rational actions in the economic, political, and social spheres. It is also, and very deeply, the focus of redemptive hopes and expectations. In an important sense, as Peter Berger (1986) reminded us in *Pyramids of Sacrifice,* "development" is also a "religious category." Even for those living on the most precarious margins of existence, development is more than a matter of improved material conditions—although that is included. Development is clearly a vision of redemptive transformation. This sense of spiritual capital is founded on an understanding that **all** resources are entrusted to people. That both individual persons and groups are called to preserve and develop a wealth of resources for which they are accountable here and later and which endowments must be managed. Thus, spiritual capital is about this entrustment of responsibility and a care for the creation it exhibits. Within various religious traditions, creative obedience or norms in economic activities are one primary way for adherents to acknowledge and demonstrate faith.

Within this frame of reference, economic development often led by the entrepreneurial acts of risk taking can be seen as a process through which persons and communities learn to care for and use the resources that sustain life.[10] Economic development can be viewed as creative management of endowed resources by stewards who act on their faith commitments. Here, genuine economic growth is guided by normative laws, character, and principled habits and practices that take into account the preservation needs of human beings, their environments, and their physical, mental, social, cultural, and spiritual lives. In the ultimate sense, spiritual capital may be the third or missing leg in the stool which includes its better known relatives, namely: human and social capital.

International Relations theory and development economics since the 1980s have similarly argued that as more advanced (West/North) nations progress with respect to technology, capital formation, growth, and diversification of economic sectors, in an era of rapid globalization and greater "interconnectivity" and interdependence across national boundaries, a "feedback" effect on culture, politics, and society occur.[11] To what extents are spiritual variables or spiritual capital the missing component ignored in much of recent academic inquiry and policy analyses of global economic growth? Of entrepreneurial activity that commence such growth?

One can rightly ask which factors and issues economists and practitioners should add to their future studies to gauge this missing link. In other words, can we operationalize spiritual capital so that the concept and empirical findings can be made more plausible and evident? Since the notion of spiritual capital is closely connected to on-going debates on trust, corruption, governance, sustainability, and entrepreneurship, this is a critical next step. Some things to look at include:

- The role and scope of personal religious ethics on private economic decisions, which face all persons and groups;
- The exegetical, economic, and historical roots and traditions which give rise to contrasting work ethics and economic systems;
- The role of societal institutions based on faith ranging from companies to trade unions to political parties to non-governmental and intermediating structures;
- Interpretations and practices concerning interest, investment, inflation, growth, government authority, charity, and trade in various spiritual worldviews;
- The impact of religion on conduct and rules as employees and employers, consumers and producers, and citizens at every level of existence;

- The degree to which religious practices and policies directly or indirectly affect economic behavior, choices, and economic policy; and,
- The role of spiritual capital as the basis for entrepreneurship.

There may be no one set of religious principles regulating any given economic polity, but all religious peoples, regardless of their faith community, make individual and collective choices in which personal faith colored by longstanding and deeply rooted historical religious traditions are highly relevant and important factors. Given the importance of entrepreneurs in the economy, it can be argued that their spirituality is given amplified expression in the business activity they commence and sustain over time.

Spiritual capital can become a useful concept and term for a vital feature of economic development that has been largely overlooked in modern theories of development. Indeed, the often used terms social capital and human capital themselves are based to a large extent on the existence of good faith, trust, stewardship, a sense of purpose, and other moral characteristics which cannot persist in the absence of the piety, solidarity, and hope that come from religion and spiritual sentiments. When this is lost, societies and economies often decline rather than grow. When this abounds, societies, economies, and companies prosper.

Notes

1. See on this topic: Van Dyke, Fred (1996). *Annotated bibliography.* Madison, WI: AuSable Institute.
2. The many works of Glen Loury.
3. The works of Pierre Bourdieu.
4. The many works of James Coleman.
5. Nan Lin's three works are: Social capital: *A theory of social structure and action* (2002, Cambridge University Press); *Social capital: Theory and research* (2001, New York: Aldine De Gruyter); and *Foundations of social research* (1976, McGraw-Hill).
6. And other works.
7. Works by Richard Crawford on management.
8. See "Planetheonomics" Papers on Economics, Ecology and Christian Faith, AuSable Institute, 1996, which includes papers by economists such as: Mark Thomas, Robert Hamrin, Bob Goudzwaard, Herman Daly, Donald Hay, Lans Bovenberg, and Theodore Malloch.
9. W.W. Rostow, his many titles on the stages of economic growth, economic development and Asia.
10. See Bovenberg, L., & Malloch, T. R. (1996). *Development from a Christian perspective.* AuSable Institute paper.
11. See Willy Brandt on North-South and the generation of literature on sustainable economic development.

Bibliography

Becker, G. (1978). *The economic approach to human behavior.* University of Chicago Press.

Berger, P. ([1976] 1986). *Pyramids of sacrifice*. Garden City: Anchor Books.

Cohen, D., & Prusak, L. (2001). *In good company: How social capital makes organizations work*. Cambridge: Harvard Business Press.

Davenport, T. O. (1999). *Human capital: What it is and why people invest it*. San Francisco: Jossey-Bass.

Phillips, J. et al. (2001). *The HR scorecard*. New York: Butterworth.

Putnam, R. et al. (1993). *Making democracy work*. Princeton: Princeton University Press.

Putnam, R. (2000). *Bowling alone: The collapse and revival of American community*. New York: Touchstone.

Putnam, R. ed. (2001). *Democracies in flux: The evolution of social capital in contempo - rary society*. New York, NY: Touchstone.

Schultz, T. W. (1961). Investment in human capital. *American Economic Review, 51*, 1–17.

Tawney, R.H. (1998). *Religion and the rise of capitalism*. New Brunswick: Transaction Books.

The World Bank (1985). *World development report*. Washington, D.C.: The World Bank.

Weber, M. (1905). *The Protestant ethic and the spirit of capitalism*. London: Penguin.

Business, Religious Spirituality and the East European Experience

Ryszard Legutko

I.

The claim that there may be religious spirituality in business practice sounds bizarre. Is there any occupation that needs such spirituality except, of course, priesthood? Scientists and politicians, doctors and lawyers—associated with spirituality in the past—have long ceased to be regarded as representatives of spiritual occupations. They are now trained in the arts of politics and scientific research, of medicine and law, with no reference to religion or metaphysics. We have grown accustomed to it and few of us find it objectionable. What is so special about businessmen that makes us, again and again, return to the question of the religious context of business practice? Why should we care?

The probable answer is precisely that businessmen are the only major group among those who substantially contributed to the growth of our civilization that from the very beginning was denied any link with spirituality. In this they differed from educators, doctors, lawyers, politicians, and scientists. This denial was made on the following grounds:

(i) the object of business activity—wealth—was considered to be of a lower order; in classical tradition—from Aristotle to Aquinas—wealth was thought to be an instrument to other higher goods, not a good in itself;

(ii) business activity too often has a morally suspect source in human nature, which is greed; true, there are other motivations, some of them nobler, and greed may have some positive consequences too, but business activity unleashes greed on an unknown scale and absolves what has been rightly considered to be a morally dubious human temptation;

(iii) business activity too often destroys the basic moral rule which is self-limitation; from the classical writers we have learned that all good in human conduct comes from *sophrosune* (moderation) while all evil from hubris; business activity is essentially hubristic because it sets no limits on human ends other than the means, these being constantly made more efficient.

These objections are serious ones, and I know no argument that ultimately refuted them. They show that whatever the blessings business practice bestowed on the human race, whatever fortitudes of character the businessmen proved to have, and regardless of with what motivations men succumb to the temptations of success in business, people in general cannot refrain from thinking that business activity is in itself, if not morally flawed, at least in its essence not as pure as other human occupations. This distrust is not against people practicing business, but against business practice as such. One can imagine a situation in which we have a majority of honest businessmen and an entirely corrupted academia—a not unlikely development and probably not particularly shocking to those with sufficient experience—but this would not lead to the belief that there is something essentially wrong in the academic practice and something essentially right in business practice.

The best known argument that linked business with religion was that formulated by Max Weber with respect to Protestantism, and later repeated in various versions, for instance, by Werner Sombart with respect to Judaism. One can sum it up in three theses countering the above mentioned criticisms:

(i) the object of business in capitalism was not wealth—wealth has been the aim of human striving from time immemorial—but rational, long-term activity; consumption was in fact prohibited as essentially sinful;

(ii) the source of human motivation in capitalism was not greed but loneliness resulting from a deep spiritual agony—no one knows if he/she will find himself/herself among the saved or the condemned, and economic activity becomes the obvious means to forget about the tormenting uncertainty; work as calling results precisely from this;

(iii) business practice does not loosen up the appetitive aspect of human nature and does not generate hubris; on the contrary, it imposes discipline—not only resulting from the capitalistic logic which does not tolerate arbitrariness and irrationality—but also as an expression of piety.

II.

Let us leave aside the evaluation of the Weberian hypothesis. Whatever its merits, one thing is clear: it is little helpful in establishing any structural link between business and religion. What this hypothesis in fact says is that at a certain historical moment a certain type of religion stimulated a certain form of activity which accelerated the growth of market economy. In other words, Weber and others succeeded in indicating a historical correlation between a religious state of mind and an economic practice. They did not succeed in finding, and they never meant to find, an argument defending business practice as having an intrinsic—no matter how historically precarious—spiritual dimension. They never found what one can easily find in the case of scientists who, however imperfectly, strive to solve the ultimate mysteries of human life, or lawyers who imitate God grappling with the justification of what is right and wrong.

The Weberian hypothesis does not allow for any of these. One can be tempted, however, to treat this connection between religion and economy in a causal way. If, one might speculate, we could recreate a similar form of religiousness, we would be able to generate similar economic results. Thus, a society that happens to find itself or rather be induced to be in a state of quasi-Protestant spirituality may—hypothetically—produce a vibrant economic order. Obviously, this tampering with the spirit of society is hardly possible, and certainly undesirable. One might sometimes however at least express regret that the society one lives in does not have the Protestant spiritual background and that had it passed through the Protestant experience, it would have developed a better, more stable and sound economic system.

Such sentiments occasionally come to the fore. In France in the 1970s, a book by Alain Peyrefitte, *Le mal français,* produced some stir, as bemoaning the fact that France did not have the benefits of the countries with the Protestant past. Peyrefitte claimed that the tension between the Catholic and Protestant Europe—which he called, alluding to St. Luke 10, the Europe of Mary and the Europe of Martha respectively—continue to shape the social and economic culture of today. In St. Luke, Mary who listened to Jesus "hath chosen the good part," while Martha who "was cumbered about much serving" and was "careful and troubled about many things" lost that most important part. But the French author reversed the conclusion: it was Martha, the working woman, the patroness of Protestantism that made a good choice, not Mary, the patroness of Catholic Europe, being too spiritual and therefore too idle.

A similar idea appeared in Eastern Europe in the 1980s and 1990s. The debate started at a time when it became clear that communism as an economic system would not survive and that even if the communists retained their political monopoly they would have to make considerable concessions to market economy. The question that emerged was whether the societies—

such as Polish—have the cultural conditions that would make it possible for a capitalist economy to develop. The Weberian hypothesis was used as a warning that in a Catholic society—and 95 percent of Poles would in one way or another qualify to this category—there might be some deep social and psychological impediments having as an ultimate source the frame of mind shaped by the Roman Catholic heritage.

These warnings did not produce any serious intellectual analyses, and mostly appeared in moralistic enunciations of politicians, journalists, and academics who took the assumption that modernization of the society could be achieved only on the ruins of the Catholic Church and most of the ideas she stood for. Yet though I do not think much of what was said at that time in Eastern Europe, I believe that the argument when properly reformulated cannot be easily dismissed. The difference between the Protestant and Catholic spirituality is real, and it may have a lot to do with how Protestant and Catholic societies organized their economic order.

In the Protestant spirituality, and specifically in the Protestant notion of freedom, there is indeed something that may harmonize with business activity. If we take Martin Luther as an authority, particularly what he said in his reply to Erasmus, we will have the following picture of human nature and the following dynamics of freedom and necessity. Man—says Luther—is free over things beneath him, while subject to necessity in the things above him. "Beneath" means our practical actions, in work, commerce, and production; "above" means the things pertaining to salvation. We are thus free in practical matters while totally unfree in the matter of salvation. Not being able to attain salvation through good works we are thus unable to essentially change our status of a sinner. But impossibility to attain salvation also implies impossibility to achieve greatness, i.e., to transcend the human limits, to aspire to sainthood, and to attain superhuman, quasi-divine ends. Man's aspiration to greatness was a common motif among Italian writers at the time Luther was writing his work. Whatever similarities between the philosophers of the Italian Renaissance and Luther, in this respect they differed radically.

The above explains why in the Catholic countries some writers envied the Protestant experience and its formative power. The economic energy that animated a Protestant businessman was doubled or tripled, when compared to his Catholic counterpart, because—to use Luther's imagery—there was no upward channel, that is, there was no other obvious earthly way except economic that could organize human efforts. This also explains why the classical arguments against the business activity applied to the Protestant entrepreneur in a limited way: with no freedom to move upward the hubris was contained while discipline and rational action—practical expressions of piety—neutralized the possibly demoralizing influence of wealth and greed. The Catholics were less fortunate in this respect. They—the argument runs—

did not and, in fact, could not invest so much energy in economic activity because they did not feel to be subject to necessity over the things above. They could thus be tempted to have higher aspirations—to sainthood as should be their proper calling—or to more secular forms of Messianism or Promethean ideologies. For a Catholic it was a more obvious role to be a political prophet, a national liberator, a savior of mankind than to be only a successful businessman and to see in his success only an imperative of piety. In essence, Roman Catholicism was potentially more hubristic. A Catholic soul, especially when isolated from religion, was largely undisciplined and could be said to be more easily lured by the lust for power and for all sorts of superhuman ideals.

It might be interesting to note—as an indirect corroboration of the above argument—that in Poland in the second half of the 19th century when the society—after a series of unsuccessful national uprisings to gain the independence it had lost at the end of the 18th century—became, suddenly, fascinated with the idea of work, work ethic, industry, and economic modernization; all these ideas and objectives were presented as new versions of the old chivalrous military virtues. The new entrepreneur was believed to be also a warrior and a national liberator, albeit in different costumes and performing different functions. His motivation and his purpose was claimed to be the same. The task he was called upon to perform was described in the language more consonant with the Europe of Mary than with the Europe of Martha. Work—in other words—belonged to the realm of the things above, not to that beneath. The call to work was a call to adventure, to war, to a moral revolution of a nation, and not a call to a quiet, disciplined long-term rationality of an individual life.

The longing for Martha qualities stopped in the late 1990s, as it turned out that religious heritage did not play a decisive role in Eastern Europe. Protestant (now overwhelmingly atheistic) Czech society had similar economic achievements as Catholic Poland. On the whole, free market was equally successful in both countries; also it brought similar disillusionment and was criticized for similar failures. Mary and Martha no longer seemed to be the patronesses of two different traditions and mindsets. Since religion appeared to be no longer an important factor, the question of religious spirituality and business practice should have been declared obsolete. But it was not.

III.

If we look at the end of Weber's book, we find the following conclusions:

> Today the spirit of religious asceticism ... has escaped from the cage. But the victorious capitalism, since it rests on mechanical foundations, needs its support no longer and the idea of duty in one's calling prowls about in our lives like the ghost of dead religious beliefs. Where the fulfillment of the calling

> cannot directly be related to the highest spiritual and cultural values, or when, on the other hand, it need be felt simply as economic compulsion, the individual generally abandons the attempt to justify it at all. In the field of its highest development, in the United States, the pursuit of wealth, stripped of its religious and ethical meaning, tends to become associated with purely mundane passions, which often actually give it the character of sport. No one knows who will live in this cage in the future, or whether at the end of this tremendous development entirely new prophets will arise, or there will be a great rebirth of old ideas and ideals, or, if neither, mechanized petrification, embellished with a sort of convulsive self-importance. For of the last state of this cultural development, it might well be truly said: "Specialists without spirit, sensualists without heart; this nullity imagines that it has attained a level of civilization never before achieved."

The no-one-knows statement should not deceive us. Weber was indeed convinced that capitalism was doomed to become materialistic and that its instrumental rationality would be largely self-sustaining, carrying little or no spiritual and ethical message. If this description of capitalism is correct, that is, if capitalism has become solely a profit-generating mechanism, then the above counterarguments in defense of the spiritual dimension of the market are no longer valid. And without this dimension the market would be indeed focused on wealth, motivated by greed, and destructive of sophrosune. The market society would then be without spirit, without heart, the nullity imagining itself to be the peak of civilization. The new entrepreneur could be a brilliant innovator, but he would certainly bear little resemblance to his pious Protestant predecessor. There would be in him no sense of the necessity to succumb to the things above as contrasted with the freedom to take care of the things beneath. There would be no above and no beneath. The new entrepreneur would be pure activity shaped by the needs of the consumers, and not by his own sense of religious duty.

This picture of capitalism, whatever its resemblance to reality, is not unattractive, and has been very much present in the minds of its apologists and critics. The latter would deplore the fact that capitalism would do away with the classical notion of human nature and human aspirations, abolishing a distinct hierarchy or the high and the low, and of the noble and the base. They accused capitalism of being a great equalizer which has been depriving us from the edifying pressure of moral hierarchies. The apologists, on the other hand, believed that the new capitalism brought life and freedom to society, which meant more fun, more sportsmanship, more pleasure, more consumption, more light-heartedness, and less of anachronistic seriousness of the Platonic type with its pursuit of the ideal at the expense of the material.

In Eastern Europe, this view of capitalism was also found attractive, precisely because of its materialistic implications. In the early 1980s, one of the Polish anti-regime intellectuals suggested the following strategy. It is pointless to strive for a democratic reform under communism since any democratic concessions would be suicidal to the ruling party. A far better way would be to soften the system from within by destroying its major pillar which is communist ideology. This could be done if the communist *nomenklatura* becomes interested in business, economic profit, and material success.

Philosophically speaking, the strategy was as follows. Ideology is a self-contained system which produces a false picture of the world and prevents those who are affected by it to see the world as it is and to benefit from experience. Its claims are always true, non-verifiable, and non-falsifiable. No experience can invalidate what the Party considers as ideologically correct. In other words, the mind affected by ideology is a degenerate form of the classical model (or, as Alain Besançon maintained, a perverted form of a Christian soul): it has its above and its beneath, but the things above are artificial constructions that make it impossible to make anything sensible with the things beneath. By concentrating on the things beneath, i.e., by becoming business-oriented, the mind will regain its contact with reality and sooner or later is bound to reject the ideological superstructure. It will eventually turn into a purely hedonistic mechanism, which—though not spiritually elevating—is far more humane and socially beneficial. It will change the *nomenklatura* from the anti-civilizational force into a group that could and would contribute to the process of modernization.

Yes, one might deplore the fact that wealth became the main objective of the new business class, but this is definitely preferable to political monopoly and to the total control of social life which they had before. Yes, one might express regret that greed and not some nobler causes became the sole motivation of the new class, but this was preferable to communist and Marxist ideology which organized their thoughts and actions before. Yes, it was on the whole unfortunate that the new business class let themselves be carried by the materialistic hubris, indulging in all sorts of extravagant enterprises, but this was far less dangerous than the communist hubris which made the Party reverse the current of the Siberian rivers, undermine the laws of nature and economy, abolish the centuries of experience, and radically reshape human nature.

IV.

These two projects—Protestantization of the Catholic soul and changing the *nomenklatura* into a business class—had some differences and some similarities. The intended effect of the first project (to call it a "project" would be probably too much; it was simply an idea) was to have a large and stable middle class, an active group that not only would animate the society with the spirit of entrepreneurship but also would bring work ethic, self-discipline, decency, and a sense of propriety to social life. The intended effect of the second project (and a project indeed it was) was to domesticate a highly dangerous political force, by appealing to its lower instincts in order to finally incorporate a group of cynics into a modern civilization. Their wealth, not their morals, was expected to benefit the society. On the contrary, it was believed or tacitly assumed that the morals of the society and the contact with the objectivity of the market would gradually turn the cynics into morally responsible businessmen.

But these two projects had one thing in common. Both removed the element of spirituality from the actual practice: in the Protestant model it was placed in the realm of salvation, in the other model it was abolished and liquidated. Of course, the Protestantization of the Catholic soul was a pure speculative idea and it could not be implemented, having its only place in the books and articles written by the disenchanted intellectuals. Recreating the experience which came into being in different circumstances was from the beginning bound to be a fantasy. Whether such a change will ever occur, we do not know, but it would most likely require a revolution similar to that carried out by Luther and others. Changing the *nomenklatura* into a business class—on the other hand—was not a fantasy at all. This change in fact took place as a result of both the deliberate political plan and spontaneous evolution of the communist system. Fifteen years after the fall of the system practically no one talks any more about the Protestantization of the Catholic soul, the old debate being almost forgotten, whereas the appropriated *nomenklatura* has become a major factor in social life which in a decisive way determines the picture of today's business class in Poland and elsewhere in Eastern Europe. Whoever wants to see the business class as wealthy cynics, without any redeeming qualities, he/she should study the social changes in Eastern Europe during the last two decades. He/she could see people entirely horizontal, moving only in the sphere of the "things beneath," with no trace of awareness there might be some things above, no matter how ambiguously and unclearly understood.

If one interprets this evolution of the communist class as a crucial experiment which should prove the claim that the market mechanism as such can make people better, ennoble them, give them dignity, push them in the right direction, thus opening them to some form of spirituality, then the East European experience will be most disappointing. One can hardly imagine more soulless people than the former apparatchiks. Even the anti-capitalist literature of the 19th and 20th centuries could not create more spiritually deformed characters.

The critics of capitalism might thus find in the East European experience an ample material to confirm their critical diagnosis: having concluded that the Protestantization of the Catholic soul is nothing but a fantasy of a group of intellectuals, and that these societies could not but generate a class of soulless businessmen, one might be inclined to agree with those who—as Paul Tillich in his youth—believe that capitalism is daemonic in nature.

V.

But this is not the whole story. Those who were worried about Catholicism as an anti-capitalist force were certainly proved wrong, considering the success of the economic transformation. How or whether Catholic religion contributed to this success or affected it somehow, positively or negatively, I do not know, and there is too little information to make any plausible hypothesis. What one can see, however, is that the Polish Church nowadays does not see free economy as a moral enemy, partly because a majority of businessmen are Catholics, go to Church, and should be in the spiritual care of their priests, and partly because some intellectual work has been done to shed a new light on the problem. The best known is of course John Paul II's encyclical *Centesimus Annus,* which developed the ideas to be found in the pope's earlier writings, both philosophical and poetical.

What we find in these writings does not resemble the Weberian pattern. There is no implication of a possible causal relation between a form of religiousness and economic performance. There is no historical or sociological argument that would explain the coexistence of religion and economy. Instead we have a theological and philosophical reflection on work. The pope sees business practice as a form of work, particularly important at that. Treating business practice as work and not as anti-work, or a perverted form of work, or a morally inferior form of work, marks a change in the Catholic perspective, though not as radical as some suggest. The Church was not as hostile to free economy as she is often believed to have been.

If business practice is a form of work, it has all the good sides and bad sides potentially attributed to it. It may be dehumanizing or it may be morally elevating, depending on how it affects the human soul. What is remarkable, however, is that by qualifying business as work, the pope and other Catholic writers seemed to indirectly dismiss the first of the above anti-capitalist arguments. Business—they imply—is not essentially and intrinsically about wealth. It is action, or rather a form of human creativity. If this or that particular business activity is solely about wealth, then it should be regarded as a deformed type of work. But wealth is certainly not its essence. Some make an even more radical position arguing that the new Catholic approach permits to claim a stronger link between business practice and religious message: if this practice is creativity, then business can be a sort of imitation of divine creativity, i.e., giving existence to things and values that did not exist before. I do not see much ground for it unless we interpret creativity in a very particular way, but then it will refer not to business in general but to very few of its representatives, as it will to very few artists, doctors, and lawyers.

I think that the pope's position, and the position of many who identify themselves with the Church, is in fact a modified version of the standard Catholic view of the human nature, which following the Greeks, envisages human being vertically: there are things above and things beneath, and the proper development of the human soul is upward. Some Catholics admit that in the communist ideology the model was used in a caricatural and grotesque form, but this is no reason to reject it. On the contrary, it is necessary to understand the anthropological error of Communism and to grasp the essential difference between spiritual striving for sainthood or perfection and ideological striving for a secular utopia. After the fall of Communism, the Catholics are even firmer in their view that taking "things beneath" as the only basis for the man's relation to the world—as it was done with the *nomenklatura* to free them from the bond of ideology and to make them good businessmen—would be unacceptable, and the economic-moral experiment in Eastern Europe only confirms it. No strategy based on the alleged beneficial consequences of human vices is to be legitimized.

The Catholics, in short, reiterated their conviction that Mary "hath chosen the good part," adding perhaps that Martha did a good job being "careful and troubled about many things," but that doing them she should somehow follow her sister. Martha's work has been appreciated, but she is denied the model status of human existence. Moreover, when left alone, without the example of Mary to look up to, Martha would sooner or later lose contact with everything her sister represents.

This does not necessarily diminish the role of the businessmen. They are nowadays perceived as a particularly important group of people, important as those who influence the modern world as no other group and who have exceptionally powerful instruments at their disposal to determine which way the societies will go. This implies both great potential and high risk. Potentially, businessmen can achieve much more than most other people, including politicians, but they can also misuse or abuse their power. In a way modern businessmen play the role that in the past was played by the warriors or the aristocrats. They too had exceptional possibilities in the old societies and ran high risks. Some of them performed admirably, others failed. In the market civilization, the situation of businessmen is no different.

This makes it possible to reply to the remaining two charges against business practice—those of greed and hubris. Greed is indeed a part of businessmen's experience, as pride and vanity were a part of the chivalrous and aristocratic societies. There is little spiritual substance in business, but this does not mean that those who practice it are by definition morally condemned. Their conduct may be determined by morally dubious motivations, but it may be also determined by noble goals. Those objectives—some of them undoubtedly qualified as "higher things"—give them opportunities to find nobility in what they do, as the knights and warriors could find "higher things" in the goals they strived for. In other words, the importance of business people should make them aware that they are more than providers of wealth. If the structure of human nature is vertical, then there is nothing in business practice that condemns people to a horizontal perspective. We have been used to see the business action in this way, partly because there were empirical reasons for this, and partly because we have accepted—as have a lot of businessmen—a wrong, horizontal, view of human nature. But looked at from a different angle and from a different notion of human nature, the business practice presents itself differently. This does not mean that we will immediately find spirituality. In this the businessmen do not differ from the representatives of most other occupations: very few of us see ourselves and are seen by others as doing something spiritual.

The most difficult to answer is the third objection. The hubris is indeed as frequent today, as sophrosune is rare. And the hubris is usually a natural consequence of power, fame, wealth, and status. Even Protestant piety which in the Weberian picture seemed effective in neutralizing it quite often turned out helpless, though the Protestants were of course right when they maintained that a profound sense of sinfulness might contain our hubristic tendencies. For the Catholics who believe in the attainability of higher things, the hubris is more difficult to combat. In a way the Catholics face the same difficulties with which the Greeks were confronted when they taught about the divine elements in the human soul. Once we believe that we are more in some respects than human, we are on a dangerous path. At the same time, one can say that once we are able to perceive the more-than-human element, that element may become a tribunal to discipline our human motives and to develop an attitude of modesty which is proper to the human status. This dynamics of vanity and humility is very much present in the Catholic thought as it was present in ancient Greek philosophy.

But the problem of hubris and sophrosune is a general problem of our times, not a problem limited to business practice. The secularized societies are no freer from it than were the Christian societies, both Protestant and Catholic. Some even say—and let us mention Ortega y Gasset as an example–that our hubris is unparalleled, and that the modern man has lost any understanding of and need for sophrosune. Whether this is really the case need not bother us here. It suffices to say that if the modern business people suffer from the hubris, and thereby lose all higher sense of what they do, it is probably not because of the business practice per se, but of the general climate of modern times. For better or worse, the businessmen reflect the prevailing ideas, and not create them. The guilty party—if there is a guilty party—is to be looked for elsewhere.

American Free Enterprise as an Enterprise in Freedom Abroad

E. R. Klein

> The freer the flow of world trade,
> the stronger the tides of human progress
> and peace among nations
> *Ronald Reagan*

Bosnia

Following the death of the communist leader of Yugoslavia, Josip Broz Tito—a man still viewed as a hero by many people of the former Yugoslavia as a unifying force that created peace and economic prosperity—Bosnia/Herzegovina held its first free elections and communism fell. However, instead of a new beginning as a free nation, each of the three ethnic groups decided that their own tribe must be in control of the government. At first the Croats and Muslims united against the Serbs and declared their independence from the rest of Yugoslavia. But when the UN jumped in to recognize the newly declared independent Federation of Bosnia/Herzegovina, the Serbs protested, headed into the hills, and declared war on the now predominantly Muslim population of Sarajevo.

The siege of Sarajevo began in 1992 as Soviet-made tanks rolled down the road just behind the apartment I used to live in, in the part of town known as Grabavitsa. The building I lived in during my Fulbright Scholarship in Residence at the University of Sarajevo was one of the first in which Serbs went apartment by apartment forcing Muslims out of their homes and either shooting them dead in the street or forcing the men into work camps and the women into rape camps. In addition, the Serbian army forcibly conscripted Bosnian Serbs who were often made to fight against their own family and friends.

It was not long after that the Croats and Bosniaks retaliated in kind and by the end of the war it was clear that no group was innocent. In addition, according to the *9/11 Commission Report,* it was during the years of 1992 and 1995 that several of the terrorists who participated in the 9/11 terrorist attacks had met in Sarajevo.

Today, Bosnia is still a country divided. At its heart is the capital city of Sarajevo; a city that at one time symbolized international good will as the host of the 1984 Winter Olympics only to become the nucleus of a war that echoed the horrors of Nazi genocide. The war has ended but ethnic and political battle lines still split the country into two acrimonious entities: The Federation of Bosnia/Herzegovina and the Republic of Srpska.

Business Ethics Spring 2003

But at the University of Sarajevo, in my Business Ethics course during the spring of 2003, there was peace and cooperation as my students—Muslims, Croats, and Serbs—gathered to learn about American business ethics.[1]

Though the connection between democracy and free enterprise (manifesting itself even in self-proclaimed communist countries like China[2], and even Islamic countries like Turkey[3]) is something I have always believed in and taught, it wasn't until I lived and taught in Bosnia that I really felt the practical power of my theoretical commitments.

About 20 students as well as the university's business ethics professor attended the course. Professor Babiç-Avdispahiç had been to the United States and believed not only in the goodness of capitalism, but also in the need to imbue students with a good background in ethics. At her request, I used my own text *People First: Professional and Business Ethics Without Ethics* that provides a simple overview of the field of business ethics while weaving in an argument for viewing persons, all persons simultaneously, as the minimum component for stakeholder considerations. The students embraced the text, and were quite open to the arguments for both the goodness of capitalism and the need for certain constraints. In addition, Professor Babiç-Avdispahiç attended every class, absorbing new ideas of capitalist dynamics. Though the interactive Socratic style of the classroom, as well as the use of case studies and group work is the norm in the United States, all of these techniques were new in Bosnia. Because of the combination of its Austro-Hungarian heritage and recent communist past, the teaching style was completely top-down. The students were expected to be completely deferential to the professors, and any questions that challenged the professors' ideas were unacceptable. Fortunately, Professor Babiç-Avdispahiç moved seamlessly into the new style, and this made for not only a dynamic and productive course for everyone, but also a special bond and friendship for the two of us.

Several other unique experiences added to the success of the course. One was that I was fortunate to have made numerous connections with the international community and was able to host a guest speaker, Dora Bentsen, International Expert in Procurement Legislation with the EU, who offered my students an actual BiH case study in corruption. The example: the *Elektoprivreda* electric company, in which a culture of fraud and mismanagement had developed, the scope of which had only recently been revealed at the time I was teaching. Although several senior managers had been removed, the problem was actually much deeper than the corporate greed of a few individuals. The company was incredibly inefficient, it was overcharging its customers in the Federation, and it had acquired several new companies without sound financial reasons, actually using the borrowed money to fund the Sarajevo Football Club (a world renowned soccer team.)[4]

We used this infamous local example to offer the students a way to rethink the use of public funds in recently privatized public corporations such as a large utility company. We discussed free markets in general, the need for transparency, equal treatment protection and non-discrimination, and finally the need to get the public involved in the process of building an economically viable future for Bosnia by drafting procurement legislation and "watch dog" groups.[5] The students were clearly engaged and truly excited about the possibility of becoming not merely the future entrepreneurs and managers of their country, but leaders in its move toward a freer, more open, and morally sound corporate culture.

Reading and discussion alone, however, has never been my idea of applied ethics, so I looked for ways to get my students out of the classroom and into the boardroom.[6] Though Bosnia was still new for me, being an American Fulbright Scholar[7] afforded me certain privileges. For example, I was able to meet with the president of the American Chamber of Commerce in Sarajevo and was given the names and phone numbers of dozens of CEOs in and around town. I contacted most of them, but only one corporation returned my calls, Coca-Cola.[8]

Coke is, of course, an American corporation, but the Sarajevo plant was actually financed by a group from Greece and managed on-site entirely by Bosnians. The fact that all of the management, as well as the workers, were Bosnian afforded my students the opportunity to see how a modern global corporation operated, and the progress it had accomplished locally in the area of business ethics.

Not only were the students given a complete tour of the plant, dozens of souvenirs, a copy of Coke's *Mission Statement*, and ample opportunity to ask questions, but many of the students also inquired about, and were encouraged to, apply for jobs as soon as they graduated.[9] Having been on many on-site tours of numerous companies throughout the United States, I expected this kind of gracious treatment from the company. What I did not expect was to be so impressed by Coke's actualized commitments not only to its employees and customers, but also to the overall business, social, and political climate of the region. Coke's determination to produce a high quality product through excellence in production, marketing, delivery, display, etc. was simply remarkable, especially given an overall economic culture that has not yet learned to value such standards. For example, management carefully explained how Coke worked diligently to avoid importing most materials in order to encourage other Bosnian companies to produce goods they needed in production, but never at the expense of Coke's strict standards of quality control. In so doing, they were able to put pressure on all of the companies they worked with to live up to product excellence, environmental standards, and equal treatment of employees unheard of in this region.

Even more encouraging was the fact that Coke was the only corporation at the time to coexist and operate successfully in both the Republic of Srpska and the Federation of Bosnia and Herzegovina. Although the local lore had it that only the Prevno Sarajevsko company, the local brewery, was allowed to operate continually throughout the war given that none of the three sides wanted to bomb it, once the war ended Coke did not hesitate to begin operating.

Coke, Sarajevo, is the only corporation that has built two brand new plants across the borders that work in complete harmony with one another. This has not only forced peaceful economic interaction between Serbs and Bosniaks, but has ensured that both sides maintain American style ethical standards including protection against any form of ethnic or religious discrimination.[10] The ability for all three ethnic groups to work together in business is essential for the future health of the country.[11]

In addition, given that Coke is flourishing in Bosnia, this example may be the case in point business ethicists have been looking for when arguing that "there are sound business reasons as well as ethical reasons for certain Multinational Corporations to adopt uniform moral codes."[12]

Free Enterprise

Traditional political wisdom has it that the dimensions of democracy are free elections, rule of law, civil-political rights, civil society, and economic liberation. This last condition, however, seems to require that some forms of political liberalization are already in place, but some scholars claim that the reverse is also true. Speaking about the Arab world, for example, Gary Gambrill claims that:

> Economic liberalization usually necessitates some form of political liberalization for several reasons. First, the regime itself has increased incentives to provide some kind of political opening in order to co-opt beneficiaries of econom-

> ic reforms who were hitherto excluded from the decision-making process. Second, economic liberalization...demands greater political participation from the business community, which has a stake in increasing government accountability. Moreover, economic liberalization in the 21st century requires a modern telecommunications infrastructure and the free flow of information, eroding the walls of ignorance that authoritarian regimes have historically built to suppress dissent.[13]

Naturally the question arises: Which has to be liberalized first, the political chicken or the economic egg?

First, it is important to note that the recognition that the concepts of democracy and capitalism[14] are interconnected is not new. The 18th century philosopher and Member of Parliament Edmund Burke used this connection to argue against the heavy taxation of the American Colonies. Even our contemporary concept of a "civil society" "owes much to the tradition of reflection on social questions that began only with the growth of commercialism."[15] The most cursory look at the concepts of property, tort law, or contracts shows that legal justice and commerce are intimately interconnected.

In today's political environment, however, the modern culmination of global free enterprise—multinationals—are assumed to be evil, and are demonized and caricatured by anti-globalists and most academics as a "rapacious force that delays the demise of capitalism in the United States and harms innocents abroad."[16] While such attitudes often misguidedly interpret free enterprise ideology as being only helpful to the rich at the expense of the poor, conservatives view free enterprise with suspicion for entirely different reasons. In a world filled with postmodern criticisms denigrating any claims that attempt to be normative and universal, theorists often take the pragmatic route to moral justification sidelining the soul of ethics.

Despite this burden, some academics (from all areas of scholarship)[17], argue that free enterprise, in the form of a "market-based economy" is a necessary condition for democracy. For example, when talking about the political history of the world, Robert Dahl claims that, "the record is amazingly unambiguous. Polyarchal democracy has existed *only* in countries with predominantly market-capitalist economies[18] and *never* (or at most briefly) in countries with predominantly non-market economies."[19] Free enterprise, it seems, is as important to democracy as democratic and civil law is to economic growth.

And this view far outreaches the scope of academia. "Democratization is seen in Washington as advancing free enterprise abroad and economic liberalization is seen as advancing democracy, [for] there has never been a constitutional democracy without a market economy."[20] America's post 9/11 foreign policy with respect to Arab states is driven, I believe correctly, most fundamentally by the belief that the two forces—democracy and free enterprise—go hand in hand. In a very broad stroke, many argue, it is money, jobs, opportunity, and private property that are the keys to establishing a secularized middle class in the Middle East and, therefore, an end to the overwhelming popularity of extremist Islamic ideology. And although the Palestinian/Israeli issue is often cited as the cause of cultural stagnation and diplomatic gridlock in the Arab world, many scholars believe that solution is economic given that the "sense of despair and hopelessness [are] rooted in poverty...the soil in which fundamentalism can grow and flourish."[21] By nurturing a robust and open economy in Muslim countries[22], it is argued, there is great possibility that the fever of anger, resentment, and hopelessness among Muslims will break, and there will be no one left to turn a sympathetic ear to those whose only means of expression is violence.[23]

Conclusions

In Bosnia—a former communist country inhabited by a large Muslim population—I witnessed a corporation using its economic clout as a multinational to win the hearts and minds of people. I witnessed a group of students—the future of Bosnia—shocked and awed by the modern technology and humanitarian working conditions that existed in their own country. Although I realize that free enterprise, let alone the way it has been abused by large global corporations, is not without serious criticism, there is no reason to believe that economic freedom and opportunity is not the best road to political freedom and personal opportunity. Free enterprise need not mean ceding large corporations the "freedom to go anywhere and do anything to people and planet,"[24] but rather allowing people anywhere on the planet the freedom to become participants in the global economy.[25]

Pending right now are three very important social experiments: "India will be the most significant test case for whether democracy and capitalism can deal effectively with mass poverty...Turkey is the wall that could stop Islamic fundamentalism from reaching into Europe...South Africa will show whether racial harmony and democratic capitalism can coexist."[26]

Bosnia, as test case, combines all three. My teaching experience in Bosnia may be one small anecdotal piece of evidence of the power of the market as weapon for freedom but given its communist history and its Islamic reality, Bosnia may be the most important emerging democracy to keep our eye on. As we look forward to the reconstruction of Baghdad, we must remember to keep looking over our shoulder at Bosnia to see if a burgeoning system of free enterprise can deliver on important social agendas.[27] In the meantime, we must not forget that even if the experiment is successful, it will be neither quick nor easy:

> New democracies tend to be chaotic, because they do not have the underlying foundations—a history or elections, the presence of skilled government bureaucracy to provide efficient services without corruption, or an effective judicial system—that give mature democracies stability. Countries opening their markets for the first time create another form of chaos, as government

controls are lifted and business experiences a free-for-all without sound regulations or other established rules of the game. On top of this simultaneous political and business chaos is the fact that newly freed people demand more from their governments than can possibly be delivered, leading to widespread popular disillusionment and a backlash against both democracy and free markets. [28]

The United States is not only the world's most advanced military power it is also the world's greatest source of wealth and economic development. In our bid to spread democracy throughout the world, we must keep in mind that military solutions may be necessary, but they are not sufficient. Perhaps what is also necessary is an enduring commitment to the symbiosis of free markets and free societies. This takes patience and a willingness to stay the course through chaotic times on the part of both government and business leaders. A decade after the guns have fallen silent in Bosnia the seeds of liberal democracy and economics have only recently taken root, but the coming season bodes a plentiful harvest.

Notes

1. The students were very willing to learn, however, this was not the case with the leaders of the local business community. Because I was a member of the Filosofski Fakultet (Faculty of Philosophy), and also because I am an American, I was invited to numerous conferences and even asked to speak on business ethics at the *World Bank "Roundtable" on Company Social Responsibility and Sustainable Competitiveness,* at the university's business school, the Ekonomski Fakultet. There was much criticism of American style economies and corporations, but little that could be considered traditional business ethics.
2. While some scholars claim that China is a communist country, others claim that the economic reality is that they are an emerging capitalist market. Jeffrey E. Garten, "Who Are the Big Emerging Markets, and Why Are They Important?," *The Investor's Direct of the New York Times,* 1997. "No market holds more long-term potential for America than China...China is the only BEM "Big Emerging Market" which includes Mexico, Brazil, Argentina, South Africa, Poland, Turkey, India, Indonesia, China, and South Korea) without a democratic foundation. The pressures for a more open political society are building, creating great tensions which could burst into a crisis for the country, the region, and the international financial system." Robert A. Sirco, "Free Trade and the Human Rights: The Moral Case for Engagement, Trade Policy Briefing Paper No.2," *Cato Institute,* July 1998. "Supporters of free enterprise have observed that, though the Chinese leaders still maintain that China is a communist state, they have, in fact, completely redefined the term. Tax rates have been slashed (and in some regions are actually lower than those of the United States), industries have been privatized, labor markets have been freed in relative terms, housing ownership is encouraged and growing, and joint ventures with Western companies are increasing rapidly and the Chinese stock market invites wide participation. China has moved from a society totally dominated by one of the world's most murderous regimes to one of increased material prosperity, freedom of movement, rising

commercial opportunity, and relative abundance."

3. Jeffrey E. Garten, "Who Are the Big Emerging Markets, and Why Are They Important?," *The Investor's Direct of the New York Times,* 1997. America, claims Garten, is counting on Turkey "to be a bulwark against the spread of Islamic fundamentalism into Europe."
4. Translated press releases from OHR (Office of the High Representative), Sarajevo, February, March, and May, 2003.
5. Ms. Dora Bensten, "Key Concepts," *International Expert in Procurement Legislation, EU,* Spring 2003.
6. E.R. Klein, "From Classroom to Boardroom: Teaching Practical Ethics Outside the Academy," *Teaching Philosophy,* 1992, 5:3, pp.123-131.
7. Fulbright is, at heart, a way of spreading democracy in a way many scholars claim is the best way: "In a free society, the only appropriate means for trying to change other people's conduct is through reason, persuasion, and example…The depoliticization or privatization of foreign intervention means an approach analogous to the private institutions of voluntary association for the handling of domestic 'social problems.' " Richard M. Ebeling, "Practicing the Principle of Freedom—At Home and Abroad," *Freedom Daily,* 2002.
8. An earlier version of my experience with Coca Cola Bosnia, is available on the online journal *Ethics Matters,* Bentley College, Spring 2004, http://ecampus.bentley.edu/dept/cbe/research/newsletter/newsletter_collection/2004apr_newsletter/2004apr_newsletter.html
9. Although I am not sure how many students from the class will join the Coke team (most have not yet graduated), I am sure that at least one of my students from the course has just been given a management position at another multinational corporation (German) in the area due to having taken the business ethics course.
10. Jeffrey E. Garten, "Who Are the Big Emerging Markets, and Why Are They Important?," *The Investor's Direct of the New York Times,* 1997. South Africa as an example of a country trying to use its "powerful trading partnership with the U.S." as a way of reconciling and overcoming ethnic divisions at home.
11. Murray Sole, "The Social Contradictions of Japanese Capitalism," *The Atlantic Monthly,* June 1998. The point is that every distinguishing feature of Japanese economics "comes from the national theory of unity through ties of blood…" In addition, it may be that even Japan's "prized ethno-economic" (based on the family as the most important value) has led them into the economic trouble they are in right now and has seen its last days.
12. Norman Bowie and Paul Vaaler, "Some Arguments for Universal Moral Standards," in (ed) George Enderle, *International Business Ethics: Challenges and Approaches.* Notre Dame: University of Notre Dame Press, 1998.
13. Gary C. Gambrill, "Explaining the Arab Democratic Deficit," *Analyses,* September, 2003.
14. Adam Smith, *The Wealth of Nations,* is, of course, the patriarch of American Free Enterprise.
15. Samuel Gregg, "Markets, Morality, and Civil Society," *The Intercollegiate Review,* Fall 2003/Spring 2004, pp.23-30, p.29.
16. Jadish Bhagwati, "Coping with Antiglobalism," *Foreign Affairs,* January/February, 2002, pp.2-7, p.3.

17. Charles Edward Scott, Jr., "'Capitalism is freedom' speaker proclaims," *Daily Illini,* April 24, 2003.
"Dr. Andrew Bernstein, Pace University novelist and philosopher, said people's freedom and prosperity are greatly increased when capitalism is introduced on any continent in any era..." Robert A. Sirco, "Free Trade and the Human Rights: The Moral Case for Engagement, Trade Policy Briefing Paper No.2," *Cato Institute,* July 1998. "The best policy for promoting human rights remains economic and moral engagement."
18. Economic liberalization does not always guarantee a more democratic and free environment. In addition, large amounts of capital may be a double-edged sword in places like China (and maybe even certain Arab countries) where they may predominantly invest newfound wealth money in military development.
19. Robert A. Dahl, *On Democracy.* New Haven, Conn.: Yale University Press, 1990, p.166-16.
20. Gary C. Gambrill, "Explaining the Arab Democratic Deficit," *Analyses,* September, 2003.
21. Louis Pojman, "The Moral Response to Terrorism and Cosmopolitanism," in James Sterba (ed.) *Terrorism and International Justice.* New York: Oxford University Press, pp. 135-157, p.140.
22. Of course the true root causes of the problems in the Muslim world may be more fundamental. For example, citing the *2002 Arab Development Report,* the *9/11 Commission Report,* suggests that Islamic culture itself, especially its endemic sexism, may actually be the cause of many of the regions economic problems. "The repression of women has not only seriously limited individual opportunity but also crippled overall economic prosperity," p.53.
23. Gary C. Gambrill, "Explaining the Arab Democratic Deficit," *Analyses,* September, 2003. "The September 11, 2001 terrorist attacks led to a shift in official American thinking about democratization in the Middle East by discrediting the idea that American-backed autocratic regimes can serve as a bulwark against radical Islamist terrorism. U.S. officials and policy experts have increasingly come to believe that the absence of democracy has radicalized Islamist movements by denying them peaceful channels of expression and that the attendant economic costs of authoritarian governance have swelled their ranks. Moreover, in Riyadh and Damascus, elements of the ruling elite have been directly implicated in terrorism abroad. Beneath their tough veneers, governments in the Arab world were revealed to be corrupt and easily penetrated by those who wish harm to befall the United States."
24. Kevin Danaher and Jason Mark, "Free Enterprise Is Dead, Long Live Free Enterprise!," *Alternet.org,* January 2004.
25. There are numerous anecdotal stories of being able to give someone begging in the streets in China (in the 50s) an American quarter and seeing them two weeks later with their own fruit stand; the truth is that there are many documented cases of modern microfinance from Third World and developing nations. See, for example, Rebecca N. Coke, "Gender and Microfinance Business Choice: Evidence from the Philippines," *Ethics Matters: Online Magazine of the Center for Business Ethics,* Bentley College,
http://ecampus.bentley.edu/dept/cbe/research/newsletter_mainpage.html#
The main point of the article was that the programs that alleviated poverty did

so not by simply giving out credit, but by encouraging long-term development through the promotion of entrepreneurial attitudes and opportunities for better education.

26. Jeffrey E. Garten, "Who Are the Big Emerging Markets, and Why Are They Important?," *The Investor's Direct of the New York Times,* 1997.
27. Jadish Bhagwati, "Coping with Anti-globalism," *Foreign Affairs,* January/February, 2002, pp.2-7, p.6. Many of the Bosnians living in the United States have expressed impatience with their financial status which may simply be a product of their first generation immigrant status—while the parents have "blue collar" jobs, their children are attending college.
28. Jeffrey E. Garten, "Who Are the Big Emerging Markets, and Why Are They Important?," *The Investor's Direct of the New York Times,* 1997.

Islam and Capitalism: A Non-Rodinsonian Approach

Irfan Khawaja

What is the relationship between Islam and capitalism? The most celebrated answer to that question is the one advanced by the French Orientalist Maxime Rodinson in his 1966 book, *Islam and Capitalism.* Rodinson wrote, "the search for profit, trade, and consequently, production for the market, are looked upon with no less favour by Muslim tradition than by the Koran itself" (Rodinson, 1974, p. 16; see also pp. 53-54). So, Rodinson argued, Islam was compatible with capitalism, understanding "Islam" in essentially non-scriptural terms and interpreting "capitalism" along Marxist lines.

But suppose that one understands both Islam and capitalism differently? In that case, I argue, we reach a different and more complex answer to our question. In this paper, I try to put discussion of the topic on a new footing by offering a scripturally-based, non-Marxist account of the relationship between Islam and capitalism.

Why a Non-Rodinsonian Approach?

Rodinson's book, as I have suggested, is the best-heralded study of the subject. It would be impossible, given constraints of space, to argue here in any detail against Rodinson's view; for present purposes, I merely describe it and contrast it with the classical liberal conception I intend to adopt.

The lynchpin of Rodinson's Marxism is his allegiance to an explicitly deterministic version of the materialist theory of history and class struggle

(Rodinson, 1974, pp. x, xii, xv, xvi). The classical version of this theory discusses the dialectical interplay between feudal, capitalist, and socialist economies in the European context, but with the possible exception of India, has little to say about economic forms falling outside of it (Rodinson, 1974, pp. 58-68). Rodinson's guiding question, then, was where Islam fit within the classical Marxist framework.

A corollary of Rodinson's Marxism is his conception of capitalism. Capitalism, in his terms, is a social system in which "formally free labor" is bound up with "a legal separation between economic and domestic activity," accompanied by "a rational system of accounting" (Rodinson, 1974, p. 9). Its distinguishing feature is a society dominated by what Marx called "merchant" and "financial" capital, along with the ideological superstructure necessary to justify (or rationalize) capital's claim to legitimacy. Rodinson's question thus becomes: How did Islam become compatible with such a system and ideology?

That leads us to Rodinson's characterization of Islam. Early in the book, he writes:

> The most usual way of dealing with the problem under examination is to ask whether what the Muslim religion prescribes has the effect of favouring, hindering or forbidding those practices which make up the capitalist (or some other) mode of production, or whether these prescriptions are neutral in relation to the practices in question. As will become apparent, this is not in my opinion the most important issue. Nevertheless, it is one that arises and that is of some interest in connection with the problem as a whole. I shall therefore take a quick look at it (Rodinson, 1974, p. 12).

The "usual way of dealing with the problem" takes the prescriptions of the Islamic religion as relatively autonomous of the mode of production in which they arose, and asks whether, in practice, adherence to those prescriptions would be compatible with capitalism. Rodinson, by contrast, takes the prescriptions more or less to have been determined by their means of production, and so bypasses the strictly propositional content of the prescriptions to examine Islamic *praxis* (my term, not his) in this or that historical epoch.[1] His question then becomes: How did Islam, considered as a historical *praxis*, become compatible with capitalism, understood as a bourgeois ideology?

It can't be stressed enough that this latter question structures Rodinson's book as a whole; to decouple the book's thesis from this question is to decouple it from the problem that Rodinson set out to solve. Obviously, then, if one rejects the terms or presuppositions of Rodinson's question, one will reject both the starting point of his inquiry as well as those aspects of his answer influenced by his ideological presuppositions. As I see it, the most objectionable feature of Rodinson's analysis is his "Marxianization" of both capitalism and Islam.

From a classical liberal perspective of the sort I adopt, Rodinson's account of capitalism suffers from two interconnected deficiencies: on the one hand, it focuses on non-essential as opposed to essential features of capitalism; on the other, it abstracts entirely from the normative presuppositions on which classical liberals have taken capitalism to rest (Rand, 1967, pp. vii-ix and 11-34). While it is true that capitalist economies rely on so-called merchant and financial capital, it isn't true that capitalist ideology is a mere superstructure built on that economic base. On the classical liberal view, the moral principles a population adopts are the basis of its social system and modes of production, not the other way around. So a definition of capitalism ought to be based on the fundamental normative ideas that undergird it as a social system—the very things missing from Rodinson's definition.

In my view, Ayn Rand's definition gets the normative priorities right, and in so doing, focuses on essentials. A "social system," she writes, "is a set of moral-political-economic principles, embodied in a society's laws, institutions, and government, which determine the terms of association among the men living in a given geographic area" (Rand, 1967, p. 18). Capitalism, then, "is a social system based on the recognition of individual rights, including property rights, in which all property is privately owned" (Rand, 1967, p. 18). This highly moralized conception of capitalism differs fundamentally from the one that Rodinson had in mind.[2]

Similar problems arise for Rodinson's conception of Islam. Unless we assume that the author of the Qur'an was determined by his mode of production—an assumption that neither Muslims nor non-Muslims need accept—the issue that Rodinson dismisses as unimportant is in fact all-important. The content of Islam's distinctively theological and moral claims constitute its identity as a doctrine. Reduce the doctrine to economics, and Islam goes out of existence. This, of course, is partly Rodinson's point: He wants to "explain" Islam, in effect, by explaining it away. But given this, we can see how deceptive is his claim to have reconciled "Islam" with "capitalism." From a classical liberal perspective, what he's done is to reconcile an un-Islamic Islam with an un-capitalist capitalism.

My assumptions here are just the reverse of Rodinson's. Contrary to Rodinson, I reject the Marxist theory of history, and accept Ayn Rand's conception of capitalism. Though, like Rodinson, I am not a Muslim believer, I intend here to offer a sympathetic reconstruction of the ethico-economic claims of the Qur'an that I think a Muslim believer could accept, and that I regard as a necessary preliminary to an inquiry into the non-scriptural sources of Islamic belief (*sunnah, fiqh,* etc.).[3] That approach gives us a radically different way of formulating Rodinson's question, namely: *Are the prescriptions of the Qur'an, understood as an orthodox Muslim might understand them, compatible with capitalism, understood as a defender of capitalism might understand it?*

Salvationist Egoism

As a first approach to our question, we need to step back and consider it in a broader context. Recall Rand's definition of a social system, which implies that capitalism, though defined in terms of rights, rests on a broader and more integrated moral conception than respect for rights alone. One crucial feature of this moral conception will be an account of self-interest. Since commerce requires a great deal in the way of self-interested action, it seems reasonable to think that an ethics positively disposed toward commerce would have to have a positive orientation toward and conception of self-interest. And so, it seems reasonable to ask what the Qur'an has to say on that score.

The answer, I think, is somewhat surprising. Alain Besançon has recently drawn attention to what he calls "the pagan" features of Islamic ethics, by which he means not a tendency to idolatry, but a glorification of this-worldly values:

> [Islam bears]…some similarity with pagan conceptions, and specifically with pagan ethics. Islamic civilization is a civilization of the good life, and it offers a certain latitude in the realm of sensory pleasure. Asceticism is foreign to the spirit of Islam. There is a Muslim spirit of *carpe diem*, a this-worldly contentment that often fascinated Christians who may have seen in it a dim echo of the ancient, classical world….Much fun has been made, wrongly, of the Muslim notion of paradise. Admittedly, it is not like the Jewish or Christian notion, which envisions an eternity participating in the life of the divine. In the other-world of Islam, God remains separate and inaccessible, but man finds there forgiveness, peace, 'satisfaction'. If biblical religion suggests a road map that originates in a garden, Eden, and finishes in a city, the heavenly Jerusalem, the Qur'an charts a return to the garden (Besançon, 2004, p. 46).

This is, I think, an astute and underappreciated point, and one that goes a long way toward illuminating much of the text of the Qur'an. What we find there, I think, is a more straightforwardly self-interested conception of moral motivation than might otherwise be expected. I call this conception salvationist egoism (for further discussion, see Glasgow, 1970; MacDonald, 1990; and Rogers, 1997).

A word of caution is in order here. The term "egoism" generally has a negative connotation in everyday speech and in moral philosophy; to be an egoist, it's often thought, is *ipso facto* to be insensitive to or even subversive of the good of others. But there is no defensible reason for taking the term that way (see Machan, 1979). "Egoism," as I'm using the term, is the principle that each moral agent ought to be the ultimate intended beneficiary of his or her actions. In other words, every action an egoist takes conduces, in some way, to his or her overall benefit. Salvationist egoism, then, is the doctrine that each moral agent ought to take salvation as his or her ultimate aim in life, and regard that aim as defining the content of his or her self-interest. If salvation is my ultimate good, in other words, that which promotes my salvation promotes my self-interest.

Though I don't have the space to argue the point here, this interpretation is in my view well supported by the text of the Qur'an. Anyone doubting this is invited to do a search of the Qur'anic text on the Arabic words denoting personal benefit or reward—*ajr, ahsan, falah,* etc. What one finds is that on the Qur'anic conception, virtue brings its practitioner a reward in this life and / or the next, while vice harms its practitioner in the same way. Moreover, a Muslim is enjoined to do good *in order to* earn the relevant reward, and to avoid evil *in order to* avoid the relevant punishment. So it's not an exaggeration to say that the Qur'an enjoins self-benefit—the desire to be rewarded for one's virtue—as a fundamental and morally legitimate motivation (e.g., Qur'an, 3:276, 4:160, 4:40, 28:84, 30:39, 39:10, 42:20; tr. A.Y. Ali). As the Qur'an puts it, "Is there any reward for good but what is good?" (Qur'an, 55:60). What is striking about this conception—and perhaps discomfiting to some—is the unapologetic attitude toward gain that it expresses, both in this world (*fi'dunia*) and in the next (*al akhira*).

It's important to qualify this point. The desire for reward, on the Qur'anic view, is intrinsically tied to virtue: one is rewarded for virtue in proportion to one's merits, but one cannot expect remuneration for what one hasn't earned, much less for vices. On the other hand, it is perfectly natural to want a reward *if* one has earned it. Indeed, as Surah Al Rahman suggests (Surah 55), it would be perverse to refuse the benefits to which one is entitled. That, after all, is what Satan does in the Qur'anic story of the Fall: He denies himself the benefits to which he is entitled because he takes himself to have achieved a status he hasn't earned (Qur'an, 2:34-39, 7:19-25).

These facts have important implications for a discussion of the Qur'anic ethics of commerce. Whereas many ethical systems, secular and religious, face the seemingly insuperable difficulty of reconciling self-interest with altruism—and then of reconciling this with the realities of commerce—the Qur'an faces neither problem, because it never enjoins altruism. While the Qur'anic ethic can accommodate norms of justice and benevolence that simultaneously bring good to benefactor and beneficiary, it cannot accommodate or even make sense of norms that require one person's sacrificing his / her genuine interests for the sake of another. Think in this light of the difference between the Christian and Muslim conceptions of Christ. Christians think it makes perfect sense for Christ to have sacrificed himself on the cross; Muslims don't think it makes sense for Christ to have been on the cross at all (Qur'an, 4:157-158). Whereas self-sacrifice is at the very center of Christian ethics, the Qur'an goes out of its way to reject it.

All of this makes Islam more obviously compatible with commerce than many rival moral conceptions. As long as commerce itself is a legitimate activity and legitimately undertaken, the motive underlying it is not only legitimate, but an instance of the fundamental motivation at the heart of Islam.

Wages, Labor, and "Unfailing Commerce"

A positive attitude toward self-interest is a necessary but not sufficient condition of a positive attitude toward commerce. An ethical system may take a friendly view of egoistic motivations generally but go on to exclude specifically *commercial* motivations from the list of the ethically permissible or praiseworthy. To get from a general egoism to a positive conception of commerce, we need scriptural evidence for regarding commercial self-benefit as an instance of the sort of worldly self-benefit that the Qur'an sanctions. As it happens, however, the scriptural evidence of this is as strong as evidence can get: The Qur'an doesn't just "sanction" commercial motivations, but puts God at the very center of them.[4]

This may at first blush seem a bizarre thing to say. Can it make sense to ascribe commercial motivations to God? How could God buy or sell anything, or expect remuneration for his "labors"?

Reasonable as these objections may sound, however, they get things backwards. To be sure, God doesn't expect remuneration for his labors, but he remunerates us for *ours*, both in this life, by creating the causal relations that lead us to earthly rewards, and in the next, by allowing us to earn salvation. What is interesting here is the metaphor that the Qur'an adopts to describe its system of otherworldly reward: The reward is a wage or payment calculated by an act of measurement performed on some equivalent of a balance (Arabic: *meizan*; Qur'an, 21:47, 23:101-4). In short, we labor; God weighs our actions in the balance and determines their worth; He then pays us the equivalent of our worth in what the Qur'an calls "spiritual prosperity" or "spiritual sustenance." Elsewhere, the Qur'an describes the transaction as a sort of "unfailing commerce" (Qur'an, 9:111, 10:59, 16:73, 19:62, 42:12, 51:57, 56:10-11, 67:31, 91:9-10).

This last phrase—*unfailing* commerce—is crucial. Divine commerce, unlike its human counterpart, is perfect, implying a perfect weighing of the merits of an action, and perfect remuneration for labor undertaken. Thus God gives us "full measure" for our actions in the sense of a reckoning utterly unaffected by human defect or worldly contingency. In the Qur'anic phrase, God measures the worth of our actions and pays us down to the "atom" (e.g., Qur'an, 21:47, 54:52-55, 99:6-8).

Obviously, humans, though enjoined to give full measure in their commercial dealings, cannot hope to achieve or even approximate the divine. Nor are they required to: The Qur'an endorses a version of the "ought implies can" principle (Qur'an, 2:286, 7:42, 23:62). We can be enjoined, however, to *do our best* to give full measure, and rule out actions that egregiously violate it. So the divine principle of full measure regulates human affairs without demanding the superhuman of us.

This rationale explains the Qur'an's more obvious stipulations against covetousness, theft, fraud, miserliness, and excessive accumulation, and its injunctions to generosity, fair dealing, and punishment for economic crimes (see especially Qur'an, 83, Surah Al Mutafifin). In more subtle ways, however, I think it also explains the Qur'an's otherwise puzzling prohibitions on *riba* (often translated as "usury" or "interest," but closer in meaning to "loan sharking")[5] and gambling. Both gambling and *riba* depend at some level on the arbitrary—on sheer, non-measurable and ungoverned vicissitude. Gambling depends on pure chance; *riba* depends on pure will. What is wrong with them from a Qur'anic perspective is that they generate profits ungoverned by *any* principle of limitation or conception of desert. The gambler has done nothing to earn his profits; the practitioner of *riba* sets an interest rate ungoverned by the measurable value of his services. (On *riba,* see Qur'an, 2:274-280; on gambling, see 2:219, 5:93).

The principle here is that while monetary reward is in one's interest, and ought to be sought under that description, profits only meet that description when they are genuinely earned, and are only earned when we can specify what was done to earn precisely *that* profit.

The upshot of this view is once again to identify a complex but genuine affinity between the precepts of the Qur'an and an aspect of the capitalist ethos. Many religious and ethical systems think of commerce as something low and unworthy, in part because their paradigm examples of it meet that description. Islam doesn't face this problem. On the Islamic view, God himself has adopted the wage-labor system, and God's adoption of it is its paradigm instance. The result is a sort of sanctification of commerce, when constrained by principles of justice. As a *hadith* puts it, "If you profit from doing what is permitted, your deed is *jihad*" (quoted in Rodinson, 1974, pp. 16-17). In short, commerce, properly circumscribed, can be a means of salvation.

Sovereignty, Viceregency, and Rights

I've so far been telling a story that gives Islam an affinity of sorts with capitalism. Recall, however, that I defined capitalism in terms of rights, whose Islamic credentials I have yet to discuss. We therefore have to deal with that issue: What does the Qur'an say directly or indirectly about rights, and how does that bear on its conception of capitalism?

We need to begin by clarifying the relevant concept of rights.[6] A right as understood by classical liberals is a claim of absolute sovereignty over something: It is a kind of dominion. What I have a right to is mine, not yours, and mine to dispose of regardless of what you may want or think. A right to life is dominion over one's life; a right to liberty is dominion over one's capacities and actions; a right to property is the moral authority to use and control one's resources for one's own purposes. Central to this conception of a right are the ideas of inviolability, inalienability, and exclusive control. I control what I have a right to, and no one else can or does.

Given this conception, rights can in principle protect actions that are in fact immoral. If I have a right to use my property, I am exclusively at liberty to decide its disposition, and if I decide badly or wrongly, it is my liberty to do so without interference from others—even from someone of greater wisdom.

This conception of rights points to a serious incompatibility between Islam and capitalism. Rights are norms that give the agent a form of dominion or sovereignty over himself/herself and things in the world. They protect what classical liberals see as the need for an *untrammeled* exercise of reason in thought and in action. But by Qur'anic standards, man has no such dominion or sovereignty over himself or the things in the world. And he lacks it precisely because the Qur'an *forbids* the untrammeled exercise of reason in human life. The exercise of reason, on the Qur'anic view, is a divine gift whose scope is circumscribed by the imperatives of faith in the supernatural (e.g., Qur'an, 2:1-20). There is thus no need to give reason unlimited scope and no rationale for a norm to protect its unlimited exercise.

In fact, by classical liberal standards, God's insistence on faith amounts to a sort of rights-violation that sits at the very heart of the Qur'an: Either we are to believe on faith and submit unconditionally to divine rule *or* we are damned to eternal punishment in Hell (e.g., Qur'an, 2:165-167). This ultimatum structures the context within which reason is permitted to operate in the life of a Muslim, and thus subordinates human autonomy to divine will.[7]

It follows that the full-blooded liberal conception of a right is incompatible with Islam. To demand such rights is literally Satanic: It is to reject one's unalterable status as God's vicegerent (*khalifa*) and to demand a dominion of one's own within the dominion of God. It is not an accident, I think, that man's status as vicegerent is described in the Qur'anic story of the Fall, and that Adam and Eve's transgression there consists precisely in violating their vicegerential status by disobeying God about a matter of jurisdiction: "Dwell thou and eat of the bountiful things," God commands, "but approach not this tree or ye will run into harm and transgression" (Qur'an, 2:35). Notice that God does not make the command because he claims that the tree is *His.* What He says is that they are not to approach it because it is *not theirs.* Whose is it? No one's; the issue is jurisdiction, not property. The Qur'an here is denying the idea that man is at liberty to appropriate the commons at will. He is only at liberty to do so subject to God's will.

As a matter of abstract principle, this implies that no Islamic social system can be based on a literal adoption of liberal rights. An Islamic system can perhaps loosely appropriate the language of rights in the way that utilitarians sometimes do, but it cannot take the concept fully on board. The very language of rights in English connotes a notion of individual sovereignty or dominion that is difficult to express in classically Muslim languages. The Arabic *haq* (like the Latin *jus* and the Greek *dike*) refers to what is right, not to individuals' rights (see MacIntyre, 1991).

In practical terms, this means that while an Islamic social system may be quite commerce-friendly, it must draw the line at adopting the sort of strong property rights distinctive of classical liberal capitalism. The potential restrictions fall into two categories, regulation and redistribution.

Regulation. Since Islam rejects the principle of an absolute right to property, it has no difficulty in endorsing far-reaching regulations on the use of property. One set of regulations might pertain to unfair but non-coercive economic transactions. Another might regulate "excessive" rates of interest or capital accumulation. A third might regulate the sale of goods whose consumption is forbidden in the Qur'an: e.g., intoxicants, foods violating the dietary laws, pornography, and the like. And a fourth might regulate transactions that weakened commitments to divine commandments, e.g., work stoppages for prayer, fasting, and the like.

Redistribution. On the classical liberal conception, my right to my property supersedes your need to have property: one person's need is not by itself a claim on another person's wealth. On the Islamic conception, however, need *is* a claim on wealth because the wealth ultimately belongs not to us, but to God. In other words, Islam endorses the idea that the worse-off have a positive right to the goods of the better-off, and thus licenses some form of redistribution.

The clearest evidence for this in the Qur'an comes from a passage in Surah al Hashr (Qur'an, 59:7-9) that makes explicit what elsewhere is implicit.[8] Here we are told that what God has bestowed on the Prophet belongs to God, and by extension to the needy, so that one is to take what one is assigned and part with the rest. This verse coheres with the traditional idea that *zakat* (as opposed to *sadaqa*)[9] is an ethical constraint *on* ownership; that is, one can't be said fully to own one's assets until one gives a part of them away.

This severing of the connection between earning and ownership suggests that, ultimately, on the Qur'anic conception, we do not fully own anything: After all, if our actions gave us full title to our earnings, we wouldn't have to give our earnings away in order to acquire title to them; but if we have to give part of our earnings away in order to acquire title to the remainder, our *actions* clearly do not confer full title to what we acquire in the first place. And if our actions don't confer title, clearly, nothing else does. In short, what we possess in the way of earnings, we possess in trust from God. But a trust is not a *right* in the liberal sense, and in my view, is not compatible with one.

Islam and Global Capitalism

We can gauge the influence on contemporary Islamic studies of Rodinson's *Islam and Capitalism* by considering the book's influence on an even more influential text in the field, Edward Said's *Orientalism.* In discussing what he calls "modern Anglo-French Orientalism in fullest flower," Said writes:

> Although he never thoroughly studied Islam, Weber nevertheless influenced the field considerably, mainly because his notions of type were simply an "outside" confirmation of many of the canonical theses held by Orientalists, whose economic ideas never extended beyond asserting the Oriental's fundamental incapacity for trade, commerce, and economic rationality. In the Islamic field those clichés held good for literally hundreds of years—until Maxime Rodinson's important study *Islam and Capitalism* appeared in 1966. Still, the notion of a type—Oriental, Islamic, Arab, or whatever—endures and is nourished by similar kinds of abstractions or paradigms or types as they emerge out of the modern social sciences (Said, 1979, p. 260).[10]

This passage summarizes, in three sentences, the essential misconceptions I've been at pains to contest in this paper. Said asserts here that pre-Rodinsonian scholarship on the subject was "essentialist" in its assumptions—i.e., overly focused on the "essence" of Islam—and being essentialist, naturally assumed that Islam was incompatible with "trade, commerce, and economic rationality." Along came Rodinson's *Islam and Capitalism,* to whose "methodological self-consciousness" we owe a non-essentialist reconciliation of Islam with capitalism (Said, 1979, p. 326). The moral of the story? Dispense with the very idea of what "Islam as such" has to say about capitalism, while insisting all the while that Islam is perfectly compatible with capitalism. Meanwhile, insist on understanding "capitalism" on the "methodologically self-conscious" model of French Marxism circa 1966.

In fact, every one of these claims is the exact reverse of the truth. As can be inferred from Rodinson's own discussion, pre-Rodinsonian scholarship was *in*sufficiently focused on the essence of Islam. In any case, a more assiduously essentialist account would *not* have claimed that Islam was incompatible with "trade, commerce, and economic rationality." It would, on the contrary, have asserted that trade, commerce, and economic reasoning were at the very heart of the Qur'an's ethic of social relations.

Further, Rodinson's book is *not* "methodologically self-conscious," and does *not* reconcile Islam with capitalism in the relevant sense of either of those terms. It is, instead, a stodgy and inconsistent attempt to apply orthodox Marxist precepts to an ill-defined archive of material arbitrarily denominated "Islamic." Besides, to demonstrate Islam's capacity for "trade, commerce, and economic rationality" is *not* to demonstrate its doctrinal compatibility with *capitalism,* at least as understood by capitalism's classical liberal defenders. As we've seen, the Qur'an's attitude towards commerce is not the same as its attitude toward classical liberal rights. Finally, it makes no sense on the one hand to reject an essentialist approach to Islam, and on the other to insist on "Islam's" compatibility with "capitalism"; the first claim merely denies what the second asserts.

In short, a more confused approach to Islam and capitalism can hardly be imagined—and yet one finds the Rodinsonian analysis taken for granted as far to the Left as Said's work, and as far to the Right as the polemics of a free market think-tank (Bartlett, 2001).

The question of Islam's relationship to capitalism is bound to take on increasing importance in the post-9/11 world. We desperately need an explanation for underdevelopment in the Islamic world, as well as an assessment of Arab/Muslim economic grievances against the West, and strategies by which the Arab/Muslim world might better cope with the inevitable stresses of globalization. A necessary condition of getting that debate right, however, will be to challenge the terms of the Rodinsonian analysis of Islam and capitalism, and to replace it with a better one. A better analysis will have to begin, unapologetically, by identifying the *essence* of Islam and of capitalism. I have merely scratched the surface of that task here, but if I'm right, the claims I've defended are a better foundation for inquiry than those advanced by Rodinson, and those taken for granted for the past several decades.

Notes

1. Actually, Rodinson's approach to the issue discussed in the text is inconsistent and rather confusing. In the passage just quoted in the text, he tells us that the content of Islam's normative precepts is *in*essential to the issue he means to discuss in the book. In the next chapter (Chapter 3), he proceeds to discuss "economic practice in the Muslim world of the Middle Ages," using the modifier "Muslim" to refer inclusively to practices consistent with and required by Islamic precepts, as well as those in violation of and completely unrelated to them. In Chapter 4, Islam's normative precepts abruptly become *central* to the discussion. So, in discussing Max Weber's famous thesis about the connection between Protestantism and capitalism, Rodinson turns to "the influence of Muslim ideology" in economics, rebutting Weber by way of a (somewhat idiosyncratic and uneven) interpretation of the precepts of the Qur'an, *sunnah* (way of the Prophet), and *fiqh* (jurisprudence). The last 120 pages of the book, however, return to the method of Chapter 3, essentially equating the practices of "Muslim countries" with that of "contemporary Islam," mostly in abstraction from the content of Islam's normative claims.

   In general, Rodinson seems not to entertain the possibility that *Islam as such* might have normative content autonomously of the various modes of production and historical epochs in which it finds expression (e.g., Rodinson, 1974, pp. 227-228). As a result, he seems not to have any consistent principle in mind when he uses "Muslim" or "Islamic" as adjectives or "Islam" as a proper noun. In a sense, then, it is utterly unclear what Rodinson takes himself to have established in demonstrating the compatibility of "Islam" with "capitalism."
2. Rodinson does not discuss the notion of a right as such anywhere in his book,

and what he says about property rights is highly problematic. At one point, he claims that "the capitalist mode of production in the strict sense" existed in "the Muslim world of the Middle Ages" (1974, p. 50). But at the time to which he refers, slavery and serfdom were well in operation in the Islamic world, and Muslim governments regularly enjoyed eminent domain over all the land in their jurisdiction (see Rodinson, 1974, p. 15); none of these institutions is compatible with classical liberal capitalism. Later, Rodinson asserts that "the pure concept of private property as an absolute right to use and abuse...is rarely if ever encountered" (1974, p. 64). But by classical liberal strictures, this claim flatly contradicts Rodinson's assertion that "capitalism in the strict sense" has ever *existed,* much less that it existed throughout the Islamic Middle Ages.

In his most extensive discussion of property rights (1974, pp. 172-176), Rodinson asserts that to understand capitalism in terms of absolute property rights is "totally unjustified," because in doing so, we would be led to the supposedly absurd claim "that Christianity is unadapted to exclusive private property" (1974, p. 174; see also pp. 15-16). But this last claim is hardly the absurdity that Rodinson takes it to be: Both Christian critics of capitalism (e.g., MacIntyre, 1991) and capitalist critics of Christianity (e.g., Rand, 1967, pp. 297-319) have explicitly affirmed it.

3. My claim is not that the Qur'an exhausts the sources of Islamic belief, but that given the primacy of the Qur'an among those sources, a discussion of "Islamic belief with respect to x" must exhaust what the Qur'an has to say about x before proceeding to non-Qura'nic sources of belief.
4. Rodinson (1974, p. 81) mentions this fact in a different context, citing a passage from Charles Torrey's study, *The Commercial-Theological Terms in the Koran* (1892, p. 48).
5. Since I reject the traditional equation of *riba* with interest, I leave *riba* untranslated in the text.

   Rodinson claims inconsistently that "we do not know for certain" what *riba* means (Rodinson, 1974, p. 14, 18), but then insists throughout the book on equating it with interest (e.g., Rodinson, 1974, p. 35). This eventually leads him to the view that "Islam did not prevent anyone from taking up, out of self-interest, an attitude that was directly contrary to its precepts on the question of *riba,*" where the precepts in question rule out the taking of interest (Rodinson, 1974, p. 171). The claim is triply false—first in asserting that Islam tolerates the violation of its own precepts; second in claiming that a Muslim's self-interest can be advanced in the violation of those precepts; and third in claiming that *riba* means "interest."

   I thank Aftab Khawaja and Imad-ad-din Ahmad for helpful discussion on this issue.
6. My account of rights relies heavily on Rand (1967), Smith (1995), and MacIntyre (1991).
7. Contrast Rodinson (1974, 78-99).
8. In fairness, I should emphasize that it *is* implicit. As Rodinson correctly points out (1974, p. 14), while the Qur'an's claims are consistent with a redistributionist outlook, it says little (if anything) explicitly in favor of redistribution. Indeed, Surah al Hashr (discussed in the text) refers to the redistribution of *battle spoils,* not peacetime production; one could conceivably argue that its claims are spe-

cific to that context but inapplicable beyond it.

9. Strictly speaking, *zakat* refers to the official and compulsory tithe administered by an Islamic government; *sadaqa* refers to private, voluntary charity.
10. Apparently oblivious to the self-contradiction involved, Said elsewhere writes that his account of Orientalism uses "the British and French experiences of and with the Near Orient, Islam and the Arabs" as "privileged *types*," and that his book eschews "a narrative chronicle" to offer a "portrait of the *typical structures*...constituting the field" (Said, 1979, p. 201; my emphases).

Bibliography

Ali, A. Y. (1938). *An interpretation of the Holy Qur'an with full Arabic text.* Third Edition. Lahore, Pakistan: Shaikh Muhammad Ashraf.

Bartlett, B. (2001). *Islam and free market capitalism* [Online]. Available: http://www.ncpa.org/edo/bb/2001/bb091901.html

Besançon, A. (2004). What kind of religion is Islam? *Commentary, 117*:5, 42-48.

Glasgow, W.D. (1970). Metaphysical egoism. *Ratio, 12*, 79-84.

MacDonald, Scott. (1990). Egoistic rationalism: Aquinas's basis for Christian morality. In: Michael Beaty (Ed.) *Christian theism and the problems of philosophy* (pp. 327-354). Notre Dame: University of Notre Dame Press.

Machan, T. (1979). Recent work on ethical egoism. *American Philosophical Quarterly*, 16:1, 1-15.

MacIntyre, A. (1991). Community, law, and the idiom and rhetoric of rights. *Listening: A Journal of Religion and Culture*, 26, 96-110.

Rand, A. (1967). *Capitalism: The unknown ideal.* New York: Signet.

Rodinson, M. (1974). *Islam and capitalism*, tr. Brian Pearce. Ludhiana, India: Allen Lane. (First published 1966 in French. Paris: Editions du Seuil).

Rogers, K. (Ed.) (1997). *Self-interest: An anthology of philosophical perspectives.* New York: Routledge.

Said, E. (1979). *Orientalism.* New York: Vintage. (First published 1978. New York: Pantheon).

Smith, T. (1995). *Moral rights and political freedom.* Lanham, MD: Rowman and Littlefield.

Torrey, C.C. (1892). *The commercial-theological terms in the Koran* (Strasbourg thesis). Leiden: Brill.

The Role of Hinduism in Global India and Her Business Ethics

Himanshu Rai

> If there is ever to be a universal religion, it must be one which will have no location in place or time; which will be infinite like the God it will preach, and whose sun will shine upon the followers of Krishna and of Christ, on saints and sinners alike; which will not be Brahminic or Buddhistic, Christian or Mohameddan, but the sum total of all these, and still have infinite space for development.
>
> *Swami Vivekananda*

Religion and business have co-existed since time immemorial and while it would be short sightedness to associate religion merely with the way to worship, there is little empirical evidence to show the effect of religion on business. Religion is a way of life and it is likely that with its cumulated experience and pervasiveness, it would affect men, life, and the world including business and its various aspects. Specifically in the context of business ethics, researchers suggest that religious role expectations, internalized as a religious self-identity, may influence ethical behavior. Moreover, technology, global competition, downsizing, and reengineering have led to employees seeking religious and spiritual meaning at their workplaces as well. While religion and religious texts may not directly address the issue of business and commerce, they have been an important force in the shaping of business-related values and ethics.

Researchers have looked at business ethics and other aspects of the world religions in the context of Christianity, Islam, Confucianism, Shintoism, Judaism, and Hinduism. However, the studies in the Indian and specifically the Hindu religion context have looked at the cultural connotations and manifestations of the religion rather than the meaning of religion itself and the way it shapes individual ideologies and business ideologies. Earlier studies have misinterpreted the concept underlying the Vedic literature probably due to loss of meaning in translations and interpretations. Their arguments on the origin of caste system and the underlying concepts of Hinduism are far removed from truth. Hinduism is built on the pillars of *Dharma* (way of life), *Artha* (wealth and prosperity), *Kaam* (desires), and *Moksha* (nirvana) and is based on the teachings of *Vedas, Smriti* (especially *Manusmriti*), the two epics, *Ramayana* and *Mahabharata*, and other religious literature. This paper attempts at interpreting the deeper nuances of the Hindu religion and religious texts and their role in shaping individual and organizational value systems and ethics in India, especially in the context of globalization.

Religion

Derived from the Latin word "*religio*," meaning something done with overanxious or scrupulous attention to detail, religion binds people together and draws them into a common fold of life. Reflections into the past would reveal that natural sciences were originally embedded into this concept and only in the last few hundred years have they parted ways to independently seek answers to life and its philosophy. Religions may differ in terms of concentrating on inner explorations related to enlightenment and peace (e.g., Jainism, Buddhism) to outer explorations establishing the constant existence of a higher authority (e.g., Christianity, Judaism, Islam); and from cohesively organized in terms of hierarchy and control (e.g., Roman Catholicism) to loosely bound (e.g., Hinduism). However, despite such differences, religions create codes of behavior that enable people to live with confidence and have significant impacts on all aspects of human life.

Role of Religion in Business and Ethics

With its cumulated experience and by virtue of being an integral part of a person's life, religion is a part of the total truth which people in administrative positions have to address. It forwards the theory of the common good of the community, which in turn can be said to have three components viz. particular goods, patterns of cooperation, and values. Stebbins (1997) suggested that particular goods refer to things, which meet human desire and need and include objects in all categories relevant to human living, while patterns of cooperation are the processes involving the interaction between the members of a community to produce these particular goods. Value, on the other hand, is the measure of the worth of particular good or a pattern of cooperation. Given that the purpose of a business is to produce an economic standard of living that reflects prioritized values, it is the responsibility of the business leaders to ensure that the goods and services they produce and the way in which they do so enhances the comprehensive good of the society. This becomes all the more significant given the influence religion has on the thinking, attitude, and behavior of its constituents.

The new WTO regime has brought about significant changes both in the social and the corporate worlds. The process of globalization the world over has had far reaching impacts not only on the human resource practices the world over, but indeed, on life and attitude itself. Culture is an aggregate of traditions and values, which shape the structures of groups and societies. These patterns, in turn, shape and influence attitudes and behaviours of individuals in that society, which then determine interpersonal relationships both at work and otherwise. Although organizational managers may attempt to create a shared sense of features of their organization landscape, it is indeed the indigenous culture that has the most significant impact on the employee relations. More often than not, this culture is shaped by the dominant religion in that country.

Studies (e.g., Weaver and Agle, 2002) point out that research has established that religiosity is related to personality, cognition, stress coping mechanisms, overall health, marital patterns, political behavior, voting behavior, use of illicit or illegal substances, and business ethics. They contend that religious role expectations involving particular religion dependent themes, taken together and internalized as a religious self-identity, may influence ethical behavior, and the relationships of religious role expectations to behavior are moderated by religious identity salience and religious motivational orientation. Also, with the evolution of culturally diverse workplaces, greater spiritual and religious accommodation would be required to achieve desired behaviors from the employees. Given that various religious sermons and business organizations are reaching a consensus on the basic tenet of making the world a better place, the study of effect of various religions and religious studies on business aspects becomes significant and beneficial to both religious leaders as well as business leaders.

World Religions and Business

While honesty, trust, acceptance of responsibility, appreciations of the work of others, and sensitivity to the human needs of a situation are the inspired insights of Christianity (Kennedy, 1968), they are also the essential elements of business. In fact, scholars suggest that subtle issues like creativity, imagination, and perseverance also originate from a positive outlook of man towards the beauty of God's creation. Insights of growth originating from one's worship get transferred to one's workplace as well. Unfortunately, the Christian clergy have enhanced the separation between religion and workplace religious discussion by ignoring business and condemning it for promoting inequality. Specifically, the Protestant concepts of work, grace, and reward have lost their intrinsic interconnections resulting in a lack of standards of excellence for evaluation of the self and others in the corporate world. This has further eroded general moral standards and has led to a lack of quality measuring criteria for products and performance.

Unlike Christianity, which has seen a deliberate separation of religion from political and economic activity, Islam provides an integrated guidance for daily living including guidelines for the constituents of sound economic practice. Islamic positive values include instruction to be just and fair, to value generosity or magnanimity, and to demonstrate honesty and cooperation, while the negative values include cheating, lying, depriving others of their due rights, malice and hatred, amassing wealth or hoarding, greed, niggardliness, and excessive indebtedness (El Kahal, 2001). These have direct impact on corporate ethics in countries following Islam and influence decision-making processes in a business situation. Ethics govern all aspects of a Muslim's life since Islam teaches its followers not to indulge in unethical or immoral activities in affairs of their lives including the affairs of business. Scholars have provided evidence from the scriptures bringing in the concepts that correspond to modern business practices. These include honesty and truthfulness, merit and competency in hiring, sincerity and honesty in business dealings, avoidance of corruption, consultative decision making, responsibility, written contracts and witnesses, allowing status and prestige ranking and income inequalities, necessity of managerial hierarchies, group and team working, globalization, performance-based rewards, equality in opportunities, information gathering before making decisions, disclosing defects, fairness in contract negotiation, excellence and quality of work, productivity, and fair wage systems. The tenets of Islam also look at protecting consumers and thus provide an all-encompassing framework to regulate the affairs of human lives including business. It encourages liberalization where all economic decisions are passed through the filter of moral values and ethics before being subjected to the market. However, some of the other aspects of Islam, specifically its direction to surrender before God's will, result in relaxed work attitudes (Wilkins, 2001) and overlooking of deadlines.

Bjorkman and Lu (1999) have discussed four features of Chinese culture that impact Chinese management practices. These are respect for age and hierarchy, face and harmony, group orientation, and personal relationships. They discuss the problems faced by managers in implementing western human resource practices in China due to the social realities that exist in the country. Citing the case of China Steel Corporation in Taiwan, Chao (990) illustrated how the system of managerial philosophy and practices based on the Chinese culture as manifested by the Confucian traditions and ethos has been successfully applied to the integration of its labour force thereby upgrading their morale, performance, and productivity. This involved putting into practice a tradition of thoroughness in work and performance, strict discipline on rules and regulations, emphasis on credibility, and inclusivity of expectations. Jou and Sung (1990) developed a typology of four managerial patterns in Taiwan, viz. the grassroots type, the mainlander type, the specialist type, and the transitional type. The grassroots and the mainlander types represent an approach typical of Chinese value orientations in family concept, paternalistic authoritarianism, and precedence on morality before capability, and humanity before materialistic concern. However, the grassroots type included some features of Japanese culture like emphasis on communication and harmony, priority on internal communication, and disregard of formality. The specialist type included some western logic of rationalism while the transitional type included both western and Japanese features. A comparison of several empirical studies suggests that Confucian virtues like loyalty to the organization, working hard, maintaining interpersonal harmony, etc. are likely to manifest in organizations where formal regulations of western-style management were enforced. With reference to overseas Chinese managers, some researchers traced present day beliefs of paternalism, personalism, and a defensiveness derived from insecurity, to the socio-historical legacy of China.

The Shinto-driven notions of relationships between superiors and inferiors, the sense of obligation between employer and employee, between citizen and country, and between the family and its members, the shame on not achieving objectives, face saving, and communication of one's honest perceptions and beliefs shape Japan's approach to business besides helping explain wealth and economic expansion as a national necessity along with the importance of the role played by groups and women. Further, Shintoism places a huge premium on maintenance of harmony, loyalty to leaders, and apologies and atonement for breaches of responsibility. Moreover, religio-cultural aspects also have their impact on the ethics governing people and organizations. Scholars suggest that the propensity of Japanese people to work hard originates from their roots in agriculture-centred society. Having needed to obey nature and not overpower it, they are submissive to change and can adapt easily. Considering work to be the source of moral culture, there lies no distinction in their minds between physical labour, spiritual training, and character building.

With its concepts of communitarianism, fairness, equal treatment, honesty, and privacy, Judaism has a distinct impact on the business environment and the expectations of all stakeholders in the process. Scholars (e.g., Tamari, 1997) point out that in the Jewish tradition, business is seen as a path to sanctity, wealth is seen as originating from God, the weaker sections are protected against theft and fraud, charity is seen as an obligation, and mercy towards debtors is tempered with justice.

It can be safely concluded that business and religion impact each other significantly. Whether religion acts as an obstacle to business in the wake of globalization or plays a positive role depends on the specifics of particular religions and their accepted interpretations.

Hinduism: Impact on Global India and Business Ethics

While the socialization process in western cultures is based on individualism that promotes greater need for autonomy and personal achievement requirements, the cultures in developing countries usually promote a sense of collectivism and stress on social and security needs. Given that globalization has had a profound effect on the social life as well as the corporate world, it is imperative that the effect of religion on these processes be seen and analyzed. In the Indian context, in the face of the new WTO regime, there is a mixed acceptance to the series of steps taken by the government and the industry to restructure the prevalent practices and norms. Structural adjustments would provide an impetus to efficiency and growth while generating resources that could be proactively used to sustain and enhance the social expenditures. In the following discussion, I will look at the role religion plays in formulating the business values and ethics in this global India.

Hinduism, on its own, has no origin but has unfolded through stages and is based largely on the Vedic scriptures. The primary scriptures of Hinduism, the *Vedas,* derive from the root word "*Vid*" meaning knowledge and according to Hindu tradition, have existed in unwritten, eternal, and perfect form from the beginning of time. Although the *Vedas* contain a variety of literature within them, the *Rig Veda* primarily consists of knowledge, both physical and spiritual, the *Yajur Veda* talks of *Karma,* the commentary on action, duties, and responsibilities, the *Sam Veda* contains prayers and commentary on fine arts, while the *Atharva Veda* contains sciences including arithmetic, geology, life sciences, physical sciences, and medicine. Earlier studies have misinterpreted the concept underlying the Vedic literature probably due to loss of meaning in translations and interpretations given the fact that they derive predominantly from Weber's work which itself is twice removed from the original scriptures. For instance, Bennion argues that "Veda…gives no idea of its content…In fact there is practically nothing concerning man or God in it. It particularly denounces the Dharma (ritual duties)" (1992: 51). In fact, one of the several hymns of the *Yajur Veda* quoted below talks of man's prayers to God:

> "*Vishwani dev savitarduritaani paraasuva. Yad bhadrantann aasuva.*" (Yajur Veda: 30/3)
>
> O creator of the universe, bearer of all wealth, giver of all happiness; please take away from me all that is bad, immoral, and cause of sorrow; give me all virtues, attitudes, and things which are good.

Further, the *Yajur Veda* lays down the duties and responsibilities of the king/leader of the community/organization as thus:

> "Namo vinyaaya cha kakshyaaya cha namah shravaaya cha pratishravaaya cha nama. Aashushenaaya chashurthaaya cha namah shooraaya chavabhedine cha." (Yajur Veda: 16/34)
>
> The leader should shower more wealth and riches specifically on teachers, scholars, army officers, and diplomats to keep them motivated for performing better.

Thus, the scriptures clearly lay out not only the duties and responsibilities of people in various positions but also surrender and pray to the almighty for his blessings. Bennion also errs in the understanding of the origin of the caste system. Examples such as "*Vratam iti karmanaam vranoti iti satah varno vranotah*" (Nirukta: 2/3) (Qualities and actions determine the caste of a person); "*Chaturvarna maya srishtam guna karma vibhagashah*" (Gita: 4/13) (Qualities and actions determine the four castes); and "*Acharya tavasya yam jaati mutpaadayati savitrayah*" (Manusmriti: 2/148) (Based on the qualities, education, and actions, the teacher determines the caste of the students during graduation) amply indicate that the caste system as laid down by the Hindu scriptures was based on the qualities of the person rather than the virtue of being born to someone of the same caste.

Hinduism is built on the pillars of *Dharma* (way of life), *Artha* (wealth and prosperity), *Kaam* (desires), and *Moksha* (nirvana) and is based on the teachings of *Vedas, Smriti* (especially Manusmriti), the two epics, *Ramayana* and *Mahabharata,* and other religious literature. *Dharma,* according to the Hindu tradition, is a way of life and should not be seen as a ritual or a means of prayer. As defined in *Manusmriti, Dharma* lays down the 10 moral values required of a person: "*Dhriti khsamaa damosteyam shauchamindriyanigrah dheervidyaa satyamakrodho dashkam dharmalakshanam.*"

The 10 elements of *Dharma* are "*dhriti*" (patience), "*kshama*" (forgiveness), "*dam*" (control over desires), "*asteya*" (no stealing), "*shauch*" (physical and spiritual cleanliness), "*indriyanigrah*" (control over sense organs), "*Dheeh*" (wisdom), "*vidya*" (education and learning), "*satya*" (truthfulness), and "*akrodha*" (anger management). These 10 elements form the basis of the ethical framework in Hinduism and have had a significant impact on the fundamental disposition of its constituents. The details charted out in these scriptures on the value systems, duties and responsibilities, attitudes and behaviors, work ethics, and general life management are several and beyond the scope of this study. The study would touch upon some of the salient philosophical issues that have affected the work life and workplace behavior of employees and the moral and ethical dimensions of organizations.

"*Karma*" (action) is one of the salient features of Hinduism, and the teaching of *Gita* viz. "*Karmanyevadhikaraste maa faleshu kadachan*" (A person has the right to do his karma but not to think of its fruits) has often been misinterpreted by scholars. Kanungo (1990) related it to the personal ethic of helplessness and surmised that it leads to a passive attitude towards environment. The philosophy, however, talks about action with a sense of detachment and selflessness where the fruits of the action are subservient to the goal of common good and fundamental duties of the human beings. In fact, the second line of this shloka clearly states, *"Ma karma phala hetur bhur ma te sango stvaakarmani"* (You shall not be the producer of the fruits of *karma* nor shall you lean towards inaction), negating the concept of helplessness lucidly. Riehm puts the idea into perspective when in a paper of his he suggests that Hinduism regards *Karma* as the life force of all the creations in the universe. He makes comparisons of the Hindu philosophy of considering all things as interdependent and inseparable parts of the cosmic whole and the same reality to the corporate context where all the different functions within a corporation have to work together to achieve effectiveness. Similarly, the interpretations of the philosophy of *Karma* in terms of creating a time perspective that has an emphasis on the past rather than the present is flawed since the philosophy clearly talks about the importance of the present and rejects dwelling in the past as the works of an idle mind. Also, the Hindu scriptures lay emphasis on equal participation of men and women in all contexts. *"Upop me paraa mrish maa me dabhraani manyathah sarvahamasmi romshaa gandhaarinaamivavika"* (Rig Veda: 1/126/7) (Just like you make decisions for the men of your kingdom I may have the ability to make decisions for the women of my kingdom) amply demonstrates the extent of women's participation in decision making at the highest levels. The role of the leader is critically examined since *"yadyadacharati shreshthastdevetaro janah. Sa yat pra - maanam kurute lokastadanurvartate"* (Mahabharata: 3/59) (It is important that leaders take special care of their behaviours since they are followed by others). All these ethical and behavioural aspects have important implications for the modern organizations and their functioning.

The study of *"Artha"* (wealth and prosperity) is one of the important facets of the Hindu religion and scriptures. *"Sarveshaam shauchanaam artha shauchanaam param smritam"* (Manusmriti: 5/106) (Of all the scruples, the ones in dealing with money are the most important). Based on the Vedic scriptures, *"Arthashastra"*, the work of Kautilya, needs a special mention. The book bases the art of governance on the two pillars of *nyaya* (justice) and *dharma* (ethics). Thus, it explained in Fourth century B.C.E., what is now propounded as the organizational justice theory and the study of ethics. For instance, in the area of public services, *Arthashastra* indicates that records should be audited for all government employees on a weekly basis and assignments should be task oriented, not target oriented. Intelligence should be kept on key government officials to check against allurements of religion, money, amour, and fear. Reward systems and promotions should be linked to performance with provisions for demotions, cuts in salaries, etc. in case of unsatisfactory performance. Cooperative undertakings should be taken up in rural areas and if need be, coercion may be used to get desired results.

Administrators should be responsible and accountable for implementation of tenancy laws, sanitation, individual sanctity, control of gambling and prostitution, care of orphans and disabled, control and inspection of food grains and related products, irrigational works, water supply, community projects, public transport, spiritual cooperation, highways, traffic, security, and work during natural calamities. An omission in carrying out any of these activities should have penal implications. On the issues of salaries, concurring with the Vedic philosophy *Arthashastra* suggests that highest salaries should be payable to the council of ministers, highest-ranking government officials, heads of the armed forces, and teachers. For public finance, the work suggests provisions for gold reserves, sources of revenue, income and expenditure details, other sources of revenue, rate of taxation, remissions, policy in times of financial stringency, and accidental sources of revenue. Rich parallels can be drawn from this study and the other studies for the modern organizational context.

It would be worthwhile to discuss the case of an Indian business group in the light of the above discussion. With 80 companies operating in the sectors of Services, Materials, Engineering, Energy, Consumer Products, Chemicals, Communication and Information Systems, the Tata Group is among the most respected business house in India. Having created institutes of excellence both in the Indian industry and the social world, the Tata Group symbolizes the true essence of Indian ethics. To begin with, 63 percent of the capital of the parent firm, Tata Sons Limited, is held by Tata (Philanthropic) Trusts, which have sponsored and promoted a variety of public institutions of excellence including hospitals, education and research centres, and scientific and cultural establishments. The five core Tata values that underpin the way they describe their business processes include:

Integrity: To conduct business fairly, with honesty and transparency such that everything done stands the test of public scrutiny. This is in line with the teachings of Hinduism which require all leaderships to be based on the tenets of honesty, truthfulness, and straight dealing and the organizations to be scrutinized publicly.

Understanding: To be caring, show respect, compassion, and humanity for colleagues and customers around the world and always work for the benefit of India. This is in perfect harmony with the teachings of Hinduism which suggest that everything is subordinate to the cause of the country. The elements of compassion and humanity are manifested in the first two elements of *Dharma* viz. *Dhriti* and *Kshama* as explained before.

Excellence: To constantly strive to achieve the highest possible standards in their day-to-day work and in the quality of goods and services they provide. This is a variation of the fundamental philosophy of *Karma* which talks about giving one's best come what may.

Unity: To work cohesively with colleagues across the group and with customers and partners around the world, building strong relationships based on tolerance, understanding, and mutual cooperation. This value is amply encouraged in Vedas in the form of *Sangathan Sutras* (formulae of unity), which demonstrate the value and need of unity both in thought and action.

Responsibility: To continue to be responsible, sensitive to the countries, communities, and environments in which they work, always ensuring that what comes from the people goes back to the people many times over. This demonstrates the fundamental teaching of Hinduism, that of selfless action with a sense of detachment for personal greed or good.

Discussion

Hinduism provides a rich framework within which the dimensions of business and business ethics find their own footing. Moreover, it has a special role to play in the process of globalization. The paradigms governing the employee relationships have changed in the post reforms world. Earlier, employees enjoyed the comforts of lifetime employment, company sponsored health programmes, and retirement pensions, but post reforms, these relationships have undergone a sea change. Employees are now expected to work in multi-faceted teams, and update their skills continuously. Globalization has led to restructuring, which in turn may lead to job insecurity and an increase in the number of organizational changes anticipated in the organization. This usually leads to a greater number of somatic complaints, intention to leave, lower organizational commitment, lower trust, reduced job satisfaction, and lower performance and lower work effort. This is where religion not only provides guidelines for organizational behaviour but also acts as a buffer to absorb stress and the other negative fallouts of the globalization processes. The salient ethical dimensions of sharing, respect for age, social networks, selfless work, honesty and truthfulness, performance, scrupulous business dealings, equality, discipline and punitive provisions, necessity of hierarchical levels, role and responsibility of leader, financial management, wage distributions, and interpersonal relationships have a significant impact on the personality of its constituents and these in turn are likely to manifest at the workplace as attitudes and behaviors. As can be seen in the Indian organizations, hierarchical perspective, the power play, preference for personalized relationship, social networking through own-other dichotomy, and collectivistic orientation, play a significant role in determining organizational effectiveness in India. Further, nurturance of subordinates by supervisors, organizational expectation of universalism, and peer leadership are some other issues whose roots can be traced to the features of Hinduism. These ethical dimensions as suggested through reflections on religion, and religious scriptures need to be assimilated with the values of industrial democracy to make Indian organizations more effective. An empirical study to look at the model of Hinduism and its effect on organizational behavior and ethics should provide interesting results to say the least.

Bibliography

Bennion, Lowell L. (1992). The business ethic of the world religions and the spirit of capitalism. *International Journal of Politics, Culture and Society, 6,* 1, 39-73.

Chao, Y. T. (1990). Culture and work organization: The Chinese case. *International Journal of Psychology, 25,* 583-592.

El Kahal, Sonia. (2001). Culture and business in Asia Pacific. *Business in the Asia Pacific,* 125-145.

Jou, J. Y., & Sung, K. (1990). Chinese value systems and managerial behavior. *International Journal of Psychology, 25,* 619-627.

Kanungo, R. N. (1990). Culture and work alienation: Western models and eastern realities. *International Journal of Psychology, 25,* 795-812.

Kennedy, Rev. Dana Forrest. (1968). Lovers together. *Training and Development Journal,* April, 16-22.

Riehm, Stephen R. (2000). The Tao of forecasting. *Journal of Business Forecasting Methods and Systems, 19,*1, 22-25.

Stebbins, J. Michael. (1997). Business, faith and the common good. *Review of Business, 19,* 1, 5-8.

Tamari, Meir. (1997). The challenge of wealth: Jewish business ethics. *Business Ethics Quarterly, 7,* 1, 45-56.

Weaver, Gary R., & Agle, Bradley R. (2002). Religiosity and ethical behaviour in organizations: A symbolic interactionist perspective. *Academy of Management Review, 27,* 1, 77-97.

Wilkins, Stephen. (2001). International briefing in training and development in the United Arab Emirates. *International Journal of Training and Development, 5,* 2, 153-165.

The African Traditional Religion's Business Ethics: A Paradigm for Spirituality in the Global Business Ethical Standard

Celestina O. Isiramen

Introduction

Discussions concerning globalization are hardly complete without consideration or mention of the global ethical standard. The emergence of globalization, international trade, and an instant communication system has resulted in increased pressure for the formation of global business ethical standards. Although several business ethical standards have sprung up, the question that often arises concerns the yardstick for determining the best and universally acceptable ethical standard for the business sphere. This is again compounded by the presence of conflict generated by varying cultural values.

However, the importance of religion in the standardization of a global ethical standard cannot be overemphasized. Although there are several religions, there seem to be embedded in these religions some positive ethical values, which can be harmonized towards a pragmatic global business ethical standard. The fact is that any business ethical standard devoid of spirituality is bound to be biased and cannot meet a universal objective standard. In this sense, Brunner (1947, p. 53) says: "all man-centered ethical systems are deemed to fail. Only what God does and wills is good and all that oppose God is bad."

We are, in this paper, attempting to expose the business ethical values of the African traditional religion towards establishing the importance of spirituality in a concrete global business ethical standard. The emphasis of the African indigenous religion on gregariousness and community consciousness that recognizes both the spiritual and human entities in the business sphere is considered to constitute a genuine base for the establishment of a global business ethical standard.

To be able to arrive at our objective, this paper will present the chaos exemplified in the modern Nigerian market that has jettisoned the traditional religion's business ethical standard. It will examine the gains that accrued to the society at a time the traditional religion's business ethical standard held sway on the business persons, and this will lead us into our suggestion towards incorporating the type of spirituality of the African traditional religion's business ethical standard in the global market.

What Is African Traditional Religion?

For reasons of time and space, generalization on African traditional religions has become spurious. For instance, it is a fact that the indigenous religions have been affected by their co-existence with other religions. Although there exist some threads of continuity, the elements of discontinuity cannot, however, be ignored. In spite of this, the factor of discontinuity seems to be minimal since the traditional religions of the people of Africa continue to survive in modern societies. A correct understanding of African traditional religions in modern Africa can only be achieved when the religions are appreciated as part of a social system, which no longer exist in their pure forms. This is largely a part of the focus of this paper.

Again, to speak or write about Africa as if it were homogenously religious will be misleading. The different traditions and systems have been modified in a variety of ways reflecting the impact made by historic figures and historic contacts between ethnic groups. The result is a bewildering variety of religions.

In spite of this pluralism, certain vital regularities in the religion are discernible. Thus, the possibility in accentuating these vital regularities gives us the impetus to refer to them generally as African traditional religions. It is in this sense that we can refer to the indigenous religion of the people of Nigeria (a country in the western part of Africa) as African traditional religion.

The Modern Nigerian Market

The modern Nigerian market presents a gory picture of business devoid of spiritual ethical standard. In the modern Nigerian market, business transactions have no recourse to the spiritual.

Prior to the total exposure of the Nigerian nation to foreign influences occasioned by commerce, colonialism, and foreign religions, the business ethical standard of the people was basically religious. Although people have argued on the basis of separation of religion from culture, the dividing line between religion and culture in the traditional African society is quite slim. Referring to the people of sub-Saharan Africa, A.C. Leonard (1968, p. 409) reports: "They are in the strict and natural sense of the word, a firmly and deeply religious people of whom it can be said, as it has been said of the Hindus; they eat religiously, dress religiously and sin religiously. In a few words, the religion of these natives… is their existence and their existence is their religion."

Thus, the indigenous religion was the sole world-view within which events were explained and behavior patterned. It permeated every facet of life of the people. It was particularly significant in inculcating and promoting discipline in all spheres of human endeavors. Thus, the chosen items to be sold were such that put into consideration the growth of the human person morally, spiritually, and physically; such that could relate man positively to his community and his creator.

Events in the business sphere took a different turn in modern Nigerian society at the incursion of foreign influences. The traditional religion lost its exclusive dominance and control over the lives of the Nigerians. Thus, the prevailing economic dispositions in the contemporary Nigerian society have lost every sense of spiritual discipline. The traditional religion's ethics and its impact on business have significantly diminished. Certain beliefs, customs, and taboos have been outlawed and classified as cruel, barbaric, and timid in modern Nigerian society. The foundation of the traditional belief, which incorporates the vital roles played by the ancestors and other spiritual patrons, has been considerably shaken. Consequently, the potency of the religion in inculcating and promoting morals in the business sphere in modern Nigerian society has diminished if not completely disappeared.

Our submission is that the problems associated with business in the contemporary Nigerian society with regard to doing what is right result from the abandonment of traditional religious values of reverence for the human person and the spiritual beings. This enviable philosophy has metamorphosed into ungodly philosophies such as individualism, humanism, and materialism. The contemporary Nigerian has gullibly swallowed these philosophies and allowed them to replace the cherished business philosophy of community life.

In light of the above, business transaction in Nigeria today is moving increasingly into the unexplored and potentially dehumanizing realms. Business policies are becoming ungodly, anti-family, and anti-human. The depravity of the community has become the order of the day and profit making has taken over soul making in society. In evidence of this, many heart-aching experiences have evolved in the business circle. Sexually explicit magazines are openly displayed on the shelves of stores and pornographic films are consumed by both old and young. Companies' internal policies and practices hardly take into consideration the family and the community. There is obviously a considerable decline in civility and morality. Thus, in modern Nigerian society, there exist advanced fee fraud, drugs peddling, cheating, embezzlement of public funds, and many others. Long-standing relationships based on trust and honesty have been swept aside in a cultural revolution neglecting the hitherto religiously-based business ethical standard for standards devoid of religion. The craze for wealth has become neurotically insatiable. As far as business is concerned, "things have fallen apart" in modern Nigerian society. Community sharing has been taken over by monolithic business interests and the idea of co-responsibility and co-operation has undergone considerable strain. Nigerians have revolted against the fear of God in business transactions. With the relegation of religion, a separation of man from man has begun and along the line, community strings have been broken with the aftermath in the business life being chaos and anarchy. This is grossly at variance with what was in operation in the traditional Nigerian society whose business ethics was basically spiritual as we shall see in the next sub-chapter.

Business Ethics and African Traditional Religion in the Traditional Nigerian Society

Like other Africans, traditional Nigerians possess the basic instinct of gregariousness. Intrinsically, the people have a community lifestyle. The common sharing of life by them is intense. There exist community farmlands, streams, economic trees, barns, markets, shrines, squares, masquerades, ritual objects, and festivals, among others, geared toward the purpose of ensuring sanity in commerce. Closeness to nature, the crucial need for security, and better livelihood combine to deepen the natural instinct for gregariousness and sense of community among different peoples of traditional Nigeria (Ejizu, 2003, p. 1).

For traditional Nigerians, community is not understood as a simple social grouping of people who are bound together by reasons of natural origin or common interest and values; rather, community is understood as "both a society as well as a unity of the visible and the invisible worlds; the world of the physically living, on the one hand, and the world of the ancestors, divinities and souls of children yet to be born to the individual kinsgroups" (Ejizu, 2003, p. 1). The community to the Nigerian, therefore, represents the world of experience and the world of spirits.

For traditional Nigerians, the norm is the extended family system. The nuclear family model is alien and it is believed to be inimical to the values of the community. The invisible members of the community, including ancestors and spiritual beings, are reckoned to be powerful and superior to human beings. Their presence and reality are usually acknowledged and honored in the community. Neglect or disobedience is capable of spelling doom for the people. Different types of symbols like carved objects, shrines, and sacred altars, represent these spiritual beings. They are considered to be benevolent and powerful representatives of the community in the spiritual world. Several taboos found in various Nigerian communities also direct attention to the reality and presence of the spiritual members. For example, most traditional Nigerian communities prohibit cheating and exploitation in business. Anyone who violates this runs the risk of impoverishment, frustration, ostracism, or even incurable sickness that could be spelt on him or her by the gods of the land. Reverence for the land and reverence for the Almighty God are also part of the religious and business milieu of the people.

For the traditional Nigerian, the idea and structure of human society essentially form a total worldview that is fundamentally holistic, sacred, and highly integrated. The lives of people only become meaningful and significant within the transcendental center of ultimate meaning. Human beings must maintain the equilibrium between the visible world and the invisible world. Thus are the happiness and prosperity of the individuals and the community assured.

In the traditional Nigerian background, religion is considered the most important aspect of life. Pervading all aspects of life, it provides significance and meaning for the ethical dimension of business and forms the basis of business ethics. Traditional religion determines the norms of acceptable behavior, taboos, and prohibitions in business.

African traditional religion plays a crucial role in the ethical dynamics of the people. It portrays a basic reality that is ethical in content and orientation. There are norms and taboos that address the comportment of individuals in business towards a harmonious growth of the community and reverence of the spiritual. Communal farmlands and economic interests like the markets are surrounded by taboos.

Traditional Nigerian leaders make moral pronouncements and invoke divine sanctions on anyone who dares to disobey. Therefore, traditional priests, individual deities, and ancestral spirits who are agents of divinities actively participate in the execution of business ethics. They bear the responsibility to impose sanctions and fines on defaulters. African traditional religion actively plays a distinctive role as the ultimate source of supernatural power and authority that sanctions and reinforces public morality. Traditional Nigerians believe that success in business and prosperity are derived from God, the gods, and ancestors. "They accrue to people who work hard and who strictly adhere to the customs and traditional norms of morality of the community; people who strictly uphold the community ideals of harmonious living" (Ejizu, 2003, p. 1) as stipulated by the traditional religion. Only such people could be hopeful to achieve the highly exalted status of ancestorhood in the hereafter. Thus, the crux of business ethics in traditional Nigeria is its traditional religion, which emphasizes harmony in community life over and above individualism. Business ethics, in this sense, remains the arena where the ethereal transcendent teachings of holiness and spirituality confront the often grubby business of making money and the rat race agreement that often confront the market place. In business ethics, African traditional religion points to a shared sense of community. To be faithful in undertaking is regarded as becoming mature.

In traditional Nigerian existence, the community is not torn apart by g reed and insatiable desire to amass wealth by exploiting others and engaging in dangerous commercial endeavors; on the contrary, there exists community labor which enables members of the community to engage in helping one another as directed by the sacred, i.e. the leaders. The ideal of good life is to share and have good company and in a society where cooperative production and common consumption is the norm; it is then virtually impossible for a poor class to exist. Reverence for the sacred and fear of negative repercussion caused the people to be well comported in business transaction.

A Paradigm for Spirituality in Global Business Ethics

The question that arises is whether the driving principles of free market, the most obvious of which in modern times is profit making, are incompatible with the ethical stipulations of the African traditional religion? Can the business ethical standards of the African traditional religion be incorporated into the spirituality of global commerce?

The bane of global commerce today is relegation of morals in all its ramifications. The world seems to be going into a doldrums. In fact, there seems to be something religious about the financial recession of the world of today. There is no doubt that the fact of the naïve conception of civilization based on material achievements has intensified the problem of finding a worthwhile global business ethics. The result is the loss of personal dignity and community sensitivity. A business ethical standard that must be functionally suitable for use in a global sense has to incorporate the spiritual qualities of the business ethical standard found in the African traditional religion as spelled out above.

We suggest here a denationalization of this indigenous religion's ethical standard for global purposes. Anything short of the emphasis on gregariousness and spirituality in global business ethics will certainly fail.

What we feel is needed right now in the world in regard to business ethics is to recover, reenact, and reestablish some basic criteria and understanding of the ethical values of the indigenous African religion towards a purposeful global business ethics.

African traditional religion is undoubtedly anthropocentric in character with a capacity to solve complex problems. African traditional religion must be appreciated as an element for the construction of a global identity of sanity in commerce. The birth of business ethics founded on the rediscovery and elaboration on the traditional religious phenomena of Africa as practiced in traditional Nigerian society is imperative. Thus, some dynamic policies on the legitimization of African traditional religion in global business transactions should be enacted. In this respect, love of community life and the sacred remain the strength with which the African traditional religion can enforce moral sanity into business ethics in the global market. The profound problems in the global business sphere today demand a religious response towards the generality of human interest especially as it concerns business crimes, drug abuse, and illegitimacy. Such a religion whose essence is a harmonious community life among the living, the sacred, and the dead would ensure that corporate executives are more family friendly, respectful of the dictates of the sacred, and thereby more scrupulous and responsible. The present individualistic tendencies in global business transactions and their attendant bizarre experiences make it right for us to conclude that the philosophy of business ethics embedded and enforced by African traditional religion is the answer to the present predicament. In this sense, the conflict of interest at the core of the global financial system would be resolved. That may mean unbundling the business sector into focused business geared towards serving wider social interest.

African traditional religion takes into consideration the individual benefits, the community and institutions, and the promotion of the global good. It promotes the desire to avoid evil in dealings with one another. Now is the time to evaluate the value that the African traditional religion will bring to the global business ethical standard. Specifically, the African traditional religion will make business transactions devoid of deontological or utilitarian extreme positions prevalent in the global business sphere. Because when the ethical and the spiritual dimensions are eliminated from the concept and goal of civilization, the result is bound to be a business ethics of disaster as experienced today all over the world.

The emphasis of the African traditional religion on loyalties to the community, rather than the self, and the sacred, rather than the mundane, remains a panacea for sound business ethics in the global market place. In this sense, civilization has to be embraced as "a product of an optimistic-ethical spiritual conception of the world." It becomes the sum total of all the progress made towards the moral and spiritual perfection of the individual within the various societies of the world. With a sound business ethics developed along the line of the African traditional religion, sanity will surely become a part of the business sphere, and global development will be achieved in its proper direction.

Conclusion

Our attention has been on the assessment of the global business ethical standard which seems to be morally battered. This has seriously affected the positive global economic advancement of world nations. Civilization must not be understood to represent mere advancement in knowledge and power without due regards to the spiritual. Business must reflect on the danger to which the world is being exposed by the diminished value allotted to the spiritual element that ought to be the bedrock of global business coherence. It is dangerous to surrender completely to a naïve satisfaction of individualistic material achievements and go headlong into an incredible superficial conception of wealth and its accumulations. The consequence could be quite disheartening, as we have seen with the Nigerian situation. Greed would take over the place of civility and morality. Individualism in business transaction would destroy the global business ideal.

The African traditional religion could be a watchdog for global business morality. It emphasizes that for business ethics to be worthwhile, there has to be equilibrium between the ethereal transcendent teachings of holiness and spirituality and the grubby business of moneymaking. Thus, the African traditional ethics recognizes the fact that God coexists in the business world rather than God and Godliness being separate and apart. It reflects a communal relationship between the individual, the community, and the spiritual beings of the invisible world. Business ethics in this sense is a matter of shared sense of community life. Business ethics has its strength in the promotion of people in the community and reverence for the taboos and sanctions on business ethics as emphasized by the ancestors, deities, and God. We advocate a business ethics of this kind to be the only panacea for a worthwhile business ethics that would put into consideration the enhancement of the moral, spiritual, physical, and material growth of the human individual in the global business sphere. In this respect, the focal points of the African traditional religion—community life and reverence and recognition of the spiritual—must be studied along the line of modern establishments in order to construct a modern business ethics for today's globalized world of commerce.

Bibliography

Brunner, E. (1947). *The divine imperative: A study of Christian ethics,* trans. Wyon. Philadelphia: Westminster.

Ejizu, C. (2003). *African traditional religion and the promotion of community living* [Online]. Available: www.africaworld.net/afrel/community.htm

Leonard, A. (1968). *The Lower Niger and its tribes.* London: Frank Cass.

Faith-Correlated Responses to Rural Assistance in a Globalizing Brazil

Paul Chandler and Bartolomeu Romualdo

Introduction

The process of globalization in Brazil's *Zona da Mata* [Bush Zone] is statistically visible in its rural-to-urban exodus. The region went from a roughly 50-50 rural-urban distribution in the late 1970s to one in the mid-1990s when more than 75 percent of the population lived in urban areas. During this period, children to be educated dominated the contributions of rural "have" households to this exodus. Urban labor attracted the younger males from the same communities' much more common "have-not" households.

Related to this exodus are two other widely visible manifestations of globalization in the *Zona da Mata*. The first is a decline of allegiance to local Catholic churches and an accompanying rise of allegiance to the many, varied and growing Protestant Evangelical, especially Pentecostal, churches. Second, Protestantism is also visibly correlated to new and existing small businesses and other pursuits of economic independence.

Acknowledgements: The authors thank the Committee for the International Exchange of Scholars - Fulbright Commission for their financial support and Sr. Sebastião Araújo de Oliveira and the Universidade Federal de Viçosa for their logistic support of this research.

The need to focus on these two changes was the unanticipated result of research originally designed as an applied, class-based study of non-participation in rural development assistance in Brazil's *Zona da Mata.* Its primary subjects during its 1999, 2001, and 2003 field seasons were those households that seem to defy Bergdall's assumption that "rural people can be agents of their own development;" i.e., those households that choose not to participate in rural assistance efforts. Its goals were twofold.

The qualitative part of the research was designed for discovery; that is, to elicit and verify the reasons why some households make the choice not to participate in rural development assistance. Efforts to realize this goal necessitated the 2001 and 2003 field seasons. The quantitative part of the research was guided by two class-based hypotheses designed to correlate household participation and non-participation statistically to measures of need and resources to meet that need. The overall guiding hypotheses of this second part were that greater rates of participation would be (1) positively correlated with greater household need, and (2) negatively correlated with household means to meet that need. This goal was met in the 1999 season, with limited support for the hypotheses.

Materials and Methods

Site Identification

To begin the research it was necessary to identify a suitable site. Suitability required several conditions. Most broadly, the site must present aggregate conditions of poverty and landlessness exceeding comparable existing measures of such conditions within the *Zona da Mata.* These conditions were selected for the specific purpose of minimizing the economic and infra-structural impacts of Brazil's globalization. Chandler and Romualdo detailed these conditions more fully in 2001. The site eventually located comprised 14 rural hamlets scattered along the drainage of the Ribeirão das Almas and known collectively as Prudentes. In 1999, Prudentes had a total population of about 850 persons in 175 households (Table 1).

Assistance Project Identification

Next, it was necessary to identify, design, and implement a rural assistance project offering, as close as possible, universal utility and desirability to the study community. In early 1999, Chandler interviewed a sample of 38 of the 175 households following methods detailed by Spradley designed to make possible analyses of the cognitive domains of (1) the greatest needs of the household and the community, and (2) possible solutions to those needs.

The most cited solution-"*coisas como Zilda trouxe*" [things like Zilda brought]-matched one commonly cited problem, a lack of good garden seed. Zilda, a popular former rural extension agent, often brought to homes packages of soon-to-be or freshly expired garden seed. As all 38 households interviewed had or had access to existing summer wet-season home gardens and all had at least one year-round water supply, this "Zilda project" offered both the broad applicability needed to identify non-participant households as well as the opportunity to utilize an idle resource, household gardens in the winter dry season.

What evolved was a no-cash-or-debt-cost package of fertilizer, lime, micronutrients, and each household's choice from 18 species of current dry-season and all-season vegetable and medicinal garden seed. This package was offered door-to-door at each household in Prudentes between late March and early May 1999. No upper limit was placed on how much area could be prepared for the package and a minimum of six weeks, more in practice, was guaranteed to each household before the authors would return in June and July to deliver and install the package themselves.

All interviewees were cautioned, and frequently reminded during the following weeks, that no part of the package would be provided if seedbeds were not prepared when the authors returned. The operational definition of participation thus became a household meeting the single donor requirement of having at least one seedbed prepared to receive the package when the authors returned.

Identification of Household Type and Reasons for Non-participation

Participating and non-participating households were each categorized in practice as one of four broad types. In the March-May interviews, households could identify themselves as non-participants by a refusal of this initial offer of the package. These households are called Type 1 Non-Participants. Their reasons for refusing the package were usually volunteered, but easily elicited and verified even if not. Most of these households were called Type 1a to distinguish them in later analysis from several other households, Type 1b, newly formed by marriage and continuing to use a parent's garden. All the Type 1a households were offered the package at least once more before the March-May interviews were completed.

In those same March-May interviews, households might also identify themselves as what was called Type 2 by agreeing to accept and prepare for the package contingent on resolution of some obstacle (always water availability) to maintaining a garden.

In June and July 1999, except for those committed Type 1 households, all remaining households had the garden package delivered to them.

At that time, all three Type 2 households, having failed to resolve their water availability problems, declined the package and so were re-classified as Type 1 for all subsequent analysis and discussion.

Despite repeated reminders and an abundance of time to prepare, some households had made no preparations of any form. When the package was withheld, several members of these households expressed, often adamantly, desire to receive the package despite failure to prepare a seedbed, the single donor requirement. These households were called Type 3 Non-Participants. In Type 3 cases, verifiable reasons for the household's failure to prepare were

Table 1: Distribution of Prudentes Household Types

Community	Households (Population)		Participants (Community %)		Non–Participants		
					Type 1a	Type 1b	Type 3
Boa Vista	12	(72)	9	(75%)			3
Lopes	36	(198)	25	(69%)	2	2	7
Assombração	3	(15)	2	(67%)		1*	
Folha Larga	25	(111)	20	(80%)	3	1	1
Inhame	8	(48)	5	(63%)	1	1	1
Prudente	16	(70)	10	(63%)	3*		3
Fumal	2	(15)	1	(50%)	1		
Bom Successo	9	(35)	8	(88%)	1*		
Barro Branco	24	(113)	15	(63%)	5	1	3
Bateia	16	(80)	16	(100%)			
Vieiro	7	(30)	5	(71%)		1	1
Castigo do Anta	4	(17)	3	(75%)	1		
Trovão	2	(1)	1	(50%)	1		
Coimbra	11	(30)	5	(45%)	4	1	1
Totals	175	(835†)	125	(71%)	22	8	20

* Includes one temporary Type 2 delayed non-participation household.
† Excludes population of four households refusing to be interviewed.

Table 2: Measures of Household Wealth

Unit of Analysis		Probability of Ownership	Land Area Owned	Area of Housegarden	Probability of Remittances
Total Community	(175)	.36	77.6L	120.7m^2	.40
Type 0 Participants	(120)	.34	68.4L	96.4m^2	.35
Super Participants	(5)	1.0 **	425.5L**	499.4m^2**	.60+
Type 1a Non-Participants	(22)	.73 **	155.3L*	295.5m^2*	.59 +
Type 1b Non-Participants	(8)	.00 **	0.0L**	3.0m^2**	.1
Type 3 Non-Participants	(20)	.25	3.1L**	74.8m^2	.40

Note: 1 hectare = 16 L (litros)

When compared by Wilcoxon sign-test to Type 0 Participant households:
** Indicates highly significant statistical difference (P </= 0.01)
* Indicates significant statistical difference (P </= 0.05)
+ Indicates noteworthy statistical difference (P </= 0.10)

elicited with great difficulty, usually proving impossible until Romualdo's 2001 and 2003 follow-ups.

Most other households had existing garden plots turned and ready to be seeded and fertilized. Almost all were called Type 0 Participants. A small number had greatly multiplied their gardens' areas and so were called Super Participants and analyzed separately from the much more numerous Type 0 Participants.

Statistical Analyses

All data on household land ownership, gardens, remittance potential, health, and demographics, but not religious allegiance, were collected during the March-May 1999 package-offering interviews. In 2001 and 2003 visits to P rudentes, Romualdo measured continuing participation rates, estimated attendance at the various churches, identified specific attendees, and sought answers to other questions that had emerged since the 1999 field season. Statistical analyses to compare the various categories of Participant and Non-Participant households for differences in wealth and need characteristics, and later religious allegiance, employed a Wilcoxon Sign test or, if normally distributed, a t-test with un-pooled variance, both executed by Microsoft Excel.

Results and Discussion

Household Types

Ultimately, 125 of the 175 households participated in the project, a total community rate of just over 71 percent (Table 1), one of the highest in the current literature. Of these, five Super Participant households had greatly expanded an existing garden, laid out an entirely new garden, or both, increasing already large garden areas by a factor of at least four. The other 120 Type 0 Participants rarely expanded any garden by more than a few square meters.

[See Table 1]

Of the remaining 50 Non-Participant households, Type 1 ultimately absorbed the three Type 2 households to total 22 Type 1a and eight Type 1b households (Table 1). Type 1a Non-Participants tended to be the wealthier, but not the wealthiest households of Prudentes (Table 2).

The remaining 20 Type 3 households (Table 1) had all accepted and agreed to prepare for the package, but none had a single seedbed ready for either seed or fertilizer when the authors delivered the package in June and July 1999.

[See Table 2]

Rejection of Both Needs and Means Hypotheses

Rejection of the hypothesis that participation rates would decline as household means increased was indicated by data from both the Super Participants, five of Prudentes' richest "have" households, and Type 3 Non-

Participants, 20 of the very poorest "have-not" households (Table 2). The hypothesis that participation rates would increase as household needs increased found support in the household membership data, but was contradicted by both the highest fertility and highest mortality rates occurring among the Type 3 Non-Participant households, and by just the opposite among the five Super Participants (Table 3).

[See Table 3]

Among Type 3 Non-Participants, despite the 42 to 56 days available, half the reasons these households cited for their failure to prepare for the package were variations on the theme of inadequate time to prepare (Table 4). The reasons offered for their failure to meet the single donor requirement had to be accepted, even if not necessarily verified, as true in only five of the 20 cases by the end of the 1999 field season. For example, to explain his failure to prepare, the male head of one Type 3 household first said, *"O tempo nào deu"* [The time doesn't give]. When engaged in follow-up questions, he ultimately sighed and stated that while the problem was not *"preguisa mesma"* [laziness itself], there was within the household a *"falta de vontade"* [lack of will]. When then asked, this man explained that the difference between "lack of will" and "laziness itself" was "very small." Unlike this case, the reasons offered by 15 other Type 3 Non-Participant households were verifiably false, often absurdly so. Verifiable reasons for most Type 3 Non-Participants' contradictions to the two guiding hypotheses were found during the 2001 and 2003 field seasons, were discovered to be working exclusively within the Catholic community, and to be directly reinforced by the Super Participants.

[See Table 4]

Of Prudentes' 14 hamlets (Table 1), only Bateia's 16 households achieved 100 percent participation, simultaneously creating a total lack of correlations to either needs or means variables, thereby making Bateia a complete contradiction to both class-based hypotheses.

The means hypothesis did find narrow support within the smaller but growing set of Pentecostal households: The eight landless Pentecostal households' participation was 100 percent, while the five landed households' participation was nil. However, except for probability of land ownership (Table 2) and land area owned (Pentecostal holdings averaged 4.4 *litros*, barely more than the Type 3 average), Pentecostal Participant and Non-Participant households were statistically indistinguishable from their respective Catholic Type 0 or Type 1 neighbors.

Household Religious Allegiance

Catholicism was the dominant faith in Prudentes in 2001, with members of at least 122 households present at one or more local Masses a month and a half-dozen more, all Type 1a households, at Masses "in the city," the small prefecture seat of Senhora de Oliveira. Also in Prudentes, as in the rest of Brazil, Pentecostalism had arrived by 1999 and by 2001 included at least 13

Table 3: Measures of Household Demographics and Health

Unit of Analysis		Household Membership	Household Fertility	Household Mortality	Medical Limitations
Total Community	(175)	4.90	4.91	0.85	1.0
Type 0 Participants	(120)	5.38	4.98	0.88	1.06
Super Participants	(5)	4.50	4.50	0.00**	0.60
Type 1a Non-Participants	(22)	2.91**	4.41	1.00	0.59
Type 1b Non-Participants	(8)	3.00**	1.59**	0.50	0.75
Type 3 Non-Participants	(20)	4.50*	5.85+	1.75*	1.05

When compared by t-test to Type 0 Participant households:
** Indicates highly significant statistical difference (P </= 0.01)
* Indicates significant statistical difference (P </= 0.05)
+ Indicates noteworthy statistical difference (P </= 0.10)

Table 4: Reasons for Type 3 Non-Participation (*n*=20)

Reason given	households citing
Variations on inadequate time	
the time didn't give	6
today is for leisure	6
no adequate period of time	2
intended to do nothing	2
Variations on physical inability	
no one to do the work	3
health does not permit	3
Unique reasons	
weather has been too wet	1
cannot divert stream	1
does not mess with gardens	1
prefer to play football	1
no one authorized to use a hoe	1
can acquire from Little Sebastian	1
wife and daughter are crazies	1
A lack of will	2
Total	32

Note: Totals exceed *n* due to multiple responses given by several households.

households. By 2003, with a net increase of only three households in all of Prudentes, no more than 110 households were represented at the local Catholic church, at least 22 at the local Pentecostal church, up to six at a small local "Evangelical Temple" formed after the initial 1999 field season, and only four of the original six attending Masses "in the city" of Senhora de Oliveira.

Responses to Development Assistance Among Catholic Households

Verifiable reasons for Type 3 non-participation surfaced during 2001 and 2003 follow-up surveys by Romualdo. While all 20 Type 3 Non-Participants were found among the 122 nominally Catholic households, most Catholic households accepted the package. Readiness to seize the opportunity presented by the research test and reduce future dependence on assistance was the rule rather than the exception.

Romualdo's follow-up visits found that 16 of the 20 Type 3 households had "solved" their 1999 non-participation by repeated visits (usually by the households' children) to ask for food from one or more of the five Super Participant households, all prominent organizers or financial supporters of the local Catholic church. With no verifiable reciprocal exchange beyond church attendance as the other half of what Scott called a "moral economy," at least 16 of the 20 Type 3 Non-Participant households must be regarded as a "parasite class" within Prudentes' Catholic community, and the Super Participants' charity as the "moral hazard" that perpetuates it.

When asked during the 1999 interviews, all five Super Participant households gave *"para os outros"* [for the others] as a reason for expanding their gardens, but three first volunteered *"obrigações Cristões"* [Christian obligations] as their reason. By contrast, most "in the city" and two other wealthier Catholic Type 1a Non-Participants cited greater likelihood of their poor neighbors' requests for food as a salient reason for their own non-participation. Both arguments reflected accurate expectations of the results encountered in the research, but through exactly opposite responses to the research's test instrument.

Responses to Rural Assistance Among Pentecostal Households

The 2001 and 2003 visits revealed the absence of a similar "moral economy" within the growing Pentecostal community. In Prudentes, as in much of Brazil, Pentecostalism and the variety of other rapidly growing Evangelical allegiances reflect Protestantism's decentralizing tendency, as was phrased in one conference session, to "divide like *paramecium.*" In the work presented here, such growth is an adaptive and increasingly common response to the pressures and uncertainties of globalization within Brazil's economy and society. Planning for or assertions of self-sufficiency were the common responses among Prudentes' Pentecostal households. The landed among them politely declined by saying, *"Não por enquanto"* [Not for the meantime], while the landless accepted the offer with numerous questions about any limits on the garden area eligible, the fertility of the garden crops' seed, the time available before the package's arrival, and so on.

By contrast, Prudentes' Type 3 Catholic Non-Participants all accepted the package without questions, or apparently any intent to prepare to receive it, but with plenty of complaints and accusations when their failure to prepare resulted in no package. While the Type 3 strategy of sending household children to beg may seem to justify Super Participant Catholic households' "Christian obligations" to expand their gardens, it hardly justifies continuing traditional patron-client relations by, in effect, giving fish to those who have refused to fish.

Romualdo's 2001 and 2003 visits support the self-sufficiency thesis by documenting the concentration of growth of small business activity throughout Prudentes among its small number of Pentecostal households. In 1999, Catholic households owned the local *alembique* [cane distillery], both of two commercial dairy farms, the bigger of two general stores, the bigger (and satellite television equipped) of two bars, the local coffee roaster, and its commercial truck garden selling into Senhora de Oliveira from Coimbra (Table 1). In 1999, Pentecostal households owned the local brick-making operation, the smaller bar and general store, and the only irrigated rice field. By 2003, Pentecostal households had added, along with eight previously Catholic households to their congregation, a new commercial egg-and-chicken farm, two single-truck commercial hauling operations, and three first-time land ownerships, all by purchase from Catholic households. Over the same four years, the Catholic congregation had declined by at least a dozen, two more of the larger landholdings became absentee-owned, one dairy farm sold its herd, no new businesses were added, and in 2000, its wealthiest and first university-educated son, once mayor of Senhora de Oliveira, lost his bid for a comeback after trying a similar garden seed (and political campaign) project through Prudentes' Catholic church.

Family Values and Full Participation

By sharing labor, materials, and information, only Bateia [gold pan] achieved 100 percent participation in the project (Table 1). The residents of Bateia usually explained their reasons by asking, "Why not? It's an opportunity." Other hamlets attributed Bateia's 100 percent participation to its residents being "competitive": "If one does something, the others all have to do it too." With one regularly attending Catholic household and no Pentecostal households, religious allegiance explained no more of Bateia than class membership, or their neighbors.

Bateia was best explained by its unique family structure. Although a theoretical maximum of 32 family names was possible within the senior generation of its 16 households, only eight family names occurred, and just three family names accounted for 24 of the theoretical 32. While competitiveness might be a trait with positive consequences for Bateia, severe birth defects were a decidedly negative trait of its degree of endogamy. Six of the 16 households had one generation, usually more, with members suffering endogamy-related birth defects including autism, mutism, lower body deformity, paralysis, and moderate to profound mental retardation. As if these problems were not enough, chronic alcoholism occurred among the senior male generation of all landowning households, and most others, within the hamlet. With all these factors working against it, Bateia nonetheless provided a local example of the emptiness of most if not all of the reasons offered for Type 3 non-participation in the other hamlets. Bateia also stands as an example of the economic value of family cooperation, collaboration, and cohesion in the face of the stresses of globalization.

Conclusions

As long as Prudentes' Super Participants maintain their presence and means within the community, they can be expected to continue to act upon their "Christian obligations" to provide at least some of what their poorest neighbors have not provided for themselves. "Not very" is the best answer to the question of how long these traditional patron-client dependencies can be maintained. Change promises to increase Prudentes' rural-to-urban migration, including absentee ownership, as Brazil is further integrated into the global economy. Both the urban atomization of individuals or nuclear family units and the absence of charitable Super Participants in rural villages would make traditional patron-client dependency untenable. In the face of such change, investments in individualized self-sufficiency are increasingly adaptive.

The failure of Type 3 households to prepare seedbeds and thus assume a very minimal responsibility for themselves means Bergdall's assertion that "rural people can be agents of their own development" is hardly universal. Type 3, unlike most other households in Prudentes, have not learned the value of one of Cameron's "lessons of history": An efficient use of both new and existing capital is necessary for economic and social development. Ignoring the capital value of the available garden package, Type 3 households exhibit a failure to appreciate the use value of time, and a low frequency of verifiable truthfulness in accounting for their use of time. This last finding is made more disturbing by the seeming absurdity of some of that accounting, not to mention the irate insistence on nonetheless receiving something for nothing. The question is not whether or not these persons deserve assistance, but whether or not they will in fact act as "agents of *their own development*." At least some of the poorest of the poor will not, and globalization is unlikely to change the preference for parasitism as a part of their livelihood.

While Type 3 households were absent among the original 13 and later 22

Pentecostal households, the growing wealth and dominance of small local businesses by econometrically indistinguishable Pentecostal households suggests that this cultural change is a case suggesting how, in fact, "rural people can be agents of their own development." Whether and how Pentecostalism might be the agency by which people achieve their own development, and what exactly are the differences between Catholic and Pentecostal expressions of faith that result in different responses to new opportunities are questions the authors leave to scholars of comparative religion and philosophy. However, were Martin Luther alive today and working as a rural economist, the presence among the Catholic community of willing intermediaries between its Type 3 households and their "salvation" would certainly be taken into consideration.

Bibliography

Bergdall, T.D. (1993). *Methods for active participation: Experiences in rural development from East and Central Africa.* Nairobi: Oxford University Press.

Cameron, R. (1967). Economic development: Some lessons from history. *American Economic Review* 57(2): 312-324.

Chandler, P. & Romualdo, B. (2001). Reasons for non-participation in rural development assistance in Minas Gerais, Brazil. *Proceedings of the 27th Annual Third World Conference.* Chicago: Third World Conference Foundation.

Scott, J.C. (1975). *The moral economy of the peasant: Rebellion and subsistence in Southeast Asia.* New Haven: Yale University Press.

Spradley, J.P. (1979). *The ethnographic interview.* New York: Holt, Rinehart and Winston.

Spradley, J.P. (1980). *Participant observation.* New York: Holt, Rinehart and Winston.

The Worldly Failures of Liberation Theology

Armando de la Torre

A specter was haunting America—the specter of the 'Theology of Liberation.'

This paraphrase of one of the initial statements of *The Communist Manifesto* by Karl Marx and Friedrich Engels in 1848 comes to my mind readily, as I try to summarize the present bankruptcy of a theory which threatened to revolutionize Latin America once more in the late 70s and did contaminate increasingly larger segments of the Catholic clergy in the United States as well.

There were several doctrinaire political movements of presumed Christian inspiration grouped under the term "Theology of Liberation," which had in common a curious and unprecedented blend of solid philosophical, and even theological, contemporary thought, and a Hegelian, as well as increasingly rather Marxist analysis of society and history.

Roughly, one can distinguish three main lines of thought, all grouped under the heading of the ambiguous term "Liberation":

The first, most eloquently advocated by Cardinal Pironio, and the closest to the traditional point of view, equates "liberation" with the cleansing of the soul of sin, the latter being the root of all human misery in the Pauline interpretation.

The second, put forward by the Brazilian Hugo Assman, is the exact opposite, barely disguising militant Marxist thought under superficially taken religious terms in between.

The third we find in the best known stream of Liberation Theologians headed by Father Gustavo Gutiérrez, of Peru, followed closely by the Brazilian brothers Leonardo and Clodoveo Boff, Franciscan priests, and Father José Luis Segundo, from Uruguay.[1]

In this short essay, I will try to analyze Gutiérrez' work, which I consider to be the most representative. But before going into a more detailed discussion of his thinking, I wish to offer some preliminary considerations which might give Anglo-Saxon Catholic observers of Latin American society a better understanding of the evolution of the so-called "Theology of Liberation."

Since roughly the mid-16th century, Latin America had depended on Europe, and to a lesser extent on the United States during the last 50 years, for the growth and vitality of its religious life. Spanish missionaries, as eager and hardworking as they were to win souls for God, brought with them a European centered vision of the Catholic world, which accounts for the Spanish traditional lack of trust in native Americans until well into the 19th century.

This ethnocentric attitude was passed on to the children and grandchildren of the Conquistadores, who were expected to live and behave as native Spaniards in a foreign land and more often than not failed to live up to these expectations. Therefore, the Catholic Church in Latin America has been to a certain extent bereft of a native **inborn** dynamism to sustain its growth with its own human resources. This is apparent still in the inordinately high percentage of foreign-born priests and nuns at the service of the local Catholic hierarchy.

The Church was seriously wounded by two historical upheavals: one, the expulsion of **all** Jesuits from the lands subject to the Bourbon kings between 1764 and 1773, which robbed the Catholic community of Spanish-speaking America of thousands of its most energetic and successful spiritual leaders and missionaries. The other, at the beginning of the 19th century, was the violent separation from the mother country of almost all its Spanish provinces in America (Cuba and Puerto Rico were exceptions until 1898).

The hostile anticlerical animus of the French Revolution greatly influenced the Latin American movement towards independence from Spain, especially under the clad of secret freemasonry, and certainly did not strengthen the position of the Church in the newly sovereign nations. The latter was compounded by the refusal of the popes to name new bishops for almost a third of a century after independence from Spain, under the pretext that as the pope recognized the already fictitious suzerainty of the kings of Spain over these lost lands, any bishop named by him would still be considered bound by an oath of loyalty to the kings of Spain. Due to this policy, the Church suffered prosecution under the governments of the self-styled "liberal" republican parties in varying degrees in different parts of Latin America, and did not start to make a comeback until the beginning of this century.

The colonial Spanish heritage can boast of some truly magnificent accomplishments; but it also left behind a feeble rate of growth in native priests and members of religious orders, an unhealthy reliance on those coming from abroad for spiritual nourishment, and a rather languid and superficial religious life among the masses of peasants and urban workers.

This sorry history explains to some extent the impact that a few bright and enterprising native priests, such as the ones mentioned above, exerted with their "Theology of Liberation" upon the least educated of the laymen (usually to be found among the fast reproducing working class members of society).

This impact very easily spilled over into violent and subversive action, more often in the rural areas (as in the Mexican uprisings during the second decade of the 20th century, and more recently in Nicaragua, for example), posing a serious threat to the chain of command of the official hierarchy of the Church through the multiplication of *comunidades de base* (community cadres), often, particularly in Brazil, in a mood defiant of the same hierarchy.

To be taken into consideration also is the fact that violent politics—or whatever goes under this guise—loomed, unfortunately, larger than ever in Latin America since Fidel Castro took over power in Cuba in 1959. Presently, it is receding, but varieties of populism (Venezuela under Chávez), and narcoguerrillas (as in Colombia) might trigger resurgence in political violence at any moment.

One important reason for all this is traceable to the enormous growth of the public sector in almost all the Latin American countries since the end of World War II. Many large enterprises were transferred over to the government-run sector, and a hemorrhage of regulations fell on the private sector at the same time taxes were being raised everywhere. Soon, the region was subjected to the moral hazard of the Kennedy-Johnson commanding heights in foreign policy, which, through the Alliance for Progress, proceeded to reinforce the trend of pumping up the Latin American public sectors.

Another reason, closely linked with the first, was the advent of the so-called "dependency theory," the only genuine Latin American "contribution" to the explanation of its well known poor rate of economic growth since the mid-60s as compared to the Asian tigers in the Pacific rim (Hong Kong, Taiwan, Japan, South Korea, Singapore, Malaysia, and Thailand).

The whole theory was built up in the early 50s particularly by the Argentinean Raúl Prebish and his associates at the Economic Center for Latin America, in the regional branch of the United Nations (CEPAL), headquartered in Santiago, Chile. It rested on a wrong reading of the terms of trade exchange between more developed and less developed economies (understanding as such those which export mainly manufactured goods and those which export raw materials).

This theory, which runs parallel to the one suggested by Lenin 30 years earlier, starts from the assumption that the world capitalist system entails a developed center (actually, the U.S.A., Western Europe, Japan) and the exploitation of a backward and underdeveloped broad periphery (mainly former European colonies in Africa, Asia, and to a lesser extent Latin America).

At certain points this "macro" view overlaps and reinforces the interventionist, authoritarian, and "caudillistic" trends among Latin American "strongmen," and as such is felt to be by their mass constituencies in closer accord with Latin American idiosyncrasies.

No mention is made by liberation theologians, who took over this approach, of the system of free prices as a means of information for producers and consumers about the most rational allocation of resources (by definition always scarce). Neither is the "micro" principle of marginal utility, or of the law of decreasing returns discussed.

None among them showed any understanding of the nature of credit, capital, savings, investments, and particularly profits. They evidently were not acquainted with the key role of the entrepreneur among the other factors of production (land, labor, capital), and still less with competitive business ethics. None quoted recent trends in economic thought, like the school of rational expectations or the economic analysis of public choice. They were, for all theoretical purposes, economic illiterates.

For them, politics is a struggle over power between classes intent on exploiting each other. But the Kingdom of Heaven must resemble a classless society. Therefore, given that the wave of the future ("a providential sign") pointed to an unavoidable triumph of socialism, and even of communism, Christians should join forces with all those proletarians organized to depose the dominant bourgeoisie, even, if necessary, by violent means, and suppress the root of all social evils: private property.

One more point of importance: the Catholic Church has recently been undergoing its most serious crisis since the Protestant Reformation. For 35 years, the aftermath of the Second Vatican Council has been widely and severely felt all over the Catholic world, but nowhere as strongly or anxiously as in Latin America.

The doors suddenly were thrown open to the winds of change, in essence secular and humanistic, that had been blowing outside for so long. This shocked the rigid structure of the Latin American Hierarchy to its foundations, almost as badly as when these countries gained their independence from Spain.

French-speaking theologians, in particular, provided Latin American bishops and priests with the mental tools of critical analysis, which in the explosive atmosphere of post-Castro Latin America have been proven to be fuses to time bombs.

Together with the new approved guidelines for the liturgy of worship and the pastoral duties owed to the grey, new theological approaches to history, philosophy, and the social sciences flooded into Latin America. Many of these approaches have much in common with traditional Marxist dialectics and, by the same token, are completely foreign to the individualist and empirical philosophy upon which most of the democracies of the Anglo-Saxon societies have been founded.

These radical winds of change had their official beginnings in the *Gaudium et spes* (Joy and Hope)-Constitution on "the Church and the World," issued by the Second Vatican Council in 1965. Two years later, Pope Paul VI abandoned the traditional caution of papal social teaching by advocating the taking of concrete political and economic steps by the industrialized nations in behalf of the nations of the Third World in his encyclical, "Populorum Progressio."

The following year, 1968, all the bishops of Latin America convened in the city of Medellín, Colombia, for the Second Conference of Latin American bishops. For the first time, concepts such as "liberation," "evangelization," and "human promotion" were interchangeably incorporated into the official language of the Latin American Church. A few months previously, the prototype of the new radical and political Latin American priest, Father Camilo Torres, had died, machinegun in hand, fighting the legitimately-elected government of his country, Colombia.

That same year, the military took power in neighboring Peru through a military coup, and immediately launched an ambitious land reform program, as well as the socialization of trade and industry.

Simultaneously, Fidel Castro since 1965 attempted to reconcile the manifold leftist movements in Latin America under his personal leadership. That was also the never-to-be-forgotten year of student unrest on campuses protesting the Vietnam War, in Europe as well as the United States.

Five years later, the Peruvian priest Gustavo Gutiérrez finished his "opus magnum" under the telltale title "The Theology of Liberation." It rapidly went through successive printings in Latin America and was translated and widely distributed in the United States through the auspices of the Orbis Printing Press belonging to the Maryknoll Guild.

In his landmark book, Father Gutiérrez synthesized the critical reflections of the European theologians and the native Latin American social scientists. The main themes of his philosophy can be summarized as follows:

1. Theology as a rational effort to understand the tenets of Christian faith is not valid anymore. Instead, theology has to take on a critical function (he calls it a "prophetic call"), aided in this endeavor by the contemporary social sciences, particularly sociology and history. In a word, theology is to be emptied of its traditional metaphysical underpinnings and become more "scientific."

2. Most theological reflections should start from a "praxis," i.e. a decision to involve oneself in the unavoidable struggle of classes, which reflects itself in the political struggles of our days. Such an involvement will allow the Christian no other choice than the one in behalf of the exploited and impoverished "Proletariat" (the true "people of God"). From political involvement in the here and now will spring the theological enlightenment of the Christian.
3. The traditional dichotomy between sacred and worldly history is no longer tenable. There is only one history, only one human nature, graciously called to supernatural life by God-made-man in the person of Jesus Christ. Hence, all worldly history is also sacred history and all human progress is supernatural progress.
4. The Kingdom of God lies in the future, but it cannot be realized without the purification of the human heart and sinful social structures, the former meaning the Christian options toward the poor, and the latter-the building of a classless society.
5. All those who work for a more just society are working for the Kingdom of God, even if they are not consciously aware of it, and even when they might be consciously opposed to it; such is the case with the Marxists.
6. In the case of Latin America, specifically, this translates into a revolutionary and subversive struggle against international and domestic capitalism. The Church too long in silent complicity with the oppressors must take an active role. In this universal struggle, not even the Church can be neutral.
7. The main reason for the injustice and rampant backwardness all over Latin America is its dependency on the centers of capitalism in Europe, the United States and Japan. This dependency is not a historical accident; it is a built-in part of the structure of capitalism, which must rest on a developed center and an underdeveloped periphery.
8. History marches on dialectically in the direction of the Kingdom of God at the end of time. There will be "a new heaven and a new earth" that will boast of the same traits as a Marxist classless society, where "each will give according to his ability and each will receive according to his need."

Father Gutiérrez' message, stated in elegant prose with a thorough knowledge of contemporary theology, did made a tremendous stir in the theological world, the first time that a Latin American theologian has encountered a worldwide echo.

After him, the floodgates were open for a torrent of similar critical analysis almost everywhere: Father Enrique Dussell in Argentina, Father Jon Sobrino in El Salvador, and many others. Bishops' conferences in Peru and Brazil did openly turn toward the Theory of Liberation. In Central America, liberation theologians were in the forefront of subversive and bloody movements. Many others have followed sympathetically at a prudent distance, so as not to incur the wrath of the Vatican. The debate has been joined with vigor and fury from both sides.[2]

Following are some statements, which illustrate the point. Father Juan Segundo, in his book *A Theology for the Builders of a New Humanity*, wrote: "The only truth that is the truth is the one which works for the liberation of man." Father Gutiérrez, in his *Marx and Jesus* added: "We must put an end to certain kinds of theologians whom we call 'idealists'-i.e., theologians who have no concrete commitment. No matter how much goodwill they possess nor how much St. Augustine they have read, this kind of theologian will always be as idealist... I am using the word 'idealist' in the Marxist sense because only theologians who are pastorally committed can match the true definition of a theologian."

After a milder call to attention to the bishop congregated at Puebla, México, in 1979, the pope answered the challenge of the Theology of Liberation on August 6, 1984, through the Sacred Congregation for the protection of the Doctrine of the Faith headed by his friend, Cardinal Joseph Radzinger.[3]

The pope severely condemned the use of Marxist terms and tools such as the struggle of the classes as a means of Christian evangelization. This was followed by another letter of instruction a year and a half later, in which he appeared to make some concessions to the Brazilian bishops who had been clamoring in favor of a milder rebuff of the Theology of Liberation, especially of Father Leonard Boff.

The fallacies in the Theology of Liberation are many:

1. From a theological point of view, the pope is right when he insists that Marxist analysis is not a "scientific" tool for a theologian who wishes to investigate the process of social progress in particular.

He is also right when he points out that the selective use of isolated scriptural quotes, mostly from the Book of Exodus and the "Magnificat," is not consonant with an in-depth perception of the whole of the Revelation. Furthermore, he is also unassailable when he states that there cannot be a correct "praxis" without a previous correct "belief."

He points out that class struggle is antithetical to the universality of Christian love, the same as the moral relativism of Marxist dialectics is irreconcilable with the absoluteness of the truth of the moral law as founded on the Word of God.

He warns of the fallacy of equating the people of the New Covenant with specific social strata, namely "the proletariat."

Last, but not least, the pope energetically condemns reducing the spiritual message of Jesus Christ to that of a political agitator against the Romans. At the same time, the pope has shown that he is well aware of the brutal challenge to the hierarchical structure of the Church innate in the concept that class struggle must invade all levels of the Church, which leads to a "popular Church" opposite of the official one headed by the Bishop of Rome.

2. In economic and political terms, the Theology of Liberation does a disservice to Latin American communities by co-opting the so-called "theory of dependency" wholesale. This theory has been a welcome pretext everywhere for uneducated leftist agitators to attack multinational corporations, who have the capital and technical knowledge so sorely needed by Latin Americans.

These people show their absolute ignorance about how markets work; they also show a snobbish clerical contempt of the common sense of common people. Worst of all, they project into the community at large their own private biases and misunderstanding about the institution of private property and the allocation of scarce resources, thereby irremissibly damaging the most helpless and defenseless of all: their own peasant followers.

What can be expected if this trend continues in the future?

The Theology of Liberation movement is receding all over Latin America but remains strong among several countries such as El Salvador, Peru, Brazil, and Guatemala. In the latter, the current vice-president of the Republic is a former liberation theologian. In Honduras, the Cardinal Archbishop of Tegucigalpa has echoed some of its main tenets. Aristide, in Haiti, was one of them.

The Theology of Liberation has lost followers in some other countries such as Nicaragua, Argentina, Mexico, and Chile, but it is still gaining in overall strength among the younger clergymen, and recently appears to have also infected those in the United Sates, Africa, and the Philippines concerned with development issues.

Only a resourceful and courageous stand in the face of this challenge by the Latin Americans themselves, as well as the Church authorities, can stem definitely the tide. There are many factors involved, each of which might prove decisive in the struggle, but none will be more important than the Christian will to be free. Men and women who have everything to lose must be convinced that what they do not do for themselves, no one will do for them and their children.[4]

Notes

1. Bibliography on this issue grows by leaps and bounds. Some of the main works are the following (in Spanish):

Assmann, H. *La Idolatría del Mercado,* Seminario, San José, Costa Rica.

__________ (1976). *Teología desde la praxis de liberación.* Ensayo teológico desde la América dependiente, Sígueme, Salamanca.

Boff, C. (1980). *Teología de lo polìtico, Sus mediaciones,* Sígueme, Salamanca.

__________ (1978). *Comunidad Eclesial-Comunidad polítiau,* Ensayos de Eclesiología Política, VOZES, Petropolis.

Boff, L. (1975). *Teología desde el cautiverio,* Indo American Press Service, Bogotá.

__________ (1981). *Jesucristo y la liberación del hombre,* Cristiandad, Madrid.

__________ (1981). *La fe en la periferia del mundo. El caminar de la iglesia con los oprimidos,* Sal Terrea, Santander.

__________ (1982). *Iglesia, Carisma y Poder. Ensayos de eclesiología militante,* Sal Terrea,

Santander.
_________ (1980). *Eclesiogenesis. Las comunidades de base reinventan la iglesia,* Sal Terrea, Santander.
Bonino, J. (1977). *La fe en busca de eficacia. Una interpretación de la reflexión teológica lati - noamericana,* Sígueme, Salamanca.
Comision Teologica Internacional (1978). *Teología de la liberación,* BAC, Madrid.
Ellacuria, I. *Tesis sobre la posibilidad, necesidad y sentido de una teología latinoamericana,* en Universidad Pontifica Comillas, *Teología y Mundo Contemporáneo.*
_________ (1975). *Homenaje a K. Rahner en su 70 cumpleaños,* Cristiandad, Madrid, 325-350.
Gutierrez, G. (1970). *Teología de la Liberación,* Lima, Perú.
Lopez, T. A. (1978). *Teología liberadora en América Latina,* Paulinas, Bogotá.
_________ (1974). *Liberación Marxista y liberación cristiana,* BAC, Madrid.
Scannone, J.C. *Teología de la Liberación,* en Floristan, C. & Tamayo J.J, *Conceptos Fundamentales de la Pastoral.*
Sobrino, J. (1977). *Cristología desde América Latina. Esbozo a partir del seguimiento del Jesús histórico,* CRT, México.
_________. (1982) *Jesús en América Latina. Su significado para la fe y la Cristología,* Sal Terrea, Santander.
_________. (1981). *Resurrección de la verdadera Iglesia, Los pobre, lugar teológico de la eclesi - ología,* Sal Terrea, Santander.
Torres, S. (Ed.) (1982). *Teología de la liberación y comunidades cristianas de base,* sígueme Salamanca.

2. The "preferential option for the poor" has been a popular catchphrase of Liberation Theologians since it was officially consecrated at the Medellín Conference of Latin American Bishops in 1968. In this respect, Cardinal Joseph Hoeffner, in his opuscule *Church Social Doctrine or Liberation Theology* (Fulda, 1984), comments:

   "Leonardo Boff says that if poor and rich alike come jointly to the table of the Lord, they use indeed the same symbol, but "with a different content, according to their class situation"; in the Church, communion, and in the Factory, excommunion. It is reported that of 3,387 Seminarians polled in Brazil, only 20 showed any disposition to work among influential people, and only 17 to work among intellectuals."

3. The main official documents are the following:
   Cf. Pastoral Constitution *Gaudium* et spes and Declaration *Dignitatis humanae* of the Second Ecumenical Council; Encyclicas *Mater et Magistra, Pacem in terris, Populorum progressio, Redemptor hominis y Laborem exercens;* Apostolic Exhortations Evangelii nuntiandi and Reconciliatio et Poenitentia; Apostolic Letter *Octogesima adveniens.* John Paul II has dealt with this issue in his Inaugural *Adress to the Third Conference of the Latin American Bishops,* Puebla, México, AAS 71 (1979), 187- 205; *Instruction about some aspects of Liberation Theology,* Libertatis Nuntius, by AAS 76 (1984), 876-877; Instruction on *Christian Liberty and Liberation,* by the Congregation for the Doctrina of the Faith, Rome, March 22, 1986.

4. The Liberation Theology movement is not as original as claimed by their leaders. A similar approach was faced by Anglo-Saxon Christianity at the height of the "social Gospel" movement during the first decade of the present century. The difference now lies in the more explicit use of Marxist and Neo-Marxist categories, and the open call for the violent overthrow of the present social structures, along with the traditional "revolutionary" cries of Latin American politicos.

Globalization: Insights from Catholic Social Teaching

Samuel Gregg

To say that the topic of globalization is controversial, both within and outside the Catholic Church, is surely a profound understatement. Around the world, we see Catholics and non-Catholics debating fiercely among themselves and with others about the meaning of the emergence of a variety of political, social, and economic phenomena collectively corralled in popular and intellectual discourse under the word "globalization." For some, it represents the slow breaking down of barriers that prevent the poor from entering into the world market. For others, it represents what they believe to be the slow and steady diminution of particular cultures that have existed for centuries.

There are many today who are especially interested in what the Roman Catholic Church thinks about the process of globalization, and the role that it plays in this world. As a body of believers, the Catholic Church continues to grow globally, with its numbers embracing more than one billion people. Its mission of evangelizing the world in the name of the Father, and of the Son, and of the Holy Spirit is, by definition, global in its aspirations. No man, no woman, no child in any time, place or culture is, from the Catholic standpoint, to be denied the opportunity to know the Way, the Truth, and the Life that is Jesus Christ. The small community of apostles left behind by the Christ who had truly risen from the dead was not told to stay perpetually in

Jerusalem. It was commanded to spread the Word of Christ to all the nations, indeed, to the very ends of the earth.

As part of its global mission of evangelization, the Catholic Church proclaims that every Christian, indeed, every person, should seek to walk the way of Christ by living in accordance with the truth, especially the moral truth, proclaimed by Christ and His Church throughout the centuries. At the core of this moral teaching is the axiom that human persons have the liberty and responsibility to transforming ourselves from the person we are into the persons that we ought to be. It is primarily in this way, by building up ourselves, that men and women contribute to the building of the Kingdom of God.

One part of this moral teaching is what many people describe as "Catholic social teaching." My task today is to elaborate, albeit briefly, on how this social teaching helps Catholics to think about, and comprehend, the phenomenon of globalization. My object, as such, is therefore not to focus on the questions of whether globalization is, overall, beneficial or detrimental to humanity. Rather, it is to think about how we think about and comprehend globalization. I will, however, offer some closing reflections about the engagement between Catholicism and a globalizing world on some of the underlying philosophical questions that require, in my view, continuing reflection and discussion, not least because they touch on the engagement between Catholicism and the phenomenon that we call modernity.

What Is Catholic Social Teaching?

But before we do this, we need to consider what Catholic social teaching is. Contrary to much received opinion, Catholic social teaching did not begin in 1891 with Leo XIII's social encyclical *Rerum Novarum*, any more than some Catholics seem to think that the Catholic Church began in 1966. There has always been a social dimension to Catholic teaching, precisely because the moral life is intimately linked with our nature as social beings.

The central proclamation of the Catholic Church and other Christians to the world—that Jesus Christ is Lord—has profound implications for Catholic involvement in public life. In making such a statement, Christians assert that our Kyrios is *already* Lord of heaven and *all* the earth. Fr. Richard Neuhaus may therefore be correct when he states that Catholics do not believe it essential for the state to declare that Jesus Christ is Lord. The same proclamation, however, means that Christ's demands cannot somehow be confined to one's private life. For while the Gospel contains important directives about how we should order our personal lives, the same moral commandments have implications for how we try to order the social and political world. The demands of the Gospel message are, of course, of a profoundly moral nature. But the Christian life is not limited to the proper ordering of personal moral life. It also has a social dimension not least because social life presents people with dilemmas to which they must respond by freely acting in ways which meet the Gospel's demands. Thus, whatever is meant by the widely used expression "separation of church and state," it does not mean, as George Weigel notes, that Catholics believe in or accept "the separation of religion from public life, or the proscription of religiously-grounded argument from public life."

We may also posit, however, that Christian involvement in public life should have a different content and set of priorities from that of secular programs. The priority of Catholic social teaching is not, for example, "effectiveness." As the Protestant theologian Stanley Hauerwas states, instead of "attempting to make the world more peaceable and just" the "first social ethical task of the church is to be the church." This primarily means that the Church should tell its story and witness to the Truth about God. Hence, while Catholics should care for the needy and the poor (who are not, as the Church reminds us, confined to the materially poor), we should do so according to the Church's distinctive priorities rather than those of "the world." One would therefore expect Catholics heavily involved in justice issues to avoid speaking almost exclusively, for instance, about material poverty and instead also say a great deal about *moral* and *spiritual* poverty. Otherwise they may leave themselves open to the charge of providing nothing more than vague theological glosses to various secular agendas.

In light of our discussion thus far, what can we say about the general approach of Catholic teaching about the social, political, and economic order? The first point is that those Catholics who disdain the Church's moral teaching, while celebrating its social teaching are effectively living a schizophrenic existence. The Church social teaching flows from both the Church's understanding of itself as the Body of Christ and the People of God, and the moral teaching and moral absolutes that are the basis of Christian love and Christian life.

The second point is that Catholics should affirm, against all utopias, that there is no paradise on earth. We are here only as pilgrims. The goal of our life is not here, but "there"—in God's eternal Kingdom. The *provisional* character of all earthly realizations is something that we must never forget. Perfect freedom, complete justice, and total peace do not exist in this life, not least because of the reality of original sin. Surely this is one Christian teaching for which Christian faith is not necessary because, in the words of the ex-Marxist philosopher Leszek Kolakowski, it is so amply confirmed by human history. Against all resignation, however, Catholics should also insist that *relative* joy, *relative* success, and relative justice (relative in comparison to eternal life) *can* exist in this life. Hence, we must strive to create space for love and for the opportunity for all to self-realize and freely participate in the basic moral goods so that, even in the midst of great deficiencies and miseries, something of God's Kingdom is made manifest on earth.

Thirdly, we can say what Catholic social teaching is not. Catholic social teaching is not an ideology; it is not a political or public policy program; it is not a "third way;" it is not "liberal;" it is not "conservative." Nor is it based on that contemporary intellectual disease of the morality of feelings; it is not utilitarian; it is not consequentialist. At its heart is the articulation of principles and basic demands of morality derived from both Catholic faith and the natural law. These principles might be summarized as the dignity of the human person as the Image of God, the protection of the human rights and human duties that express this dignity, the virtue of solidarity, the principle of subsidiarity, the virtue of justice, and the love of preference for the poor. All of these, I might add, are derived from reflection upon Scripture, Tradition, the Church Fathers, the Natural Law, the Magisterium, and the lives and writings of the Church's saints and scholars throughout history. They are also derived from serious reflection on what the Church considers to be the nature of the person: that is, the reasoned conviction that man is an embodied creature graced with reason and free will, capable of discerning and choosing material, scientific, moral, and metaphysical truth, but also capable of choosing the opposite because he is marked by the disorder of original sin.

Fourthly, Catholics need to discern how they apply these principles to the social and political order, and to recognize that, in many cases, Catholic social teaching allows tremendous room for prudential judgment. On issues such as minimum wages and affirmative action, it is entirely possible for Catholics to arrive at quite different judgments and yet remain in good standing with the Church. There are, of course, a number of subjects where Catholic moral and social teaching translates into very specific, non-negotiable demands, most of which in our present age are concerned with the promotion and protection of the culture of life over and against the culture of death.

What is Globalization?

So, having summarized what Catholic social teaching is, and is not, we need to briefly describe what we mean by globalization. On one level, globalization is a new paradigm for describing the new way in which the human family can relate has emerged in the wake of the collapse of the previous Cold War paradigm. This is not to say that the world is no longer divided; it is. But the idea of globalization does reflect the end of Marxist-Leninist systems in most of those countries where it prevailed.

There are, of course, various features of globalization that we can identify without entering into a polemical discussion of its significance. Some of the features include:

- the proliferation of transnational organizations and movements both of a "private" (e.g., multinational corporations) and "public" (e.g., interna-

tional judicial bodies) nature;
- the emergence of planetary dimensions to business, finance, trade, technological, and information flows;
- the diminution of many hitherto common political and economic barriers such as tariffs;
- an increasing degree of cultural homogenization; and
- the unparalleled expansion of personal relationships beyond the level of the family, local communities and associations, and even nations.

Generally and simply put, globalization is the increased interconnectedness of all peoples on the face of the earth. While interaction between peoples is hardly new to human history, more and more people can now more easily, rapidly, and cheaply than ever move—and thus share—themselves and their material and human capital with others.

I also think that there are at least two developments, beyond the demise of Communism, that are driving much of this increased interconnectedness. The first is the technological revolution that has emerged from the natural sciences. Specifically, two areas of technological progress have made globalization possible. One is rapid advances in communications technology. The rise of the personal computer in the 1990s and its interface with the Internet has created the ability to process, store, and move large amounts of information and ideas with unprecedented and ever-improving ease, speed, and economy. The other technical area promoting the globalization phenomenon is transportation. Again, with unprecedented and ever-improving ease, speed, and economy, we can move ourselves and our capital.

The second development underlying globalization is the "social dimension" of modernity. This is sometimes called "liberalism" because of its association with the idea of liberty, although as we all know, the number of contrary and even contradictory positions that claim the title of liberalism raises questions about the usefulness of the term.

Economic liberalism stipulates that the real wealth of nations would be greatest in an economy marked by private property and a relatively free market. Political liberalism is concerned with economics, but goes on to assert that a variety of freedoms—ownership, trade, association, speech, religious—are due each person, and should thus be protected as (negative) "rights" by the state. It is also concerned with particular institutions such as constitutional order and rule of law.

The Catholic evaluation of liberalism has been, and continues to be, complex. My point is simply to note that it is not only technology that makes our new interconnectedness possible. Cardinal Francis George of Chicago has noted that technology would not carry our ideas, people and things without a philosophical premise that such exchanges are beneficial. Globalization, particularly its economic aspect, has thus, George states, proceeded not only because we possess the requisite technology, but also because it is held that certain freedoms are beneficial to all the human persons who inhabit the globe.

Globalization and Catholic Social Teaching

Having established, then, the nature of globalization as well as the character of Catholic Social Teaching, the challenge becomes how Catholics can apply the principles of the Church's teaching in ways that help to direct the process of globalization towards the service of the human person rather than his degradation. For it is not a matter of thinking that the Church can somehow "stop" globalization. Globalization is a social process that reflects man's social nature and thus has been going on for centuries as people throughout the world come to know each other. The difference is the accelerated pace, as countries in the developing world go through a process of change that took European countries centuries to achieve.

The question is how Catholics apply the insights of the Church's social teaching so that globalization reflects the full truth about the unique dignity of man. Broadly speaking, there are three areas in which this requires attention: the economic, the political, and the cultural. In this regard, as in any other area of the social order, there is tremendous room for prudential judgment. Catholics can say, for example, that we want a globalization that reflects the virtue of solidarity and the principle of subsidiarity. But discerning what this means in concrete terms can be, in many cases, very much a matter for prudential judgment.

One area which I do think will demand more and more attention from Catholics, as the processes of globalization speed up, is the area of the rapid growth and spread of biotechnology. By this, I do not primarily have in mind the use of technology to genetically enhance food products. Rather, I have in mind the work that is occurring in the area of human genetics and the reproduction and altering of the human species, either through direct intervention to either fix disordered genes or what some people believe is necessary to enhance their off-spring. While I will refrain from entering into the discussion about the specific morality of various possibilities, the process of globalization means that these and other issues must be discussed, considered, and then acted upon by Catholics at a global level, precisely because of their implications about what it means for our understanding of ourselves as human beings and possible changes in the meaning of what it is to be human. While science now has the capacity to allow us to do various things, science is simply incapable of saying in any authoritative way that we ought to do various things. Appeals to undefined, content-less notions of progress for the sake of change are simply inadequate for discussing these questions in a coherent and reasonable way. It is surely essential that the insights of theology and moral philosophy be brought to bear. In this regard, I would highly recommend that people read Leon Kass's latest book, *Life, Liberty, and the Defense of Dignity,* for a profoundly reasonable treatment of the issue. I would, however, also suggest that reflection upon Catholic social and moral teaching would help the process of a reasoned discernment upon an aspect of globalization that will only grow in importance.

Catholicism, Modernity, and Globalization

This subject of biotechnology brings us to the concluding point of this lecture which I foreshadowed at the beginning: that the pace of globalization makes ever more urgent a serious reflection by Catholics through the lens of Church teaching upon some more fundamental questions that concern the way that Catholics think about and regard the modern world. Globalization reflects in so many ways the spread of what the second Vatican Council called the modern world or what others call modernity to the rest of the globe. Technological progress, as well as the emergence of political democracy, the spread of economic liberty, and the institutions that underlie it such as private property, rule of law, and free markets, are all regularly associated with the idea of modernity. All of these things, incidentally, have their roots in Judeo-Christianity and pre-modern European Civilization. Nevertheless, there is also little question that the various Enlightenments, all of which were ambiguous developments, have given a particular tone and meaning to all of these ideas, processes, and institutions, and it is a tone and meaning that much of globalization spreads around the globe as these ideas, processes, and institutions spread around the world. There are unresolved matters here that Catholicism, and Catholic social teaching, must continue to grapple with.

In many senses, the Catholic Church began grappling with these matters long before the Second Vatican Council. Many trace the Church's engagement with the modern world to Leo XIII's 1891 social encyclical, *Rerum Novarum.* It is, of course, a difficult engagement, because it involves Catholics establishing themselves equidistant between those who hold that all was darkness before 1789, and those who hold that nothing but darkness has followed after 1789. The inability of many Catholics to do so has relegated them to the irrelevance of romantic nostalgia or the triviality of aping secular modernity. In the case of the latter, the virtual disintegration of most mainline Protestant churches in Western Europe and North America that has followed their embrace of a rather uncritical view of modernity in the form of theological liberalism should be a salutary warning about the potential dangers involved.

There is, of course, no alternative to a Church engaged with the modernity that the processes of globalization continue to spread. But if such an engagement is to be meaningful, then Catholics should maintain no illusions about precisely what they have been called upon to engage. For while modernity has helped to create a world that is unquestionably more materially prosperous and scientifically advanced, it has spawned some terrible beasts. The following list, I would suggest, many of which have been outlined by the Catholic theologian George Weigel, summarizes some of the tensions between Catholicism and the modernity being spread by globalization.

1. Modernity insists that God-talk is, at best, metaphorical and at worst, irrational. Catholicism teaches that the Creed professed by Catholics every Sunday is the truth of the world.

2. Modernity's view of history remains that of the Enlightenment: that is, one of an "automatic" linear forward movement achieved almost by passage of time and without enormous personal effort. Catholicism, however, maintains that historical change is not necessarily benign. It insists that without a shared knowledge, understanding, and belief in the objective moral order that transcends time, place, and culture, there can be no coherent, believable, or effective knowledge of how to improve either oneself or society.
3. Modernity imagines that salvation is a matter of achieving one's human potential. Catholicism holds that while such achievement is important, salvation is ultimately a question of communion with God, in which our human potential is realized in an unsurpassable way by our free obedience to the truth.
4. Modernity understands evil primarily in social terms and largely as the result of disordered structures. Catholicism holds that, in the final analysis, evil and structures of evil proceed from original sin as well as the personal choice of human persons to do evil rather than good.
5. Modernity insists that all religions are equally valid. Catholicism honors other faiths, but teaches that God has revealed Himself and His purposes definitively in the life, death, and resurrection of Jesus Christ, thereby changing the world's history and restoring it to its proper trajectory. It also states, in the words of Vatican II's Declaration of Religious Liberty Dignitatis Humanae that the "one true religion [*unicam veram religionem*] subsists in the Catholic and Apostolic Church, to which the Lord Jesus committed the duty of spreading it abroad among all men."
6. Modernity insists that the hope of life after death is, if not a nonsense, irrelevant to human liberation in this world. Catholicism teaches that the Christian hope of life after death liberates us in the most radical way and thus makes a genuinely liberating transformation of the world possible in ways that mere politics cannot even begin to imagine.
7. Modernity conceptualizes reason in instrumental, technical terms. Catholicism also understands reason to be capable of knowing moral, metaphysical, philosophical, and theological truth.
8. Modernity understands morality in terms of externalities, that is, the effects of one's actions upon others. It speaks of "the greatest good of the greatest number," and is profoundly utilitarian. Catholicism disputes the consequentialist notion that the good is quantifiable. Intentions may be noble, people may claim to be acting in good conscience, and circumstances may mitigate personal responsibility. Nonetheless, Catholicism teaches that many human acts remain *everywhere* and *always* evil.
9. Modernity conceptualizes freedom as freedom of choice. Catholicism underlines free will as a sign of our dignity as the *imago Dei,* but insists that one is only truly free when one lives in truth. As Deuteronomy states: "I set before you life or death, blessing or curse. Choose life, then, so that you and your descendants may live" (Dt 30:19). This leads to a particular vision of freedom

so aptly captured by Lord Acton's statement that liberty is "not the power of doing what we like, but the right of being able to do what we ought."

Reflection upon these points soon indicates that a genuine conversation between the impulse of modernity that underlies much contemporary globalization, and Catholicism is bound to be difficult. It should also remind Catholic intellectuals that a conversation between the Church and the modern globalizing world is not necessarily one in which the world sets the agenda for the Church. A genuine conversation is a two-way process, and more than one observer would agree that in recent decades too many Catholic intellectuals have simply articulated pale imitations of whatever happens to be the latest transitory secular intellectual fashion.

Conclusion

Certainly, in some of the areas that I have listed above, it seems clear to me that there is room for some dialogue and less room in other areas. A conversation is, however, essential and inevitable. Globalization holds out great promise for humanity, the promise of making, as the Second Vatican Council taught, human life more humane. The expansion of free trade and of institutions such as the rule of law and private property throughout the world presents us with tremendous opportunities for helping the developing world to raise its living standards. But the challenge for Catholicism in the midst of a globalizing world is to make sure that in the midst of ever-increasing change that the great dignity of the human person, the only creature who God made for His own sake, is not lost sight of. The spread of what some people call "liberal institutions" such as market exchange, private property, limited government, constitutional order, and rule of law throughout the world through globalization hold out tremendous promise, both materially as well as morally, for humanity. Ultimately, however, what matters from a Catholic standpoint is whether or not these institutions are based on an anthropology of man reflecting the truth about the human person. One need only read the writings of St. Thomas More, the greatest Englishman, in my view, over the past two millennium, to see that these institutions can be based upon an authentically Christian humanism: a Christian humanism that tells us that, by virtue of our humanity, by virtue of our status as the Image of God, we transcend our culture and place; a Christian humanism that shows us how to take advantage of the immense opportunities that globalization offers humanity in ways that accord with our dignity; and a Christian humanism that shows respect for the rich variety of cultures and yet also teaches us, as Vatican II reminds us, that none is or ought to be considered a prisoner of his/her culture and that the evils that are present in any culture ought to be identified and dispensed with. It is this Christian humanism that is at the basis of Catholic social teaching, and this Christian humanism that can provide us with the principles we need for a truly harmonious globalization to emerge—principles that speak forever about the innate dignity of man and at all times and places express the spiritual grandeur of the human person.

CONCLUSION

The Archbishop of Canterbury: On the Facts and Values of Religion and Globalization

Gordon Lloyd

The Problem of Globalization

In December 2002, Rowan Williams, the newly selected Archbishop of Canterbury, delivered his "provocative" lecture on the appropriate relationship between religion and public policy in the "globalized" 21st century.[1] "Let me put it provocatively," he said. "We are no longer confident of educating children in a tradition," that teaches a shared vision (Williams, 2002, p. 10). Traditional religion, concludes the archbishop, must fill the "moral vacuum" that currently exists in the creation of public policy.

For the archbishop, the central public policy question is: "Why should we do what the government tells us?" (Williams, 2002, p. 1; see also pp. 12, 14, 15.) Translated to the 21st century, the archbishop wants to know what makes it legitimate for "modern governments" to "order you around?" There is urgency to Williams' question: we are living in a time when the "basic assumptions" about legitimate authority are shifting. The 21st century market state, argues the archbishop, is replacing the 20th-century nation state, with the result that a moral and political vacuum has been created. The nation state's legitimacy is based in a social contract, by which Williams doesn't mean a contract among individuals who create a society where they lay down rights and write constitutions. No, a Williams' social contract is a "bargain" made between the "people" and their "government." *We* obey the *government* because it delivers a "high degree of internal stability" (Ibid. p.2). Williams' social contract has little to do with securing individual freedom and much to do with guaranteeing public welfare.

Thus, says Williams, we need a new social contract, and that is where the revival of traditional religion enters the equation. Traditional religion must now fill the role once held by the welfare state to provide the eternal context within which the market state ought to operate. Traditional religion, operating within the geographical boundaries of the former nation state, is the solution to the problem of economic globalization; it provides a national religion or moral compass for an identifiable "homogeneous community" in a world occupied by solitary individuals who go to market to buy a fat pig and then go home again jiggerty jig, and, moreover, don't give a fig. We need a rejuvenated traditional religion, he chides, one that presses the case for community standards in a world that has lost its collective compass. We need the value of traditional religion to trump the fact of the market state.

The Archbishop's Paradox

There is a fundamental tension at the heart of Williams' analysis of moral action and public policy. On the one hand, he calls for a renewed confidence in "the strength of non-governmental communities that support and nourish the sense of continuity, the sense of the story, which I have been suggesting is vital for reasonable moral action that looks beyond the immediate scene" (Williams, 2002, p. 10). And he has in mind traditional religious organizations as *the* critical non-governmental organizations. This is promising, for it could involve a partnership between religious organizations and business enterprises based on an active social sphere, independent from the administrative state. On the other hand, he is so critical of "the consumer culture" of the market state that we are left wondering about what his "third way" of "moral action" might look like. He rightly observes that in education, "we are very much at sea over what concrete moral content we want to see in our children's education." The schools aren't providing the moral culture and the best they can do is encourage general respect and tolerance. But he blames the market state for this concern with "procedural education," when in fact this drift is due to the actions of the nation state itself over the last 50 years. I wonder also where the status of the individual fits into his solution. He wants a robust social order, but an organic and planned group order rather than a decentralized order created by individuals to meet the twin objectives of individual freedom and community responsibility.

The archbishop exaggerates the extent to which 1) the welfare state[2] actually provided for public morality; it certainly provided for an individual dependency on the state for basic services from womb to tomb, even from jowel to bowel, as well as nationalizing personal responsibility, 2) the market state undermines the personal morality of self-reliance and encourages self-indulgence, greed, and "piggishness;" the archbishop has uncritically accepted the criticism that the market is responsible for self-indulgent behavior when this unruly behavior may well have been caused by what Prime Minister Tony Blair calls "the liberal consensus of the 1960s," 3) traditional religion is still capable of providing the solution which he seeks. The 20th century nation state encouraged indifference, perhaps a hostility, toward traditional religion.[3] All major studies on religiosity in Britain and Europe show an alarming indifference to church attendance and religious belief over the last 25 years. In Britain, fewer than 10 percent of the population attend church more than once a month, and in Western Europe, 50 percent of the population have given up on going to church all together. In fact, there are more practicing Muslims in Britain than there are practicing Anglicans, 4) the social contract is a "bargain" between government and citizen, rather than an arrangement between individuals. Only the latter aims to retain a robust private sphere while at the same time providing for the public good.[4] And, finally, he underestimates the extent to which the nation state still interferes in our day-to-day lives.

Many of the archbishop's market-orientated critics point out that it is perverse to argue that contemporary Britain is in fact a market state. In the 21st century, Health, Education, and Welfare are very much under the control of the central government and more than 50 percent of the government budget is devoted to these three social issues. Interestingly, however, these market-based critics of the archbishop's thesis appear to be more worried about what they see as his call for the return of an intolerant religious state than they are about the persistence of the welfare state. They would rather stick it out with the secular values of the welfare state than even consider Williams' call for a rejuvenation of religious values. Such is the dysfunctional condition of the conservative movement in Britain.

I wish to make two points about the archbishop's claim that the welfare state has collapsed and that it is time for the religious sector to be revitalized.

First, Williams misses the opportunity to foster a robust private sector and instead simply replaces the mechanism of the welfare state with the mechanism of traditional religion without altering the fundamental goals of the welfare state. His premise seems to be that the religious ethic and the spirit of capitalism are locked in mortal combat and with the factual victory of capitalism over the welfare state, the religious ethic must rise to do battle once again, but now on behalf of the values of the deceased welfare state.

Second, nevertheless, Williams' call for a vigorous role for the religious sector can be rescued from Williams himself; like the good archbishop, I think traditional religion should work to reestablish the severed connection between the community and the individual, and the religious ethic and the market spirit. But he assumes that the market is amoral, perhaps even immoral, and that individualism, even properly understood, is an illegitimate moral horizon. Thus, for Williams, morality must be imposed from the outside on both the market and individuals. And the only institution that can impose that kind of collectivist disposition, he claims, is the established church.

Contrary to the archbishop, I suggest that the only way that traditional religion can provide an ethical guide in the era of globalization is by rejecting, rather than by endorsing, the principles of the welfare state, and by invigorating the links within the private sector. I agree with the archbishop that we need to restore what I will call value-based political economy. It was once a beacon for all lovers of self-reliance, personal autonomy, risk taking, and, yes, community responsibility. But the idea of value-based political economy was tarnished by a religious, political, and economic critique from both the left and the right. There is an unfortunate value-free predominance in the social sciences these days.

I also agree with the archbishop that there is a vital role for traditional religion to play in the restoration of moral political economy. But we disagree on the nature of that role. I believe traditional religion should inspire a new love of individual freedom and communal responsibility, instead of repeating the old, and tired, desire for individual security and communal paternalism.[5] We need a good dose of Alexis de Tocqueville's "self interest rightly understood."[6] And we need this even more in a world that seems to have embraced the market far more than ever.

The Archbishop's Case Against the Market State

Here is Archbishop Williams's concern: The welfare state had a "clear public morality," but it "no longer has the power to keep up its side of the bargain." Economic globalization has arrived and the independence of the nation state has departed. The nation state is no longer able to secure its side of the bargain: stable employment patterns and manageable welfare levels at home (Williams, 2002, p. 3). The "social contract," whereby the citizens obey the law in exchange for government delivering "internal security," has collapsed. The nation state, which attempted to "give shape to society," has been replaced by the market state where individuals are given "maximum choice" to determine their own life-style. The market state substitutes the importance of immediate personal concerns for the traditional interest in the long-term community well being.

Williams sees the arrival of the market state as a bad bargain. Following the lead of Philip Bobbitt[7], he sees the role of the government of the market state as one that clears "a space for individuals or groups to do their own negotiating, to secure the best deal or the best value for money in pursuing what they want" (Williams, 2002, p. 4). In this deregulated state, based on "the consumer model," individual comforts take precedence and individuals ask for maximum choice with respect to purchasing power to determine one's own life-style. In short, the market state, or the consumerist-insurance model, emphasizes short-run, even immediate, gratification and "insurance issues" at the expense of long-run community good. Politics takes the following form: how rapidly will the government respond to the "surface needs" of the "consumerist or insurance model?"

Life under the market state becomes "just a game" (Williams, 2002, p. 9) and that is his litmus test of a rotten society. If politics is simply a game, then "arguments about the nature of the story, mine and ours, becomes a waste of time—whatever the political party" (Ibid.). The market state government "abandons the attempt to give shape to society." Put differently, government and culture part company and we risk "reducing freedom in the name of increasing choice." He thinks this emphasis on "choice" (Ibid.) actually is a parody rather than the ideal of democratic life.

The archbishop claims that the market state has abandoned "a clear morality for the public sphere," once prevalent in the welfare state. The market state asks us to recognize its legitimacy in terms of "its capacity to maximize varieties of personal insurance." But in doing so, it undermines "the very idea of reasonable politics, the rule of law, and the education of active citizens" (Ibid.). So here is Williams' proposal: Religion was made private by the welfare state, but the welfare state at least had a public morality. The market state has no public morality, so religion must go public again. But how is traditional religion going to persuade people to change their lives if a) it is antagonistic to the market state, and b) few people go to churches of traditional religion any more?

He wants traditional religion to fill the void abandoned by the replacement of the nation state by the "button pushing" market state. Traditional religion is based on the "bold claim that there is a story of the whole universe without which your own story won't make sense." The market state doesn't care about "educating children in a tradition." But, excuse me dear archbishop; didn't this abandonment of tradition occur on the watch of the welfare state and traditional religion?

What he has in mind is this: "For the religious believer—very particularly in the Jewish, Christian, and Muslim worlds—each of us, and each item in our environment, exists first in relation to something other than me, my needs, my instincts. They are related…to the eternal; to God. To see or know anything adequately is to be aware of its relation to the eternal" (Williams, 2002, p. 11). To the archbishop, the commercial spirit is in a sort of mortal combat with the eternal spirit rightly understood. Yet over the centuries, there has been sufficient evidence to demonstrate the compatibility of the religious ethic and the genius of commerce. The facts suggest that the values of religion and commerce can be, and ought to be, reconcilable.

A Third Way Home?

The archbishop worries: "What does a reasonable (individual) decision look like in this context" of the market state (Williams, 2002, p. 7)? When we let individuals make their own decisions, aren't we really abandoning the idea of a grand narrative, the longer story of the fuller life, one that tunes into the "cumulative experience?" Only traditional religion can overcome the defects of the market state: it alone can make "the bold claim that there is a story of the whole universe without which your story won't make sense" (Ibid. p. 8). In the end, the market state destroys our ability to make human decisions in the context of a larger story. The market state, he fumes on, is only interested in "maximizing varieties of personal insurance." Again, we are left wondering about the status of the individual in Williams' model. Isn't there a grand human narrative that incorporates the individual into, rather than subjugates the individual to, the community? The answer is, "yes," and it is to be found in religion and commerce marching together to promote a vigorous social sphere.

But we are left wondering just how robust, and spontaneous, Williams actually wants the social sphere to be. In the 1980s, Williams took part in a raid of RAF facilities where cruise missiles were being stored, and he is proud of this defiance of the government. I'm surprised, then, that this crusader should see the "populist protests" in 2000 against high fuel taxes across Britain as the activity *par excellence* of what is wrong with globalized modernity! So what is the response of the church to these concerns, which sound very familiar to the 18th century call of no taxation without representation? Williams is hostile to their claims. This action, he says, shows the dangerous nature of the market state: Here "the individual confronts the state, asking for ...maximal choice, purchasing power to determine a lifestyle." Thank goodness, he says, that the British government held its ground and told the protestors to do what the government tells them to do. Consumer demand and instant action, he says, are undermining long years of carefully constructed environmental and transportation policy.

And yet, there is the other more hopeful side to Williams' approach. He talks about a joining together—"a partnership"—of the market state and traditional religion so that we join the immediate with the eternal. This is a new opportunity created by the collapse of the nation state. Although Williams wants religion to go public again, it must be in opposition to personal liberty and the market state. "Fragmented and deprived" communities "need brokers," and local churches can organize electoral forums. The church can create "a space where reflective politics is still possible because it belongs to a tradition whose interests are more than political." But is the church a place where individuals learn from each other by reflecting on what is to be done or is it a place where an advocacy group can press their public claim—a "moral vision" of course—upon the rest of the uneducated citizens?

Williams leaves me thinking that his model is the latter rather than the former.

Self-Interest Rightly Understood

Archbishop Williams, following the footsteps of continental philosophy, emphasizes the commercial vices of modernity and expresses an embarrassment and an outrage—two critical components of prejudice—with respect to the modern project. Modernity seems so banal, non-heroic, and piggish. And now this amorality has been globalized. To Williams, there is something abhorrent about the hallmarks of modernity and globalization: an advocacy of the economic market system and the promotion of the idea of limited political government. But, dear archbishop, modernity is, as you say, what we have, and individual self-interest rightly understood is, as I say, what we must do to improve the human condition. Religion is a value, but currently in Britain and Western Europe, it is not a fact. To bring value and fact together requires that we listen closely to the wise advice of Tocqueville who teaches us the valuable lesson that public virtue can be personally useful.

True, we need to make sure that we do not replace "the prejudice of the nation state," namely, that the state is the most authoritative actor in our social life, with "the prejudice of the market state," that the market ought to be the exclusive authoritative source for the distribution of values. The archbishop's third way attempts to correct the prejudice of the market state, but it embraces the prejudice of the nation state. Instead, we need a third way that corrects the prejudice of the market state without duplicating the prejudice of the nation state. We need a non-prejudicial solution. We agree with the archbishop, the issue is not to make the world safe for globalization. Rather the task is to make globalization safe for the world. But the archbishop is trapped; he rejects globalization in principle, or as a value, while accepting globalization in practice, or as a fact. And in the process, Williams is promoting a public interest wrongly understood.

We need a Tocquevellian modern *public action* solution for the problems of globalized modernity, one that retains decentralized and spontaneous human initiative and yet appeals to the civic dimension of human existence. Tocqueville warns that reliance on ancient sacrifice, and contemporary paternalism, is inappropriate. But he also warns that the market system may well encourage self-interest wrongly understood: by helping myself, I help others. Tocqueville argues instead for self-interest rightly understood: by helping others, I help myself. By promoting restraint, modesty, and determination, and doing good for others, traditional religion can provide the ethical framework for global capitalism. What we do *not* need today is the following ethical precept: if you do something good for me, then I'll do something good for you. Instead we need the following: I'll do something good for you, and perhaps you will do something good for me. That is capitalism rightly understood, because it reminds us that moneymaking is the necessary, but not the sufficient, condition for the good life. Being a good shepherd is the sufficient condition, even if we have to be reminded that virtue is useful as well as good in itself.

Self-interest rightly understood, says Tocqueville, is not "a sublime doctrine," one that is among the highest of public virtues. But it is reliable, it brings out the best in modern man; it produces "orderly, temperate, moderate, careful, and self-controlled citizens." These are virtues that religion encourages, and there ought to be nothing embarrassing about embracing these "bourgeois values" of self-reliance and generosity to others. Most importantly, Tocqueville's self-interest rightly understood provides an alternative to the worst features of both the paternalistic state and the market state. It does not encourage an attachment to the prejudice of traditional religion or the nation state, nor does it encourage us to abandon the fact that we are, by nature, at least partly communal creatures. The doctrine that "virtue is useful" leads humans "to help one another and disposes them freely to part of their time and wealth for the good of the state." And when we support this practical approach with the dissemination of the "sublime utterance" of Christianity—"we must do good to our fellows for love of God"—we have the grounds for a reliable moral political economy that is absent in both the paternalistic model and the market alternative. The doctrine of self-interest rightly understood makes us neither perfect nor angelic. But nor does it make us nasty, solitary, poor, piggish, or brutal. We can, perhaps, remain free and responsible, and perhaps we can become decent and human. Perhaps we might even become autonomous in fact and philanthropic in our values.

Notes

1. Williams, Rowan (2002). *Archbishop of Canterbury: The Richard Dimbleby Lecture* [Online]. Westminster School, London: 19 December 2002. Available: http://www.archbishopofcanterbury.org
2. I use the nomenclature "nation state" and "welfare state" interchangeably because that is what the archbishop does.
3. The Church of England itself is no doubt partly responsible for the growth of indifference to traditional religion. The archbishop's speech was reported in *The Times* to be "one of the most intellectually ambitious and far reaching speeches from an Archbishop of Canterbury for thirty years." See Ruth Gledhill, Religion Correspondent, *The Times,* December 19, 2002. See also Ferdinand Mount's comment that the speech was one that "tickled up the body politic like no archbishop ever did in the whole of the last century…. Anything is better for the Church of England than quiet diplomacy and the genteel management of decline." See *The Sunday Times,* December 29, 2002.
4. This view of the Social Contract is grounded in thought of John Locke and the American Founders, neither of whom, in contrast to the architects of the welfare state, understood the separation of church and state to be the same as the sepa-

ration of religion and politics.

5. The archbishop's call for a revitalized role for religion in politics received a swift rebuke from secularists, including those who are friendly to a robust market and limited state. See Minette Marrin, The Sunday Times, December 22, 2002.
6. Alexis de Tocqueville, *Democracy in America,* vol 2, part 3.
7. Williams relies on Philip Bobbitt's claim that a "consumerist" approach to politics turns politics into "a matter of insurance," where "voters look for what will guarantee the maximum possible freedom to buy their way out of insecurity." See Lecture, p. 5. In *The Shield of Achilles: War, Peace and the Course of History,* Bobbitt argues that the market state is "indifferent to norms of justice, or for that matter, any particular set of moral values." Bobbitt focuses on the impact of globalization on the foreign policy of individual nation states; Williams focuses on the impact of globalization on domestic policies.

Contributors

Imad-ad-Dean Ahmad is president of the Minaret of Freedom Institute, an Islamic think tank in the Washington, D.C. area.

Stephen V. Arbogast is treasurer for ExxonMobil Chemical Company in Houston, Texas, EMC's worldwide chemical division.

Rev. John Michael Beers currently teaches at Ave Maria University in Naples Fl. He also serves as President of the Annecy Institute for the promotion of Virtue and Liberty.

Walter Block is the Harold E. Wirth Eminent Scholar and Endowed Chair and Professor of Economics at the College of Business Administration of Loyola University in New Orleans.

Rev. David Boileau teaches philosophy at Loyola University in New Orleans.

William F. Campbell is emeritus professor of economics at Louisiana State University and currently serves as secretary of the Philadelphia Society.

Art Carden is a Ph.D. candidate at Washington University in St. Louis where he studies economic history and development.

James C. Cavill is a retired executive from the oil industry. He is currently studying religion at Wilfrid Laurier University in Waterloo, Ontario.

Alejandro Chafuen serves on the Boards of several U.S., European and Latin American institutes including the Atlas Economic Research Foundation and the Hispanic American Center of Economic Research.

Paul M. Chandler was a Peace Corps volunteer in Brazil and presently teaches environmental history, resource conservation and development challenges at Ball State University in Indiana.

Krishna S. Dhir is professor of business administration and dean of the Campbell School of Business at Berry College in Georgia.

James R. Edwards, Jr., is principal and co-founder of Olive, Edwards, & Brinkmann, a Washington, D.C. public affairs firm.

Samuel Gregg is director of research at the Acton Institute and adjunct professor at the John Paul II Pontifical Institute for Marriage and the Family within the Pontifical Lateran University in Rome.

Celestina Isiramen teaches philosophy, religion, and management studies at Ambrose Ali University in Nigeria.

Joseph F. Johnston, Jr., is a partner in the Washington office of Drinker Biddle & Reath. He also serves on the Board of the Liberty Fund.

Harold B. Jones, Jr., is a Methodist pastor and currently teaches at Mercer University's Stetson School of Business and Economics.

Joseph Keckeissen is a brother of the Salesians of Don Bosco and professor of economics at Francisco Marroquin University in Guatemala.

Irfan Khawaja is adjunct professor of philosophy at the College of New Jersey, lecturer in politics at Princeton University, and member of the Institute for the Secularization of Islamic Society.

Ellen Klein was a Fulbright Scholar in Bosnia and is a professor of philosophy at Flagler College.

H. C. Peter Koslowski is a professor of philosophy and the philosophy of management at the Free University of Amsterdam. He was the founding director of the Hanover Center for Ethical Economy and Business Culture.

Rabbi Daniel Lapin is the president of Toward Tradition, a noted columnist and the host of a radio show.

Ryszard Legutko is professor of philosophy at the Jagellonian University in Krakow, Poland and president of the Center of Political Thought.

Leonard Liggio is executive vice president of the Atlas Economic Research Foundation, and is serving this year as president of the Mont Pelerin Society.

Gordon Lloyd is a Professor at the School of Public Policy of Pepperdine University.

Tibor Machan is a prominent libertarian philosopher and the R.C. Hoiles Chair in Business Ethics and Free Enterprise at the Argyros School of Business & Economics of Chapman University.

Michael C. Maibach is the vice chairman of the board of the World Affairs Council of Washington, D.C. and is the president and CEO of the European American Business Council.

Theodore Roosevelt Malloch is chairman and chief executive officer of the Roosevelt Group, a leading strategic management and thought leadership company.

Mark Markuly is the director of the Loyola Institute for Ministry.

Robert Nelson is professor of environmental policy at the School of Public Affairs of the University of Maryland.

Seth W. Norton is Norris A. Aldeen Professor of Business at Wheaton College.

Jean-Francois Orsini is founder and president of the Saint Antoninus Institute of Catholic Education in Business.

Gary Pecquet is a visiting assistant professor of economics at Tulane University.

Himanshu Rai is a doctoral student in the field of personnel and industrial relations management at Indian Institute of Management, Ahmedabad, India.

Peter Redpath is professor of philosophy at St. John's University in New York.

Bartolomeu Romualdo is an independent consultant in Brazil who assisted Paul Chandler.

Rev. Stephen C. Rowntree, S.J., teaches philosophy at Loyola University in New Orleans, and he has spent a number of years in Zimbabwe.

Gerald J. Russello is senior attorney with the Securities and Exchange Commission in New York.

Kevin E. Schmiesing is a research fellow in history at the Acton Institute in Grand Rapids, Michigan.

Armando de la Torre is professor of philosophy at Francisco Marroquin University in Guatemala.

James R. Wilburn is dean of the School of Public Policy at Pepperdine University and professor of strategy in Pepperdine's Graziadio School of Business and Management.

Index